Crown and People

George William Cullen Gross

Crown and People

British Coronations and the Shaping of National Identity 973–2023

palgrave
macmillan

George William Cullen Gross
King's College London
London, UK

ISBN 978-3-032-20785-2 ISBN 978-3-032-20786-9 (eBook)
https://doi.org/10.1007/978-3-032-20786-9

This Palgrave Macmillan imprint is published by the registered company Springer Nature Switzerland AG.
The registered company address is: Gewerbestrasse 11, 6330 Cham, Switzerland

For Elizaveta and Anastasia
As the saying goes and infinitely more
'Live a century—learn a century'

Preface and Acknowledgements

It is rare to be able to write about history that is still being made. A coronation at Westminster Abbey is one at the same time an event of a thousand years of history and more, going back into the Anglo-Saxon, and also of the present, in having taken place most recently in 2023. A coronation generates political, religious, cultural, and sociological questions and reaches far beyond the royal peculiar at Westminster overlooking the Houses of Parliament. It is hard to think of an area of historical study that cannot be found within the study of coronations—it is all encompassing. The ceremony in many ways takes the audience through the British constitution, with the key players of the nation present to oversee the marriage of the monarch to the state. At the centre of this event are fundamental issues of national identity and of the values of the country, with concepts of justice and mercy at the core of proceedings from the very earliest tradition.

By way of acknowledgement, I would like to begin by thanking His Majesty the King and her late Majesty Queen Elizabeth II for graciously granting me access to the Royal Archives at Windsor and permitting the British Coronations Project to feature on the official Coronation 2023 website. To cover such a vast array of sources and timeframe has led inevitably to innumerable questions, and I am greatly indebted to the support of friends, colleagues, and students over many years, from conversations over the phone, to dinner discussions post Institute of Historical Research (IHR) seminars, in particular, and for reviewing chapters and providing guidance and suggestions and recommended secondary reading. There are too many people to individually thank, but I would like to name those that have made this project possible in providing tremendous support during the crucial writing-up phase, most particularly Professor Linda Woodhead MBE, Professor Susan Doran, Professor Kenneth Fincham, and Dr Elizabeth Evenden-Kenyon. For helping focus on impact and widening the reach of the overall King's College London (KCL) project, my deepest thanks go to Ana Rita Claro Rodrigues and Yiannis Vassilakis. Likewise I wish to thank all at the KCL communications team, most particularly Sian Young and Julie Wheldon, who have gone above and beyond, now over many years. I am indebted to Ann Kennedy, Emeritus Fellow and former Law Tutor at Lady Margaret Hall, Oxford, for her guidance on the constitution and many a discussion over contract; The Rt Hon. Lord Murphy of Torfaen for his fascinating political insight, friendship, and encouragement; Professor Sir Iain Torrance for discussions on the ongoing importance of the Stone of Destiny and the Scottish Honours more generally; Rebecca Lamont and Simon Field MW on royalty and wine; and so too, to Hristina Ivanova. It is not too much to say that the British Coronations Project would never have got off the ground without Hristina's support and input, most particularly with the surveys—I am hugely grateful. Likewise to all members of the Socratic Club, both past and current students, and parents too, I send my thanks for listening to ideas and contributing yet further points to our debates and discussions with such panache.

I am also very thankful for the facilities provided by the Maughan Library at King's College London, and the expert guidance received from its staff. My research has also drawn upon amenities available at the British Library, the IHR, the Bodleian Library, the College of Arms, and many other repositories, and I am hugely appreciative of the time taken by so many dedicated archivists and librarians to help with my inquiries. This book could not have been completed in the present form without such tremendous support. I should also like to thank in particular for their valuable assistance: Canon Vernon White, Dr Tony Trowles, and the staff at Westminster Abbey Library and Archives; Ingrid Thomson at Glamis Castle; the Earl and Countess of Mansfield and Mansfield; Ralph Allwood MBE for his splendid insight into the musical worlds of George Frideric Handel, Hubert Parry, and Henry Purcell; the pupils and staff of West Ham Church of England Primary School; Dr Lynsey Darby at the College of Arms; and archivists at the Folger Shakespeare Library, Washington DC, the Morgan Library, New York, Chatsworth House, Castle Howard, and the John Rylands Library. To Victoria Gray at Lambeth Palace Library, and to Ulrike Hogg of the National Library of Scotland, I wish to add an extra note of thanks for their assistance in clarifying various source references and providing yet additional suggestions and ideas. Archivists and librarians both here and abroad have been so very helpful in providing further information on records held, many for the love of the subject alone—a reminder of how precious humanities learning remains and how at risk.

Further thanks are due to Elizabeth Bray at British Museum Images and Karen Lawson of the Royal Collection Trust for their co-operation in supplying and licensing illustrations.

To my beloved late wife Ekaterina—'Katya'—missed every second of every day, you thankfully knew of this book's completion in draft form, and you helped so much in the long days and nights of writing, whilst manging the lives of our little girls, my gratitude is eternal. To my family, I owe the greatest debt of thanks for their continuing and unwavering support and in putting up with 'coronations' for so many years, and for raising challenging ideas and concepts, enhancing elements of the chapters in this book. To my Mother (Lady Gross)—huge thanks—for dedicating so much time in checking the typescript prior to submission. I do of course, take responsibility for any remaining errors.

I am also immensely grateful to Palgrave Macmillan for their support and to two people in particular in the History section, without whom this project would not have been possible and with whom it has been a pleasure to work: Lucy Kidwell, senior editor, and Sasikala Thopu, production editor.

London, UK George William Cullen Gross
10 December 2025

Conventions

With particular reference to the early modern period, dates are Old Style, that is in accordance with the Julian Calendar, but with the beginning of the calendar year taken to have been 1 January. Dates after September 1752 are New Style (i.e. follow the Gregorian Calendar).

Where individuals mentioned here receive an entry in the *ODNB*, the spelling of personal names has been standardized to usage there; life-dates also conform to what is given in that work. If they exist, then English forms of foreign place-names are used.

In quotations from primary sources, I have retained original spellings as they appear in manuscript form, but for ease of the reader, capitalisation has generally been modernised, along with punctuation, and 'i' and 'j', 'u' and 'v', and 'y' or thorn have silently been altered where appropriate to match current practice. Further editorial changes are enclosed within square brackets.

In terms of titles, aristocrats are mentioned under the titles that they held at the point in time to which the reference belongs; some titles may subsequently have changed.

To provide a rough estimate of what the sums of money quoted might accord in today's currency, the online National Archived currency converter: 1270–2017 has been used.

Many sources used here are now online. Consequently my references do not always give the page references which are in the hard copies and instead provide either the document number or the online reference. For instance, various newspaper articles now only appear in online versions. To prevent the book being impossibly long, wherever possible references have been abbreviated and full details of works cited can be found in the bibliography.

Contents

About the Author

George William Cullen Gross (@drgeorgegross) is a visiting research fellow at King's College London, and founder of the British Coronations Project there. He was educated at KCL and the University of Cambridge (Sidney Sussex) studying Theology and Early Modern History. His work has featured on the BBC (*BBC Coronations*, https://www.bbc.co.uk/news/uk-65031625), CNN, *The Times*, *The Daily Telegraph*, and *History Hit Podcasts*: Gone Medieval (https://shows.acast.com/gone-medieval/episodes/ceremonial-elements-coronations). He is a co-convener at 'The Religious History of Britain, 1500–1800' seminar held at the Institute of Historical Research (IHR) in London. He has given papers at *inter alia* Westminster Abbey, UCL, and the British Academy. Publications include a co-edited book *Reformation Reputations (2020)* (https://link.springer.com/book/10.1007/978-3-030-55434-7); *The Last Coronation in Scotland 1651* (https://www.tandfonline.com/doi/full/10.1080/14629712.2021.1996947#:~:text=The%20last%20Scottish%20coronation%20occurred%20at%20Scone%20in%201651) in the Court Historian; and articles on Coronation perceptions and Anglo-Russian communications between Tsar Ivan IV ('The Terrible') and Elizabeth I.

Abbreviations

APC	J. R. Dasent (ed.), *Acts of the Privy Council of England*, New Series, 32 vols (London, 1890–1907)
BL	The British Library, London
BM	The British Museum, London
Bodl.	The Bodleian Library, Oxford
CP	G. E. C[okayne] et al. (eds), *The Complete Peerage of England, Scotland, Ireland, Great Britain and the United Kingdom, Extant, Extinct or Dormant*, 14 vols in 15 parts (2nd edn, London or Stroud, 1910–1998)
CSP, Venice	R. Brown et al. (eds), *Calendar of State Papers and Manuscripts, Relating to English Affairs, Existing in the Archives and Collections of Venice, and in other Libraries of Northern Italy*, 38 vols (London etc., 1864–1947)
CUL	Cambridge University Library
EHR	*The English Historical Review*
KJV	King James Version of the Bible (1611)
LPL	Lambeth Palace Library, London
NRS	The National Records of Scotland, Edinburgh
ODNB	*Oxford Dictionary of National Biography, Online*
OED	J. A. Simpson and E. S. C. Weiner (preparers), *The Oxford English Dictionary*, 20 vols (2nd edn, Oxford, 1989)
SR	*The Statutes of the Realm*, 11 vols (London, 1810–1828)
TNA	The National Archives, Kew
WAM	Westminster Abbey Muniments

List of Figures

List of Tables

Introduction: Past, Present, and Future

And let Zadok the priest and Nathan the prophet anoint him there king [.][1]

Then on midwinter's day [1066] Archbishop Aldred hallowed him [William the Conqueror] to king at Westminster, and gave him possession with the books of Christ, and also swore him, ere that he would set the crown on his head, that he would so well govern this nation as any before him best did, if they would be faithful to him.[2]

On 11 May 973 at Pentecost, Bath Abbey played host to the consecration of Edgar,[3] what is often seen or described as the first English coronation. For coronations are not unique to the British Isles; indeed, the idea or concept of crowning or inaugurating a reign can be found ubiquitously in history, the world over. Yet, Edgar's coronation was recorded in the *Anglo-Saxon Chronicle* and was the basis for the earliest extant order, with the anointing central to the rite.[4] This service or liturgy would provide the benchmark for English and later British coronations.[5] King Edgar also saw in an English monastic revival in combination with the work of Dunstan, Archbishop of Canterbury.[6] Edgar became 'king of the English' in 959, uniting a fractured land, and his period of rule has been seen 'a golden age of peace and plenty, exemplified by the epithet Pacificus, which first appears in the twelfth-century chronicle of John of Worcester'.[7] Nevertheless, why Edgar's coronation took place so many years later in 973 remains unclear. Or indeed, the fact that the chronicle records it at all is itself perhaps significant, for Alfred, Edward the Elder, and Edmund, amongst others, are not mentioned, and of his successors, only Æthelred II, Edward the Confessor and Harold II are cited. There is also debate as to whether there was some form of claim to governance over 'all the nations of Britain'.[8] Edgar's consort Ælfthryth was also crowned and anointed as queen, in itself creating precedent, which has survived to the present, 'a near contemporary account pictures her feasting after the coronation with abbots and abbesses in a silken gown sewn with pearls and precious stones'.[9]

On 6 May 2023, His Majesty King Charles III became the 40th reigning monarch to be crowned at Westminster Abbey since 1066. The famous Abbey is, of course, now one of the symbols of London and the UK, and has witnessed numerous key events in British history. 40 monarchs were crowned in the Abbey, 16 royal weddings took place there, and for 30 British kings and queens, it became their final resting place.[10] However, if Bath was the location for Edgar's coronation, why then did the event become synonymous with Westminster Abbey?

In the 1040s, the Anglo-Saxon King Edward (later St Edward the Confessor) created a royal palace near the present-day Palace of Westminster on the banks of the River Thames. Nearby, there was a Benedictine monastery, founded around 960 by King Edgar and St Dunstan. Following restructuring work, it was greatly enlarged and became known as 'west minster'.[11] Edward the Confessor was buried there in 1066, and his brother-in-law Harold, Earl of Wessex, was crowned the next day.

> Godwineson, having obtained the support of a group of English magnates who were in London, had himself crowned as king, as it would seem by Aldred, archbishop of York, in the Confessor's new Abbey of Saint Peter of Westminster.[12]

William the Conqueror, the Norman ruler who defeated King Harold at the Battle of Hastings and ended Anglo-Saxon rule, nevertheless, wished to be associated with Edward the Confessor. He was crowned at Westminster Abbey on Christmas Day in 1066.[13] The coronation combined the Anglo-Saxon tradition of the Witan (leading advisors of the country who would elect the monarch) and the Norman idea of a coronation where the ruler was selected based on inheritance, uniting the government, the monarchy and the church in Westminster for the first time.[14]

King Edward the Confessor was made a saint in 1161. His canonisation was essential in creating the holiness of Westminster Abbey as a house of Kings or Queens. On 13 October 1163, Edward the Confessor's body was moved to a special shrine within the Abbey. Since then, every Westminster

Abbey coronation has taken place in the vicinity of his shrine and, therefore, in the saint's presence. Successors were placed in St Edward's Chair, famously known as the Coronation Chair, and typically crowned with St Edward's Crown.

Coronations of the past united the two cities of London, with the royal and political centre in Westminster and the financial one in the City. The new monarch would traditionally process from the Tower of London to Westminster Hall, and then on to Westminster Abbey for the coronation. By the nineteenth century, this procession had evolved, and as with that custom, King Charles III's procession began from Buckingham Palace rather than the Tower of London. In the medieval and early modern worlds, Westminster Hall was of crucial significance in the inaugurating of a new reign, with its hammer-beam roof, commissioned by Richard II in 1393, the largest medieval timber roof in northern Europe.[15] Westminster Hall was also the home of the central law courts (King's Bench, Chancery, and Common Pleas), before the creation of the Royal Courts of Justice in the Strand, and featured famous trials, such as Sir Thomas More's in 1535 and Charles I's in 1649.[16]

Of course, today it is most readily thought of in connection with the ends of reigns—with the lying-in-state of sovereigns from Edward VII in 1910 (the first) to Elizabeth II in 2022, and in 1965 for Britain's 'Greatest Britain' Sir Winston Churchill. It has also received distinguished visitors when addressing both Houses of Parliament, for instance, Nelson Mandela in 1996, Pope Benedict XVI in 2010, and Barack Obama in 2011.[17]

In Medieval times, and for some of the early modern period, Westminster Hall hosted a secular inauguration 'ritual', a sign of the Anglo-Saxon elective tradition before primogeniture determined succession.[18] The Witan, replaced by the later leading Magnates and landowners of the Middle Ages, elected the sovereign who was placed in the built-in ancient 'marble' throne or 'The King's Bench', situated up a short flight of steps in the centre at the south end.[19] The monarch was then invested with a sceptre as a symbolic act of having taken possession of the realm. Following enthronement, the coronation regalia was then conveyed to Westminster Abbey in the hands of leading bishops and nobles, along a walkway lined with cloth. Under a canopy of cloth of gold held aloft by the barons of the Cinque Ports, the sovereign processed to the Abbey.[20]

Coronations involved processions on a grand scale. They played an important part in the build-up to the ceremony, particularly the well-known triumph through the City of London on the eve of the great day,

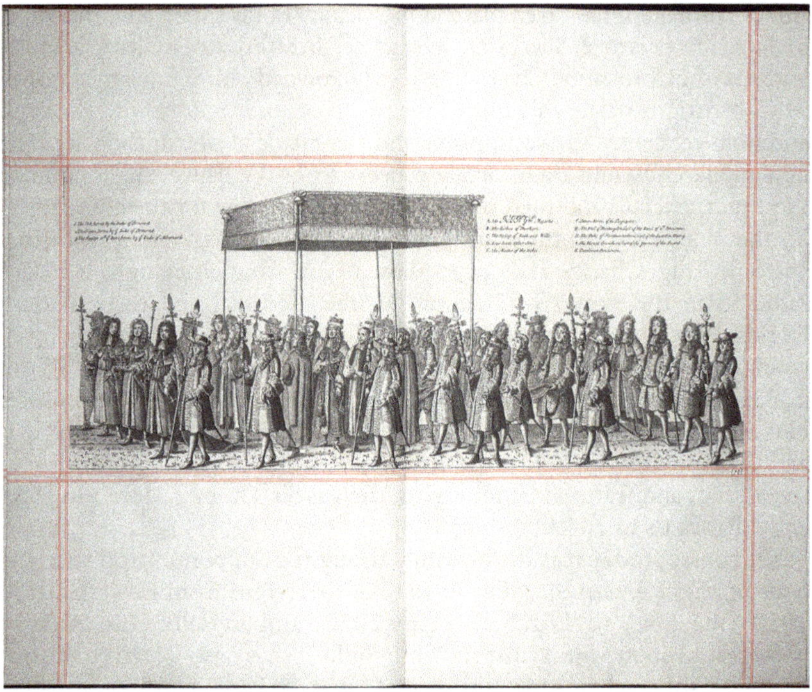

Fig. 1 Part of the formal procession for the coronation of James II in 1685: The Royal canopy. As baron of the cinque ports, Samuel Pepys was allocated a place of honour, holding the nearer of the front poles supporting the canopy. (Sandford, *History*, no. 18) (from the British Library archive, G.8188, +136)

as well as the cavalcades from and to Westminster Hall and within the Abbey itself. These were all magnificent spectacles for the wider coronation audience too, not just those inside the Abbey but also those lining the streets and observing from windows, as the diarist Samuel Pepys did; a vivid impression could additionally be gained from the elaborate depictions printed by John Ogilby and Francis Sandford (see Fig. 1).[21]

Referencing a mythical ancient past, originating in the Old Testament and the Orient, a canopy of almost celestial significance took a prominent position, covering and protecting the royal personage from the elements and from the crowds. This miniature marquee was a transient object, playing its part on the journey to the Abbey and inside the holy walls. The canopy brought the stage outside to the public precincts of the metropolis, in the sense that it marked out a mobile area of special space, and thereby linked the monarchical focus of these events to an expectant public, in a variety of locations, whether the Tower of London, Westminster Hall, Whitehall, or the Abbey. There was, of course, an important difference in these processions before and after the service. Immediately preceding the coronation, on the route to the Abbey, royalty and nobility were not yet in their full pomp: the sovereign was uncrowned, and the nobility had still to put on their coronets. However, when the people witnessed their post-coronation departure from the Abbey, all the trappings of Crown and State were brilliantly manifest. In an age in which the visual was a major feature of social relations, this contrast must have made a telling impact on bystanders, who could perceive their ruler's transformation. Such a canopy required notable personages to carry it. In 1189, these positions were assumed by the barons of the Cinque Ports for Richard I's coronation.[22] The barons were the freemen of the major ports of Kent and Sussex, namely Dover, Hastings, Hythe, New Romney and Sandwich; Rye and Winchelsea were later additions. The Cinque Ports constituted the maritime defensive positions for England (and later Britain) in the south east. They provided annually 57 ships for the Royal Navy. Besides being points of entry and exit, some remained vital commercial markets. The monarch was England's embodiment, and so the barons of the Cinque Ports symbolically represented their naval capacities to protect the country and the economy by guarding the sovereign during coronation processions. The tradition began that the Ports sent sixteen bearers.[23] This number was unusually expanded to '32 barons [being] assigned 16 to each canopy' for the coronation of James II and Mary of Modena in 1685.[24] The honour of carrying the canopy also brought with it the perquisite of receiving portions of the awning and the staves, normally for a monetary exchange that went to the individual towns. This privilege became a right;[25] in contrast to those selected to hold an object of the regalia purely out of royal favour, the barons still needed to obtain legitimation from the Court of Claims in exercising their entitlement.[26] Another part of the perquisite was the right to attend the Coronation Banquet: they occupied a principal position, on the right-hand side, below the royal table. On the left sat the lord mayor, aldermen, and citizens of London. The procession also included unusual customs, for instance, the role of the herb stewer, which was revived in discussion in 2023.[27] In 1901, Miss Beatrice Fellowes, daughter of Rear Admiral Butler Fellowes, became a victim of a new court ruling to abandon outdated offices (armour-bearer and bow-bearer). She had been selected as chief herb strewer for Edward VII's impending coronation, based on hereditary responsibility. Her predecessor, another Miss Fellowes, had performed the task, along with six of her assistants, at the coronation of George IV when she cast rosemary and other sweet-smelling herbs across his path as he walked between Westminster Hall and the Abbey in the procession. Miss Fellowes wore a costume consisting of a white gown, scarlet mantle with gold lace, and a wreath of laurel and oak leaves. She was assisted or attended by six other women, attired in white, adorned with flowers and foliage, and each carried a two-handled basket. Alice Bell was the herb strewer for George I, and as with the coronation robes for peers, her outfit was lavish and expensive, as records reveal 'two yards of scarlet cloth for a livery'. Mary Dowle was the herb strewer for James II's coronation in 1685, depicted in Francis Sandford's *History of the Coronation … of James II*, published in 1687. On this occasion, the procession was lined with yards of 'cloth … [and] strewed with nine baskets full of sweet herbs and flowers, by Mary Dowle, strewer of herbs in ordinary to his majesty, assisted by six women, two to a basket, each basket containing two bushels'.[28]

Following the coronation, the royal party would return to Westminster Hall for a banquet, the last in 1821 for George IV (subsequent banquets have taken place at St James's Palace or Buckingham Palace). This lavish tradition, as will be discussed in more detail in Chap. 5, was often a sign of things to come; Henry VIII's concluding banquet was described as 'greater than any Caesar had known'.[29] Part of that tradition included the champions challenge, a right held by the Dymoke family.[30] The 1661 challenge is recorded in the neglected diary of Richard Boyle, 1st Earl of Burlington and 2nd Earl of Cork (1612–1698). This is a particularly good example of surviving accounts of coronations and the before, during, and after of these occasions, in that Cork covers the entire programme, both at Westminster Hall, the coronation, and the return to Westminster Hall following the service in the Abbey.

> The ceremony[s] ended wee returned to Westminster Hall, where the king dined and all the Lords at another table, the kings second course was ushered in by the l[or]ds high constable steward and marshall all on horseback and afterwards they brought in the kings champion Dimock … on horseback who threw downe his gantelet, chalenging any that denied the title of the king to [be] undoubted, That performed he advanced neer the king his

> launce being carried before him … his ma[jes]ty having drunke in a cup of gold, did send it to him who after hee had pledged him has the cup as a reward: The dinner ended, it lightned and thundred excessively [.][31]

In 1821, an additional highlight, for some, lay in the fact that the champion (Dymoke) was accompanied by the Duke of Wellington, the victor of the recent Battle of Waterloo. Both took part on horseback.[32]

Whilst a large part of this book's originality lies in its geographical scope, the role of Westminster Abbey in constituting an immediate context can scarcely be ignored. It is truly the house of kings and queens for this 'Sceptred Isle'—once the precedent had been set by William the Conqueror, 'from that day to this [,] every sovereign, except Edward V and Edward VIII, has been crowned at Westminster'.[33] The scholarship on this famous building is extensive, with the great contents of the Abbey muniments and library fully exploited. Edward Carpenter, Penelope Hunting, Richard Mortimer, Tony Trowles, James Wilkinson, Charles Knighton, and Richard Jenkyns have all produced excellent material.[34] However, this coverage of coronations can be characterised as Westminster centred. Nevertheless, as discovered during a private visit to the Abbey in 2013, it quickly became apparent that the triforium ('The Queen's Diamond Jubilee Galleries') has received less attention.[35] The triforium is a gallery, rather like an attic, located above the nave side aisles, going much of the way around the Abbey, and often said to afford one of the greatest views in Europe. Indeed, from the triforium, almost everything not obscured by a cover within the Abbey can be observed. Two immediate questions come to mind: one, is there any evidence of the triforium being used in a coronation? And second, if it was used, then for what? Contemporary engravings take us only so far, in that the Abbey is often depicted with temporary seating extending up to the triforium, but it is unclear whether or not the triforium is being used for extra capacity.[36] Given the need for seating, it would seem highly likely that it was used by spectators.[37] Such a consideration may lead to some intriguing new possibilities. Take, for example, Elizabeth I's coronation of January 1558/1559. This coronation has attracted considerable interest, not least because of uncertainty about what exactly happened, due to the lack of suitable first-hand testimony, and also because the religious stakes were so high.[38] Many have argued that her coronation 'anticipated her settlement of religion'.[39] The chief problem in knowing what took place is that much of it occurred shrouded from public view; one cannot be sure precisely what she or her dean of the Chapel Royal, George Carew, did about the mass, as it was 'communicated in secret' within a 'traverse', that is a temporary curtained enclosure positioned in the sacrarium. Roger Bowers's analysis of the coronation mass reveals that Elizabeth caused a modification of the conventional Latin service in three crucial respects. First, the epistle and gospel were read in English. Second, following the Latin consecration, Carew did not elevate the host, offering Elizabeth a vernacular ritual of preparation prior to her reception of the Eucharist. Third, 'and in plain contravention of law, she received in both kinds.'[40] Yet these claims may need re-assessment once the existence of the triforium is recognised, for the triforium offered an uninterrupted view of the 'coronation theatre', or stage, located before the high altar, on which the main acts of the service, including the anointing and crowning, took place.

In order to properly assess thematically coronations, it is first necessary to dis-aggregate 'The Coronation'. In essence, there exists that shorthand term, and because it is usually taken to refer to a single event that has become rooted in Westminster Abbey, the complexity of what is really a process—that is to say, a sequence of events of varied origins and purposes—has become lost. Indeed, the rationale for any particular component is likely to have become obscure, not least because, until 2023, we lived in the longest ever gap between coronations.

Why Have a Coronation At All? Is Not the Monarch Already Sovereign?

When the sovereign dies, the heir inherits the throne immediately, hence the famous dictum, 'The king is dead, long live the king!' The transfer of power is seamless. Yet monarchs of England, and later Britain, that have not been crowned do not seem fully king or queen, for we view uncrowned (and of course 'un-sworn'—not having taken the Coronation Oath)—sovereigns as being in part not fully sovereign. The often-forgotten Edward V (one of the Princes in the Tower) reigned for just seventy-seven days and was murdered shortly after his deposition. Lady Jane Grey (the nine-day queen)[41] has always been seen as a usurper, yet had she taken the Coronation Oath and been crowned, what then would Mary Tudor have done?[42] As it happened, she led the only successful *coup d'état* of the sixteenth century. In a modern context, Edward VIII (of the abdication crisis and Wallis Simpson fame) did swear the Scottish Oath immediately upon accession (as Charles III has already done), but the royal family was relieved that Edward VIII did not abdicate post coronation. Reflecting on the 1936 Abdication, the late Queen Elizabeth ('The Queen Mother') stated that it was fortunate 'he was never crowned, and that was one of the good things he did. If he was going to make up his mind to go away, to do it before'.[43] Thus, a coronation has taken on a constitutional significance, for a monarch who has not undergone a coronation does not seem to be fully sovereign, notwithstanding their legal status and the concept of '*le roi est mort, vive le roi*!' This constitutional significance is further reinforced by the analogy of engagement and marriage. When the king or queen inherits the throne, they can be seen to be engaged to the state; when they are crowned, this is the formalisation or marriage of the sovereign to the country. This marital comparison is matched within the coronation service, with vows in the Coronation Oath and a special Coronation Ring. This ring came to symbolise the indivisibility of the Crown from the sovereign, but also the king's marriage to the kingdom. The coronation-marriage tradition, originating in medieval times, survived through the Tudors to the present era and 2023, when Charles III received the 'Sovereign's Ring'.[44] Mary I, in 1533, referred to her coronation as a marriage, and Elizabeth I maintained a similar position, declaring that 'I am sworn when I was married to the realm not to alter the laws of it'.[45] This symbolism was of such transparent importance that it registered with eyewitnesses: Celia Fiennes noted in 1702 for Queen Anne's coronation, that 'the ring is put on her finger to witness she is married to the kingdom'.[46] Such a bond being anchored in the popular mind, when a sovereign failed to meet expectations, as in the cases of Edward II, Richard II, Charles I, and James II, then it was to the vows—the Coronation Oath—to which people returned.

Throughout the UK's history, transitions of power between sovereigns and even more so between dynasties have been complex to say the least. A coronation fully legitimises an uncrowned head of state and provides a very public framework in which a monarch and a regime signal the new priorities of the reign about to unfold. The Coronation Oath has bound the monarch to the Constitution in vows and helped secure the liberties of the subject and underlined the central importance of justice. Given the dangers of arbitrary rule in the world today, this is something that remains a cornerstone of how the UK projects itself, as a country steeped in and governed by the rule of law.

Coronations Anatomised

This subject caught my imagination when I was a schoolboy reading a rather obscure Sherlockian tale, 'The Musgrave Ritual', involving 'the ancient crown of the kings of England'. From that day, I have been fascinated by what one might term the *Kind Hearts and Coronets* aspect of this event;[47] and, as most people are aware, crowns do indeed play a significant role in coronations—the centrality of the imperial diadem and 'imperial status' is uppermost within the service itself. As Joseph Hone has argued in writing on the Stuarts, the 'coronation was the most important ceremony in any monarch's life. It formalized the process of succession within a set of ancient ritual conventions centred on a royal oath, the crowning, the presentation of the regalia, and other features such as a sermon and the distribution of medals'.[48] Yet, Hone goes on to say that 'some coronations, such as those of Elizabeth [I] and Charles II, were accompanied by elaborate civic pageantry on the eve of the ceremony. But this display should not be confused with the coronation itself, which was the religious ritual occurring in the Abbey'.[49] In terms of the liturgy, of course, Hone is correct, but as this book will make clear, a coronation is more than just the religious service. There is so much more to a coronation than the crowning; it is a focal point of the service, surrounded in turn by many other important elements or layers. Moreover, what takes place in Westminster Abbey is at the heart of further crucial events and rituals on coronation day—and these proceedings on coronation day are preceded and followed by additional events and processes, sometimes by several months (Fig. 2).

Given that this work adopts a thematic approach, it would be easy to lose sight of the chronological integrity of each coronation; unless a 'typical' coronation is anatomised, the diversity and inter-relationship of its components would be difficult to fully appreciate. For these reasons, set out below, in list form, is the make-up of a coronation from the Demise of the Crown to commemorations. In the interests of clarity, this scheme has been split into three parts, comprising stages leading up to a coronation; those occurring on the eve of coronation day and during the day itself; and those coming after. It should be understood that not all of these stages (or aspects) apply to every coronation, for example a parliamentary grant of taxation. Moreover, they did not always occur in the same chronological order—in fact, several elements must have occurred simultaneously, especially when the time-lapse between accession and coronation was short.

Fig. 2 King Charles III and Queen Camilla in the Gold State Coach, as part of the post-coronation procession, 6 May 2023, Rod Olukoya/Alamy Stock Photo

Even so, it will be helpful, for making sense of the remainder of this book, to keep the following basic breakdown in mind.

A. Before Coronation Day
- Demise of the Crown
- Proclamation of accession
- Proclamation announcing coronation date
- Creation of Court of Claims by letters patent
- Proclamation announcing membership of Court of Claims and inviting submission of petitions
- Searches for precedents
- Preparations at Westminster Abbey
- Commissions, for example for art, music, robes, etc.
- Meetings of Court of Claims: decisions about tenure of coronation offices
- Preparation of order of service
- Dispatch of invitations *via* Earl Marshal

- Preparations in London/Westminster: Infrastructure
- Act of Parliament granting taxation for coronation

B. Eve of Coronation and Coronation Day

- Sovereign proceeds to Tower of London (for Early Modern and Medieval coronations)
- Creation of Knights of the Bath and peers (for Early Modern and Medieval coronations)
- Public procession from Tower of London to Westminster Hall, normally through the streets of the metropolis (for Early Modern and Medieval coronations)
- Presentation of regalia to sovereign in Westminster Hall and its distribution to those chosen to carry items in procession to the theatre in Westminster Abbey
- Procession from Westminster Hall into Westminster Abbey (for Early Modern and Medieval coronations)/or Procession from Buckingham Palace to Westminster Abbey
- Coronation service:
  - Recognition and Acclamation
  - *Presentation of the Bible*
  - Sermon *(in 2023, the Sermon followed the Oath)*
  - Oath
  - Anointing
  - Investiture with regalia (orb, sceptre, swords, etc.)
  - Crowning
  - Fealty and Homage
  - Crowning and Anointing of Consort if applicable
  - Mass/Communion
- Procession from Westminster Abbey into Westminster Hall/or to Buckingham Palace
- Coronation Banquet in Westminster Hall/or at Buckingham Palace
- Eye-witness accounts:
  - Journalism
  - Ambassadorial dispatches
  - Private correspondence
  - Diaries
- Celebrations outside London/Westminster—'Street Parties'

C. After Coronation Day
- Court of Claims: Proof of service and authorisation of distribution of perquisites
- Coronation Fleet Review (Royal Navy)
- Souvenirs
- Official commemorative publications (e.g. those written by John Ogilby in 1661 and Francis Sandford in 1685)
- Bills and debts
- Anniversary commemorations

The Problems of 'The State': English/British Definitions

The idea of a coronation conjures up so many different images and concepts. In a British context, it is a word encapsulating an extraordinary history, a recent present, and the interest of yet more to be written in the future as the ceremony evolves. Few historical subjects with 'a thousand years of history' have the ability to add yet more pages to what is a journey, not just for the topic in question, but the country and nation too. This book is focussed on coronations since 973, and most especially in a Westminster Abbey setting. Before 1707, it might perhaps be better to describe those coronations as 'English', although that in itself doesn't necessarily reflect contemporary descriptions. With the Union of the Crowns in 1603, James VI of Scotland and I of England's accession changed forever the language of discussion. In the first instance, by the act of a Scottish monarch acceding to the English throne, and in the second, by his efforts to change the vocabulary of 'Great Britain' and the politico-legal structure too, with as Susan Doran expertly explores James I's 'British Project'. James did not succeed with his aims, but he was most definitely a 'contingent influence' in the idea of 'Britain' as we might know it today.[50] As Lawson-Peebles has also discussed with James's accession, 'James prepared the way for his "Pronouncement" with an improvement on John of Gaunt's deathbed speech. Because of the Union, he claimed that this

> Island, compassed with one sea [...] like a little World within it self, being intrenched and fortified round about with a natural, and yet admirable strong pond or ditch', need not concern itself with 'former feares'.[51]

It is also important to note that until 1651, there were distinct coronations taking place in Scotland. As we have seen, the changing definition of the geographical and legal entity of which the sovereign became head evolved over time. Much of coronation tradition is rooted in Anglo-Saxon practices, developed before 'England' was even unified, with one king, although as Williams and Molyneaux have discussed, English monarchs, even in the tenth century, considered and expressed the idea of being a ruler of Britain. After the Acts of Union 1707, the term British can be more readily applied, and it would therefore be anachronistic to continue to speak of 'English coronations'. Nevertheless, this is not a straightforward English/British split, for individual monarchs themselves understood the ceremonial nexus between Crown and peoples differently. For instance, when being crowned, kings and queens of England and later Britain claimed sovereignty over France long after they had ceased to possess any territory there. The last claimant was George III, whose proclamation on 26 October 1760 still included the title 'King of France', as Andrew Roberts puts it, 'a fiction dating back to Plantagenet days when the kings of England really had ruled much of the territory of their great rival'.[52] The change formally took place in 1801 as a result of the Act of Union with Ireland, with George III becoming king of the United Kingdom of Great Britain and Ireland. The *fleur de lis* (the traditional French heraldic symbol) was also dropped from the royal arms.[53] Likewise, English rulers claimed sovereignty over Scotland, even though they did not practically enjoy it. Conversely, at the Scottish coronation of Charles II at Scone in 1651, the king was crowned, asserting sovereignty over England, when he barely had control of Scotland—and Oliver Cromwell was on the march to drive him from the British Isles altogether.[54] In summary, this book relates to the Westminster Abbey tradition of coronations, which began in an Anglo-Saxon and later 'English' setting and from 1707 onward may be more readily termed 'British', but in cases where this distinction remains of further contextual importance, it will be clearly enumerated.

Having established how this book will look at the geographical or politico-legal scope of Westminster Abbey coronations, a second point also needs to be considered in relation to 'The State'. More or less everyone knows that the sovereign is Head of State in the UK. For our purposes, however, it is important to note the transformation of 'The State', from a personal to a constitutional monarchy: the transition, in other words, from the position in which the sovereign was conceptualized as having an 'estate' and ruled directly through the various organs of government to the position in which 'The State' is an abstraction independent of the person of the monarch, who no longer has a role in day-to-day governance. Even to this day, there persists, if anything, a continuing muddle in the notion of 'The Crown', and indeed 'The Crown Estate'. Members of the public are often at a loss as to what belongs to the monarch or to the State.[55] Again, where applicable or where there was (and remains) uncertainty to contemporaries, this will be made clear in the context of a coronation. The ongoing complexity of this point is made all the more so, in that monarchs have had and continue to have a direct hand in the planning of coronations, from the earliest inception of these occasions to long after the sovereign ceased to be a law-maker in any personal capacity.

Public Interest and Post-Modern Significance

King Charles III's coronation in 2023, Royal weddings, Buckingham Palace accession and coronation commemorations, the birth of new heirs to the throne, the late Queen's Platinum Jubilee celebrations, exhibitions, plays and award-winning films and drama (*The Queen*, *The Young Victoria*, *The King's Speech*, *The Crown*)—all highlight the continuing fascination with Britain's monarchy, both here and abroad.

The British public remains interested and indeed cares about the Royal family—as part of our heritage and cultural identity. This combination has created an ongoing formula for the success, and therefore importance, of royal ceremonial. Despite a fear of irrelevance, Royalty has somehow always managed to keep itself in the spotlight, or perhaps just be kept there by the general public, and thus we can find that royal events matter, most of all because we want them to matter. Relevance is maintained by intrigue—in people wanting to know about the traditions. A very clear example of this is the fascination held by other nations, particularly the USA, with all the cultural differences that exist in a presidential system. American audiences make up very large numbers indeed, an estimated 29 million television viewers for the marriage of Prince Harry and Meghan Markle.[56]

Television viewing figures/statistics are important indications of modern trends. The coronation of Elizabeth II, 1953, had 20 million viewers, outnumbering radio listeners for the very first time.[57] Approximately 10 million radio listeners were present, just over half the number of TV watchers.[58] 10.4 million watched in the homes of friends and neighbours, and 1.5 million watched in public places. In the USA, 85 million people tuned in to watch recordings of highlights. In 1973, Princess Anne and Mark Phillip's wedding had an estimated 500 million viewers worldwide.[59] Prince Charles and Lady Diana Spencer's wedding in 1981 saw 28.4 million viewers (in the UK) and up to 750 million viewers worldwide.[60] It has been argued that public interest has waned in more recent years and that people are not as enthusiastic as they once were to such occasions.[61] Yet Prince William and Kate Middleton's wedding in 2011 saw approximately 27 million viewers (just shy of 1981) and almost 23 million in the USA.[62] Prince Harry and Meghan Markle's wedding in 2018 also saw significant viewing numbers, with 18 million viewers (UK) and an estimated 29 million viewers in the USA.[63] Millions continue to view, even when there are so many viewing possibilities these days. It is one thing to watch the only programme available or from a selection of 3 or 4 stations. It is quite another when satellite TV and the internet permit innumerable streaming options. Princess Diana's funeral, in 1997, saw 32.1 million viewers in the UK alone,[64] with over 2 billion viewing the procession globally.[65] Prince Philip's funeral had more than 13 million UK viewers,[66] and the Platinum Jubilee Party had 13.3 million UK viewers.[67] We should also not forget those at the Mall or participating in celebrations up and down the country. A tradition long held. In 1838, for Queen Victoria's coronation, up to 400,000 people gathered in the London streets nearby to celebrate.[68] These are staggering statistics and all the more so when placed in a wider context. The Finale (and most-watched episode) of Game of Thrones received 13.6 million live viewers.[69] The 1966 FIFA World Cup Final—32 million viewers; the 2012 Summer Olympics Closing ceremony—24 million viewers.[70] The 2019 ICC cricket world cup had 1.6 billion live coverage viewers across the world, with 15.4 million in the UK. Queen Elizabeth II's funeral had an average of 26.5 million television viewers, and King Charles III's coronation viewing figures exceeded 18 million; this, of course, does not take into account radio, viewing in person across London, or other streaming services.[71] We can therefore see that royal spectacle is to be viewed—if it did not matter, it would not stand as some of the most-watched events in the UK and indeed globally.

A coronation stands above all other royal events. Precisely because they are infrequent, normally inaugurating reigns, coronations are momentous occasions when a monarchy and its subjects re-assess themselves, projecting their beliefs and aspirations. Connecting Crown, Church, and peoples, they therefore become crucial constitutional, political, religious, social, and cultural barometers. Take, for instance, the period 1661–1714—a mere 53 years, which encompassed the re-creation of an intolerant episcopal Church of England, the efflorescence of Protestant dissent, the Exclusion Crisis, the Glorious Revolution, a novel joint monarchy (William III and Mary II), and continental military success under Queen Anne.[72] The state was transformed: Parliamentary sovereignty, the Act of Union, the Bank of England, and the National Debt all came into being. Over five coronations, the Crown passed from the Scottish Stuarts through the Dutch House of Orange to the German Hanoverians.[73] So too in modern times, 1911–2023, has seen four coronations, two world wars, the creation of the NHS, female suffrage, and a transformation in technology across every aspect of our lives. A coronation is a snapshot in time, a window into national identity, encapsulating change and continuity and highlighting the priorities of the age. This is perhaps all the more significant or portentous given the past decade taking in referenda, with a vote on Scottish independence, and Britain's position with regard to the European Union, as well as questions on values, and an introduction of Fundamental British Values within the education system. In addition, questions have been, and continue to be, raised on Anglican disestablishment.

Historiography

Yet for all of the change and discussion that a coronation may showcase or enunciate in society, in the state, and in the concerns of the age, much of the coronation's core (set out in the manuscript *Liber Regalis* of *c.*1390) has remained essentially a medieval Roman Catholic rite—arguably quasi-sacramental—notwithstanding the tumultuous Protestant Reformations of the sixteenth century. Why was that? Clearly, many must have invested the ancient kernel with new significance. What was it? In addressing these questions, how narrow it would be to follow well-trodden research paths and to focus merely on the world of Westminster. In answering these questions, the intention is not, however, to ignore what took place in Westminster itself. On the contrary, that lies at the heart of my analysis. Despite popular myth-making about timelessness, Westminster Abbey coronations have in fact always been a dynamic amalgam of change and continuity.

The methodology is thus holistic, looking on the one hand at the ways in which Crown and Government sought to manage coronations, with particular emphasis on patronage and the projection of monarchical magnificence, and on the other hand at the ways in which different social groups and localities were drawn into proceedings—and what those experiences meant for them. 'The people' could be active, not least as consumers, and ought not to be seen as passive observers.

The key point is that it represents a new approach. Each coronation stimulates a flurry of historical inquiry into precedents, generating much in the way of publication of different forms. However, it could be said that coronation-related writing has suffered from antiquarianism (particularly in the Victorian/Edwardian period); a concentration on central, official sources; the reissuing of former works, due to lack of time; and a nearly exclusive concern with events at Westminster Abbey.[74] At times, too, it could be argued that some of these works have also been uncritically monarchist. Publications have generally tended to be limited in scope,[75] and modern, wide-ranging syntheses are rare. The standard reference work amazingly remains Leopold Wickham Legg's old-fashioned edition of 1901,[76] followed in the 1930s by Percy Schramm's account of 1937 vintage.[77]

Coronations are 'iconic' events to deploy an apt but rather overused term. Therefore, it is perhaps unsurprising that there is a vast array of primary and secondary source material associated with them. The primary source material available—whether manuscript, printed or in the form of material objects, especially works of art—is considerable and is the bedrock for this book. Secondary sources touching upon coronations, whether directly or indirectly, are also plentiful. There are numerous books on aspects of coronations, and many tangential references appear in biographies of monarchs and in works on periods that happen to have included a coronation. Although much has been written, there is, as this introduction indicates, a clear path and opportunity for offering an original and distinctive analysis of British coronations in thematic form.

Early Accounts with an Heraldic Basis

Given what could be written about coronations, especially in the light of the connections and contexts outlined above, what in fact was written? We have seen that vast arrays of relevant manuscripts exist; nevertheless, there are some surprising gaps. One major gap is that of unpublished histories of coronations in the medieval and early modern worlds. It seems likely that some once existed, but persistent searches have so far drawn a blank. On the other hand, there were probably not many—a possible explanation for the paucity (and perhaps non-survival) is that the field was so dominated by heraldic writers that there was no room for other authors. We are therefore thrown back onto the work of the heralds, some of which was printed—and this heraldic material forms a main category of printed primary evidence. Such evidence is plentiful, as the Bibliography indicates.

It is for these reasons that the historiography of coronations begins with early printed material. The books emerging from an heraldic background are fundamentally antiquarian and consist of much that might be characterised as a form of journalism, but perhaps a description as 'eyewitness' or 'contemporary historical accounts' is nearer the mark. It is not quite journalistic, in the sense that an opinionated, critical edge is lacking. These publications do not necessarily offer analysis akin to history as practised today, but they are not written without regard to what had come before, the authors also being aware of historical context. Since these pieces have proved remarkably influential in the study of coronations, it is important here to assess their significance.

Perhaps because of the remarkable nature of the Restoration—its extraordinary political impact on the British Isles, and the revelry involved in celebrating the return of monarchy—three major printed accounts deal with the 1661 coronation. Sir Edward Walker's book (see below) is perhaps the best known, but arguably more important are the works of the Scot John Ogilby. He began life in the world of dance, as a master and teacher, and eventually became master of the Revels in Ireland. Linked to the production of masques, he was heavily involved in developing theatre in Dublin before the Civil War. Following the Restoration, he climbed the greasy pole to become Charles II's leading cosmographer, geographer, and printer. He was a pioneer in publishing history, combining texts with lavish illustration. As the king's leading printer, he secured the patent granting him exclusive rights to publish commemorations of the procession and coronation. His work on the coronation exists in three very different states.[78] The earlier accounts, entitled *Relation* (London, 1661) and *Entertainment* (London, 1662), were published on either side of the coronation. The much later account, a revised version, including Charles's passage from the Tower of London to Whitehall, entitled *The King's Coronation*, emerged posthumously in 1685, seemingly intended to support the monarchy and particularly the succession of James II, with whose coronation it coincided. It was also reprinted in 1689, conceivably to fit with the coronation of William III and Mary II.[79]

As Charles Withers has argued, Ogilby drew on 'earlier traditions of triumphal royal processions', such as those of ancient Rome and the amphitheatre or stage that London became during such events.[80] The pageantry of these coronation processions had been a constant theme of Tudor monarchy, and so what happened in 1661 was a backward glance by the executive and a reminder of the sovereign's power. It was also an optimistic look to the future, with the coming together of Court and civic wealth, highlighting both royal authority and the prosperity of the City, but looking to prospective collaborative success. Ogilby was not merely producing an 'official programme book' of the processional, but one set within a classical historical context.[81] This would include numerous references to Cicero and Virgil and much poetry—something not unsurprising given both the classical themes of the triumphal arches, but also his own scholarly background, having translated and published works of Virgil from as early as 1649 and Homer's *Iliad* in 1660. His *Entertainment* is divided into two sections: the procession and the coronation. For the latter, Ogilby procured the assistance of Elias Ashmole, the famous astrologer and antiquary who was then Windsor Herald at the College of Arms. Ashmole's precise role is unclear, but, according to Michael Hunter, he amassed various accounts of past coronations and may have assisted Sir Edward Walker in the official planning of the main ceremony.[82] This second section, entitled 'A brief narrative of his Majestie's solemn coronation', is indeed a descriptive account and aims to do nothing more or less than report details of the event and the following feast in Westminster Hall. Ogilby's account lists no manuscript sources and provides nothing in the way of analysis. However, it is an exceptionally useful illustrated guide to the day's proceedings. His text was dedicated to Charles II and approved by Sir Edward Walker in his capacity as Garter Principal King of Arms; in these respects, it was clearly an official publication.[83]

The third major contributor to early coronation history was the Irish herald and genealogist Francis Sandford, with his *History*.[84] Sandford's heraldic career began in 1661 when he assumed office as Rouge Dragon Pursuivant in the College of Arms. In the 1670s, he was involved in the planning and rebuilding of the College of Arms, following the 1666 Great Fire of London. Royal appointment came in 1676 as Lancaster Herald. At the same time as this promotion, Sandford's major genealogical work, *A Genealogical History of the Kings of England and Monarchs of Great Britain … from the Conquest, Anno 1066, to the Year 1677* (London, 1677), was published, with illustrations of royal tombs and portraits.

When it came to writing on royalty, Sandford had expertise. Thus, following James II's coronation in 1685, he worked with 'fellow herald Gregory King',[85] better known as a political economist—who was by 1684 registrar of the College of Arms and had worked under Ogilby in the 1670s. Sandford's *History* was eventually published in 1687. With the coming of the Glorious Revolution, it is perhaps unsurprising that, according to Peter Sherlock, the book only just covered the author's expenses, and that includes a gift of '£300 from James II', which also highlights the publication's official nature. Whilst it is not an analytical history of the events, and tends towards propaganda, incorporating 'twenty-seven lavish engravings', it is nevertheless crucial groundwork for this coronation.[86] The illustrations include items of regalia, a plan of the Abbey, scenes of the service, and map-style layouts of Westminster. This is not merely a study of the coronation itself, but of preliminaries (including the Court of Claims) and the feasting, fireworks, and processions too.

Key printed primary evidence also includes work by the herald Sir Edward Walker,[87] whose detailed manuscript account of Charles II's coronation was published in 1820.[88] Walker was knighted in Oxford on 2 February 1644/1645, following which he was appointed Garter King of Arms. With the Restoration, he was re-installed in his position and played a major role in the organisation of the 1661 coronation. One of his other tasks was to oversee commemorations of the occasion, and he produced his own work in manuscript. However, it was not published contemporaneously, seemingly being superseded by the combined work of Ogilby and Walker's fellow herald Ashmole. It is not entirely clear why Walker's work failed to see print at the time. The most likely explanation is that Ogilby's account, with its royal patent of monopoly, had captured the market and thus appears to have rendered Walker's efforts superfluous. Nevertheless, the text is very important because not only does it include an account of the coronation itself, but significantly also details the preparations for it; Walker locates the coronation within the context of the Restoration, including the king's physical arrival in London, and his work also encompasses the importance of royal patronage.

What is striking about the early work on coronations from Ogilby, Sandford, and Walker is the inclusive nature of their projects. Coronations were seen by such heralds and contemporaries as clearly spread across three days; the civic celebrations were as important to note as the ritual of crowning itself. This approach of looking outwards from the 'Westminster bubble' to the procession and to the City of London was important for the people of the time and therefore provides a model for this book. So too these writers reached consumers beyond London. For example, Ogilby's *King's Coronation* was published in Edinburgh in 1685.

These three major contemporary contributors to early coronation history in this period are exceptionally helpful in setting out the formal arrangements in print. Other noteworthy materials exist, though falling into a different category, namely programmes; they are emphatically not historical syntheses. Examples come from 1689 (William and Mary) and 1702 (Anne) and continued to the twentieth century.[89] However, the account for William and Mary is nearer to the character of Walker's work and provides a very good base from which to assess the primary source material extant from that double coronation.[90] An important point to be noted here is that some of this material, particularly these anonymous *Forms* and Ogilby's first piece,[91] were published prospectively—they are not descriptions, but guides to what was expected to happen. Other items were published retrospectively and presumably more accurately.[92] These works are really descriptive and narrative rather than analytical, and must be treated, given the heralds' positions close to the Crown, as potential propaganda. Nevertheless, they are excellent starting points, and the genesis for coronation history, out of which the founding fathers of the secondary literature, to be considered next, built their efforts.

Founding Fathers

Our journey beyond the world of contemporary historical accounts begins with what one will term the 'Founding Fathers' of coronation history. Five writers—Christopher Wordsworth;[93] Leopold Wickham Legg and to a lesser extent John Wickham Legg; John Crichton-Stuart, 3rd Marquess of Bute; and Schramm—make up this select band, and the history of British coronations owes them a great debt.

The most notable and enduring work is that of Leopold Wickham Legg, but in chronological order of publication, the rather less well-known piece by Wordsworth, *The Manner of the Coronation of King Charles the First ... at Westminster 2 Feb. 1626 ...* (London, 1892), is our starting point. Printed posthumously, this book was one of the earliest publications of the newly founded Henry Bradshaw Society for the propagation of knowledge of the liturgy of the Church of England. Though on nothing near the same scale as Leopold Wickham Legg, Wordsworth still compiled a fascinating edition of primary sources, principally surrounding Charles

I's February 1626 coronation, but also including invaluable details on James II's 1685 coronation and Archbishop William Sancroft's notes about it. According to Margaret Pawley, he remained, like his father, 'constant to the high-churchmanship of the seventeenth- and eighteenth-century tradition, rather than that of the Tractarians'. Perhaps, therefore, the reason for his choice of subject matter was his position as an Anglican bishop, and a high churchman at that—this made it fitting for him to assess Laudianism under Charles I and to wish to address the issue of the Church of England crowning a Roman Catholic king, in the person of James II. The main line of argument (perhaps unsurprisingly given his Establishment status) is to underline the crucial episcopal role in the various coronations. This point is important (and will be explored fully in Chap. 3) because it emphasises a coronation as an event of huge significance for the Church of England itself. Moreover, it was an opportunity to set the religious agenda at the beginning of each reign.

Over a century on, Leopold Wickham Legg's *Records* (London, 1901) remain a crucial resource for coronation research. It is a testament to his diligence in the archives that his editorial efforts continue to contribute to nearly every modern piece of scholarship on this subject. These records include coronation orders, letters, and notes from before the Norman Conquest right up to Queen Victoria. His reproduction of the *Liber Regalis* in full paved the way for future historians to be able accurately to ascertain coronation procedure from Henry IV onwards, on the basis of the scheme (technically known as the fourth recension) to which each one adhered. In the later Middle Ages, the volume containing this rite was in the custody of Westminster Abbey, and the Abbey Library still houses the *Liber Regalis* (MS 38), which is the classic version of the medieval text. The *Liber Regalis* (a Latin composition of *c.*1390) sets out: the presentation of the monarch to the people, the Coronation Oath and anointing, the offering of the ornaments to the sovereign (including the sword, bracelets, mantle, ring and sceptre), the crowning and trumpet fanfare, and, lastly, the mass. The *Liber Regalis* was extended into an all-encompassing order, entitled the 'Little Device', for Richard III's coronation, detailing not only the office but also the events of the day before; the latter order provided the model for all coronations that have followed.[94] However, Legg's reproduction of the *Liber Regalis* has been allowed to stand without question until now. This lack of critical scrutiny is of tremendous importance in relation to the Coronation Oath, for Legg, although he translated the rest of the service into English, failed to translate the oath itself, instead referring the reader to the oath as embedded in the English coronation service for Charles I, printed later in his edition. This editorial practice was both eccentric and misleading because the Caroline oath differs in important particulars from that of *c.*1390. In the light of this revelation, therefore, any analysis of the oath section of the *Liber Regalis* must be revised.

The *Liber Regalis* aside, Legg's *ad fontes* approach, a precursor to the Eltonian ethos, stands up to examination because it is founded on rich veins of primary source material. Bute, with his *Scottish Coronations* (London, 1902), continued this empirical tradition, which culminated in Schramm's *A History of the English Coronation* (Oxford, 1937), translated by none other than Legg.[95] John Wickham Legg's work also deserves brief mention. His contribution on James I's coronation has been particularly useful for piecing together the puzzle of the Stuart Coronation Oath, as will be revealed in Chap. 4.[96] Legg's short article on the Coronation Ring was exceptionally helpful in drawing out the idea of a coronation as being akin to a marriage ceremony, symbolised by the customary receiving and wearing of a ring.[97]

Whilst these 'founding fathers' produced works that are more accurately characterised as 'antiquarian', they were, nevertheless, meticulously researched for the time in which they were written, using the available resources, and in many cases are reproductions of texts. It could also be said that some of the lack of critical assessment rests more on a failure to ask the questions that really are the questions of today and not those of the 1901 British Empire in Leopold Wickham Legg's case. Nevertheless, it is remarkable, given his influence, that a figure whose father was a distinguished liturgical scholar, and who was an early editor of the *Dictionary of National Biography*, remains unnoticed in the new *Oxford Dictionary of National Biography*.[98]

Furthermore, there has tended to be a failure to ask a key question: what of coronations for those beyond Westminster Abbey? No one has attempted a systematic and detailed analysis of the records available from the length and breadth of the British Isles. Schramm's excellent work, and all the more interesting given its 1930's Germanic background, tacitly admits, regarding his own efforts, the danger of 'swamping':

> ... we must bring this study to a close – not, however, because there is no more to be said, for the subject is wellnigh inexhaustible.[99]

This book has not merely reproduced primary sources, nor has it been willing to shy away from the voluminous records available; but rather, it provides (*inter alia*) a detailed analysis of the significance of the trickle or ripple effect of this most archaic, steadfast, and essential of royal ceremonies. We now turn from contributions that were editions of primary sources to those that are secondary sources, attempting to provide a synthesis (Schramm) or to address aspects of coronations (David Sturdy *et al.*).

It is worth noting that as one of the major contributions to English coronation history, Schramm's 1937 book was not a home-grown enterprise, but instead emerged out of German interest. His conclusion includes a striking passage comparing a British coronation to the festivals being constructed in connection with the rise of twentieth-century Fascism in Italy and Germany.[100] Schramm could little know the devastation that such a political philosophy would bring, but his comparison demands attention. Fascist parades and other meetings held in Berlin, Munich, and Nuremberg sought to invent new traditions, in much the same vein as the phenomena discussed in *The Invention of Tradition*.[101] Allusions to Ancient Rome were a key part of the propaganda. Coronations likewise invented traditions and drew links to forefathers, as well as to biblical and other ancient civilizations. However, what is so very different about a British coronation is that, in many respects, it transcends the political philosophy of a Fascist or indeed Communist parade. This is no Red Square party or Nuremburg rally. On the contrary, we find a deeply spiritual, indeed sacramental, tradition that is born less of political philosophy and more of pragmatism and political expediency. Whatever the changing nature of royal and later parliamentary politics, of Whig or Tory party, of Liberal, Labour, or Conservative Party, British coronations remained essentially constant: adapted to be sure, but in their fundamentals immutable from their medieval origins—not 'instant' history.

However, Schramm is absolutely correct in suggesting that a coronation 'is a day on which past, present, and future meet'. It is worth quoting his very words:

> This is to-day more than ever true, now that the inventions of modern science turn us all into spectators and listeners. The courtly and elaborate consecration service in which but few could have a direct share has become the celebration of a people numbered by the million – a popular festival in the

> more profound sense that on that day all members of the Empire, becoming conscious of their common life, remember that the history of a thousand years is their common heritage, that an individuality which this history has formed binds them together, and that a living representative, the king of Great Britain, Ireland, and the British dominions beyond the seas is their own in common.[102]

Nevertheless, findings presented in this book indicate that, in some respects, Schramm is very wide of the mark. Well in advance of photography, the wireless, or even the internet, coronation celebrations were taking place across the realm. It is this hitherto barely explored dimension of coronations that is a particular focus of this project.

Later Scholarship

Beyond the founding fathers, Sturdy was the most recent historian to delve in detail into aspects of coronation history. For our purposes, two short articles are notable: one on sermons and the other on historiography. The earlier essay, on coronation sermons 1603–1689, reveals how the Established Church used these keynote speeches to project its views of kingship and its religio-political aims for society. Sturdy's work crucially reveals the continuity of Divine Right ideology throughout the period, in that 'the first four coronation preachers showed themselves to be devotees of the idea of the divine right of kings' and even as late as 1689, 'Burnet did not deny the proposition'. Yet Sturdy does not pursue this fascinating insight, claiming that whilst seventeenth-century sermons played important roles as broadcasts for new regimes, eighteenth-century coronation sermons, by contrast, were brief pitches lacking content. Chapter 2 will reveal a different picture. It is true that the disquisitions of 1702 and 1714 may not have approached the length of George Morley's 1661 effort, but they still had significant messages to proclaim—and they continued to express similar themes, especially in projecting the idea of a divinely sanctioned monarchy.[103] Sturdy's later work provides a rare and perceptive analysis of coronation historiography over the last 120 years. It is particularly valuable in drawing attention to the problems in assessing change versus continuity in a topic especially characterised by tradition. He sets out the importance of a coronation in terms of its impact on society and the legitimacy afforded to a sovereign, for

> the coronation was an occasion that united all the cultural and celebratory impulses of society into one great carnival with a single point or focus: the king and queen. The ceremony of crowning and anointing the monarch served the legitimation process in respect of tradition and custom and of legality; its attendant festivities served the cult of the charismatic leader.[104]

Coronations are therefore essential 'topics for historical inquiry', but they have a significance 'beyond the minutiae of the ritual itself' because 'their history can augment and refine our understanding of themes in constitutional, political and social history'. Sturdy offers the simile of a 'blood test', in that a coronation gives one a sense of the general condition of the state, and of the position of the monarch, at the outset of each reign. In this regard, coronations, 'if they are understood in the widest sense of comprising processions and festivities as well as the crowning of the monarch, can inform us as to the temper of a community, even of a nation'. Just as with the context of the typical coronation sermon, the entire complex of events can be seen to project, 'either consciously or unconsciously', the 'aspirations and concerns' of the country at that juncture.[105] Yet, as Sturdy rightly points out, that does not mean that it is easy to construct an 'all-embracing' theory in relation to coronation history:

> To the question 'what happened?' in the case of an individual coronation, rarely is it possible to supply a precise and detailed answer. The surviving evidence often is too fragmentary or self-contradictory to sustain dogmatic interpretations.[106]

Those who have propagated such interpretations may have had an agenda or 'been inspired by aspirations other than a dispassionate pursuit of historical research'.[107] An example is the Whig interpretation of history, maintaining that Divine Right ideology ended with Charles I's execution, and, if not at that point, then certainly with the Glorious Revolution. Nevertheless, this claim oversimplifies and misconstrues the evidence available. For as this book will argue, the Divine Right of Kings lived on within coronation ritual long after these events and became coupled to an evolving constitutional monarchy. However, a note of caution is needed in regard to Sturdy's own analysis. Having made clear the dangers of generating overarching, catch-all theories, he falls into exactly that trap by branding post-1689 coronations as 'shadows of the great ceremonies of earlier periods'. No substantive evidence is furnished to support this bold assertion, even though it looked beyond the specific timeframe that he had set for his inquiry. His analysis emphatically does **not** fit the coronations of 1702, 1714, and 1821, or the coronations of the twentieth century or indeed 2023.[108]

Finally, and perhaps most importantly, Sturdy made clear the contractualism inherent in the medieval Coronation Oath, and therefore, by extension, the whole coronation rite. In doing so, he is one of the few historians to have used John Brückmann's unpublished thesis. As will become apparent in Chap. 3, the development of the Coronation Oath in the Middle Ages was immensely complex and has generated considerable controversy. Brückmann's contribution, examining the oath in the context of the whole *ordo*, is significant because it underlines the contractualism present within the promises and thus stresses the limitations on royal power.[109]

Since writing about coronations tends to proliferate around them, it follows that the last major outpouring (prior to 2023) was in 1953. These include, for instance, Randolph Churchill's *The Story of the Coronation* (London, 1953) and Lewis Broad's *Queens, Crowns and Coronations* (London, 1937, revised edition 1952)—a work intended for the crowning of Edward VIII, but in the end first produced for King George VI.[110] As the death of a monarch is not 'predictable', it follows that many of these works have to be hastily put together in order to meet the timeframe of a coronation, as in Broad's case. Similar works accompanied the accession and coronation of Charles III in 2023, including an array of biographies.[111]

As remarked at the start of this Introduction, coronations are rare occasions on which the monarchy and its subjects re-assess themselves, projecting their beliefs and aspirations. Although there are set components that have become traditional, a monarch is no automaton, and in many respects becomes an actor—in the sense that the sovereign is actively involved in 'playing a part' and can therefore directly influence the outcome. There is also an element of theatricality, in that a role can be laid down in a script and yet performed very differently depending on the actor and the quality of the acting. So too in a coronation, a monarch takes on a well-defined role, but how they perform it may rest on the exigencies of the moment and could alter perceptions, in the context of expectations. Ronald Hutton, writing about Charles II, stated that 'the overall impression was one of royal confidence and magnificence, and, of course; everybody agreed that the monarch himself played his part wonderfully'.[112] Alice

Hunt's work on Tudor coronations looks directly at this theatrical side, comparing the ceremony to the drama of contemporaneous playwrights.[113] Building on Hunt's insights in establishing such a link, this book considers the dramatic dimension to what was 'staged', both inside and outside Westminster Abbey, for a later period.

Sir Roy Strong's 2005 book, *Coronation: A History of Kingship and the British Monarchy* (and reissued in 2022), is the most well-known book-length survey in recent decades and exceptionally rich in visual material, from illuminated manuscripts to television stills, but with Westminster Abbey as the central focus of the project. This book looks to go beyond those walls, taking into account material from across the UK (and abroad)—in essence, a reception history.

Reception History

Anybody who sees coronations as exercises in hidebound ceremonialism only involving the sovereign and the social elite, and of interest merely to traditionalist political and constitutional historians, is much mistaken. The global interest in the 2023 ceremony is a case in point, as discussed above. On the contrary, it is now possible, given recent historiographical trends, to ask exciting, fresh questions, and to use sources unknown to our predecessors, many of which this project has identified for the first time and which make up the substantial body of archival material used in this book. Ongoing cataloguing at the National Archives (Kew) and elsewhere in London is uncovering a profusion of government material unknown to previous generations of scholars. So too, and arguably even more importantly, the post-war creation of local records offices, enriched through the deposit of family, municipal, and ecclesiastical documents, and now furnished with searchable electronic catalogues, has facilitated the addition of an exciting new dimension, potentially challenging received interpretations. That new dimension is the overall significance of a coronation as its impact spread, ripple-like, outward from Westminster Abbey, nationally and internationally. In short, this can be termed reception history. How was a coronation marked provincially and, later, in the empire and the commonwealth? Who was the driving force, and why? What did remote celebrations mean to participants and observers? To what extent were they reported? How far did they foster a sense of British identity?

Such a project, with the overarching aim of delineating changing national identities, contributing to debates stimulated by the work of

Linda Colley[114] and on the ramifications of the Royal Supremacy,[115] is only feasible with considerable contextualization, on various levels. Indeed, that contextualization may itself only be achieved by adopting a multidisciplinary approach, which is to recognize the many-sided nature of English–British coronations. The high-point may indeed be the crowning, but that act is surrounded by processions, sacred rituals, preaching, feasting, artistic activity, music-making, and (from the seventeenth century) a pervasive commemorative commercialism.

Using a wealth of unexploited archival material, much of it unique—letters, diaries, dispatches, newspapers, sermons, poems, plays, musical compositions, drawings, paintings, photographs, films, medals, costumes, menus, warrants, memoranda, financial accounts, and civic muniments—this book uncovers the extraordinary creativity unleashed by the need to stage an English–British coronation and then assesses the impact and significance of the resulting concatenation of events, wherever they may have occurred. Importantly, objects are treated on a par with documents. This book traces developments **across** coronations thematically, not in a reign-by-reign approach, but recognises the conscious harking back to St Edward the Confessor that is a feature from 1066 onward. The Coronation Oath and the parallelism with matrimony of a coronation—the idea, indeed argument, that the coronation is the monarch's symbolic marriage to the state—is set out fully. Above all, this book asks (and seeks to answer) searching questions. What (from various perspectives) are coronations for? Does an anointed sovereign become a quasi-sacerdotal figure? What is revealed about changing values? Have coronations engendered a bringing together of the nation? Do they still matter? In all of this, for the very first time in the history of coronations, this book presents findings from two surveys of school children across the UK (as part of this research project), with particular reference to what they think about such events, and notably the 2023 coronation, and how that impacts or impacted their views on monarchy.

The main argument of this book, and something of a counter-intuitive one, is that coronations, whilst undoubtedly of vital importance to the person or persons being crowned, were of even greater importance to their subjects, and critical too (in various ways) for the state, when it makes sense to speak of the state as an abstract entity distinct from the monarch on one hand and from the people on the other. Moreover, the significance of the coronation to the sovereign (or queen consort) lay less in the act of crowning than in what had preceded it, not only during the service itself but also during the weeks of preparation leading up to the sacred rite. Correspondingly, there was massive royal investment—politically, artistically, and (latterly) commercially—in all that came next, once the service had ended, and for weeks, possibly months, thereafter. Yet those efforts were dwarfed by local initiatives and by speculative concerns. The economic ramifications were huge. More than events at the heart of the nation, stirring though those were, it was the holding of myriad celebrations far and wide, plus the emergence of a vibrant commemorative culture, which lent to diverse peoples a sense of shared identity under the auspices of the Crown.

Overview of Some Types of Primary Sources

In view of the important role that manuscript sources have played in the Coronation Project at King's College London, and given the discussion above of relevant secondary literature that uses some of this material, certain general remarks are appropriate here. The first point concerns the enormous diversity of what survives: there are numerous items, ranging from detailed notes on the coronation procession, for example on the role of the barons of the Cinque Ports, to heraldic instructions on coronation offices; from draft oaths to letters of summons (invitations), and from private correspondence to bills of account.[116] Of material objects, coins and medals feature widely. One does not have to look far to uncover tremendous deposits of data relating to these extraordinary occasions. Besides the predictable London, Oxford, and Cambridge archives, research has been undertaken in many libraries, private collections, and county record offices across the country and indeed internationally, from Scottish and Irish archives to the USA. This approach has helped further understand the reach of coronations, of the pervasive way these events have permeated every corner of the land (and beyond). Important information on key aristocratic families involved in coronations, such as the Howard dukes of Norfolk, the Cavendish dukes of Devonshire, and the Howard Earls of Carlisle, was obtained in private collections at Arundel Castle, Chatsworth House, and Castle Howard.[117] The heralds, who had extremely important roles in coronation organisation and reportage under the Earl marshal's jurisdiction, left behind an immense body of miscellaneous manuscripts in the College of Arms, some related items having migrated to the Society of Antiquaries of London. Institutionally and topographically, the City of London played a significant part in these events; material relating to those dimensions can be found in the London Metropolitan Archives. A wider metropolitan perspective was gained from holdings in the National Army Museum and the National Art Library. Provincial corporation records were also brought into view. For example, material to do with coronations can be found in Warwickshire, in the Stratford-upon-Avon borough muniments deposited in the Shakespeare Centre Library and Archive. Coronations impacted far and wide, with a ripple factor spreading outwards from the Westminster Abbey epicentre. As should now be clear, with respect to coronations, there is not, and there never was, one organic archival core. This situation is unlike that for many other topics in which State participation is central. The reason for the anomaly boils down to a combination of infrequency and multiplicity of players, not all State servants, with the first factor perhaps the more important. The rarity of coronations—for example the huge gaps between February 1326/1327 and 1377, between 1509 and February 1546/1547 and between January 1558/1559 and 1603—prevented the creation of a responsible department with its own single record store, of the kind that tends to occur as a result of routine processes. Even today, the Coronation Roll does not capture the event beyond Westminster Abbey or indeed the wider discussion of planning.[118] In other words, precisely because the turnover of sovereigns was so unusual, no bureaucratic system of recording details in series form (and then of carefully preserving those records) ever emerged, and this has continued to this day. There was little to be gained by doing so, for (given average life spans in the Middle Ages and under the Tudors and Stuarts) few people were likely to see more than one coronation. No great incentive to diligent record-keeping existed. The most that was expected was that (at least from Edward II's reign) a formal account (including Court of Claims adjudications) was to be deposited in Chancery, but the fact that C 57 contains major gaps tells its own story.[119] What is left to us, therefore, survives haphazardly and is often widely dispersed. It is this lack of a coherent documentary base that makes any comprehensive efforts at coronation study ambitious but worthwhile for what can be uncovered, for it has been necessary to piece together myriad fragments in order to reconstruct what took place in the examples and themes covered in this book, and why.

A major theme of this work is that there were far more facets to a coronation than one might assume, that those facets sometimes involved groups of people beyond the obvious ones, and that they inevitably had broad implications, not least for patronage and cost. Those facets generated their own documentation. As noted above, it is impossible, in the scope of one book, to explore all aspects of interest, but these themes delve further than ever before.

Challenges

Given the scale of the British Coronation Project, it is not inappropriate to acknowledge that it has faced a number of significant challenges. These challenges can be grouped into the following categories: archival, source-related, and practical. On the archival front, the most significant problem is scale—the vastness of what is available, both in the UK and globally. In many archives, volumes of miscellaneous items often provide items relating to coronations, without any meaningful cataloguing, categorisation, order, or dating. In essence, more is and will be found. In terms of source-related challenges, the most notable have been the gaps. It will come as no surprise, given what has already been said about the Court of Claims, that many of its internal papers seem to have disappeared. Another important gap is the Coronation Oath of Elizabeth I. The text has never been found, which means that we hypothesise about what was said, but the precise form of words is left open to question. The implications of this situation are severe: we cannot be entirely certain whether James I was therefore an innovator, or whether he merely continued a radical step taken by his predecessor. Thirdly, there is the practical challenge of length and scope (as will be covered below). Perhaps the best that can be said is that, as with almost all historical inquiry, there is much more to be done: this book should be seen as the first part of the British Coronation Project's analysis.

Timeframe and Scope

A book looking to cover chronologically the history of each and every coronation in Britain, with contextualisation and asking searching questions, would render itself unwieldy simply in terms of length. Yet, the scope of this work in referencing a timeframe going back to the Anglo-Saxons allows us to thematically explore what our forebears looked back to. For coronations have always sought to reflect on precedent, whilst highlighting the priorities of a new age. This is not a final word on coronations and further publications are intended, but rather the first of a number of complementary publications. As such, I am fully appreciative that it cannot examine all that is important. Nevertheless, this thematic approach allows for the exploration of so many of the most important questions that surround coronations. Because each coronation references its predecessors, recalling in various respects even medieval precedents, it is crucial to range back and forth between periods so as to highlight crucial changes and continuities. In many instances, case studies have been selected so as to provide exemplars for the wider picture.

Conclusion

In nearly all chapters of this book, it has been necessary to take a backward glance at the medieval and, in turn, the Tudors (with the creation of the Royal Supremacy during the Break with Rome in the 1530s and its re-creation in 1559) and the Stuarts (because of the Civil Wars, the 1651 coronation and the Protectorate). We see, for example, that the Roman Catholic heritage mentioned above survived the worsening factionalism in the early Stuart Church of England.[120] Was Divine Right ideology destroyed, or merely modified, by the crisis of military conflict? What, for instance, should one make of the fact that a 1656 coin, showing the Protectorate's coat of arms, also displays an imperial crown?[121] How far were these events truly symbolic of a changing nation? How adaptive was royalty and who pushed adaptation? Consider the issue of cost, for a coronation involves huge expenditure. Writing about the conventional procession from the Tower of London to Westminster, Schramm wondered 'how large a proportion of the year's revenue must have been squandered on this one day. An extravagance, yet ... the records of contemporaries reveal ... the deep impression made on every occasion by this ride.' A 1660 source gives (not necessarily accurately) an abstract of the financial accounts for several coronations, recording total disbursements of £17,285 (Mary I), £14,338 (Elizabeth I) and £9,492 (James I). The extraordinary cost begs various questions: Is such a thing 'worth it'? Did sovereigns have to borrow extensively (how much? from whom?) to pay for coronations? If so, then how long did it take to clear the debts? Or if some finance came *via* taxation, then with what willingness was it granted and paid? And how was the money administered: by the Exchequer, the Chamber, the Privy Purse, or by some other department(s)?[122] But as we shall see, it is important not to conceptualize outlay purely in terms of cost to the Crown and to central government; local events also necessitated expenditure. And the profusion of events itself raises further questions relating to perception. Chapters 5 and 6 deal with exactly some of these questions and explore in detail for the first time coronation finances for the period 1661–1714. What were the perceptions of those, lay and clerical, present in the Abbey? How was a coronation viewed at Weymouth, Manchester, or Edinburgh?—places all known, for example, to have hosted major celebrations in 1661. In other words, it is crucial to look outwards from the London–Westminster nexus and to consider not only what happened but also how it was understood. In Chap. 9, we take this to the present with the first ever nationwide polling of school children and their views of monarchy and the 2023 coronation. In so doing, we also see the ongoing relevance or importance in their eyes of the Coronation Oath.

The earlier reference to a commemorative coin hints at the striking range of sources that are available and at the different disciplines that have been brought to bear upon them: documentary analysis, theology, political thought, art history, and economics, to name only some. Such a multiplicity of disciplines is unsurprising given the many-sided nature of coronations themselves: processions, sacred rituals, preaching, patronage, music, and art. Therefore, this book has taken an imaginatively thematic approach, exploring what royal occasions—in planning, execution, reportage, and commemoration—reveal more broadly about the British past. Complex questions like these cannot be answered unless one breaks free from the confines of an antiquarian, Westminster-centric mentality. Cataloguing at the National Archives (Kew) and elsewhere in London has uncovered a wealth of government material unknown to previous historians, which has been analysed. However, the post-war emergence of county record offices, enriched through the deposit of family and parochial records, and now furnished with searchable electronic catalogues, has made possible the addition of an exciting new dimension, perhaps making received interpretations vulnerable to challenge. In exploiting these unofficial and local records, the broader significance of a coronation has been revealed, as the impact of these events spread, ripple-like, outward from Westminster, nationally and even internationally. As David Cressy has shown, royal events and their commemoration have profound implications for the country at large.[123] Moreover, coronations involve the creation of original music and art; the art-historical dimension of the topic is substantial, as highlighted (in a general sense) by John King and (more particularly) by Bruce Lenman.[124] Using many unique manuscript sources—eye-witness testimony, diaries, correspondence, sermons, poetry, plays, newspapers, financial accounts, and civic muniments—the processions, feastings, artistic activities, music-making, and commemorative commercialism permeating society have been exposed. Coronations were massive events whose influence filtered into so many aspects of society in the early modern world. In investigating all of these questions, brief indicative comparisons will be made with Protestant, Catholic, and Orthodox European countries, though a fuller comparative analysis must await another occasion.[125]

It is, of course, impossible in a project of this length to cover every aspect of a coronation, and in a number of instances, case studies have been used to render the project accessible in length. Therefore, this book has taken key themes to analyse, within which individual chapters explore key elements of a coronation, some often underinvestigated or at times misunderstood. Part I: 'Rituals & Religion' accesses the central role of religion within a Westminster Abbey coronation and its enduring presence from the Anglo-Saxon to the present era, with chapters on the Anointing and British Coronation Sermons. The latter seeing a return to the service for the first time since 1911, a reminder that whilst much endures, the coronation ceremony has been an evolving tradition through centuries. Coronation sermons provide valuable insights into the priorities of each new reign and the influence that a coronation had beyond Westminster (with sermons countrywide). A rough indication of duration has been established for the first time, on the grounds that this may well have had a bearing on impact, and the emphases of each sermon set out. These keynote speeches also underscore continuities and changes that took place, for example the importance of the nation whether English or British; the desire for justice and the rule of law; the providentialist beliefs that accompanied each accession; and the shift from a post-Regicide nation state to a rapidly expanding imperial power. This books argues that within the coronation rite, Divine Right ideology persisted, long after it has been suggested to have lessened or died, and that the rite of coronation, particularly in the anointing, was a form of consecration that was as important for Elizabeth II or Charles III as it was for William of Orange and for the Lutheran George I or their medieval forebears. Building on the work of Kevin Sharpe, this chapter challenges the argument alleging a demystification of monarchy, pointing out that touching for the King's Evil was revived by Queen Anne and that there were surprising continuities in terms of sacral relic symbolism in the shape of St Edward's Staff, and new objects and symbols created even in the twenty-first century.[126] Chapter 1 also explores to what extent a monarch was seen as akin to a priest, in other words, elevated to a quasi-sacerdotal position, and the popular support for these ideas. Nevertheless, changes did take place, and it will be shown how the status of the Bible was elevated within the service, particularly from 1689 onwards through Bishop Compton's revisions, and how Divine Right concepts evolved into a providentialist Divine Right theory, readily attuned to the dramatic growth of Britain as a burgeoning Empire. Part II: 'Oaths & Objects' looks at the tangible items of a coronation in Swords—so often referenced in 2023, and other relics of coronations past. Chapter 3 of this section examines the Coronation Oath in light of contract and the analogy of marriage to the state, something expressed globally during media coverage of Charles III's coronation.[127] This chapter also shows just why this oath was so immensely important for the British Constitution and, indeed, has remained so to the present day. This book argues that the Coronation Oath should be seen as akin to a contract and as a development of Magna Carta. Crucially, the oath is contextualised within the rest of the coronation rite, which places it, according to tradition, after the contractual acclamation and before the sacral (consecration) stages of anointing and crowning. Also highlighted is the fact (significantly neglected) that by 1714, there were two distinct Coronation Oaths, one for England (later distinguishable as the British oath) and one for Scotland. Part III: 'Senses, Expenditure & Participation' showcases the feasting and street party nature of these events, far beyond London, and in Chap. 6 sets out the cost of these remarkable occasions, in an original approach, 'to follow the money', for no aspect of a coronation, whether central or local, was cost-free. Indeed, the costs were huge, especially for the coronation banquet. Who was spending the money, why funds were spent in a certain way and why they were perhaps spent differently from one coronation to another are important questions to be explored, with conclusions, which are indicative of wider changes during so many eras of flux, including novel patterns of thought. Michael Braddick's work on 'the birth of the tax state' during the seventeenth century,[128] and his analysis of parliamentary taxation, and the relationship between central government and 'locality' during the rise of an 'increasingly powerful' State, is wonderfully researched and provides the foundation on which to explore (in Chap. 6) the main financial themes of this book.[129] Part III therefore brings together an appreciation of national identity linked to coronations *via* celebration and expense. By revealing the true magnitude of costs, this book further undermines the argument that spending on coronations declined and that these events mattered less to the Crown, the State, and the public at large. Furthermore, this chapter indicates how widespread was the impact of coronations, with examples of celebrations drawn from up and down the country, from urban environments, such as Bath, Bristol, Chester, and Nottingham, to rural parishes in Gloucestershire and Sussex. The financial commitment and jubilation did not end there, with celebrations beyond the British Isles, for instance in the colony of Leghorn (now Livorno) on the Tuscan coast in 1714, which were also reported in the English press. This book argues that coronations had become days of national rejoicing preceding the Act of Union—what had changed was that they had become days financed by the nation too. The final thematic section, Part IV: 'Material Remembrance & Responses' looks at coins and medals that endure far beyond the time in which they were made, providing a longevity and link to coronations past. Chapter 8 looks significantly at what went wrong, from major incidents to rioting and critiques of these events. The concluding Chap. 9 draws many of these threads together and breaks fresh ground in providing new research on what school children think of such history and such events, thus allowing for an exploration and analysis of impact even to the present day.

Coronations mattered to contemporaries and continue to matter. If the coronation was of considerable moment in any era, to both rich and poor, governed and ruler alike, then we need to try and find out why. This research is also valuable because knowledge of the permeation of regal power beyond the political and administrative centre can impact other historical debates about the country. The widespread nature of this filtration, seemingly spontaneous since signs of coercion prove elusive, suggests that we need to re-consider Britain's character, in respect of the idea of a nation state. We should question the notion that there was a separation between major Court and metropolitan events on the one hand and the concerns of provincial society on the other. This book is therefore, in a sense, building upon a confessionalization paradigm used of the religio-political interdependence of state-building initiatives, but now applied to a whole country under the auspices of the Royal Supremacy.[130] Long before the Act of Union, but with a greater sense of nationhood than before the Reformations, we see the development of a nation, with a providentialist protestant Anglican outlook at its heart. The topic of coronations is utterly distinctive, for few, if any, other event, or series of events, whether courtly or civic, combined and continues to combine state resources, holy sanction through the national Church, the involvement of the social elite (in the post-modern world—celebrity), and the participation of the general populace. Coronations may not have happened very often, but they made up for that with their unique power.

Appendix I: Coronation Timeline since 1066

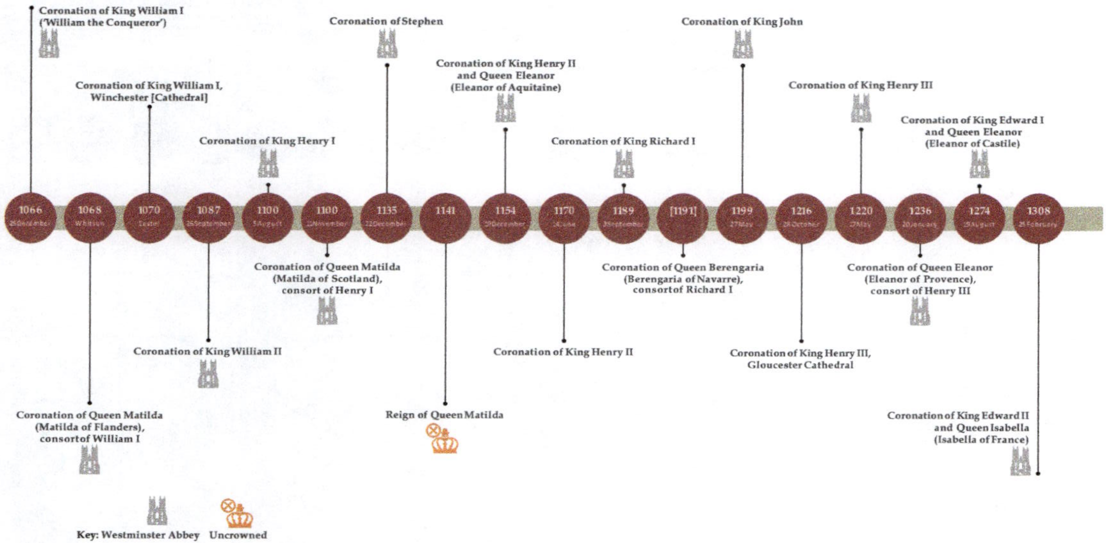

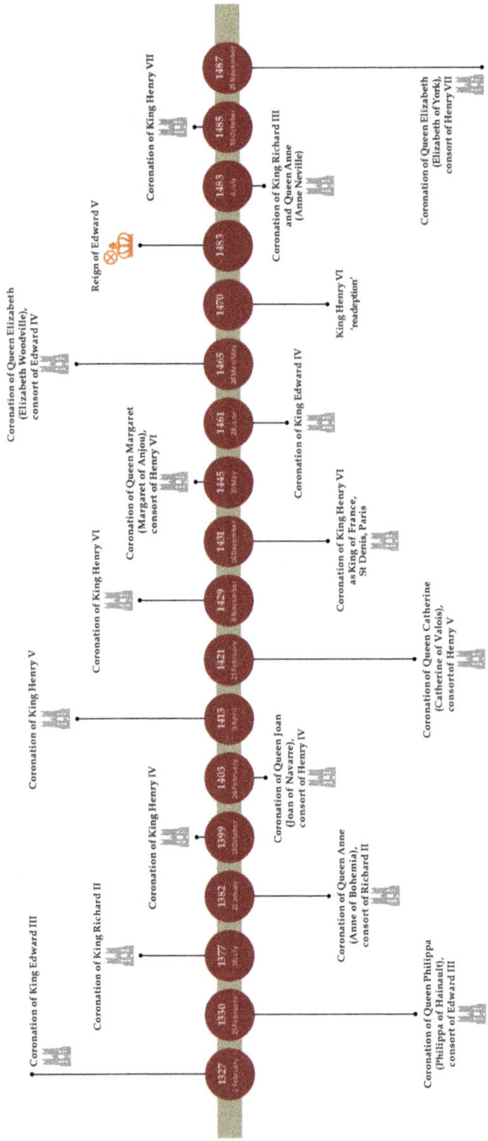
1327
Coronation of King Edward III
1330
Coronation of Queen Philippa (Philippa of Hainault), consort of Edward III
1377
Coronation of King Richard II
1382
Coronation of Queen Anne (Anne of Bohemia), consort of Richard II
1399
Coronation of King Henry IV
1403
Coronation of Queen Joan (Joan of Navarre), consort of Henry IV
1413
Coronation of King Henry V
1421
Coronation of Queen Catherine (Catherine of Valois), consort of Henry V
1429
Coronation of King Henry VI
1431
Coronation of King Henry VI as King of France, St Denis, Paris
1445
Coronation of Queen Margaret (Margaret of Anjou), consort of Henry VI
1461
Coronation of King Edward IV
1465
Coronation of Queen Elizabeth (Elizabeth Woodville), consort of Edward IV
1470
King Henry VI 'readeption'
1483
Reign of Edward V
1483
Coronation of King Richard III and Queen Anne (Anne Neville)
1485
Coronation of King Henry VII
1487
Coronation of Queen Elizabeth (Elizabeth of York), consort of Henry VII

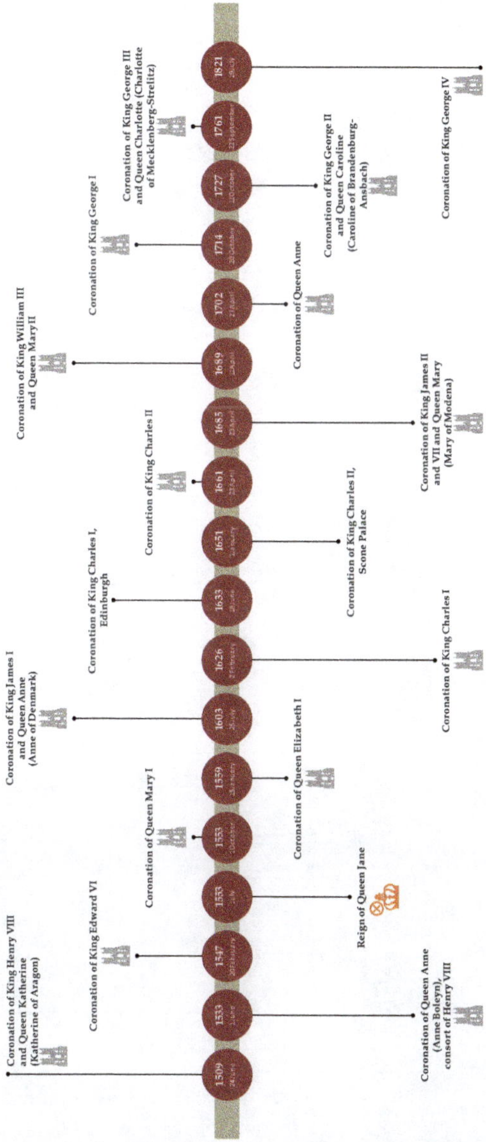
1509
Coronation of King Henry VIII and Queen Katherine (Katherine of Aragon)
1533
Coronation of Queen Anne (Anne Boleyn), consort of Henry VIII
1547
Coronation of King Edward VI
1553
Reign of Queen Jane
1553
Coronation of Queen Mary I
1559
Coronation of Queen Elizabeth I
1603
Coronation of King James I and Queen Anne (Anne of Denmark)
1626
Coronation of King Charles I
1633
Coronation of King Charles I, Edinburgh
1651
Coronation of King Charles II, Scone Palace
1661
Coronation of King Charles II
1685
Coronation of King James II and VII and Queen Mary (Mary of Modena)
1689
Coronation of King William III and Queen Mary II
1702
Coronation of Queen Anne
1714
Coronation of King George I
1727
Coronation of King George II and Queen Caroline (Caroline of Brandenburg-Ansbach)
1761
Coronation of King George III and Queen Charlotte (Charlotte of Mecklenburg-Strelitz)
1821
Coronation of King George IV

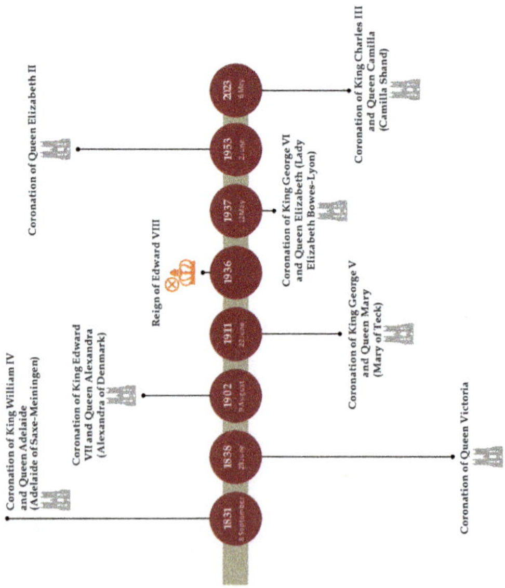
1831
Coronation of King William IV and Queen Adelaide (Adelaide of Saxe-Meiningen)
1838
Coronation of Queen Victoria
1902
Coronation of King Edward VII and Queen Alexandra (Alexandra of Denmark)
1911
Coronation of King George V and Queen Mary (Mary of Teck)
1936
Reign of Edward VIII
1937
Coronation of King George VI and Queen Elizabeth (Lady Elizabeth Bowes-Lyon)
1953
Coronation of Queen Elizabeth II
2023
Coronation of King Charles III and Queen Camilla (Camilla Shand)

Notes

1. KJV (1 Kings 1: 34).
2. https://avalon.law.yale.edu/medieval/ang11.asp (*The Anglo-Saxon Chronicle: Eleventh Century*), accessed 13 March 2025, from the first entry referring to 'A.D. 1066'.
3. A. Williams, 'Edgar [called Edgar Pacificus] (943/4–975), king of England', *ODNB*.
4. https://avalon.law.yale.edu/medieval/ang10.asp#b43 (*The Anglo-Saxon Chronicle: Tenth Century*), accessed 13 March 2025, see entry referring to 'A.D. 973'.
5. See also L. G. Wickham Legg (ed.), *English Coronation Records* (London, 1901), pp. 3–13. See also H. G. Richardson and G. O. Sayles, 'Early Coronation Records', *Bulletin of the Institute of Historical Research*, XIII (1935–1936), pp. 129–45 and XIV (1936–1937), pp. 1–9, 145–8; H. G. Richardson and G. O. Sayles, *The Governance of Mediaeval England from the Conquest to Magna Carta* (Edinburgh, 1964), Appendix 1. For more recent discussion see A. Jones, 'The Significance of the Royal Coronation of Edgar in 973', *Journal of Ecclesiastical History*, 33 (1982), pp. 375–90; S. Keynes, 'Edgar, Rex Admirabilis', in D. Scragg (ed.), *Edgar, King of the English, 959–975: New Interpretations* (new edn) (Woodbridge, 2008), pp. 3–59; G. Molyneaux, "Why were some Tenth-Century English Kings presented as Rulers of Britain? 'The Alexander Prize Essay.'" *Transactions of the Royal Historical Society*, 21 (2011), pp. 59–91.
6. M. Lapidge, 'Dunstan [St Dunstan] (d. 988), archbishop of Canterbury'. *ODNB*.
7. Williams, 'Edgar', *ODNB*. See also P. McGurk, 'John of Worcester (*fl.* 1095–1140), Benedictine monk and chronicler monk at Worcester', *ibid.*
8. Williams, 'Edgar', *ibid.* See also Molyneaux, 'Tenth-Century English Kings', pp. 59–91.
9. P. Stafford, 'Ælfthryth (d. 999x1001), queen of England, consort of King Edgar'. *ODNB*.
10. See Appendix I: Coronation Timeline.
11. H. Summerson, 'From Legend to History: *c.*604–*c.*1100', in D. Cannadine (ed.), *Westminster Abbey: A Church in History* (London, 2019), pp. 16–17.
12. D. C. Douglas, 'The Conquest of England January 1066–March 1067' in D. C. Douglas, *William the Conqueror: The Norman Impact Upon England* (New Haven, Connecticut, 1999), p. 182.
13. BL, Royal MS 15 E IV/2, fol. 236r (depiction of the crowning).

14. On the Witan or 'Witanagemot', see T. Cole, *The Norman Conquest: William the Conqueror's Subjugation of England* (Stroud, 2018), pp. 24, 106, 109. See also J. Crick, '*Pristina Libertas*: Liberty and the Anglo-Saxons Revisited', *Transactions of the Royal Historical Society*, 14 (2004), pp. 47–71; and B. O'Brien, 'Conquest and the Law' in L. Ashe and E. J. Ward (eds), *Conquests in Eleventh-Century England: 1016, 1066* (Woodbridge, 2020), pp. 41–64.
15. On Westminster Hall, see two volumes from The British Archaeological Association Conference Transactions by W. Rodwell and T. Tatton-Brown (eds), *Westminster I & II. The Art, Architecture and Archaeology of the Royal Palace* (Abingdon, 2016–2017); R. Beech, 'The Hammer-beam Roof of Westminster Hall and the Structural Rationale of Hugh Herland', *Architectural History*, 59 (2016), pp. 25–61; G. Waddell, 'The Design of the Westminster Hall Roof', *Architectural History*, 42 (1999), pp. 47–67; D. Gerhold, *Westminster Hall: Nine Hundred Years of History* (London, 1999), *passim*; https://www.parliament.uk/about/living-heritage/building/palace/westminsterhall/architecture/the-hammer-beam-roof-/, accessed 20 March 2023.
16. S. House, 'More, Sir Thomas [St Thomas More] (1478–1535),' *ODNB*; M. Kishlansky, & J. Morrill, 'Charles I (1600–1649), king of England, Scotland, and Ireland.' *ODNB*. See also C. V. Wedgwood, *The Trial of Charles I* (London, 1964).
17. J. Clarke, 14 September 2022, https://www.bbc.co.uk/news/uk-62875864, accessed 20 November 2025; https://www.parliament.uk/globalassets/documents/parliamentary-archives/Churchill-for-web-Mar-2014.pdf, accessed 20 March 2024; see also https://www.bbc.co.uk/pressoffice/pressreleases/stories/2002/11_november/25/greatbritons_final.shtml (Press Office release, 25 November 2002), accessed 20 March 2024; and https://www.londonmintoffice.org/blog/384-the-greatest-briton-24, accessed 20 November 2025.
18. C. A. Edie, 'The Public Face of Royal Ritual: Sermons, Medals, and Civic Ceremony in Later Stuart Coronations', *The Huntington Library Quarterly*, 53 (1990), p. 311.
19. C. A. J. Armstrong, 'The Inauguration Ceremonies of the Yorkist Kings and Their Title to the Throne', *Transactions of the Royal Historical Society*, 30 (1948), pp. 59–60.
20. *Ibid.*, pp. 64–5.
21. R. Latham and W. Matthews (eds), *The Diary of Samuel Pepys*, 11 vols (London, 1971), II p. 83 (22 April 1661). Cf. Sir Edward Walker, *A Circumstantial Account of the Preparations for the Coronation of His Majesty King Charles the Second, and a Minute Detail of that Splendid Ceremony, with all the Particulars Connected with it; Including the*

Installation of Knights, Creation of Peers, &c., to which is Prefixed, an Account of the Landing, Reception, and Journey of His Majesty from Dover to London (London, 1820), p. 22; J. Ogilby, *The Entertainment of His Most Excellent Majestie Charles II, in his Passage Through the City of London to his Coronation: Containing an Exact Accompt of the Whole Solemnity; the Triumphal Arches, and Cavalcade, Delineated in Sculpture; the Speeches and Impresses Illustrated from Antiquity. To these is Added, a Brief Narrative of His Majestie's Solemn Coronation: with his Magnificent Proceeding, and Royal Feast in Westminster-Hall* (London, 1662); *ibid.*, *The Kings Coronation: Being an Exact Account of the Cavalcade, with a Description of the Triumphal Arches, and Speeches Prepared by the City of London for His Late Majesty Charles the Second, in his Passage from the Tower to Whitehall. Also the Narrative of his Majesties Coronation, with his Magnificent Proceeding, and Feast in Westminster-Hall, April the 23th* (Edinburgh, 1685); and F. Sandford, *The History of the Coronation of the Most High, Most Mighty, and Most Excellent Monarch, James II. By the Grace of God, King of England, Scotland, France and Ireland, Defender of the Faith, &c. and of His Royal Consort Queen Mary: Solemnized in the Collegiate Church of St. Peter in the City of Westminster, on Thursday the 23 of April, being the Festival of St. George, in the Year of Our Lord 1685* (London, 1687). For a depiction of the procession of William III and Mary II, showing the barons of the Cinque Ports, see The Folger Shakespeare Library, Washington DC, USA, ART: Vol. d105 no. 41, fol. 34r (dated 21 April 1689; the coronation was on 11 April).

22. For the history of the Cinque Ports and their involvement in coronation services, see FSL, MS V.b.277, fols 60r–61r. Cf. Kent Archives, Maidstone Branch, MS CP/C1, fols 10r–v (Translation of Elizabeth I's charter); 24r–v (Law and customs, Sandwich); 44r–v (Notes on composition and purses as means of raising money); 46r–v (Memorandum regarding James I's coronation); 70r–v (Copy of Elizabeth I's charter); and East Sussex Record Office, Lewis, Rye Corporation Records, MS RYE/47/164/23; Sir Thomas Mantell, *Coronation Ceremonies and Customs Relative to the Barons of the Cinque Ports as Supporters of the Canopy* (Dover, 1820); T. Ross, 'Coronation Services of the Barons of the Cinque Ports', *Sussex Archaeological Collections*, XV (1863), pp. 178–210; C. Dawson, *The Services of the Barons of the Cinque Ports at the Coronation of the Kings and Queens of England, etc.* (Lewes, 1901); K. M. E. Murray, *The Constitutional History of the Cinque Ports* (Manchester, 1935), pp. 19–21; P. E. Schramm, (trans. L. G. Wickham Legg), *A History of the English Coronation* (Oxford, 1937), pp. 68–9; and Historical Manuscripts Commission, JP5: *A Calendar of the White and Black Books of the Cinque Ports, 1432–1955* (London, 1966), pp. xxxiii–xxxv.

23. BL, Add. MS 31043, fol. 74v (Canopy borne by sixteen barons of Cinque Ports).
24. KA, MS NR/CPh3/11 (W[illia]m East to John Mascrall, jurat, New Romney, 15 April 1685). For 1661 see ESRO, Ashburnham Papers, MS ASH AMS3705, and for 1689 see *ibid.*, MS ASH AMS3715. See also J. M. Baines, 'The Cinque Ports and Coronation Services', *Hastings Museum Publication*, No. 18 (3rd edition, 1968).
25. West Sussex Record Office, Chichester, Add. MS 54975, fols 1r–2r (copy). The barons of the Cinque Ports were to play their role at every coronation up to and including George IV's. William IV removed the posts on financial grounds. The barons resurfaced for Edward VII's coronation in 1902.
26. See for example commission creating the Court of Claims in 1509: J. S. Brewer *et al.* (eds), *Letters and Papers, Foreign and Domestic, of the Reign of Henry VIII. Preserved in the Public Record Office, the British Museum, and Elsewhere in England*, 23 vols in 37 parts (London, 1862–1932), I item 164.
27. V. Low, 3 March 2023, https://www.thetimes.com/uk/royal-family/article/king-charles-coronation-downton-abbey-herb-strewer-jkxw8g-zzf, accessed 4 March 2023.
28. Sandford, *History*, pp. 80–2. For other unusual claims, including one to present falcons at the coronation of James II in 1685, see Lancashire Record Office, Preston, Cunliffe Shaw Collection, MS DDS/acc 1175/41.
29. J. J. Scarisbrick, *Henry VIII* (London, 1968), p. 18.
30. The Dymokes retained the role of champion at every coronation between Richard II's coronation (1377) and Edward VII's in (1902). This was not in fact a hereditary claim, but rested on ownership of the manor of Scrivelsby; it just so happened that Dymokes tenaciously held on to that manor. G. H. White, 'Coronation Claims', *The Genealogists' Magazine*, 7 (1937), pp. 512–13. Cf. T. C. Banks, *History of the Ancient Noble Family of Marmyun; Their Singular Office of King's Champion, by the Tenure of the Baronial Manor of Scrivelsby, in the County of Lincoln: also, Other Dignitorial Tenures, and the Services of London, Oxford, &c. on the Coronation-Day. The Whole Collected at a Great Expense from the Public Records; Illustrated by a Variety of Notes and Remarks, and Embellished with Several Curious Engravings* (London, 1817).
31. Chatsworth House, Derbyshire, MS 29 (23–4 April 1661). On Cork, see T. Barnard, 'Boyle, Richard, first Earl of Burlington and second Earl of Cork (1612–1698)', *ODNB*.
32. See https://www.wellingtoncollection.co.uk/wellington-stories/new-exhibition-coronation-robes/, accessed 5 March 2025; See also

R. Holmes, *Wellington: The Iron Duke* (London, 2003); N. Gash, 'Wellesley [formerly Wesley], Arthur, first duke of Wellington (1769–1852)', *ODNB.*

33. L. E. Tanner, 'Coronations in the Abbey', in E. Carpenter (ed.), *A House of Kings: The History of Westminster Abbey* (London, 1966), p. 409.
34. Carpenter, *House*; P. Hunting, *Royal Westminster: A History of Westminster Through its Royal Connections* ([London], *c.*1981); R. Mortimer, *Guide to the Muniments of Westminster Abbey*, Westminster Abbey Record Ser., 7 (Woodbridge, *c.*2012); T. Trowles, *Treasures of Westminster Abbey* (London, 2008); J. Wilkinson and C. S. Knighton, *Crown and Cloister: The Royal Story of Westminster Abbey* (London, 2010); and R. Jenkyns, *Westminster Abbey* (revised edn, London, 2011).
35. https://www.westminster-abbey.org/visit-us/the-queens-diamond-jubilee-galleries, accessed 2 December 2025.
36. For engravings, see e.g. FSL, D 219 I8 and London Metropolitan Archives, SC/PZ/WE/02/1373 (both 1685); and *ibid.*, SC/GL/PR/L/22/2/P7488105 (for 1689).
37. Or it may have been used by those working backstage. For the 1953 coronation the triforium played host to some of the BBC television and lighting crews: http://www.bbc.co.uk/blogs/aboutthebbc/entries/6e258b7f-3b29-399e-9356-c538706ff933.
38. Early twentieth century debate: C. G. Bayne, 'The Coronation of Queen Elizabeth', *The English Historical Review*, XXII (1907), pp. 650–73; H. A. Wilson, 'The Coronation of Queen Elizabeth', *ibid.*, XXIII (1908), pp. 87–91; G. L. Ross, 'Il Schifanoya's Account of the Coronation of Queen Elizabeth', *ibid.*, pp. 533–4; C. G. Bayne, 'The Coronation of Queen Elizabeth', *EHR*, XXIV (1909), pp. 322–3; A. F. Pollard, 'The Coronation of Queen Elizabeth', *ibid.*, XXV (1910), pp. 125–6; and C. G. Bayne, 'The Coronation of Queen Elizabeth', *EHR*, XXV (1910), pp. 550–3.
39. D. Hoak, 'The Coronations of Edward VI, Mary I, and Elizabeth I, and the Transformation of the Tudor Monarchy', in C. S. Knighton and R. Mortimer (eds), *Westminster Abbey Reformed 1540–1640* (Aldershot, 2003), p. 138.
40. R. Bowers, 'The Chapel Royal, the First Edwardian Prayer Book, and Elizabeth's Settlement of Religion, 1559', *The Historical Journal*, 43 (2000), p. 327, which cites the relevant literature of this famous controversy; see also BL, Egerton MS 3320, fol. 22r.
41. See A. Plowden, 'Grey [married name Dudley], Lady Jane (1537–1554)', *ODNB.*

42. E. W. Ives, 'Tudor Dynastic Problems Revisited', *Historical Research*, 81 (2008), pp. 255–79; E. Ives, *Lady Jane Grey: A Tudor Mystery* (Chichester, 2009).
43. L. Goldman, 'Elizabeth [née Lady Elizabeth Angela Marguerite Bowes-Lyon] (1900–2002)', *ODNB*; W. Shawcross (ed.), *Counting One's Blessings: The Selected Letters of Queen Elizabeth The Queen Mother* (London, 2012), p. 230. See also discussion on 'The Abdication Crisis' in P. Williamson and E. Baldwin (eds.), *Baldwin Papers: A Conservative Statesman, 1908–1947* (Cambridge, 2004), pp. 387–425. See also H. Matthew, 'Edward VIII [afterwards Prince Edward, duke of Windsor] (1894–1972)', *ODNB.*
44. The 2023 Coronation Roll, https://www.coronationroll.gov.uk/further_info/the-ring/, accessed 22 November 2025.
45. Quoted in M. Levine, *Tudor Dynastic Problems 1460–1571* (London, 1973), p. 177.
46. C. Morris (ed.), *The Journeys of Celia Fiennes* (revised edition, London, 1949), p. 301.
47. 'The Musgrave Ritual', in Sir Arthur Conan Doyle, *The Complete Sherlock Holmes; With Illustrations by Sidney Paget* (London, 2005), p. 367; Robert Hamer's 1949 masterpiece.
48. J. Hone, 'The Last Stuart Coronation' in P. Kewes and A. McRae (eds), *Stuart Succession Literature: Moments and Transformations* (Oxford, 2019), p. 132.
49. *Idem.*
50. S. Doran, *From Tudor to Stuart: The Regime Change from Elizabeth I to James I* (Oxford, 2024), p. 429 (see pp. 390–429 'Union and Empire').
51. R. Lawson-Peebles, 'The Implications of the Accession of James VI and I', in *The Yearbook of English Studies*, Vol. 46, Writing the Americas, 1480–1826 (2016), pp. 56–74 (Modern Humanities Research Association), p. 68 quoting James I, 'Speech to parliament of 19 March 1604', in J. P. Sommerville (ed.) *King James VI and I: Political Writings* (Cambridge, 1995), pp. 135–36. On the elision of English and British nationalism in Gaunt's speech, see P. Schwyzer, *Literature, Nationalism, and Memory in Early Modern England and Wales* (Cambridge, 2004), pp. 4–6.
52. A. Roberts, *George III: The Life and Reign of Britain's Most Misunderstood Monarch* (London, 2023), p. 57. See for Charles II Anon., *A Proclamation* [8 May 1660], *of both Houses of Parliament, for Proclaiming of His Majesty King of England, Scotland, France, and Ireland, Defender of the Faith, &c.* (London, 1660).

53. See J. Black, *George III: America's Last King* (New Haven, Connecticut, 2008), p. 379. Black notes the newspaper report from *The Courier* of 2 January 1801 mentioning the royal carriages altering the coat of arms to take account of the changes heraldically. See https://www.britishnewspaperarchive.co.uk, accessed 6 March 2025.
54. See R. Douglas, *The Form and Order of the Coronation of Charles the Second, King of Scotland, England, France, and Ireland. As it was Acted and Done at Schoone, the First Day of January, 1651.* (Aberdeen, 1651), pp. 4–5. See also the proclamation of Charles II in Scotland at the Mercat Cross of Edinburgh, 5 February 1649, declaring Charles II as 'king of Scotland, Great Britain and Ireland': K. M. Brown et al. (eds), *The Records of the Parliaments of Scotland to 1707* (St Andrews, 2007–2020), 1649/1/71. On the challenge of finding a safe location to crown Charles in Scotland with Cromwell's ensuing invasion, see NRS, Kerr family papers, GD40/2/19/1/22, fol. 1r (John Campbell, first Earl of Loudoun, Chancellor, Edinburgh, to Charles II, 16 August 1650). Cf. NRS, GD40/2/19/1/22–25: for further correspondence between John Campbell, first Earl of Loudoun and Charles II (16 August–13 September 1650).
55. For discussion on the complexity see for examples: M. Loughlin, 'The State, the Crown and the Law', in M. Sunkin and S. Payne (eds), *The Nature of the Crown: A Legal and Political Analysis* (Oxford, 1999), pp. 33–76; J. McLean, "The Crown in Contract and Administrative Law." *Oxford Journal of Legal Studies*, 24 (2004), pp. 129–54; C. Shore, 'The Crown as Metonym for the State?: The Human Face of Leviathan', in: C. Shore, and D. V. Williams (eds.), *The Shapeshifting Crown: Locating the State in Postcolonial New Zealand, Australia, Canada and the UK.* (Cambridge, 2019), pp. 53–74.
56. S. Berger, 21 May 2018, https://www.cnbc.com/2018/05/21/ratings-for-prince-harry-and-meghan-markle-royal-wedding.html, accessed 23 November 2025.
57. https://www.bbc.com/historyofthebbc/anniversaries/june/coronation-of-queen-elizabeth-ii/, accessed 23 November 2025.
58. J. Moran, 2 June 2013, https://www.radiotimes.com/books/why-elizabeth-iis-1953-coronation-is-the-day-that-changed-television/, accessed 23 November 2025.
59. https://www.parliament.uk/about/living-heritage/evolutionofparliament/parliamentwork/offices-and-ceremonies/collections/parliamentary-collections-royal-weddings/princess-annes-wedding-/, accessed 5 March 2025, (Parliamentary Archives, PUD/15/4).
60. https://www.bbc.com/historyofthebbc/anniversaries/july/wedding-of-prince-charles-and-lady-diana-spencer, accessed 6 March 2025.

61. https://www.economist.com/britain/2022/05/26/britain-celebrates-a-jubilee-again: 'The Platinum Jubilee: Land of hops and glory' – the argument being that 'Britain is celebrating jubilees more often, but less confidently', 26 May 2022, accessed 6 March 2025.
62. N. Andreeva, 30 April 2011, https://deadline.com/2011/04/so-how-were-the-royal-wedding-ratings-126926/, accessed 6 March 2025.
63. S. Berger, 21 May 2018, https://www.cnbc.com/2018/05/21/ratings-for-prince-harry-and-meghan-markle-royal-wedding.html, accessed 6 March 2025.
64. T. Douglas, 22 January 2012, https://www.bbc.co.uk/news/entertainment-arts-16671101, accessed 10 April 2023.
65. J. P. Rotondi, 13 November 2009, https://www.history.com/this-day-in-history/september-6/some-2-5-billion-tv-viewers-watch-princess-dianas-funeral, accessed 10 March 2023.
66. A. Sherwin, 18 April 2021, https://inews.co.uk/culture/television/prince-philips-funeral-watched-more-than-13-million-uk-viewers-961811, accessed 11 March 2023.
67. N. Duffy, 5 June 2022, https://inews.co.uk/news/entertainment/platinum-party-palace-jubilee-becomes-most-watched-tv-event-of-the-year-thirteen-million-tune-in-2022-1669735, accessed 11 March 2023.
68. https://www.londonmuseum.org.uk/collections/london-stories/long-reign-queen-victoria/, accessed 11 March 2023; https://www.royal.uk/royal-archives-coronation (Queen Victoria), accessed 11 March 2023; https://www.bl.uk/collection-items/material-relating-to-the-coronation-of-queen-victoria, accessed 11 March 2023; see also The National Library of Ireland, Dublin, MS 49,034/1 (1838 coronation procession).
69. C. Gartenberg, 20 May 2019, https://www.theverge.com/2019/5/20/18633136/game-of-thrones-got-season-8-finale-hbo-most-watched-show-all-time-viewership-numbers-live, accessed 10 March 2023.
70. https://web.archive.org/web/20051122221448/http://www.bfi.org.uk/features/mostwatched/1960s.html, accessed 10 March 2025.
71. https://www.trentbridge.co.uk/news/2020/january/2019-cricket-world-cup-confirmed-as-most-watched-ever.html, accessed 11 March 2023; A. Rhoden-Paul, 7 May 2023, https://www.bbc.co.uk/news/uk-65518360#:~:text=King%20Charles%20III's%20Coronation%20watched%20by%20more%20than%2018%20million%20viewers,-Published&text=The%20King's%20Coronation%20was%20watched,UK%2C%20overnight%20figures%20have%20shown, accessed 12 May 2023.

72. The Exclusion Crisis (1679–1681) saw significant parliamentary attempts (though ultimately unsuccessful) to exclude Charles II's brother, James, duke of York, from the line of succession, because of his conversion to Roman Catholicism. See P. Seaward, 'Charles II (1630–1685)', *ODNB*; and W. Speck, 'James II and VII (1633 – 1701)', *ibid.*
73. See also M. Kishlansky, *A Monarchy Transformed: Britain 1603–1714* (Harmondsworth, 1996), *passim.*
74. E.g. J. H. T. Perkins, *The Coronation Book ... Illustrated by Mrs Temple Perkins, etc.* (2nd edn, London, 1911).
75. E.g. E. M. R. Ditmas, E. M. R., 'The Curtana or Sword of Mercy', *The Journal of the British Archaeological Association*, 3rd Series, XXIX (1966), pp. 122–33, and E. Halfpenny, '*The Cities Loyalty Display'd*: A Literary and Documentary Causerie of Charles II's Coronation "Entertainment"', *The Guildhall Miscellany*, 1 (1959), pp. 19–35.
76. Legg, *Coronation Records.*
77. Schramm, *Coronation.*
78. C. Withers, 'Ogilby, John (1600–1676)', *ODNB.*
79. J. Ogilby, *The Relation of His Majestie's Entertainment Passing Through the City of London to his Coronation etc.* (London, 1661); *Ibid.*, *Entertainment*; *Ibid.*, *Kings Coronation.* See also T. Claydon, 'William III and II (1650–1702)', *ODNB*; W. A. Speck, 'Mary II (1662–1694)', *ibid.*
80. C. Withers, 'Ogilby, John (1600–1676)', *ODNB.*
81. Halfpenny, '*Cities Loyalty*', p. 21.
82. M. Hunter, 'Ashmole, Elias (1617–1692)', *ODNB.* See also E. Ashmole and F. Sandford, *The Entire Ceremonies of the Coronations of ... Charles II and ... Queen Mary, Consort to James II,* ... (London, 1761).
83. For Charles II's concerns for Walker to authorise publication, see TNA, SP 29/122/27; *ibid.*, SP 44/7, fol. 25r–v; and *ibid.*, SP 44/48 fol. 20r–v. See also Halfpenny, '*Cities Loyalty*', p. 28.
84. P. Sherlock, 'Sandford, Francis (1630–1694)', *ODNB*; Sandford, *History.*
85. J. Hoppit, 'King, Gregory (1648–1712)', *ODNB.* On heraldic coronation material, see also Inner Temple Library, London, Petyt MS 531 Vol. A.
86. P. Sherlock, 'Sandford, Francis (1630–1694)', *ibid.*
87. Walker's 'detailed account of the event in fifty-two manuscript folios dated 25 May 1661, [was] subsequently published in 1820': H. Chesshyre, 'Walker, Sir Edward (1612–1677)', *ODNB.*
88. A copy of Walker's account (dated 25 May 1661) of Charles II's arrival at the Restoration and also of his 1661 coronation survives in BL, Add. MS 30195. Either that or another MS was used as the basis for Sir Edward Walker, *A Circumstantial Account of the Preparations for the Coronation of His Majesty King Charles the Second, and a Minute Detail of that*

Splendid Ceremony, with all the Particulars Connected with it; Including the Installation of Knights, Creation of Peers, &c., to which is Prefixed, an Account of the Landing, Reception, and Journey of His Majesty from Dover to London (London, 1820). Further coronation material exists in other MSS associated with Walker: BL, Add. MS 37998, Hargrave MS 497 and Stowe MS 580; Bodl., Carte MS 129; and The Society of Antiquaries of London, Burlington House, London, MS SAL/MS/455.

89. Anon., *The Form of the Proceeding to the Coronation of … King William and Queen Mary, etc.* ([London], 1689); Anon., *The Form of the Proceeding to the Royal Coronation of Her Most Excellent Majesty Queen Anne, the Twenty Third Day of this Instant April, 1702* (The Savoy, 1702). Cf. for further examples *The Form and Order of Service that is to be performed, and of the Ceremonies that are to be observed, in the Coronation of their Majesties King George III. and Queen Charlotte, in the Abbey Church … Tuesday the 22[n]d of September 1761 …* (London, 1761); *The Form and Order of Service that is to be performed and of the Ceremonies that are to be observed in the Coronation of their Majesties King Edward VII. And Queen Alexandra …* (London, 1902); *The Form and Order of Service that is to be performed and of the Ceremonies that are to be observed in the Coronation of their Majesties King George V. and Queen Mary in the Abbey Church … Westminster, on Thursday … 22nd day of June, 1911* (London, 1911); *The Form and Order of Service that is to be performed and the Ceremonies that are to be observed in the Coronation of their Majesties King George VI and Queen Elizabeth …* (London, 1937); and *The Form and Order of the Service. Coronation of Her Majesty Queen Elizabeth II, 2 June 1953* (London, 1953).
90. Anon., *An Exact Account of the Ceremonial at the Coronation of Their Most Excellent Majesties King William and Queen Mary, the Eleventh Day of this Instant April, 1689* (The Savoy, 1689).
91. Ogilby, *Relation.*
92. See also Halfpenny, '*Cities Loyalty*', pp. 20–1, 23, 27–8.
93. Christopher Wordsworth, bishop of Lincoln, was born at Lambeth Palace, see M. Pawley, 'Wordsworth, Christopher (1807–1885)', *ODNB.*
94. Cf. Legg, *Coronation Records*, pp. 81–131 (*Liber Regalis*), 219–40 ('Little Device'). See also Anon., *A Collection Out of the Book Called Liber Regalis, Remaining in the Treasury of the Church of Westminster. Touching the Coronation of the King and Queen Together, According to the Usual Form* (London, 1661).
95. On Schramm's *oeuvre*, see J. M. Bak, 'Medieval Symbology of the State: Percy E. Schramm's Contribution', *Viator*, 4 (1973), pp. 33–64. See also J. Cooper, *Four Scottish Coronations (The Coronation of James VI – The Coronation of Anne, Queen of James VI – The Coronation of Charles I – The Coronation of Charles II)* (Aberdeen, 1902).

96. J. Wickham Legg (ed.), *The Coronation Order for King James I* (London, 1902).
97. *Idem*, 'The Queen's Coronation Ring', *The Archaeological Journal*, 54 (1897), pp. 1–9.
98. S. Ollard (revised G. M. Murphy), 'Legg, John Wickham (1843–1921)', *ODNB*. Strangely, there is no *ODNB* entry on his son, Leopold George Wickham Legg (1877–1962), who was arguably even more important in research on coronation history.
99. Schramm, *Coronation*, p. 230.
100. *Ibid.*, p. 231.
101. D. Cannadine, 'The Context, Performance and Meaning of Ritual: The British Monarchy and the "Invention of Tradition", *c.*1820–1977', in E. Hobsbawm and T. Ranger (eds), *The Invention of Tradition* (Cambridge, 1983), pp. 101–64.
102. Schramm, *Coronation*, p. 231.
103. D. J. Sturdy, 'English Coronation Sermons in the Seventeenth Century', in H. Duchhardt (ed.), *Herrscherweihe und Königskrönung im Frühneuzeitlichen Europa* (Wiesbaden, 1983), pp. 72–3 and 69 (n. 2).
104. D. J. Sturdy, '"Continuity" versus "Change": Historians and English Coronations of the Medieval and Early Modern Periods', in J. M. Bak (ed.), *Coronations: Medieval and Early Modern Monarchic Ritual* (Berkeley and Los Angeles, California, *c.*1990), p. 242.
105. *Ibid.*
106. *Ibid.*, p. 243.
107. *Ibid.*
108. *Ibid.*
109. *Ibid.*, pp. 236–8: J. J. Brückmann, 'English Coronations, 1216–1308: The Edition of the Coronation "*Ordines*"', PhD thesis, University of Toronto (1964). Strong references Brückmann's work, but does not engage with it: R. Strong, *Coronation: A History of Kingship and the British Monarchy* (London, 2005), p. 506.
110. See also W. H. C. Le Hardy, *The Coronation Book. The History and Meaning of the Ceremonies at the Crowning of the King and Queen* (London, 1937); and M. Bowen, *Crowns and Sceptres: The Romance and Pageantry of Coronations* (London, 1937). For 1902 see M. F. Johnston, *Coronation of a King, or the Ceremonies, Pageants and Chronicles of Coronations of all Ages … With Illustrations, etc.* (London, 1902).
111. See for examples C. Pepinster, *Defenders of the Faith: The British Monarchy, Religion and the Next Coronation* (London, 2022); C. Andersen, *The King: The Life of Charles III* (Waterville, Maine, 2022); A. James, *Charles III: A Modern Monarch* (Solihull, 2023); C. Jackson, *Charles III: A King and His Queen* (New York, New York, 2023); G. Knappett, *King Charles*

III (London, 2023); and R. Hardman, *Charles III: New King. New Court. The Inside Story* (London, 2024).

112. R. Hutton, *Charles the Second: King of England, Scotland and Ireland* (Oxford, 1989), p. 165.
113. A. Hunt, *The Drama of Coronation: Medieval Ceremony in Early Modern England* (Cambridge, 2008).
114. L. Colley, *Britons: Forging the Nation, 1707–1837* (New Haven, Connecticut, and London, 1992); cf. B. R. O'G., Anderson, *Imagined Communities: Reflections on the Origin and Spread of Nationalism* (1st edn, London, 1983; 2nd edn, London, *c.*2006); M. J. Braddick, *State Formation in Early Modern England, c.1550–1700* (Cambridge, 2000).
115. J. Rose, *Godly Kingship in Restoration England: The Politics of the Royal Supremacy, 1660–1688* (Cambridge, 2011).
116. For examples Northamptonshire Record Office, Northampton, MS FH2411(Summons for Christopher Hatton, 1st baron Hatton of Kirby, to attend coronation of Charles II, 1 February 1660/1661 (sign manual)); CUL, Hengrave MS 90/98 (Summons for Francis Browne , 4th viscount Montague, to attend coronation of James II, Whitehall, 23 March 1684/1685 (sign manual)); NRS, Strathallan Papers, MS RH15/123/71 (Summons for William Drummond, 4th viscount Strathallan, to attend coronation of George II, 19 August 1727 (sign manual)); and NLI, MS 38,811 (Summons to coronation of George VI in 1937 for Viscount Richard De Vesci).
117. See for examples Arundel Castle, West Sussex, MS BN and MS MD/1590 and MSS GI/99–105.
118. https://www.coronationroll.gov.uk/roll/, accessed 10 March 2025.
119. See also TNA, C 195.
120. The literature is vast, but see, e.g., N. Tyacke, *Anti-Calvinists: The Rise of English Arminianism c.1590–1640* (paperback edn, Oxford, 1990); K. Fincham (ed)., *The Early Stuart Church, 1603–1642* (Basingstoke, 1993); and K. Fincham and N. Tyacke, *Altars Restored: The Changing Face of English Religious Worship, 1547–c.1700* (Oxford, 2007).
121. BM, E.3442.
122. Schramm, *Coronation*, pp. 94–6; Bodl., MS Carte 73, fol. 505r–v – fuller financial accounts survive at TNA; M. J. Braddick, *Parliamentary Taxation in Seventeenth-Century England: Local Administration and Response* (London, 1995); M. J. Braddick, *The Nerves of State: Taxation and the Financing of the English State, 1558–1714* (Manchester, 1996).
123. D. Cressy, *Bonfires and Bells: National Memory and the Protestant Calendar in Elizabethan and Stuart England* (London, 1989).

124. J. N. King, *Tudor Royal Iconography: Literature and Art in an Age of Religious Crisis* (Princeton, New Jersey, 1989); B. Lenman, 'The Exiled Stuarts and the Precious Symbols of Sovereignty', *Eighteenth-Century Life*, 25 (2001), pp. 185–200.
125. Useful literature includes S. Bertelli, (trans. R. Burr Litchfield), *The King's Body: The Sacred Rituals of Power in Medieval and Early Modern Europe* (University Park, Pennsylvania, 2003); R. A. Jackson, *Vive le Roi! A History of the French Coronation from Charles V to Charles X* (Chapel Hill, North Carolina, 1984).
126. K. Sharpe, *Image Wars: Promoting Kings and Commonwealths in England, 1603–1660* (New Haven, Connecticut, and London, 2010). See also A. Somerset, *Queen Anne: The Politics of Passion: A Biography* (London, 2012), pp. 226–8.
127. See for examples: https://x.com/KingsCollegeLon/status/1654788387058876416, 6 May 2023, accessed 7 May 2023; L. Potts, 20 April 2023, https://www.bbc.co.uk/news/uk-65031625, accessed 2 May 2023;

     G. Rayner, 5 May 2023, https://www.telegraph.co.uk/royal-family/2023/05/05/queen-camilla-second-wedding-king-charles-coronation/#:~:text=According%20to%20the%20Liturgy%20for,to%20the%20public%20in%20service, accessed 10 March 2024.
128. Braddick, *Taxation*, p. 298. Cf. Braddick, *Nerves of State* and J. Brewer, *The Sinews of Power: War, Money and the English State, 1688–1783* (London, 1989).
129. Braddick, *Taxation*, p. 21.
130. The literature on the confessionalization paradigm is now extensive, but for sample works by leading protagonists, see H. Schilling, 'Confessionalization in the Empire: Religious and Societal Change in Germany Between 1555 and 1620', in H. Schilling, *Religion, Political Culture and the Emergence of Early Modern Society: Essays in German and Dutch History*, Studies in Medieval and Reformation Thought, L (Leiden, 1992), pp. 205–45; and W. Reinhard, 'Pressures towards Confessionalization? Prolegomena to a Theory of the Confessional Age', in C. S. Dixon (ed.), *The German Reformation: The Essential Readings* (Oxford, 1999), pp. 169–92. Discussion of wider applicability can be found in A. Pettegree, 'Confessionalization in North Western Europe', in J. Bahlcke and A. Strohmeyer (eds), *Konfessionalisierung in Ostmitteleuropa: Wirkungen des Religiosen Wandels im 16. und 17. Jahrhundert in Staat, Gesellschaft und Kultur* (Stuttgart, 1999), pp. 105–20; and U. Lotz-Heumann, U., 'Confessionalization', in D. M. Whitford (ed.), *Reformation and Early Modern Europe: A Guide to Research* (Kirksville, Missouri, 2008), pp. 136–57.

PART I

Rituals & Religion

CHAPTER 1

Cleansing and Anointing: The Hallowing

The association of monarchs with divinity originates in the ancient world: from the pharaohs of Egypt to the Shang Dynasty of China, from the Obas of Benin (present-day Nigeria) to the *Shahnameh*[1] of Persia, from the emperors of Japan to the Dalai Lama in Tibet. In classical tradition, one need not look further than the Roman Empire with Caesar, and the investment of Julius Caesar with god-like status; such were the symbolic powers of the double-headed eagle and laurel, that these images perpetuated themselves in Byzantine tradition, and later in Muscovy. The list goes on and is diverse. These examples of rule by godly approval, rule as a god or goddess, and rule with divine sacerdotal power were age-old concepts long before the birth of Christianity.[2] It is therefore not surprising that the Bible continued such themes, but wove the thread in a monotheistic direction, something that had already been 'fostered', to some degree, under Akhenaten (Amenhotep IV, 1352–1336 BC), the Egyptian 'heretic king', with his 'sun-disc' god (the Aten). This deity 'was simply the hypostasis of divine kingship, a … reflection of his [i.e. Akhenaten's] own on earth, projected heavenwards'.[3] Power thus rested in one God alone, and kings and queens derived their authority from one single Almighty and not multiple sources. The idea of reinforcing this power by ceremonial, such as a coronation, lay not in Western tradition but in pre-biblical times too. Ancient Egyptian pharaohs underwent re-investing ceremonies in the presence of their people. For example, Ramesses II (*c.*1304–1237 BC)

G. W. C. Gross, *Crown and People*,
https://doi.org/10.1007/978-3-032-20786-9_1

was to celebrate fourteen such rituals, known as the *heb sed*, or 'royal jubilee'.[4] Japan provides a far-eastern example of continuity, in which the theory remained intact, traversing ancient and modern. Right up until their defeat in the Second World War and the establishment of a new democratic constitution, Japan retained the principle that its emperor was the 'Sun God'—an entirely divine figure and absolute ruler. Tsarist Russia offers an interesting point of comparison to the ideology that developed in Britain, particularly in relation to the monarch's patrimonial position. To what extent was the realm and its people the estate of the potentate?[5] French rulers, traditionally crowned at Reims and invested with the conventional emblems of sovereignty, are notable for their healing powers: their supposed ability to cure scrofula.[6] This efficacy was also found in the British monarchy. Even closer to home, the Stone of Scone would become an intrinsic coronation element, incorporated in St Edward's Chair. The swords of the regalia, carried at a coronation, signified all-powerful sovereignty, coupled with justice and mercy. Along with *Curtana* (Sword of Mercy), they were associated with the almost magical nature of Arthurian legend and kingship, with Lancelot and Excalibur, and also the Celtic tale of Tristan and Isolde.[7] Thus, the crowning, anointing, and inaugurating of monarchs, by religious figures, in holy buildings, using sacred symbols, and imbuing them with majesty has existed for thousands of years across an array of differing cultures.

This long history is also apparent in the anointing of English monarchs, with some dating the origins to the eighth century.[8] Amongst other Anglo-Saxon monarchs, Edgar the Peaceful, Æthelstan, Edmund Ironside, and Edward the Confessor were all anointed or 'consecrated' kings.[9] This custom continued under William the Conqueror, who sought to legitimise his succession by laying claim to the inheritance of the Confessor king. Even the 1170 coronation of 'Young King' Henry, 'the first – and last – king of England since the Norman Conquest to be crowned in the lifetime of his father [Henry II]', involved anointing, for 'young Henry was now hallowed, set apart and above other men as *Christus Domini* – the anointed of the Lord'.[10] With the fusion of Anglo-Saxon and Norman ideas within this service, the anointing has remained ever since.[11]

This sacred tradition was reaffirmed in 1953 and 2023, in that the only moments of the service 'deliberately' not to be broadcast on television were those of the anointing. The act of Anointing or Consecration, with its biblical origins in the anointing of King Solomon, is seen as the most holy part of a British coronation. The monarch is imbued with sacredness by the act of Anointing, almost akin to the ordination of a priest or bishop. It is about changing the monarch's character by consecration—as Shakespeare wrote,

> Not all the water in the rough rude sea
> Can wash the balm off from an anointed king. (*King Richard the Second*, Act III Scene ii)[12]

The religiosity of a coronation was of central importance, as recorded by Roger of Howden. Young King Henry's coronation involved both 'the great joy of the clergy and the people'.[13] In the procession for the medieval coronation (and continued to the present day) was a 'solemn train' of clerical figures, 'crucifers, torch bearers and censors ... followed by the priors and abbots. Next came the bishops, while behind them came magnates each bearing elements of the regalia, including the rod and sceptre'.[14] In the early modern period, James I went so far as to argue that only a monarch 'could claim to represent God's own majesty, and 'only a king [or queen] unlike other non-ecclesiastical office holders, was anointed'.[15] His son Charles I continued this theme, as Sharpe contends his piety was made manifest in 'practices and performances', and as Ronald Asch argues, when he was 'crowned in February 1626 ... the ceremonies emphasized the almost sacramental character of the coronation and the special relationship between the king, represented as both *rex* and *Sacerdos*, and the clergy'. Bishop Laud also 'revived' from the *Liber Regalis* a prayer drawing 'a parallel between Aaron, the priest of the people of Israel, and the anointed king'.[16] With the Restoration in 1660, Charles II renewed this tradition; indeed, his entire coronation in 1661 underlines 'the idea of sacral monarchy'.[17] The extent or importance of consecration was not lost hundreds of years later, even in wartime, in 1944, when according to Sir Alan 'Tommy' Lascelles (the King's (George VI's) private secretary)[18] recorded in his diary 'Monty['s][19] project for an elaborate service to be held in St Paul's on the anniversary of the coronation, for the "hallowing" of the fighting men who will be engaged in "Overlord". The proposed form of service was adapted from that of the Coronation'.[20] Lascelles was to meet with Archbishop Cosmo Gordon Lang,[21] who was 'horrified' to see the 'Coronation service being re-hashed in this way, and justly remarked that it, and the regalia, were consecrated to a unique purpose'. There was also concern as to the idea of 'hallowing' those in the cathedral, given that 'ninety per cent of whom would not be fighting men', but the emphasis on hallowing and consecration is significant.[22] A coronation was a religious moment above all others for Lascelles and the archbishop, and not one for "gaudy fancy or the wanton blandishments of theatrical enchantment"'[23]

In a similar vein to the religiosity of baptism, the ceremony of anointing was hidden from television cameras during the 1953 coronation of Queen Elizabeth II to preserve the mystery surrounding it.[24] In this instance, four Knights of the Garter held the canopy of gold over and around the monarch to shield the act from view. During the act of Anointing, the monarch disrobes from their crimson robes and takes off any jewellery, giving up all symbols of their status. They are seated on St Edward's Chair (the Coronation Chair), clothed in a simple white tunic or vestment. The ceremony is presided over typically by the Archbishop of Canterbury, although this was not the case for Elizabeth I.[25] The Archbishop is then handed the Ampulla containing special 'holy' oil or chrism.[26] An eagle-shaped flask in solid gold, it dates back to the remade crown jewels for the coronation of Charles II in 1661. The Archbishop is then presented with the Coronation Spoon of twelfth-century origin, and possibly made for Henry II.[27] The Archbishop pours the chrism into the spoon and anoints the monarch on their head, hands and breast/chest, with the accompanying words (much unchanged since the seventeenth century):

> Be your hands anointed with holy oil. Be your breast anointed with holy oil. Be your head anointed with holy oil, as kings, priests, and prophets were anointed. And as Solomon was anointed king by Zadok the priest and Nathan the Prophet, so may you be anointed, blessed, and consecrated King[/Queen] over the Peoples, whom the Lord thy God has given you to rule and govern [...].[28]

In the Middle Ages, French kings were anointed with oil from the Sainte Ampoule, which legend claimed had been brought from heaven by an angel for the baptism of Clovis. Given their historic rivalry, it is hardly surprising that Englishmen found that privilege unacceptable. Consequently, documentary 'evidence' was produced in 1318 to the effect that in his exile, Thomas Becket had been given, by the Virgin Mary, a golden eagle containing a phial of heaven-sent oil for the consecration of English kings. This miraculous oil seems not to have been deployed in the fourteenth century—Richard II, re-discovering eagle and phial in the Tower in 1399, requested re-anointing, but was refused by Archbishop

Arundel. Nevertheless, the oil undoubtedly came into play during the coronations of Henry IV, Henry V, Henry VI, and Richard III. Mary I did not wish to be anointed by oil 'consecrated by schismatic hands' and therefore acquired what she perceived to be properly consecrated chrism from the bishop of Arras, three phials of 'acceptable unction'. This provides one of the more amusing accounts of coronation rituals: in 1559, the same chrism was used; Elizabeth, ever fastidious, reportedly thought it 'was grease and smelt ill'. Dale Hoak poses the question: did the Queen also think that its use reeked of superstition? 'Perhaps she remembered what the reform-minded Edwardine, John Coke, had written in 1550 about the '"holy oyle"' used in the French coronation ceremony, that it was nothing but Spanish olive oil, '"very good for salettes"'.[29]

The recipe for the Coronation Oil has been kept secret throughout history. For the coronation of George I in 1714, the anointing oil mixture was created by James Chase and Daniel Malthus, the apothecaries in ordinary, for £206. According to Exchequer accounts held in the National Archives, it was 'a very large composition of rich, essentiall, chymical, odoriferous oyles, balsams and spirits highly perfumed'.[30]

In the 2018 documentary featuring the late Queen Elizabeth II, it was revealed that the oil used during Her late Majesty's coronation included sesame and olive oil, ambergris, civet, orange flowers, roses, jasmine, cinnamon, musk and benzoin.[31] This secret formula was similar to the one used for Charles I in 1626. It was originally prepared from a mixture used by Peter Squire for the coronation of Edward VII in 1902, King George V in 1911 and King George VI in 1937. A phial with remaining oil, carefully hidden in the Deanery, was destroyed in a bombing raid in May

Fig. 1.1 The Coronation Spoon, second half twelfth century, Royal Collection Trust/ © His Majesty King Charles III 2024

1941, so the new batch had to be made for the coronation of Queen Elizabeth II.[32] Peter Squire's firm of chemists, who had mixed the last known anointing oil, had been purchased by a new company, *Savory and Moore Ltd*. They were asked by the Surgeon-Apothecary to mix a new supply, based on the ancient recipe. *Savory & Moore* took over *John Bell & Croyden*, and they were in turn bought by *Lloyds* in 1992. To this day, the *John Bell & Croyden* pharmacy in Marylebone also holds two bottles of sacred oil.[33]

In a break with tradition, the oil used for King Charles III's coronation was consecrated in Jerusalem, at a special ceremony in The Church of the Holy Sepulchre.[34] It has been created from the olive groves of the Mount of Olives and has been perfumed with similar oils to those of 1953, including sesame, rose, jasmine, cinnamon, neroli, benzoin, amber and orange blossom. This is a reference to the King's late father, the Duke of Edinburgh, whose mother, Princess Alice, is buried at the Mount of Olives near her aunt, Grand Duchess Elizabeth.[35] The choice of anointing oil from Jerusalem was also a pointer to the King's interest in world religions and inter-faith dialogue, in this case the Abrahamic religions, with Jerusalem being a city of great importance and significance for Christians, Jews and Muslims alike.[36] In the history of British coronations, the link, or attempted analogy of Britain as Israel and Westminster as Jerusalem, was a longstanding trope of early modern coronation sermons (as will be seen in Chap. 2), and the idea of a New Jerusalem will be explored below. The idea of a secular twenty-first-century age is very far removed from an anointing oil being specially requested from Jerusalem—pluralism perhaps, but clearly not in the eyes of Lambeth or King Charles any sense of secularism. The 2023 coronation saw a distinct affirmation of religiosity or sacredness with such a move.

Divine Right

At the heart of British coronation ritual lay the concept of Divine Right, implied, figured and enacted, although not explicitly stated. At the centre of the coronation service is the anointing. This ancient custom, the spiritual anointing of the sovereign, raised hugely significant questions about his or her status as a consecrated person. This chapter explores to what extent we should see the coronations as imbuing the sovereign with a sacerdotal or quasi-sacerdotal status, and will ask how far and in what terms the concept of Divine Right was consciously projected by those participating in a coronation, or understood in the country at large. Before going further, it is necessary to clarify what we mean by 'Divine Right ideology', for scripture was used to affirm the thesis that kings derive their authority from God alone. The term 'Divine Right' is open to differing interpretations. For our purposes, it is taken generally to signify something having either the sanction or the inspiration of God. More concretely, it is a right conferred by God or based on God's ordinance. In its most extreme form, the doctrine of the 'Divine Right of Kings' claims that legitimate sovereigns derive their power from God alone, unlimited by any rights on the part of their subjects.[37] This has often been elided with absolutism.[38] The Whig Interpretation of History may well be responsible for such an approach. This tendency to conflate the terms is incorrect for two reasons. Firstly, according to the *Oxford English Dictionary*, absolutism, as a noun, did not exist until the mid-eighteenth century. Secondly, that usage emerged, in a theological context to mean 'the doctrine of God's absolute sovereignty, especially that salvation is preordained absolutely'.[39] The word absolutism, in a political sense, is not attested until 1824; 'absolute', on the other hand, appears *c.*1475 in an authoritative sense. In the period covered by this book, the term commonly employed was 'despot', used from 1562; 'despotism' did not arrive linguistically until 1728. Therefore, historians have applied the terms absolutism and despotism both anachronistically and abstractly, in that the words have been transferred from their original personalised focus to describe instead a political system or ideology.

James Daly's examination of exactly these points has been surprisingly overlooked. He explores the usage of the terms 'absolute' and 'absolutism' by numerous figures, such as Sir Thomas Smith, Shakespeare, Henry Parker, Philip Hunton, Hobbes, George Starkey, Sir Edward Coke, Sir George Mackenzie, John Milton, and John Dryden. His etymological inquiry reveals how medieval and early modern notions varied widely. For some, the word 'absolute' equated to a pure form of rule; for others, it veered into the perilous territory of arbitrary government, often exemplified by the old enemy—France. He astutely argues that there has been a danger in modern scholarship of a 'not … very careful terminology': one that 'risks reading an essentially modern opinion' of absolute rule 'back into historical evidence'.[40] Moreover, he is wary of the use of Divine Right as a qualification of absolutism, pointing out that it 'is a source of even greater confusion'.[41]

Fig. 1.2 The anointing of Queen Alexandra at the coronation of Edward VII, 1902, by Tuxen Laurits (1853–1927)

This is not a general study of Divine Right ideology; instead, this chapter focusses on its **realisation** in the context of English coronation ritual. This is crucial because historians have generally suggested that the concept of Divine Right was in decline and had vanished altogether following the Glorious Revolution. Yet, this chapter would suggest otherwise, not least because even in 1953, and in 2023, priests, members of the public and the monarchs themselves talked of a sense of elevation, or appeared profoundly moved beyond the ordinary with this service, and particularly the anointing. Many commentators have spoken of the sense that the late Queen Elizabeth II felt she had been 'divinely assigned' to her role.[42] This, of course, is not the same as a Tudor or Stuart monarch arguing that they can make a change to the law, believing they had direct power from God. Nevertheless, a sense of providentialism, of a Divine Right in their role as Head of State and of Supreme Governor of the Church of England seems to have survived the evolving constitutional changes to the monarch's position over the centuries.[43] This chapter tackles the subject by focussing on what contemporaries saw as the practical realities of this subject. In discussing such a complex topic, a range of important issues are involved, from dealing with the foundations of Divine Right ideology to millenarianism and providentialism. In addressing these questions, we will explore the way in which these concepts are anchored in, and projected from, certain objects and are given further 'reality' in the creation of the knights of Bath, the anointing, and their connection to touching for the King's Evil. In essence, this project revises our understanding by challenging the received wisdom that coronations became increasingly secular in a linear fashion.

Much has been written about the development of 'Divine Right' ideology in the Tudor and early Stuart periods, particularly with the transformation of the 'State' in terms of government and of bureaucracy in relation to the Reformations.[44] Of special interest are the comparisons of nations and kings, and the nature of the king's 'two bodies'—the 'twin-born majesty', as analysed by Ernst Kantorowicz and Marie Axton.[45] It is well known that a theory of 'Divine Right' was a long-standing polemical motif of James I, appearing in many of his pronouncements. One example is this: 'The state of MONARCHIE is the supremest thing upon earth: for kings are not only GODS lieutenants upon earth, and sit upon GODS throne, but even by GOD himselfe they are called Gods'.[46] Early modern English monarchs embraced both the concept of 'Divine Right' and their coronations with fervour. 'Divine Right' took on a greater potency not only as enshrined in coronations but also as expressed through concepts of hegemony and as central to confessionalizing imperatives, which had the aim of edifying the nation. As these ideas developed, they in turn absorbed a new language connected with absolutism, providentialism of a 'Whig' style English and later British imperialism, and the power and influence of Louis XIV (1638–1715), the Sun King.[47] The field has been covered at length in terms of Political Thought, the existence of such concepts with the emergence of the political party system, so there is therefore no need for a recapitulation here, other than to note the extensive work by amongst others, Quentin Skinner,[48] John Kenyon,[49] Tony Claydon,[50] Harry Dickinson,[51] and Mark Goldie.[52] Greater emphasis is put on the increasing emergence of providentialism, yet we should note that providentialism had always been a key component of the Divine Right of Kings, most obviously from the Tudor age, but it is hard to think of monarchs in earlier epochs who did not claim providential backing for their positions. To argue that this perspective emerged as a theory in 1689 and was not, for example, already firmly in existence under Elizabeth I, particularly following the defeat of the Spanish Armada, would not seem to sit too easily with the facts. The point is not that it was something new, but rather the degree to which providentialism was stressed. Much of the political thought discussion around Divine Right is centred on the fall of James II. Ultimately, 'loyalty to the church overrode loyalty to the king … and thus the most Royalist of all seventeenth-century political groups [the Tories] helped to usher James VII & II into exile, and to shut the door behind him'.[53] This is a line similarly argued by William Speck, in that Tory 'loyalties lay with the Church of England more than with the exiled king'.[54] What is quite clear is that the responses to the crisis of 1688/1689, and the question of authority, were undoubtedly influenced by the Regicide of 1649 and the Commonwealth that followed.[55] The coronation was a key tool in the resulting settlement, a mechanism for binding the nation together, of uniting Church and State, Whig and Tory, under a new joint monarchy. Edward Vallance goes further in exploring the implications for Britain, in that Scotland and Ireland were heavily involved too. This recognition is important, for by 1685, a Westminster coronation had become the sole one for Britain—there were no longer separate Scottish coronations, as there had been in 1633 and 1651. Moreover, by 1689, two distinct Coronation Oaths had developed: one for Scotland and one for England; the latter, in effect, applied to the rest of Britain. As for England, his analysis leads to the conclusion that the settlement was

> much less a peaceful transfer of power from one dynasty to another than one important stage in a protracted and messy struggle over the royal succession.[56]

However, this insight does not quite fit the facts, given that Anne succeeded to the throne with relative ease in 1702. Of course, Vallance is keen to underline the point that what emerged in 1688–1689 was a 'unique phenomenon' in English history, namely a 'dual monarchy'. He adds that although

> executive power was officially lodged with the King, the fact that William and Mary ruled as joint monarchs was vitally important to legitimating the Revolution. Mary's hereditary claim to the throne helped ease the consciences of Tories in giving their allegiance to the new monarchs.[57]

The coronation provided the praxis for this legitimation in ceremonial terms, symbolically crowning and anointing the new regime, and, in the acclamation and oath, binding monarchy and people together. In terms of a developing nationalism, Vallance sees the events of 1688/1689 as those in which the 'English people were deeply involved', for it

> was ordinary people, not the gentry, who first flocked to William's cause in the west of the country. It was the London crowd, so virulent in its anti-popery, which played a large part in James's decision to flee his kingdom rather than attempt to stay and fight.[58]

Vallance also underlines the way in which the political changes of 1688/1689 were interpreted as 'an opportunity to return divine blessings upon the nation in terms of its salvation from popery, through a thorough reformation of public morals and manners'.[59] Rightly, he sees this agenda not as heralding a new secular age, a problem with Strong's account of the alleged decline of Divine Right ideology, but quite the reverse: 'Christian religion remained at the core of public and private life'.[60] Perhaps his most interesting conclusion is that the changes of 1688/1689 started a process of passing supreme authority from the monarch to the legislature of Parliament. The Glorious Revolution may well have prevented the tyranny of an omnipotent monarch, but it did not prevent the 'possibility of legislative tyranny'; thinking of the modern era, Vallance refers to Lord Hailsham's famous dictum warning of the dangers of 'elective dictatorship'.[61]

Patrick Dillon examines the Tory standpoint on the importance of the Oath of Allegiance in the process of explaining the Tories' approach to William III and the departure of James II. For Archbishop Sancroft,

> this was an oath never to be broken, and in the heart of the Archbishop … the words reflected not just ritual but passionate belief. Only recently, Sancroft had commissioned a new edition of Robert Filmer's *Patriarcha*, the bible of English monarchists.[62]

In terms of Divine Right ideology, he notes the context of the pre-eminence of Louis XIV and his cultural impact upon Europe, for, by the Treaty of Ratisbon in 1684, the continent was 'froze[n] … in an attitude of supplication to the Sun King'. On this basis, if Divine Right monarchy was alive and thriving in France, then it seems unlikely that it would have failed to have survived the Restoration and be in decline, as suggested by Jeremy Black, Paul Monod, Hannah Smith, and Strong.[63] Nevertheless,

Dillon suggests that 'no ideology survived the Revolution intact'.[64] Whilst the concept of Divine Right may have evolved, it did not decline. Dillon's views on the coronation ceremony in general are questionable. He argues that

> two ideals had crystallised in the struggles around James's reign: the Tory dream of a paternal monarch commanding royal obedience, and the Whig model of contract government. Neither survived the Revolution intact, and neither was upheld by this ceremony.[65]

Yet the coronation oaths were precisely a form of quasi-contract (as will be explored in Chap. 3), and coronation sermons spoke of paternalism. Most notably, the Westminster Abbey sermon for Queen Anne (to be discussed in Chap. 2) talks of a 'nursing mother' to her people. Steven Pincus's research is particularly interesting in that his view shifts from one publication to another. Importantly for this book, in his earlier work, he argues that 'England's 1688 revolution was a nationalist revolution'.[66] This nationalism rested on common values, 'shared national characteristics', fear of France, but more vitally English peoples' 'love of their own nation'. It was this love that, according to Pincus, was 'so profoundly challenged by the policies and actions of James II [and] that … led them [his subjects] to insist that ultimate political authority lay in the nation'.[67] Furthermore (and perhaps a contention susceptible to attack by Vallance, given what we have seen of his interpretation), Pincus argues that 'because the English understood their revolution in … nationalist terms … it proved to be both bloodless and innovative. It was in this sense, at least, a "Glorious Revolution"'.[68] The present author would agree with regard to nationalism, but suggest that the bedrock of authority can be found in a shared quasi-contract between ruler and people, in the reciprocal acclamation and Coronation Oath. This book is also deeply mindful of the 'bloody' nature of the Revolution, most obviously in the events in Ireland. In terms of nationalism, such concepts did not develop as something new in the 1680s, but rather rested on an idea (however mythological) of an 'ancient constitution'. Furthermore, this study avoids a narrowly Anglocentric definition of nationalism, taking a broader British one. Yet for all of Pincus's focus on nationalism in 1998, in his later work, he claims that it is 'justifiable to understand the Revolution of 1688–1689 as a bourgeois revolution in a cultural and political sense'.[69] It is difficult to see how the two theories are compatible, unless his definition of 'nation' is exceptionally narrow. Clearly, this latter perception would not fit with Vallance's analysis outlined above. Pincus's later work also suggests that those holding Divine Right views were in the minority. On the other hand, this book demonstrates that such ideas were expressed in coronations throughout the early modern period, notably in sermons, and have remained in the centrality of the anointing to the present day. It seems highly improbable that set-piece sermons delivered on such high-profile public occasions would have risked being so out of touch with those listening, and likewise the religiosity of the anointing has been maintained in the twenty-first century—thus speaking to a sense of elevating the monarch above others, even in 2023. Obviously, the language of Divine Right was adopted over time in order that it would resonate, and the service has evolved, but at the core of a British coronation remains the anointing.[70]

Asch's recent analysis of Divine Right ideology stresses the providentialist nature of the British monarchy and a militaristic form of Protestantism. This was undoubtedly true and can be discerned in the coronation sermons of both William and Mary and George I. He goes on to remark that

> the future belonged to a reconfessionalized model of monarchy which downplayed the sacerdotal aspects of kingship while emphasizing the role of the monarch as a providential hero fighting for liberty and the one true faith; that is, Protestantism. This was certainly an image that William III adopted, but it was also projected onto James II's son-in-law and his wife by the supporters of the Glorious Revolution. This particular model of kingship continued to have a significant influence on the religious culture that gave monarchy legitimacy after 1714, when the Hanoverians ruled Britain. Whatever the personal and political deficiencies of the first two Georges, they both presented themselves as emphatically and often militantly Protestant; after all, their claims to the British crown were based on confessional allegiance, and not much else.[71]

British coronations did not downplay sacerdotalism, but they did stridently articulate a militant Protestantism, particularly in an age of war with France and of the demands of a burgeoning Empire. As Jonathan Clark has it, there was a shift from Divine Right based on 'hereditary succession' to one based on Protestantism, 'as demonstrated by the direct intervention of Providence'. Indeed, 'most of the clergy continued to preach the doctrines of divine right and passive obedience throughout the reigns of William III and Anne, and beyond'.[72]

Moving outside of Westminster Abbey, and considering the theme of environmental factors, Vladimir Jankovic's article is highly instructive. What have 'celestial conflagrations' to do with coronations? Further, how can unexplained happenings in the night sky in a completely different year to a coronation be at all germane to this project? Jankovic convincingly argues that the politics of astronomy in 1716 needs to be seen in the context of 'the fate of the Jacobite cause following King George's coronation' in 1714.[73] Not only does this interpretation stress the importance of George I's coronation in the battle for legitimacy against the Jacobite threat, but it also underlines the clear need to see coronations both in context and as providing a context for other developments. Moreover, his essay shows how the study of coronations extends far beyond political and constitutional history. When writing the article, Jankovic was a lecturer in the Centre for the History of Science, Technology and Medicine at Manchester University. His research was facilitated not by royal funds, or by Court studies enthusiasts, but by 'the Wellcome Trust for the History of Medicine, the Social Science Research Council, and the William Andrews Clark Memorial Library'. Certainly, his focus is political astronomy; yet, once again, one sees that coronations cast long shadows, infiltrating what might initially appear to be remote topics.[74] A further neglected perspective is presented by Gerard Reedy's intriguing essay on the 'noumenal sense' as a method used in the early modern world for 'interpreting social change as the direct effect of a noumenal transcendence'.[75] Reedy makes it very clear that the power of providence was seen in symbolic form at Charles II's 1661 coronation; the point he addresses is not whether or not people believed in such an 'outside force', but rather that of the ways in which it was to be understood. Nevertheless, whilst Reedy is absolutely right to see mystical monarchy surviving Regicide in 1649, he argues that Charles II's crowning day was the last to be held when such a conceptualisation was commonplace. His interpretation does not therefore take account of the solar and weather analogies adopted in James II's coronation sermon, nor in the reports of Queen Anne's coronation, as will be covered in Chap. 2. Far from diminishing, these ideas were part of a package of beliefs, centred on the power of 'the other', that were evoked to explain the events of the day. In other words, they were consistent elements of a providentialist Divine Right *mentalité* that was as important in Hanoverian Britain as it had been in 1661.

As introduced at the outset of this chapter, given the longevity and ubiquity of theories of divine kingship, it would seem unlikely that they would simply cease in an abrupt fashion. It has been assumed that as England and Britain moved to a more constitutional monarchy, particularly following the Glorious Revolution, Divine Right became incompatible with power sharing and therefore disappeared from a coronation. Such an argument is a *non sequitur* because the Divine Right ideology found in a coronation has nothing to do with the existing constitutional elements, present since the earliest times, in the form of an acclamation and an oath.

Background, Distinctions, and Definitions

From Kantorowicz to Glenn Burgess, much has been written about the ideology of Divine Right, whether in theology, history, or political thought, but it has tended to be narrowly conceptual. By contrast, this chapter will focus not on the idea itself, but rather on its realisation. The aim is to show how such a belief was actualised not only in the Westminster Abbey ceremony, but also in the world beyond—in communities across the country: in poems, dedications, and correspondence. The question at stake is not whether Divine Right was an important theory discussed abstractly; it clearly was. The point here is to assess significance *via* praxis[76]: the practical realities, seen in crowning; anointing with holy oil; use of St Edward the Confessor's Chair, incorporating the Stone of Scone; costumes; regalia; pomp, especially in music and art; and popular reverence in the continuation of the practice of touching for the 'King's Evil'. This chapter will highlight the importance of this practical dimension for the monarchy, the Church, politicians and the wider public.

Foundation of Divine Right Ideology

Although conceptions of kingship were given greater breadth and depth under the Tudors and early Stuarts, Divine Right ideology did not simply emerge in that period, nor was the basic doctrine unique to those dynasties. As has been indicated, this philosophy was ubiquitous. For Britain, its roots can be traced to the medieval heritage,[77] going back to St Edward the Confessor. The Confessor's reputed holiness and canonisation (1161) rendered him suitable to become the patron saint of later kings of England and gave credence to the idea of monarchical divinity.[78] Significantly, all successors at their coronations, which took place in the vicinity of his shrine and therefore as it were in the saint's presence, were first crowned with St Edward's Crown as well as being placed in his so-named chair.

This dedication to the cult of St Edward was firmly established by the Plantagenets, and in particular Henry III, who named his first son Edward as a mark of devotion. The Confessor's sacred status was essential in creating the holiness of Westminster Abbey, a royal peculiar, as a house of kings, a 'foundation in England [which] symbolised the immaterial Crown'.[79] This was equally important throughout the early modern period, as seen, for example, in Elizabeth I's coronation, records of which refer to 'St Edward's staff [and] ... an offering to St Edward's Shrine'.[80] These were the relics of royal holiness: the tangible evidence, for contemporaries, of the quasi-sacerdotal power inherent in sovereignty, and will be examined in more detail below.

The evolution of Divine Right ideology under the Tudors and Stuarts has attracted considerable scholarly attention.[81] Beyond James I's speeches and literary expositions, the theory found expression in Ruben's Apotheosis of the king. It would also appear in the early eighteenth century in Verrio's 'Apotheosis of Queen Anne as Astraea-Virgo' in the Queen's drawing room at Hampton Court.[82] Perhaps less well known is that Philip II of Spain was being portrayed as early as 1585 receiving Christ's blessing with the royal insignia, as if this was the Mass.[83] This point will be explored in more detail below. The depiction of James I of England was therefore not original, nor was the confessionalisation of Divine Right something new. However, the ideas flourished under Charles I, who assumed this inheritance and created his own sacerdotal idea of kingship, in which courtly ritual played a central role. This development was coupled with the king's patronage of Arminian divines and promotion of Laud's 'Beauty of Holiness' agenda.[84] Court sermons 'dwelt on the sacredness of kingship'; should one take public sermons and Laud's preaching before the king to be 'representative of what ... Charles like[ed] to hear', then these clerics 'filled his ears with Divine-Right theory and reference to the righteousness [of] the rulers of Israel. Kings[,] they reminded him, did God's work on earth'[85] and were '*Imago Dei*': 'the bright image of God, and the most magnificent and conspicuous representation of the divine majesty'.[86] With these ideas in mind, Cressy's work has looked at how Charles's kingship evolved in terms of the interaction between people and sovereign.[87] Charles's style of government and religious commitment foreshadowed his image as 'the martyr of the people'; that image and 'cult' did not just emerge with Regicide in 1649.[88] Andrew Lacey argues that by 1647–1648 'there was a substantial part of the nation who ... were ready to receive sympathetic images of Charles and who could identify their hopes and fears with the figure of the defeated king'.[89]

Biblical Justifications

Divine Right theory in early modern Britain was biblical in its origins and in much of its justification. Numerous scriptural texts exemplify sacral kingship:

> By me kings reign, and princes decree justice (Proverbs 8:15);
> I have said, Ye are gods. (Psalms 82: 6)

Such phrases and ideas were used throughout coronation proceedings to affirm the monarch's quasi-sacerdotalism. We see this, for instance, in the processional tributes lining the London streets, in musical anthems accompanying the litany, and in the coronation sermon. Scripture was pressed into service to validate the thesis that rulers obtained their earthly authority from God. It was an abiding Tudor trope to see the English monarchy in direct line to that of ancient Israel, and commonplace to compare sovereigns with biblical figures. Henry VIII had liked nothing better than to identify himself with 'David the destroyer of Goliath or Solomon the builder of the temple',[90] later in his reign even seeing himself as 'Typus Christi' or 'David as [a] Type of Christ'.[91] These associations continued: Edward VI was often referred to as 'Salomonem' or the young Josiah,[92] and Elizabeth I as 'gracious Debora[h], by whom God ... caused his Church of England to prosper in health, wealth, peace, policie, learning, religion, and many good gifts and graces'.[93] Elizabeth's portrayal as Deborah, by such figures as John Aylmer and John Hales, was two-fold. On the one hand, loyal subjects sought to praise their rulers by recognising their elevated status and answering opponents such as John Knox and his 1558 critique of queenship, and, on the other, wished to provide a model for princely rule.[94] There was perhaps plenty of aspiration here: Deborah of the Book of Judges defeated Israel's enemies and was at once wife, judge, prophetess, and mother. She brought forty years of peace to her people, something almost unheard of for an early modern subject.[95] Thus, emphasis on quasi-sacerdotal kingship, and a cult of royalty, embellished the Crown with a repertoire of biblical and classical *personae*; the Elizabethan cult of Gloriana entailed a profusion of images from the Virgin Mary, a second Eve, to Cynthia, Diana, and Astraea.[96]

Fig. 1.3 Queen Elizabeth I in coronation robes, by an unknown artist, oil on panel *c.*1600, National Portrait Gallery/Alamy

It is worth noting that such scriptural allegory came with the corollary that the Bible could also be used to identify weakness. For example, one writer's musings in January 1710/1711 show how, with hindsight, James II's end could be foretold from his crowning:

> Melancholick reflections for an hour, or two … made me call to my mind the story of Bernini, and his bust, burnt in Whitehall. It made me also call to mind the omens that happened at the coronation of his son James II. W[hi]ch I saw … the tottering of his crown upon his head, the broken canopy over it, and the flag hanging upon the white tower over[h]a[n]g[ing] my door, when I came home from the coronation. It was torn by the wind at the same time the signal was given to the Tower that he was crown'd: I put no great stresse upon omens, but I cannot despise them; most of them, I believe, come by chance, but some from superiour intel[l]ectual agents, especially those, w[i]ch regard the fate of kings, and nations[.][97]

The biblical allusions are clear with the torn flag being seen as the 'curtain of the temple [being] torn in two' (Mark 15:38) following Christ's crucifixion. The comparison with the holy nature of the sovereign is obvious, together with the providential conclusion that such omens are the work of a higher being.

It is possible to trace these biblical parallels across various coronations. For example, the surrounding days witnessed the delivery of speeches marking the monarch's arrival at Westminster. A case in point is that given for James I by the Recorder of London, Sir Henry Montagu, who also 'compared [the king] to Solomon', with further references to Israel and the legacy of Elizabeth I.[98] At Charles I's coronation, it was stated that he should keep his oaths in the tradition of 'Solomon and David'.[99] As will be discussed further in Chap. 2, coronation sermons abound with biblical and classical analogies. The monarch in these comparisons was easily identifiable; just as readily picked up by an early modern audience was the notion that England or Great Britain was Israel.[100] This providentialism, and Britain's dramatic military and commercial success on the world stage by 1714, was a key factor in the continuation of Divine Right ideology. How else had a sovereign been instituted to rule such a chosen nation? It is hard to beat Rosewell's 1714 coronation sermon, which will be encountered in more detail in Chap. 2. Rosewell's point was to stress George I's Divine Right in the face of a rival claimant. Though providentialism itself obviously was not exclusively Protestant, Providential Protestantism in this case had won out against the Roman Catholic Pretender. The coronation ceremony was therefore necessary: a ritual of elevation to mark off the newly crowned and anointed sovereign from the rest of the kingdom and, importantly, any remaining Stuart. All was to be consistent with God's plan.

Biblical comparisons invariably featured in coronation services, often in musical (anthem) form. Indeed, they would be prominent in the anthem to surpass all Divine Right anthems: Handel's *Zadok the Priest* (1727).[101] Those familiar with this music will know the extent to which Old Testament figures play a part; less well known, however, is that this was a new version of an old anthem. An earlier setting had been used for the 1603 coronation of James I. It was also there in Charles I's 1626 coronation: 'meanwhile the quire singeth this anthem: Zadock the Priest, and Nathan the Prophet, anointed Solomon king: and all the people rejoiced, and said, God save the king for ever'.[102] This elevation of the sovereign's status was not confined to speeches and other literary works—it was to be received firstly by the elite and then by the populace. As late as 1727, Handel's anthem struck just the appropriate Divine Right note for the occasion. In the words of one contemporary, 'the coronation … was the finest [and] most magnificent of any that ever was in England'.[103] From the early modern to the modern, the 1902 coronation 'was truly an imperial affair' and would see the music continue to match traditional scriptural themes, with the addition of Parry's 'I was glad' (words taken from Psalm 122) and 'through … publications … the coronation music became disseminated on an unprecedented scale'.[104]

Royal Saints and their Afterlives in the Age of Imperialism

Significantly, theories of Divine Right did not just rest on scripture. Royal and national saints also played a major part in affirming the sovereign's holy nature, for the ruler was not only crowned in the custom of David or Solomon, but in line with the heritage of the 'glorious king … St Edward'.[105] This inheritance, this link to the Anglo-Saxons, was all the more important in the context of the shifting sands of dynasticism and the increasing internationalism of the British monarchy. The very selection of a saint's day (or feast day) for a coronation can be seen going back to the medieval, from King Harold II on Twelfth-night/Epiphany, William the Conqueror on Christmas Day and Young King Henry in 1170 on 14 June, 'the feast of St Basil'.[106] Tudors, Stuarts, Hanoverians, and their successors alike exploited this powerful tradition. A coronation was a perfect opportunity to display these ideas in praxis, demonstrating the sovereign's 'distant elevation above the common herd'. Three figures—one real saint, one legendary saint, and one putative saint—must be considered in this connection: St Edward the Confessor, St George, and Henry VI. We begin, therefore, by considering the crucial legacy of the Confessor saint.

The cult of Edward the Confessor was firmly established with his canonisation in 1161, contributing to the belief in the 'King's Evil' (discussed below) and the mystical attributes of sovereignty itself. The chief symbols of that majesty were two magnificent crowns: that of St Edward and the 'imperial' crown of England—styled imperial after Henry V turned the open circlet into a closed diadem. Henry VI, Edward IV, and Richard III 'successively advanced the symbolism of the crown imperial' iconographically, as Hoak has shown[107]; Henry VII so magnified that symbolism that he can be said to have invented something new, 'a veritable cult of sacred imperial kingship'.[108] Henry VIII was the epitome of grandeur; his coronation banquet was a sign of things to come: 'greater than any Caesar had known'.[109] For his finale, he even planned a tomb of monumental proportions, but the project was so elaborate that it was far from complete by his death. His 'kingship had carried an imperial dimension', legally expressed in 1533–1534, which drew inspiration from his ancestors, particularly St Edward.[110] Crucially, all Henry's successors, at their coronations, were first crowned with St Edward's Crown. Thus, those inheriting the English throne could claim 'divine or saintly blood' in their lineage. St Edward was to the Crown what St George was, as patron saint, to the nation and to the Order of the Garter, famously established by Edward III.[111] No doubt there was some fluidity, but the continual coronation invocation of these figures was intrinsically linked with Divine Right ideology and with a growing providentialism: the notion that England, with its growing empire, was the new Israel.

Yet how would these key features fit with the Reformation(s)? A saintly cult would not seem to sit too readily with Protestantism. Nevertheless, in terms of change and continuity, Henry VIII did not abandon St Edward, nor would his son. Whilst the evangelical hold on England grew under Edward VI, profoundly influencing the development of imperial kingship, 'evangelicals at Court invested the symbolism of the crown imperial with new meaning'; the position of most other saints was smashed, indeed quite literally so in massive iconoclasm.[112] Edward VI personally railed against the Knights of the Garter, for example, and the traditional connection with St George: 'a saint of decidedly legendary character whom most reformers treated with frank contempt, and whom Edward himself ridiculed at the Garter ceremony of 1550'.[113] Whilst St George was abandoned,[114] as a legacy of Roman Catholicism, Edward the Confessor and, more importantly, the cult of 'imperial' kingship would survive, playing a prominent role in the young king's coronation pageants. To have such a link to this famous ancestor was clearly too valuable an asset to reject. In the 1547 pre-coronation procession, an enormous replica of Edward VI's crown imperial was shown triumphant on a 'sumptuous founteyne' at the Great Conduit in Cheapside, London's main thoroughfare. At the Little Conduit, an array of flags and banners surmounted a replica tower, opening out to display the person of 'an anncient man setting in a chere … representing Kinge Edward the Confessor' wearing, anachronistically, 'a crowne imperiall'.[115] Edward VI was therefore not rejecting divine sanction, but was interpreting it in a very different—specifically Biblical—fashion.

In this transitional period for the Church in England, various other elements of a more discernible Roman Catholic tradition remained in Edward VI's coronation. Given the reforming influences, and his own evangelical zeal, it is notable that the presence of three 'confessors of the householde' is recorded.[116] Why were they at the coronation, and why three, and where was the Reformation in all this? Such questions highlight how a coronation could be a surprising bulwark against radical change. Not only did it come at the beginning of a reign, when it might have been problematic to alter an age-old format, but it was also invested with the religious ethos of an earlier era. The coronation made manifest the link to a divine or saintly status that was of such importance that it was worth compromising a shift in religious views. Authenticity was to be found in its very traditional nature and persistence. Radical change would have lessened the power of the occasion. Although it would be difficult to prove, what is likely to have triggered thoughts about St Edward the Confessor and St George, especially for those in the Abbey, would be the objects whose names record them and the fact that many of the coronations in this period took place on St George's Day. Of course, a feast day in itself is intangible, but the objects were not, and they therefore merit extensive discussion below.

Having survived the evangelical purge of saints, the Confessor's saintly influence was extensively displayed emblematically in the crowning of the Tudor queens regnant. Mary inherited an imperial kingship merged with a royal supremacy over the Church, which she sought to dissolve in favour of the restoration of obedience to Rome. Whilst the 'imperial' dignity automatically passed to Elizabeth I, the royal supremacy had to be recreated by statute in 1559. In Elizabeth's case, Henry's 'crown imperial' played a prominent role in Richard Grafton's coronation pageantry—for the image of Edward the Confessor was seen enthroned in imperial majesty. St Edward's reputed holiness was referenced throughout Elizabeth's coronation, symbolically present in both crown and staff. Significantly, despite her Protestant credentials, Elizabeth still made the customary 'offering to St Edward's Shrine'[117]; something that continued in the shape of two formal oblations, as seen in the coronations of James II and William and Mary.[118]

On the first of those occasions, a remarkable discovery seems to have been made which emphatically proves the continuing resonance of St Edward the Confessor in the late seventeenth century. When scaffolds were being built inside Westminster Abbey for the coronation, the shrine was damaged. It was possible for a crucifix to be extracted, which was described as of very considerable value. The item could not be concealed and, having been brought to the attention of the collegiate authorities, eventually found its way to the king, and it was reported that he 'in reverence to the antient proprietor, wears this religious ornament himself'. The significance of this discovery was stressed by John Gibson in a book of 1688, where he writes

> But as the vision of St Brightwald ... assured him, the kingdom of England was the kingdom of God, and He would give it to whom He pleased. So this *Regium Cimelium*, this royal rarity was ordained for one elect of God; whom, though the numerous and powerful exclusive party in England, and a malevolent party in Scotland, would have put by; yet maugre all, He is become Saint Edward the Confessor's successor to his crown, scepter, and this religious relique, so wonderfully preserved[.][119]

Despite Edward VI's hostility to the Order of the Garter, the institution survived for the remainder of the early modern period and indeed flourished, which meant that the figure of 'St George the Holy Martyre'[120] continued to hold some prominence as England's patron saint. It is in that context, that we should understand the significance of the choice of 23 April as coronation day in 1661, 1685, and 1702. Moreover, the fact of this conjunction was stressed in several publications, such as Morley's 1661 sermon and other commemorative works.[121] Furthermore, this feast day resonance was also picked up by private correspondence. For example, Thomas Smith writing to Edward Bernard states that 'Great preparations are making at Westminster ... [for] St George's Day'.[122] Such was the reputation of this national saint that in a poem to commend George Monck (1608–1670)[123] for his services in the Restoration, he is figured as St George:

> But now without dispute it is well knowne,
> Saint George is truly England's Champion
> Henceforth, Brave Monke, weele offer to thy shrine
> All the due praises for our Charles [and] thine
> Amonge our Aprill Saints shall duly there
> George Monke be placed in our calendar.
> Knights of thy noble Order now may decke
> With thee bl[u]e ribbands worne about their necke.[124]

Interestingly, St Edward the Confessor and St George were nearly joined by a third saint with monarchical connections in that Henry VII pursued an impressive campaign to have Henry VI canonised. In doing so, the king was acknowledging the strength of the unofficial cult that had emerged, but his efforts ultimately proved abortive.[125]

Although it is obviously a very different culture, nevertheless, a comparison with Russia is instructive, not least because Peter the Great visited England in early 1698. He recognised the power of saints as the means for establishing 'a new brand of "holiness" … [to] emphasise … the sacredness of the monarchy'.[126] This is best seen in his revival of the cult of St Andrew (1688/1689),[127] which would have a standing in St Petersburg that was commensurate with that of St George in England. Indeed, he may well have picked up useful ideas during his visit, when attending the Garter ceremony; he had been offered the honour by William III, but had declined because he was in the process of founding his own chivalric order.[128]

It is clear, therefore, that special saints were harnessed to affirm quasi-sacerdotal kingship, not only in Britain but also in the Russia of Peter the Great. For the tsar, it was largely a case of inventing tradition; for British rulers, it was a case of renewing long-standing customs. In both instances, saintly power was brought to bear in order to 'bless' the Crown and strengthen monarchical ambitions. Most importantly, in terms of Divine Right, saints were thus used to highlight the divine attributes of sovereignty. Nevertheless, despite the similarities, there is no doubt that the ways in which these saints were interpreted varied in this period, as well as the motivations for interpreting them—interesting discoveries might well emerge from dedicated inquiries along those lines. However, the important point here is far from narrow—it is that, whatever the understandings and motivations, appeal was made to these figures, so that by *c.*1661–*c.*1714, there was substantial continuity, despite the strong potential for rupture during the Reformations.

Coronation Honours and Knights of the Bath

The power of royal patronage is often nowhere more evident than in the accession of a monarch and the creation of coronation peerages—a tradition going back to 1377, when Richard II created four earldoms. The average number of creations per coronation prior to 1661 was roughly the same number.[129] These creations could be a mixture of elevating commoners to the nobility and of advancing existing peers within peerage ranks. With the Restoration, Charles II had a chance substantially to strengthen the royal cause by quite literally ennobling support—this involved twelve coronation peerage creations: six earldoms (from those who had previously held baronies) and six baronies.[130] This was thus a sizeable number by coronation peerage creation standards and is therefore significant in highlighting Charles's efforts to cement his position. Two good examples of the sovereign's exercise of munificence can be seen with the Howards and the Annesleys. Charles Howard, 1st Earl of Carlisle, and Arthur Annesley, 1st Earl of Anglesey, were both elevated to earldoms in 1661. These marks of royal favour make good case studies for the Crown's efforts in political rehabilitation. The two men had been active parliamentarians in the Civil Wars, but moved to support the Restoration and were rewarded for their support. Howard had served the parliamentarians with distinction at the Battle of Worcester in 1651. From 1653, he served on the Council of State.[131] Annesley was not militarily involved in the same manner as Howard. However, he did serve as an MP on the parliamentarian side in the later 1640s, and 'the harsh treatment of his father by Lord Strafford when the latter was lord deputy of Ireland no doubt inclined him to the parliamentary side'.[132] These men had not been royalists, but the king chose to reward them for their endorsement of monarchy in 1660, in an effort to unify the country. James II and Queen Anne did not follow suit in coronation peerage creations, although there were some elevations on either side of their coronations, but perhaps they were not near enough to count as 'coronation' ones. However, the dynastic shifts in the accessions of William III and Mary II in 1688/1689 and George I in 1714 saw the creation of 11 and fourteen coronation peerages, respectively.[133] The opportunity to reinforce their positions in uncertain waters was too much to be overlooked. These examples show the monarch deploying the royal prerogative as the fount of all honour in order to give rewards and to alter the complexion of the political and social establishment.[134] Queen Victoria was doing very much the same in the nineteenth century, and the records of these coronation honours can be found in *The London Gazette*, from 20 July to 24 July 1838.[135] Turning to the twentieth century, 1953 would see the continuation, indeed propagation, of honours, with *The London Gazette* record running to numerous pages of coronation honours bestowed by Queen Elizabeth II.[136] 2023 did not see specific Coronation Honours at the time of the grand occasion in May, but rather, at the end of the year, with the Royal Victorian Order—including the impresario Sir

Antonio Pappano, conductor of the coronation orchestra.[137] Appointments continued in 2024, when in April, King Charles III appointed Lord Peach and Lord Lloyd-Webber respectively, to the Order of the Garter. The former had the duties of bearing the sword Curtana, the latter, composing music for the service. In May 2024, it was also reported that the King had presented the Duke of Norfolk (Earl Marshal) with a silver gilt cup, continuing a tradition of perquisites that ran for centuries and adjudicated over by the Court of Claims.[138] Commonwealth realms also made changes and new honours. In New Zealand, the then Prime Minister Chris Hipkins declared that the New Zealand Royal Honours List would be restyled 'The King's Birthday and Coronation Honours List 2023', including Queen Camilla's elevation to the Order of New Zealand.[139]

The process of appointment was and is equally important. In more modern times, whether at Buckingham Palace, St James's, or at Windsor, the setting can be seen to add to the occasion. In the early modern world, a list of coronation honours was one thing, but the point is that the bounty of dignities would achieve reality at the Banqueting House in Whitehall, suitably under the watchful gaze of Rubens's glorious Apotheosis of James I. These were honours deriving their prestige in two ways: through the Divine Right of the giver and the magnificence of the staging, for, like the coronation, this ceremony was a remarkable pageant, involving insignia, robes and the presence of much of the aristocracy. For example, Charles II was enthroned in state, and each appointee made three gestures of obeisance to his person, following which the letters patent were passed by Garter King of Arms to the lord great chamberlain, thence to the king, and from Charles to the secretary of state, who declaimed the patent before returning it to the king, who then handed it to the newly created peer. John Evelyn recorded this great spectacle:

> then were they robed, their coronets & collers put on by his majestie, then were they placed in rank on both sides of the state & throne: but the barons put of their caps & circles and held them in their hands, the Earles keeping on their coronets as cousins to the king.[140]

The coronation honours list was a great opportunity to garner support, but also to placate those who might be disruptive. For example, in 1689, the dukedom of Cumberland was granted to Prince George of Denmark, the husband of Princess Anne, the future Queen Anne, presumably in an attempt to soothe potential tension.[141] Another form of honour, strongly associated with coronations, was a relic of a chivalric age—the creation of the Knights of the Bath—and it is to that category that we now turn.

Acts of cleansing and anointing were the two most private rituals of the coronation process, and are perhaps amongst the least understood. Cleansing was integral to the creation of Knights of the Bath—they underwent a medieval rite of purification that traditionally took place, together with religious observances and the swearing of an oath, a few days preceding the coronation, often at the Tower of London.[142] Even by the coronation of Young King Henry in 1170, 'rituals for dubbing were well developed, [involving] … [t]he aspirant … spend[ing] the previous night in vigil in church, before taking a ritual bath of spiritual purification, reflecting the rite of baptism'.[143] How many knights were created lay in the sovereign's discretion, and to be chosen was obviously a mark of considerable favour. Unlike the Knights of the Garter, the Knights of the Bath were not originally constituted as a military Order. The last figures to be elevated according to the ancient pattern achieved that distinction prior to the coronation of 1661; a hiatus then ensued until the foundation of the Order (still extant) in 1725.[144] Today, knights of either Order may be appointed more or less at any time; installation is, however, a different matter. But for the period before the 1661–1725 gap, it is extremely rare to find evidence of Knights of the Bath being created other than in connection with a coronation,[145] and therefore, one supposes that they must have attained a degree of prominence in the remainder of those events.

Whereas ordinary knighthoods might be conferred at any time, the ancient Order of the Knights of the Bath was unusual in being replenished on the eve of a coronation, which therefore requires some attention here, though (for reasons that remain somewhat obscure) 1661 was to be the last occasion on which it occurred.[146] The election of Knights of the Bath was an important element of patronage that involved a medieval ritual of bathing, in an almost Old Testament Leviticus form of purification. The secondary literature appears to be rather slight for such an interesting topic, and we must recognise that some of it relates to the order as re-created (on different lines) in 1725. There are, of course, works in the antiquarian tradition that simply list the names of those honoured, such as that by Walter Metcalfe.[147] The order naturally features in general treatments of the chivalric orders and of the ethos to which they relate.[148] Only one recent work seems to address the Order of the Bath exclusively, and this is concerned entirely with the foundation of 1725.[149] Much work therefore remains to be done for a future study, yet it is possible here to suggest some potential avenues for inquiry. With the Restoration, expectations of such honours being distributed ran high; a letter written six weeks before the coronation suggests that up to ten new dukedoms might be created and over 100 Knights of the Bath.[150] These are exceptionally high figures, even if inflated by expectation, and go to show that not only did the build-up to coronations have a wider impact, but also that for the country elite they were potential game-changers in terms of social mobility. Whilst many figures continued from one sovereign to another to carry out their duties resulting from inherited status, this was an opportunity for the rise of new personalities in the world of Court and politics. In the end, 68 Knights of the Bath were created for the coronation of Charles II, still a substantial total.[151] Looking in more detail at the list of names published contemporaneously in *Mercurius Publicus*, we see obvious rewards for earlier sacrifices. For example, one recipient, Sir Adrian Scroop, is described as the son of Sir Gervas Scroop, 'who received nineteen wounds in one battle for his majesty'.[152] We also see multiple awards consolidating the political sway of certain families. The Egertons provide a good instance here: both Lord Brackley, the heir to the Earl of Bridgewater, and William Egerton, Lord Bridgewater's second son, were amongst those honoured. The Egertons were certainly on the ascent. By 1689, John Egerton, 3rd Earl of Bridgewater, would be cupbearer to the king.[153] Charles II was perhaps echoing his grandfather James I, whose 'liberality' saw the creation of 'sixty-two knights of the bath, more than twice as many as the twenty-seven installed by Henry VIII on the eve of his coronation and five times as many as the eleven dubbed by Elizabeth'.[154]

Millenarianism and the New Jerusalem

Divine Right ideology rested heavily on biblical foundations, whatever contested readings of scripture there may have been. In Tudor times, this became linked with other equally scripturally-based movements: millenarianism, immanent eschatology, apocalypticism, providentialism, and the notion of creating a New Jerusalem. Astrology could also be added.[155] In some respects, in practical terms, a fatalism was also present, coupled with a theistic idea of God. Perhaps this was an ancient legacy of a concept of Divine Right, rooted in Egyptian thought, that

> [t]he kingship is central, one, indivisible, and unique. It is on earth and in heaven, solar in origin and manifestation. No one can escape its power, claims, or obligation.[156]

It is clear that duty was important, but even in the revolutionary time of Akhenaten, there was a sense of predestination and providentialism. With this in mind, it is important to address the suggestion that providentialism was a new aspect of Divine Right ideology after the Glorious Revolution. Gerald Straka rightly challenges the interpretation that 'Divine Right theory died a sudden death' with James II's departure, and that the roots of providentialism in Divine Right ideology were to be found in 'medieval and renaissance political theory'.[157] By contrast, he asserts that what he calls 'Divine Right of providence' replaced 'the Stuart concept of divine hereditary right'.[158] The former point is true: that concept of providentialism was already ingrained in medieval and Tudor ideology and culture. God's supposed favour towards the British nation was a key component of the doctrine prior to 1689 and featured prominently in Elizabeth I's reign, most obviously in the triumph over the Spanish Armada. Providentialist Divine Right was not a uniquely English or British doctrine. Jason Nice has convincingly written on French parallels, showing the two countries' continued association with Old Testament Israel; France 'was a nation under God with exactly the same spiritual and providential principles'.[159]

Geoffrey Parker's analysis highlights how the early modern world was dominated by messianic and apocalyptic thought, arguing that this was prevalent across the Abrahamic religions.[160] The Shahs of Iran claimed to messianic status; the founder of the Safavid Dynasty, Shah Isma'il, regarded himself as the *Mahdi* (1494–1592 CE),[161] as did the Ottoman sultans. Sultan Selim defeated Shah Isma'il in 1514 and acquired cities of immense religious significance: Jerusalem, Mecca and Medina. In so doing, he described himself in messianic terms, and was 'compared ... with Alexander the Great, Genghiz Khan and Tamerlane'.[162] His heir, Suleiman 'the Magnificent', adopted by 1532 a 'special tiara with four crowns, symbolising the rule of the last world emperor'.[163] This crown has almost papal connotations. Suleiman's name referenced Solomon of the Qur'an, but his repertoire included biblical comparisons and mention of Alexander the Great. He was honoured as the *mujaddid* (renewer of Islam).[164] Another example of this Solomonic tradition exists in Sephardic Jewish tradition. With their expulsion by the Spanish Inquisition, Sephardic communities sought another Solomon, a 'Ben-David' or messiah. Two such figures arose: Isaac Abravanel, who emerged in Italy, and the Portuguese Solomon Molcho. Both proved unsuccessful. Although Molcho was to meet the Holy Roman Emperor Charles V, he did not persuade him of his desire to revive Judaism and retake the Promised Land, and was burnt at the stake.[165]

Turning to the Christian world, and less well known, was Philip II's messianic vision. He had assumed much of the mantle of his father, Charles V, who was often seen in a messianic light, in processions, and in his titles. A pageant celebrating Charles's entry into Bruges (1515) compared that city to Jerusalem and Charles with the Messiah. From his maternal grandparents, Ferdinand of Aragon and Isabella of Castile, Charles derived another strand of 'messianic imagery', of being a 'new David'. He also inherited the titles of 'Catholic king' and 'king of Jerusalem'.[166] Parker suggests that when it came to Philip's foreign policy, he 'expected God to provide a miracle to bridge the gap between means and ends'.[167] Philip's belief in providentialism, and his divine status, can be seen from ministerial correspondence: 'May God give you life and health, because you are engaged in His service and in mine—which is the same thing.'[168] Artists often depicted this overlap, showing the king 'in direct communion with heaven',[169] as seen in Fig. 1.4.[170]

Beyond the obvious providentialism implicit in Philip's notion of being God's instrument, there is the question of Philip as a consecrated person. Presumably, not all of God's instruments are necessarily consecrated, and not all consecrated people are God's instruments. The Elizabethans may have had difficulties in seeing Philip II in that way. It is important to recognise the distinction between these ideas. Nevertheless, even if understood in different ways, we can see that notions of Divine Right—of Philip as '*rex et sacerdos*: king and priest'—were central to early modern *mentalité*.[171] Philip's role as Mary I's consort fused *iuredivino* ideology with Tudor ideas of kingship. His responsibilities included that of joint sovereign of the Order of the Garter.[172] So enamoured was he with the regal position that he even considered recovering the title of Defender of the Faith after Mary's death.[173] Mary, in marrying Philip, had also acquired the queenship of Jerusalem.[174] This title disappeared with Mary, but the connection with Jerusalem did not. London–Jerusalem parallels became common in Protestant preaching under Elizabeth I and the early Stuarts.[175]

It is clear, therefore, that Straka's latter argument—that hereditary right became providential right—does not adequately explain the survival

Fig. 1.4 Christ invests Philip II of Spain with royal insignia: an engraving by Johannes Wierix, after Ambrosius Francken, published by Willem van Haecht, 1570–1580 (The British Museum Images)

of Divine Right conceptions, given that the notion of providence was **already** cemented in British ideology long before the Glorious Revolution. Indeed, these ideas were established across religions and far more nuanced. We can therefore conclude that Divine Right ideology was ever evolving, for different rulers and their supporters played out differing elements of the theory.

Objects

As we have seen, Divine Right kingship in Britain rested on biblical origins that were reinforced by a legacy of saintly power. These scriptural echoes, and their saintly endorsement, were given a concrete reality in the coronation: in both symbols of majesty and acts of homage. Homage will be dealt with later, but central to the visible realities of Divine Right ideology were the symbols of majesty—the regalia—shown in all their splendour on coronation day. These items were designed to highlight the biblical basis for the Crown's sovereignty and quasi-sacerdotalism and to stress the sacred link to the Confessor king. These objects held tremendous symbolic importance.[176] These remarkable, priceless objects should be accorded as much significance by historians as any document relating to Divine Right ideology since contemporaries saw them as hugely important relics, imbued with ancestral power. Of course, the objects themselves were visible chiefly in Westminster Abbey and to a limited degree in processions, but public perception must have been much wider, for iconography to do with regalia appeared in several publications.[177] If such pieces indicated the praxis of Divine Right theory in the liturgy of a coronation, then their post-Commonwealth recreation and survival show how the theory lasted in material form, long after it had been suggested that the concept had diminished. Since the Crown Jewels have received extensive scholarly attention, notably by Anna Keay, a detailed analysis is not required here.[178] We should also recognise that the regalia was substantially enlarged in the eighteenth and nineteenth centuries. What is relevant for this book is the way in which the sacred connotations of particular items were used to promote the ideology of Divine Right. The Coronation Ring will be explored below, whilst other objects will feature in Chap. 4.

Sovereign as Priest?

This question has many parts. It is a moot point to what extent a sovereign ceased to be an ordinary lay person. And if they did cease, then what did they become? It is impossible to measure how far in a coronation a 'king or queen became God' or assumed quasi-sacerdotal powers; one cannot quantify divine eminence. Nevertheless, we should acknowledge early modern perceptions of divine kingship and sacerdotalism, with reference to coronations. This section argues: firstly, that the anointing was an ordination/consecration and thus imbues the sovereign with an indelible priest-like character; secondly, that in that sense, the coronation was generally analogous to a sacrament, in terms of the transmission of grace; and thirdly, that aspects of the ceremony are suggestive of particular sacraments.

Contradictory opinions existed. One Act of Parliament spoke of: 'power given by God to princes of the earth … your grace beinge a lay man'.[179] By contrast, Henry VIII regarded himself as akin to a bishop: 'a lay bishop such as [the Emperor] Constantine had been'.[180] Here was a sovereign who was *Fidei Defensor*, 'Defender of the Faith'[181]—the title remained even after his renunciation of Roman obedience. His status as God's vicegerent, and combining temporal and spiritual powers, was represented iconographically in the famous title page to the *Great Bible* (1539). That the authority that came with the association with St Edward the Confessor and the anointing was increasingly important is suggested by the fact that Henry VIII required Anne Boleyn to be crowned with St Edward's crown. This was unprecedented for a queen consort.[182] The pattern of sovereigns as conduits for God's word was perpetuated under Edward VI: the frontispiece of Cranmer's 1550 Catechism shows the boy king handing the Bible to his bishops.[183]

These notions, once established, would continue far beyond the Tudor dynasty. Sir Henry Montagu (recorder of London) made a speech before James I's 1603 coronation, stating that 'the greate God of heaven be thanked that hath blessed us w[i]th such a god on earth'.[184] A poem commemorating Charles II's London procession on 22 April and his coronation the following day highlights God's blessing and his providential actions in the Restoration:

> God save Kinge Charles the second: let the cry
> Strike dead thy foes, which sends the ecchoinge sky.
> Let heaven's waggones through the world convey
> in thyne owne wayne the triumphs of this day:
>
> … flora to ushe[r] in thy pompe puts out
> all her enamled traine: which throwne about
> are stron'd as royall carpets in greate state,
> Thy springing honour to inaugurate.
> Thus 1 earth 2 men, nature & art, dos bye sye?
> Which shall illustrate most thy maijesty.
> Heaven (a) to is auspicious, 2 prepares to bee
> it selfe thy glorious royall canopy.
> How hath God chang'd our scene! Onely by thee
> Heaven ordaines our peace and liberty.
> The keepers of our libertyes before kept them so close ….
>
> Thanks be to heaven and you
>
> Passe on, greate sir, in triumph to adorne
> Your royall head: a prince not made, but borne.
> Ascend thy throne of State, illustrious stemme

> ordaind by heaven for a diadem.
> See how thy nobles all in order stand
> about thee with their coronets in hand,
> Deriv[e]d from thyne the fountaine: as we know
> from the vast ocean lesser rivers flow:
> Archbishop Juxton with his sacred oyle
> Anoints thy temples; sweetening thy exile.
> Whom fate from ruine next, now honoured
> To put th' imperiall crowne upon thy head.
> O God, instill such graces as may fit
> This royall head to beare the weight of it.
> Let quires of men & angells ecchoinge singe
> this musicall anthem, this, – God Save the Kinge.[185]

According to another poem celebrating his 1661 coronation, Charles II, succeeding his father, was 'the faith defender'.[186] In the anointing and crowning, Charles had been made vicegerent, a priest-like intercessor with God for his people. Regarding James II's crowning, one correspondent told Sancroft that

> the tyme of his majestyes coronation [is] at hand wherein his blood is consecrated by your grace, or some other bishop.[187]

The coronation is clearly here viewed as making the monarch sacred. To consecrate 'is to set apart (a person or thing) as sacred' to God; it is 'to dedicate solemnly for some sacred or religious purpose, and so to give the object itself a character of holiness'. The Mass, for example, is made holy when the elements are consecrated, and the host is elevated, making it 'fit for ... religious use'.[188] A coronation can be seen in that light. It is, in many respects, a sacrament and akin to the Eucharist. In this instance, the sovereign is consecrated, like a priest, who, undergoing ordination, is anointed.[189] This is key in British coronations; by contrast, Italian princes (except the pope) remained 'unanointed ... [and] did not have the status of *personae sacrae* or anointed "sacred beings"'.[190] The monarch in the British coronation service is anointed with holy chrism (oil),[191] analogously to Christ, for the Messiah was anointed king, priest, and prophet. Likewise, the adoration of the magi who came to pay homage to the infant Jesus is replicated in a coronation. Just as Jesus had a ministry, so the coronation invests the ruler with a pastoral charge. The investiture with religious vestments and symbols accentuated this dual role, paralleling the way in which a priest's clothing signifies his position. The priestliness of the sovereign was by no means unique to Britain. Turning to the continent, it was customary in France to view chrism as having been divinely sent; coupled with the power to touch for the King's Evil, this gave rise to 'the French ... insist[ing] that the consecration of their king was an eighth sacrament'.[192]

As has been adumbrated above, a coronation also has parallels with the pre-Reformation sacrament of marriage.[193] The service can be seen as confirmatory of the engagement a monarch enters into from accession; it is the public affirmation of the position and duties of the new ruler and their contract with their people.[194] This relationship is symbolised in the Coronation Ring, as presented to Mary I: 'a gold ring [was] put on her graces marrying finger'.[195] For James I, it was even ordered 'that the ring shall be set on the king's wedding finger'.[196] This convention continued and is expressed in a seventeenth-century manuscript:

> Receive this ring as a pledge of the mar[r]iage that is between the king and his people. (the ring is now put on) ... and remember, that as God has made, you, our lord and king, a husband to your people; so it is your majesties part to love and govern them [and] to provide for their welfare, as it is theirs to pay you their affection and obedience.
> And thou Lord that hast made this happy mar[r]iage by thy good providence, prosper thou thy owne handywork, keep his ma[jes]ty [and] his people together in love inviolable, [and] ... faithfull performance of all their duties to our comfort, [and] to the glory of thy name[.][197]

This was God's work: the doing of the

> Lord, who by thy good providence hast brought this our king and his people together, blast the wicked designs of all those that would put them asunder. Let it be seen that this was thy own choice. Bless, oh Lord, and prosper thy owne handy-work.[198]

Sir George Buc's *History of King Richard* of 1619, in one passage on the coronation, turns to his monarch, King James I,[199] and further enunciates the consecratory and marital analogy:

Fig. 1.5 Miniature of the coronation of Edmund, surrounded by courtiers, with an illuminated initial 'T'[he], from John Lydgate's *Lives of Saints Edmund and Fremund*, *c.*1461–1475 (from the British Library archive, Yates Thompson 47, fol. 22v)

> He hath in possession also those singular and particular monuments of empire and reign ... The one of these being the ring of the holy King Edward, the son of King Ethelred, which was consecrate and extraordinarily blessed by St John the Baptist in Palestine and sent back to the king, as old writers affirm. Which ring hath been carefully and religiously kept in the Abbey of Westminster, being, as they say, the ring which the Archbishop of Canterbury is accustomed at the inauguration and consecration of the kings to put upon their finger, called in our stories, the wedding ring of England.[200]

The tradition of a Coronation Ring can be found even earlier, in Greek and Egyptian custom. For the Romans, it can be seen in the magistracy, 'whence [according to Legg] it ... passed to the Christian bishop and the Christian king'.[201] In a British setting, the Coronation Ring has a tradition that goes back to the Medieval era. The current Coronation Ring dates from 1831 and the coronation of William IV.[202] The Ring appears to be both a very significant part of the Anglo-Saxon and also the Norman coronation tradition. The origins of the Ring can be found in early coronation orders that pre-date the *Liber Regalis* (*c.*1390). Reference is found to the Ring in the Second Recension (sometimes referred to as Æthelred II's Coronation Order) and possibly used as a guide for the coronation ceremonies of Harold Godwinson and William the Conqueror. It is also referenced in the Twelfth Century Coronation Order (sometimes referred to as the Third Recension) and in the list for Henry III's (1207–1272) regalia. Legg traces the survival of this extraordinary legacy up to (and including) Queen Victoria, and the tradition has continued to the present era. The ring is another example of a coronation as consecration, for it is an 'imitation of the ceremonies used in the consecration of a bishop. From very ancient times, a ring has been part of the ensigns of a bishop'.[203]

A similar tradition to that of the Sovereign's Ring is the Queen Consort's Ring. It also features in the early coronation records that predate the *Liber Regalis.* Legg argued that Matilda of Flanders (*d.* 1083), Queen of England and consort of William I, had received a ring of gold with a sapphire from her Westminster coronation in 1068. The rumour was that her tomb was ransacked during the Wars of Religion in the sixteenth century, and the Coronation Ring was found still on her hand.[204] As with the Coronation Ring, the current Queen Consort's Ring dates back to William IV's 1831 coronation and his Queen Consort, Adelaide. Since Edward VII's 1902 coronation, all queens consort have used this ring for their coronation ceremony. The parallels to the sacrament of marriage did not end there. Although confetti was not thrown over the newly crowned sovereign(s), in a form of reversal, commemorative medals were distributed amongst spectators. The new status of the monarch was to be 'minted' for all to see. In an age before photography, these medals were a palpable form of enduring publicity.[205]

Pulling these threads together, we can see that the sacramental theme is particularly prominent in coronations: Firstly, reminiscent of the Mass, the Coronation Chair faced the high altar; secondly, the monarch was anointed by the officiant; thirdly, and crucially, the prelate elevates the crown as if elevating the host and places it on the anointed monarch's head; and fourthly, the sovereign receives a Coronation Ring to confirm marriage to the realm. These points are best encapsulated in two quotations, the first from a poem and the second from a modern scholar:

> Kings are by God appointed,
> And damn'd are those who dare resist,
> Or touch the Lord's anointed.[206]

> Each generation has put its own stamp on the consecration of its monarch, and the rite has been adapted to cope with changed circumstances; the precise term 'consecration' [should be] used deliberately, because that is without question what the rite [i.e. the entire coronation ceremony] is about.[207]

Whilst there is no tradition of British monarchs crowning themselves, the concept of consecration was embedded in coronation ritual. Not least because a coronation was seen in a marital context, involving a special Ring. The Ring or royal signet came to symbolise the marriage of the monarch to the state and the inseparability or indivisibility of the Crown from the Sovereign. Such a link emulated episcopal consecration—the sacramental concept of episcopal marriage being conferred to the king or queen, but here acquiring a constitutional significance too, a significance that will be explored in Chap. 3 on the Coronation Oath.

Homage

Coronation homage can be understood in several ways. In the first instance, it involved the monarch presenting items to the high altar. In a technical sense, there is the tradition of homage paid by bishops and peers to the sovereign, and in the general sense of celebration by those beyond Westminster. The latter aspect is examined in Chaps. 5 and 6. In terms of the ceremony within the Abbey, those performing homage proceeded onto the dais in order to honour the enthroned king. The 1714 service records the Archbishop of Canterbury saying:

> I present unto you King George[,] king of this realm, wherefore all you who are come this day to do your homage, and service[,] are you willing to do the same?
>
> Then the archbishop[,] accompanied with the lord chancellor, lord great chamberlain, lord high constable, and Earl marshall, garter [king of arms] going before them, proceed[ed] to the south side of the theatre and repeat[ed] the same words, and from thence to the west, and after to the north in like manner, the king standing up all the while, and turning his face to each of the said sides, at such time as the archbishop at every of them speaks to the people, and at the last of them the trumpets sound.[208]

This is far from an obscure part of the ceremony. Indeed, it features in the most formal official record of each coronation, namely the Coronation Roll. Within these records (taking for examples 1661–1714), there is a complete list naming those members of each peerage rank who made their homage—this has continued with the 2023 Coronation Roll.[209] Queen Victoria regarded the 'Homage … first all the Bishops, then my Uncles, and lastly of all the Peers, in their respective order' as 'very fine'.[210]

As if homage-making was not enough to highlight the heightened religious character of this element, the 'choir s[a]ng *veni creator [spiritus]*'[211]—the invocation of the Holy Spirit. The later 'proce[ssion] in state into King Edwards Chappel' was accompanied by 'the organs playing all the while'.[212] The impact must have been tremendous, with sound reverberating around the Abbey, signifying the sovereign's elevated status and connection with God. By 1714, the organ, formerly a confessionalised instrument associated with Roman Catholicism, was once again part of the musical homage.[213] The whole coronation process—costume, music, regalia, and ritual—was designed to consecrate the new ruler. In saying that, one is challenging the argument put forward by Smith to the effect that 'Queen Anne's death brought an end to sacral monarchy'.[214] For on the contrary, we have just demonstrated, by reference to George I's coronation, that this was not the case. Indeed, 1714 was only thirteen years away from the most triumphant of Divine Right coronation anthems: Handel's *Zadok the Priest*.

For all of the changing nature of the UK in societal terms post war, 1953 would see the peerage continue the pattern of homage of their forebears; if anything, this was a doubling down of ceremonial. This, however, would be the last hurrah of the prominence of the peerage within a coronation setting in the UK (for it is highly unlikely ever to return as before). The House of Lords Act of 1999 set in motion the reduction of the number of hereditary peers sitting in the House of Lords, and there have been subsequent proposals to reform the Lords still further, with the current Labour government of Sir Keir Starmer vowing to remove all hereditary peers from the right to sit/contribute within the chamber.[215] It would therefore have been somewhat odd for the peerage to have their role reinforced in 2023. This also allowed Charles III to be able to cut down on the length of the service by reducing the role of the peerage within the homage. This did not mean it went altogether, but rather a new emphasis was placed on wider faith representation, aligning the service to a Commonwealth service style setting at Westminster Abbey.[216] 1953 had seen a change with a major role for the Moderator of the General Assembly (Scotland), the then-Moderator, James Pitt-Watson, in a British coronation, presenting the Bible to Elizabeth II with the words: 'Here is wisdom; This is the royal law; These are the lively Oracles of God'.[217] Charles III would go far further in 2023. Thus, to reflect the multi-faith nature of the UK, representatives from different denominations were not only present during the service but active participants. The then Prime Minister (the first Hindu Prime Minister of the UK), the Right Honourable Rishi Sunak MP, gave a reading from the Epistle, St Paul's letter to the Colossians 1:9–17. The presentation of the regalia was adapted by the monarch to involve

> peers from non-Christian faith traditions ... chosen because they [did] not bear explicit Christian motifs. Each contribution affirm[ing] our mutual interdependence as neighbours of whatever faith tradition or belief, and that His Majesty is invested with these 'instruments of state' by all people, not just the Christian Church.[218]

The 'Armills' were presented by the Lord Kamall, a Peer from the Muslim faith; The Robe Royal was brought from the Shrine to the monarch by The Baroness Merron, a Peer of the Jewish faith; The Orb by Archbishop of Armagh and Primate of All Ireland and Metropolitan; the Ring by The Lord Patel KT, a Peer of the Hindu faith; The Glove was presented to the

King by The Lord Singh of Wimbledon, a Peer from the Sikh faith; The Sceptre with Cross and the Sceptre with Dove by the Primus of the Scottish Episcopal Church and the Archbishop of Wales. Thus, 'in fulfilment of His Majesty's desire ... all the principal faiths of the United Kingdom ... [were] given places of honour on his Coronation Day'.[219] Also in attendance was a representative of the Humanists of the UK.[220] These changes were also a pointer to the Union, with Northern Ireland, Scotland and Wales all being represented by the various church leaders above. Furthermore, at the procession at the end of the service, by the Great West Door, the newly anointed and crowned sovereign 'was greeted by faith leaders and representatives, from the Jewish, Hindu, Sikh, Muslim and Buddhist faiths, who said':

> 'Your Majesty, as neighbours in faith, we acknowledge the value of public service. We unite with people of all faiths and beliefs in thanksgiving, and in service with you for the common good.'[221]

Of all the modifications to the service, the presence and participation of diverse faiths (and none) would be a radical shift from 1953 and those before. At the same time, this was also entirely in keeping with those accustomed to Commonwealth Day services at the Abbey, even under the late Queen. This was updating the coronation service to reflect changes that have become the norm within national services in the UK.

In addition, changing the role of the peerage and homage allowed the monarch to avoid involving Prince Harry and Andrew Mountbatten-Windsor (then Prince Andrew and both embroiled in controversy) in the coronation, for if not all the peerage would be paying homage, then they did not need to either as royal Dukes. So, by contrast, Prince William, the Prince of Wales, played an even greater role, in what many saw as a touching moment of fealty for his father as his 'liege man'—which was followed by a further tribute at the coronation concert at Windsor Castle on 7 May.[222] The public were also welcomed to take part in a pledge of allegiance or homage of the people—in a move by Lambeth Palace and Justin Welby (the then Archbishop of Canterbury) that was highly controversial and toned down on the day itself, and will be discussed further in Chap. 8.

Thus, homage still reinforced the sacred and elevated status of the monarch, but with wider faith representation, a much reduced role for the peerage, and an enhanced role for the Prince of Wales. Whilst radically different to previous coronations, this was, if anything, a reflection of the types of national service taking place for many years, involving far greater representation of the national picture.

Touching for the King's Evil

> [H]e cures, Hanging a golden stamp about their necks,
> Put on with holy prayers: and 'tis spoken,
> To the succeeding royalty he leaves The healing benediction
> (*Macbeth*, Act IV Scene iii)

One of the most obvious signs of the sacral side of monarchy was touching for the King's Evil: the sovereign's so-called ability to cure skin diseases, typically scrofula.[223] This practice was rooted in Edward the Confessor's alleged miraculous powers and continued from the reign of Henry II until 1714. Strickland also notes that 'Henry I reputedly touched for ... scrofula ... although there is little evidence that either the young Henry or his father did likewise'.[224] The ceremonial format was printed in the Book of Common Prayer, only disappearing *c.*1719–1732.[225] Since the ground has been very well covered by Marc Bloch and Stephen Brogan,[226] little need be said here. However, a few points should be made, as this phenomenon was an important example of quasi-sacerdotalism.

The main purpose of this section is to show that people believed that touching for the King's Evil indicates the persistence of a mystical belief in monarchy beyond the Restoration and Glorious Revolution. It makes sense to proceed broadly chronologically. For Charles II, the ritual of touching was part of an effort to revive monarchical mystique.[227] Simon Werrett highlights the importance of ritual in the early modern *weltanschauung*, '[f]rom the coronation to the State funeral, rituals focused on the body of the monarch and made manifest its seemingly miraculous powers and divine privileges'.[228] Charles's ostensible power to heal was significant because it was a metaphor for the return of monarchy and the hope for a more settled period of rule. Sancroft, later Archbishop of Canterbury, gave a sermon in 1660, declaring that

> the healing of the wounds of the daughter of our people ... are [now] under the cure of those very hands, upon which God hath entailed a miraculous gift of healing ... [and that] we shall ow[e] one day to those sacred hands, next under God, the healing of the Church's and the people's evils, as well as the king's.[229]

The link with Christ is clear: Charles was the longed-for Messiah, who will deliver his people, 'for blessed for ever be that God, who hath restored [unto] us such a gracious sovereign … [and] be the … repairer of the breach, and the nursing father of his Church'.[230] Asch points to the significance of the Garter Ceremony and the chivalric, priest-like status it echoed, 'the panoply of chivalry becomes an aspect of biblical priest-kingship. St George is one with King David'.[231] Charles wished to restore all of these traditions and links and 'did not hesitate to exercise the miraculous powers that his hereditary rights and position as an anointed ruler gave him. During his long reign, he assiduously touched men and women for the scrofula. He probably healed, or tried to heal, more people than any English monarch before him. Several tens of thousands, perhaps up to one hundred thousand people flocked to court to be healed by the king'.[232] As Bloch and Werrett have noted, this healing rite can readily be likened to consecration: the laying on of hands being similar to that of a priest.[233] The propaganda benefits to the Crown are obvious. Why believe in the sovereign's hereditary right and elevated status? Why should such a being be closer to Christ than a layman? Touching for the King's Evil offered an answer. Yet this concept, of medieval origin, survived not simply because it was too useful to discard, but rather because people continued to 'believe' the act was efficacious.[234] In an era in which it was difficult for most subjects to gain access to their monarch, this ceremony provided that opportunity. A proclamation advertised prospective sessions.[235] These events could bring monetary gain; beneficiaries conventionally received a token, often in gold or silver, produced by the Royal Mint. Sceptics may argue that the medallic reward kept the populace interested, perhaps rather more than the miraculous powers of healing, although there were many who undoubtedly did believe. The practice certainly worked both ways: for monarch and people. Cressy shows that whilst Charles I's 'predilections made him even more remote' from his subjects than many predecessors, he nevertheless enthusiastically embraced this healing power, and none more so than when his rule was in peril.[236]

From his return in 1660, Charles II quickly revived the ceremony, attracting almost unprecedented numbers. The chance of coming face-to-face with the monarch,[237] of being healed and of receiving 'gold ducketts', encouraged a stream of eager participants.[238] In June 1660 alone, he touched 600 people and attracted similar numbers in later years. From 1669 to 1684, 28,983 people were touched by the king, a mean of 1,900 a year.[239] Such 'ritual demonstrations of the king's miraculous powers ... consolidated his Restoration with an enthusiastic public'.[240]

> For all those joys the Restauration brought,
> For all those miracles it wrought,
> For all the healing balm thy mercy pour'd,
> Into the nation's bleeding wound,
> And care that after kept it sound.[241]

Dryden's poem neatly underlines the fact that Charles did not disappoint, and that the sacral power of monarchy, in this respect, was extremely important for many subjects.

So if Divine Right, in the form of touching for the King's Evil, did not die in 1660, then what happened? James II continued to touch—indeed was to transmit the belief in divine 'indefe[a]zible hereditary right' to the Stuart line of pretenders and Jacobites.[242] By contrast, under William III and Mary II, the practice ceased, William supposedly saying, 'God grant you better health and better sense' than have the monarch touch.[243] Nevertheless, Queen Anne was to revive the ceremony, being 'quite literally ... in touch with her people'.[244] She seems to have linked, in her mind, these ancestral powers with her coronation, for she purportedly only revived the practice after being anointed and crowned.[245] George I and George II disapproved of the custom and, according to Smith, 'firmly spurned the mantle of sacral kingship[,] [being] ... leading exponent[s] of ... enlightened initiative'.[246] Touching for scrofula never returned. However, a false connection has been drawn between sacral Divine Right monarchy and touching for the King's Evil. Historians have often been quick to associate the end of one with the discontinuation of the other. It is certainly true that touching for the King's Evil was **one way** of showing sacerdotalism, but it was not the only way, and not all monarchs touched to the same degree. Perhaps the most ardent proponent of the Divine Right of Kings was James I, yet he was sceptical of touching for the King's Evil.[247] The other key point, as regards touching for the King's Evil, is the difference between what the monarch thought and what their people felt.

Queen Anne was in tune with her public in reviving the practice, and indeed took her role very seriously.[248] It is too easy simply to assume that sovereigns touched for the King's Evil because of the legitimising propaganda benefits, although it certainly helped Anne in authenticating her position, given that there was a rival claimant. This fact is interesting because one would hardly touch for the King's Evil in order to legitimise one's position if this sacrality was not popularly recognised as an important element of queenship and of the right to the throne. Nevertheless, Anne was religiously devout and was said even to fast before the ceremony.[249] As under her ancestors, subjects came from all quarters to participate; this even included the young Samuel Johnson.[250] So it was not the case that the people either fell out of affection with this practice or lost their faith in monarchical power. George I's decision to desist, like William's, was entirely personal; it should not be equated with the end of sacral monarchy and Divine Right ideology or, for that matter, with a rejection of such ideas on their subjects' parts.[251] George I may, as Smith has argued, have been influenced by a shifting *mentalité* to do with continental Enlightenment thought, but even the great Robert Boyle (1627–1691), and many other figures of the early British Enlightenment, 'proved remarkably obdurate in their desire to retain a place for a providential and active deity in their evolving worldview'.[252] There was room for a belief in a monarch's miracle-working power. Perhaps historians erred in adopting the questionable secularisation thesis[253] and therefore in arguing that the rise of natural philosophy ended belief in the sovereign's divinity. Peter Elmer's account of the intriguing Valentine Greatrakes (1629–1683) and Werrett's work on the relationship between royal ritual and experimental philosophy have shown that the situation was far more complex—'problematic and convoluted'[254]—and that far from inhibiting scientific discovery, Charles II's touching for the King's Evil may even have 'aided' experiments in natural philosophy—in other words, that Charles's power 'was key to the legitimation of experimental science'.[255] Elmer's research convincingly draws attention to the much-overlooked fact that the power to heal was not exclusively royal and should therefore not be regarded as a fundamental element of Divine Right ideology. George I may not have shared many of his ancestors' views on touching for the King's Evil, but his coronation involved all the trappings of his predecessors. One should therefore be careful not to attribute the end of Divine Right concepts simply to the circumstance of a monarch ceasing to believe in their supposed healing powers. Crucially, George I's subjects continued to utilise the rhetoric of 'sacred' Divine Right in numerous sermons, poems, and other publications. Emphatically, this was the same under George II.[256] Did a coronation transfer the right to touch for the King's Evil? Did it maintain sacral monarchy long after the Reformations, the Restoration, and the Glorious Revolution? Not necessarily, but we can conclude that the act of anointing, and the use of St Edward's 'relics', undoubtedly added authenticity to the practice of touching for the King's Evil and hence powerfully to the divinity of the monarch crowned.

A Secular Show?

In the light of the foregoing conclusion, it is difficult to make sense of some historians' interpretations. Lorraine Madway writes on the 'majesty and accessibility' of Charles II's 1661 coronation, noting that the king 'gave his subjects a spectacular display of rank and grandeur … [that] reinforced the aura of legitimacy surrounding his restoration.'[257] However, she goes on to say that the preceding procession 'lacked the vital element of sacrality for which all the august solemnity of the service could not compensate'. Her argument is that his 'entry … was the first (and only) one to present an image of kingship largely devoid of religious content'.[258] But this claim does not quite match the rapture with which his subjects, and Charles himself, viewed proceedings. As evidence of this, we can quote Cook's retrospective assessment:

> It is very observable, that altho' it had rained for about a month before [the coronation], yet it pleased God, that not one drop fell upon this splendid triumph, which appeared in its full lustre and grandeur.[259]

The vast array of print material that emerged, as shown by Reedy, included religious and classical references, something absolutely in line with coronation tradition. The occasion's religious feel was undoubtedly different, in the sense that Charles's return heralded an end to a period of puritanical zeal. Madway argues that '[t]he imagery of restoration and stability in the pageantry transmitted a message that was immediate rather than transcendent.'[260] Nevertheless, Charles was hugely successful in his return and in reviving the monarchy. He ensured dynastic survival, even if his brother was to lose the throne. Charles may not have possessed the religious convictions of all his subjects, but then how many monarchs did? What of Henry VIII, Elizabeth I, or Charles I? A belief in quasi-sacerdotal Divine Right endured in coronations, when it might readily have disappeared. Like Elizabeth I's coronation procession of 1559,[261] 'Charles II made London a national theatre and used it in a variety of ways to help secure his crown'.[262] In so doing, he was able to re-establish 'the ancient authority of the monarchy, the right of kings and the rightness of his family's reign.'[263] To conclude: whilst it is important to acknowledge that there was more to a coronation than the crowning, it is unwise to judge the religious flavour of the confection on the basis of what does or does not feature in the preliminary procession.

Neglected Perspectives

> So glorious was the show with gold and silver,
> that we were not able to look at it[.][264]
>
> God has wrought a wonderful miracle
> in settling us as he hath done.[265]

Charles II's Restoration procession and coronation were grand affairs, recognised as such by monarch and people alike. Along with his touching for the King's Evil, Charles had 'publicly affirmed the heavenly origins of his powers'. His crowning day was 'a spectacular affirmation of his connection with the people ... attract[ing] huge crowds'.[266] One of the most celebrated rulers associated with divine and absolute power was France's Louis XIV—'the Sun King'. This cosmological vocabulary has been overlooked because its familiarity, as in this case, has caused it to be taken for granted. It was also nothing new. Akhenaten, as previously mentioned, had been compared to the sun, linguistically and pictorially.[267] Likewise, Charles II was praised in solar terms as evidence of his Divine Right to rule[268]:

> As by it genial heat the sun doth bring
> To the cold Muscovite a present spring;
> So wonders wait where e're you raise your head,
> You cheere the drooping, and revive the dead.[269]
>
> For want of such an April 23,
> Each month a showry April seemed to bee;
> The sunne now r[is]ing dryes up every care.[270]
>
> Dread sir, your happiness is now begun,
> You're crown'd with the perfections of the sun:
> Imparting light and heat, you make us live.[271]

Reedy's fascinating essay, noticing the noumenal realities of weather, argues, however, that 'the Interregnum [and Regicide] had done its work' and that in Charles II's coronation proceedings, the fabric of mystical monarchy was already under attack and that this would lead to the proponents of 'mystical moments' being associated with the 'ugly name' of Jacobites.[272] Charles II's crowning day saw, in Reedy's eyes, 'the noumenal sense [having] its last, glorious, triumphant fling at interpreting social change as the direct effect of a noumenal transcendence.'[273] Yet, as this chapter has shown, providentialism remained a central tenet of coronations and Divine Right ideology. Indeed, in accounts of James II's coronation sermon and of Queen Anne's coronation day, we find solar and weather analogies repeated:

> Blessed be the L[or]d ... God who has the h[e]arts of kings at his com[m]and; and blessed be [the] ... soveraign lord the king, for his contributing cheerfully to the same ... we did read ..., how happily the solemnities of the ... coronation, did proceed: and I read in y[ou]r printed sermon ... an excellent composure, of pious and religious eloquence and prudence; ... as a star in a constellation of heavenly lights ... my joyful congratulation at the happy dispatch ... of the coronation solemnitie[.][274]

> This day ... Q[ueen] Ann was crowned ... queen of England, Scotland, France & Ireland. The brightness of the day contributed to the splendo[u]r of the cavalcade and shewe that Heaven smiled upon the placing of the crown of her ancestors on her royall head whom God grant long to wear it[.][275]

From these perspectives, it is manifest that Divine Right concepts persisted, even in a noumenal sense.

Conclusion

What exactly the practice of anointing meant for the status of the person experiencing it is almost impossible to assess, but it remains a truly significant or 'holy' moment, and even in 2023 untelevised because of the status of that specific act. Whilst Elizabeth I may have poured scorn on the anointing oil, foolish would have been the subject to question her godly derived or ordained status. The personal transformation believed to have been wrought by the anointing was felt deeply by Richard II, for instance. When he was told that he had abdicated all kingly dignity, he replied that 'he did not wish to renounce those special dignities of a spiritual nature which had been bestowed upon him, nor indeed his anointment; he was in fact unable to renounce them, nor could he cease to retain them'.[276] Richard was alluding to the idea that the anointing was analogous to the sacrament of Holy Orders, and hence left an indelible mark of spiritual authority. In short, this consecration conferred a quasi-sacerdotal status: the king was no longer a layman, but he was not quite a priest either—he could not say Mass. That Christian rulers are God's representatives upon earth was a venerable commonplace in the medieval and early modern worlds, but the notion that the anointing was critical as a conduit for heavenly power survived the English Reformation only to become bound up (from the 1590s) with the developing doctrine of 'The Divine Right of Kings'. As we have seen, one manifestation of the ruler's imputed power was the practice of 'Touching for the King's Evil'. In broad terms, it is also clear that Divine Right ideology lived on within the service because it was intrinsically bound with anointing, and that tradition of anointing survived Regicide, to be restored in 1661, and to continue beyond the constitutional settlement of the Glorious Revolution. In that sense, the anointing within a coronation challenges the idea of a demystification of monarchy. Sharpe tackled this notion of 'demystification' for the Restoration period, and his summary is worth quoting at length:

> What such a view risks is simplification and anachronism. The historian who detects new languages and beliefs must always take care not to discount the continuing force of old words and codes. Belief in the king, the Church and the male as divine and natural authorities survived the challenges of science and scepticism, not to mention the reign of a monarch who did not entirely embody these ideals. And traditional beliefs and discourses were reinforced and revalidated by political crisis. As, in the late 1670s, England [during the Exclusion Crisis] teetered on the brink of Civil War, claims that the king was 'God's vicar on earth', that 'not only Nature but God himself affects monarchy', that 'majesty' scatters tumults as the sun does the clouds, again became common utterance. Old prophecies were reprinted and new ones published, questioning any narrative we may be tempted to posit of the triumph of reason over superstition. Men and women in 1680 and 1681 testified to portents of doom – pikemen fighting in the sky over Carmarthen, for example – and their accounts of visions were purchased by a readily credulous public. What was different was a greater willingness, and in an overtly partisan culture, greater need, to question and contest such visions.[277]

As this chapter has demonstrated, Sharpe's thesis is extendable far beyond the Glorious Revolution, provided that sacrality is not seen in a purely healing sense and that one is aware of the sacral nature of coronations. If one stays attuned to British monarchs' differing interpretations of Divine Right ideas, then variations appear more consistent than many historians have observed. The Divine Right of Kings was ubiquitous, but it meant different things to different rulers and was used diversely, depending upon context. Most importantly, judging by popular interest in coronations and in touching for the King's Evil, the public retained a tenacious grasp upon this sacral ideology well into the eighteenth century, even if in Britain the Hanoverians personally adopted a more secular interpretation. Of course, the status of warrior king, which was quickly seized upon, necessarily brought into the frame another range of religious associations, invoking the zeal of militaristic biblical figures, such as King David. Indeed, in terms of coronations, those of George I and George II 'were carried out according to precedent' and imbued those kings with the same divinity as their predecessors.[278]

Coronations ostensibly endowed sovereigns with quasi-sacerdotal powers—the anointing, the objects involved, and the claims to saintly status were a realisation of these divine right ideas. They were devised to elevate the monarch to a priest-like status. Many monarchs laid claim to this sacrality and demonstrated it through exercising the power to touch for the King's Evil. In view of Elmer's work, it is also clear that the capacity to heal was not exclusively royal and thus should not be regarded as an essential element in Divine Right ideology. Nevertheless, the coronation continued to be steeped in a religiosity epitomised by consecration and providentialism. Items of the regalia were deployed to symbolise attributes of divine rule. These objects, from crowns to chairs and swords (as will be covered in Chap. 4, effectively relics, were 'real to men's minds'.[279] Throughout these years, the public (in the majority)[280] embraced coronations and the idea of sacral kingship. Numerous pieces of evidence highlight this fact: dedications, poems, and accession and coronation literature, as well as public demand for touching for the King's Evil. Just as the sovereign was drawn in parallel to biblical and classical figures, so Britain became Israel and Westminster Jerusalem. From popular interest to a rival claimant, from patriotic fervour against a dangerous France to the possible weakness of being a 'female ruler'[281]—in all these aspects, Queen Anne (as Smith shows) reinvigorated sacral monarchy in reaction to William III's relative austerity. Nevertheless, for all the Prince of Orange's dislike of ceremonial, he wore the crown again when assenting to the Bill for the new coronation oath.[282] For William, polemical representation as divine warrior-king was far more appropriate than Anne's characterisation as nursing mother. Although this has been proposed as something new, the description of William III and George I as warrior kings recalled the style of medieval chivalrous monarchs. This was a view of monarchy that had been transfixed on James I's oldest son, Prince Henry, and conveyed no less of a Divine Right ideology, than one that was founded in a crusading view of kingship and of the mighty Henry V. Smith rightly points out that 'military kingship played to the strengths of William III and George I',[283] yet does not see this as connected to a divine, crusading and providential kingship.

Far from disappearing from the coronation and the national context, the Divine Right of Kings, like the monarchy, evolved. Admittedly, with the rise of Enlightenment thought, certain elements achieved greater prominence. Other concepts, such as justice and mercy, remained ever-present in coronations and did not emerge as 'the new idea of magisterial Divine Right'.[284] Providentialism would become a central aspect as Britain rose to dominate the European military scene. However, the majesty of coronation remained, as most clearly evidenced in increasingly grandiose musical accompaniments, as noted by contemporaries. The Hanoverians regarded Britain as their rightful hereditary home. George I certainly spoke in a language of inheritance, of the 'throne of my ancestors' and of the 'Protestant succession'.[285] A poem written to celebrate Queen Anne's coronation brings these threads together, highlighting that the Divine Right of Kings was still of fundamental importance. The monarch remained an elevated being ruling at Heaven's behest:

> Phoebus arise, put on thy brightest ray,
> To grace the triumphs of this glorious day,
> On which is plac'd, since conqu'ring William's dead,
> Th'imperial crown on Anne's illustrious head.
> And may that crown was to her merits due,
> Receive new lustre from her wearing too.
> That crown, still, by a race of monarchs worn,
> May it now long her royal head adorn;
> And may she long possess the regal throne,
> Which providence, & birth, have made her own.
> May she ne're know what are domestick jars,
> But, prove victorious in her foreign wars.

And may her arms (crown'd with success) now make,
Both the false French, & haughty Spaniard quake,
May it please heav'n to hear our prayers, & send
These glorious actions may her reign attend;
And make th'admiring world her conduct bless,
Guided by prudence, acted with success,
Protect her allies, & make France still less;
Till to her ancient bounds she be confin'd,
Who wou'd give sov'rain-law to all mankind.

J. B. [John Boevey?][286]

Elizabeth Barrett Browning picks up the Victorian notion of the change from this service taken on by the young Queen, in her poem: 'Crowned and Wedded' (1840), as she moves from 'her own fair face … [and] child-smile' to a 'solemn vow … to rule'. For Queen Victoria had undergone 'with priestly hands on high, Which bring the first anointing to all legal majesty' a moment of consecration, elevated like a sacrament. The laying on of hands reference and elevation of the host is made explicit here. 'And as the loyal shouts went up, true spirits prayed between, "The blessings happy monarchs have, be thine, O crownëd queen!" [287] So for all in the audience Queen Victoria had also changed too, not just personally but in their own eyes.

Moving to the twentieth and twenty-first centuries, and we see the continuation of this ancient idea—of Zadok anointing Solomon. Archbishop Lang (writing of the 1937 coronation of George VI) described the event as 'the culminating day of my official life, the day on which the Archbishop of Canterbury fulfils his highest office in national life, on which through him the Church of God consecrates that life in the person of its King'.[288] Queen Elizabeth, the Queen Mother, described the 'great ceremony' as 'such a spiritual and wonderful service … I was more moved & more helped than I could have believed possible'.[289] Similar themes abound in Archbishop Fisher's accounts of 1953 in terms of the sacred nature of the coronation, and on the question of televising the anointing, he stated that 'I was willing that the whole ceremony should be filmed, but that I could not agree to televisi[ng] of those entirely spiritual parts of the Service'.[290] 1953 is often seen as the pivotal moment in the world of broadcasting royal events in the UK, but in fact, the milestone began earlier with the filming of King George VI's coronation, most significantly for the BBC. This saw the progress between the complete prohibition placed on the corporation for his wedding as Duke of York in 1923 to the pomp and pageantry and display of the coronation rites (bar anointing) of Queen Elizabeth II's coronation on television—in essence, 1937 was the turning point, rather than 1953 (Fig. 1.6).[291]

The coronation of 1953 had a profound impact on Elizabeth II, and explained in Hugo Vickers mind why she carried on even with ill health to the end. Vickers, referring to the pact she had made with God during the coronation, argued that "[o]ne main reason why the Queen will absolutely not abdicate is unlike other European monarchs, she is an anointed Queen … [a]nd if you are an anointed Queen you do not abdicate".[292] The coronation provided the praxis for this legitimation in ceremonial terms, symbolically crowning and anointing the new regime, and, in the acclamation and oath, binding monarchy and people together; and arguably in Elizabeth II's eyes also binding her further to God to a sense of duty for life, admired by so many from around the world.

How to reconcile such ideas in a so-called secular age is problematic—though that perhaps is because the secularisation thesis is itself questionable if not fundamentally flawed. How to know truly what one person believes religiously—down to their inner conscience or soul—is inherently

Fig. 1.6 Photo from the balcony scene for the 1937 coronation of George VI, from a souvenir book, with George VI, Queen Elizabeth (later 'The Queen Mother'), the dowager Queen, Mary of Teck (queen consort to George V), and princesses Elizabeth (later Queen Elizabeth II) and Margaret, Alamy

difficult, and certainly a challenge in any sample poll. What we know from a coronation is that in a British, Westminster Abbey context, the anointing remained from the very earliest tradition to the present, surviving changing eras and epochs, from the medieval to Generations Z and Alpha. In May 2023, *The Standard* commented that 'Charles will emerge from this sacred ritual as a different man' and described the moment as 'the most important day in the reign of King Charles III ... with the anointing with holy oil ... the most sacred part'. Indeed, the event is seen as a 'sacred service [with] ... the whole panoply of the Coronation ... the final step for King Charles as he embarks on his reign'. This view is representative of many of the ideas and pieces expressed at the time.[293] Such a view echoed those of 1953 and reflections on 1953, as can be seen in a 2013 BBC piece by Mark Easton (Home editor) on the anniversary of Elizabeth II's coronation. Easton reflected on the anointing as the 'Act of Consecration ... the most magical aspect of an English coronation, so extraordinary that history (and the 1953 Coronation Committee) decreed it must remain out of sight' from television cameras. His conclusion gives that sense of the transformation, the 'high theatre' of the whole occasion, and is worth quoting in full:

> From the flask, the archbishop poured some "blessed oil" of orange, roses, cinnamon, musk and ambergris, and anointed the Queen in the form of a cross, on the palms of her hand, on the breast and on the crown of her head.
>
> As he did so, he whispered these words: "Be thy head anointed with holy oil: as kings, priests, and prophets were anointed. And as Solomon was anointed king by Zadok the priest and Nathan the prophet, so be you anointed, blessed and consecrated Queen over the Peoples, whom the Lord thy God hath given thee to rule and govern."
>
> In that instant, the viewing public were meant to believe that their Queen was transformed. As a newsreel commentator put it: "the hallowing - a moment so old history can barely go deep enough to contain it."
>
> When the golden pall was removed and the cameras rolled on the monarch once more, hey presto and hallelujah, Elizabeth had become associated with the divine.[294]

Such words could so easily have been made by a chronicler of Tudor times for the first Elizabeth.

Notes

1. A. Ferdowsi (trans. D. Davis), *Shahnameh: The Persian Book of Kings* (New York, 2006). See also The National Library of Scotland, Edinburgh, Adv. MS 33.2.26, fol. 84r–v ('The Coronatione of the Ancient Persian kinges').
2. For early Islamic perceptions of Divine Right kingship, see also A. Al-Azmeh, 'Monotheistic Kingship', in A. Al-Azmeh and J. M. Bak (eds), *Monotheistic Kingship: The Medieval Variants* (Budapest, 2004), pp. 9–31.
3. D. B. Redford, *Akhenaten: The Heretic King* (Princeton, New Jersey, 1984), pp. 176–8. An example of the iconography of Akhenaten's devotion to this one god can be seen in the Metropolitan Museum, New York. For a detailed explanation of Akhenaten, see also Redford, *Akhenaten*, pp. 20–1.
4. For a detailed explanation of the *heb sed*, see I. Shaw and P. Nicholson, *The Dictionary of Ancient Egypt* (revised edn, New York, 2003), p. 256; cf. Redford, *Akhenaten*, p. 178.
5. R. Pipes, *The Russian Revolution 1899–1919* (London, 1992), pp. 54, 55.
6. Jackson, *Vive le Roi*, pp. 4–5.
7. Ditmas, 'Curtana', pp. 122–33, especially pp. 126–7.
8. A. Williams, 'Edgar [called Edgar Pacificus] (943/4–975)', *ODNB*; S. Foot, 'Æthelstan [Athelstan] (893/4–939)', *ibid.*; M. K. Lawson, 'Edmund II [known as Edmund Ironside] (d. 1016)', *ibid.*; and F. Barlow, 'Edward [St Edward; known as Edward the Confessor] (1003x5–1066)', *ibid.* See also G. Garnett, 'Coronation', in M. Lapidge, J. Blair, S. Keynes and D. Scragg (eds.), *The Wiley Blackwell Encyclopedia of Anglo-Saxon England*, 2nd edn (Oxford, 2014), pp. 125–126; A. Norrie, 'The Bishop and the Queen; or, Why did the Bishop of Carlisle crown Elizabeth I?', *Northern History*, LVI:1–2, 2019, pp. 25–45; P. L. Ward,'The Coronation Ceremony in Mediaeval England', *Speculum*, XIV (April 1939), 160–178; and J. L. Nelson, *Politics and Ritual in Early Medieval Europe* (London, 1986), pp. 283–286, 296–303, 361–374.
9. S. Keynes, 'Church Councils, Royal Assemblies, and Anglo-Saxon Royal Diplomas', in G. R. Owen-Crocker and B. W. Schneider (eds), *Kingship, Legislation and Power in Anglo-Saxon England* (Woodbridge, 2013), pp. 142, 148–156; and J. L. Nelson, 'Inauguration Rituals', in P. H. Sawyer and I. N. Wood (eds), *Early Medieval Kingship* (Leeds, 1977), pp. 63–70.
10. M. Strickland, *Henry the Young King, 1155–1183* (New Haven, Connecticut, 2016), p. xi, p. 87: Strickland points out that the 'conse-

crated garments' from the anointing were preserved for 'it was customary for kings to be buried in them, as young Henry was to be'. See also W. Stubbs (ed.), *Opera Historica: The Historical Works of Master Ralph de Diceto, Dean of London*, 2 vols (Rolls Series, London, 1876), II, 20. Similarly, in 1199 Richard was buried in the regalia in which he had been crowned, and which 'he had been adorned with' (infulatus) at his crown-wearing in 1194 at Winchester (H. R. Luard (ed.), *Annales de Wintonia* in *Annales monastici*, 4 vols (Rolls Series, London, 1864–1869), II, 71). See also T. Keefe, 'Henry II (1133–1189), king of England, duke of Normandy and of Aquitaine, and count of Anjou', *ODNB*; and E. Hallam, 'Henry [Henry the Young King] (1155–1183), prince', *ibid.*

11. https://www.coronationroll.gov.uk/coronation_roll/the-coronation-service-2/the-anointing-of-the-king/, accessed 30 November 2024.
12. Shakespeare's *King Richard the Second*, Act III Scene ii. Cf. B. Wilkinson, *The Coronation in History* (London, 1953), p. 9 (arguing that the act of anointing confers upon the ruler the 'divine sanction for his [/her] kingship') and E. W. Ives, *Anne Boleyn* (Oxford, 1986), p. 224.
13. W. Stubbs (ed.), *Chronica Magistri Rogeri de Houedene*, 4 volumes, *Rerum Britannicarum Medii Aevi Scriptores*, 51 (London, 1868–1871), II, pp. 4–5; and R. Howlett (ed.), *The Chronicle of Robert of Torigni, in Chronicles of the Reigns of Stephen, Henry II and Richard I*, 4 vols (Rolls Series, London, 1884–1889), IV, p. 245, 'cum magna cleri et populi laetitia'. For Torigni, see E. M. C. van Houts, 'Le Roi et son historien: Henri II Plantagenêt et Robert de Torigni, abbé du Mont- Saint- Michel', *Cahiers de civilisation médiévale*, 37 (1994), pp. 115–18.
14. Strickland, *Henry the Young King*, p. 86. See also W. Stubbs (ed.), *Gesta regis Henrici secundi Benedicti abbatis: The Chronicle of the Reigns of Henry II and Richard I, AD 1169–1192*, 2 vols (Rolls Series, London, 1867), II, 81.
15. R. G. Asch, *Sacral Kingship between Disenchantment & Re-Enchantment: The French and English Monarchies 1587–1688* (New York and Oxford, 2014), p. 42. For the anointing of his wife, Anne of Denmark in 1590, see NRS, Cuninghame Papers, MS GD149/265; M. M. Meikle, 'Anna of Denmark's Coronation and Entry into Edinburgh, 1590: Cultural, Religious and Diplomatic Perspectives', in J. Goodare and A. A. MacDonald (eds), *Sixteenth-Century Scotland: Essays in Honour of Michael Lynch* (Leiden, 2008), pp. 277–94. For more on Scottish ceremony before 1633 see A. Thomas, 'Crown Imperial: Coronation Ritual and Regalia in the Reign of James V', in *ibid.*, pp. 44–67.
16. Sharpe, *Image Wars*, p. 252; Asch, *Sacral Kingship*, p. 68. Much discussion in the 1640s examined whether Laud had tampered with the Coronation and adjusted the wording of the oath and the ceremony more

generally, see William Prynne, *Canterburies Doome, or the First Part of a Compleat History of the Commitment, Charge, Tryall, Condemnation, Execution of William Laud, Late Archbishop of Canterbury* (London, 1646), pp. 69–70, 475–6; cf. W. Laud, *The Works ...*, 7 vols (Oxford, 1854; reprint Hildesheim, 1977), IV: *History of the Troubles and Trial of Archbishop Laud*, pp. 211–19. See also NLS, Wodrow MS 4 TO XX. On the prayer, see Legg, *Coronation Records*, p. 257; and L. L. Knoppers, *Constructing Cromwell: Ceremony, Portrait, and Print 1645–1661* (Cambridge, 2000), p. 110. See also A. Milton, 'Laud, William (1573–1645)', *ODNB.*

17. Asch, *Sacral Kingship*, p. 131.
18. H. Matthew, 'George VI (1895–1952), king of Great Britain, Ireland, and the British dominions beyond the seas, and sometime emperor of India', *ODNB*; F. Prochaska, 'Lascelles, Sir Alan Frederick (1887–1981)', *ibid.*
19. N. Hamilton, 'Montgomery, Bernard Law [known as Monty], first Viscount Montgomery of Alamein (1887–1976)', *ODNB.*
20. D. Hart-Davis, *King's Counsellor, Abdication and War: The Diaries of Sir Alan 'Tommy' Lascelles* (London, 2020), p. 212 (14 April 1944).
21. A. Wilkinson, 'Lang, (William) Cosmo Gordon, Baron Lang of Lambeth (1864–1945)', *ODNB.*
22. Hart-Davis, *King's Counsellor*, p. 212 (14 April 1944).
23. *Ibid.*, p. 213 (15 April 1944, quoting C. Whilley's, *William Pitt*, 1782 House of Commons William Pitt entry, Lascelles thought this 'seemed ... so appropriate to Monty's Coronations service that I copied it out and sent it ... to Cosmo').
24. M. Easton, 4 June 2013, https://www.bbc.co.uk/news/uk-22764987, accessed 20 May 2023.
25. See Norrie, 'The Bishop and the Queen', pp. 25–45.
26. https://www.rct.uk/collection/stories/the-crown-jewels/the-ampulla, accessed 20 May 2023.
27. https://www.rct.uk/collection/31733/the-coronation-spoon, accessed 20 May 2023.
28. *The Authorised Liturgy for the Coronation Rite of His Majesty King Charles III*, Commissioned and Authorised by The Most Reverend & Right Honourable Justin Welby, The Archbishop of Canterbury [with commentary] (London, 2023), p. 13; see also *The Form and Order of the Service. Coronation of Her Majesty Queen Elizabeth II, 2 June 1953* (London, 1953).
29. Hoak, 'Transformation', p. 138; D. Loades, *Mary Tudor: A Life* (Oxford, 1989), p. 206; Antoine Perrenot de Granvelle bishop of Arras; Hoak, 'Transformation', pp. 136–8 – from L. Pannier and P. Meyer (eds), *Le*

Débat des Hérauts D'Armes de France et d'Angleterre suivi de The Debate between the Heralds of England and France by John Coke (Société des Anciens Textes Français [xxi], Paris, 1877), p. 64.

30. TNA, E 351/567. See also *ibid.*, AO 1/410/151.
31. 'The Coronation', *BBC* (2018) featuring conversation with the late Queen Elizabeth II and royal commentator Alastair Bruce of Crionaich: https://www.bbc.co.uk/programmes/b09p1vdh#:~:text=Shedding%20an%20entirely%20new%20perspective,overwhelmed%20colleagues%20lost%20their%20voices, accessed 20 May 2024.
32. https://www.royal.uk/50-facts-about-queen-elizabeth-iis-coronation, accessed 22 November 2025.
33. https://johnbellcroyden.co.uk/blogs/about-us/who-we-are, accessed 22 November 2025.
34. AFP, 4 March 2023, https://jordantimes.com/news/region/coronation-oil-charles-iii-consecrated-jerusalem, accessed 22 November 2025; H. Khalil and M. Foster, 4 March 2023, https://edition.cnn - Charles III coronation-oil, accessed 22 November 2025.
35. https://www.yadvashem.org/righteous/stories/princess-alice.html, accessed 22 November 2025: H. Vickers, 'Alice, Princess [Princess Alice of Battenberg; married name Princess Andrew of Greece] (1885–1969)', *ODNB*. https://www.westminster-abbey.org/abbey-commemorations/commemorations/grand-duchess-elizabeth, accessed 22 November 2025. https://www.bbc.co.uk/news/uk-42651950, reflections on the life of Prince Philip, 9 April 2021, accessed 22 November 2025.
36. See for examples: http://news.bbc.co.uk/1/hi/england/1957421.stm, 29 April 2022, accessed 22 November 2025; H. Sherwood, 9 September 2022, https://www.theguardian.com/uk-news/2022/sep/09/king-charles-to-be-defender-of-the-faith-but-also-a-defender-of-faiths, accessed 22 November 2025; see also S. Sebag Montefiore, *Jerusalem: The Biography* (London, 2011).
37. *OED.*
38. J. P. Sommerville, *Politics and Ideology in England, 1603–1640* (1st edition, London and New York, 1986), p. 9.
39. *OED.*
40. J. Daly, 'The Idea of Absolute Monarchy in Seventeenth-Century England', *The Historical Journal*, 21 (1978), p. 250.
41. *Ibid.*, p. 227.
42. A. Maqbool, 18 September 2022, https://www.bbc.co.uk/news/uk-62942772, accessed 22 November 2025.
43. See also J. C. D. Clark, 'Protestantism, Nationalism, and National Identity, 1660–1832', *The Historical Journal*, 43 (2000), pp. 249–76; and S. J. Brown, *Providence and Empire: Religion, Politics and Society in*

the United Kingdom, 1815–1914 (Harlow, 2008), *passim*; and C. Kidd, 'Protestantism, Constitutionalism and British Identity under the Later Stuarts', in B. Bradshaw and P. Roberts (eds), *British Consciousness and Identity: The Making of Britain, 1533–1707* (Cambridge, 1998), pp. 321–42.

44. S. W. Haas, 'Martin Luther's "Divine Right" Kingship and the Royal Supremacy: Two Tracts from the 1531 Parliament and Convocation of the Clergy', *The Journal of Ecclesiastical History*, 31 (1980), pp. 317–25; Sommerville, *Politics*, pp. 9–33; R. Zaller, 'Breaking the Vessels: The Desacralization of Monarchy in Early Modern England', *The Sixteenth Century Journal*, XXIX (1998), pp. 757–78; A. Ryrie, 'Divine Kingship and Royal Theology in Henry VIII's Reformation', *Reformation*, 7 (2002), pp. 49–77; Al-Azmeh & Bak, *Kingship*; and G. Burgess, *British Political Thought, 1500–1660: The Politics of the Post-Reformation* (Basingstoke, 2009). For the 'deep medieval roots of the theory' see G. Burgess, 'The Divine Right of Kings Reconsidered', *The English Historical Review*, CVII (1992), p. 837, and pp. 837–61 *passim*, in discussing John Neville Figgis's 'pioneering study' *The Divine Right of Kings*, first published in 1896.
45. E. H. Kantorowicz, *The King's Two Bodies: A Study in Mediaeval Political Theology* (Princeton, New Jersey, 1957), p. 5; M. Axton, *The Queen's Two Bodies: Drama and the Elizabethan Succession* (London, 1977).
46. James I, 'A Speach to the Lords and Commons of the Parliament at White-Hall, on Wednesday the XXI of March. Anno 1609 [1610]', in James I, *The Workes of the Most High and Mightie Prince, Iames by the Grace of God, King of Great Britaine, France and Ireland, Defender of the Faith, &c.* (London, 1616), p. 529. Apart from in his writings, the idea is famously expressed in Rubens's 'The Apotheosis of James I' for the Whitehall Banqueting House: C. White, *Peter Paul Rubens: Man and Artist* (New Haven, Connecticut, and London, 1987), pp. 248–55.
47. See P. Mansel, *King of the World: The Life of Louis XIV* (London, 2022) and J. Wilkinson, *Louis XIV: The Real King of Versailles* (Stroud, 2019). See also on the concept of *Dei gratia*, 'by the grace of God', M. Range, 'Dei gratia and the 'divine right of kings': Divine legitimization or human humility', in E. Woodacre, L. H. S. Dean, C. Jones, R. E. Martin and Z. E. Rohr (eds), *The Routledge History of Monarchy* (Abingdon, 2019), pp. 130–145.
48. Q. Skinner, 'The State', in T. Ball *et al.* (eds), *Political Innovation and Conceptual Change* (Cambridge, 1989), pp. 125–6.
49. J. P. Kenyon, *Revolution Principles: The Politics of Party, 1689–1720* (Cambridge, 1977), p. 207.

50. T. Claydon, 'Latitudinarianism and Apocalyptic History in the Worldview of Gilbert Burnet, 1643–1715', *The Historical Journal*, 51 (2008), p. 20: 'Burnet greeted the Glorious Revolution with the hopes for a "New Jerusalem", and the Hanoverians with the observation that God had marked them out "with signal characters of amazing providence"'. See also T. Claydon, *Europe and the Making of England: 1660–1760* (Cambridge, 2007), p. 248.
51. H. T. Dickinson, *Liberty and Property: Political Ideology in Eighteenth-Century Britain* (London, 1977), p. 39.
52. M. Goldie, 'Tory Political Thought, 1689–1714' (Cambridge Ph.D. thesis, 1977) and M. Goldie, 'The Revolution of 1689 and the Structure of Political Argument: An Essay and An Annotated Bibliography of Pamphlets on the Allegiance Controversy', *Bulletin of Research in the Humanities*, 83 (1980), pp. 473–564. See also J. Greenberg, *The Radical Face of the Ancient Constitution: St Edward's 'Laws' in Early Modern Political Thought* (Cambridge, 2001), pp. 143–5. See also T. P. Slaughter, '"Abdicate" and "Contract" in the Glorious Revolution', *HJ*, 24 (1981), pp. 323–5, who takes a different view to Goldie on the definition of the word abdicate for seventeenth century contemporaries. See also J. Miller, 'The Glorious Revolution: "Contract" and "Abdication" Reconsidered', *HJ*, 25 (1982), pp. 541–55; and M. P. Thompson, 'Significant Silences in Locke's *Two Treatises of Government*: Constitutional History, Contract and Law', *HJ*, 31 (1987), p. 281.
53. Burgess, *Political Thought*, p. 372.
54. W. A. Speck, *James II* (London, 2002), pp. 82–3.
55. Burgess, *Political Thought*, p. 372. See also P. Dillon, *The Last Revolution: 1688 and the Creation of the Modern World* (London, 2006), p. 241, pointing out that, for Whigs and Tories, 'in the past their differences had been enough to bring the nation to war. After the Revolution, they would co-exist – to everyone's surprise – in a state of permanent, dynamic equilibrium, a controlled chemical reaction'. See also H. Nenner, *The Right to be King: The Succession to the Crown of England, 1603–1714* (Basingstoke, 1995), *passim*.
56. E. Vallance, *The Glorious Revolution: 1688, Britain's Fight for Liberty* (London, 2006), p. 17.
57. *Ibid.*, p. 225.
58. *Ibid.*, pp. 306–7.
59. *Ibid.*, p. 309.
60. *Ibid.*, p. 310. Pincus concurs with this analysis in refuting the secularisation thesis of a decline in religious belief as a product of, or factor in, the events of 1688/1689: see S. Pincus, *1688: The First Modern Revolution* (New Haven, Connecticut, and London, 2009), p. 479.

61. Vallance, *Glorious Revolution*, p. 311.
62. Dillon, *Last Revolution*, p. 5. For *Patriarcha*, see *ibid.*, p. 6 – describing a world of patriarchal authority, starting with Adam, descending to monarchs and leading up to God. See also W. A. Speck, *Reluctant Revolutionaries: Englishmen and the Revolution of 1688* (Oxford, 1988), pp. 139–41.
63. J. Black, *The Hanoverians: The History of a Dynasty* (London, 2004), *passim*; P. K. Monod, *The Power of Kings: Monarchy and Religion in Europe, 1589–1715* (New Haven, Connecticut, and London, 1999), p. 311; Strong, *Coronation*, p. 339; H. Smith, '"Last of all the Heavenly Birth": Queen Anne and Sacral Queenship', *Parliamentary History*, 28 (2009), p. 149.
64. Dillon, *Last Revolution*, p. 239.
65. *Ibid.*, p. 233.
66. S. Pincus, '"To Protect English Liberties": The English Nationalist Revolution of 1688–1689', in T. Claydon and I. McBride (eds), *Protestantism and National Identity: Britain and Ireland, c.1650 –c.1850* (Cambridge, 1998), p. 102.
67. *Ibid.*, p. 103.
68. *Ibid.*, p. 104.
69. Pincus, *1688*, p. 483.
70. *Ibid.*, p. 476. See: https://www.coronationroll.gov.uk/coronation_roll/the-coronation-service-2/the-anointing-of-the-king/, accessed 22 November 2025.
71. Asch, *Sacral Kingship*, p. 158.
72. J. C. D. Clark, *English Society 1660–1832: Religion, Ideology and Politics During the Ancien Regime* (2nd edn, Cambridge, 2000), p. 87.
73. See Shropshire Archives, Shrewsbury, MS 1536/2/1/1–18 (on coronation of George I and 1715 rebellion).
74. V. Jankovic, 'The Politics of Sky Battles in Early Hanoverian Britain', *Journal of British Studies*, 41 (2002), p. 429.
75. G. Reedy, 'Mystical Politics: The Imagery of Charles II's Coronation', in P. J. Korshin (ed.), *Studies in Change and Revolution: Aspects of English Intellectual History, 1640–1800* (Menston, 1972), p. 40.
76. As Garnett has argued, at some point 'life had to yield to logic' and it is the practical realities that we are interested in here: G. Garnett, 'The Origins of the Crown', in J. Hudson (ed.), 'The History of English Law: Centenary Essays on "Pollock and Maitland"', *Proceedings of the British Academy*, 89 (1996), p. 214.
77. Notable in the late Middle Ages are the influential writings of Marsilius of Padua (*c.*1275–1342) and his *Defensor Pacis* on the nature of rulership: G. Moreno-Riaño, 'Marsilius of Padua on Rulership', in Al-Azmeh &

Bak, *Kingship*, pp. 277–89. In terms of earlier origins in political thought, I am indebted to Ann Kennedy, Emeritus Fellow and former Law Tutor at Lady Margaret Hall, for bringing Marsilius of Padua to my attention and his influential writings in the late Middle Ages; and also Al-Azmeh & Bak, *Kingship*, pp. 9–31: for early Muslim origins of divine right and kingship.

78. For the importance of St Edward the Confessor see J. Greenberg, *The Radical Face of the Ancient Constitution: St Edward's 'Laws' in Early Modern Political Thought* (Cambridge, 2001) and *ibid.*, 'Confessor's Laws' and D. A. Carpenter, 'King Henry III and Saint Edward the Confessor: The Origins of the Cult', *The English Historical Review*, CXXII (2007), pp. 865–91.
79. Garnett, 'Crown', p. 201. See also M. Holmes, 'New Light on St. Edward's Crown', *Archaeologia*, 2nd Series, 97 (1959), pp. 213–23.
80. BL, Egerton MS 3320, fols 16r, 17r, 22r.
81. See also O. Chaline, 'The Kingdoms of France and Navarre: The Valois and Bourbon Courts *c.*1515–1750', in J. Adamson (ed.), *The Princely Courts of Europe: Ritual, Politics and Culture Under the Ancien Régime 1500–1750* (London, 1999), pp. 68–70; J. Adamson, 'The Kingdoms of England and Great Britain: The Tudor and Stuart Courts 1509–1714', in J. Adamson (ed.), *The Princely Courts of Europe: Ritual, Politics and Culture Under the Ancien Régime 1500–1750* (London, 1999), pp. 95–117; Ryrie, 'Divine Kingship'; Al-Azmeh and Bak, *Kingship*, pp. 9–31; and Burgess, *Political Thought*, espescially pp. 142–51.
82. Smith, '"Last of all the Heavenly Birth"', pp. 140–1.
83. G. Parker, 'The Place of Tudor England in the Messianic Vision of Philip II of Spain', *Transactions of the Royal Historical Society*, 6th Series, XII (2002), p. 175.
84. P. Lake, 'The Laudian Style: Order, Uniformity and the Pursuit of the Beauty of Holiness in the 1630s', in K. Fincham (ed.), *The Early Stuart Church, 1603–1642* (Basingstoke, 1993), pp. 161–85.
85. D. Cressy, *Charles I and the People of England* (Oxford, 2015), p. 215. See also J. Bliss and W. Scott (eds), *The Works of the Most Reverend Father in God, William Laud*, 9 volumes (Oxford, 1847–1860), I *passim*. See particularly W. Laud, *A Commemoration of King Charles his Inauguration; or, a Sermon* [on Ps. LXXII 1] *Preached at Pauls Crosse* ... (London, 1645): though thought to belong to 1631.
86. H. Valentine, H., *God Save the King. A Sermon Preached in St. Pauls Church the 27th of March 1639. Being the Day of his Maiesties Most Happy Inauguration, and of his Northerne Expedition* (London, 1639), pp. 5–6.
87. Cressy, *Charles I*.

88. A. Lacey, *The Cult of King Charles the Martyr* (Woodbridge, 2003), pp. 52–3.
89. *Ibid.*, p. 18.
90. D. MacCulloch, *Thomas Cranmer: A Life* (1st edn, New Haven, Connecticut, and London, 1996), p. 364.
91. P. Tudor-Craig, 'Henry VIII and King David', in D. Williams (ed.), *Early Tudor England*, Proceedings of the 1987 Harlaxton Symposium (Woodbridge, 1989), p. 198.
92. WAM, 51119, p. 11. See also D. MacCulloch, *The Boy King: Edward VI and the Protestant Reformation* (Berkeley, California, 2002), p. 35.
93. P. E. McCullough, *Sermons at Court: Politics and Religion in Elizabethan and Jacobean Preaching* (Cambridge, 1998), p. 82 (quoting a Lenten sermon given at Richmond Palace in 1575 by Richard Curteys, Bishop of Chichester).
94. Cf. A. N. McLaren, 'Delineating the Elizabethan Body Politic: Knox, Aylmer and the Definition of Counsel 1558–88', *History of Political Thought*, XVII (1996), pp. 224–52.
95. Cf. D. Hoak, 'Tudor Deborah? The Coronation of Elizabeth I, Parliament, and the Problem of Female Rule', in C. Highley and J. N. King (eds), *John Foxe and His World* (Aldershot, 2002), pp. 73–88. See also B. Usher, 'John Aylmer (1520/1521–1594)', *ODNB* and B. Lowe, 'John Hales (1516?–1572)', *ibid.* Hales was a royal office-holder and former MP, while John Aylmer's tract *Harborowe* (1559) was a response to John Knox's 1558 critique of queenship.
96. Cf. H. Hackett, *Virgin Mother, Maiden Queen: Elizabeth I and the Cult of the Virgin Mary* (Basingstoke, 1995), pp. 38–71; Zaller, 'Vessels'; King, *Iconography*, p. 266.
97. Bodl., MS Ballard 12, fol. 186r–v.
98. The Codrington Library, All Souls College, Oxford, MS 155, fols 75r–v, 76r–v. See also B. Quintrell, 'Henry Montagu (*c.*1564–1642)', *ODNB.*
99. BL, Add. MS 47184, fol. 11r.
100. Cf. P. Collinson, *The Birthpangs of Protestant England: Religious and Cultural Change in the Sixteenth and Seventeenth Centuries* (Basingstoke, 1988), pp. 1–27 ('The Protestant Nation').
101. The biblical passages are Revelation 19: 6 and 16. Handel's 'Zadok the Priest' has been played at every British coronation since George II's in 1727. A re-hearing in the light of this book is to be recommended. The interpretation by Sir Malcolm Sargent (1895–1967) is particularly impressive. See also M. Range, *Music and Ceremonial at British Coronations: From James I to Elizabeth II* (Cambridge, 2012), p. 129. For further details on music and its influence, see A. Copland, *What to Listen for in Music* (New York, 1957). On Handel's music as seen in terms of

sacralisation and embodying British religion, see T. Blanning, *The Triumph of Music: Composers, Musicians and their Audiences, 1700 to the Present* (London, 2008), p. 91.

102. Legg, *Coronation Records*, p. 258; Wordsworth, *Coronation*, p. 32.
103. Northants., RO, MS IC 2160, fol. 1r–v.
104. Range, *Music*, pp. 237–8.
105. BL, Add. MS 47184, fol. 11r.
106. Strickland, *Henry the Young King*, p. 82: A. Duggan, 'The Coronation of the Young King in 1170', in G. J. Cumming (ed.), *Studies in Church History*, vol. 2 (London, 1968), p. 165, n. 1; R. W. Eyton, *The Court, Household and Itinerary of Henry II* (London, 1878), p. 138; J. C. Robertson and J. B. Sheppard (eds), *Materials for the History of Thomas Becket, Archbishop of Canterbury*, 7 vols (London, Rolls Series, 1875–1885), VII, pp. 673, 679. As well as the feast of St Basil, it was 'the vigil of the holy martyrs Vitus and Modestus and the holy virgin Crescentia' (W. Stubbs (ed.), *Gesta regis Henrici secundi Benedicti abbatis: The Chronicle of the Reigns of Henry II and Richard I, AD 1169–1192*, 2 vols (Rolls Series, London, 1867), I, p. 5).
107. Hoak, 'The Iconography of the Crown Imperial', in *ibid.* (ed.), *Tudor Political Culture* (Cambridge, 1995), p. 57, and esp. pp 64–7.
108. *Ibid.*, 'Transformation', p. 116; *ibid.*, 'The Iconography of the Crown Imperial', in *ibid.* (ed.), *Tudor Political Culture* (Cambridge, 1995), pp. 54–103; see also W. Ullmann, '"This Realm of England is an Empire"', *The Journal of Ecclesiastical History*, 30 (1979), p. 176 and Schramm, *Coronation*, pp. 95, 96.
109. Scarisbrick, *Henry VIII*, p. 18.
110. Tudor-Craig, 'Henry VIII', p. 183.
111. For details on St George see D. H. Farmer, *The Oxford Dictionary of Saints* (5th edn, revised, Oxford, 2011), pp. 181–2.
112. Hoak, 'Transformation', pp. 121 and 116; MacCulloch, *Boy King*, pp. 71–4.
113. *Ibid.*, *Boy King*, p. 32.
114. R. C. Strong, 'Queen Elizabeth I and the Order of the Garter', *The Archaeological Journal*, 119 (1962), pp. 247–8.
115. Hoak, 'Transformation', p. 141. Cf. Hoak, 'Iconography', pp. 54–9. For further details, see also contemporary accounts of Edward VI's pageants in J. G. Nichols (ed.), *Literary Remains of King Edward VI*, 2 vols (London, 1857), I pp. cclxxxiii, cclxxxvi, cclxxxviii.
116. TNA, LC 2/3/1, p. 85.
117. BL, Egerton MS 3320, fol. 22r–v.
118. Legg, *Coronation Records*, pp. 293–4, 329–30.

119. [J. Gibbon], *Edovardus Confessor Redivivus, The Piety and Vertues of Holy Edward the Confessor, Reviv'd in the Sacred Majesty of King James the II …* (London, 1688), pp. 20, 27.
120. BL, Add. MS 6336, fol. 15v.
121. Strong, 'Garter', p. 246. In 1660, Charles II was quick to reinforce the Order: Bodl., MS Carte 73, fols 506r–507v (Charles II to Edward Montagu, 1st Earl of Sandwich, 19 February 1660/1661). See also Cressy, *Bonfires*, p. 171; L. Madway, '"The Most Conspicuous Solemnity": The Coronation of Charles II', in E. Cruickshanks (ed.), *The Stuart Courts* (Stroud, 2000), pp. 143; BL, Add. MS 15950, fols 139r–141r. G. Morley, *A Sermon* [on Prov. XXVIII 2] *Preached at the … Coronation of … Charles II, King of Great Britain, etc.* (London, 1661), title page; H. Bold, *St. Georges Day Sacred to the Coronation of His Most Excellent Majesty Charles the II* (London, 1661); Anon., *A Proclamation* [6 March 1684/1685], *Declaring His Majesty's Pleasure Touching His Royal Coronation, and the Solemnity Thereof* (London, 1684/1685); Anon., *Festa Georgiana*.
122. Bodl., MS Smith 57, fol. 37r.
123. R. Hutton, 'George Monck, 1st duke of Albemarle (1608–1670)', *ODNB*.
124. BL, Add. MS 4457, fol. 75r.
125. S. Anglo, *Images of Tudor Kingship* (London, 1992), pp. 62–3; L. A. Craig, 'Royalty, Virtue, and Adversity: The Cult of Henry VI', *Albion*, 35 (2003), pp. 187–209.
126. L. Hughes, 'Russia: The Courts at Moscow and St Petersburg *c.*1547–1725', in Adamson, *Courts*, p. 304. See also J. Fennell, *A History of the Russian Church to 1448* (London, 1995), p. 21 and L. Ash, *The Baton and The Cross: Russia's Church from Pagans to Putin* (London, 2024), pp. 35–6.
127. According to legend, St Andrew was one of the apostles who had visited Novgorod, south of St Petersburg.
128. G. Vilinbakhov, 'K istorii uchrezhdeniia ordena Andreia Pervozvannogo', *Kul'tura i iskusstvo petrovskogo vremeni* (Leningrad, 1977), pp. 144–5; A. I. Andreev, 'Petr I v Anglii v 1698', in *Petr Velikii: Sbornik statei* (Moscow and Leningrad, 1947), p. 87.
129. *CP*, II pp. 651–3 (App. F). For 1625 see Glamorgan Record Office, Cardiff, MS DF/VOL/119.
130. Appointments were given wide publicity, e.g. *Mercurius Publicus …*, 18–25 April 1661 (No. 16, London), pp. 254–6. See also *CP*, II p. 652 (App. F): the six earldoms were: Clarendon (Hyde), Essex (Capell), Cardigan (Brudenell), Anglesey (Annesley), Bath (Granville) and Carlisle (Howard). The six baronies were: Cornwallis, Crewe, Holles, Delamere (Booth), Townshend and Ashley (Cooper).

131. G. Goodwin (revised S. Kelsey), 'Howard, Charles, 1st Earl of Carlisle (1628–1685)', *ODNB*.
132. M. Perceval-Maxwell, 'Annesley, Arthur, 1st Earl of Anglesey (1614–1686)', *ibid*.
133. *CP*, II p. 653. Note that several families honoured at this time would be prominent in the political history of (at least) the next century, e.g. in 1689 Portland (Bentinck) and Marlborough (Churchill); in 1714 Halifax (Montague) and Uxbridge (Paget).
134. *Ibid*., II pp. 652–3 (App. F).
135. *The London Gazette*, 20 July 1838; 24 July 1838: https://www.thegazette.co.uk/London/issue/19637/page/1639, accessed 22 November 2025; https://www.thegazette.co.uk/London/issue/19638/page/1659, accessed 22 November 2025; https://www.thegazette.co.uk/London/issue/19639/page/1666, accessed 22 November 2025.
136. *TLG*, 1 June 1953: https://www.thegazette.co.uk/London/issue/39863/supplement/2939, accessed 22 November 2025.
137. *TLG*, 29–30 December 2023: https://www.thegazette.co.uk/London/issue/64269/data.pdf, accessed 22 November 2025. See also https://www.rbo.org.uk/people/antonio-pappano, accessed 22 November 2025.
138. E. Prescott, 19 May 2024, https://www.dailymail.co.uk/news/royals/article-13434187/prince-harry-king-charles-duke-norfolk-emily-prescott.html, accessed 22 November 2025. See for examples: T. Murdoch, 'A Silver-Gilt Cup Commemorating the Coronation of James II and the Culture of Gifts and Prerequisites [*sic*] in Stuart and Hanoverian Coronations', *V&A Online Journal*, No. 2 (Autumn, 2009) http://www.vam.ac.uk/content/journals/research-journal/issue-02/a-silver-gilt-cup-commemorating-the-coronation-of-james-ii/, accessed 22 November 2024; J. R. Planché, *Regal Records: or, A Chronicle of the Coronations of the Queens Regnant of England* (London, 1838), *passim*; and G. W. Wollaston, *Coronation Claims: Containing a Full Report of all the Cases Argued Before the Court of Claims at the Coronation of King Edward VII., with Other Matter Relating to Coronation Services in General* (2nd edn, London, 1910). For older claims (seventeenth century–nineteenth century) see also Dorset History Centre, Dorchester, MS D/WLC/F66.
139. See https://www.beehive.govt.nz/release/pm%E2%80%99s-international-travel-advance-nzs-economic-interests, 18 April 2023, accessed 22 November 2025; and https://www.dpmc.govt.nz/publications/kings-birthday-and-coronation-honours-list-2023, 5 June 2023, accessed 22 November 2025.
140. E. S. de Beer, (ed.), *The Diary of John Evelyn. Now First Printed in Full from the Manuscripts …*, 6 volumes (Oxford, 1955), III pp. 277–8.

141. *CP*, II p. 653 (App. F).
142. See J. Goodall, *The Castle: A History* (New Haven, Connecticut, 2022), pp. 188–90.
143. Strickland, *Henry the Young King*, p. 82.
144. For an early depiction of the Order (and so too the earliest known representation of Westminster Abbey's west towers), see Canaletto's painting of *c.*1749 in the Westminster Abbey collection: https://www.westminster-abbey.org/abbey-news/canaletto-painting-display/, 2 March 2020, accessed 22 November 2025. See also BL, Lansdowne MS 865 (for *c.*1603–1661 details).
145. They were sometimes created at the ceremonies for the creation of a monarch's first son as Prince of Wales and of his second son as Duke of York.
146. Matikkala provides some explanation for the ending of this ancient tradition. According to later evidence – a report submitted to Sir Robert Walpole – James II had upon his accession conceived the idea of converting the Order of the Bath 'into a kind of Religious Order for' the 'Defence of the Roman Catholic religion'. However, since the 'genius' of the 'nation' was 'otherwise inclined', the proposal proved abortive, and even the custom of creating Knights of the Bath shortly before the coronation was abandoned: A. Matikkala, *The Orders of Knighthood and the Formation of the Honours System, 1660–1760* (Woodbridge, 2008), p. 91. It might be argued that enthusiasm for further creations of Knights of the Bath may have been waning owing to the possibility of new orders being established, especially the Order of the Royal Oak: see *ibid.*, pp. 67–72.
147. W. C. Metcalfe, *A Book of Knights Banneret, Knights of the Bath, and Knights Bachelor Made Between the Fourth Year of King Henry VI. and the Restoration of King Charles II. ... and Knights Made in Ireland Between 1566 and 1698, etc.* (London, 1885). See also Bayne, 'The Coronation', (1910), pp. 550–3; F. Pilbrow, F., 'The Knights of the Bath: Dubbing to Knighthood in Lancastrian and Yorkist England', in P. Coss and M. Keen (eds), *Heraldry, Pageantry and Social Display in Medieval England* (Woodbridge, 2002), pp. 195–218; and Strong, *Coronation*, pp. 163, 252.
148. Sir Ivan De La Bere, *The Queen's Orders of Chivalry* (2nd edn, London, 1964); Pilbrow, 'Knighthood'; Matikkala, *Knighthood*, pp. 88–97. See also J. L. Nevinson, 'The Robes of the Order of the Bath', *The Connoisseur*, 134 (1954), pp. 153–9.
149. P. Galloway, *The Order of the Bath* (Chichester, 2006).
150. Staffordshire Record Office, Stafford Branch, MS D868/4/93b (W. Smith to John Langley, Drury Lane, 9 March 1660/1661). Such news also filtered out to the Venetian resident in England, who stated that the king was installing sixty-four 'deserving persons, in reward for

their services not only to the Crown in general but to his royal person and family': *CSP, Venice,* XXXII p. 284 (item 335: Francesco Giavarina to the doge and Senate of Venice, London, 29 April 1661).

151. W. A. Shaw, *The Knights of England: A Complete Record from the Earliest Time to the Present Day of the Knights of all the Orders of Chivalry in England, Scotland, and Ireland, and of Knights Bachelors,* 2 volumes (London, 1906), I, pp. 163–6. The 1661 creation of the Knights of Bath received significant publicity, e.g. *Mercurius Publicus ...,* 18–25 April 1661 (No. 16, London), pp. 248–54. Cf. BL, Add. MS 6303.
152. *Ibid.*, p. 250.
153. J. W. Legg (ed.), *Three Coronation Orders,* Publications of the Henry Bradshaw Society, 19 (London, 1900), p. 108. His coronation role is omitted from L. A. Knafla, 'Egerton, John, 3rd Earl of Bridgewater (1646–1701)', *ODNB.*
154. Doran, *Tudor to Stuart,* pp. 135–6. See also Bayne, 'The Coronation', (1910), pp. 550–3.
155. For an excellent early modern example, including horoscopes, see FSL, MS W.a.341.
156. Redford, *Akhenaten,* p. 181. Astrology and astronomy were equally essential elements in Egyptian rule and in the reign of Akhenaten.
157. G. Straka, 'The Final Phase of Divine Right Theory in England, 1688–1702', *The English Historical Review,* LXXVII (1962), p. 638. The abdication of James II posed very real problems for hereditary succession, and a belief in an acting God and of providential Divine Right helped to overcome the difficulties of rival claimants to the throne: see FSL, MS X.d.433 (arguments arising out of abdication of James II, *c.*1691 and [William] Sherlock's case of allegiance).
158. Straka, 'Final Phase', p. 639.
159. J. A. Nice, '"The Peculiar Place of God": Early Modern Representations of England and France', *The English Historical Review,* CXXI (2006), p. 1007.
160. Parker, 'Messianic Vision', pp. 167–221.
161. *Ibid.*, p. 168.
162. *Ibid.*
163. *Ibid.*, p. 169. See also Necipoglu, 'Suleyman' and Fleischer, 'Messiah'. The coronation ceremony would remain an important part of the status of a Sultan and the publication of that power to other Emperors: see FSL, MS W.b.132 (176) No. 32, fol. 218 [233r–v] (letter announcing the coronation of Suleiman as Sultan, 1099 [1687] to Imperator Leopoldo [Holy Roman Emperor]).
164. Parker, 'Messianic Vision', p. 169.

165. *Ibid.* See also H. Lenowitz, *The Jewish Messiahs: From the Galilee to Crown Heights* (Oxford, 1998), pp. 120–3 and M. Goldish, 'Patterns in Converso Messianism', in M. D. Goldish and R. H. Popkin (eds), *Millenarianism and Messianism in Early Modern European Culture*, Volume 1: Jewish Messianism in the Early Modern World (Dordrecht and London, 2001), pp. 41–63.
166. Parker, 'Messianic Vision', p. 170. See also W. A. Christian, *Apparitions in Late Medieval and Renaissance Spain* (Princeton, New Jersey, 1981) and J. Bilinkoff, 'A Spanish Prophetess and her Patrons: The Case of Maria de Santo Domingo', *The Sixteenth Century Journal*, 23 (1992), pp. 21–34.
167. Parker, 'Messianic Vision', p. 167.
168. *Ibid.*, p. 174. Parker here quotes from Bibliothèque Publique et Universitaire, Geneva, MS Favre 30/73v (Philip II to Don Luis de Requesens, 20 October 1573): 'Spero en Dios … que os dara mucha salud y vida, pues se empleara en su servicio y en el mío, que es lo mismo'.
169. Parker, 'Messianic Vision', p. 174.
170. *Ibid.*, p. 175 (Plate 2).
171. Parker, 'Messianic Vision', p. 174.
172. Strong, 'Garter', p. 248. See also H. Ellis (ed.), *The New Chronicles of England and France, in Two Parts; by R. F., Named by Himself The Concordance of Histories …* (London, 1811), p. 715; Anon. (ed.), *Holinshed's Chronicles of England, Scotland and Ireland*, 6 volumes (London, 1807–1808), IV, pp. 57, 62; and *CSP, Venice*, V pp. 524–5.
173. Parker, 'Messianic Vision', p. 182.
174. Cf. Sebag Montefiore, *Jerusalem*, pp. 216, 278 (n.). According to Sebag Montefiore, the title of King of Jerusalem remained with the Habsburg Emperors as late as 1918.
175. Collinson, *Birthpangs*, pp. 8, 10, 21, 28–31, 56, 99.
176. Cf. Lenman, 'Exiled Stuarts'. Cf. C. Blair, (general ed.), *The Crown Jewels: The History of the Coronation Regalia in the Jewel House of the Tower of London*, 2 volumes (London, 1998).
177. Edie, 'Public Face', pp. 311–36.
178. A. Keay, *The Crown Jewels* (London, 2011).
179. 37 Henry VIII c. 17: *The Statutes of the Realm*, 11 vols (London, 1810–1828), III p. 1009.
180. C. Cross, 'Churchmen and the Royal Supremacy', in F. Heal and R. O'Day (eds), *Church and Society in England: Henry VIII to James I* (London, 1977), p. 23.
181. Thomas Wolsey persuaded the monarch to write a response to Martin Luther's attacks on the Roman Catholic Church. It is almost certain that theologians produced the initial drafts of the work, which were amalgam-

ated by the editorial hand of Thomas More, and that Henry VIII merely added finishing touches. Nevertheless, the *Assertio Septem Sacramentorum* was published under the King's name in July 1521, earning him the title *Fidei Defensor* from Pope Leo X: BL, Cotton MS Vitellius B IV/1; Scarisbrick, *Henry VIII*, pp. 110–15; J. Guy, *Thomas More* (London, 2000), pp. 114–15, 149; L. Wooding, *Henry VIII* (Abingdon, 2009), pp. 108–9.

182. Ives, *Anne Boleyn*, p. 224.
183. Cross, 'Royal Supremacy', p. 23; K. W. T. Carleton, 'The *Traditio Instrumentorum* in the Reform of Ordination Rites in the Sixteenth Century', in R. W. Swanson (ed.), *Continuity and Change in Christian Worship*, Studies in Church History, 35 (Woodbridge, 1999), p. 183.
184. CLO, MS 155, fol. 75r–v.
185. BL, Add. MS 4457, fol. 74r–v.
186. *Ibid.*, Add. MS 15950, fol. 140r; Anon., *The Manner of the Solemnity of the Coronation of his Most Sacred Majesty King Charles* (London, 1660).
187. Bodl., MS Tanner 31, fol. 33r (Abraham Shapton to William Sancroft, 22 April 1685). For the consecration of James VI and I, see S. M. Jack, '"A Pattern for a King's Inauguration": The Coronation of James I in England', *Parergon*, New Series, 21 No. 2 (2004), p. 84. Cf. Monod, *Power of Kings*, p. 39.
188. *OED*. In 1559 [Carew] is 'remembered mainly for celebrating mass at the coronation of Elizabeth, no bishop being willing to do so because the queen had forbidden the elevation of the consecrated elements', in Fincham and Tyacke, *Altars Restored*, p. 75. See also, W. P. Haugaard, 'The Coronation of Elizabeth I', *The Journal of Ecclesiastical History*, XIX (1968), pp. 161–70; & P. McCullough, 'Carew, George (1497/1498–1583)', *ODNB*.
189. The iconography of the consecration of a king is too extensive to discuss here, but for a spectacular example see the ninth century MS miscellany on the life of St Edmund: The Pierpont Morgan Library, New York, USA, MSM 736. See also A. S. G. Edwards (ed.), *The Life of St Edmund, King and Martyr: John Lydgate's Illustrated Verse Life Presented to Henry VI: A Facsimile of British Library MS Harley 2278* (London, 2004). See also A. Gransden, 'Edmund [St Edmund] (d. 869)', *ODNB*.
190. M. Fantoni, 'The Grand Duchy of Tuscany: The Courts of the Medici 1532–1737', in Adamson, *Courts*, p. 268.
191. See W. Ullmann, 'Thomas Becket's Miraculous Oil', *The Journal of Theological Studies*, 8 (1957), pp. 129–33; J. W. McKenna, 'The Coronation Oil of the Yorkist Kings', *EHR*, LXXXII (1967), pp. 102–4; T. A. Sandquist, 'The Holy Oil of St Thomas of Canterbury', in

T. A. Sandquist and M. R. Powicke (eds), *Essays in Medieval History, Presented to Bertie Wilkinson* (Toronto, 1969), pp. 330–44.

192. Jackson, *Vive le Roi*, p. 32. For the French coronation consecration, see the legend of the holy flask and coronation relics at Reims Cathedral and the Palais du Tau museum, https://www.palais-du-tau.fr/en, accessed 22 November 2025. It is also worth noting Reims BM 328, fol. 72r–v, cited in Jackson, *Vive le Roi*, pp. 4–5. See also W. Ullmann (ed.), with a note on the music by D. H. Turner, *Liber Regie Capelle: A Manuscript in the Biblioteca Publica, Evora*, Publications of the Henry Bradshaw Society, XCII (London, 1961), pp. 30–31.
193. See also D. Cressy, *Birth, Marriage, and Death: Ritual, Religion, and the Life-Cycle in Tudor and Stuart England* (Oxford, 1997), pp. 231–81 on 'Courtship', including section pp. 267–76 on 'Cementing the Engagement', and pp. 283–376 on 'Marriage', including section pp. 342–7 on 'The Ring in Marriage'.
194. On contractualism, see Chap. 3.
195. BL, Royal MS App. 89, fol. 100r–v. There seems to be reference to this in Charles I's coronation order, but it is very obscure: Wordsworth, *Coronation*, p. xxv ('The Ring. ["The Linnen Gloves" struck out]').
196. Legg, 'Coronation Ring', p. 6. For medieval context, see also W. Ullmann, *Principles of Government and Politics in the Middle Ages* (2nd edition, London, 1966), pp. 181–2.
197. Bodl., MS Tanner 31, fol. 86r.
198. *Ibid.*
199. J. Wormald, 'James VI and I (1566–1625)', *ODNB*. See also A. Kincaid, 'Buck [Buc], Sir George (bap. 1560, d. 1622)', *ibid.*
200. A. Kincaid (ed.), *The History of King Richard The Third (1619) by Sir George Buc Master of the Revels* (New edn, London, 2023), p. 215.
201. Legg, 'Coronation Ring', p. 4.
202. https://www.coronationroll.gov.uk/roll/, accessed 22 November 2025.
203. Legg, 'Coronation Ring', p. 8.
204. *Ibid.*, p. lviii, see also Lee, 'Coronation Ring', , pp. 1–9.
205. https://www.coronationroll.gov.uk/roll/, accessed 22 November 2025, see also E. Hawkins (comp.) and Franks, A. W. and Grueber, H. A. (eds), *Medallic Illustrations of the History of Great Britain and Ireland to the Death of George II*, 2 volumes (London, 1885). For less well-known examples, discovered by the present author, see Oriel College, Oxford, Archives, AH 5 D1.
206. Sommerville, *Politics*, p. 35, from a sermon by 'The Vicar of Bray', quoted in W. H. Auden (ed.), *The Oxford Book of Light Verse* (Oxford, 1938), p. 260.

207. H. Everett, 'The English Coronation Rite: From the Middle Ages to the Stuarts', in H. Everett *et al.*, *Coronations: Past, Present and Future* (Cambridge, 1997), p. 7.
208. BL, Add. MS 6281, fol. 13r.
209. TNA, C 57/5–9, see also https://www.coronationroll.gov.uk/roll/, accessed 22 November 2025.
210. Queen Victoria Diary, Coronation entry: Thursday, 28 June 1838 (http://www.queenvictoriasjournals.org/, accessed 23 November 2025).
211. BL, Add. MS 6281, fol. 15r (George I, 1714). See also Anon., *The Whole Ceremony of the Coronation of His Most Sacred Majesty King George: on Wednesday the Twentieth Day of October, 1714* (Dublin, 1715).
212. *Ibid.*, fol. 22r.
213. For discussion of organ music as part of the homage-making element in coronations, see Range, *Music*, pp. 16, 36–7 and 104–5.
214. Smith, '"Last of all the Heavenly Birth"', p. 149.
215. https://www.parliament.uk/about/living-heritage/evolutionofparliament/houseoflords/house-of-lords-reform/overview/hereditarypeersremoved/, accessed 22 November 2025; T. Brown, 6 November 2024, https://lordslibrary.parliament.uk/house-of-lords-reform-government-policy-and-recent-developments/, accessed 22 November 2025.
216. https://www.royalcwsociety.org/upcoming-events/commonwealthdayservice#:~:text=%E2%80%8BThis%20annual%20event%2C%20held,particularly%20amongst%20its%20young%20people, accessed 22 November 2025.
217. https://www.westminster-abbey.org/abbey-commemorations/royals/elizabeth-ii/, accessed 22 November 2025.
218. *Authorised Liturgy for the Coronation Rite of His Majesty King Charles III* [with commentary], p. 18.
219. https://www.coronationroll.gov.uk/coronation_roll/the-coronation-service-2/the-presentation-of-the-regalia/, accessed 22 November 2025. The *OED* has the spelling as 'armil', but provides various historical examples that included a second 'l'. Both Keay, *Crown Jewels*, p. 183 and The 2023 Coronation Roll, https://www.coronationroll.gov.uk/further_info/the-armills/, accessed 21 November 2025, adopt a second 'l' in their spelling.
220. https://humanists.uk/2023/05/06/humanists-uk-to-attend-coronation/, 6 May 2023, accessed 21 November 2025.
221. https://www.coronationroll.gov.uk/roll/, accessed 22 November 2025.
222. D. Capurro, 8 January 2023, https://www.telegraph.co.uk/royal-family/2023/01/08/prince-harry-has-written-kings-coronation/, accessed 20 March 2023; L. Turner and S. Coughlan, 8 May 2023,

https://www.bbc.co.uk/news/entertainment-arts-65480420, accessed 10 May 2023.

223. A tubercular disease of the lymph nodes.
224. Strickland, *Henry the Young King*, p. 88. See also M. Bloch (trans. J. E. Anderson), *The Royal Touch: Sacred Monarchy and Scrofula in England and France* (London, 1973); N. F. Cantor, *Church, Kingship and Lay Investiture in England 1089–1135* (Princeton, New Jersey, 1958), p. 173; P. Buc, 'David's Adultery with Bathsheba and the Healing Power of Capetian Kings', *Viator*, 24 (1993), 101–20; and cf. G. Koziol, 'England, France and the Problem of Sacrality in Twelfth-Century Ritual', in T. Bisson (ed.), *Cultures of Power. Lordship, Status and Process in Twelfth- Century Europe* (Philadelphia, Pennsylvania, 1995), pp. 139–40.
225. *OED*, which disagrees on dates with H. Smith, H., *Georgian Monarchy: Politics and Culture, 1714–1760* (Cambridge, 2006), p. 96. See also S. Werrett, 'Healing the Nation's Wounds: Royal Ritual and Experimental Philosophy in Restoration England', *History of Science*, 38 (2000), pp. 379–80.
226. Bloch, *Royal Touch*; S. Brogan, *The Royal Touch in Early Modern England: Politics, Medicine and Sin* (Woodbridge, 2015). For an even earlier account, see Sir Raymond Crawfurd, *The King's Evil* (Oxford, 1911).
227. See Reedy, 'Mystical Politics', pp. 19–42.
228. Werrett, 'Healing', p. 379.
229. W. Sancroft, *A Sermon Preached in S. Peter's Westminster … at the Consecration of … John* [Cosin] *Lord Bishop of Durham, William* [Lucy] *Lord Bishop of S. David's, Beniamin* [Laney] *L. Bishop of Peterborough, Hugh* [Lloyd] *Lord Bishop of Landaff, Richard* [Sterne] *Lord Bishop of Carlisle, Brian* [Walton] *Lord Bishop of Chester, and John* [Gauden] *Lord Bishop of Exeter* (London, 1660), p. 33. See also R. Beddard, 'Sancroft, William (1617–1693)', *ODNB*.
230. Sancroft, *Sermon*. See also Reedy, 'Mystical Politics', p. 30. For the idea of Charles I as being made *imago dei*, see E. Kiryanova, 'Images of Kingship: Charles I, Accession Sermons, and the Theory of Divine Right', *History*, 100 (2015), p. 25.
231. Asch, *Sacral Kingship*, p. 132 quoting R. Knowles, 'Introduction', in John Ogilby, *The Entertainment of His Most Excellent Majestie Charles II in His Passage Through the City of London to His Coronation* [London, 1662] (New York, 1988), p. 15. For the role of the Order of the Garter in 1660 and more generally during the Restoration period see also Matikkala, *Knighthood*, pp. 62–7, 305.
232. Asch, *Sacral Kingship*, p. 132. See also A. Keay, *The Magnificent Monarch: Charles II and the Ceremonies of Power* (London, 2008), pp. 115–18, and

211–13; cf. H. Weber, *Paper Bullets: Print and Kingship under Charles II* (Lexington, Kentucky, 1996), pp. 50–87. For miraculous healings in this period see P. Elmer, *The Miraculous Conformist: Valentine Greatrakes, the Body Politic, and the Politics of Healing in Restoration Britain* (Oxford, 2013).

233. See Bloch, *Royal Touch*, p. 42. See also Werrett, 'Healing', p. 380.
234. Schramm, *Coronation*, p. 133. See also *ibid.*, pp. 116, 125–6.
235. For example, Anon., *At the Court at Whitehall the Ninth of January 1683 ... the Happiness of Their Sacred Touch ... Kings-Evil ...* (London, 1683[/4]). See also CLO, MS 222, fols 3r, 8r.
236. Cressy, *Charles I*, pp. 13, 302–4.
237. For the power of public royal ritual, see Edie, 'Public Face', pp. 311–36.
238. Bodl., MS Rawlinson D663, fols 59v–60v, 62v, 70r. See also *Mercurius Publicus*, 19–26 July 1660, p. 465; L. Picard, *Restoration London* (1st edn, London, 1997), pp. 79–81. See also Latham & Matthews, *Pepys*, I p. 182 (23 June 1660). For healing medals under Queen Anne, see TNA, Mint 6/2.
239. G. E. Aylmer, *The Crown's Servants: Government and Civil Service under Charles II, 1660–1685* (Oxford, 2002), pp. 247–8. The figure may even have been more, somewhere in the region of 100,000 people in his reign: Brogan, *Royal Touch*, pp. 149, 171 and Elmer, *Miraculous Conformist*, p. 117.
240. Werrett, 'Healing', p. 393.
241. J. Dryden, 'Threnodia Augustalis: A Funeral Pindaric Poem. Sacred to the Happy Memory of King Charles II', in J. Warton *et al.* (eds), *The Poetical Works of John Dryden; Containing Original Poems, Tales, and Translations* (London, 1862), pp. 97. See also J. Dryden, *To His Sacred Majesty* [Charles II], *a Panegyrick on his Coronation* (London, 1661).
242. BL, Add. MS 47087, fol. 88r. See also P. K. Monod, *Jacobitism and the English People, 1688–1788* (Cambridge, 1989), pp. 127–31; and B. Lenman, *The Jacobite Risings in Britain 1689–1746* (London, 1980), *passim*.
243. Smith, *Georgian Monarchy*, p. 95.
244. R. O. Bucholz, 'Queen Anne: Victim of her Virtues?', in C. Campbell Orr (ed.), *Queenship in Britain, 1660–1837: Royal Patronage, Court Culture, and Dynastic Politics* (Manchester, 2002), p. 108.
245. For the announcement of the forthcoming coronation Sermon and 'touching for the King's Evile', see Glamis Castle, Angus, NRAS885/1/Box 70/Folder 1/Bundle 3 (London, 2 Aprile 1702 [side 1 of doc]). See also Smith, '"Last of all the Heavenly Birth"', p. 145.
246. Smith, *Georgian Monarchy*, p. 95.
247. Smith, '"Last of all the Heavenly Birth", p. 145.

248. It was part of the role of the Supreme Governor of the Church of England, a responsibility that the late Queen Elizabeth II took with great assiduousness, and so too by King Charles III.
249. Smith, *Georgian Monarchy*, pp. 95–6.
250. R. O. Bucholz, *The Augustan Court: Queen Anne and the Decline of Court Culture* (Stanford, California, 1993), p. 212. Sessions were publicised in *TLG*: see *TLG*, 24–8 May 1705 (no. 4126), 28 February–1 March 1712/1713 (no. 5099), 17–19 April 1712 (no. 4993), 16–20 February 1713/1714 (no. 5200).
251. See Anon., *Great Britain's Welcome*, pp. 6, 16 and M. Kilburn, 'Royalty and Public in Britain: 1714–1789', DPhil. thesis, University of Oxford (1997), pp. 24–31.
252. Elmer, *Miraculous Conformist*, p. 7.
253. The argument that, in the passage of time, people in Britain have gradually become less religious and the country increasingly secular. The literature on this controversial topic is too vast to cite here.
254. Elmer, *Miraculous Conformist*, pp. 7–8.
255. Werrett, 'Healing', p. 378. For discussion of the medical background for touching for the King's Evil under Queen Anne cf. Weber, *Paper Bullets*, pp. 81–4.
256. See Chap. 2 and see for examples: S. Rosewell, *The King's True Divine Right. The Flourishing of his Crown: and the Shame of his Enemies. A Sermon Preach'd upon Occasion of His Majesty's Coronation: the Lord's Day after; being October the 24th. 1714. ...* (London, 1714); J. Blair, *Divine Providence, the Security of the Crown and Subject: Two Sermons Preach'd in London-Derry December 8 1714 Being a Day of Thanksgiving, Observ'd by the Presbyterians of Ulster for the Peaceable and Happy Accession of his Most Excellent Majesty King George to the Throne of these Kingdoms* (Belfast, 1715); J. Boyse, *A Sermon Preach'd on the First of March, 1714/1715. Being the Day of Publick Thanksgiving to Almighty God, for the Peaceable Accession of his Sacred Majesty King George to the Throne; and for Disappointing the Designs of the Pretender, and all his Adherents* (Dublin, 1715); J. Dennis, *A Poem upon the Death of Her Late Sacred Majesty Queen Anne, and the Most Happy and Most Auspicious Accession of his Sacred Majesty King George ...* (London, 1714); C. Beckingham, *A Poem on His Most Sacred Majesty King George the IId, his Accession to the Throne, etc* (Dublin, 1727). Although the use of the vernacular was typical, see also BL, Sloane MS 3516, fol. 6r (George I: verses on his coronation day 1714 [Latin]).
257. Madway, '"Solemnity"', p. 152. See also Wenceslaus Hollar's engraving of the ceremony, reproduced *ibid.*, p. 153. Cf. R. Pennington, *A*

Descriptive Catalogue of the Etched Work of Wenceslaus Hollar 1607–1677 (Cambridge, 1982), p. 92.

258. Madway, '"Solemnity"', p. 152. Cf. R. M. Smuts, 'Public Ceremony and Royal Charisma: The English Royal Entry in London, 1485–1642', in A. L. Beier *et al.* (eds), *The First Modern Society: Essays in English History in Honour of Lawrence Stone* (Cambridge, 1989), pp. 91–3.
259. A. Cook, *Titus Britannicus: An Essay of History Royal: in the Life & Reign of His Late Sacred Majesty, Charles II, of Ever Blessed and Immortal Memory* (London, 1685), p. 279.
260. Madway, '"Solemnity"', pp. 152–3.
261. The published account of Elizabeth I's coronation procession, cited in Hoak, 'Transformation', p. 143.
262. P. R. Backscheider, *Spectacular Politics: Theatrical Power and Mass Culture in Early Modern England* (London, 1993), p. 2.
263. *Ibid.*, p. 11.
264. Latham & Matthews, *Pepys*, II p. 83 (22 April 1661). For an account of seals, coins and medals connected with Charles's Restoration, see CLO, MS 187, fols 68r–75v.
265. Sir A. Bryant (ed.), *The Letters, Speeches, and Declarations of King Charles II* (London, 1935), p. 114.
266. Monod, *Power of Kings*, p. 226. The choice of day was important in astrological terms for the Tudors, and seems to be a particularly English phenomenon, see Jackson, *Vive le Roi!*, pp. 47–8: 'in England the dates of both the Catholic Mary's and the Protestant Elizabeth's coronations were selected by the astrologer John Dee. No such consideration was at work in the French ceremony'.
267. See, for example, images of the rays emanating from the sun disc (the *Aten*), often culminating with hands holding the life symbol, directed either at Akhenaten or members of his immediate family: Redford, *Akhenaten*, pp. 80–1.
268. Reedy, 'Mystical Politics', pp. 28–30. See also BL, Harleian MS 4129, fol. 24v.
269. Anon. [sometimes attributed to John Evelyn], *A Poem Upon his Majesties Coronation* (London, 1661).
270. Bocalini, Junior, *Iö Carole: or, An Extract of a Letter sent from Parnassus, Wherein are Contained Severall Epigrames, Odes, &c. Upon his Majesty's Coronation* ([London], 1661), p. 11.
271. Anon., *Gloria Britanica: or, A Panegyrick on His Sacred Majesties Passage thorow the City of London, to his Coronation. On the 23 of April, 1661...* (London, 1661), p. 8.
272. Reedy, 'Mystical Politics', p. 39.
273. *Ibid.*, p. 40.

274. Bodl., MS Rawlinson Letters 94, fol. 16r (Barnabas Oley to Francis Turner, Bishop of Ely, 18 May 1685).
275. GC, NRAS885/1/Box 70/Folder 1/Bundle 3, side 2 of 1 document (London, letter 23 April).
276. C. Given-Wilson (ed.), *Chronicles of the Revolution 1397–1400: The Reign of Richard II* (Manchester, 1993), p. 188.
277. K. Sharpe, *Reading Authority and Representing Rule in Early Modern England* (London, 2013), pp. 206–7, quoting J. Brydall, *Jura Coronae. His Majesties Royal Rights and Prerogatives Asserted* ... (London, 1680), p. 6; T. Bayly, *The Royal Charter Granted Unto Kings by God Himself* (London, 1682), pp. 53–4; W. Sanders, *The True and Wonderful Relation of the Dreadful Fighting and Groans That Were Heard and Seen in the Ayr, on the Fifteenth of this Instant January, in Carmarthen, in South-Wales* ... ([London], 1681). See also J. Milton, *Eikonoklastes in Answer to a Book Intitl'd Eikon Basilike* (London, 1649); T. Hunt, *The Great and Weighty Considerations, Relating to the Duke of York*, ... (London, 1680), p. 9; [T. Rymer], *A General Draught and Prospect of Government in Europe, and Civil Policy. Shewing the Antiquity, Power, Decay, of Parliaments with Other Historical and Political Observations Relating Thereunto* (London, 1681), p. 78.
278. C. L. Broad, *Queens, Crowns and Coronations* (rev. edn, London, 1952), p. 124.
279. Ditmas, 'Curtana', pp. 132–3.
280. For an interesting discussion of those who did not, see Bodl., MS Rawlinson Letters 110, fols 15v–16v (Thomas Hearne to James Tyrrell, 26 July 1709): which contains a lengthy discussion of the Romans and states that 'Emperors ... often styl'd Domini ... de-rive their authority from the people ... [and I] have always thought that coronation adds nothing to the right of any of our kings and queens'. He maintained that 'allegiance and submission' was the key point.
281. Smith, '"Last of all the Heavenly Birth"', p. 139.
282. L. G. Schwoerer, 'The Coronation of William and Mary, April 11, 1689', in L. G. Schwoerer (ed.), *The Revolution of 1688–1689: Changing Perspectives* (Cambridge, 1992), p. 111. Cf. Legg, *Coronation Orders*, p. 75 (App. 4).
283. Smith, '"Last of all the Heavenly Birth"', p. 146. See also J. M. Beattie, *The English Court in the Reign of George I* (Cambridge, 1967); R. M. Hatton, *George I* (New Haven, Connecticut, and London, 2001); and A. Thompson, *Britain, Hanover and the Protestant Interest, 1688–1756* (Woodbridge, 2006).
284. Kiryanova, 'Images', p. 25.

285. BL, Add. MS 61684, fol. 92r–v. As did the 3rd Earl of Carlisle, see Castle Howard, MS J8 1/647, fol. 1r–2r; MS J8 1/648, fol. 1r. So too did the people of York, as represented by the aldermen: York Archives, MS Y/COU/1/1/41, fols 155v–156r.
286. FSL, MS W.b.661, fol. 85r.
287. S. Donaldson, B. Taylor *et al.*, (ed.), *The Works of Elizabeth Barrett Browning*, vol. 2 (London, 2010), Chapter 31, *passim.*
288. LPL, Lang 223, fols. 247–8.
289. *Ibid.*, Lang 318, fols. 184–7 (Queen Elizabeth to Lang, 15 May, 1937). See also L. Goldman, 'Elizabeth [née Lady Elizabeth Angela Marguerite Bowes-Lyon] (1900–2002)', *ODNB.*
290. *Ibid.*, Fisher 123, fol. 8 (Coronation of Elizabeth II 1953).
291. See T. Hajkowski, *The BBC and National Identity in Britain, 1922–53* (Manchester, 2010), esp. pp. 83–93, and pp. 235–6.
292. C. Davies, 11 April 2021, https://www.theguardian.com/uk-news/2021/apr/11/she-made-a-pact-with-god-why-the-queen-will-not-be-abdicating, accessed 20 May 2021.
293. H. Vickers, 5 May 2023, https://www.standard.co.uk/comment/charles-sacred-ritual-different-man-coronation-b1079086.html, accessed 20 May 2023; see for examples Z. Campbell, 5 May 2023, https://www.dailymail.co.uk/news/article-12050535/What-happens-King-Charles-anointed-screen-for.html, accessed 8 May 2023; G. Tudor, 7 May 2023, https://www.bbc.co.uk/news/uk-england-shropshire-65518256, accessed 8 May 2023; S. Coyle, 6 May 2023, https://www.manchester-eveningnews.co.uk/news/uk-news/what-anointing-king-charles-covered-26837280, 10 May 2023.
294. M. Easton, 4 June 2013, https://www.bbc.co.uk/news/uk-22764987, accessed 20 May 2023. See also L. Gosling, *Royal Coronations* (Oxford, 2013); and for reflections in an earlier decade, J. M. Robinson, 'Patriotic Glory', *The Spectator* (May 2003), p. 42.

CHAPTER 2

British Coronation Sermons in Context

Introduction

> For the king in my text made himself his text; he made his own life the subject of an excellent sermon. He was pleased to stile himself the preacher, as well as the king in Jerusalem.[1]

The origins of this chapter lie in a discovery, in the Bodleian Library in Oxford, of a remarkable letter, dated 16 February 1685/1686, from James Fawkett, minister of St Michael's Town, Barbados, and a fellow of Trinity College, Cambridge, to Francis Turner, bishop of Ely and author of James II's coronation sermon. If one needs evidence of the reach and impact of a coronation and indeed a coronation sermon, then this is surely promising:

> I also had [th]e happiness of seeing your l[or]dships incomparable sermon at th[e] coronation, of w[i]ch I shal[l] only say, y[ou]r l[or]dship is loved and admired by all y[ou]r readers here & I fared very well in some mens opinions of me for having had the honour of y[ou]r acquaintance.[2]

This chapter has two main aims: firstly, to explain why coronation sermons are an important area of research and why they have been largely neglected hitherto; and secondly, to contextualise sermons preached at the coronations of sovereigns with particular reference to those from Charles II to George I, and then to the present era assessing as to why in 2023, the

G. W. C. Gross, *Crown and People*,
https://doi.org/10.1007/978-3-032-20786-9_2

sermon returned as part of the service, having been dropped for much of the twentieth century. The surviving texts of coronation sermons of the seventeenth and eighteenth centuries in particular are not pithy expositions, easily covered in a couple of pages, but rather substantial works. For that reason, contextualisation of whole sermons is difficult; earlier scholars therefore focussed on reading shorter passages. In this case, however, those of 1661–1714 will be analysed in closer detail to showcase change and continuity and the importance of the sermon in a coronation setting. This chapter argues that the coronation sermon epitomised a growing nationalist fervour long before it has been suggested to have existed. Moreover, we shall see how this developing nationalism was manifested countrywide, and very much beyond the 'Westminster Bubble', by exploring coronation sermons delivered either in or to some surprising locations. We shall also see that the coronation sermon evolved with the priorities of the era, highlighting the differing positions of each succession, politically, religiously, and culturally. In exploring these ideas, and answering such questions, this chapter will focus in turn (in Sections "Introduction", "The Evidence", "What Do we Mean by Context?", "Scotland: 1633 and 1651", and "1661–1714") on why coronation sermons were so important (with reference to Scotland for 1633 and 1651); on the historiographical background; on the surviving texts; and on their duration, including a detailed breakdown. This will be followed (in Section "Duration") by an explanation of why the sermons must be viewed in the full context of the coronation service. Having done that, the five coronation sermons of the period 1661–1714 will be analysed individually and chronologically (in Section "Coronation Sermons in Context"). Section "Impact" looks at the question of impact and assesses just how far the ideas articulated by coronation sermons really spread. This will be followed by Section "1661–1714 Conclusion" and a conclusion for the case studies 1661–1714. The chapter ends with (Section "Coda: 1727–2023, Modern and Post-Modern Coronation Sermons") examining the reinstatement of the coronation sermon in 2023, following an absence for much of the twentieth century, and a coda that seeks to draw these various threads together.

It is important to recognise that nationalism is a term with many differing interpretations. For the purposes of this chapter, with particular emphasis on the early modern world, we need only note that preachers used the concept in both a biblical context and a contemporaneous one. It is something akin to the nation of the Israelites of the Old Testament and of the divinely blessed English nation of Whig teleological history.[3] Throughout, writers for 1661–1714, used 'nation' interchangeably when discussing England and Britain.

In a typical coronation, the sermon sits directly after the acclamation and before the oath, anointing and investing with the regalia.[4] Subject to minor alterations (as presented in), all components of the Abbey service have been necessary over time for the sovereign to have been fully crowned, so its position is therefore significant. In essence, the sermon (a 'church' prerogative in the liturgy) involved the final words, 'the last influence heard and undergone by the king or queen before being crowned'.[5]

Given the opportunity and importance of the coronation sermon as a remarkable public occasion, it might be assumed or anticipated that research about them must be plentiful. Yet, oddly, coronation sermons have been all but ignored. The most relevant works include articles by Sturdy,[6] Carolyn Edie,[7] and Hone,[8] yet these are entirely focussed on early modern coronations, rather than looking beyond.

Sturdy's short essay examines coronation sermons from 1603 to 1689 and reveals how the Established Church used them to project its views of kingship and 'the kind of society' it thought desirable. His study demonstrates continuity of Divine Right ideology: 'the first four coronation preachers showed themselves to be devotees of the idea of the Divine Right of Kings; even Burnet did not deny the proposition'. Nevertheless, he takes this insight no further, instead claiming that whilst seventeenth-century coronation sermons 'performed a function of considerable importance [and were] … much more than decorative devices', later sermons, of the eighteenth century and beyond, 'were … slight in content'. This was certainly not true for 1702 and 1714; they may not have approached George Morley's lengthy 1661 sermon, but they did not lack for detail, and, indeed, rehearsed the same key themes of a New Jerusalem and a monarch enjoying divine sanction.[9]

Edie's comments are embedded in a broader analysis of civic ceremonies and the public face of royal ritual, also covering items of material culture, such as medals and coins. Her work on the public sphere shows how these 'ceremonies marking the crowning [developed] … over … the seventeenth century, [becoming] more and more in the public eye'. A coronation was not just 'solemn ritual', but was usually accompanied by 'public rejoicing and festivity'. Monarchs knew this, which was why the coronation should ideally be witnessed by 'foreign dignitaries … [and] ambassadors' and celebrated nationwide.[10] Edie hints at the importance of the coronation sermon, and other features, especially as essential items in the legitimisation of a new regime. She provides a good base from which to look beyond the Stuarts and to which to add archival depth.[11]

Hone's work as part of the extensive and detailed work covering *Stuart Succession Literature* focusses on the reign of Queen Anne (as with Edie looking at medals too) and seeks to correct the longstanding trope that the 1702 coronation was a 'public relations failure'. He also makes the vital point that both sermon and medals had influence (both at home and in diplomacy abroad) long after the coronation event itself, not least with 'distribution of medals and printed coronation sermons'.[12]

Beyond these articles, there are no books dedicated to them. Doran's authoritative account of the succession of James I, provides one of the most recent and thorough assessments of James I's 1603 coronation sermon delivered by Thomas Bilson, Bishop of Winchester.[13] *The Oxford Handbook of The Early Modern Sermon* touches on the coronation sermon of 1689 (William III & Mary II) but provides no overview more generally of early modern coronation sermons.[14] Strong makes only passing reference: concentrating on the 'three crucial sermons' of 1661, 1685, and 1689, he argues that 'theories of Divine Right gradually recede, although no one actually enunciates the fact'.[15] Hunt's work discusses Edward VI's coronation sermon, with its line of Edward as the young Josiah, yet caution is needed, for as Sir Diarmaid MacCulloch has revealed, what is said to be Cranmer's sermon never occurred, or rather the surviving text is fabricated.[16]

The historiography is, thus, surprisingly thin (and in some cases, working off a fabricated text) and these remarkable pulpit offerings therefore provide an opportunity to produce an original interpretation about the significance of coronations. This book seeks to put the coronation sermon back on the map of historical study and indicates that Divine Right ideology inherent in the texts did not gradually recede, but rather continued, beyond 1689. The sermon endured, to evolve into the eighteenth and nineteenth centuries, showcasing the political, religious, and cultural priorities of each era. It would then all but vanish in the twentieth century only to return for Charles III in 2023. As with a coronation, the sermon provides a snapshot in time as to the religious discussion of the day, the priorities ecclesiastically of the reign at the outset and the hopes from a clerical perspective of the new era. They are thus invaluable insights religiously, sociologically, culturally, and historically.

The Evidence

The coronation sermon had been part of the order of service from the *Liber Regalis* onwards, yet it took on a new importance in the seventeenth century in an age of Protestantism and polemical religious debate, accompanied with the power of print. From 1603 onwards, we have printed versions of coronation sermons, thus circulating religious and political ideas of monarchy beyond the Abbey to the laity. We know that in all probability George Day, Bishop of Chichester gave Mary I's coronation sermon, but no extant copy remains.[17] The authors of the sermons can be found in the table below (see Appendix 1). Authorial manuscripts seemingly do not exist, but there is excellent coverage of these sermons in print.

How do we know that what survives was actually delivered? Was the printed version later revised? Are these really the words of the speakers in question? What was the print run? Were these simply London publications? How can one measure impact?

We will return to some of these questions later in this chapter, but, on the immediate question of the status of the text, a degree of pragmatism is required. It would be surprising if sermon notes had not been transferred to print without error. Since when has a newspaper today accurately recorded a speech, word for word, without error, deliberate or otherwise? We shall therefore take these printed texts to be true reflections of the sermons given, but not necessarily the perfect article. Peter McCullough suggests that 'broadly speaking, when any sermon was altered substantially between delivery and print its author or editor usually went out of his way to say so'; this is not the case for any of these speeches. Furthermore, McCullough argues that 'readerly expectation at least until the mid-seventeenth century was that what a buyer paid for was a fair approximation of what was spoken—sermon readers were sermon hearers first, and expected the print version to be a fair substitute'.[18] This argument is reasonable. However, Arnold Hunt's excellent study, focussing on the 'hearing' of sermons, suggests that there 'were often significant differences between the sermon as preached and the sermon as printed' and comes to the 'slightly paradoxical … conclusion that if we want to get back to the oral sermon, we need to look at unauthorised editions of sermons taken from shorthand transcriptions, which were bitterly attacked by preachers for their inaccuracy but may, nevertheless, preserve elements of oral preaching in a raw, unaltered state'.[19] Ultimately, one could debate this issue to distraction: we do not have clandestine editions available and we are left with these printed versions, and must approach them accordingly, as we have no evidence to the contrary.[20]

In order fully to appreciate the nature and significance of coronation sermons, it is essential to gain a clear understanding of each context. This must include its position in the service and the contemporaneous religio-political situations. McCullough makes this point perfectly: it is 'dangerous to treat [early modern] "sermons" as an undifferentiated category to which the same kind of interpretation always apply; for what we are dealing with—whether "elite" or otherwise—were radically occasional pieces of performed writing, contingent upon the contexts in and for which they were delivered'.[21]

What Do We Mean by Context?

The word 'context' has been much used throughout this book and is vital in a deeper understanding of coronation sermons, but what do we understand by it? To study a 'source' or 'piece' of literature, or music or art form in 'context'—whether that be in a literary way, historically, culturally, sociologically, or even archaeologically—provides greater meaning, perspective and 'depth' to one's appreciation of that 'source'. Take, for example, the Fourth Symphony by Johannes Brahms (1833–1897)[22] —a bold and stirring construct of the Romantic Movement. Placing it in context, in 1884–1885, towards the end of his life, and one discovers a deeply moving reflection upon that life, but also of his expectations of the time to come—in many respects, this is a requiem symphony. Likewise, George Eliot's *Daniel Deronda*[23] tells of a love affair or triangle involving several Jewish characters, yet, placed in context, it is a striking tale of anti-Semitism, of class and of the division in Victorian Orientalism between East and West. The study of coronations is no different; the significance of context can be seen in Dan Beaver's essay. Whilst that study does not directly hinge on the 1661 coronation, it does investigate the importance of Charles II's 'semi-divine status', and his position in the 'social and political hierarchy', arguing that such beliefs need to be recognised in order properly to understand the reactions to the Popish Plot nationwide.[24] His contribution is very significant as it builds upon Kantorowicz's classic work on the nature of the king's 'two bodies'—the 'twin-born majesty'.[25] Whether it be sermons or oaths, this book does not seek to remove sources, idea, or events abstractly from the greater whole.

The Tudors to Charles II

For all of the polemical debates of the Tudor era, the religious flux that would change the cultural and ecclesiastical landscape of Britian forever, it is striking that Tudor coronation sermons do not survive in print or manuscript form, other than Cranmer's address for Edward VI, and this has been shown to be a fabrication. At no point between 1485 and 1559 did a coronation sermon move beyond the confines of the Abbey and possibly did not even take place in 1547 (to shorten the service for the young monarch Edward VI).[26] In addition to the *Liber Regalis*, we have various 'Little Device' documents that provide accounts or plans for the coronations of Henry VII and Henry VIII. It is suggested that the Bishop of Lincoln was to 'make a sermon' at the coronation of Henry VII.[27] It is not known whether Henry VIII had a coronation sermon or indeed the preacher of any given text, but 'The Little Device' does set out that at the pleasure of the archbishop 'som short sermon [is] to be seyde' by a different bishop.[28] However, frustratingly given the compelling narrative of Cranmer's text and changes made both to the service and the ensuing reformation, given MacCulloch's revelation for Edward VI, we move to Mary I and 1553 and a reign that sought to return England to the old religion. In this instance, according to the Patent Rolls George Day, the Bishop of Chichester was given the honour by the monarch for the occasion. Again we have no extant text of a sermon, but we have some sense of the theme for it is also corroborated by Commendone that one was 'pronounced' and 'on the subject of the obedience which is due to the King'. The writer, the papal envoy, Giovanni Francesco Commendone, means the Queen in this instance.[29] A fitting text and a subject that will reappear in sermons for the Stuarts. Yet again with a pivot back to Protestantism, we have no surviving text of a sermon or the name of the preacher for Elizabeth I's much analysed coronation. Again it is surprising given the opportunity after the Marian exile for so many preachers, that a more prominent text was not made and then distributed in print, but none survives, and perhaps highlights the fragile nature of such moments and of the succession.[30] 1603 would be the turning point for the coronation sermon, not only ushering in the new Stuart dynasty but also publicising the words of Thomas Bilson, Bishop of Winchester far beyond the bounds of Westminster Abbey, and highlighting the Protestant focus of the ceremony with the central role played by the Word. As with earlier sermons, the speaker was close or spoke the language of the monarch, to be thus entrusted with such a moment of public speaking. Bilson as Doran puts it was a 'safe pair of hands',[31] having produced 'treatises against Catholicism and Presbyterianism' and perhaps even more importantly, he was an ardent supporter of the concept of divine right of kings for the function of monarchy 'is established by God' and 'their power ... ordained and confirmed of God'—using the context of verse 1 of Romans 13.[32] Bilson spoke openly against 'Romish Error' and at further length of the distinct power of a King, all music to James's ears.[33] As with the importance of objects (to be discussed in Chap. 4), Bilson 'gave the regalia a precise symbolism. The sceptre represent[ing] righteousness, the oil gladness'

> a sword in sign of power, a crown in shew of Glory, a sceptre for a token of direction, a throne for a seat of justice and judgement and In unction as a pledge of outward protection and inward infusion of grace.[34]

1603 also saw the ushering in of the Stuart dynasty, and it was 'in this ceremony that English was first used instead of Latin'.[35]

In 1626, Richard Senhouse, Bishop of Carlisle (*c.*1570–1626) would preach for Charles I.[36] Senhouse 'had been chaplain both to James I and to Charles when Prince of Wales'.[37] Sturdy is overhasty to suggest it was 'long', it is certainly no longer than subsequent sermons (see Appendix 1), but it was nevertheless a 'closely-argued sermon, taking scriptural reference from Revelation 2:10 'I will give thee a Crowne of life', which sought to make telling constitutional points and to reinforce scriptural authority'. It was printed in 1627 as part of a four-sermon collection.[38]

Scotland: 1633 and 1651

Although not taking place at Westminster Abbey, it is worth noting here two other coronation sermons from this period, from the Scottish coronations of Charles I (1633) and Charles II (1651). The 1633 Scottish coronation of Charles I was in many ways a turning point or stepping stone towards Archbishop Laud's[39] plans for a 'new prayer book and canons for Scotland', setting 'the tone' for their 'development'.[40] For the 1630s saw Laud '[i]n his pomp' and 'more powerful than any other bishop since the days of Cardinal Wolsey in the 1520s, a consequence of the steadfast support he received from Charles I. If Laud's voice carried weight, it was because he was an informed and tireless presence in government who stood high in the king's favour'.[41] Bishop Lindsay[42] gave the sermon using the 1 Kings 1: 39, 'And all the People said, God save King Solomon'.[43] Whilst the coronation might be viewed as pivotal in the religious policies of Charles I and his archbishop north of the border and more generally towards civil war in England, the sermon was less significant, other than like that of the Westminster Abbey setting it was again placed before the crowning of the service, and thus was required listening before the monarch could proceed further. By contrast, the coronation sermon of 1651 has acquired notoriety as a highly critical rebuke to monarchical (Stuart) rule from not a bishop, but the Moderator of the General Assembly, Robert Douglas. As I have commented on elsewhere, it needs to be seen within the context of the time and service more generally.[44] For many modern historians, Douglas's coronation sermon is often cited as proof that the young king (Charles II) resented his Scottish coronation,[45] one of the main criticisms being that it was exceptionally long at 'one hour in length'.[46] Yet, other examples of sermons given by Douglas suggest a man capable of remarkable skill in biblical reference, and long sermons were by no means unusual in this period—not least other coronation sermons as Appendix 1 indicates. It would seem particularly strange if length had been the central issue, that Charles II would permit an equally long sermon for his Westminster Abbey coronation ten years later.[47] It is true that the content of the sermon included a warning about monarchical dynasties falling, those straying from the path and lacking respect for the presbyterian and Covenantal cause and is liberally scattered with examples of the 'misdeeds of his father', yet given the changing nature of the times and disastrous nature of Charles I's fall, the martial context, with the imminent arrival of Cromwell's forces, perhaps a sermon of a serious and solemn tone was the order of the day. It might not have been the most pleasant sermon to hear, but it was set firmly in the context of the moment. Indeed, Douglas went on to stress that the central purpose of this magnificent ceremony was to bind the Scottish people to their young sovereign.[48] Referring to 2 Kings 11, verse 17, Douglas sought to compare the young king to Joash and saw himself as the high priest Jehoiada, for

> They crowned the young king, to endeare the peoples affections to their own native Prince, and to alienate their heartes from her that had usurped the kingdome ... [t]he same is observed in our case ... it is our necessarie duetie to crowne the king upon all hazards, and to leave the successe God.[49]

The more 1651 is viewed within the wider context of coronations more generally, and within the context of the challenges faced by the royalist cause in Scotland at the time, the more it should be viewed as an event as significant within the Stuart crowning occasions as any other. Financial accounts reveal a coronation and accompanying feast of considerable expense, rendering it far from anomalous to other seventeenth-century coronations.[50]

1661–1714

All five sermons are similarly structured, with unifying aspects, yet the political and religious context was often wholly different. They all begin with Providence.[51] The omnipotent, omnibenevolent, omniscient Almighty is the most essential point of all: what will take place is divinely sanctioned, and it is to God that praise and prayer is required. This is most interesting in Turner's sermon for James II: how to reconcile Providence with something that seemed at odds with its recent workings: a Roman Catholic monarch for the Protestant nation. In general, the monarch is compared to various biblical or classical figures, or both. The immediate context is uppermost in the sermon; even if not explicitly stated, it would have been clear to the audience. The strengths of each sovereign are unveiled in flattering tones. Conclusions are drawn and the audience is invited to share in prayer for the monarch. At last, the speaker finishes and the service continues. These are consistent themes, but each piece must be considered in its own right, not as building on a canon of former works. Interestingly, they make no reference to previous coronation sermons. Text and context should not therefore be separated. These pieces were designed for a highly specific location, time, and audience and thus one must not underestimate 'the importance of place and circumstance in determining meaning'.[52] To undertake an exegesis that looks at text without context, or *vice versa*, would be to miss the greater whole and obscure instructive results. One aspect of my approach has been to envisage, indeed to essay, the role of the bishop preacher. I have accordingly read and timed each sermon. The exercise usefully suggested the answer to a question posed earlier in this chapter, namely why these sermons have slipped under the radar of historical research. The answer: length.

Duration

It may seem an obvious thing to do, but it is unclear from the historiography whether or not anyone has attempted accurately to time these sermons.[53] Sturdy estimates that they 'must have lasted at least forty to forty-five minutes, occupying a solid portion of the entire coronation ceremony'.[54] However, a glance at the print versions makes the first part of this statement seem misleading, as they did not all appear to be of similar length. As Appendix 1 indicates, I have established approximate durations, and it will be observed that these varied considerably—far more than Sturdy evidently supposed. We can imagine, therefore, that the impact of these sermons will have varied accordingly.

Re-enacting delivery generated: (a) insights that would not otherwise have arisen—the slowly evolving thesis, the hidden drama, the subtleties, the arguments and climaxes; and (b) key moments, pithy sayings, memorable styles—in essence, the drama of the piece. It also allowed one time to ask basic questions. Was it an easy read? Was it perhaps something easy to listen to? Was it funny? Serious? Interesting? Was the argument lost? One was left in no doubt that the papacy, Roman Catholics and, most importantly, 'the French', were enemies. They leap out of Sharp's 1702 sermon for Queen Anne in a way that only becomes obvious when his text is read as a whole. We shall return to the issue of duration as we proceed through the various sermons.

Coronation Sermons in Context

Charles II: A Restoration Coronation

The Restoration provided ample opportunity for the sprouting forth of sermon-making. The 1661 celebrations throughout Charles's kingdoms far exceeded even modern royal jubilee festivities. Contrary to what we might know or expect, they were as much an Edinburgh scene as they were a Westminster/London event. From feasting, toasting, and bonfire-making at Holyroodhouse, such festivity took place across the board and a religious element, *via* preaching, was at the heart of these public displays of affection.[55] Ceremony was all important for contemporaries: as William Cavendish, duke of Newcastle, asked, 'what preserves kings more than ceremony?'

> The cloth of estates, the distance people are with you, great officers, heralds, drums, trumpeters, rich coaches, rich furniture for horses, guards, martialls men making room, disorders to be labored by their staff of office and cry 'now the king comes' ... even the wisest though he knew it and was accustomed to it, shall shake off his wisdome and shake for fear of it ... you cannot put upon you too much king.[56]

Hutton is right to regard Charles II's 1661 coronation as a 'staged' event.[57] This was indeed a stage management on a terrific scale: from the magnificence of the costumes to the re-making of the crown jewels, following their melting down by the commonwealth regime.[58] The sovereign, although following detailed preparations, could have had little say in the ordering of the occasion based on the medieval *Liber Regalis* and recognised traditions, but the sermon stands out, with the monarchs' direct involvement.[59]

Charles was anointed and crowned by William Juxon (*bap.* 1582, *d.* 1663),[60] the aged archbishop of Canterbury, but he chose to have his sermon preached by George Morley, bishop of Worcester (later of Winchester), which was not only to overlook the primate of all England but also the bishop of London, Gilbert Sheldon—perhaps the more obvious alternative.[61] Why? This was very much the king's choice: Hutton argues that following the City election, Charles wished Sheldon to be 'less visible'. Another reason, perhaps more in keeping with the essence of the 1660–1661 celebrations, was that Charles sought to spread his patronage as far as possible. This was an opportunity to re-connect the Crown with the elite, whether the nobility, gentry, or senior clerics.[62]

Perhaps it was just that 1660–1662 saw Morley 'everywhere': from Oxford, as canon of Christ Church, to interviewing (at Court) Anne Hyde over the legitimacy of her son by James, duke of York, to 'represent[ing] the episcopalian interest at the Worcester House discussions which fleshed out the plan for a comprehensive Church settlement'. Consecrated bishop of Worcester on 28 October 1660, he was more importantly also dean of the Chapel Royal. Morley had served as a chaplain to Charles's father and participated in negotiations with Parliament in the 1640s. Having been deprived, he had gone into exile, remaining amongst royalists on the continent. He had thus 'shared the hard times experienced by Charles'.[63] Furthermore, although Calvinist in theology, his support for episcopacy and his 'zealous[ness] for the Church' counted strongly in his favour, and because of that '[s]hortly before the Restoration he had been sent to

England to hold a series of meetings with Presbyterians to calm apprehensions over a return of the Stuarts'.[64] This was not, therefore, a surprise choice, but rather a commendation for loyalty, a culmination of two excellent years and long-term service to the Stuart cause.

Given the importance of this unique context, and Morley's obvious suitability, what then did he say? While in essence he argues that, thanks to Providence, Charles's example of having returned from exile could do more than any sermon for 'publick Reformation both in Church and State', his contribution is nevertheless by far the longest of these five sermons, lasting approximately an hour. This was long by coronation standards, though not out of place with the tradition of the hour glass, but certainly not as long as the 'hour and [a] half' claimed by Strong, without citing any evidence.[65] The sermon was published in the same year. Given the unprecedented nature of the occasion, the lengthy planning, the time invested on the day, a short sermon would perhaps have been inappropriate.[66] As Sturdy argues, Morley's speech 'blends his theoretical propositions on monarchy with current circumstances ... directed both at Charles II and ... [his] subjects ... supported by ... biblical and historical precedents'; and throughout he is 'a protagonist of Divine Right monarchy'.[67] The clergy more generally 'also placed great emphasis on the sacral aspects of kingship in 1660', and 'many sermons and pamphlets praised Charles as a biblical David who had returned to claim his kingdom, and Charles himself ordered that the litany which was used to celebrate Saint George's Feast (the king was crowned on Saint George's Day, and St George was also the patron saint of the Order of the Garter) be modified so that it was mostly based on the Psalms of David'.[68]

However, returning to Morley's sermon, as this chapter will highlight, Morley's considerable focus on nation and nationalism is ignored by Sturdy, and barely noticed by Madway.[69] Morley's sermon was a celebration of the renewal, indeed survival, of 'this nation of ours, which was so neer perishing under the conduct of many ... [and will be] recovered from its former distempers and dangers for the present ... and the state thereof prolonged ... for the future'. It was also a calling for the settlement of 'Church and ... State' so that they could 'flourish'.[70]

In contrast to Thomas Bilson's 1603 sermon for James I, or Richard Senhouse's 1626 sermon for Charles I, in which the nation is only mentioned once, Morley talks continually of 'this nation of ours'. Expressions of nationalism would now become a constant presence in coronation sermons of the period 1661–1714, articulating a sense of nationhood long before 1707 when, according to Colley's thesis, it began.[71] This is a very significant development, challenging a key component of the received historiography, and the implications will become increasingly apparent throughout this chapter.

It is perhaps hard in our times to envisage the monarch possessing supernatural powers. Yet, for many people of the seventeenth century, the sovereign was very much a deified force, endowed with healing powers.[72] This was gold dust for the Restoration Crown, and Charles II never hesitated to exploit such opportunities. From the very iconography of the regime to touching for the King's Evil, Charles sought to cement this popular view of royal potential: stressing kingship, militarism, and ceremonial over the humanity of the laity.[73] This emphasis on Divine Right is present throughout Morley's text in referring to both Charles II and his father, Charles the Martyr, who had been rejected by the populace and 'who onely had right by all lawes humane and divine to reign over us'. For 'monarchy is more natural and more according to divine institution, and consequently a better form of government[,] then any other'.[74] This was a glorious occasion for royalists, requiring words to match. The Restoration was, of course, also a celebration of Providence; just as David had been tested and then crowned, so it was

> the very case of our present SOVERAIGN … and therefore I doubt not but God had the same design in the breeding of them both; namely, to make them as glorious afterwards by their actions, as they had been formerly by their sufferings: neither do I doubt, but our David will do, as that other David tells us he did, he will rule us prudently with all his power. Psal. 78.71.[75]

On 29 May 1661, just over a month after the coronation, a day set aside as a national holiday, being both Charles's birthday and the anniversary of his return to London, Morley's Davidic theme was continuing to strike chords with other preachers. Addressing a packed chapel in Westminster, Chaplain Peter Heylyn, reminded his congregation of how the king had been driven into exile, 'like a partridge by a falcon', and had returned to his land 'not with an army to besiege it, to smite it with the edge of a sword, but as a Prince of Peace, or the Son of David'.[76] Morley's sermon was an affirmation of the Restoration and of the fruits of Providence. It is an assertion of the dualism of Church and monarch, of the Church of England and its Supreme Governor, though not perhaps relaying the deep complexities underlying the reconstruction 'of an Anglican identity that was richer and more paradoxical than that conveyed by the notion' of a restored Church of England.[77] It is nevertheless suffused with Divine Right ideology, which had manifestly survived the Regicide. Perhaps, though, the most interesting aspect is the emergence of a sense of nationhood, a theme not previously covered in quite the same way in the coronation sermons for Charles's immediate predecessors.

James II: A Catholic King for the Protestant Nation

The coronation sermon for James II may be half the length of Charles II's, though it is anything but half the interest, since it contains some fascinating arguments and notable instances of casuistry. Nevertheless, John Miller's *James II* (1978 and 2000)[78] does not reference the sermon even with the existence of the highly detailed contemporary account published by Sandford.[79] John Callow's *James II* (2005) is similarly silent on the sermon.[80] Given the attempt to alter the coronation in a Roman Catholic direction, it is perhaps odd that what was expressed on such a public occasion has been left in the shadows. Essentially, James II radically sought the removal of Holy Communion, as he attempted to balance a service conducted by the Church of England episcopate with his Catholicism. The key point for James was that a coronation was not worth an Anglican Eucharist. The archbishop of Canterbury, William Sancroft, was therefore given the difficult job of condensing the order of service. However, Sancroft had no intention either of diminishing it or of moving in a Roman Catholic direction. Instead, music would play a key role in padding out the proceedings. This was the start of a tradition of glorious coronation anthem music that would lead to the most famous of all in 1727: Handel's *Zadok the Priest*.[81] In 1685, the preliminary procession from Westminster Hall to the Abbey was accompanied by *O Lord, grant the king a long life*, composed by the royal musician William Child (1606/1607–1697). On arrival at the great west door, the king and queen were greeted with *I was glad*, not the famous Hubert Parry setting, of course, but a new setting composed for 1685 by Henry Purcell, displaying magnificent counterpoint.[82] This piece was followed by another traditional anthem, *Let thy hand be strengthened*, but newly arranged as a full choral work by John Blow (*c.*1648–1708). This, then, was the tremendous musical introduction to the recognition, the acclamation (the congregation's positive vocal response to the new monarch) and then the keynote speech: the sermon. Great music would follow it, but the sermon was the climax to an audible crescendo. The sermon is all the more significant as it remained intact within the revised service and offered the Church of England an opportunity to set out its stall, binding James II to support the Established Church, in the holiest of rites for a king, a coronation in the Abbey of kings. Lasting approximately thirty minutes, the sermon is deeply rooted in the religious politics of the 1680s and particularly the Exclusion Crisis: the efforts to prevent James's accession. One must thank Providence, asserted Turner, 'after his majesties deliverance, as well as ours, from that abominable excluding Bill'.[83]

Francis Turner, bishop of Ely, was perhaps not an unexpected choice to preach now as he had long been a favoured supporter of James. He had acted on his behalf in negotiations over the Episcopal Church in Scotland while James governed there and in the 1681 ecclesiastical promotions commission. Following installation as dean of Windsor in July 1683, he was consecrated bishop of Rochester in November 1683 and became lord almoner. This was an impressive rise, promotion continuing with translation to Ely in July 1684. Hopkins reiterates Beddard's conclusion, namely 'that Sancroft was advancing him not only as the Church's agent at Court, using the political skills and *savoir-faire* which Sancroft himself lacked, but as his own eventual successor at Canterbury. James also, still committed to the Anglican alliance, was believed to have the same intentions'.[84] It would seem, therefore, that Turner was an obvious choice to deliver this sermon. Their relationship would first be strained and then broken as James's religious policy unfolded, but, for 23 April 1685, it was as positive as could be.

On the back of the Exclusion Crisis, and with the fearful possibility of a revolt by the duke of Monmouth, the sermon was a warning against rebellion and a reminder of the dangers of the Civil War, the Wars of the Roses and, more generally, of 'faction[s]':

> the fatal dispute between York and Lancaster … rent the kingdom in pieces between them: They made our poor countrey an *Aceldama,* a field of blood … till the woful controversy was happily ended by that auspicious marriage, from which a race of kings with undoubted right, and our present gracious sovereign is lineally descended.[85]

As so often occurs in coronation sermons, out of warnings we have a reminder of the qualities and rights of the new ruler, in this case James's hereditary claim. Yet, Turner also sought to bind James to the Church of

England with a sophistry that cannot have escaped his auditory. Solomon of the Old Testament features in nearly all of these coronation sermons as a guide to wisdom and success, but, in this instance, as an example of the fall from grace: 'King Solomon in his declining age fell, so as no Christian prince can ever fall, unless he renounce his baptism'.[86] This statement could be seen as an attempt at a veiled criticism of James's Roman Catholicism (though perhaps deliberately, not very covert). On the other hand, this was perhaps an effort by Turner to be cleverer than that: since James was baptised into the Church of England, therefore as long as he did not renounce that distinction, even as a Roman Catholic convert, his baptism should have kept him in check. However, in practical terms, this was anything but binding, and was yet another Tory argument that would soon be seen to fail. His conversion was renunciation.

Nobody could have missed the clear unhappiness that many felt with James's accession. Turner had the immensely difficult task of reconciling the 'congregation ...[as] the king-makers' during the recognition and the acclamation with the widespread belief in Protestant Providentialism, given the emergence of a Roman Catholic king. What did God have in mind for His elect Protestant nation? The answer is simple: 'God's choice and the people's are not always the same'. Furthermore, just as in the Old Testament, this is the nature of a kingdom that 'was to be hereditary ... from the conclusion of those provisional statutes Deut 17'. Just as 'Solomon's right to empire was thus visible', so too was James's. Yet, additional use is made of the story of Solomon. If the people are unhappy, why should they be loyal? The Israelites 'were eminently loyal' because they had been given a 'famous good governor'. His other 'royal qualifications[,] ... his supernatural gifts [and] ... wisdom' were 'most conspicuous' and thus, through wise council and government Solomon, and likewise James, should expect national loyalty. Moreover, Turner warns of the danger of disloyalty and of worse: 'rebellion', as something abhorrent to 'Religion'. It is a fascinating argument that begins by reminding all present that Charles I 'the best of kings [!] was most vilely cast away, as if he had not been anointed with oyl[.] How dear these kingdoms have paid for the murder of that blessed king, is too grievous a reflection at this time'.[87] Blame here is attributed to a people wanting in obedience and unwilling to be 'rul'd by a gentle hand'. If those anxious about James's religion thought that rebellion could be sanctioned, then Turner had other ideas:

> Though the maintenance of religion is commonly made the most plausible pretence for rebellion … yet rebellion almost constantly proves (as that last prov'd) the means to destroy religion.[88]

For Turner argues that 'as ever men begin to be rebels, they cease to be inwardly religious, and truly good men; but I drive it farther, that to rebel is the ready way to ruine the constitution of the outward, profest, and establish religion in a nation'.[89] This is strong stuff and one can almost see the finger pointing at anyone in the congregation who might be thinking of jumping ship to a Monmouth camp. Loyalty was demanded not just because the obverse was so dangerous but also because James had royal blood underpinning his sovereignty. There are references to his brother and to his father, Charles the Martyr. As suffering servants, these Stuart relations had according to Turner, an even greater claim to sovereignty: James was

> the sharer of his royal brothers cares … and [the] picture of Charles the Martyr … [and] his living sacred image on this day.[90]

Every syllable of this sermon is saturated with hereditary Divine Right ideology, but it is not without warning: the people's obedience is not automatic. A contract links people and king, just as the Israelites served in the Old Testament, 'as freemen, not as slaves'.[91]

Turner's sermon may well have done much to shore up James's support, reminding all of the dangers of disloyalty and of the king's qualities, albeit in the most splendidly sycophantic way:

> We have a king that has not been bred up at ease in the Court of his father, but in the school of hardship and affliction; (as the Apostle tells us) worketh patience, and patience experience. Sure I may say without imputation of flattery, no prince within the memory of man has come to a Crown with so vast a stock of experience.[92]

Yet, his conclusion was peculiarly dark, with a warning to James II and his queen: 'his sacred majesty' should take the coronation as 'a powerful motive … to act well his sovereign part for the good of this great people', for he is to be crowned and

> will be presented anon with all the regalia set in the seat of Empire, and made the anointed of God; the place which is the royal Golgotha, the burying place of kings; where we have lately deposited the venerable remains of majesty.[93]

This peroration should have put James 'in mind, from the royal prophet; though kings are made as Gods, they shall dye like men'.[94] Turner's final comments seem to have been a call for unity, that, in death, royal opponents face judgement together. It is an extraordinary form of heavenly counter-confessionalization in an age of religious polarity and hatred:

> Think how much royal dust and ashes is laid up in yonder chappel; there the Houses of York and Lancaster rest quietly under one roof, there does Queen Mary & her sister Q[ueen] Elizabeth lye close together, their ashes do not part ... their smoke divided into two pyramids as it ascended from one funeral pile: But here these dusts do as kindly mingle.[95]

Turner's sermon powerfully continues the motif of Divine Right of Kings, using the concept as an essential argument in support of James. The nation is still a prominent theme, parallels being drawn with Israel in the Old Testament, but perhaps the most striking idea is encapsulated in his closing remarks on a 'general resurrection [and] ... judgement'.[96] It would not be for another 144 years, until the 1829 Catholic Emancipation Act, that such an idea could realistically be expressed.

The Glorious Revolution: William III and Mary II

The coronation of William and Mary as joint sovereigns was a unique occasion in British history. It is all the more breathtaking when one considers that there was an existing crowned sovereign, and that this was a patriarchal age in which a married women's rights and property became her husband's. Precisely because of this complex situation, if ever there was a need for a coronation, then this was it. Here was an essential ceremony in order to establish William and Mary as legitimate monarchs ahead of James II. This, then, was the conundrum. Central to planning the new royal government was Gilbert Burnet, bishop of Salisbury. Shortly before the Convention Parliament of 22 January 1688/9, Burnet wrote and published anonymously *An Enquiry into the Present State of Affairs*, delineating this unprecedented scenario and arguing against the idea of a regency, a potential solution.[97] Once Parliament was in session, William made it clear that he would neither support a regency nor assent to playing second fiddle to Mary as consort; in fact, he went further in arguing that sovereignty should rest with him alone. This proposal proved too much for Burnet and Parliament. Thus, a unique compromise was effected whereby the Crown would be shared equally, William III and Mary II being proclaimed rulers on 13 February 1688/9.[98]

With the benefit of hindsight, much seems obvious, but it was by no means straightforward lawfully to bypass an existing monarch whilst maintaining the institution of monarchy. The solution was to argue that James had subverted the throne and abandoned his constitutional responsibilities. In such a case, the nation had a right to protect itself with secure government. Having played such a significant role in the creation of this new regime, it was Burnet who would be chosen to preach the 'set-piece' coronation sermon on 11 April 1689 and, in so doing, have the opportunity to justify this glorious compromise.[99] Although the occasion was unprecedented, biographies do surprisingly little to analyse it incisively. Bryan Bevan's *William III* unaccountably ignores the sermon.[100] John Van Der Kiste sketches parts of the ceremony but delves no deeper.[101] Surely what was expressed at this unique double coronation should have warranted more detailed inquiry? To what extent, for example, was the novel constitutional reality borne out in the sermon?

At approximately twenty-five minutes, Burnet's sermon is fractionally shorter than that of James II's, and of the five stands out as the most interesting in terms of constitutional history: a 'must read' for students of Edmund Burke and Albert Venn Dicey.[102] Burnet's concise turn of phrase allows him to include many more themes than Turner, and the brevity of the sermon is clearly part of his general attitude to preaching, as articulated in another book published soon after. In *A Discourse of the Pastoral Care* (London, 1692), Burnet argues that shorter sermons 'are generally both better heard, and better remembered'.[103] The desired political and constitutional compromise having been achieved, Burnet's sermon justifies Parliament's actions in support of William and Mary, amid 'fears' of tyranny: of 'wisdom, when it is not guided by justice'.[104] Burnet begins with a powerful affirmation of humanity as *imago dei*. As such, this carries responsibilities to act as wisely and as justly as possible. This imperative applies to ruler and subject alike. There are the usual classical and biblical analogies, as well as continual indirect references to James's failings, in an effort to banish a bad memory. The abuse of power is a constant theme:

> Here are the true measures of government; it is a rule, and not an absolute dominion; it is a rule over men, and not a power, like that which we have over beasts. In a word, it is the conduct of free and reasonable beings, who need indeed to be governed, but ought not to be broken by the force … of power.[105]

Absolutism, the dangers of standing armies, the failure of 'just' government—all are starkly spelt out, both as a reminder of the inadequacies of the last regime, but also as a warning for the future. In a theology that is almost Paley-esque, good government is described in natural terms, as a 'temperate air, and a clear sky; a fair morning, and an unclouded sun … [as] things which do not only please, but animate'.[106] Sturdy highlights Burnet's emphasis on the dangers of 'despotic government' and on the need for the 'balanced constitution by which England is ruled … [with] the sense of justice displayed by the new king and queen'. This was a sermon as much prospective as reflective: as Sturdy points out, 'England can look forward to just government, the implication being, of course, that it had suffered unjust government under James II'.[107] However, although Sturdy argues that Burnet does 'not deny … the idea of the Divine Right of Kings', he does not accord it the weight that he does in his assessment of Morley's sermon.[108] Nevertheless, it is still present. Moreover, Sturdy ignores the stress on the concept of the 'nation', as will emerge in the rest of this chapter.[109] As in Charles II's and James II's sermons, importance is placed on monarchical divinity, but very much 'up to a point'. Sovereigns may be God's 'vicegerents', yet they 'should not exceed those limits' of 'just' government, according to 'the sacred oath of this great day', which had been revised through an Act of Parliament.[110] This emphasis on justice has much to do with James's tinkering with the judiciary and with the conduct of the infamous Judge Jeffreys.[111] For a wise monarch is 'just likewise to every one of their subjects, sheltring them all under an impartial protection; neither perverting justice themselves, nor suffering it to be perverted, as far as in them lies, by any that act in their name'. Coupled with this is the necessity for mercy, for

> he understood government well, that said, mercy and truth preserve the king, and his throne is upheld by mercy. This is the character of a just prince, who sitteth on the throne of judgment, and scattereth away all evil with his eyes.[112]

These striking words, celebrating the ideals encapsulated as the 'rule of law' in the British constitution, conclude with a magisterial passage inspired by the beautiful words of Amos[113]: 'justice and righteousness issue out from the throne in so free a course, that they run down like a river'.[114] Burnet's profound providentialism, which needs to be seen as part of a package also including his apocalypticism and internationalist perspective, has been valuably stressed by Claydon, though deriving that interpretation from a wider field of work than this coronation sermon specifically.[115] Nevertheless, we see it powerfully reflected here too. Burnet offers a warning that Providence can bring a monarch down just as quickly as up: 'this fear of God will make princes often remember, even in the pride of all their glory, that though then they look like Gods, yet they must die like men' and their actions 'will be weighed in the scales of impartial justice'. Here is another reminder of the essential nature of sound justice: impartiality.[116] Burnet's views of Roman Catholicism are made transparent in a passage underlining the nation's course: the Church of England, 'the Church of God'. The former king's religious position was a false one: an 'Hypocrisie'. Yet, Burnet explained why much of the world was still under its spell, for at 'times the praying and preaching with appearances of fervour and devotion, has a charm that carries nations after it'. However, proper government is the 'encouraging … of a vigorous piety, and sublime vertue, and the maintaining and propagating of true religion … without superstition [and] … tyranny'.[117] James II and Roman Catholicism are implicitly identified in the foregoing passage as 'tyranny' and 'superstition', respectively, and are seen as setting about the 'converting [of] the world … by dragoons [and] cruel edicts'. The only evils that rival this are, intriguingly, 'atheism and impeity' (interestingly distinct in this text) and 'drunken[ness]'.[118] It would seem that in many of his ideas, Burnet anticipated much Christian theology and important features in British constitutional theory. The task for William and Mary was to act as 'vertuous' and 'Christian philosophers', ruling in the 'fear of God'. As a result, the nation can 'expect to see the City of God, the *New Jerusalem,* quickly come down from Heaven to settle among us'. If the two sovereigns govern as was hoped, then much could be achieved, for 'kings examples have an efficacy which few can resist'.[119] The examples of virtuous Platonic philosopher kings are taken from the classical world, as Marcus Aurelius over Caligula and Nero. It is strikingly clear that James was to be consigned to history as one of the 'monsters'; William and Mary, by contrast, are hailed as 'you, GREAT SOVERAIGNS' and are enjoined to follow Marcus Aurelius and his way, giving it their 'best light and utmost force'.[120] Much is expected from the Glorious Revolution, but rather more 'yes you can' than 'yes we can':

> From you … we expect the glorious reverse of all cloudy days. You have been hitherto our hope and our desire: you must now become our glory and crown of rejoycing: ordinary vertues in you, will fall so far short of our hopes, that we shall be tempted almost to think them vices. It is in your persons, and under your reign, that we hope to see an opening to a glorious scene, which seems approaching.
>
> May your fleets be prosperous, and your armies victorious. But may you soon have cause to use neither; by settling both at home and abroad, a firm and just peace, and by securing the quiet of Europe from those who have so often, with so little regard to the faith of treaties, and now at last beyond all former examples, disturbed it.[121]

Interestingly, 'fleets' come before 'armies'. Already it was clear that the Navy was the strength of the kingdom. 'The quiet of Europe' is a phrase that could have been lifted from any Victorian passage seeking the maintenance of the *status quo*. Once a European ruler in William III takes to the throne, Europe has become unavoidable in a coronation sermon.

This sermon, these thoughts, this 'auditory' are not just confined to Westminster Abbey, 'but the whole nation', who are roused in Burnet's finale to 'join with united voices, and inflamed hearts, in saying God Save King William and Queen Mary'.[122] It was published in 'three London editions and one Scots … by the end of 1689'.[123] Burnet's sermon is thus wonderfully put together—a model argument for how to govern. He sets up the system of how not to do it under James and then points William and Mary in the direction of justice and mercy. What intrigues most are his comments on the rule of law. Would he have said such things to this congregation had they not been expected to strike a profound chord? This sermon therefore tells us something very important about the forging of a nation, and one that was increasingly aware of its rights. It is perhaps not coincidental that this statement came ten years after passing of the Habeas Corpus Act of 1679, which had been heavily wrapped up in the Exclusion Crisis and concerned about arbitrary government over the rights of subjects.

Queen Anne

John Sharp's coronation sermon for Queen Anne, on the theme 'kings shall be thy nursing-fathers, and queens thy nursing-mothers', is by far the shortest of these five sermons, at approximately fifteen minutes.[124] Providence is again at work for this chosen nation: 'and blessed be God this promise hath for many ages, from time to time, been made good to abundance of nations and peoples: But to none more apply, more signally than to us of this kingdom'.[125] According to Till, Sharp 'was the only one of the seven churchmen recommended by Burnet to William for bishoprics who was consistently a high-churchman and usually on the side of the Tories in Parliament'. Although not a favourite of William III, with Queen Anne it was different and he quickly rose at Court. It was at the queen's personal request, and despite his poor health, that Sharp was selected to deliver this sermon.[126] We have now reached the eighteenth century: does ceremony remain important? In Sharp's eyes, the coronation was still a 'solemnity' and, indeed, this particular coronation was judged in one account to have been 'more magnificent than any in England till that time'.[127] Sharp's opening lines are a variant on a theme that is still prevalent today in public speaking: brevity; he was 'very sensible that the shortness of my sermon will be the best recommendation of it'.[128] Unlike James II, William III, and later George I, Anne's 'right to the Crown was not at issue' and she acceded peacefully on 8 March 1701/2.[129] That circumstance perhaps explains, along with Sharp's eagerness for pithiness, why the sermon is considerably shorter than its predecessors. Yet, like many a short speech, Sharp's sermon does not lack for weight. Much was nevertheless still at stake: over religion, over the French threat, and over the War of the Spanish Succession. The accession of a female sovereign in a time of conflict was a sensitive point. Anne's position as 'nursing mother' to Church and people brought obligation: 'kings and queens … [as] natural parents… should submit their scepters to … Jesus Christ'. Likewise, the rest 'of this nation' was expected to submit to her and God: whether male or female citizens or male or female rulers, submission to faith was the key point, not the gender of the person.[130] This was not unlike ideas explored in 1598 by James VI of Scotland (later I of England), as Asch and Lake have argued when examining James's, *The True Law of Free Monarchies* (1598), with James's 'emphasis on the paternal character of kingship'—yet James also links this to 'divinely ordained status' and explores the idea of rule 'without' the 'consent' of a monarch's subjects, 'though not as tyrants who disregard their subjects' welfare'.[131] Just over a century later, Sharp's sermon in a similar vein emphasises maternalism, but not without the consent of Anne's subjects.

Edie argues that 'the image of monarchy … presented was curiously impersonal' and that 'Sharp [presumably] meant to hono[u]r the queen and to enhance her authority. [However,] in fact, [by recounting the tradition to which Anne was heir], the heroic images [of] "the immortal Elizabeth", of Charles II, and even of Mary, overshadow that of Queen Anne, whose own particular direction and disposition Sharp all but ignored'. However, Sharp's sermon can be understood entirely differently. Edie's interpretation can be viewed differently or even reassessed when one reads the five case study coronation sermons for this chapter of 1661–1714. It was standard for these sermons to remind both auditories and monarchs about hereditary succession, and to draw parallels with past heroic figures, from Solomon and classical figures, to Elizabeth, as Gloriana. As Hone points out, 'four historical British figures' are used: 'King Lucius, Emperor Constantine, Henry VIII, and Elizabeth. The importance of those figures was religious. Lucius was, in Sharp's words, "the first Christian King in Europe", and Constantine the first Christian emperor of Rome, and of supposedly British descent'. The comparison here was to argue 'that the Church would once again flourish under Anne. Equally importantly, by recalling these figures from British history, Sharp appealed to Tory nationalists who celebrated Anne as a "native" queen after the reign of a Dutchman'.[132] The new monarch's virtues are often mentioned, but this is rarely in any more detail than as guidance on just governance. Indeed, as Edie highlights, 'Anne was drawn as a pattern of propriety and virtue, a moral exemplar, the image of the queen as nursing mother to her people'. She argues that 'she was not drawn as a driving force in English political affairs'.[133] However, this characterisation of an impersonal detached monarch from politics, does not match the text, for Sharp celebrated Anne's personal virtues, something that one might have thought had become irrelevant with the new constitutional settlement of 1689:

> Her firmness to the English Church, and English interest, in the most difficult times … her zeal for the supporting of the common cause of Europe, against the exorbitant power of France: … her tender love to her people … her concern for our religion, our laws, our liberties for the continuance of

> the Crown in the Protestant line; for the Government in Church and State as by laws establish'd.[134]

Again, the French are the great enemy, and it is Anne's virtues that will counter that threat. Despite her critique, Edie surprisingly concludes that even if Anne's appeal was different to that of Charles II, the sermon was no less suitable to the occasion than that of 1661, in efforts to 'unify and to encourage her people'.[135] The good example expected of the sovereign is consistent with the Reformation of Manners[136] and almost anticipates Victorian evangelical expectations[137]: the queen must be the personification of 'piety and devotion, of temperance and moderation'. This perception is connected with the important biblical analogy of David and psalm 101. Just as William and Mary were called to bring justice and righteousness in the tradition of Amos, so Anne is expected to bring 'impartial justice ... as it is tempered with mercy' in the tradition of Proverbs 20:28. In a phrase that would fit Dicey's work, the rule of law is invoked as essential: 'in such a constitution as ours, where the people have their fixed rights and liberties and properties, the standing laws of the kingdom would always be the rule of their actions'. A contrast is drawn with the 'fears of despotick or arbitrary proceedings', implicitly referring to James II, French rule, and Stuart absolutism.[138]

Sacral monarchy and Divine Right theory survived the Glorious Revolution and Anne's succession, for 'princes ought to be above all others. For by this, they truly imitate God, and make good their character of being his representatives upon earth'.[139] The role of vicegerent was as applicable in 1702 as it was in 1661 or, indeed, in 1603: 'The one is Gods ordinance as well as the other, for God hath not put princes in his place, and given them his power, to be despised or disobeyed, but to be honoured and served as his ... vicegerents here on earth'.[140] Anne's role as Supreme Governor of the Church of England was of tremendous importance for Sharp, for this was the Church of Apostolic Succession.

Sharp also celebrated the English-ness of the occasion, and it is a far more Anglo-centric sermon than any of the others. This fact can be explained by his concerns with Scotland, which can be seen in his initial opposition to the Union. However, that emphasis on English-ness also came from a desire to highlight Anne's national claim in contrast to the House of Orange. This kingdom, which had been 'oppressed by the papacy; and Christianity ... corrupted by superstition and idolatry', was first saved by 'an English king that ... threw off the foreign yoak; and it was an English king also, that first began the Reformation of religion'.[141] Not only is the path of a providential Protestantism shown, but the Roman Catholicism of Anne's father is indirectly attacked here as being foreign. Coupled with this, Anne's hereditary right is reinforced by her Stuart birthright, but also her Tudor blood of Henry VIII and Edward VI. Sharp then draws out the benefits of having a queen regnant by extolling the virtues of Elizabeth I, for 'the honour of perfecting that great work [of Reformation] was reserved for a queen'. Anne was a rightful successor: 'And such another QUEEN we trust God has now given us'. A female ruler was thus not to be feared on account of supposed weakness, but rather to be celebrated.[142]

The fear of faction, a constant motif of the earlier sermons, is evident in Sharp's work too:

> Even then when our constitution was not long since (not so long since but that many here present may remember it) quite subverted by factions at home; yet in a little time did he [God] restore our lawful king and with him our Church, and laws, and liberties.[143]

Thus, Providence prevailed with the Restoration, and the nation was allowed to advance following again God's plans with the Glorious Revolution, to 'continue upon the same bottom we were: we had still the same religion, the same Church, the same government: we still enjoy the same rights and liberties, and properties, that ever we did'. This is strikingly Burkean in political terms: keeping the state afloat whilst sailing a boundless and bottomless sea. Yet, this sermon is prospective as well as retrospective: 'O may they for ever be continued to us and our posterity'.[144] So what is the nation called upon to do? 'To thank God heartily for all the repeated instances of his favour to us' and to remain unified. In an age of division, Sharp called for unity, using the words of St. Paul in Galatians 5:13:

> If … [the] bite and devour one another, have a care that the be not consumed one of another. Nothing can ever so much endanger this kingdom as our own divisions.[145]

Anne had come to the throne, according to Sharp, with a tremendous outpouring of support, for no other sovereign in his eyes had acceded 'with a more general satisfaction, and with more good wishes of the people ... [and] Parliament['s] ... sincere affection'.[146] Far from looking to the end time and Anne's final judgement, as Turner did in his 1685 sermon, Sharp calls for longevity: 'And as the QUEEN will rejoice in her people; so it will be her peoples daily prayer that God would long long preserve QUEEN ANNE'.[147]

Sharp's sermon is both a warning and a commendation. It warns of the dangers of internal 'divisions' and 'faction[s]', and of the external threat from France. Simultaneously, it is one of praise for the Queen's virtues and of thanksgiving to Providence, for 'such is his goodness that he hath preserved to us another branch of the same royal stock'.[148] It continues the theme of civil liberties discussed by Burnet in 1689, building on the notion of nation. For, aligned with domestic threats, the French menace was now already a unifying factor for nationalism, as argued by Colley, except that this was 1702, whereas Colley's thesis holds that nationalism emerged in 1707 with the Act of Union.[149]

George I: The Hanoverian

The coronation of 20 October 1714 had a very different role. This was now a battle for legitimacy, and the coronation sermon would be at the centre of the propaganda campaign against the Jacobite Pretender, James Francis Edward Stuart (1688–1766). Yet, amidst this great fear of the Pretender's invasion 'arriv'd ... [the] Protestant heir'.[150] William Talbot, bishop of Oxford and dean of the Chapel Royal, was appointed preacher (later bishop of Durham). At approximately twenty-two minutes, this sermon is marginally longer than that of 1702, but fits the fashion for brevity. Although the contemporary antiquary Thomas Hearne 'dismissed [Talbot] as a "republican"',[151] it is hard to see how this sermon could be interpreted in that light. If anything, this text is an even stronger thanksgiving for providential Protestantism: 'the Providence that seated him [George I] upon his throne, are as remarkable [as] ... those which brought King David to his'. This was a continuation of the affirmation of God's actions in 1689, 'deliver[ing] for us, the great WILLIAM ... delivering us from popish tyranny and arbitrary power ... [and] establishing a ballance of power in Europe'.[152]

All five coronation sermon case studies are extraordinary indicators of change in Britain and provide insights into the political, religious, and constitutional questions of the time. In this instance, Talbot highlighted Britain's role as a nation ascendant and, by 1714, as a burgeoning imperial power; this contrasted with 1661, for Britannia was now dealing the cards as much as playing them. Crucially, God had restored 'our envy'd legal establishment in Church and State'.[153] The origins of a Whig teleology are by 1714 increasingly evident. Just as William and Mary's 1689 sermon had called for the nation to prosper, so Talbot appealed to God, quoting Psalm 118: 24–35: 'O Lord, I beseech thee send now prosperity'. It is a striking similarity, given the foreign nationalities of the male monarchs in question. George I was ushered in with a zealous Protestant welcome. Talbot even continued to foster an anti-Catholicism rooted in the tradition of John Foxe's 'Book of Martyrs', noting the 'woeful experience of two popish reigns since the Reformation'. He continued dramatically:

> Had this succession been defeated, by a successful attempt by him, who pretends a right to the Crown; one educated in the maxims of French tyranny, and the principles of popish superstition … [the nation would have suffered the] … worst slavery of body and mind. The spiritual government … submitted to the most monstrous absurdities in doctrine … idolatry … ancient methods of fire and faggot, or [even] convinced by the more modern ones of dragoons, dungeons, and galleys.[154]

Talbot's Britain had thus been saved, but by 1714, the Crown embraced not just the kingdoms of the British Isles but also the colonies; George would bring 'gracious government in his dominions abroad, … he will answer the ends of magistracy here, by being the minister of God to us for good'.[155] Whilst not explicitly called 'vicegerent', George was certainly seen as chief minister, and Divine Right ideology continued to dominate even with this new royal house, for the 'crown, which is now to be put on the sacred head of his majesty' was a sacral not just a lay one.[156] Why such a celebration for a German king? Yes: Protestant and not the Pretender, but George brought one other great asset to the throne that had not been seen for generations: dynastic continuity. In Talbot's eyes, this fact completed 'this great mercy', since the benefits of his accession would be continued 'to our children, and children's children'. For 'his royal highness is also bless'd with hopeful issue, by a princess of the brightest character … [and these children are] … pledges of the lasting happiness of these kingdoms'.[157] This was Protestant security. Not since Charles I's 1626 coronation had the realm experienced a guaranteed succession.

In past ages, prayer was the necessary popular obligation. This remained true for the coronation sermon of 1714, but a Protestant work ethic emerges too. The peoples' 'constant prayers to God [should be] second[ed] with our sincere endeavours'. Collective endeavour was a new theme, rooted in the present. The medieval soteriological world, of the life to come, was gradually being downgraded for 'this present world'. For in 1702, Anne's coronation sermon` reflected the Reformation of Manners and the foreshadowing of the Evangelical Revival, living here and now did not just mean 'sincere obedience to … laws', but also 'living soberly [and] righteously' too.[158] Talbot exemplified the tendency for preachers of coronation sermons to adopt a nationalistic language, drawing Britain in parallel to Israel:

> Their history is chiefly made up of the many remarkable interchanges of national blessings, or national judgements, upon prince and people, as they proved obedient or disobedient to God. And it will ever be so, righteousness will exalt a nation, but sin will be the reproach, the ruin of any people.[159]

Unity and confessionalization,[160] in a political as much as in a religious sense, was needed to avoid the 'fatal tendency … [of] ruin [to] societies', that of 'factions and divisions'.[161] For Providence, 'the umpire and director', has made the British 'a peculiar people' and 'members of the most happily constituted society in the world'. God is seen in state-like judicial terms: the acting night-watchman of society, 'reach[ing] to every subject of these dominions'.[162]

Talbot's conclusion is, in part, something as accessible to a modern audience as to that of 1714—timeless in words that would be familiar to the Victorian Empire and in places is still relevant today:

> May he [George I] long continue the Defender of our Faith, and maintainer of our civil rights; may the happy influences of his glorious government, extend as widely as those of the sun … The protector of the liberties of Europe, the guardian of the Protestant interest, the refuge of the oppressed …, and a common blessing to mankind.[163]

Yet, having struck powerful chords—in terms of asylum for refugees, of civil rights, of liberties—Talbot finishes with words that are more consonant with a Russian Tsarist ideology of saintly monarchy: 'And when, being full of years, and full of glory, he shall be gathered to his fathers, to take possession of an eternal crown; may his temporal crown descend peaceably upon his ROYAL SON'. In this, George I was to be elevated with death to an eternal sacred status, forever deified, whilst his son would inherit by Divine Right.[164]

The anti-Jacobite rhetoric continued after the coronation. Its sermon provided a base for other preachers to mount attacks on those of wavering loyalty, who made 'mighty and clamorous pretences of loyalty to his prince' while hankering after 'a spurious Pretender'. By contrast, echoing the coronation sermon, George I was a 'true loyalist ... loyal to GOD, whose authority is most ancient and paramount, and ... one of his ministers and vicegerents'. Simon Browne's London preaching in 1715–1716 called for obedience to the realm's lawful governor. Those of proper loyalty should thus 'honour lawful governours, and be obedient to their lawful commands'.[165] Such a demand would arguably have rung rather hollow without the legitimacy that the coronation in general gave to George I and especially without the words of the sermon, which provided the theological heft to support the ceremonial dimension.

Impact

How does one measure impact? That is extremely hard to quantify, but a couple of possible means are to look at the print run of the Westminster Abbey coronation sermons and the character of the coronation sermons given around the country concurrently. What did these say of providence, of nation, of Divine Right? Did such concepts travel beyond the metropolis? Shapiro, working on assize sermons (*c.*1600–1688), shows how these ideas spread out 'into the countryside', and that theories of the Divine Right of Kings were prevalent both 'prior to the Civil War and again after the Restoration'.[166] It is therefore not unlikely that the ideas expressed in coronation sermons would have filtered out too. The coronation sermon delivered in the Abbey was printed in London and then often in Edinburgh and Dublin editions. Was this the same version or was it adapted for different kingdoms? As a test case, the text consulted for Sharp's coronation sermon for Queen Anne, the Dublin 1702 impression, has been compared with the London 1702 edition; it is identical. Sharp's sermon would go through four editions in seven years, the fourth published in 1709, and reappear in a collection of Sharp's sermons in 1749. Perhaps it was reissued then to coincide with the Peace of Aix-la-Chapelle, which ended the War of the Austrian Succession in 1748 and Handel's composition of 'The Royal Fireworks'.[167] A reasonable argument can therefore be made that his text (Isaiah 49:23)—kings and queens being nursing fathers and mothers—resonated with the public. The market justified multiple editions. One might speculate that the circumstances of a female ruler, in a time of war with France and the existence of a rival claimant to the throne, meant that the queen and her advisers encouraged the further distributions of approved works.

What is significant is that although coronation sermons were designed for a specific context, they could, as in this instance, achieve longevity, functioning as royalist propaganda even after the specific monarch had been succeeded. They could also call into question a monarch's status by upholding the legitimacy of the Stuart line. For instance, John Morphew, a successful publisher, had Morley's sermon for Charles II republished in London in 1714, thus coinciding with George I's accession. Morphew is thought to have had Jacobite sympathies and was arrested for those in 1717. The republication seems more than coincidental, being rather an act of Jacobite propaganda, to point to the Old Pretender's existence.[168] However, simply to examine Westminster Abbey sermons would be to miss a crucial dimension, namely the phenomenon of coronation sermons delivered nationally and published soon after. Three examples, the fruits of a preliminary enquiry, may be given.

The first example is a sermon preached by John Winter at East Dereham (Norfolk) on 29 May 1661. It addresses the very questions of service and honour discussed by Morley. Winter, quoting 1 Peter 2:17, calls for people to 'fear God: [and] honour the king'; indeed the nation must 'serve God and the king; God with fear, the king with honour: God above all, the king next under God, in God, and for God'. Unsurprisingly, this is a sermon of restoration, but, importantly, as in Morley's work, Solomon is the exemplar. It is also a sermon of fulfilment: 'and now that royal prediction is abundantly fulfilled. Thus gloriously in our horizon appears Charles the second, for vertue and piety second to none, but Charles the first'.[169] Again, five weeks after the coronation, the echoes of the Westminster Abbey sermon are remarkably strong.

Moreover, in Oxford, in 1685, it was reported that 'the coronation [of James II] was celebrated … with great solemnity, both at St Mary's & the Theatre; Dr Hall was appointed to preach, who gave us a very excellent sermon, upon Rom[ans] 13:5'. The text links with the coronation sermon and the theme of submission to authority, though this was more out of blind obedience, than to 'just and merciful' authority, 'wherefore the must needs be subject, not only for wrath, but also for conscience sake'.[170]

The final example is a sermon preached by Luke Beaulieu at Gloucester Cathedral purportedly on the same day as Queen's Anne's coronation at Westminster.[171] How is it that Beaulieu's text is none other than Isaiah 49:23, 'kings shall be thy nursing-fathers, and their queens thy nursing-mothers'? There is no reference to Sharp, or to the Abbey. It is, nevertheless, roughly the same length as his sermon, at eighteen minutes. It rehearses important themes that have appeared in the five coronation sermons that I have discussed: 'providence'; the 'nation', as compared with the Jewish people of the Old Testament; the construction of 'our Christian Jerusalem'; 'obedience', not as something 'passive', but rather as 'submission to the laws'; a divine 'crown of immortal glory'; and monarchs who have received 'power … from above'. This is a sermon calling for prosperity: 'may her government over these kingdoms be long and prosperous'. These are all concepts familiar from the Abbey sermon, but now expressed in Gloucester, also on 23 April. So far, no evidence of state orchestration has been discovered. Nevertheless, one might conjecture that if Beaulieu was advancing these concepts in Gloucester, whilst they were being expounded in the Abbey, then they arguably carried weight beyond London. In a sense, therefore, Sharp was deliberately preaching to a much wider audience, relating his work to the issues of the moment, and was not simply writing on a whim—he was anything but 'out-of-touch'. Taking this point a little further, Beaulieu was far from a conformist. His background as a French Huguenot refugee comes out in his sermon. He talks of 'all Christians' being included in the Church, of a unity with the 'Reformed churches abroad' and the desire for a Church that involves religious freedom of conscience: 'This takes in all that are truly Christians, and not ashamed to declare what they believe and after what manner they worship their God and saviour'.[172] It is an extremely moving text in thankfulness for sanctuary and in praise for the queen. His conclusion is compelling:

> Let none fear persecution who peaceably follow their conscience, though in a wrong way: the queen is too sincere a worshipper of God, to think religious persuasions, or true devotion, can be forc'd'.[173]

1661–1714 Conclusion

The years 1661–1714 saw five very different coronation sermons, delivered by five very different preachers. On the surface, the only unifying aspect is that of location. Yet, delving into the texts, one finds striking parallels and continuities across a period of tremendous flux: the Restoration, the Exclusion Crisis, the Glorious Revolution, Jacobinism, the War of the Spanish Succession, and the Hanoverian succession. Britain in 1714 was a country transformed, with an altered place in the world, compared to the three kingdoms of 1661. Nevertheless, the same concepts abound in all these sermons. Concentrating on the coronation sermons of 1661–1689, Strong suggests that 'theories of Divine Right gradually recede'.[174] However, a close examination reveals Divine Right ideology permeates them all with enhanced emphasis. The providentialist thrust grows, perhaps partly explained by increasing national prosperity; but it is intriguing that this aspect was rooted in God's direct involvement with England, in a likeness to the Israelites of the Old Testament. There is no question at any stage of a passive God. Sturdy is right in suggesting that it is in Burnet's concept of 'the New Jerusalem' that we see historical significance in a form of 'messianic vision' to be fulfilled in England.[175] Yet, he goes on to argue that '[e]ighteenth and nineteenth-century coronation sermons are banal by comparison with those of the seventeenth; they express little more than polite expressions of good will towards the monarch about to be crowned'. This chapter has shown that, at least for the first two eighteenth-century coronations, that is far from true. The audience at Gloucester Cathedral in 1702 was enjoined to build this 'Christian Jerusalem' as much as Talbot would celebrate the Britain's 'national blessings' in 1714. Crucially, print culture allowed for the wider distribution of these sermons, spreading the message far beyond the confines of the Abbey, as Edie has argued for the 'four later Stuart coronation sermons made an apt and cogent political statement; each defined clearly the particular character of the reign it inaugurated. Copies of the sermons were printed at once and made available for sale to the public. In this way the message reached all parts of the kingdom'.[176]

At the centre of this analysis has been the concept of the nation and the sense of a burgeoning nationalism. The semantics of the term are easily debated; it has many connotations. However, this chapter has shown that a form of collective feeling—whether towards (interchangeably) England, the three kingdoms or Britain—was being expressed in 1661, in a way that had not been the case in 1603, and barely so in 1626. From Morley's sermon to Talbot's, this concept is constantly elaborated. These themes were not merely articulated in the Abbey, to the social elite, but across the country too, with similar and even identical biblical texts being used. They were then published, often running to several editions. Does this suggest state orchestration? Probably not, though this possibility requires more research. Certainly, the coincidences are intriguing, and, at the very least, show that preachers of different religious hues were talking to their congregations about the nature of royal governance in similar ways, albeit in diverse environments.

It is fitting to finish with extracts from a 1714 sermon given by Samuel Rosewell four days after George I's coronation. The very title highlights a powerful continuation of Divine Right ideology: '*The King's True Divine Right. The Flourishing of his Crown: and the Shame of his Enemies. A Sermon Preach'd upon Occasion of His Majesty's Coronation* ... '[177] This is a sermon in which the 'influence of providence' is paramount, with 'the hand of God' placing George I on the throne. Like Sharp, Rosewell calls for the rejection of 'popery and arbitrary power', highlighting the dangers of 'France and Rome' and the 'Pretender'.[178] The power of John Foxe's work is seen in the reference to 'the perfidious behaviour of the Bloody Q[ueen] Mary towards the Suffolk Protestants'.[179] Throughout, there are comparisons with David and Solomon. In line with Burnet in 1689, 'civil rights and liberties' are seen to be vital for the country.[180] As with all five Westminster Abbey coronation sermons assessed here, the terms 'the nation' and 'nations' feature prominently. Most interestingly, in commemorating William III, we find expression that memory is 'precious' not to all the people, or to every subject, but 'to every Briton': for the Britain of 1714 was a country of the 'brave and successful general, the duke of Marlborough'.[181] From 1661, a strengthening notion of 'nation' had been expressed in all these coronation sermons. Now, after a period of extraordinary flux and with an assured Hanoverian succession, this sceptred isle was a land of 'British people' and 'noble patriots'.[182]

Coda: 1727–2023, Modern and Post-Modern Coronation Sermons

Sturdy has argued that the coronation sermons of the eighteenth and nineteenth centuries 'are banal by comparison to those of the seventeenth', for

> they express little more than polite expressions of good will towards the monarch about to be crowned. Those of the seventeenth century, by contrast, not only examine monarchy, or the reasons for the ills of society, but urge a messianic vision which is capable of being realised in this world if certain conditions are fulfilled; it is the purpose of the preacher to keep that vision before the King and the nation, but even more, to point the way to its realisation. The sermon gave to the ceremony as a whole, a powerful declaration that the ritual that was about to unfold represented the interpretation of the divine and the secular; the coronation not only was a constitutional exercise, but potentially represented yet another stage whereby the God of History could fulfil His will to bring among fallen men that City of God which their sin and corruption so far had denied them.[183]

Sturdy goes further in addressing all of coronation ceremonial, when he states that

> coronation ceremonial itself was treated in cavalier fashion in the 1700s and 1800s: Hanoverian coronations lacked the attention to detail that characterized those of earlier periods, the nadir probably being reached with the crowning of George III whose coronation was reduced almost to a shambles as one mishap followed another; on that occasion even the sermon scarcely could be heard above the clatter of cutlery and popping of corks as the congregation used the opportunity to take lunch! The coronations of George VI and William IV were mean affairs; that of Victoria only marginally better. In short, after 1685 the constitutional and social significance of the coronation went into decline.[184]

Sturdy is right to recognise the extraordinary significance and detail of the seventeenth- century coronation sermons, but goes too far in labelling all that follows as mere polite rhetoric. Likewise, he is correct that mishaps abound in many of the coronations that followed (although they of course had occurred before), and this will be covered in Chap. 8 but goes too far in labelling this as a total decline without social significance. 2023 being a case in point—a coronation watched by millions globally and celebrated by many millions too around the United Kingdom and abroad. Dixon has also shown for the period 1761–1838, that whilst those 'British coronations ... have conventionally been dismissed as tawdry pageants with little religious significance' they in fact 'were perceived to retain a religious and political significance'.[185] The concept of a form of contract between the sovereign and their people continued in the coronation sermon, for instance in 1821, for George IV's coronation sermon

> Archbishop Venables-Vernon (later Harcourt) of York, said that the coronation was intended 'to inspire the Subject with reverence for the authority and person of the Sovereign, and to impress on the Sovereign his obligations of duty to his People', enforcing 'the performance of that duty by the sanctions of Religion'.[186]

This continued at William IV's coronation in 1831, when the Bishop of London, Charles James Blomfield talked of the coronation as

> 'the formal ratification' of a 'contract between king and people ... on the part of the king, to govern according to law; to execute judgement in mercy; to maintain the true religion: on the part of his subjects, to render a willing and conscientious obedience'.[187]

By the time of Queen Victoria's coronation in 1838, the power of cheap print (and of the newspaper) allowed for far greater circulation of the service and of the liturgy for the clergy to follow across parishes up and down the country (and across the empire). John Gurney spoke of the "liturgy" as "much less known and read than it deserves to be" and echoes the religious contract note with reference to the presentation of the Bible to the sovereign, arguing "if that is the book for princes to rule by, it is the book for subjects to serve by".[188] Samuel Allen also referenced the coronation service in a sermon, 'regretting that it had not been distributed among Sunday school children, who would thereby "have seen at once the folly of those, who....ventured to pronounce it 'an idle and barbarous pageant,'—'an unmeaning ceremony,' and the like"'.[189] Bishop Blomfield's coronation sermon for Queen Victoria in 1838 seemed to combine a new wave of (perhaps Tractarian or wider ideas about anointing and spiritual sanction) when he stated

> The diadem, which encircles the brow of royalty, may be placed there by human hands, and after the letter of human compacts: but it bespeaks a majesty of a more exalted transcendent kind than any human agency can confer. As to the person, who is entitled to our allegiance, man's ordinances may be our guides; but the right motive to loyal obedience is this, that the power, which claims it, is of God.[190]

Ideas that were very much the order of the day in early Stuart coronations, but in this case restoring or continuing the idea of the mystique of majesty. With this element coupled with an emphasis on contractualism (also seen within the oath as will be covered in Chap. 3), we have the hallmarks of a twentieth and twenty-first century ceremony—the constitution, legally and religiously played out in the drama of the service. As Dixon has argued

> Anglican clergy developed a formidable response to arguments that the ceremony was an outmoded superstition. They placed coronations firmly in the context of hegemonic notions of "providential economy" and consensual constitutionalism and posited a coherent sacramental symbolism in the anointing, investiture, and communion. Successive archbishops of Canterbury made the coronation liturgy distinctively Protestant and Anglican while retaining the outward appearances of the past to emphasize their church's venerability. In their dealings with the state, clergy tenaciously defended their ancient rights in relation to the ceremony and were far from reticent in using the occasion to question authority. The picture emerges of a church neither Erastian nor lethargic.[191]

Edward VII's ill health saw the coronation sermon swept aside in 1902 when the reconvened day of 9 August came to pass. Although the clergy more generally had prepared texts, with particular emphasis on education for children, to explain the service and the purpose of the occasion, with titles including 'The Significance of a Coronation'; 'The Crown of Precious Stones'; 'The True Inwardness of a Coronation'; 'A Coronation Sermon'; 'King of Kings'; 'From Above'; 'The Pure Crown'; and 'The Coronation Service Interpreted to Children'.[192] Beyond the Christian faith, 1902 would also see a Coronation Sermon from Rabbi I. H. Daiches delivered at Beth Hamedrash Hagodel in Leeds on 9 August 1902.[193] The coronation sermon reappeared in the 1911 ceremony for George V, in 'abbreviated form' in Strong's view, yet closer inspection sees a text full of carefully chosen words with the 'hallowing' at the core of the message as well as the

Fig. 2.1 The Coronation of Queen Victoria, 28 June 1838, George Hayter (1792–1871), Alamy

'sovereignty of service' and the monarch as 'servant of God' and 'servant of the people' and

> For the national life as well as for its representative this is a day of consecration. May this great people make an seal this day a covenant of service with our fathers' God [...].[194]

A coronation sermon would have been due to take place in 1937 but with the abdication of Edward VIII, it was not reinstated for George VI's coronation. The abdication crisis threatened the very foundations of monarchy in Britain and across the empire, and it was again the coronation that archbishop Cosmo Gordon Lang sought to utilise to 'reaffirm Chrisitan public morality ... as a moment of national spiritual renewal'.[195] Although there would not be a coronation sermon for 1937, in order to 'amplify his vision of a nation congregated in support of their rulers, the archbishop also oversaw the publication of three special forms of service that were distributed nationally, one of which was used as part of the evening service on the Sunday before the coronation'. At the BBC concert hall, Lang would also preach a sermon entitled 'The King Comes Not Alone' to an audience of special guests and, *via* the wireless, to British listeners gathered in their homes and at church services around the country'.[196] 1937 would also see a publication of a 'King George VI Coronation Sermon by The Chief Rabbi Dr. J. H. Hertz'—showing how far times had come from the horrors of coronations for the Jewish people of England in the medieval era, as will be covered in Chap. 8.[197]

For all of the late Queen Elizabeth II's undoubted faith, 1953 did not see a return for a coronation sermon, in what Strong argues was 'a radical diminution of the ministry of the Word, an integral part of any Christian liturgy'.[198]

So whilst religion had remained a cornerstone of the coronation service, as also seen in Chap. 1 the twentieth century had seen just one coronation sermon out of a possible four opportunities. A precedent had assumed to be set for modern or 'post-modern' ceremonies. It is therefore all the more intriguing that it returned in 2023 for the first time since 1911, something Strong had called for when he wrote

> At present the communion service fall shorts on the ministry of the Word, and the sermon, however brief, should certainly be restored.[199]

Lambeth's official commentary to the liturgy stated that '[w]ith very few exceptions a sermon has always been part of the Coronation service'.[200] Yet, as we have just noted, this was not the case for the twentieth century and all the more significant given the publicised requirement of a shorter service in 2023.[201] King Charles III's own spirituality will have been important in the final decision, but the Lambeth official commentary text provides all one needs to read to see the former archbishop of Canterbury's desire to use the coronation as a platform:

> This is an opportunity for the Archbishop to address Their Majesties, the congregation, and those participating elsewhere, drawing on and contextualising what we have already seen, and setting out the themes and desires of the Coronation, and how they relate not only to Their Majesties but to all people. A sermon is an essential aspect and feature of Anglican liturgy. It is a moment to reflect on Scripture readings, to learn, to be challenged and to explore the core themes and motifs of a Eucharistic service, to hear the call of God's Word, and discover within our own context how we are being called to serve.[202]

The sermon which took Colossians 1:9–17 and Luke 4:16–21 as key texts did much to stress 'unity'. It is not a long sermon, running to *c.*3 mins, but the choice of words for all of the ecumenical or even pluralistic nature to the service is fascinating, for Welby states

> This is promised by Jesus who put aside all privilege, because, as the first reading tells us, God will give all things for our sake, even His own life. His throne was a Cross. His crown was made of thorns. His regalia were the wounds that pierced his body. Each of us is called by God to serve. Whatever that looks like in our own lives, each of us can choose God's way today.[203]

The proselytising call to a Christian way of life is at odds with much of the rest of the introductions to the service and one wonders whether such a coronation sermon would return in the future or be as evangelical as this.[204] In any view, the coronation sermon returned to a key role within the coronation service, as it has been for centuries preceding the twentieth, and as a reminder of the religiosity of this occasion, whether in the heat of the reformation(s), the Restoration, the Glorious Revolution or indeed in our so-called secular era.

Appendix 1: Westminster Abbey Coronation Sermons, 1603–2023, with Reference to Duration (Dates from *ODNB*)

Year	*Monarch*	*Preacher*	*Estimated duration (minutes)*
1603	James I	Thomas Bilson (1546/1547–1616)	35
1626	Charles I	Richard Senhouse (*d.* 1626)	27
1661	Charles II	George Morley (1598?–1684)	60
1685	James II	Francis Turner (1637–1700)	30
1689	William III & Mary II	Gilbert Burnet (1643–1715)	25
1702	Anne	John Sharp (1645?–1714)	15
1714	George I	William Talbot (1659–1730)	22
1727	George II	John Potter (1673/1674–1747)	15
1761	George III	Robert Hay Drummond (1711–1776)	15
1821	George IV	Edward Vernon-Harcourt (1757–1847)	10
1831	William IV	Charles James Blomfield (1786–1857)	8
1838	Victoria	Charles James Blomfield (1786–1857)	10

(*continued*)

Year	*Monarch*	*Preacher*	*Estimated duration (minutes)*
1902	Edward VII	Arthur Foley Winnington-Ingram (1858–1946) but not delivered	N/A
1911	George V	William Cosmo Gordon Lang (1864–1945)	10
1937	George VI	No sermon	N/A
1953	Elizabeth II	No sermon	N/A
2023	Charles III	Justin Welby (1956–)	3

Notes

1. F. Turner, *A Sermon Preached Before their Majesties K. James II. and Q. Mary, at their Coronation in Westminster-Abby, April 23. 1685. …* (London, 1685), p. 4.
2. Bodl., MS Rawlinson Letters 94, fol. 94v.
3. D. Loades, 'The Origins of English Protestant Nationalism', in D. Loades, *Politics, Censorship and the English Reformation* (London, 1991), pp. 39–47; Braddick, *State Formation*; Collinson, *Birthpangs*, pp. 1–27; P. Collinson, *This England: Essays on the English Nation and Commonwealth in the Sixteenth Century* (Manchester, 2011).
4. See Chaps. 1 and 4.
5. Sturdy, 'Sermons', p. 69.
6. *Ibid.*, *passim.*
7. Edie, 'Public Face'.
8. Hone, 'The Last Stuart Coronation', pp. 132–145.
9. Sturdy, 'Sermons', pp. 72–3 and n. 2.
10. On foreign representation, see below pp. 222–3.
11. Edie, 'Public Face', pp. 311–12.
12. Hone, 'The Last Stuart Coronation', p. 133.
13. Doran, *Tudor to Stuart*, pp. 139–9. See also Jack, 'Coronation of James I'.
14. McCullough, *Sermons.*
15. Strong, *Coronation*, p. 339.
16. Hunt, *Drama*, pp. 83–4, 93. See also Fincham and Tyacke, *Altars Restored*, p. 9 'a "second Josiah" … who would "see idolatry destroyed … and images removed"'. See D. MacCulloch, 'Foxes, Firebrands, and Forgery: Robert Ware's Pollution of Reformation History', *The Historical Journal*, 54 (2011), pp. 307–46, on the fabrication of this much referenced text. Cf. MacCulloch, *Boy King*, p. 62 (illustration of gold and silver medal commemorating Edward VI's coronation. The inscriptions, although in Latin, Greek and Hebrew, all have identical texts, all stressing

the royal supremacy; a similar medal had been struck for Henry VIII in 1535: cf. MacCulloch, *Cranmer*, pp. 364–5). Caution is needed over Edward VI's coronation, for, as MacCulloch has revealed, what is said to be Cranmer's sermon never occurred, or rather the surviving text is fabricated: MacCulloch, 'Firebrands'. Therefore, we cannot be as certain as Strong that 'monarchy was thus rendered seemingly absolute' by these supposed changes: Strong, *Coronation*, pp. 200–1.

17. *Calendar of Patent Rolls Preserved in the Public Record Office: Philip and Mary* (London, 1937), I, p. 339, stating that 'the Quenes Heighnes hath specially appointed hym to make the sermon on … Coronation Daye …'. See also M. Kitch, 'Day, George (c. 1502–1556)', *ODNB*.
18. P. McCullough, 'Preaching and Context: John Donne's Sermon at the Funerals of Sir William Cokayne', in P. McCullough *et al.* (eds), *The Oxford Handbook of the Early Modern Sermon* (Oxford, 2011), p. 215.
19. A. Hunt, *The Art of Hearing: English Preachers and their Audiences, 1590–1640* (Cambridge, 2010), p. 12.
20. In our case, we have to be even more careful given that the much discussed and analysed version of Cranmer's 1547 sermon or address for Edward VI's coronation has been proven to be false, with no historical grounding.
21. McCullough, 'Preaching', p. 213.
22. The 1957 EMI interpretation by Herbert von Karajan (1908–1989) of Brahms's *Symphony No. 4* (1884–1885) and the Philharmonia Orchestra was particularly impressive. For further details on music, its context and influence, see Copland, *Music*.
23. George Eliot (1819–1880), *Daniel Deronda* (1876). See also E. Said, *Orientalism: Western Conceptions of the Orient* (1st edn, London, 1978).
24. D. Beaver, 'Conscience and Context: The Popish Plot and the Politics of Ritual, 1678–1682', *The Historical Journal*, 34 (1991), p. 297. On wider public reception, see P. Hinds, *'The Horrid Popish Plot': Roger L'Estrange and the Circulation of Political Discourse in Late Seventeenth-Century London* (London, 2010), *passim*. The Popish Plot began in 1678, and centred on the alleged conspiracy to assassinate King Charles II and reintroduce Roman Catholicism. Whilst the plot was fictitious (conspired by Titus Oates), it was widely believed, and many innocent Roman Catholics were put on trial and executed. See A. Marshall, 'Titus Oates (1649–1705)', *ODNB*.
25. Kantorowicz, *King's Two Bodies*, p. 5; cf. S. Bertelli, '*Rex et Sacerdos*: The Holiness of the King in European Civilization', in A. Ellenius (ed.), *Iconography, Propaganda, and Legitimation* (New York, 1998), pp. 123–45 and Bertelli, *King's Body*; P. Hammarol, 'The King's Two Bodies: Representations of Charles II', in J. Black and J. Gregory (eds),

Culture, Politics and Society in Britain, 1660–1800 (Manchester, *c.*1991), pp. 13–48.

26. See MacCulloch, 'Firebrands'. See also FSL, MS L.b.8.
27. M. Bowker, 'Smith [Smyth], William (d. 1514)', *ODNB*. 'Little Device for the Coronation of Henry VII', p. 230. See also: BL Additional MS 18669, fol 1r. The manuscript, Legg claims, dates from early in the reign of Henry VIII, so it is either a copy of the original or an earlier version (p. 220). The three other versions of the Device are BL Add. MS 18669, BL Harleian MS 5111, fol. 77, and W. Jerdan (ed.), *Rutland Papers. Original Documents Illustrative of the Courts and Times of Henry VII. and Henry VIII. Selected from the Private Archives of His Grace the Duke of Rutland*, Camden Society, Old Series, XXI (London, 1842), pp. 1–24. There are subtle variations between all the manuscripts, see for instance, BL Cotton MS Tiberius E VIII, 'The coronacion of king henry the viiith', fols. 90r–99v; see also The College of Arms, MS Vincent 24, fol. 144, and CA, MS 1.7, fol. 21.
28. BL Cotton MS Tiberius E VIII, 'The coronacion of king henry the viiith', fol. 94v; see also CA, MS Vincent 24, fol. 144, and CA, MS 1.7, fol. 21. See also Hunt, *Drama*, p. 26; Scarisbrick, *Henry VIII*, pp. 17–18; and MacCulloch, *Thomas Cranmer*, p. 94 on Anne Boleyn's coronation, but no mention of a sermon: 'The following day, Whit Sunday 1 June, the Archbishop played the principal role in the actual coronation ceremony, praying over Anne, anointing and crowning her and delivering her sceptre and ivory rod; afterwards his old Lincolnshire friend William Benson, the newly appointed Abbot of Westminster, took over to star as celebrant of high mass'.
29. *CPR: Philip and Mary*, I, p. 339: 'A nother letter to the Bisshopp of Chichester, doing hym to make sermon on the Coronation Daye at Westminster.' On Day's recovery of this office, see D. Loades, *The Reign of Mary Tudor: Politics, Government and Religion in England, 1553–58* (London, 1991), p. 47; and C. V. Malfatti (trans. and ed.), *The Accession, Coronation and Marriage of Mary Tudor as Related in Four Manuscripts of the Escorial* (Barcelona, 1956), p. 33 'Events of the kingdom of England beginning with King Edward VI until the wedding of the most serene Prince Philip of Spain and the most serene Queen Mary as related by Monsignor G. F. Commendone: an Italian Manuscript in the Library of the Monasterio de San Lorenzo El Real Dl Escorial'; Cf. Hunt, *Drama*, p. 132 and Whitelock, A. and MacCulloch, D., "Princess Mary's Household and the Succession Crisis, July 1553." *The Historical Journal*, 50 (2007), p. 276.
30. See also Norrie, 'The Bishop and the Queen', pp. 37–39. Starkey, *Apprenticeship*, p. 271, leaves the door firmly open to the idea of a ser-

mon by Oglethorpe: 'Then the Queen and bishop descended towards the altar. The Queen made the traditional offerings to the altar and then sat in the southern throne to hear the sermon.' See also R. L. Brown and G. C. Bentinck (eds), *Calendar of State Papers and Manuscripts, Relating to English Affairs Existing in the Archives and Collections of Venice, and in Other Libraries of Northern* Italy, Volume 7: 1558–1580 (This edition first published 1890; this compilation published Cambridge, 2013), pp. 11–19.

31. Doran, *Tudor to Stuart*, p. 138.
32. T. Bilson, *A Sermon Preached at Westminster Before the King and Queens Maiesties, at their Coronations on Saint Iames his Day* ... 1603 (London, 1603), p. 37. See also *ibid.*, *The True Difference between Christian Subjection and Unchristian Rebellion* (Oxford, 1585).
33. *Ibid.*, *A Sermon ... at their Coronations on Saint James his Day*, p. 3.
34. Jack, 'Coronation of James I', p. 87.
35. Sturdy, 'Sermons', p. 69. See also Eton College Archives, Windsor, Political Miscellany Vol. (1603–1625).
36. R. Senhouse, *Foure Sermons Preached at the Court upon Severall Occasions, etc.* (London, 1627). See also Wordsworth, *Coronation.*
37. Sturdy, 'Sermons', p. 70.
38. *Ibid.*, pp. 69–70. See also Senhouse, *Foure Sermons.* On the importance of 'crownation day' and the continuing relevance of early Stuart coronation and accession sermons see Kiryanova, 'Images'; and D. Colclough, "I have brought thee up to a Kingdome': Sermons on the Accessions of James I and Charles I', in P. Kewes, and A. McRae (eds), *Stuart Succession Literature: Moments and Transformations* (Oxford, 2018), pp. 205–221.
39. A. Milton, 'Laud, William (1573–1645)', *ODNB.*
40. L. James, *'This Great Firebrand': William Laud and Scotland, 1617–1645* (Woodbridge, 2017), p. 80.
41. K. Fincham, 'William Temple and William Laud', *Theology*, 125 (2022), p. 279.
42. D. Stevenson, 'Lindsay, David (c. 1575–1639/40)', *ODNB.*
43. https://www.british-history.ac.uk/rushworth-papers/vol2/pp175-244, accessed 22 November 2025. See also Cressy, *Charles I*, p. 168; & R. J. Lyall, 'The Medieval Scottish Coronation Service: Some Seventeenth-Century Evidence', The Innes Review, 28 (1977), pp. 3–21; D. M. Bergeron, 'Charles I's Edinburgh pageant (1633)', Renaissance Studies, 6 (1992), pp. 173–84.
44. G. W. C. Gross, '1651: The Last Coronation in Scotland – An Anomaly?' *The Court Historian*, 26 (2021), pp. 229–245: https://www.tandfonline.com/doi/full/10.1080/14629712.2021.1996947#:~:text=The%20last%20Scottish%20coronation%20occurred%20at%20Scone%20

in%201651, accessed 22 November 2025. See also K. Holfelder, 'Douglas, Robert (1594–1674)', *ODNB*.

45. R. Douglas, *Sermon Preached at Scoone, January 1st 1651, at the Coronation of Charles the Second* (Edinburgh, 1651). As Moderator of the General Assembly, Douglas took the coronation sermon to be his due on this occasion.
46. A. Fraser, *King Charles II* (London, 1979), pp. 98–9. Keay, *Magnificent Monarch*, pp. 46–7.
47. Cf. Edinburgh University Library, DC.5.30–31: Papers of Robert Douglas vol. 1–11, for other examples of his Sermons and of note his remarkable skill including in biblical reference. For 1661 see Morley, *Sermon*. See also D. Shaw, 'The Coronation and Monarchical Culture in Stuart Britain and Ireland 1603–1661' (unpublished PhD dissertation, University of Cambridge, 2002). One must have caution when dealing with Shaw's work on the Coronation Sermon of Douglas as he draws comparison with Cranmer's Sermon for Edward VI's Coronation on idolatry as a form of precedent. Yet as MacCulloch has revealed what is said to be Cranmer's sermon never actually took place or rather the details of what we have are a forgery. Douglas's Sermon was therefore a unique Presbyterian Sovereign's Coronation Sermon for the British Isles without precedent; and if there is any comparison to be drawn with Cranmer it cannot be from a forged Sermon. Cf. MacCulloch, 'Firebrands'.
48. *Correspondence of Sir Robert Kerr; first Earl of Ancram and his son William, third Earl of Lothian 1616*, 2 vols (Edinburgh, 1875), vol. I, p. 93.
49. Douglas, *The form and order of the coronation of Charles the Second … January, 1651*, p. 7.
50. Gross, '1651: The Last Coronation in Scotland': https://www.tandfonline.com/doi/full/10.1080/14629712.2021.1996947#:~:text=The%20last%20Scottish%20coronation%20occurred%20at%20Scone%20in%201651, accessed 22 November 2025.
51. A. Walsham, A., *Providence in Early Modern England* (Oxford, 1999).
52. Hunt, *Hearing*, p. 292. On political context, see pp. 292–342.
53. Nothing suggests that the authors of these works, when discussing coronation sermons, have attempted accurately to time them: Strong, *Coronation*, pp. 237–8, 339–41, 356; T. Harris, *Restoration: Charles II and his Kingdoms, 1660–1685* (London, 2005), pp. 69, 94–5, 109; Schwoerer, 'Coronation', pp. 114–15; and Schramm, *Coronation*, pp. 96–112.
54. Sturdy, 'Sermons', p. 69.
55. Harris, *Restoration*, pp. 109–11. Cf. W. L. Sachse, (ed.), *The Diurnal of Thomas Rugg, 1659–1661*, Camden Society, 3rd Series, XCI (London,

1961), pp. 179–80; *The Kingdomes Intelligencer* ..., 29 April–6 May 1661 (No. 18, London), pp. 270–71; D. Laing, (ed.), J. Nicoll, *A Diary of Public Transactions and Other Occurrences, Chiefly in Scotland, from January 1650 to June 1667* (Edinburgh, 1836), p. 327; R. Wodrow, *The History of the Sufferings of the Church of Scotland, from the Restauration to the Revolution, Collected from the Public Records ... and ... Well Attested Narratives*, 2 volumes (Edinburgh, 1721–1722), I p. 106. Cressy, *Bonfires*; N. E. Key, 'The Political Culture and Political Rhetoric of County Feasts and Feast Sermons, 1654–1714', *Journal of British Studies*, 33 (1994), pp. 223–56; and B. Shapiro, 'Political Theology and the Courts: A Survey of Assize Sermons c1600–1688', *Law and Humanities*, 2 (2008), pp. 6–9.

56. J. S. Uglow, *A Gambling Man: Charles II and the Restoration, 1660–1670* (London, 2009), p. 112. On ritual, see also E. Muir, *Ritual in Early Modern Europe* (2nd edn, Cambridge, 2005), especially pp. 252–93.
57. Hutton, *Charles the Second*, p. 164.
58. M. J. R. Holmes, *The Crown Jewels in the Wakefield Tower at the Tower of London* (3rd edition, London, 1961);T. Rose, *The Coronation Ceremony of the Kings and Queens of England and the Crown Jewels* (London, 1992); and Keay, *Crown Jewels*. See also R. Lightbown, 'The King's Regalia, Insignia and Jewellery', in A. MacGregor (ed.), *The Late King's Goods: Collections, Possessions, and Patronage of Charles I in the Light of the Commonwealth Sale Inventories* (Oxford, 1989), pp. 257–75.
59. James II is the obvious exception to this rule, but traditionally, the monarch was heavily involved in the selection of office holders.
60. B. Quintrell, 'Juxon, William (*bap.* 1582, *d.* 1663)', *ODNB*. Juxon's coronation chair and footstool survive at the Victoria and Albert Museum, London: J. Yorke, 'Archbishop Juxon's Chair', *The Burlington Magazine*, 141 (1999), pp. 282–6.
61. J. Spurr, 'Sheldon, Gilbert (1598–1677)', *ODNB*.
62. Hutton, *Charles the Second*, p. 165.
63. Sturdy, 'Sermons', p. 71.
64. *Ibid.*; see also Spurr, 'Morley, George (1598?–1684)', *ODNB*, omitting information on Morley's Interregnum career in the original *DNB*: Sir Leslie Stephen and Sir Sidney Lee (eds), *Dictionary of National Biography*, 22 vols (original edn, reissued, London, 1908–1909), XIII pp. 971–2. On Morley, see also F. Bussby, 'George Morley: Bishop of Worcester, 1660–62', *Transactions of the Worcestershire Archaeological Society*, New Series, XXXVII (1961), pp. 11–23 and A. Wood, *Athenae Oxonienses. An Exact History of all the Writers and Bishops Who Have Had Their Education in the Most Ancient and Famous University of Oxford, From ... 1500 to the End of ... 1690* ..., 2 volumes (2nd edition, London, 1721), II pp. 768–74.

65. Strong, *Coronation*, pp. 340–1.
66. Bodl., MS Rawlinson Letters 108, fol. 85r (Thomas Mason to John Peirson, London, 20 March 1660/1661), which talks of 'great prepirations for his mai[es]tes coronatio[n]'.
67. Sturdy, 'Sermons', pp. 75–6.
68. Asch, *Sacral Kingship*, pp. 131–2. See for examples Joseph Swetnam, *David's Devotions upon his Deliverances: Set Forth in a Sermon [on Psal. xxiv. 3] June 28, 1660, Being the Day of Publique Thanksgiving for his Majesties Happy Restauration* (London, 1660); Francis Gregory, *David's Returne from his Banishment, set forth in a Thanksgiving Sermon [on 2 Sam. Xix. 30] for the Returne of [...] Charles II* (Oxford, 1660); William Creed, *Judah's Return to their Allegiance and David's Returne to his Crown and Kingdom. A Sermon Preacht at St Mary Woolchurch upon June 28. 1660, Being the Day of Solemn Thanksgiving for the Happy Return of His Majestie* (London, 1660). See also James Heath, *The Glories and Magnificent Triumphs of the Blessed Restitution of His Sacred Majesty King Charles II from his Arrival in Holland 1659–1660 till this Present* (London, 1662).
69. Madway, '"Solemnity"', pp. 145–6.
70. Morley, *Sermon*, p. 61.
71. Bilson, *A Sermon ... at their Coronations on Saint James his Day*; Senhouse, *Sermons*, p. 23; Colley, *Britons*, p. 1 and *passim*; cf. Anderson, *Nationalism* and Braddick, *State Formation*.
72. On the King's Evil, see also Bloch, *Royal Touch*; Brogan, *Royal Touch*.
73. Sharpe, *Image Wars*. Note Charles II's coronation portrait in the Royal Collection.
74. Morley, *Sermon*, p. 33.
75. *Ibid.*, p. 54.
76. Uglow, *Gambling Man*, p. 118; P. Heylyn, *A Sermon Preached in the Collegiate Church of St Peter in Westminster, on Wednesday May 29th. 1661. Being the Anniversary of his Majesties Most Joyful Restitution to the Crown of England. ...* (London, [1661]), pp. 26–7.
77. S. Taylor and K. Fincham, 'Episcopalian Identity, 1640–1662', in A. Milton (ed.), *The Oxford History of Anglicanism. I: Reformation and Identity c.1520–1662* (Oxford 2017), p. 479.
78. J. Miller, *James II: A Study in Kingship* (Hove, 1978); *Ibid.*, *James II* (New Haven, Connecticut, and London, 2000).
79. Sandford, *History*.
80. J. Callow, *James II: The Triumph and the Tragedy* (Kew, 2005).
81. For details on 1685 coronation music, see 'Coronation Music for King James II (1685) Choir of Westminster Abbey and Orchestra on Authentic Instruments' (Polydor International GmbH, Hamburg, 1987). Cf.

'Coronation Anthems: Anthems Composed and Sung at the Coronations of James II in 1685, William and Mary in 1689, Anne in 1702, George I in 1714, George II in 1727, and George III in 1761' (Decca, 2002). See also M. Range, 'The 1685 Coronation Anthem *I Was Glad*', *Early Music*, 36 (2008), pp. 397–408; M. Range, '"With Instrumental Musick of all Sorts"–The Orchestra at British Coronations Before 1727', *Acta Musicologica*, 82 (2010), pp. 87–104; Range, *Music*.

82. On British music, nationalism and Purcell's role, see Blanning, *Music*, pp. 240–5. For the continuing influence of this theme within coronations, see the music of Queen Victoria's coronation in *The Order of the Music, &c. to be performed at the Coronation, June 26, 1838* (London, 1838). For modern political and musical analogies and uses of counterpoint cf. D. Barenboim and E. W. Said (ed. A. Guzelimian), *Parallels and Paradoxes: Explorations in Music and Society* (London, 2004); E. W. Said, *Musical Elaborations* (London, 1991); E. W. Said, *Culture and Imperialism* (London, 1993); Copland, *Music*. The power of music as a force for peace is evident in the creation of the West-Eastern Divan Orchestra by Barenboim and Said *c*.1999. In an historic concert at Ramallah, in 2005, Barenboim poignantly underlined the necessity to recognise the different 'narratives' and 'voices' of the 'one' and the 'other'.
83. Turner, *Sermon*, p. 15.
84. P. Hopkins, 'Turner, Francis (1637–1700)', *ODNB*.
85. Turner, *Sermon*, p. 10.
86. *Ibid.*, p. 12.
87. *Ibid.*, p. 11.
88. *Ibid.*
89. *Ibid.*
90. *Ibid.*, p. 15.
91. *Ibid.*, p. 8.
92. *Ibid.*, p. 14.
93. *Ibid.*, p. 16.
94. *Ibid.*
95. *Ibid.*
96. *Ibid.*
97. M. Greig, 'Burnet, Gilbert (1643–1715)', *ODNB*. See also L. G. Schwoerer, 'The Transformation of the 1689 Convention into a Parliament', *Parliamentary History*, 3 (1984), pp. 57–76. See also NRS, Campbell Papers, MS GD112/39/145/2 (on the conversion of the Convention into a Parliament).
98. *TLG*, 11–14 February 1688/1689 (no. 2427). See also Schwoerer, 'Coronation', pp. 107–11. For the proclamation declaring William and

Mary joint rulers of Scotland, see Anon., *A Proclamation* [11 April 1689], *Declaring William and Mary, King and Queen of England, to be King and Queen of Scotland* (Edinburgh, 1689).

99. T. Claydon, 'The Sermon Culture of the Glorious Revolution: Williamite Preaching and Jacobite Anti-preaching, 1685–1702', in McCullough, *Sermon*, p. 484.
100. B. Bevan, *King William III: Prince of Orange, the First European* (London, *c.*1997), p. 114.
101. J. Van Der Kiste, *William and Mary: The Heroes of the Glorious Revolution* (new edn, Stroud, 2008).
102. Both, of course, important constitutionalists: P. Langford, 'Burke, Edmund (1729/30–1797)', *ODNB* and R. Cosgrove, 'Dicey, Albert Venn (1835–1922)', *ibid.* See also A. V. Dicey, *Introduction to the Study of the Law of the Constitution* (9th edition, London, 1945).
103. McCullough, *Sermon*, pp. 533–4 (App. I).
104. G. Burnet, *A Sermon Preached at the Coronation of William III. and Mary II. King and Queen of England, ... France, and Ireland ..., April 11. 1689* (London, 1689), p. 2. See also S. Taylor, 'State formation, political stability and the revolution of 1688', in T. Harris, & S. Taylor (eds.), *The final crisis of the Stuart monarchy. The revolutions of 1688–1691 in their British, Atlantic and European contexts* (Woodbridge, 2013), pp. 273–304.
105. Burnet, *Sermon*, p. 5.
106. *Ibid.*, p. 6.
107. Sturdy, 'Sermons', pp. 76–7.
108. *Ibid.*, pp. 72–3.
109. Burnet, *Sermon*, p. 29.
110. *Ibid.*, p. 10. For details of the Act of Parliament see T. Harris, *Revolution: The Great Crisis of the British Monarchy, 1685–1720* (London, 2006), pp. 356–7 (on the Coronation oath). See 'An Act for Establishing the Coronation Oath' (1 William & Mary c. 6, printed in *SR*, VI pp. 56–7).
111. P. D. Halliday, 'Jeffreys, George, 1st baron Jeffreys (1645–1689)', *ODNB.*
112. Burnet, *Sermon*, p. 12.
113. 'But let justice roll down like waters, and righteousness like an ever-flowing stream' (Amos 5:24). Agatha Christie's *Nemesis* (1971) quotes this beautiful passage. The desire of the novel is for 'justice' to be done whatever the results: a father desires to know whether his son is guilty or not, even if it may cause his son's punishment. For translation to a legal context, see T. Bingham, *The Rule of Law* (London, 2010).
114. Burnet, *Sermon*, p. 12.

115. Claydon, 'Burnet'. On 'hijacking the calendar of Stuart legitimacy' for 'dual Protestant providences' see also Claydon, 'The Sermon Culture', p. 485.
116. Burnet, *Sermon*, p. 16.
117. *Ibid.*, p. 19.
118. *Ibid.*, p. 23.
119. *Ibid.*, p. 20.
120. *Ibid.*, p. 26.
121. *Ibid.*, p. 28.
122. *Ibid.*, p. 29.
123. Claydon, 'The Sermon Culture', p. 484.
124. J. Sharp, *A Sermon [on Isa. xlix. 23] Preach'd at the Coronation of Queen Anne, in the Abby-Church of Westminster, April 23, 1702* (London, 1702), p. 2.
125. *Ibid.*, p. 8.
126. B. Till, 'Sharp, John (1645?–1714)', *ODNB*; G. V. Bennett, *White Kennett, 1660–1728, Bishop of Peterborough: A Study in the Political and Ecclesiastical History of the Early Eighteenth Century* (London, 1957), p. 113. Cf. Edie, 'Public Face', pp. 324–5.
127. N. Menin, *The Form, Order and Ceremonies, Used at the Investiture of all the Sovereign Princes of Europe: With the Whole Ceremony of the Grand Anointing and Coronation of the Present King of France ...* (London, 1727), p. 221. Cf. BL, Add. MS 6336; Anon., *Form of Proceeding*.
128. Sharp, *Sermon*, p. 2.
129. Edie, 'Public Face', p. 327: 'Staunch Jacobites, of course, recognized James II's son James III at his father's death in September 1701. But they were few and in 1702 posed no serious threat to Anne's accession. There was a flurry of activity in Scotland at William's death, but there the issue was not so much Queen Anne as her potential successor and the proposed union with England'.
130. Sharp, *Sermon*, p. 3; G. J. Schochet, *Patriarchalism in Political Thought: the Authoritarian Family and Political Speculation and Attitudes Especially in Seventeenth-Century England* (Oxford, 1975), p. 218.
131. Asch, *Sacral Kingship*, p. 42 and P. Lake, "The King (The Queen) and the Jesuit: James Stuart's 'True Law of Free Monarchies' in Context/s." *Transactions of the Royal Historical Society*, 14 (2004), p. 259. See also Sommerville, *Political Writings*, and *Political Works*; see also A. Pečar, *Macht der Schrift. Politischer Biblizismus in Schottland und England zwischen Reformation and Bürgerkrieg (1534–1642)* (Munich, 2011); and D. Fishclin and M. Fortier (eds), *Royal Subjects: Essays on the Writings of James VI and I* (Detroit, Michigan, 2002). See also J. Wormald, 'James VI and I, *Basilikon Doron* and *The Trew Law of Free Monarchies*: The

Scottish Context and the English Translation', in L. L. Peck (ed.), *The Mental World of the Jacobean Court* (Cambridge, 1991), pp. 36–54.

132. J. Hone, 'The Last Stuart Coronation', p. 140. See also F. Heal, 'What Can King Lucius Do For You? The Reformation and the Early British Church', *English Historical Review*, 120 (2005), 593–614. See also E. Gregg, *Queen Anne* (2nd edn, New Haven, Connecticut, and London, 2001), p. 154.
133. Edie, 'Public Face', p. 325.
134. Sharp, *Sermon*, p. 11.
135. Edie, 'Public Face', p. 327.
136. R. von Friedeburg, 'Reformation of Manners and the Social Composition of Offenders in an East Anglian Cloth Village: Earls Colne, Essex, 1531–1642', *JBS*, 29 (1990), pp. 347–85, and R. Hutton, *The Rise and Fall of Merry England: The Ritual Year 1400–1700* (Oxford, 1994), pp. 111–52.
137. Cf. D. W. Bebbington, *The Dominance of Evangelicalism: the Age of Spurgeon and Moody* (Leicester, 2005); I. C. Bradley, *The Call to Seriousness: The Evangelical Impact on the Victorians* (London, 1976); M. A. Noll, *The Rise of Evangelicalism: the Age of Edwards, Whitefield and the Wesleys* (Nottingham, 2004).
138. Sharp, *Sermon*, p. 7.
139. *Ibid.*
140. Bilson, *A Sermon … at their Coronations on Saint James his Day*, sig. [B5].
141. Sharp, *Sermon*, p. 9.
142. *Ibid.*
143. *Ibid.*, p. 10.
144. *Ibid.*
145. *Ibid.*, pp. 13–14.
146. *Ibid.*, p. 14.
147. *Ibid.*
148. *Ibid.*, p. 10.
149. Colley, *Britons*, *passim.*
150. W. Talbot, *A Sermon* [on Ps. cxviii. 24, 25] *Preach'd at the Coronation of King George, … October the 20th, 1714* (London, 1714), p. 17.
151. M. Johnson, 'Talbot, William (1659–1730)', *ODNB*, citing C. E. Doble, *et al.* (eds), *Remarks and Collections of Thomas Hearne …*, 11 volumes, Oxford Historical Society, 2, 7, 13, 34, 42, 43, 48, 50, 65, 67, 72 (Oxford, 1885–1921), IV p. 422.
152. Talbot, *Sermon*, p. 14.
153. *Ibid.*
154. *Ibid.*, p. 19.
155. *Ibid.*, p. 21.

156. *Ibid.*, p. 29.
157. *Ibid.*, p. 22.
158. *Ibid.*, p. 23.
159. *Ibid.*, p. 26.
160. See above p. 27.
161. Talbot, *Sermon*, p. 28.
162. *Ibid.*, p. 27.
163. *Ibid.*, pp. 30–1.
164. *Ibid.*, p. 31.
165. S. Browne, *Religion and Loyalty. A Sermon Preach'd January 30, 1715/16, etc.* (London, 1716), pp. 24–5. Cf. M. McCormack, 'Rethinking "Loyalty" in Eighteenth-Century Britain', *Journal for Eighteenth-Century Studies*, 35 (2012), pp. 407–21.
166. Shapiro, 'Assize Sermons', pp. 1, 8.
167. D. Burrows, 'Handel, George Frideric (1685–1759)', *ODNB*.
168. L. Laborie, *Enlightening Enthusiasm: Prophecy and Religious Experience in Early Eighteenth-Century England* (Manchester, 2015), pp. 135–7.
169. J. Winter, *A Sermon Preached at East Dearham in Norf. May 29 1661. Being the Day of the Coronation of our Most Gracious Soveraign Lord King Charles the Second, &c.* (London, 1662), p. 38. On John Winter MA, who was curate at East Dereham, see Clergy of the Church of England Database Person ID 129188.
170. Bodl., MS Eng. letters e. 29, fol. 8r (J. Tyleton to Matthew Henry, Trinity College, Oxford, 6 May 1685). The preacher was rector of St Aldate's Oxford and Lady Margaret professor of divinity, on whom, see W. Marshall, 'Hall, John (1633–1710)', *ODNB*.
171. L. Beaulieu, *A Sermon on the Coronation-Day, April 23 1702. Preach'd in the Cathedral Church of Glocester, before the Mayor and Corporation* (London, 1702). See G. Goodwin (rev. E. Major), 'Beaulieu, Luke de (1644/5–1723)', *ODNB*.
172. Beaulieu, *Sermon*, p. 13.
173. *Ibid.*, p. 19.
174. Strong, *Coronation*, p. 339.
175. Sturdy, 'Sermons', p. 81.
176. Edie, *Public Face*, p. 312.
177. D. L. Wykes, 'Rosewell, Samuel (1679–1722)', *ODNB*; Rosewell, *Sermon*.
178. *Ibid.*, p. 10.
179. *Ibid.*, p. 13.
180. *Ibid.*, p. 12.
181. *Ibid.*, p. 21 (my emphasis).
182. *Ibid.*, p. 24.
183. Sturdy, 'Sermons', p. 81.

184. Sturdy, "Continuity", p. 243.
185. N. Dixon, 'The Church of England and the Coronation Rite, 1761–1838', *Church History*, 90 (2021), at 'abstract' p. 98.
186. *Ibid.*, p. 102, quoting E. Venables-Vernon, *A Sermon preached at the Coronation of King George IV. in the Abbey Church of Westminster July XIX, M.DCCC.XXI* (London, 1821), pp. 6–7.
187. Dixon, 'The Church of England and the Coronation Rite', p. 102, quoting C. J. Blomfield, *A Sermon preached at the Coronation of Their Most Excellent Majesties King William IV. and Queen Adelaide in the Abbey Church of Westminster September VIII. MDCCCXXXI* (London, 1831), pp. 7–8.
188. Dixon, 'The Church of England and the Coronation Rite', pp. 106–7, quoting J. H. Gurney, *A Sermon, preached in Lutterworth Church, on Thursday, June 28, 1838, being the Day of Her Most Gracious Majesty's Coronation* (Leicester, 1838), pp. 12–18.
189. Dixon, 'The Church of England and the Coronation Rite', p. 107, quoting S. J. Allen, *A Sermon, preached at Burnley Church, on Sunday, July 1, 1838, on occasion of the Coronation of Her Most Gracious Majesty, Queen Victoria* (London, 1838), p. 16.
190. Dixon, 'The Church of England and the Coronation Rite', p. 107, quoting Blomfield, *A Sermon preached at the Coronation*, pp. 6–7. See also N. Dixon, 'The Evolution of the British Coronation Rite, 1761–1953' in A. Kalinowska, J. Spangler and P. Tyszka (eds), *Power and Ceremony in European History: Rituals, Practices and Representative Bodies since the Late Medieval Age* (London, 2021), pp. 54–55.
191. Dixon, 'The Church of England and the Coronation Rite', p. 115.
192. F. W. Farrar and J. B. C. Murphy *et al.*, *Sermons for The Coronation of King Edward VII* (London, 1902).
193. Rabbi I. H. Daiches, *Sermon on the Coronation of Their Gracious Majesties, King Edward VII. and Queen Alexandra … On Saturday, August 9th, 1902 …* (Leeds, 1902).
194. LPL, Lang 288, p. 138. See also reference to the sermon in *Dominion*, 4 (Issue 1161) (23 June 1911), p. 5 & *Supplement to TLG*, 26–27 September 1911 (referencing 22 June 1911), https://www.thegazette.co.uk/London/issue/28535/supplement/7077, accessed 22 November 2025; and on Lang, see R. Beaken, *Cosmo Lang: Archbishop in War and Crisis* (London, 2012).
195. E. Owens, *The Family Firm: Monarchy, Mass Media and the British Public, 1932–53* (London, 2019), p. 156.
196. *Ibid.*, p. 157 – citing LPL, Lang 22, fol. 372, C. Bardsley to C. G. Lang, 16 Apr. 1937; & '[o]ne of the 3 main distributors claimed to have sold 1.5 million copies of the forms of service, which included servicing one

tenth of all the parishes in England' (LPL, Lang 22, fols. 308–9, W. K. Lowther Clarke to A. C. Don, 31 May 1937 and reply).

197. Dr J. H. Hertz, *King George VI: Coronation Sermon* (London, 1937).
198. Strong, *Coronation*, p. 477.
199. *Ibid.*, pp. 499–500.
200. *Authorised Liturgy for the Coronation Rite of His Majesty King Charles III* [with commentary], p. 13.
201. See for examples: C. Davies, 9 April 2023, https://www.theguardian.com/uk-news/2023/apr/09/king-charles-iii-coronation-procession-route#:~:text=In%20keeping%20with%20the%20king's,about%205%20miles%2C%20taking%20in, accessed 22 November 2025; S. Coughlan, 11 October 2022, https://www.bbc.co.uk/news/uk-63172425, accessed 22 November 2025; H. Dixon and G. Narwan, 13 September 2022, https://www.telegraph.co.uk/royal-family/2022/09/13/charles-coronation-prince-king-monarchy-when-plans-cost-living/#:~:text=Sources%20have%20said%20that%20the,was%20only%20announced%20this%20year, accessed 22 November 2025.
202. *Authorised Liurgy for the Coronation Rite … Charles III*, p. 13.
203. https://www.archbishopofcanterbury.org/speaking-writing/speeches/archbishop-canterburys-sermon-coronation-king-charles-iii#:~:text=The%20unity%20you%20show%2C%20the,give%20our%20lives%20to%20others, accessed 22 November 2025.
204. *Ibid.*

PART II

Oaths & Objects

CHAPTER 3

Contracting: *Recognitio*, Acclamation and the Coronation Oath

The crowning is perhaps the most famous part of British coronations.[1] Yet, easily overlooked —and equally important—is the coronation oath, which has been a fundamental component of the rite since medieval times.[2] The coronation oath is of such significance that the remainder of the ceremony cannot take place unless it has been sworn. Why? It is because the oath is the essential counterpart to the *recognitio* or recognition and acclamation. The recognition is the moment at the beginning of the ceremony when the monarch is presented to the people for approval, and the acclamation is the moment in which the people correspondingly accept the new monarch. These three elements, the three acts of the coronation drama, combine to establish a contractual relationship between monarch and peoples. By public commitment to the promises and values enshrined in the oath, the sovereign is forming a bond to the state, and to the largely uncodified British constitution.

The English oath was enshrined in statute in the 'Coronation Oath Act 1689', calling upon William III and Mary II, as joint sovereigns, to swear to the revised text and this was also made a legal requirement in further legislation: 'The Act of Settlement 1700/1' and the 'Accession Declaration Act 1910'; both oblige the ruler to take the Coronation Oath.[3] In order properly to contextualise this oath, it is necessary to go back to the Middle Ages. The English Coronation Oath is startling in its basic immutability—there have been many subtle alterations since the days of Edward the Confessor, but the core promises remain. Nevertheless, the path to change

G. W. C. Gross, *Crown and People*,
https://doi.org/10.1007/978-3-032-20786-9_3

was dramatic and the nuances of considerable significance, as this chapter will reveal.

What was established in 1689 would endure, and well over two hundred years later Elizabeth II swore an almost identical version in 1953, and so too King Charles III in 2023. Yet few people are aware of the oath's exact nature, fewer still that it is one of the world's greatest legal obligations, akin to a contract, with origins dating as far back as the Anglo-Saxons, and perhaps even fewer that the monarch swears not one, but two Coronation Oaths: one for Great Britain and the Commonwealth (the English oath) and a separate one for Scotland. In fact, these oaths, at their heart, cement the religious and political positions of the Churches of England and Scotland, laying the foundations for the Church and State settlements of both countries. The division of the oaths is all the more intriguing given the great constitutional debates of the 2010s. There is nothing new in what we are seeing: political manoeuvring, discussions about power sharing and questions about the royal prerogative.

The sovereign's oath is one of the shortest elements in a Westminster Abbey coronation service, uttered in a moment, and perhaps barely remembered by those near enough to hear it (in the days before radio and television), yet it is of fundamental constitutional importance. The recension emerging from the Middle Ages had a complicated transmission history: modified either actually or abortively, either overtly or secretively. For some coronations, the precise text is altogether obscure. Nevertheless, the oath has been invoked at moments of acute political crisis. Controversy has long swirled around its meaning and status. Nothing about it is inconsequential. Moreover, Presbyterian Scotland generated its own highly distinctive oath, with significant ramifications, not least given the 1603 union of the two Crowns and, in time, the union of the two nations. In tracing key historical developments, this chapter reinforces the importance of contract within a coronation and the significant analogy of the sovereign marrying the state, for the Coronation Oath should be seen as akin to a contract, and as a development of Magna Carta.

To understand the Coronation Oath, it is crucial that the oath be contextualised within the rest of the coronation rite, which places it, according to tradition, after the contractual acclamation and before the sacral (consecration) stages of anointing and crowning. Yet, despite these quasi-democratic roots, we shall see that there were also Divine Right elements ever-present in the oath, and that this was not incompatible to the contractual elements. This book therefore disputes the Whig theory that 1689 saw a total shift to a constitutional oath and monarchy. The developments that were seen were reinforcements of an existing tradition, but brought up-to-date to deal with Stuart absolutism (not the concept of Divine Right) and Roman Catholicism under James II. As often neglected in the history of British coronations, and so too relegated in discussion of the 2023 coronation, this chapter highlights the fact that by 1714 there were two distinct Coronation Oaths. The development of this tradition long before (and surviving after) the Act of Union rested on the changes that took place in the Tudor and early Stuart dynasty.

Introduction

Let us turn first to 'breach of contract', for even before we reach the Glorious Revolution of 1688–9, the charge that the Coronation Oath had been broken was prominent in proceedings for the removal of three kings of England.[4] Although some readers may have been taught that Edward II 'abdicated' the throne in 1327, the best modern reconstruction of events, by Valente, convincingly shows

> not only that a deposition did take place, but [also] that some contemporaries reinvented it as an abdication, recognizing the need to fit the sometimes ugly practice of politics into more acceptable paradigms of kingship and consultation.

The first overt suggestion that Edward be forced out came when the lord mayor and citizens of London wrote to the magnates and prelates orchestrating affairs at Westminster urging them to crown the king's eldest son 'and to depose his father for frequent offences against his oath'. Sure enough: that the oath had been flouted features in the formal list of accusations levelled against Edward II.[5] While legitimate doubts have been cast over some elements of the 'official' account of Richard II's deposition in 1399, the essential truth of the thirty-three charges is not in question. It has been argued that the 'pre-eminent theme' running through the lengthy document is the king's faithlessness: five charges deal with his contravention of the Coronation Oath (the text of which prefaces the entire list) and another of having disregarded Magna Carta. Overall, says Theilmann, twenty-one of the charges 'addressed Richard's deceit in general, lies to specific individuals and violation of the laws and customs of

England'. He singles out one charge (the twenty-fifth) for full quotation because it is so devastatingly all-encompassing. It bears repetition here:

> Item: the king was so variable and dissimulating in both word and letter, and so inconstant in his behaviour, especially in his dealings with the pope, and with kings, and with lords and others both within and beyond his own kingdom, that virtually no living person who came to know him could or wished to trust him. Indeed, so faithless and deceitful was he reputed to be, that he was a scandal not just to his own person and to the whole realm, but above all to foreigners throughout the world who heard about him.[6]

Such lines are a worthy reminder for those that decry the modern politician, that it has perhaps been ever thus!

The charges laid against Charles I in 1649 begin by declaring that he had been

> **admitted** king of England, and therein trusted with a limited power to govern by and according to the laws of the land, and not otherwise; and by his trust, oath, and office ... **obliged** to use the power committed to him for the good and benefit of the people, and for the preservation of their rights and liberties[.]

Yet, Charles Stuart had allegedly pursued

> a wicked design to erect and uphold in himself an unlimited and tyrannical power to rule according to his will, and to overthrow the rights and liberties of the people, yea, to ... make void the foundations thereof, and of all redress and remedy of misgovernment, which by the fundamental constitutions of this kingdom were reserved on the people's behalf in the right and power of frequent ... Parliaments, or national meetings in Council[.][7]

In all three cases, the crux of the problem was the clash between a strong monarchy and an incompetent monarch. Monarchical government had developed earlier and more rapidly in England than in most medieval European realms, so that, by the beginning of the fourteenth century, English kings 'were at the head of a highly centralized legal and policing system which was the chief peacekeeping agency right down to village level'. Indeed, in many respects, 'the State' had become too impressive. As Carpenter explains,

> the king's power to do harm or good was so great that it simply was not possible to manage without him, as was effectively the case under Stephen in the mid-twelfth century, or even as late as the early 1270s, during the absence of Edward I on crusade. ... A deeply fallible or dangerous king was too dangerous to be endured indefinitely.[8]

It should come as no surprise to learn that at moments of political crisis in the seventeenth century, commentators sought medieval precedents. In 1629, their relationship having seriously deteriorated, a furious Charles I dissolved Parliament for what would turn out to be the eleven years of 'personal rule'.[9] That same year, Sir Francis Hubert published his verse *Historie of Edward the Second*, which contains these telling lines:

> And therefore, though we have Prerogatives,
> Yet there are certaine limits to the same.
> Which keepes not Kings from being Superlative
> To sway (as Gods Lieue-tenants) this faire frame
> And those Aspirers merit death and shame,
> That doe repine against those supreame powers
> Whom God hath made his underlings, not ours
>
> Yet grant their State free from coercive force,
> That gives not lawlesse libertie in all,
> Kings must observe a just and rightfull course.
> God is their King, by whom they stand or fall.
> Who all their acts to strickt account will call.
> Besides, their Oath, their vertue, their Renowne
> Are Diamantine chaines to tye a Crowne.[10]

In 1689, there appeared a book on the depositions of Edward II and Richard II, printing (from the Parliament Rolls, translated into English where necessary) the official articles exhibited against both kings; a vernacular version of the Coronation Oath is also reproduced.[11] One common factor linking Edward II, Richard II, and Charles I (at least) was the problem of what Conrad Russell called 'diminished majesty'. Under the last of these rulers, respect had dissipated to such an extent by 1642 that, as Lord Brooke put it, even some of the king's closest servants had 'had the courage almost to despit him to his face'.[12] There were many reasons, specific to each context, why majesty had become diminished, but at the centre of the phenomenon was the perception that the king could no longer be trusted. He could no longer be trusted because, above all, he was seen to have broken the Coronation Oath sworn solemnly at the High Altar of Westminster Abbey. Until the Glorious Revolution, this was the only oath ever sworn by a sovereign. Now there are three.

Conversely, what can be said of those monarchs who were never sworn and crowned as already discussed in the introduction? In the twentieth century, for the few in the know, Edward VIII was perhaps well on the way to diminishing majesty without the help of Wallis Simpson. What kind of man, for the sake of the visibility of his hair parting, ignores the tradition whereby the direction of portrait profiles on the coinage alternates by reign? Although he swore the Scottish Oath immediately upon accession, the royal family was relieved that the process of inauguration did not go much further than the abortive design of new coins.[13]

Clearly, the Coronation Oath is of considerable constitutional significance: on the one hand, it has been deployed effectively against delinquent kings; on the other, monarchs who have not undergone coronation do not seem fully sovereign, notwithstanding their legal status. A qualitative transformation occurs in the service. In fact, two transformative moments may be isolated, very important in different ways: the swearing of the oath and the anointing. This Chapter is concerned with the first moment (the earlier Chap. 1 with the latter). It seeks to explain why the Coronation Oath has constitutional ramifications. Before those ramifications can become clear, however, one must locate the oath-swearing within the broader framework of a normative Westminster Abbey coronation.

Context

When one thinks of a coronation, one perhaps immediately thinks of the crowning as the most important element of the complex of events, whereas, in fact, the three most important aspects of a British coronation are arguably the acclamation, the Coronation Oath and the anointing. Why?

The Coronation Oath is of immense significance because it is a conditional element with which a monarch must comply if they are to proceed with the rest of the ceremony. It is the crucial follow-up to the acclamation. The danger in a discussion of the Coronation Oath is that it potentially isolates it from the rest of the service. To see the full implications of its role, we must be aware of its place. The oath comes at the heart of the service, before the anointing and crowning, and investiture with the regalia and needs to be seen in quasi-contractual terms, as will be explained shortly. No monarch crowned in Westminster Abbey has avoided this requirement. To break with this tradition would be a 'radical' step. Intriguingly for all of the critical importance and statutory requirement for the Coronation Oath, it receives little more coverage than the presentation of the Bible in the official Lambeth commentary for the liturgy, with no mention of contract.[14]

Having located the oath within the context of a typical coronation service, we are now better able to see its role as a form of contract. The acclamation or recognition involved a question from the officiating archbishop/bishop that asked the Abbey congregation if it recognized the person(s) about to be crowned as monarch(s). Those present then, in response, quite literally acclaimed the new sovereign as their monarch with the cry of 'God save the King/Queen'. Hence, both spiritual and temporal authorities combined for this authorization of rule. One must therefore keep in mind, when we turn to the question of contract, that the Coronation Oath is the follow-up to this acclamation and only takes place on the basis of popular consent. For now, we turn to the medieval background which helped cement this contract tradition.

The Medieval Background

The history of the English Coronation Oath begins with the fusion of the Anglo-Saxon custom of the Witan 'election' of a monarch with the Frankish, Norman tradition of an oath.[15] According to Schramm, it was this assimilation that led to 'permanent success' and 'the adoption of the oath of allegiance', beginning with King Edmund (920/1–946).[16] This early oath bound both parties together: loyalty from the people and a *mandatum regis* from the monarch. In Schramm's words,

> the fundamental obligations of ... Teutonic kingship [were] ... the preservation of peace, the removal of wrongdoing, and the establishment of justice.[17]

It was from these beginnings that the English tradition of an oath was born and with time, like common law, it evolved, accumulating precedent. Although its origins can be found in the feudal election of a monarch, perhaps thanks to the depiction in the Bayeux Tapestry and William the Conqueror's success over King Harold—following Harold's alleged abandonment of an oath—the Coronation Oath became a cornerstone in the making of an English and later British monarch. As this was coupled with the presence of key representatives of the country, it assumed even greater significance, drawing all parts of society together in the making of a sovereign and in 'binding the conscience' of that person in their 'outward … acknowledgement of [their] obligation' to the realm.[18]

In the case of Young King Henry in 1170, after 'the oath came the *recognitio*, whereby one of the bishops asked the people if they were willing to submit him as their ruler and obey his commands, to which they replied, "We wish it and grant it so (*Volumus et concedimus*)"'.[19] Such a moment

> reflected the element of election inherent in the king-making process. Kingship in England was less truly elective than in the empire, yet it was not nominal, as the circumstances of both King Stephen's accession in 1135 and the dramatic events of 1141 had so forcefully revealed. Blood right and designation by the previous ruler did not always guarantee a smooth succession, and the support of a majority of the nobility was essential.[20]

There are numerous coronation *ordos*, all showing the fusion of various elements, whether Anglo-Saxon tradition or Frankish influence or papal continental ideas. An *ordo* is a ceremonial directory, a collection of rubrics to order a service or office and for a coronation 'comprises a liturgical sequence of prayers and blessings by which various actions are given sacramental significance, in particular by invoking divine sanction, blessings and the descent of the gifts of the Holy Spirit upon the person chosen as king'.[21] For our purposes, four need discussion.[22]

(a) The 'Fulrad' *ordo* takes its name from Abbot Fulrad of the Abbey of St Vaast at Arras, a friend of St Dunstan (responsible for early Anglo-Saxon *ordines* and the *mandatum regis* for King Edgar's 973 coronation) and was created *c.*980. It was adopted as the main rite for French coronations *c.*1100. It remained as the model for French coronations until the end of French monarchical rule; although with significant alterations, as late as 1825 Charles X's oath ultimately derived from this source. For countries that would be at war for centuries, it is perhaps rather ironic that the very rites according to which their sovereigns would be crowned were born of Anglo-Saxon and Frankish influences.[23]

(b) The 'Anselm' *ordo* developed out of a battle over clerical and lay power, notably between Henry I and Archbishop Anselm

Fig. 3.1 Nineteenth-century stained glass showing the coronation of King Edgar, Bath Abbey. Edgar was the first king of England, crowned in AD 973 by St. Dunstan, Alamy

(*c*.1100–1107). It was possibly used for Henry I's coronation in 1100, almost certainly for that of Stephen in 1135 and from 1154 onwards. The papacy did not wish to see priests relegated to an inferior position in relation to monarchical authority: a coronation seemed to elevate the status of a layperson above the clergy. Thus, the 'Anselm' *ordo* saw the further encroachment of continental tradition. The papal German *ordo* of Mainz (961)[24] was used as the basis for substitutions for those Anglo-Saxon traditions not consistent with clerical aims, notably the anointing of the monarch's head with chrism, which was revised to encompass hands, shoulders, and arms. The oath, although possibly enlarged, was not permanently redrawn.[25]

(c) The *Leges Anglorum Saeculi XIII Ineuntis Collectae* is a legal book, compiled *c*.1100–*c*.1250 'apparently in London', in substance containing the jurisprudence of coronation *ordines.* It includes a paragraph entitled *quid sit officum regis*, developed into a chapter *de iure et appendicitis corone regni Britanniae*. The chapter specifies a series of fresh rules governing the Coronation Oath, insisting that it be sworn on the gospels and holy relics, in the eyes of the people. The content may be summarised thus: (1) 'The property of the Crown cannot be alienated: if alienated, it must be recovered'; (2) 'The king must rule right, that is to say according to law, and not according to his own will nor arbitrarily, but *per iudicium procerum regni*'; (3) 'The king must fear God, keep his laws, protect the Church according to her ancient right; and (4) 'The king must maintain good laws and customs and abolish bad ones. He must further render true justice and maintain equity *per consilium procerum regni sui*'. These alterations owe their genesis to French traditions and the constitutional arrangements surrounding the rule of King John (1167–1216),[26] not least the signing of Magna Carta (1215).[27]

(d) The Fourth Recension[28] has received considerable coverage owing to better record survival, enabling us to 'trace without great difficulty the stages of its development'. It has also been debated whether or not the oath was taken in Latin or French.[29] According to Richardson, French was replaced by English in the fifteenth century, as can be seen from material connected with Richard III's coronation, which includes an abbreviated English rendering of the text.[30] The final decisive shift to English came with Edward VI's crowning[31] and the round is thought to have been completed with Elizabeth I's coronation, which, according to Bowers, contained biblical readings and the Eucharist in the vernacular.[32] Importantly, the fourth recension refers to the duties of key officers on coronation day, such as the almoner, pointing to the significant role of the Court of Claims. This recension emerged as the 'Lytlington' *ordo* (*c*.1377).[33] The oath here was based on that of Edward II and made provision for an addition by the archbishop.[34] It also set out that 'either the metropolitan or another bishop should officiate over the coronation ceremony', underscoring the religious nature of proceedings.[35] A fifth clause was included in the form of a call by the bishops to reinforce clerical rights. Phillips argues that the controversial fourth clause was part of a wider goal of 'reconciliation' by Edward II, in which he would offer to 'maintain future legislation provided that it was properly approved by himself and the community of the realm', in essence a form of 'charter'.[36] Here, we clearly see the oath as a type of contract. This revised Coronation Oath also emphasised 'the sacred quality of [the] monarchy' by placing significant emphasis on St Edward: existing laws were 'described symbolically' as his and Edward II was to take his oath close to the Confessor's shrine; the regalia was also connected with the royal saint.[37] These traditions would endure into the early modern era and to the present.

As can be seen, the Middle Ages saw considerable developments regarding the Coronation Oath. Two legacies were that the oath was a type of contract between ruler and people and that the ceremony was as much religious as secular. The most detailed scholarship on the medieval English Coronation Oath remains that of Richardson.[38] His analysis shows how this evolution was anything but systematic, instead involving sporadic bursts of change, followed by long periods of continuity; essentially, there was an organic unfolding, rather than a carefully planned and executed maturation. Richardson points to Edward I's coronation for an example of an addition to the accustomed vows, namely an undertaking that the sovereign would 'preserve the rights of the kingship ... unimpaired, and that nothing affecting the rights of the Crown would be done without the counsel of the prelates and great men of the realm'.[39] Although this addition may have been used for Edward I's coronation and that of Henry III's previously, the 'Anselm' *ordo's* oath remained ever present. More pressing was the matter of anointing, which had been radically recast following the clash between Anselm and Henry I; the former had endeavoured permanently to remove the use of unction, thereby diminishing the monarch's divinity.[40] Unction is 'the action of anointing with oil as a religious rite or symbol'.[41] Anointing, which is dealt with in Chap. 1, is mentioned here because it was an essential part of the sacred nature of the coronation service, thereby further sanctifying the oath owing to its biblical origins: not only the obvious example of Zadok the Priest anointing Solomon, but also the precedent of Melchizedek as priestly sovereign.[42]

We should also note Sturdy's work on continuity and change within medieval and early modern coronations, specifically the February 1307/1308 Coronation Oath.[43] He explains that (against much misunderstanding) the new fourth clause was designed to stop the king reneging (as Edward I had done) on his undertakings; it was not committing him in the first place to accept whatever the people would choose—his veto remained, but the point is that it was future legislation that was at issue. This was definitely a quasi-contractual obligation and the barons held him to it.[44] Furthermore, Sturdy summarizes Brückmann's work, which has been ignored by modern scholarship, probably because it was unpublished.[45] His *précis* shows that Brückmann strongly endorsed the idea that the February 1307/1308 oath imposed (to quote Sturdy) 'severe limitations on the power of the king'.[46]

In addition to the four *ordos*, Richardson highlights the frequent issuing of coronation charters, from Henry I to Henry III, and suggests that Magna Carta should be interpreted in this light, as a form of coronation charter, since it was re-issued in 1216 at the start of Henry III's reign.[47] The Coronation Oath became more important precisely because it replaced a charter. This is especially true with regard to the oath's first clause—referring to laws and customs—since Magna Carta was taken to have been absorbed into common law. Such a practice further indicates the contractual nature of the medieval oath—holding the king in check both by the barons and by the papacy: the very things that Henry VIII would later seek to revise.[48] It is also worth noting linguistic change, from a Latin and a French text to a Coronation Oath in English.

For the early modern period, the codification of coronations is to be found in the authoritative *Liber Regalis* (*c.*1390). It was rather limited in scope, generic and in Latin and was therefore extended into an all-encompassing English order, entitled the 'Little Device', for Richard III's coronation, detailing not only the coronation, but also the events of the day before.[49] What we might recognise as the Coronation Oath in the present owes its creation, in relation to the Gospel, to revisions considered under the Tudors and implemented under the early Stuarts, and it is to the first of those royal houses that we now turn.

The Early Modern Era: The Tudors

Henry VII's Coronation Oath in his 'Little Device' follows the 1483 English text, combining what is found in the 'Lytlington' *ordo* with the French tradition of the 'Fulrad' *ordo* and the *Leges Anglorum*. The last section, the 'bishops' admonition',[50] sets out a crucial tenet for our purposes, that of confirming Church rights:

> Keepe to us and to eche of us the privilegis of lawe canon and of holye chirch and due lawe and rightfulnesse and us and theim defende as a devoute

> Christen kinge ought to do and in like wise to graunt and do thorough alle your realme to every bysshop abbot and to all the chirches to theim committed.[51]

This was an exceptionally important adage, for it would ultimately permit a phraseology that could disjoin itself from asserting the freedoms granted by the papacy to the clergy, and recognised by former kings, to uphold instead a national Established Church. Referring to the whole text, and not just this last part, Schramm usefully concludes:

> The underlying meaning of the coronation oath at the end of the Middle Ages … [was] … that the ruler recognizes … that he is under the law.[52]

The Coronation Oath as found in the *Liber Regalis* and derivatives such as the 'Little Device' was clearly not satisfactory for Henry VIII and a new draft was prepared, though it was seemingly never used. Indeed, according to Schramm, 'the text that Henry corrected … was not the traditional coronation oath, but a form allied to it' and was therefore 'never authoritative'.[53] Nevertheless, the king's corrections are still significant because they reveal his view of the contractual nature of the oath in relation to royal power. In the latter section, corrected by Henry, the document states, his insertions here printed in italics:

> And that he shall graunte to holde lawes and *approvyd* customes of the realme and *lawfull and not preiudiciall to hys crowne or imperiall juris*[diction] to his power/kepe them and affirme them which the *noblys* and people have made and chosen *w*[ith] *hys consent* …[54]

These adaptations clearly show an attempt to move from a contractual basis. As Maitland put it,

> the interpolations are very remarkable: they seem to point to the notion of an indefeasible royal power which laws cannot restrain; the king will not bind himself to maintain laws prejudicial to his Crown.[55]

Schramm's premise was that a medieval monarch, bound by the oath, was below the law.[56] It is in Henry VIII's revisions (of the 1530s) that we witness the beginnings of the struggle between the Crown and the law being worked out.[57] In part, this can be attributed to his needs and that of the

English Crown, but Henry's adaptations also reflected changing early modern attitudes to temporal and spiritual authority, and, most importantly, to the concept of the Divine Right of Kings.[58] Although this revised version was not used for his own coronation, where the oath confirmed ecclesiastical privileges, the 1530s version may have been intended for his children.[59]

The Coronation Oath of the *Liber Regalis* and the 'Little Device' was still of such value as to become the foundation for Edward's VI's February 1546/7 coronation, but modifications occurred. We do not have an extant copy of Edward's oath, but Privy Council records indicate what was planned. Several important points can be made. Firstly, the drafting was executed by Protector Somerset and other privy councillors.[60] Secondly, the oath's initial question was reduced so that the king promised 'to kepe to the people ... laws and liberties of this realme', but it now included 'and others your realmes and domynions'.[61] The addition was therefore intended to encompass Ireland, as Henry VIII had declared himself king of Ireland. The major subtraction was reference to the laws and customs of St Edward. Further limitations were removed so that the Crown remained as arbiter over what could be defined as law and liberty. Edward's coronation was thus an opportunity for Reformation, and, as Schramm states, 'it was not mere accident that peace and concord were promised only to Church and people and not to the clergy', and that the bishops' admonition was deleted. The fourth question was radically altered, so that what had required the king 'to observe the laws of the people's choice' was substituted by a clause more in keeping with the royal prerogative[62]:

> Do you grawnte to make no newe lawes but such as shalbe to thonour and glory of God, and to the good of the commen wealth, and that the same shalbe made by the consent of your people as hath been accustumed[?][63]

On this basis, it was no longer the sovereign, but rather the people, who had to consent to new laws. Legislative initiative and authorisation had been switched. Thus, the February 1307/1308 oath and the 1483 English text had been substantially changed.[64] If one looks more closely at the 1483 English text, the point of the fourth clause is not to bind the king to accept whatever the 'community of the realm' decides, but rather it is to commit him to uphold Acts of Parliament. The king must already have agreed to Bills in order to transform them into Acts. Hence, whatever the monarch has turned into statute law he must stand by. This clause was therefore about committing the sovereign to uphold and enforce laws past and future; arguably, the first clause is about the past and the fourth clause is about the future. This February 1546/7 revision makes it exclusively about law creation. It is recognising the king's inherent absolute rule: he could theoretically make law unilaterally, but by this clause permitted himself to creating law only with the consent of the people (i.e. Parliament) and in the public interest. Nevertheless, it is still a constitutional check on the king, but there has been a shift in emphasis from enforcement to creation.[65] Although Henry VIII was the architect of a new oath, the first Tudor actually to adapt the oath for their own coronation was therefore Edward VI. Nevertheless, Edward's changes (and those of the Privy Council) did not become authoritative, as can be seen from Mary I's accession.

The new ardently Roman Catholic queen would, like her half-brother, adapt the oath, but her modification was minimal, amounting to an addition of a line intended to preserve her goodwill and integrity. Her reasoning here was, however, significant. According to Hunt, Mary understood the oath of Edward VI to have made reference to the 'new religion' (though it is hard to see how it did so directly, judging by what is recorded in the Privy Council register).[66] Instead, Mary wished to revert to the 'old and accustomed' form, which must have meant Henry VIII's 1509 oath, and added the words 'just and licit laws': this was particularly odd, given that it is tautological—one cannot have illicit laws![67] Although we do not have an extant copy of Mary's oath, we do have a reliable source in the form of Henry Penning, Cardinal Pole's secretary, who refers to it:

> Her majesty gave me the copy of the oath taken by her at the coronation, which she had thoroughly considered beforehand, and added a few words having for object to maintain her majesty's integrity and good-will; as may be seen by the identical copy.[68]

Mary's actions show just how important the oath could be for a new monarch, particularly in the religiously charged atmosphere following the Reformation(s). Moreover, the queen requested special chrism for her anointing: 'holy oil, which she had sent to obtain at Brussels from the Emperor'.[69] However, her additional words and the use of continental (Roman Catholic) oil were not to endure beyond her reign.

What did, or did not, take place at Elizabeth I's coronation has been open to plentiful debate, not least because there is no surviving record of her oath.[70] January 1558/1559 could well have been a moment of change, but we can only guess what happened. Elizabeth's Coronation Oath is as interesting as it is problematic—and Sir William Cecil's role is of particular note.[71] Primary evidence suggests that Cecil had a hand in recasting the oath, and 'delivered … a booke' containing the text at the appropriate moment in the ceremony to the officiating bishop of Carlisle, Owen Oglethorpe.[72] Hoak argues that figures such as John Aylmer, Cecil and Richard Grafton were aware of the elevated status of the Privy Council under Edward VI, particularly its crucial role in the Edwardian Reformation, and sought to mould the situation under Elizabeth in a similar fashion. Nevertheless, such a stance (even taking account of his minority) fails to consider Edward's connivance in the schemes of Cranmer and the Privy Council, as highlighted by MacCulloch. Furthermore, it assumes that Elizabeth was malleable and lacked authority, given the absence of a husband and her inexperience in leadership—yet such a view is based on a gross misunderstanding of a Tudor monarch.[73] This argument assumes that Elizabeth was crowned analogously to the scheme of 1546/7, reasserting the royal supremacy in the queen's Coronation Oath. The point of the exercise would have been to 'allow her godly advisors to complete the aborted Reformation of Edward's reign, a Reformation that some of them, such as Cecil, had actually helped script under the duke of Northumberland'.[74] However, there is a strong counter-argument to be made: that, given the fractious nature of both the succession and the religious situation, events did not take that radical a turn. In all of these coronations, tradition cannot be underestimated in matters of legitimacy.[75] With this background in mind we are able to turn to the question of contract and the discussion of changes to the oath under the Stuart dynasty.

Promises, Oath and 'Contract'

Discussion of the Coronation Oath is bedevilled by two problems: imprecision and anachronism. The authors of many of the primary sources, as well as modern historians, have been happy to write of the 'Coronation Oath' without saying exactly what they mean. In fact, the term is a shorthand description which casually assimilates the two main components under the heading of the second of them. When most people cite the 'Coronation Oath', what they really have in mind is a series of promises. This set of promises (articulated in French, but also officially recorded in

Latin) was recast for Edward II in 1308, slightly modified (uniquely) for Richard II in 1377 and translated into English for Richard III in 1483. It should have stayed the same thereafter. However, we know that Henry VIII, very likely in the aftermath of the Break with Rome in 1534 and consistent with his by then stridently 'theocratic' conception of kingship, drafted a new oath designed to enhance the royal prerogative, though it was never used. We also know that changes to the old oath (almost certainly implemented temporarily) were prepared by the Privy Council for Edward VI in 1547; and that mysterious alterations, which the House of Commons in the Long Parliament later saw as both unauthorized and dangerous, took place subsequently, probably for James VI and I in 1603. That early Stuart text survived until the complete overhaul in 1689. What, then, are the original four promises of 1308? Translated from the more authoritative French manuscript, they read thus:

> Sire, are you willing to grant and preserve and by your oath confirm to the people of England the laws and customs granted to them by former kings of England, your righteous and godly predecessors, and particularly the laws, customs and liberties granted to the clergy and the people by the glorious king St Edward, your predecessor[?]
> *Response*: I grant and promise them.
>
> Sire, will you for God and holy Church and for the clergy and for the people keep peace and accord in God, to the best of your ability, intact?
> *Response*: I will.
>
> Sire, will you in all your judgments have impartial and proper justice and discretion done in compassion and truth to the best of your ability?
> *Response*: I will.
>
> Sire, do you agree to maintain and preserve the laws and rightful customs which the community of your realm shall have chosen and will you defend and enforce them to the honour of God to the best of your ability?
> *Response*: I agree and promise.[76]

For Richard II's coronation in 1377, Clause 4 was revised to read 'which the community of your realm shall **justly and reasonably** have chosen'.[77] That change did not stick, however, and it was the text used at the coronations of Edward II and Edward III that was imported (albeit in Latin) into Westminster Abbey Library MS 38, better known as the *Liber Regalis*, which was made during the 1390s and became the standard coronation *ordo* until an English recension was executed for James I in 1603.[78] When the *Liber Regalis* was created, a fifth clause was added, termed 'the admonition of the bishops' in the relevant rubric, according to which the king confirmed episcopal privileges.[79]

Amazingly, none of these sources gives what was, strictly speaking, the Coronation Oath. Not until a document prepared for Richard III's coronation does the utterance itself— the invocation of God as witness— appear on paper:

> Alle thise thingis and every of theim I Richard kinge of Engelond promitte and conferme to kepe and observe, so helpe me God and by thise hooly evangelistis by me bodely touched uppon this holy aulter.[80]

In short, the oath was sworn to the officiant, normally the archbishop of Canterbury, but it related to the preceding promises, which had been declared to the people. These distinctions are important because it is often claimed that the 'Coronation Oath' was sworn to God. That claim betrays a fundamental misconception: vows are sworn **to** God, but oaths are sworn **before** God.

It is difficult to avoid anachronism creeping into any attempt to interpret the 'Coronation Oath' (now taken chiefly to mean the promises) because many of the concepts with which we are familiar today either did not yet exist or were in a process of evolution or meant something quite different. Garnett, for instance, has traced the medieval emergence of the abstract concept of 'the Crown' as distinct from both king and object.[81] Similarly, Skinner has elucidated how the idea of 'the State' passed through a number of stages of conceptual development during the Renaissance.[82] The challenge we face is that of understanding the constitutional significance of the 'Coronation Oath' in relation to two epochs—the later Middle Ages and the Early Modern period—when there was barely any notion of 'a constitution'. There were, however, extremely sophisticated legal systems: common law practised in most secular courts, canon law practised in the ecclesiastical courts and civil law (i.e. Roman law) practised in certain specialized courts, such as the High Court of Admiralty, yet exercising a much wider influence. In addition, there was the equitable jurisdiction of (for example) the Court of Chancery. Many folk viewed relationships of various kinds legalistically, and litigation increased dramatically under the Tudors and Stuarts.[83] Centuries before Henry VII won his throne, it had become legal doctrine that the king was above the law and could do no wrong: he could not be prosecuted. It is within this legal context that the 'Coronation Oath' should be understood.

In analysing contractualism in political thought, for instance, Höpfl and Thompson note that it was common for the Coronation Oath to be understood as such a contract or as evidence of a contract.[84] Their examples range from France to England and Scotland, and from the 1570s to the early eighteenth century. Although a coronation may appear to be the apogee of pure monarchy, in British tradition it was also the contractual ceremony binding the sovereign to the other three pillars of the unwritten constitution. In Charles I's mixed monarchy, the pillar comprising the body politic was largely centred upon the House of Commons and the House of Lords, the latter possessing an important judicial capacity. This fact is crucial, because a coronation provided the legal framework, *via* the oath, to hold the new ruler to account. The people, in their representatives in the Abbey,[85] first acclaimed the monarch, and the sovereign then limited his or her powers (in normal circumstances) by agreeing to swear a prescribed oath. This is not to say that monarchy was not absolute in terms of potential powers, which could be invoked in emergencies, but rather that absolute rule was checked by the sovereign undertaking to limit their full powers, so that authority would be exercised in accordance with the law.[86] In failing to appreciate contractualism, Weston elides Divine Right ideology with absolutism, yet it is essential to distinguish between them. It was perfectly possible for a monarch coming to the throne by Divine Right to avoid absolutism by entering into a contractual relationship with the people. For example, in taking his oath like his predecessors, Charles II bound himself to the law and to his subjects—a solemn contract with the nation. This was not 'incompatible with the theory of Divine Right of Kings with which Charles I is commonly associated'.[87]

What this chapter and indeed book highlights is a form of binding constitutional arrangement at the heart of the English (and later British) monarchy, long before 1649, 1661 or even 1689. The Coronation Oath was a mechanism to restrict absolutism, for the people's delegation of immense power to the sovereign at a coronation was effected only on the basis that they had taken the oath. As Strickland has argued, for as early as the coronation of Henry the Young King in 1170

> The coronation oath formed a deeply significant element in the ceremony, for by it the king entered into a contract with his people and with the Church to rule as a just and lawful sovereign.[88]

Absolutism in an English context was therefore never compatible with the oath, for the ruler was held in check by the requirement to agree to the terms of the promises; to this degree, Divine Right ideology and royal authority were restricted. Although an attempt was made to weaken its power, probably in 1603, the oath nonetheless in general remained constitutionally quasi-contractual.

When James I acceded to the English throne in 1603, there had not been a coronation for over forty years. A search for precedents was therefore needed. As Doran highlights, 'James's respect for the traditional form was deliberate. Participating in England's long-established coronation rituals was essential for his legitimation and—equally important—demonstrated his commitment to English customs'.[89] Legg details the process surrounding the creation of James's oath.[90] There are four important points to be made. Firstly, that '*quas vulgus elegerit*' (referring to the laws and customs 'which the people shall have chosen') was dropped. The novel fourth clause of 1308 was changed to read 'will you graunt to hold and keepe the lawes and rightfull customes, which the comminaltie of your kingdome have, and to defende and upphold them'.[91] The sense has been completely altered. It now means the laws possessed currently, not those to be enacted in the future. This squares with James's idea of kingship. The change was perpetuated for Charles I.[92] Legg shows that Parliament (in later complaining about the deletion) noticed that '*elegerit*' does not mean only 'have'.[93] Amazingly, however, the modified version was re-used for Charles II[94] and James II.[95] Here, therefore, was a potential path to absolutism.[96] Secondly, and intriguingly, it seems that Parliament was also unaware of an English translation prior to 1603. As Schramm puts it, 'whether the formula used at [James I's] coronation was drawn up for the occasion or whether it was copied from a draft made in the sixteenth century must remain an open question; the text is, at any rate, a new and independent translation of the … 1308' oath.[97] Thirdly, and significantly, there was an addition to the first clause, explicitly referring to the Gospels. The first clause asks whether or not the king promises to

> grant and keepe, and by your oath confirme to the people of England the lawes and customes to them granted by the kinges of England your lawfull and religiouse predecessors, and namely the lawes, customes and ffranchisez granted to the clergie, and to the people by the gloriouse King Saint Edward your predecessor?[98]

These lines were then followed by the interpolation:

> according and conformable to the lawes of God and true profession of the Gospell established in this kingdome.[99]

Placed firmly within the Coronation Oath, this insertion was a clear product of the Reformation(s) and so too that the coronation was the first in the vernacular, and in addition 'James took communion in both kinds', that is the bread and the wine, 'as customary in all Protestant Churches'.[100] It would also fit with James I's later sponsorship of a new authorised English translation of the Bible. Fourthly, this mark of confessionalization was not 'the only real novelty [in] the Coronation Oath', as Schramm states, for one more crucial line was included in the first clause in a fashion 'reminiscent of Henry [VIII]'s addition'.[101] In a move designed dramatically to strengthen the royal prerogative, the words 'agreeing to the auncyent customes of the realme and the prerogatives of the kinges thereof' were incorporated. It was these very changes that William Laud, archbishop of Canterbury, was later accused of having made in Charles I's Coronation Oath, which runs almost identically:

> the true profession of the Gospell established in the Church of England, and agreable to the prerogative of the kinge thereof, and the auntient customes of this realme.[102]

Laud was not helped by the fact that 'the addition is not in all the manuscripts' that preserve a text of James I's Coronation Oath, 'but it is ... in some of King James' Order; in which the archbishop could not have had a hand'.[103] Therefore, 1603 saw significant developments to the Coronation Oath and not 1626. According to Legg, the latter year witnessed only one change of note:

> There is indeed one serious alteration in the Coronation Oath of Charles I. It is that the words *and to the people* have been left out of the first section. They are omitted in all known copies of the oath; but in one, the words *and people* have been interlined. It is quite possible that the omission was unintentional; the words *the people of England* occur immediately above.[104]

Legg goes on to point out that had a studious Parliament actually perceived this alteration, a 'very formidable attack might have been organised in view of the omission of these words'.[105] This was not to be the case.

One final change, came with the acclamation when the monarch is presented to the people by the archbishop and they are asked for their consent. As Doran notes with reference to Legg, 'James was determined that this acclamation should not be construed as an election or in any sense conditional' thus 'he decided upon a form of words that denoted his position as "the rightfull inheritour of the crowne" without any need for his people's consent'. Yet, Archbishop Whitgift, still continued the custom of the presentation of the sovereign to all four corners of the Abbey, speaking the 'novel lines in that they required "the people" merely "to make acknowledgement of their allegiance to his Majesty", whilst there was no explicit 'mention of consent. Those present, "signifieng their willingness", cried out in one voice "Yea, yea, God save King James".[106] Even if the language had been modified, the very fact this process was carried on retained a sense of election, in crude modern language, 'why bother?' to ask the people for any form of sign if it was not needed at all or if it did not matter. James would reference this episode in a 1620 work, where he 'explained his thinking about this part of the ceremony' for "a monarchie or hereditary kingdome cannot justly be denied to the lawfull successor, what ever the affections of the people bee; yet it is a great signe of the blessing of God, when he enters in it with the willing applause of his subjects".[107] Nevertheless, as if to emphasise the point made about the inclusion of this acclamation, for all of the delicate changes made, 'the subtlety' of the revised language, it was noted by 'a lawyer from the Inner Temple who attended the ceremony' that it 'was designed "to shewe the cause of that solemne assembly of the state of the common wealth to elect their king".[108] Election was thus retained for all of James's efforts.

Given these changes, the question remains as to the place of the Coronation Oath, within the context of the service, as a form of binding agreement, in which the people held the sovereign in check. Cressy contests the importance of the acclamation which crucially preceded the oath, in that a small hierarchy represented the people, and were not likely to reject the call to recognize the new sovereign—'as if there was any choice in the matter'.[109] Nevertheless, it is highly significant that they were asked at all. If it was not needed, why include it? Russian serfs were never asked their consent to recognize the new tsar. Furthermore, although only a tiny elite was present in the Abbey, those figures nevertheless represented the key elements of the British constitution at that time; this was much closer to some form of 'representation' than can be found in other countries contemporaneously. As Samuel Pepys recorded for the momentous Restoration coronation of Charles II in 1661:

> The king in his robes [entered], bare-headed, which was very fine. And after all had placed themselves, there was a sermon and the service; and then in the Quire at the high altar, the king passed through all the ceremonies of the coronacon … The crown being put upon his head, a great shout begun, and he came forth to the throne, and there passed more ceremonies: as taking the oath … And three times the King at Arms went to the three open places on the scaffold, and proclaimed, that if any one could show any reason why Charles Stewart should not be king of England, that now he should come and speak.[110]

Pepys's feelings at seeing his sovereign stand out and moreover, the acclamation and rejoicing for the crowned monarch is emphasised, as is the central importance of the oath. What is intriguing is the question—akin to a wedding—as to whether or not anyone objects to the king as sovereign. Perhaps Pepys has merged this idea with the acclamation, for the recognition is not put in this way. What can we conclude? Arguably, it underlines the real contractual character that people recognised (or at least Pepys did) in a coronation. There was a legitimate sense that those present were consenting to this new monarch; it was not a *fait accompli*.

In the acclamation and those being asked to recognise the sovereign we have the evolution of the important role of the Privy Council that emerged from the Witan of Anglo Saxon days. The Witan had of course helped elect a monarch. The development of that tradition fused with divine right kingship created this contractual compromise.[111]

As Hunt argues, this oath, sworn in the presence of the people, meant that the 'constitutional purpose of the ceremony remained paramount'.[112] Therefore, the question is: was this a contract? Cressy states that

> These questions and answers constitute an oath, but not a contract. Though performed before the people (at least an elite fraction of them), the oath was sworn not to them, **but to God**. King Charles staked his immortal soul on his fealty to these words, which bound him to strict obligations. The obligations, however, like everything else in these utterances, were subject to interpretation.[113]

However, as we have already shown, this was not the case. The words were sworn **before** God; they were not a vow, but rather an oath. Legal scholars have debated *ad absurdum* what constitutes a contract. Seventeenth-century folk certainly did so, with many arguing that in 'taking the Coronation Oath the king accepted contractual obligations which had been imposed upon his ancestors'.[114] Interpretation of such an agreement dominates commercial law even today and, indeed, contract law was undergoing significant change in the seventeenth century, being 'tidied up in 1677'.[115] It is certainly the case that this was an oath, with promises made to the people, and with God as witness and final arbiter. Anthony Milton discusses this point with reference to the crisis of the 1640s and the bishops' admonition. Only they (it was maintained by several commentators) could release the king (Charles I) from the acceptance of their petition in the Coronation Oath's fifth clause: 'this promissory oath could not be broken without the consent ... of the bishops'.[116] The same logic applies to the rest of the oath: if bishops were the other party to the fifth clause, then the people must have been the other party in Clauses 1–4. If it is not a contract, then it comes remarkably close to one. Such an oath could not readily be broken under the prevailing *mentalité*, for to make this kind of promise was to bind one's conscience: 'there was no stronger bond than an oath', Spurr argues.[117] Cressy is right to highlight the question of interpretation, but that is true of contracts as much as it is of oaths. Placed in the context of the coronation ceremony, the oath looks every bit contract-like, in that the sovereign cannot proceed to be anointed and crowned until it is sworn. This chapter therefore argues that the Coronation Oath is quasi-contractual; the service in which it is embedded is similar to a wedding ceremony, with the vows. The marital analogy is all the more real because a coronation involves a special ring:

> The appearance of the ring is a significant feature: we should recall that in all medieval royal coronation *ordines* (English and continental) the ring formed an essential emblem.[118]

The 'royal signet' came to symbolise 'the inseparability of the Crown from the king, but also the meaning of the king's marriage to the kingdom'. Such an act emulated episcopal consecration: 'the essential point is that the sacramental idea of the episcopal marriage was transferred to the king and here assumed constitutional and ... practical importance'.[119] This coronation-marriage tradition continued under the Tudors right through to the present era and the 2023 coronation.[120] Mary I referred to her coronation 'as a marriage', and in a speech reminded her audience of this contractual relationship between people and ruler, stating that

> at my coronation[,] when I was wedded to the realme and to the lawes of the same (the spowsall ring whereof I have on my finger, which never hetherto was, nor hereafter shall be[,] left of) the [i.e. thee] promised your allegeaunce and obedience unto mee, and that I am the right and true inheritor to the Crowne of this realme of Englande.[121]

Just as the monarch marries the realm and promises to uphold the laws, so too the people must honour their part of the agreement *via* oaths of allegiance. When of course a monarch, such as Richard II or Charles I, fell short of their obligations (as perceived by the populace) then it was the Coronation Oath and those sacred vows, that were held up as evidence of a contract reneged. James I certainly saw the oath as defining the terms of his kingship and grappled with the question of contract.[122] Although he denied that the oath was one, his rationale is fascinating and comes close to defining it quasi-contractually, as Sommerville mentions:

> Whatever the powers of monarchs considered abstractly might be, any good king was obliged to act within the law. 'Therefore all kings that are not tyrants or perjured will be glad to bound themselves within the limits of their laws, and they that persuade them the contrary are vipers and pests, both against them and the commonwealth'.[123]

James was therefore admitting that crucial monarchical obligations were cemented in the Coronation Oath. Sommerville highlights the king's speech to Parliament of 21 March 1611 that underlines that the monarch's 'duty to rule in the public interest entailed a further duty to abide by the constitution. The king was bound to maintain the laws "by a double oath" — firstly in virtue of the duties of kingship itself, and secondly because he swore to do so at his coronation'.[124] James, of course, sought to avoid notions of an 'election', or that there could be 'legitimate resistance' to the monarch, but he came exceptionally near, defining the oath as a binding agreement. This statement is all the more remarkable given his Divine Right claims:

> As to this contract alledged made at the coronation of a king, although I deny any such contract to bee made then, especially containing such a clause

> irritant as they alledge; yet I confesse, that a king at his coronation, or at the entry to his kingdome, willingly promiseth to his people, to discharge honourably and trewly the office given him by God over them.[125]

Perhaps the two perspectives can be reconciled—a reconciliation in which the Coronation Oath is analogous to a covenant in biblical terms, but that too, legally speaking, can be viewed as a form of contract. It is clear, therefore, that by 1649 a broad understanding of the Coronation Oath existed, yet its legal status *vis-à-vis* the monarch was still open to discussion. Apart from the obvious sacral sense, it was certainly discussed in legal terms too, which is itself significant. After the Republic, there would be a fresh opportunity either to re-affirm or to adjust ancient concepts, yet it would not be until 1689 that radical change took place. With the Restoration of Charles II and subsequent succession of James II in 1685, there came a series of fresh questions on the position of Scotland and the Scottish Coronation Oath. It is to those developments that we now turn, before going on to discuss the Glorious Revolution.

Scotland

As we have seen, the Coronation Oath is highly complex. Few people are aware of its exact nature, fewer still that it is one of the world's greatest legal obligations, akin to a contract, with origins dating as far back as the Anglo-Saxons, and perhaps even fewer that the monarch swears not one, but two Coronation Oaths: one for Great Britain and the Commonwealth (the English oath) and a separate one for Scotland. In fact, these oaths, at their heart, cement at the personal level the religious and political positions of the Churches of England and Scotland, reinforcing the statutory foundations of the Church-State settlements of both countries. The division of the oaths is all the more intriguing given the great constitutional debates of the moment. There is nothing new in what we are seeing: political manoeuvring, discussions about power sharing and questions about the royal prerogative. Indeed, the 2014 Scottish independence referendum, and the resulting re-evaluation of the preserved Union, has its roots in the period 1567–1707, when both the stability and the instability of the Union originated. Given this duality, any significant discussion of the Coronation Oath must involve consideration of the Scottish oath too. Set out below is a brief history of the steps to the 1707 Union that encapsulated this dual system.

In order to see the development of the distinct Scottish and English Coronation Oaths, we must go back to the 1603 Union of the Crowns. James VI and I had been crowned in Scotland in 1567, when a new Scottish oath (see Appendix 1) had been enshrined in parliamentary legislation,[126] and then in England in 1603. As he saw it, he was the first king of 'our kingdome of Great Britaine'.[127] The Union of the Crowns continued with Charles I, who was crowned in England in 1626 and then in Edinburgh in 1633. Charles II was crowned at Scone Palace in 1651 and then in 1661 at Westminster Abbey. This background therefore left open the question of whether or not James II would follow suit. Yet James saw no need for a Scottish crowning. Harris's interpretation is that the 'omission [was] perhaps understandable', on the basis that, since the Union of the Crowns, England had become the Stuart powerbase and visits 'to Scotland [were] regarded as luxuries ... [taking] the monarchy away from the important task of running England.'[128] This is the key point; indeed, something more controversial than just 'understandable', for James II's inheritance highlights the permanent geo-political shift that had occurred. James I was a Scot who felt that he was king of Great Britain. His surviving son was an Englishman aware of his Scottish heritage. James II, like his older brother Charles, was a Briton. In essence, this was second generation immigration at work – and the realization of what his grandfather had envisaged. At the back-end of the Exclusion Crisis, the Scottish Succession Act (1681), passed in the Scottish Parliament, affirmed the principle of 'the king is dead, long live the king': that with the sovereign's death, the next-in-line automatically inherits. Such a move undermined the need for a coronation as a declaration of authority; indeed, James did not even take the separate Scottish Coronation Oath. Perhaps because he had governed Scotland successfully as his brother's representative, and because he was a Stuart, he felt no need to do so, and this omission passed more or less unnoticed at the time.[129] By contrast, with a new dynasty on the throne in 1689, this constitutional anomaly would flare up dramatically.

Although there is no such oath for either Wales or Northern-Ireland, there developed separate Coronation Oaths for England and Scotland, and these were still sworn in 1953.[130] This historic separation was cemented by James II's departure and the manner in which the Scottish Crown was offered to William III and Mary II. With the arrival of the Williamite regime, and the exile of a Scottish Stuart, the Scots pressed for certain demands (the Articles of Grievances). This determination followed directly from James VII's (and II's) actions, his Roman Catholicism and how that had threatened Presbyterian Scotland. William and Mary were offered the Crown—it was not conferred as an automatic right—in the Claim of Right (11 April 1689). In many respects, this was a Scottish form of the English Declaration of Rights, a vindication and 'asserting [of] ancient rights and liberties'.[131] Much of this constitutional re-alignment was based on grievances dating back to the reign of Charles I, the ambitions of the Covenanters and the Civil Wars. The Glorious Revolution was an opportunity for Scotland to draw up a more formalised mechanism for the Union of the Crowns. The central tenet arose from the twinned fears of arbitrary government and Roman Catholicism:

> By the law of this kingdome[,] no papist can be king or queen of this realme, nor bear any office whatsoever therin; nor can any Protestant successor exercise the regall power, until he or she swear the Coronation Oath.[132]

Debate rested, as it had done for Charles I, on how far a Scottish ruler was an 'absolute' one: how much did parliamentary sovereignty restrict, or work compatibly with, the Scottish monarchy? The essential question remained whether or not a monarch of both England and Scotland needed a Scottish coronation too; indeed, did any king or queen of Scotland legally require a coronation so as to validate their rule? According to the Whig lawyer Sir John Lauder of Fountain Hall, it was not a legal prerequisite. However, the swearing of an oath **was** an essential requirement, presumably because it was statutory.[133] The issue was not a live one when the *status quo* of rule was maintained. Nevertheless, when Charles I and James II sought to interfere, and particularly on religion, then the degree to which royal authority was absolute was questioned; in fact, a more basic problem emerged: whether or not a form of authorization was needed for the inheritance of the throne to be possible. In an English coronation, even if it was only as a *fait accompli*, at least in the ceremony, popular consent was needed in order to validate sovereignty. A Coronation Oath was exactly the form of contract that served as the response to the acclamation, and could be seen as a binding legal undertaking in case of either despotic or negligent rule. With James II's departure from mainland Britain, leaving a vacant throne, the need for such an oath in Scotland became paramount; a crucial consideration was the maintenance of the privileged position of the Scottish Kirk, as established following Charles I's demise. The Scottish Convention (a gathering of the Scottish estates) was organised for the purpose of establishing the means for the settlement of the

Scottish Crown.[134] The Convention devised a new Coronation Oath for William and Mary, containing the obligation to swear to uphold and

> maintain the true religion of Christ Jesus, the preaching of his holy word and the due right ministratione of the sacraments now receaved and preached within the realme of Scotland; [abolish] all false religion, contrary to the same; [rule] according to the loveable lawes and consitutiones receaved in this realme; [and] roote out all hereticks and enemies to the true worship of God that shall be convicted by the true Kirk of God [from Scotland].[135]

It is unclear as to whether or not William and Mary really did need to swear this new oath and the Claim of Right and Articles of Grievances before they could receive the Crown: '[s]cholars disagree over whether the offer ... was made conditional upon their acceptance'.[136] It certainly seems to have been an essential requirement. A new dynasty, facing a rival claimant overseas, had little choice but to follow this new mandate. The central point again is that a coronation (or at least, in this case, a central element of a coronation, namely the oath) was of key significance in the creation of royal authority. For William and Mary, full regal power was only attainable, indeed conditional, upon the taking of the Coronation Oath. The offer of the Scottish Crown was formally made on 11 May 1689 by a tripartite group representing the Convention: for the nobility, the duke of Argyll; on behalf of the knights, Montgomery of Skerlmorlie; and for the burghs, Sir John Dalrymple. The delegation travelled to London, again highlighting the geo-political shift since 1603. The offer took place at the Whitehall Banqueting House and was made up of the Claim of Right, the Articles of Grievances and the new Coronation Oath. The three commissioners also asked that William and Mary turn the Convention into a Parliament in order to pass the necessary legislation concerning the demands laid before them. William was guided by his chief Scottish adviser, the Earl of Melville, who 'strugled hard to defear the grivances' until after the Coronation Oath had been sworn. However, on this matter, the delegation won. The only aspect about which William demurred was a demand in the new oath for the monarch to deal with heretics. The king objected to becoming a 'persecutor', but was put at ease by the commissioners along the lines that this was simply a formal anachronism and that in reality 'no man was to be persecuted for his private opinion' under Scottish law. Perhaps that was debatable, but the clarification seemed to settle the matter for William and he consented to all:

> They shall find me willing to assist them in every thing that concerns the weal and interest of that kingdom, by making what laws shall be necessary for the security of their religion, property, and liberty, and to ease them of what may be justly grievous to them.[137]

The revised Scottish Coronation Oath was continued for Queen Anne.[138] By 1702, it was seen as a compromise between the Presbyterian Kirk and the Church of England, as a letter from Thomas Smith to Samuel Pepys reports:

> The Scotch Whigs triumph in the Coronation Oath in that it assures the Presbyterian government in their Kirke. The Ch[urch] of England also rejoices at having a Ch[urch] of England queen on the throne, which encourages the clergy who have suffered so much for her father King James II to hope for some relief from their troubles.[139]

The matter was of such importance that it was enshrined in the twenty-fifth article of the 1707 Act of Union, and so there would continue to be different oaths for England and Scotland. Nevertheless, George I's accession put the Scottish Coronation Oath under further scrutiny, with discussions taking place between the Scottish and English judiciaries. Yet again, the key point was the securing of Presbyterian rights. With the Act of Union already on the statute book, and following these further discussions, the oath was settled and no longer controversial.

As we have seen, 1688–9 saw dramatic changes to the Scottish Coronation Oath and the accession of dual sovereigns for England and Scotland. For Scottish Presbyterians, the Coronation Oath certainly constituted a contractual agreement, enabling them to secure an enduring position—it must be taken by, and is binding upon, any monarch acceding to the throne. Given the current heightened political atmosphere in Scotland, any alteration to such an important and longstanding oath should only be made with immense caution. This duality in terms of oath was an important factor in cementing the Union, in that it clearly recognized Scotland's position under the Crown. To tinker with such a successful resolution may have significant implications for the rest of the Union; what of oaths for Wales and Northern Ireland? On 24 June 1953, in the same month as her Westminster Abbey coronation, the Queen took part in a ceremony in which she was presented with the Honours of Scotland. The crown (at least) is brought before her when she opens the Scottish

Parliament. Much has been done, therefore, to accommodate sensitivities to Scotland's proud history in these ceremonial acts. To change the oath may precipitate the need for a separate Scottish coronation, which might also have an impact on the stability of the Union, embroiling the Crown in nationalistic debate.

Having outlined the development of the Scottish Coronation Oath, we now return to the English Oath and the Glorious Revolution.

The Glorious Revolution

Perhaps of any historical period covered in this chapter, it was the Glorious Revolution that generated the most important change to the English Coronation Oath. This watershed resulted in a double coronation: as Celia Fiennes noted,

> King William and Queen Mary … were set joynctly on the throne, anoynted both and sworne by the Coronation Oath.[140]

James II's reign, in particular his Roman Catholicism and actions towards the Church of England, triggered a desire by the Establishment to fashion an oath that could prevent future incursion against Protestant hegemony, not dissimilar to the agenda just discussed *vis-à-vis* Scotland.[141] Although changes were made to the 1685 coronation ceremony under Archbishop Sancroft's careful direction, the oath (as mentioned earlier) remained unaltered. Precisely because James had so readily sworn to uphold the rights of the 'churches … [and all their] canonical privileges … and [to] defend the bishops and churches' under his rule, and had then proceeded in the eyes of many to renege on his oath, the old setting would be dramatically changed through the Revolution. Not surprisingly, for something of such huge constitutional significance, the issue caused heated debate in Parliament between Whigs and Tories.[142] The oath texts up to that point display differing levels of Anglican emphasis. James I's 1603 oath refers to matters 'conformable to the lawes of God and true profession of the Gospell established in this kingdome',[143] but Charles I's oath says 'the true profession of the Gospell established in the Church of England'.[144] Charles II's oath reverted to James I's formula, which meant that an adherent of Rome might readily swear to

> confirme to the people of England the lawes & customes to them granted by the kings of England your lawful & religious predecessors, & namely the lawes, customes & franchises granted to the clergie by the glorious King St Edward your predecessor, according to the lawes of God, the true profession of the Gospel established in this kingdome, and agreeing to the prerogative of the kings thereof & to the antient customes of this realme.[145]

Regarding the first part of this interrogation, a Roman Catholic could reasonably contend that these laws and customs had not be subsumed into the Church of England settlement, but rather that the Church was still part of the Roman family; and, as per the second part, no Roman Catholic would object to the ancient customs of the kingdom. It was therefore necessary for the oath to be altered, affording an opportunity in the amended version to guard against future arbitrary, absolute rule. In order to achieve this aim, the traditional preliminary interrogation, ensuing three clauses and concluding bishops' admonition were completely altered. As can be seen in Appendix 1, the result barely resembles the structure of the oath that went back to Edward II's coronation in 1308.

The opening provision, for the first time, explicitly requires the monarch to rule 'according to the statutes in Parliament'.[146] The second clause retains a fundamental component of all Coronation Oaths: the exercising of law, mercy and justice in all the ruler's judgements. In essence, it fuses the third clause of the early basic form and the second clause of the version contained in the *Liber Regalis*; it lasted until 1953. The final clause of the 1689 recension is exceptionally carefully devised. It marries the medieval bishops' admonition to the Stuarts' innovative reference to the Gospels, but the combined formula now asks the monarch to preserve and

> maintain the laws of God, the true profession of the Gospell and the Protestant reformed Religion established by law.[147]

This new stipulation offers little room for the **in conscience** agreement of a Roman Catholic. As intended, no future equivalent to James II would be able freely, in good faith, to assent to the revised Coronation Oath. This provision has remained intact ever since. Of course, the Act of Settlement (1701) would in any case prevent a Roman Catholic from inheriting the throne, so this revision, post-dating Anne's accession, is weakened; its central role lay in the period 1689–1701. Nevertheless, in that time it was highly significant, as nobody could know when William and Mary would die. After 1701, it continued to function as a double 'lock': preventing the possibility of a Protestant inheriting the throne and then converting to Roman Catholicism. In such circumstances, the heir could not proceed without breaking the Coronation Oath. Celia Fiennes grasped the significance of this 'promise', commenting in 1702 that the

> oath is very large in three articles, relateing to all priviledges of the Church and State to which she promised to be the security and to maintaine all to us; then she kiss'd the Bible, then a Bible was presented to her to maintaine the true Protestant religion.[148]

Once again, we see the ever-increasing contractual nature of this declaration. 1689 was not the final alteration in the Coronation Oath's remarkable development in this period: for that, we must look to Queen Anne, last of the Stuarts to rule England and Scotland. In line with changes under her predecessors, Anne was to make a statement on what had become, arguably, the most important theological difference between Roman Catholics and Protestants —the doctrine of transubstantiation. This statement of rejection would not endure as part of the coronation *ordo* and from 1761 it became traditional for the monarch to read the declaration in the House of Lords. Legg argued that that connection 'is certainly more seemly, as it prevents the taint of religious controversy from being introduced into the service'.[149] Such an explanation is debatable, given the controversial nature of the subject; it is more likely to have been a time-saving measure. Furthermore, there was no historical precedent, and therefore little merit, in incorporating this declaration into Westminster Abbey proceedings. George I, of course, continued to swear two oaths, the Scottish and the English, but there would be no alteration to the wording in 1714.[150]

In concluding this section, it is helpful to turn to Speck's summary regarding two of the key results of 1688–9, showing just how important a coronation was following the turmoil of the Revolution:

> What triumphed in the Revolution Settlement was a version of the rule of law which saw the king as beneath and not above it. This concept found concrete expression in the significant changes made to the Coronation Oath in 1689. Where James II had sworn to 'grant and keep' the Laws 'granted by ye Kings of England' William and Mary undertook 'to govern the people

> of this kingdom of England … according to the statutes in parliament agreed on, and the laws and customs of the same'.[151]

This settlement was not necessarily incompatible with Divine Right concepts, precisely because the Coronation Oath had always held an important contractual role at the heart of such a sacral ceremony. What changed was that, in many respects, the Coronation Oath became even more significant. For, as Pocock states, this contract, this feature of an 'immemorial constitution' invented by common lawyers, was 'identified with the coronation oath, an oath to observe the ancient constitution—which … binds the people as well as the king'.[152] This ancient link was all-important. As Pocock continues, 'Whigs – and all Englishmen who took their stand on the principles of 1688—clung to the habit of appealing to a supposedly actual English past not less and perhaps more than to abstract principles of government'.[153] It is the praxis found in a coronation arising from this perception of the supposed English past with which this book is concerned.

Implications

The implications of these developments necessarily arise in large part from contextualization. It is important to contextualize the English Coronation Oath by recognizing that it originated in the feudal era, when relationships of many kinds were predicated upon the idea of mutual obligation, and that it developed as feudalism declined, during the late medieval and Early Modern periods, when oaths generally proliferated. Those societies could barely have functioned without the web of commitments sealed by oath. As John Digby, Earl of Bristol, explained in 1647, oaths are

> the highest and strongest obligations that can pass from man to God, from nation to nation, from subjects to their prince, or prince to their subjects, or from man to man, and this is not only so declared in scripture, but was undoubtedly part of that natural and moral law which was by God planted in the hearts of man even from the creation.[154]

Charles I, the ultimate earthly guarantor of justice, was executed on 30 January 1649. It is probably no coincidence that at about that time—George Thomason annotated his copy with a purchase date of 13 February—somebody enterprisingly published a great compendium of oaths: had not oaths now become, in the topsy-turvy world of the Interregnum, the only mundane guarantees available? Admittedly, the compiler, in full antiquarian mode, indiscriminately hoovered up anything remotely oath-like, so we find here the oaths of the mythical Knights of the Round Table and of the lieutenant of Calais, long after Calais had ceased to be English territory. Nevertheless, the book includes the perfectly authentic oaths of countless officers high and low, such as:

Attorney of the Court of Wards
Clerk of the Parliament
Churchwarden
Chancellor of the Exchequer
Freeman of London
Justice of the Peace
Marshall of Berwick-upon-Tweed
Scavenger of London
Sheriff
Verderer of a forest

The work runs to over 400 pages.[155] Revised editions appeared in 1689[156] and 1715.[157] The scholarly literature on the Tudor and Stuart culture of oath-taking is now extensive.[158] However it was phrased, therefore, the Coronation Oath should be understood as coming out of an environment in which the swearing of oaths was as serious as it was commonplace.

In addition it is important to note that Coronation Oaths are not the only oaths to have descended to the present day. Parliamentarians of either House must swear an Oath of Allegiance to the monarch before they may take their seats. Cabinet ministers are invariably appointed to the Privy Council, which means that they are obliged to swear a special oath (sixteenth century in origin) that was secret until 1964. Judges are required to swear both an Oath of Allegiance and the Judicial Oath. Senior members of the judiciary also become Privy Councillors. Those joining the Army, the Royal Air Force, the scouts and the girl guides must all swear oaths, as must those becoming police officers. Each of these oaths mentions allegiance or loyalty or service to the sovereign. It would be absurd if the sovereign, at the summit of the constitutional pyramid, swore no oath, or one so watered down as to be meaningless. To put the matter differently: given our predominantly unwritten constitution, and the fact that the sovereign is above the law, what links the monarch to the rest of the constitution? It is the Coronation Oath.

Significantly, European states which have adopted written constitutions have found it necessary to specify in those documents a mechanism according to which the sovereign can personally be connected to everything else. For example, Article 91 of the Belgian Constitution (as at 2014) states that the king cannot assume the throne until he has sworn an oath before both Chambers of the federal Parliament. It reads:

> I swear that I will observe the constitution and laws of the Belgian people, preserve the country's independence and protect its territorial integrity.

Article 5 of the Constitution of Luxembourg prescribes something very similar, adding the grand duke's undertaking to maintain 'public and individual liberties'. Two countries have kept (one optionally) overt reference to the religious dimension. In the Netherlands, under Article 32 of the Constitution and as soon after taking office as possible, the sovereign swears thus:

> I swear (affirm) to the peoples of the Kingdom that I will always observe and uphold the Statute for the Kingdom and the Constitution.
>
> I swear (affirm) that I will defend and preserve, with all My power, the independence and territory of the Kingdom; that I will protect the freedom and the rights of all Dutchmen and all residents, and will employ for the maintenance and promotion of the welfare, all the means which the laws place at My disposal, as a good and true King should do.
>
> So help me, God Almighty!
>
> (This I affirm!)

Article 9 of the Constitution of Norway stipulates that, immediately upon his accession, the king must take this oath:

> I promise and swear that I will govern the Kingdom of Norway in accordance with its Constitution and Laws; so help me God, the Almighty and Omniscient.

These quotations underline a basic point: where a written constitution provides for a royal oath, that oath refers to the constitution—a harmonious circularity locks in the sovereign. It follows that in the United Kingdom, largely lacking a written constitution, there can be no such simplicity. Our Coronation Oath must not only bind the monarch to the people and to the apparatus of governance that has evolved but also enunciate some of the principles upon which that governance is founded.

As we have seen, the Coronation Oath was not simply akin to a legalistic contract, but was also analogous to a marital vow: it was a sacred bond too. In the order of service, the monarch, having publicly made the promises, then went to the High Altar to seal them by the solemn oath proper. Until the fifteenth century, this appears to have been done by swearing on the Gospels, but then there was a shift to swearing on the eucharistic elements, laid out on the altar, which served to emphasise the sacramental nature of the transaction. According to Legg, these 'customs doubtless arose from confusion excited by the term *cum sacramenti confirmatione*'; previously, this had meant to confirm by oath, but was ultimately taken to refer to the Eucharist.[159] Such was this sacral importance that it endures and, for the modern era, the monarch kisses the Gospels and subscribes the oath at the altar, uttering the phrase: 'The things that I have here promised, I will perform, and keep. So help me God'.[160] Any change to the oath would also require consideration of its place within the service and of the role of the Church of England, which, unless disestablished, remains the State Church.

Perhaps it is partly thanks to the sixteenth-century French legist Jean Bodin that Coronation Oaths are of particular interest to historians of political thought; he certainly engaged heavily with the problem of Coronation Oaths and their limitations on absolutism, his chief subject. Yet, he neatly summarised a widely held view that an English monarch is not fully incumbent if they have not sworn the Coronation Oath. In the modern era, the abdication, without coronation, of Edward VIII if anything cemented this theory; such an idea is encapsulated in this Bodinian quotation:

> Kings of England are not consecrated unless they swear to keep the ordinances and customs of the country.[161]

Given this long background, the trauma of the Abdication and the absence of an oath-taking, questions would certainly arise as to where this would leave any future sovereign who abandoned the oath, or indeed the coronation.

In a rapidly changing world that is also often obsessed by change, ceremonies based on tradition, and affording continuity, provide points of stability. They are opportunities to reflect, to collect our thoughts, to remind ourselves of our priorities, and to pause to assess the direction of travel in which, as a society, we go. A coronation is undoubtedly symbolic; the royal prerogative is unrecognizable from the days of the first Queen Elizabeth, and the relevance of such ceremonial can be questioned in the modern age. Nevertheless, we must be mindful of the power of symbolism. Such power takes many years to generate, but can be thrown away in an instant. To have the head of State swear to uphold certain core values, such as law, justice and mercy, speaks for the entire nation, and sends a message to the rest of the globe – a message of what the United Kingdom is about. In an environment where news is created in seconds, and technologies develop overnight, the constancy of an oath of such longevity has much to commend it. By the same token, if such ingrained symbols are to be cast away, it leaves open the troubling question of whether or not other such symbols are needed at all. Why have a flag? A national anthem? The opening of the legal year? We should always question what we do and adapt customs, where necessary, to meet the reasonable requirements of the times, but we must also stop to wonder why such traditions have survived. Why did others not reform or remove them? Perhaps, just perhaps, it was because they were (and are) of tremendous, but unquantifiable, intrinsic value.

Fig. 3.2 King Charles III taking the Coronation Oath, touching the bible engraved with his sovereigns cypher and date, 2023, Ian Shaw/Alamy

Conclusion and 2023

Thus, the Coronation Oath has undergone much development since 1308. While there has essentially been continuity since 1689, it was in the period *c.*1603–*c.*1714 that the foundations for a binding national settlement were laid. On each occasion, the oath (and, in time, oaths) has been at the heart of the coronation ceremony and part of the State's anatomy, linking two nations and two national Churches under one ruler. Each oath does so in the form of a contract-like agreement. Concurrently, the ruler was restrained by the oath's promises; Divine Right ideology and royal power were limited. Crucially, the Scottish and English Coronation Oaths were not so fossilised as to fail to evolve, given the pragmatic needs of the moment— they were at the same time conduits of tradition and sources of both authority and legitimacy. As Bogdanor has suggested, perhaps this is a metaphor for the monarchy itself:

> The survival of monarchy may indeed be said to symbolize this process of evolutionary change.[162]

In the build-up to the ceremony there was much constitutional and historical debate on the value, meaning and nature of the Coronation Oath in modern times. Robert Hazell and Bob Morris of the Constitution Unit have presented papers setting out potential alternatives or modifications, so too the likes of Norman Bonney and C. L. Berry have questioned and been concerned with the question of religion in such an Oath in a contemporary setting.[163] Most of these, however, have assumed to some degree the need for an Oath of some form within the framework of a type of ceremony. The questions have therefore centred on potential alterations for the future and the religious nature of the Oath. Several wider or broader questions have also been asked now we are in the context of the reign of a new sovereign and a recent coronation: why have a Coronation Oath at all—or indeed a coronation? How can we understand this ceremony given the concept of 'the King is dead long live the King'— what is the place of the Oath within that framework? This chapter and indeed book seek to answer these questions, explaining why the Coronation Oath remains important in a twenty-first century setting, what has changed in more recent history and how we might view or understand the coronation and the Oath—through the prism of contract and of marriage.

Technically, any form of the Coronation Oath which does not match the wording set out in the 1688 Act is contrary to law. In practice, however, several changes have been made without amending the original Act. These changes have generally reflected constitutional territorial developments. The oath as set out in the Act referred to the "Kingdom of England", so in later oaths this was changed to "Great Britain" and then to the "United Kingdom".

Other alterations took account of the fact that after 1931 (and the Statute of Westminster)[164] the King or Queen was separately monarch of various Commonwealth Realms, such as Canada, Australia and New Zealand. In the oath taken by King George VI in May 1937, he swore to govern all those realms (which were listed) according to their "respective laws and customs". Queen Elizabeth II's oath took account of the fact that India and Ireland—both Commonwealth Realms in 1937—had become independent republics by May 1953.[165]

In 1953, Churchill and Attlee agreed in Parliamentary debate for modifications to be made to reflect territorial changes and this was in turn covered by agreement between the United Kingdom and other Commonwealth Realms.[166] The Coronation Oath has therefore constantly evolved to reflect changes to the territorial composition of the United Kingdom and wider Commonwealth. Thus, it was updated in 2023—as there could no longer for example be reference to South Africa, Pakistan and Ceylon (now Sri Lanka) —all now being republics. Modifications going beyond such territorial reference, would have been a major step and surprising if they did not require legislation or much greater discussion in Parliament and more generally.

2023 saw little in the way of dramatic change to the existing Oath, but rather additional preamble to tackle King Charles III's desire to be a defender of faith[167]—it thus included the lines read by the Archbishop of Canterbury:

> Your Majesty,
>
> the Church established by law, whose settlement you will swear to maintain, is committed to the true profession of the Gospel, and, in so doing, will seek to foster an environment in which people of all faiths and beliefs may live freely. The Coronation Oath has stood for centuries and is enshrined in law.[168]

The commentary accompanying this inclusion noted:

> The wording before the Oath explains that the Church of England seeks to foster an environment where people of all faiths and beliefs may live freely. In the words of Her Late Majesty Queen Elizabeth II "gently and assuredly, the Church of England has created an environment for other faith communities and indeed people of no faith to live freely". King Charles III, at a reception at Buckingham Palace days before his late mother's funeral, drew attention to this same fact. He reflected that his Anglican Christian confession committed him to the common good of freedom for all faith and belief traditions, as articulated in this wording.[169]

It goes on

> This Oath is prescribed by the Coronation Oath Act 1688, an Act of Parliament. An innovation in this service is that the Oath is preceded by a short paragraph in which the Archbishop reflects that the church will continue to seek to foster an environment where all people may live freely. This reflects the words of Her Late Majesty in 2012, when she said 'The concept of our established Church is occasionally misunderstood and, I believe, commonly under-appreciated. Its role is not to defend Anglicanism to the exclusion of other religions. Instead, the Church has a duty to protect the free practice of all faiths in this country.[170]

Thus Elizabeth II was utilised as a justification from the Church of England perspective for this addition. Perhaps the reference to a monarch held in such high regard by so many across the UK, the Commonwealth and wider world, allowed for the smooth passage of this change, with little in the way of debate.

In 2017, the barrister Graeme Watt argued that the oaths taken in 1937 and 1953 "lacked statutory authority" and were therefore unlawful on the basis that Queen Elizabeth II's oath did not include the lines 'according to the statutes in Parliament agreed upon'.[171] In the commentary of 2023, it is noteworthy that the Act is explicitly referenced. Yet Watt sets out that the absence in 1953 was almost certainly to avoid a conflict with Parliament no longer having a continuing right to legislate for the dominions given the 1931 statute and that 'laws and customs of the same' remained in the Oath—which clearly nuanced the necessary references to different jurisdictions/countries including Parliament in the United Kingdom. The idea that the monarch or the late Queen Elizabeth II lacked statutory authority was in the politest way thrown out by judges in a case in 2000 cited by Watt.[172] In 1937 and 1953, senior legal advisers to the government argued that most changes were "implied" amendments which had legal authority from other statutes. Nevertheless, Lord Hailsham (the then Lord Chancellor) said future revisions must "be limited to what was essential to give effect to the alteration in the [UK or Monarch's] constitutional position".[173] Most recently, in a written statement Oliver Dowden, the then Chancellor of the Duchy of Lancaster, confirmed that the Government intends to follow this approach. He said "that no express legislative authority is required to make the changes on the basis that they are to ensure consistency with the position regarding the Realms and Territories, as reflected in legislation".[174]

F. D. Maurice spoke of the spirit of judgement as some of the most complex thoughts and words of his life and yet judgement as the most beautiful in the whole Word of God.[175] The Coronation Oath speaks to that spirit of judgement. It is rooted in the tradition of Solomon. The monarch is the chief judge of the country—the fountain of justice. Our judges are his majesties judges. In the United Kingdom, the Coronation Oath in conjunction with the prior Recognition-Acclamation serves not only to bind consensually the monarch to the people, and to the apparatus of governance as it has evolved, but also to enunciate some of the principles—law, justice and mercy—upon which that governance rests. These principles or rights have been arduously attained and should be strenuously upheld. This is more than symbolism, not least in an era of extreme turbulence, when democracy can seem increasingly fragile and with an ongoing war in Europe and when leaders across the world are prepared to break the rule of law. This was brought ever more home to me when doing a 2023 interview with Ukrainian tv on the Oath and the purpose of a coronation in the twenty-first century and we were interrupted by an air raid warning.[176] Why I asked was a coronation of interest to Ukraine? To which the response came back—"it is difficult for you to understand, but what we wouldn't give for a chance to celebrate in such a way or pronounce on our values rather than thinking about war—we are interested because these moments are moments of celebration and we need such light in this darkness". We forget so easily here in the United Kingdom just how important the rule of law is in maintaining our way of life and also how such symbolism and such celebration is not available to all but can be a beacon of hope for those in peril in the world.

The oath has therefore been at one and the same time a conduit for tradition, a constitutional pillar, a source of authority and legitimacy and a marker of national values. The coronation oath binds monarch to peoples and to the governmental system of the state and the constitution, but it also communicates some of the principles—law, justice, and mercy—upon which that governance rests. Oaths are still an important part of employment in the British armed services, police force, parliament, privy council and law courts amongst others. Each of those oaths mentions allegiance, service or loyalty to the sovereign. How incongruous it would be if the person at the summit of the constitutional pyramid had no oath to swear themselves. Thus, 2023 saw the Coronation Oath continue with a central role within the service as it has been for time immemorial, with additions yes, but remaining ever-present.

Appendix 1: Coronation Oath Texts

A. **English Coronation Oaths**

(i). Text Found in the *Liber Regalis*, *c.*1390 (modern English translation of Latin original)[177]

[The metropolitan asks]

Whether he will be willing to grant and to preserve the laws and customs granted by ancient just and God-fearing kings to the people of England with confirmation by oath to the same people, and especially the laws, customs and liberties granted by the glorious King Edward to the clergy and people.

The said prince, however, promising to grant and preserve all the aforesaid, the metropolitan will then expound to him the things he has sworn to in so saying.

Will you preserve intact the peace of the Church of God for the clergy and people and union in God so far as in you lies [according to your powers].

He will answer. I shall preserve them.

Will you ensure in all your statutes [judgements] equal and true justice and discretion in mercy and truth so far as in you lies [according to your powers].

He will answer. I shall do so.

You will grant that just laws and customs which the people shall have chosen are to be observed, and will promise that they will be protected by you, and strengthened to the honour of God so far as in you lies [according to your powers].

He will answer. I grant and promise as much.

There follows the admonition of the bishops to the king and there shall be read by one bishop in the presence of all in a clear voice speaking thus:

[My] lord king we ask to be pardoned [considered?] by you so that you will preserve for each of us and to those churches in our trust the canonical privilege and due law and justice, and will deliver defence [for us] as the king in his kingdom owes to every bishop, to the abbots and the churches entrusted to him.

He will answer. Willing and sincere [devoted] in mind I promise and remit to you that to each of you and to the churches committed to you that I shall preserve canonical privilege and justice, and that I shall show with the help of God, so far as I can, as much as a king ought to show to each bishop, to abbots and to the churches committed to him by right.

(ii). Text Found in the Coronation Order for James I, 1603 (English Original)[178]

Sir will you grant and keepe, and by your oath confirme to the people of England the lawes and Customes to them granted by the Kinges of England your lawfull and Religiouse predecessors, and namely the Lawes, Customes and ffranchisez granted to the Clergie, and to the people by the gloriouse King Saint Edward your predecessor **according and Conformable to the lawes of god and true profession of the Gospell established in this Kingdome and agreeing to the Auncyent Customes of the Realme and the prerogatives of the Kinges thereof?**[179]

Rex. Resp. I grant and promise to keepe them.

Episcopus. Sir will you keepe peace and godly[180] agreement entirely (according to your power) both to god, the holie Church, the Clergie, and the people?

Rex. I will keepe it.

Episcopus. Sir will you ~~grant~~[181] to your power cause Lawe, iustice, and discretion in mercye and truth to bee executed in all your iudgmentes?

Rex. I will.

Episcopus. Sir will you graunt to hold and keepe the Lawes and rightfull Customes, which the Comminaltie of your Kingdome haue,[182] and to defende and vpphold them to the honor of god, so much as in you lye?[183]

Responsio Regis. I grant and promise so to doe.

[In Legg's source, the text continues with the admonition of the bishops, but this portion was oddly not translated into English]

(iii). Text Found in the Coronation Oath Act, for William III and Mary II, 1689 (English Original)[184]

Archbishop Will you solemnly promise and Swear to govern the People of this Kingdome of England, and the Dominions thereto belonging, according to the Statutes in Parliament agreed on, and [th]e Laws and Customs of [th]e same?

King and Queen I solemnly promise so to do.

Archbishop Will you to yo[u]r Power cause Law and Justice in Mercy to be Executed in all yo[u]r Judgments?

King and Queen I will.

Archbishop Will you to the Utmost of yo[u]r Power maintain the Laws of God, the true Profession of [th]e Gospell and the Protestant Reformed Religion Established by Law; and will you preserve unto [th]e Bishops and Clergy of this Realm, and to [th]e Churches committed to their Charge, all such Rights and Privileges, as by Law do or shall appertain unto them or any of them.

King and Queen All this I promise to do.

... laying their right hands upon the holy Gospels in the great Bible, ... and saying these words each of them ...

The things which I have here before promised, I will perform and keep; so help Me God.

Then each of them kisseth [th]e book.

(iv). Text used for Elizabeth II, 1953 (English Original)[185]

The late Queen was asked by the Archbishop:

Will you solemnly promise and swear to govern the Peoples of the United Kingdom of Great Britain and Northern Ireland, Canada, Australia, New Zealand, the Union of South Africa, Pakistan, and Ceylon, and of your Possessions and other Territories to any of them belonging or pertaining, according to their respective laws and customs?

Response:

I solemnly promise so to do.

Archbishop:

Will you to your power cause Laws and Justice, in Mercy to be executed in all your judgements?

Response:

I will.

Archbishop:

Will you to the utmost of your power maintain the Laws of God and the true profession of the Gospel? Will you maintain and preserve inviolably the settlement of the Church of England, and the doctrine, worship, discipline, and government thereof, as by laws established in England? And will you preserve unto the Bishops and Clergy of England, and to the Churches there committed to their charge, all such rights and privileges, as by law do or shall appertain to them or any of them?

Response:

All this I promise to do.

Laying her hand on the Bible, the Queen confirmed her oath, saying:

The things which I have here promised, I will perform, and keep. So help me God.

(v). Text used for Charles III, 2023 (English Original)[186]

The King was asked by the Archbishop:

Your Majesty,

The Church established by law, whose settlement you will swear to maintain is committed to the true profession of the Gospel, and in so doing, will seek to foster an environment in which people of all faiths and beliefs may life freely. The Coronation Oath has stood for centuries and is enshrined in law. Are you willing to take the Oath?

Response:

I am willing.

Archbishop:

Will you solemnly promise and swear to govern the Peoples of the United Kingdom of Great Britain and Northern Ireland, your other Realms and the Territories to any of them belonging or pertaining, according to their respective laws and customs?

Response:

I solemnly promise so to do.

Archbishop:

Will you to your power cause Laws and Justice, in Mercy, to be executed in all your judgements?

Response:

I will.

Archbishop:

Will you to the utmost of your power maintain the Laws of God and the true profession of the Gospel? Will you to the utmost of your power maintain in the United Kingdom the Protestant Reformed Religion established by law? Will you maintain and preserve inviolably the settlement of the Church of England, and the doctrine, worship, discipline, and government thereof, as by laws established in England? And will you preserve unto the Bishops and Clergy of England, and to the Churches there committed to their charge, all such rights and privileges, as by law do or shall appertain to them or any of them?

Response:

All this I promise to do.

The things which I have here promised, I will perform, and keep. So help me God.

Archbishop:

Your Majesty, are you will to make, subscribe, and declare to the statutory Accession Declaration Oath?

Response:

I am willing.

I Charles do solemnly and sincerely in the presence of God profess, testify, and declare that I am a faithful Protestant, and that I will, according to the true intent of the enactments which secure the Protestant succession to the Throne, uphold and maintain the said enactments to the best of my powers according to law.

B. **Scottish Coronation Oaths**

(i). Text used for James VI, 1567 (English Original, Modernised)[187]

Concerning the King's Oath to be Given at his Coronation

Item, because that the increase of virtue and suppressing of idolatry craves that the prince and the people be of one perfect religion, which of God's mercy is now presently professed within this realm, therefore it is statute and ordained by our sovereign lord, [*James Stewart, Earl of Moray*], my lord regent, and three estates of this present parliament that all kings and princes or magistrates whatsoever holding their place, which hereafter in any time shall happen to reign and bear rule over this realm, at the time of their coronation and receiving of their princely authority, make their faithful promise by oath in presence of the eternal God that, enduring the whole course of their life, they shall serve the same eternal God to the utmost of their power accordingly as he has required in his most holy word revealed and contained in the New and Old Testaments; and according to the same word, shall maintain the true religion of Jesus Christ, the preaching of his holy word and due and right administration of the sacraments now received and preached within this realm; and shall abolish and gainsay all false religion contrary to the same; and shall rule the people committed to their charge according to the will and command of God, revealed in his aforesaid word and according to the loveable laws and constitutions received in this realm, in no way repugnant to the said word of the eternal God; and shall procure to the utmost of their power to the kirk of God and whole Christian people true and perfect peace in all time coming, the rights and rents, with all just privileges of the crown of Scotland, to preserve and keep inviolated, nor shall they transfer nor alienate the same; they shall forbid and repress in all estates and degrees robbery, oppression and all kind of wrong; in all judgements, they shall command and procure that justice and equity be kept to all creatures, without exception, as the Lord and father of all mercies be merciful to them; and out of their lands and empire they shall be careful to root out all heretics and enemies to the true worship of God that shall be convicted by the true kirk of God of the aforesaid crimes; and that they shall faithfully affirm the things above-written by their solemn oath.

(ii). Text used in 1689 (English Original)[188]

Coronation Oath: Voted and Approved
The Oath to be Administered to the King and Queen at their Acceptance of the Crown

The form of the oath to be taken by their majesties the king and queen, at their acceptance of the crown, being twice read was voted and approved by the estates, of which oath the tenor follows:

We … faithfully, promise and swear, by this our solemn oath in presence of the eternal God, that during the whole course of our life, we will serve the same eternal God to the utmost of our power, according as he has required in his most holy word revealed and contained in the new and old testaments, and according to the same word shall maintain the true religion of Christ Jesus, the preaching of his holy word, and the due and right ministration of the sacraments now received and preached within the realm of Scotland, and shall abolish and withstand all false religion, contrary to the same, and shall rule the people committed to our charge according to the will and command of God revealed in his aforesaid word, and according to the loveable laws and constitutions received in this realm, in no way repugnant to the said word of the eternal God, and shall procure to the utmost of our power to the kirk of God and whole Christian people true and perfect peace in all time coming, that we shall preserve and keep inviolate the rights and rents, with all just privileges of the crown of Scotland, neither shall we transfer nor alienate the same, that we shall forbid and repress in all estates and degrees, plunder, oppression, and all kinds of violation, and we shall command and procure that justice and equity in all judgements be kept to all persons without exception, as the Lord and father of all mercies shall be merciful to us, and we shall be careful to root out all heretics and enemies to the true worship of God that shall be convicted by the true kirk of God of the foresaid crimes out of our lands and empire of Scotland, and we faithfully affirm the things abovewritten by our solemn oath.

Notes

1. https://www.rct.uk/collection/stories/the-crown-jewels/st-edwards-crown, accessed 18 November 2025.
2. A. Spencer, "The Coronation Oath in English Politics, 1272–1399," in B. Thompson and J. Watts (eds), *Political Society in Later Medieval England: A Festschrift for Christine Carpenter* (new edn) (Woodbridge, 2015), pp. 38–54; H. G. Richardson, 'The Coronation in Medieval England: The Evolution of the Office and the Oath', *Traditio*, 16 (1960), pp. 111–202.
3. 'An Act for Establishing the Coronation Oath' (1 William & Mary c. 6, printed in *SR*, VI pp. 56–7); 'An Act for the further Limitation of the Crown and better securing the Rights and Liberties of the Subject' [the Act of Settlement] (12 & 13 William III c. 2, printed *ibid.*, VII pp. 636–8), and cf. Lord Mackay of Clashfern (ed. in chief), *Halsbury's Laws of England* (5th edn, London, 2008–), 8(2), paragraph 39 for statutory conditions of the descent of the Crown. 'An Act for an Union of the Two

Kingdoms of England and Scotland' [the Act of Union, in the English Parliament] (6 Anne c. 11, printed in *SR*, VIII pp. 566–77) sets out a declaration and requirement for the monarch to swear an oath to maintain the Church of Scotland. This swearing does not take place in the coronation, but rather follows almost immediately upon accession, and is done in the Privy Council's presence: *Second Supplement* (*c*. 8 February 1952) *to TLG Extraordinary* (no. 39463), p. 839; *TLG*, 12 February 1952 (no. 39467), p. 861.
4. It is also worth thinking of Harold (II's) supposed oath breaking of Bayeaux Tapestry fame with William the Conqueror, see D. Bates, *William the Conqueror* (New Haven, Connecticut, 2018), p. 255; see also B. O'Brien, "Conquest and the Law," in L. Ashe and E. J. Ward (eds), *Conquests in Eleventh-Century England: 1016, 1066*, (new edn) (Woodbridge, 2020), pp. 41–64; F. Leneghan, "Royal Wisdom and the Alfredian Context of 'Cynewulf and Cyneheard.'" *Anglo-Saxon England*, 39 (2011), pp. 71–104; G. Garnett, 'Coronation and Propaganda: Some Implications of the Norman Claim to the Throne of England in 1066: The Alexander Prize Essay.' *Transactions of the Royal Historical Society*, 36 (1986), pp. 91–116; M. W. Campbell, 'Earl Godwin of Wessex and Edward the Confessor's Promise of the Throne to William of Normandy.' *Traditio*, 28 (1972), pp. 141–58.
5. C. Valente, 'The Deposition and Abdication of Edward II', *The English Historical Review*, CXIII (1998), pp. 853, 855–6, 880.
6. Given-Wilson, *Chronicles of the Revolution 1397–1400*, pp. 168–89; J. M. Theilmann, 'Caught Between Political Theory and Political Practice: "The Record and Process of the Deposition of Richard II"', *History of Political Thought*, XXV (2004), pp. 599–619.
7. S. R. Gardiner (ed.), *The Constitutional Documents of the Puritan Revolution 1625–1660* (3rd edition, Oxford, 1906), pp. 371–2 (my emphasis).
8. C. Carpenter, 'Resisting and Deposing Kings in England in the Thirteenth, Fourteenth and Fifteenth Centuries', in R. von Friedeburg (ed.), *Murder and Monarchy: Regicide in European History, 1300–1800* (Basingstoke, 2004), pp. 100, 101, 103.
9. Cressy, *Charles I*, p. 19.
10. Sir F. Hubert, *The Historie of Edward the Second* … (London, 1629), p. 6.
11. Anon., *A True Relation of the Manner of the Deposing of King Edward II Together With the Articles which were Exhibited Against Him in Parliament. As also, an Exact Account of the Proceedings and Articles Against King Richard II* … (London, 1689), especially pp. 13–14 (Coronation Oath).
12. C. Russell, *The Causes of the English Civil War* (Oxford, 1990), p. 23.

13. Shawcross, *Selected Letters of Queen Elizabeth The Queen Mother*, p. 230. See also discussion on 'The Abdication Crisis' in Williamson and Baldwin, *Baldwin Papers*, pp. 387–425.
14. *Authorised Liurgy for the Coronation Rite ... Charles III*, pp. 7–8.
15. A. Williams, 'Edmund I (920/1–946)', *ODNB*. Cf. A. J. Robertson (ed.), *The Laws of the Kings of England from Edmund to Henry I* (Cambridge, 1925) and R. P. Abels, *Lordship and Military Obligation in Anglo-Saxon England* (Berkeley, California, 1988).
16. Schramm, *Coronation*, p. 17 and particularly pp. 177–227.
17. *Ibid.*, pp. 17–18.
18. J. Spurr, '"The Strongest Bond of Conscience": Oaths and the Limits of Tolerance in Early Modern England', in H. E. Braun and E. Vallance (eds), *Contexts of Conscience in Early Modern Europe, 1500–1700* (Basingstoke, 2004), p. 151.
19. Strickland, *Henry the Young King*, p. 87, quoting Legg, *Coronation Records*, p. 31.
20. Strickland, *Henry the Young King*, p. 87.
21. Strong, *Coronation*, p. 23. See also *OED*.
22. There is evidence of a second oath from Richard I's coronation, taken shortly before his crowning. This involved the archbishop imploring the king not to assume governance unless he promised to rule to the utmost of his powers. The king responded that with God's help he would. According to Legg, this was perhaps not so much an oath as a 'private pact between the archbishop and the king': Legg, *Coronation Records*, p. xxviii and n. 2. There seems to have been a similar oath for King John's coronation: Bibliothèque Nationale, Paris, MS lat 6048B, fol. 148v.
23. Schramm, *Coronation*, p. 24. See also Jackson, *Vive le Roi!*, pp. 57–61, 192, 196 (especially pp. 58–9: 'In France [this *ordo* were still being] used, basically unchanged, at the coronation of Louis XVI nine hundred years after it had first been formulated'; alterations did take place for Charles X, but the origins of the oath rested on this former *ordo*). Interestingly, the French tradition was used as the *ordo* for the kingdom of Jerusalem: Sebag Montefiore, *Jerusalem*, pp. 211–12, 214–16, 278.
24. The coronation *ordo* for the Holy Roman Emperor, the *Pontificale Romanogermanicum*, at the Abbey of St Alban's, Mainz, 961: Schramm, *Coronation*, p. 36; Strong, *Coronation*, p. 43.
25. Cf. *ibid.*, pp. 42–6; Richardson, 'Oath', pp. 130–2; and Schramm, *Coronation*, pp. 34–9.
26. Richardson, 'Oath', pp. 196–7. See J. Gillingham, 'John (1167–1216)', *ODNB*.
27. Magna Carta is perhaps the one other English medieval document that paralleled the Coronation Oath in limiting royal power: V. Bogdanor, *The*

Monarchy and the Constitution (Oxford, 1995), pp. 3–4; Spencer, 'Coronation Oath', p. 40, quoting Carpenter as saying that the Coronation Oath was 'one of the two most fundamental documents of the [medieval] constitution' and adds that the other one was, of course, Magna Carta.

28. A. Hughes, 'The Origins and Descent of the Fourth Recension of the English Coronation', in J. M. Bak (ed.), *Coronations: Medieval and Early Modern Monarchic Ritual* (Berkeley and Los Angeles, California, *c.*1990), pp. 197–216.
29. Richardson & Sayles, 'Records', p. 134. This is a non-issue, given that French was the language of Court culture, in which case either language would have been sufficient. Had the oath been taken in English, then that would have been significant: S. Phillips, *Edward II* (New Haven, Connecticut, 2010), p. 55.
30. BL, Add. MS 18669, fols 1r–10v; A. F. Sutton and P. W. Hammond (eds), *The Coronation of Richard III: The Extant Documents* (Gloucester, 1983).
31. *APC*, II p. 30.
32. For fuller discussion on Elizabeth I's coronation, see above p. 5.
33. Richardson & Sayles, 'Records', p. 138. Lytlington/Litlington was abbot of Westminster 1362–1386.
34. B. Wilkinson, 'The Coronation Oath of Edward II', in J. G. Edwards *et al.* (eds), *Historical Essays in Honour of James Tait* (Manchester, 1933), pp. 405–16.
35. Richardson & Sayles, 'Records', p. 136.
36. Phillips, *Edward II*, pp. 142–3.
37. *Ibid.*, p. 143. See also H. A. L. Fisher (ed.), *The Constitutional History of England: A Course of Lectures Delivered by F. W. Maitland* (Cambridge, 1908), pp. 98–100 and Greenberg, 'Confessor's Laws'. She stresses that Edward the Confessor's laws (or those associated with him) were hugely venerated, and that this connection was re-established at every coronation *via* the oath.
38. Richardson, 'Oath'; *H. G. Richardson*, 'The English Coronation Oath', *Speculum*, XXIV (1949), pp. 44–75; and *idem*, 'The Coronation in Medieval England: The Evolution of the Office and the Oath', *Traditio*, 16 (1960), pp. 111–202. See also Richardson & Sayles, 'Records'.
39. Richardson, 'Oath', p. 131. His evidence is an anonymous note in a BL MS which he misleadingly calls the *Liber Regalis*, thereby fostering possible confusion with the later *Liber Regalis* at WA. Crucially, alteration did occur, but the core three promises remained. For Richardson's *Liber Regalis*, see *ibid.*, p. 143 (n. 3).

40. This battle of *c.*1100–1107 was part of a wider conflict between Church and State (the Investiture Contest) and was not fully settled until the murder of St Thomas Becket, Henry II's archbishop of Canterbury, in 1170.
41. *OED*. See also Strong, *Coronation*, p. 9.
42. Ultimately, a compromise was achieved, whereby the monarch was anointed (with a different form of chrism) on hands, shoulders and arms, but not head. Chrism was used in Tudor coronations, but this tussle is significant in that, for clerical authorities, a coronation raised the idea of anointing a sovereign as being commensurate to that of a spiritual figure. It was fear of an overly priestly status that led to this revision: Cantor, *Kingship*, pp. 131–5, 174–6 and P. L. Ward, 'The Coronation Ceremony in Mediaeval England', *Speculum*, XIV (1939), pp. 160–8. Within the context of the full coronation ceremony, the oath is essential precisely because a monarch could not be anointed without the oath-taking. Equally, there was reciprocity, in that the oath acquired additional significance by being part of a ceremony that involved the sanctification of sovereignty, through the use of unction.
43. Sturdy, '"Continuity"'.
44. *Ibid.*, p. 237.
45. Excepting Strong, who cites it as a source, but does not engage with it: Strong, *Coronation*, p. 506.
46. Sturdy, '"Continuity"', p. 238, summarising Brückmann's thesis.
47. Richardson, 'Oath', p. 129. On coronation charters, see C. H. McIlwain, 'Due Process of Law in Magna Carta', *Columbia Law Review*, 14 (1914), pp. 27–51, reprinted in C. H. McIlwain, *Constitutionalism and the Changing World: Collected Papers* (Cambridge, 1939), pp. 94–8. See also R. S. Hoyt, 'The Coronation Oath of 1308', *The English Historical Review*, LXXI (1956), p. 358.
48. Richardson, 'Oath', pp. 157–8. On the 'non-alienation clause', King John's 'oath of homage to the Pope' and the role of the papacy in relation to the Coronation Oath, see Schramm, *Coronation*, pp. 194–8, 200. See also Strong, *Coronation*, pp. 62–3, 186–7; Kantorowicz, *King's Two Bodies*, pp. 347–9: 'a non-alienation oath of some kind was customarily taken by a king at his coronation ... in other words ... certain royal obligations towards the impersonal Crown – analogous to the obligations of a bishop towards his See'.
49. Legg, *Coronation Records*, pp. 81–131 (*Liber Regalis*), 219–40 ('Little Device', for Richard III, modified for Henry VII).
50. As defined in the *Liber Regalis*.

51. F. R. H. Du Boulay (ed.), *Registrum Thome Bourgchier Cantuariensis Archiepiscopi A.D. 1454–1486*, The Canterbury and York Society, LIV (Oxford, 1957), p. 61.
52. Schramm, *Coronation*, pp. 214–15. See also Sutton & Hammond, *Richard III.*
53. Schramm, *Coronation*, pp. 215–16. Perhaps the text was discarded because Henry VIII discovered the unofficial character of this source.
54. BL, Cotton MS Tiberius E VIII, fol. 89r–v. See also *ibid.*, fols 90r–100r (copy of Henry VIII's coronation order). The text of Henry VIII's revisions is also given in Legg, *Coronation Records*, pp. 240–1 and Tudor-Craig, 'Henry VIII', pp. 187, 199 (rejecting Ullmann's 1509 dating) and Ullmann, '"Empire"', p. 183.
55. Maitland, *Constitutional History*, pp. 286–7; Tudor-Craig, 'Henry VIII', pp. 187–8.
56. Schramm, *Coronation*, pp. 88–91, 214–17.
57. Another aspect was the problematic status of royal proclamations (and a proclamation has some affinities with an oath in the sense of being declamatory): R. W. Heinze, *The Proclamations of the Tudor Kings* (Cambridge, 1976), pp. 30–54; F. A. Youngs, Jr, *The Proclamations of the Tudor Queens* (Cambridge, 1976), especially pp. 27–58.
58. Cf. Kantorowicz, *King's Two Bodies*, p. 5; Axton, *Queen's Two Bodies*; Haas, '"Divine Right"'; Sommerville, *Politics and Ideology*, pp. 9–54; Burgess, 'Divine Right'; Zaller, 'Vessels', pp. 757–8; Ryrie, 'Divine Kingship'; Al-Azmeh & Bak, *Kingship*, *passim*; and Burgess, *Political Thought*, pp. 142–52.
59. Strong, *Coronation*, pp. 185–6.
60. *APC*, II pp. 29–33; Zaller, 'Vessels', p. 759; from the 'Little Device' for the coronation of Henry VII in Legg, *Coronation Records*, pp. 228–9. Cf. MacCulloch, *Boy King*, p. 62 (illustration of gold and silver medal commemorating Edward VI's coronation. The inscriptions, although in Latin, Greek and Hebrew, all have identical texts, all stressing the royal supremacy; a similar medal had been struck for Henry VIII in 1535: cf. MacCulloch, *Cranmer*, pp. 364–5). Caution is needed over Edward VI's coronation, for, as MacCulloch has revealed, what is said to be Cranmer's sermon never occurred, or rather the surviving text is fabricated: MacCulloch, 'Firebrands'. Therefore, we cannot be as certain as Strong that 'monarchy was thus rendered seemingly absolute' by these supposed changes: Strong, *Coronation*, pp. 200–1.
61. *APC*, II p. 30.
62. Schramm, *Coronation*, p. 217.
63. *APC*, II pp. 30–1.

64. Schramm, *Coronation*, p. 217 and Maitland, *Constitutional History*, p. 286.
65. Ullmann, '"Empire"', pp. 183–4.
66. Hunt, *Drama*, p. 128. See also Schramm, *Coronation*, pp. 217–18.
67. *CSP, Spain*, XI pp. 239–40.
68. *CSP, Venice*, V p. 431. See also T. F. Mayer, 'Pole, Reginald (1500–1558)', *ODNB*.
69. *Ibid.* See also *CSP, Spain*, XI p. 220 and Hunt, *Drama*, p. 129. Cf. Hoak, 'Transformation', pp. 136–8: Mary did not wish to be anointed with oil 'consecrated by schismatic hands' (Cranmer's), and therefore acquired properly consecrated chrism from the bishop of Arras – three phials of 'acceptable unction': Loades, *Mary*, p. 206.
70. See Haugaard, 'Elizabeth I'; Hoak, 'Tudor Deborah?'; Hoak, 'Transformation'. For early twentieth century debate, see above p. 54 (n. 27).
71. Cf. W. T. MacCaffrey, 'Cecil, William, 1st baron Burghley (1520/1–1598)', *ODNB*.
72. TNA, SP 15/9, fol. 18v.
73. Hoak, 'Transformation', pp. 149–51; MacCulloch, *Boy King*, *passim*.
74. Hoak, 'Transformation', pp. 149–50. We should not underestimate Privy Council power: D. J. Crankshaw, 'Ecclesiastical Statesmanship in England in the Age of the Reformation', in D. Wendebourg (ed.), *Sister Reformations: The Reformation in Germany and in England* (Tübingen, 2010), pp. 271–303.
75. On the one hand, only one bishop (Oglethorpe) had been willing to crown Elizabeth and even he might have refused if the oath had been too radical. On the other hand, perhaps the reason for Cecil producing the oath at the last minute (in the ceremony) was to stop Oglethorpe having time to reject it on grounds of any radical content, but would Cecil and the Privy Council have been so radical at this delicate juncture? Perhaps only the emergence of Elizabeth's Coronation Oath can solve this conundrum.
76. D. C. Douglas (general ed.), *English Historical Documents*, 10 volumes in 11 parts (London, 1953–1977), III p. 525.
77. T. Rymer and R. Sanderson (eds), *Fœdera* ..., 4 volumes in 7 parts (London, 1816–1869), IV p. 9 ('*justo & rationabiliter*').
78. Strong, *Coronation*, p. 84. See also G. O. Sayles, *The King's Parliament of England* (London, 1975), pp. 96, 105–8, 115–17; and B. Wilkinson, 'The Coronation Oath of Edward II and the Statute of York', *Speculum*, 19 (1944), pp. 445–69.
79. Legg, *Coronation Records*, p. 88 (Latin).
80. Du Boulay, *Registrum ... Cantuariensis Archiepiscopi ...*, p. 61.

81. Garnett, 'Crown', pp. 171–214.
82. Skinner, 'The State', pp. 90–131.
83. C. W. Brooks, *Pettyfoggers and Vipers of the Commonwealth: The 'Lower Branch' of the Legal Profession in Early Modern England* (Cambridge, 1986), pp. 48–131.
84. H. Höpfl and M. P. Thompson, 'The History of Contract as a Motif in Political Thought', *The American Historical Review*, 84 (1979), p. 932.
85. With the Glorious Revolution, the House of Commons was first invited for the first time *en bloc* to attend the coronation. In 1689, King William III and Queen Mary II granted the 'request of the House of Commons, to see their ma[jes]ties Crown[e]d' (CA, MS L.19, p. 88) – so, importantly, the contract was agreed before both Houses of Parliament in the Abbey; members of the House of Lords were, of course, present by personal invitation.
86. As Ullmann explains, even in theocratic kingship, although a king was above the law of the populace, he was nevertheless subject to God's law: Ullmann, *Principles*, p. 139.
87. C. C. Weston, 'The Theory of Mixed Monarchy Under Charles I and After', *The English Historical Review*, LXXV (1960), p. 429.
88. Strickland, *Henry the Young King*, p. 86.
89. Doran, *Tudor To Stuart*, p. 137.
90. J. W. Legg (ed.), *The Coronation Order for King James I* (London, 1902), pp. xcvi–cii. See also Schramm, *Coronation*, pp. 218–20; Fisher, *Constitutional History of England: Maitland*, pp. 286–7; and Strong, *Coronation*, pp. 238–41. Yet for all the importance of these changes, and James I's discussion of the Coronation Oath, they are omitted in P. Croft, *King James* (Basingstoke, 2003).
91. Legg, *Coronation Order … James I*, p. 16.
92. Legg, *Coronation Records*, pp. 250–1.
93. Legg, *Coronation Order … James I*, p. xcix.
94. Walker, *A Circumstantial Account of the Preparations for the Coronation of His Majesty King Charles the Second …*, pp. 95–7.
95. Sandford, *History*, pp. 88–9. See also Schwoerer, 'Coronation', pp. 128–30.
96. J. P. Sommerville, *Royalists and Patriots: Politics and Ideology in England 1603–1640* (2nd edition, London and New York, 1999), pp. 169–70, 173–4.
97. Schramm, *Coronation*, p. 218.
98. Legg, *Coronation Order … James I*, p. 15.
99. *Ibid.*, p. 90.
100. Legg, *Coronation Order … James I*; Doran, *Tudor to Stuart*, p. 137; A. Hunt, 'The Bright Star of the North: James I and his English

Coronation', in M. Twycross, S. Carpenter *et al.* (eds), *Medieval English Theatre 38: The Best Pairt of Our Play. Essays Presented to John J. McGavin. Part II.* (Woodbridge; 2017), pp. 23, 27–9; Contemporary accounts include SP14/2, fols 208–11r; BL, Additional MS, 4712, fols 59r–68v; The Huntington Library, California, Ellesmere, 1222 (35/B/32); Bodl., Rawlinson MS, B40; T. Milles, *Catalogue of Honour ... of all the free monarches ... kinges of England ... Scotland ...* (1610), pp. 59–60; There is also a much later version in print coinciding with the year of James II coronation: *The Ceremonies, Form of Prayer and Services used in Westminster Abbey at the Coronation of James I* (London, 1685) – however, Jack, 'Coronation of James I', p. 76 (n. 48) regards this as 'unreliable' given a 'polemical aspect' to it; *CSPVen*, 10, no. 105; and W. B. Rye, 'The Coronation of King James I, 1603', *The Antiquary*, 22 (1890), pp. 18–23.

101. Schramm, *Coronation*, p. 218.
102. Legg, *Coronation Records*, p. 251.
103. Legg, *Coronation Order ... James I*, p. c. See also *ibid.*, pp. xcix–cii for discussion of the charge against Laud and his denial.
104. *Ibid.*, p. cii.
105. *Ibid.*
106. Legg, *Coronation Order ... James I*, pp. liv–lv, 11; Doran, *Tudor To Stuart*, pp. 137–8. See also W. C. Taylor, *Chapters on Coronations* (London, 1838), p. 99 and pp. 180–1 (on accusations of novelties).
107. Doran, *Tudor to Stuart*, p. 138 quoting James I, *A Meditation Upon the 27.28.29. verses of the xxvii Chapter of Saint Matthew. Or a Paterne for a King's Inauguration* (London, 1620), pp. 117–19.
108. Doran, *Tudor to Stuart*, p. 138 quoting Legg, *Coronation Order ... James I*, p. lxxviii.
109. Cressy, *Charles I*, p. 72.
110. *Ibid.*
111. See Cole, *The Norman Conquest*, pp. 24, 106, 109. See also O'Brien, "Conquest and the Law"; Leneghan, "Royal Wisdom and the Alfredian Context"; Garnett, 'Coronation and Propaganda'; Campbell, 'Earl Godwin of Wessex and Edward the Confessor's Promise'.
112. Hunt, *Drama*, p. 14.
113. Cressy, *Charles I*, p. 74 (my emphases).
114. Sommerville, *Royalists and Patriots*, p. 63.
115. Picard, *Restoration London*, pp. 240–1.
116. A. Milton, 'Sacrilege and Compromise: Court Divines and the King's Conscience, 1642–1649', in M. J. Braddick and D. L. Smith (eds), *The Experience of Revolution in Stuart Britain and Ireland: Essays for John Morrill* (Cambridge, 2011), pp. 138–40.

117. Spurr, '"The Strongest Bond of Conscience"', p. 156. See also Shapiro, 'Assize Sermons', pp. 24–7 (discussing importance of oaths in law courts).
118. Ullmann, *Principles of Government …*, p. 181.
119. *Ibid.*, p. 182.
120. https://www.coronationroll.gov.uk/further_info/the-ring/, accessed 22 November 2025.
121. Quoted in Hunt, *Drama*, p. 133. See also R. Grafton, *A Chronicle at Large and Meere History of the Affayres of Englande and Kinges of the Same …* (London, 1569).
122. [James I], *The True Law of Free Monarchy, or The Reciprocall and Mutuall Duty Betwixt a Free King and his Naturall Subjects* (London, 1642).
123. Sommerville, *Royalists and Patriots*, p. 124.
124. *Ibid.*
125. James I, *The Workes of the Most High and Mightie Prince, Iames by the Grace of God, King of Great Britaine, France and Ireland, Defender of the Faith, &c.* (London, 1616), p. 208.
126. K. M. Brown *et al.* (eds), *The Records of the Parliaments of Scotland to 1707* (St Andrews, 2007–2016), A1567/12/7. See Appendix 1.
127. Croft, *King James*, pp. 54, 58–61.
128. Harris, *Revolution*, p. 44.
129. *Ibid.*, pp. 44–5. This is based on absence of evidence, but it is equally not unlikely that there were complaints.
130. On the 1953 coronation as 'a significant cultural indicator in 1950s Wales', see M. E. Wiliam, 'Monarchy and National Identity: Wales and the 1953 Coronation', *Cultural and Social History*, 19 (2022), pp. 301–322.
131. Brown, *Records of the Parliaments of Scotland*, 1689/3/105–9. See also Anon., *The Declaration of the Estates of the Kingdom of Scotland, Containing the Claim of Right, and the Offer of the Crown to Their Majesties, King William and Queen Mary: Together with the Grievances Represented by the Estates; and Their Majesties Oath at Their Acceptance of the Crown* (Edinburgh, 1689).
132. Harris, *Revolution*, p. 395.
133. *Ibid.*, p. 396.
134. *Ibid.*, pp. 386–91, 406. The Convention was turned into a Parliament on 5 June 1689: Brown, *Records*, 1689/6/6.
135. *Ibid.*, 1689/3/131–3.
136. Harris, *Revolution*, pp. 404–5.
137. *TLG*, 13–16 May 1689 (no. 2453); Brown, *Records*, 1689/3/160.
138. A. Boyer, *The History of the Reign of Queen Anne, Digested into Annals*, 11 volumes (London, 1703–1713), I pp. 3, 26.
139. Bodl., MS Smith 65, fol. 57r–v (28 March 1702).

140. Morris, *The Journeys of Celia Fiennes*, p. 299.
141. Legg, *Coronation Records*, pp. xxviii–xxix.
142. See Fisher, *Constitutional History ... Maitland*, pp. 283–8.
143. Legg, *Coronation Order ... James I*, pp. 89–90.
144. Legg, *Coronation Records*, p. 251.
145. Walker, *A Circumstantial Account*, pp. 95–6.
146. That Parliament was meant in the 1308 oath even if it is not stated explicitly is indicated by the draft English translation made for Richard III's coronation, where the word was written and either underlined or deleted (the MS is ambiguous). The idea in 1308 of popular choice is also an implicit reference to parliamentary consent for statutes.
147. Legg, *Coronation Records*, p. 326 (my emphasis).
148. Morris, *The Journeys of Celia Fiennes*, p. 301.
149. Legg, *Coronation Records*, p. xxx.
150. NLS, MS 9255; NRS, Erskine Papers, MS GD124/10/486/3 (Copy of report on Coronation Oath by attorney-general of England to lords justices of Great Britain; letter to Archibald Campbell, 1st Earl of Ilay, from Joseph Addison on behalf of lords justices and reply thereto by Charles Hay, 3rd marquess of Tweeddale, and others, 1714); and NRS, Clerk Papers, MS GD18/3151.
151. Speck, *Reluctant Revolutionaries*, p. 165.
152. J. G. A. Pocock, *The Ancient Constitution and the Feudal Law: A Study of English Historical Thought in the Seventeenth Century* (Cambridge, reissue 1987), p. 231.
153. *Ibid.* See also T. P. Slaughter, 'Abdicate' and 'Contract' Restored', *The Historical Journal*, 28, pp. 399–403.
154. Quoted in J. Spurr, 'A Profane History of Early Modern Oaths', *Transactions of the Royal Historical Society*, Sixth Series, XI (2001), pp. 41–2.
155. Anon. (ed.), *The Book of Oaths, and the Severall Forms Thereof, Both Antient and Modern. Faithfully Collected out of Sundry Authentike Books and Records, not Heretofore Extant, Compiled in One Volume. Very Useful for all Persons Whatsoever, Especially those that Undertake any Office of Magistracie or Publique Imployment in the Common-Wealth* (London, 1649).
156. Anon. (ed.), *The Book of Oaths and the Several Forms Thereof, Both Ancient and Modern Faithfully Collected out of Sundry Authenticke Books of Records, not Heretofore Extant. Very Useful for all Persons Whatsoever, Especially those that Undertake any Office of Magistracy or Publique Imployment* (London, 1689).

157. Anon. (ed.), *The Book of Oaths, and the Several Forms Thereof, Both Ancient and Modern, Faithfully Collected out of Sundry Authentick Books of Records* (London, 1715).
158. For some important contributions, see C. Robbins, 'Selden's Pills: State Oaths in England, 1558–1714', *The Huntington Library Quarterly*, XXXV (1972), pp. 303–21; J. Spurr, 'Perjury, Profanity and Politics', *The Seventeenth Century*, 8 (1993), pp. 29–50; D. M. Jones, *Conscience and Allegiance in Seventeenth Century England: The Political Significance of Oaths and Engagements* (Rochester, New York, 1999); E. Campbell, 'Oaths and Affirmations of Public Office under English Law: An Historical Retrospect', *The Journal of Legal History*, 21 (2000), pp. 1–32; Spurr, 'Early Modern Oaths', pp. 37–63; Spurr, '"The Strongest Bond of Conscience"', pp. 151–65; and C. Condren, *Argument and Authority in Early Modern England: The Presupposition of Oaths and Offices* (Cambridge, 2006).
159. Legg, *Coronation Records*, p. xxx.
160. J. Hall, *Queen Elizabeth and Her Church: Royal Service at Westminster Abbey* (London, 2012), p. 13.
161. J. H. Franklin (ed. and translator), Jean Bodin, *On Sovereignty: Four Chapters from The Six Books of the Commonwealth* (Cambridge, 1992), p. 21. See particularly pp. 1–45.
162. Bogdanor, *Monarchy and the Constitution*, p. 2.
163. R. Hazell and B. Morris, *Swearing in the New King: The Accession and Coronation Oaths,* The Constitution Unit (London, 2022); N. Bonney, 'The Evolution and Contemporary Relevance of the Accession and Coronation Oaths of the United Kingdom', *The British Journal of Politics and International Relations*, 13 (2011), pp. 603–18; C. L. Berry, 'The Coronation Oath and the Church of England', *JEH*, 11 (1960), pp. 98–105.
164. https://www.legislation.gov.uk/ukpga/1931/4/pdfs/ukpga_19310004_en.pdf, accessed 10 March 2025.
165. TNA, https://webarchive.nationalarchives.gov.uk/ukgwa/+ /https:/www.nationalarchives.gov.uk/jubilee/gallery/queen-elizabeth-second-highlights/coronation-oath/, accessed 18 November 2025.
166. https://hansard.parliament.uk/commons/1953-02-25/debates/8218c895-c62e-4918-b23c-0c4b83edd819/CoronationOathChanges, volume 511, debated on Wednesday 25 February 1953, accessed 18 November 2025; https://api.parliament.uk/historic-hansard/commons/1953/feb/25/coronation-oath-changes-1, accessed 18 November 2025.
167. H. Sherwood, 4 May 2023, https://www.theguardian.com/uk-news/2023/may/04/defender-of-all-faiths-coronation-puts-focus-

king-charles-religious-beliefs, accessed 10 May 2023; C. Murray, 5 May 2023, https://www.forbes.com/sites/conormurray/2023/05/05/king-charles-iiis-people-of-all-faiths-pledge-why-theyve-introduced-new-inclusive-language-as-more-crown-critics-emerge/#:~:text=As%20Britain%20has%20become%20more,religions%20in%20the%20United%20Kingdom, accessed 5 May 2023; J. Cooper, 8 May 2023, https://www.telegraph.co.uk/news/2023/05/08/charles-iii-is-a-21st-century-philosopher-king/#:~:text=In%201994%2C%20he%20seemed%20to,the%20epithet's%20prior%20Anglican%20exceptionalism, accessed 10 May 2023.

168. *Authorised Liturgy ... Coronation Rite ... Charles III*, pp. 7–8.
169. *Ibid.*
170. *Ibid.*
171. G. Watt, 31 August 2017, https://www.cambridge.org/core/journals/ecclesiastical-law-journal/article/coronation-oath/F83079759125218B8D97BA1722954CBC#fn51, accessed 10 May 2023.
172. G. Watt, 31 August 2017, https://www.cambridge.org/core/journals/ecclesiastical-law-journal/article/coronation-oath/F83079759125218B8D97BA1722954CBC#fn54, accessed 10 May 2023.
173. TNA, https://discovery.nationalarchives.gov.uk/details/r/D7730541, accessed 10 May 2023.
174. D. Torrance, 19 April 2023, https://commonslibrary.parliament.uk/changes-to-the-coronation-oath/, accessed 20 May 2023.
175. B. Reardon, 'Maurice, (John) Frederick Denison (1805–1872)', *ODNB*; https://www.kcl.ac.uk/events/the-british-coronation-oath-why-an-age-old-custom-still-matters-lecture-1, F. D. Maurice Lecture I, KCL, 2 May 2023, accessed 10 June 2023.
176. Ukrainian TV 1+1 - two episodes on the history of Coronations (1–2 May 2023): https://www.youtube.com/watch?v=x97CzPkglkQ, accessed 10 May 2023.
177. Legg, when translating the *Liber Regalis*, failed to translate the oath and instead cross-referenced to the oath of Charles I, thereby hugely misleading readers, for that oath is different: Legg, *Coronation Records*, p. 117. I am very grateful to Dr Elisabeth Leedham-Green who has taken the time to provide a proper translation.
178. Legg, *Coronation Order ... James I*, pp. 15–16. It is not clear whether the 1603 translation was executed from a Latin or a French source. Legg shows that both texts were available in his own source (see *ibid.*, pp. 13–14 and 14–15): the Latin probably from the *Liber Regalis* (or a source ultimately derived from it) and the French from the 1308 Close Roll (or a source ultimately derived from it). Whatever the original language used, the point is that the translation was defective, and that this translation was used in 1626, 1661 and 1685.

179. Legg, *Coronation Order … James I*, pp. 89–90.
180. Omitted *ibid.*
181. Omitted *ibid.*
182. 'comminalties of your kingdomes haue': *ibid.*
183. 'lyeth': *ibid.*
184. Legg, *Coronation Records*, pp. 325–6.
185. Hall, *Queen Elizabeth … Westminster Abbey*, pp. 12–13.
186. *Authorised Liturgy … Coronation Rite … Charles III.*
187. Brown, *Records*, A1567/12/7.
188. *Ibid.*, 1689/3/131.

CHAPTER 4

Swords and Objects: Old and New

One of the most talked about moments of the 2023 coronation involved the then Leader of the House and Lord President of the Privy Council The Rt Hon Penny Mordaunt MP holding the Sword of State and then later in the service the Jewelled Sword of Offering (Fig. 4.1).[1] Even in the twenty-first century, swords have the power to capture the imagination of the public, both within the Abbey and to audiences far beyond.[2] As we have seen coronations are not unique to Britain and the use of ceremonial objects to confer a status on a particular ruler has been ubiquitous. Perhaps one of the oldest known jewels or royal relics in British history is that of the Alfred Jewel, housed in the Ashmolean Museum, Oxford, thought to be linked to King Alfred the Great (r.871–899).[3] Within the Westminster Abbey service, the Stone of Scone would become an intrinsic coronation element, incorporated in St Edward's Chair. The Coronation Ring as already discussed, provided a tangibility to the conceptualisation of a coronation as a marriage. The swords of the regalia, carried at a coronation, signified all-powerful sovereignty, coupled with justice and mercy. Along with *Curtana* (Sword of Mercy), they were associated with Arthurian legend, medieval concepts of kingship, and the Celtic world of Tristan and Isolde.[4] These objects, effectively relics, were 'real to men's minds', with their accretion of history and legend: of 'Tristram, King Arthur[,] … the Fellowship of the Round Table … [and] Charlemagne'.[5] Whether it was the Angevins[6] or Henry VIII the medieval and early modern world were

G. W. C. Gross, *Crown and People*,
https://doi.org/10.1007/978-3-032-20786-9_4

Fig. 4.1 King Charles III with the then Lord President of the Council, Penny Mordaunt, carrying the Sword of State, during his coronation at Westminster Abbey, 6 May 2023, Richard Pohle/*The Times*, PA Images, Alamy

fascinated by and sought to retain their links to his legendary status. Henry VIII had King Arthur's Round Table freshly painted at Winchester for visiting European nobility in 1522—as 'a unique example of public propaganda' for it 'radiated an aura of antiquity [as] a … relic of Britain's glorious past'. To link his dynasty to this famous table, the centre included a Tudor rose.[7]

Across different cultures, the crowning, anointing, and inaugurating of monarchs, with the use of sacred symbols to invest them with majesty, has existed for millennia. The earliest known English crown dates from *c.*200–150 BC, and is associated with the 'Mill Hill Warrior'—for it was found on a skull of an Iron Age ruler discovered in 1988 (27 December) 'above the bleached sands of Deal' in Kent.[8] Yet more importantly for our purposes, given the status of swords within British coronations, the crown 'was not the only treasure in the tomb' of remarkable finds, 'but just one element in a collection of precious objects. On the skeleton's right arm rested a long iron sword with a bone handle, still in its leather and bronze scabbard … and over his body were the remains of a magnificent ceremonial shield'.[9] Significantly, as Keay points out, 'the Mill Hill warrior demonstrates, there was a tradition of crown-wearing in Britain before the arrival of the Romans' and this custom continued.[10] It should not be in anyway unexpected that in a world dominated by might and the often sheer physical force of an individual ruler, that swords should have attained a key status amongst rulers and that this would endure long into the medieval and beyond. The sense of leading the army and indeed nation into battle is captured in words in the famous and extraordinary Tilbury Armada speech of Elizabeth I in 1588.[11] As late as the eighteenth century, both George I and George II have been described as 'soldier-kings in the German tradition' and indeed George II 'identified closely with his army, keeping a brown coat for civil business and a red one for military, and maintaining a notebook in which he recorded officers' characters and achievements. He was the last English monarch to command an army in battle, at Dettingen in 1743'.[12] Even within the ancient world, the 'sword as a piece of regalia—something with a ceremonial as much as a practical function—belonged more to the northern European tribes than to the Roman or Greek empires, and a number of richly made early English swords and shields survive'—such examples including the 'Battersea Shield' can be found in the British Museum.[13] Swords were not just for military use and they became synonymous with heroism and heroes, attaching to them 'miraculous properties. To Beowulf, the warrior of the eponymous Anglo-Saxon poem, belonged the great sword Hrunting … to Charlemagne the magical Joyeuse, which changed colour thirty times a day; and to King Arthur, Caliburn or Excalibur'.[14]

The presence of a monarch's sword during a major ceremony should not be surprising—at least within the context of the ancient world, or indeed chivalric medieval era. Long before 1821, the two swords of Justice and Curtana, and the Sword of State were 'established elements of the regalia, whereas the sword that the sovereign offered on the altar during the service in act of alms-giving was normally his own weapon'.[15] Given such an opportunity, George IV had an entirely new and bejewelled item made (at the staggering personal cost of *c.*£6,000), which survives to this day as the Sword of Offering.[16] The sword represented both the royal presence, but also the sovereign's military might as heard of the armed forces (a role that continues to the present day). The sword 'was carried aloft by one of the nobility so that all might see the symbol' of the power of the ruler, and presented to the sovereign during royal ceremonial 'with an exhortation to use it in defence of his people'.[17] In a modern and post-modern coronation this sword 'ritual now takes place after the sovereign has been anointed and robed in the Colobium Sindonis and the Supertunica.[18] First the spurs are presented to the sovereign, then the Sword of Offering (in early times the king's own sword) is brought to him and by him offered at the altar from which it is redeemed by payment of one hundred shillings. Thereafter the Sword of Offering replaces the Sword of State and is borne naked before the sovereign for the rest of the ceremony'.[19]

However, for all of the logic (at least within a feudal culture) of the near-absolute power of the ruler and thus the presence of a sword within a ceremony, what is perhaps surprising is the number of swords used within a British coronation service as part of a procession.

Exchequer records provide us with the earliest written material of English coronations, referring to the crowning of the 'Young King' Henry in 1170[20]—a ceremony that took place during the reign of his father Henry II, 'in the great Abbey of Westminster, built by his ancestor Edward the Confessor and the site of royal inaugurations from the time of Harold II'.[21] This includes notes on the refurbishment of swords for that coronation, as well as payments for robes amongst other items.[22]

More detail on a coronation service and the planning involved can also be seen for Queen Eleanor in 1236, wife of Henry III.[23] Roger of Hoveden's account of Richard I's coronation in 1189 supplies us with the earliest 'eye-witness' description of swords being referenced in conjunction with an English coronation, in this case 'three swords'. Ditmas points out though, that Geoffrey of Monmouth's work on the coronation of King Arthur—'when four swords were borne before him by four kings'—establishes an already exciting precedent and this would seem to concur with the 'Mill Hill Warrior' find.[24] This can also be seen in the Great Seals of Henry I (1100–1135) indicating a ceremonial occasion—with the king shown enthroned, with crown, orb, and sword.[25] Again, the custom of a processional sword was not bespoke to England—the custom was also part of a tradition seen with the Holy Roman Emperor and in Denmark and Poland too.[26] Neuschel reveals, in an 'image from an illuminated gospel book depict[ing] the coronation of Holy Roman Emperor Otto III, [the ruler] holds a staff with an eagle, echoing Roman precedent, as well as an orb ... [and importantly present too, is a] courtier bearing his sword standing to his left'.[27] Strickland also provides an example of a 'bearing sword, used for the imperial coronation of the Young King's nephew Otto

IV in 1198, [being] ... extant, complete with its gold repoussé scabbard depicting great Old Testament kings, and with a verse from the *Laudes regiae* inscribed on its hilt—"Christus vincit, Christus regnat, Christus imperat"'.[28]

It is clear, therefore, that in the medieval world, a custom emerged of swords being present for ceremonial occasions—'as early as 1099, the King of Scotland [William the Lion] carried a sword before William Rufus when the latter held his court in London'.[29] This tradition then became part of a coronation setting. In England, this developed into a number of swords being present, not just the sovereign's personal sword.

> The account of Richard I's coronation definitely mentions three swords in gold-covered scabbards, carried respectively by David, the brother of the King of Scotland, Earl of Huntingdon, John, Earl of Moreton, the king's brother, and by Robert, Earl of Leicester, Wickham Legg infers that the middle one, carried by the king's brother, was in fact the Curtana though none of the swords are named.[30]

Strickland argues that given the precedent of 1154 and 1189 involving the new king being presented with 'the sword of the realm with which he was to repress evildoers against the Church' that it seems more than likely given Henry II's 'insistence on the Young King's royal status and their regal equality' that this also occurred in 1170.[31] Whilst we lack precise records for King John's coronation, the Patent Rolls for 1207 reveal 'significant reference to two state swords ... [with] Peter des Roches, Bishop of Winchester, attest[ing] the receipt of them, with other important items of the regalia including the 'German' crown, at the Royal Palace of Clarendon'.[32] Intriguingly, we have no details of swords being present for the 1216 coronation of Henry III at Gloucester.[33] This coronation—of note as it did not take place at Westminster Abbey—was the king's first coronation aged just nine. The flux of the time, with King John's sudden death may have meant not all of the regalia featured in this coronation. Henry III would later be crowned with full regalia in London in 1220.[34]

The Curtana's association with the name 'Sword of Mercy' appears as early as Richard III's coronation in 1483. The link is thought to relate to the shortened nature of the sword. Though as Ditmas points out, it did not suddenly become shorter, so why it took so long for this link to be written down is perhaps surprising.[35]

Whilst there is perhaps a contemporary sense that coronation regalia have been fixed as the same set items for generations and only remade at the Restoration, with one or two minor alterations and additions, it seems that the medieval regalia was more open to change. Delving into the Wardrobe accounts of the Tudor dynasty provides evidence to prove 'that new Curtanas were ... made for Henry VIII, Edward VI, and Elizabeth I'.[36] Keay argues that 'until the 17th century the three processional swords were generally provided new for each coronation', however, this ended with Charles I. Following his coronation in 1626, 'the king "gave into ye Hands of ye B[ish]p ye curtana, and the two other Swords, yt wear carryed before him, w[i]th Scabberds of Cloth" and these were "to be kept w[i]th ye other Regalia att Westminster"'.[37] The Curtana 'was found and entered on the inventory of the regalia made by order of Cromwell in August 1649 being one of three swords with scabbards of cloth of gold ... in an iron chest and valued at £3'.[38] Regicide heralded not only the destruction of the monarchy, but also that of its emblems. The crown jewels were broken up and melted down. Into 'the Mint melting pots ... went the queen's crown, Edward VI's crown, the orb, two sceptres, and the coronation bracelets. The liquid gold was then pressed into hundreds of small blank discs. Sandwiched between engraved metal dies and struck by the mintmen's hammers, the once-hallowed gold became money, emblazoned with the simple words "The Commonwealth of England"'.[39]

With the Restoration, Charles II had an opportunity to start afresh, with completely new designs and names, yet he evidently chose to order the re-creation, as faithfully as possible, of what had been lost. Why? Surely, he did so because of the significance of the link to St Edward the Confessor and his sacred power. Thus, St Edward's Crown was remade in 1661 and was popularly believed to have been the Confessor's and 'King Alfred's before him'.[40] At a time of considerable uncertainty, following the Civil Wars and Commonwealth, Charles II sought legitimacy in Britain's historical and mythical past. St Edward's Crown was designed for the sole purpose of crowning the sovereign.[41] Under Charles II's orders, Garter King of Arms, Sir Edward Walker, set about re-establishing the crown jewels and what would be required in this collection, including most significantly coronation and state crowns, 'St Edwards Crowne, & the other an Imperiall Crowne', as well as orb and sceptre, Coronation Ring, spurs, bracelets, and swords.[42] Remarkably, the three swords carried in the procession before the monarch at a coronation did not need to be remade as they had survived from Charles I's reign and continue to this day. Sitwell's work provides a detailed overview of these swords and this has been elaborated further by Keay's compendium of *The Crown Jewels*.[43] All three swords 'are straight, two-edged swords with plain hilts and guards but, in contrast to the Sword of Justice to the Spirituality and the Sword of Justice to the Temporality, the blade of the Curtana has a flat broken end and is shorter, measuring only 3 ½ in. as against the 39 ½ in. of the other two'.[44] All three swords also contain a trademark of 'a running wolf incised on the blade' (used by the renowned Passau and Solingen), 'the blades were the work of the famed Italian swordsmiths Andrea and Giandonato Ferrara and were imported into England in the 1580s. The leather scabbards have been made periodically; the current velvet covering was created for the coronation of King George VI in 1937'.[45] 1953 had seen no lesser personage than the Earl of Home, later Prime Minister,[46] carrying the Sword of Spiritual Justice, or Second Sword and in 2023 as discussed the then Leader of the House The Rt Hon Penny Mordaunt MP held the Sword of State and then later in the service the Jewelled Sword of Offering.[47]

Delving more deeply and as I have commented elsewhere on the Coronation Chair, the religious element of a coronation can also be seen from these objects, for there is 'a sense of the ancient chair having acquired its own sacred status—as a "deeply mystical relic" … [seen by some] as "emitting a form of spiritual radioactivity"'.[48] This takes us into the realm of Divine Right kingship. The power of these objects continued to amaze and fascinate another generation in 2023—long after the Divine Right of Kings of James I or Charles I has any sense of political reality—and yet the elevation of the crown within the service and the enthronement and procession and presentation of objects were all carried out as if each item and act had some form of religious or holy significance. As discussed in the Chap. 1, if such objects indicated the praxis of Divine Right theory in the liturgy of a coronation, then, their post-Commonwealth re-creation and survival to the present, shows how the theory lasted in a material form, long after it has been suggested that the concept had diminished. Since the crown jewels have received extensive scholarly attention, notably by Keay, a detailed analysis of all items is not required here.[49] What is relevant and searching for this book is the way in which the sacred connotations of particular items were used to promote the ideology of Divine Right.

In a coronation, the costume is not simply for pomp: it can indicate office and also point to ideas. Even the king's special attire carried important associations, though that might not have been apparent to observers. For instance, according to a description of Charles II's coronation published shortly after his death, his ceremonial vestments were called 'St Edward's robes'.[50] Royalty has long been associated with ermine—'the king then putting on his velvet cap turned up w[i]th ermin[e]'[51]—and often the colour purple: '[t]he robes of estate of purple velvet'.[52] It was not just sovereignty that was made so conspicuous: at James II's coronation, the solicitor-general and attorney-general wore 'gowns of black velvet', while the barons of the Exchequer, the master of the rolls, the lord chief justice of the Kings Bench and other judges wore 'robes of scarlett'.[53] These judicial figures were clearly important, but above them was of course the monarch as supreme judge, a biblical concept and a key component of Divine Right kingship. The magnificence on display can only have enhanced what Kiryanova terms 'magisterial Divine Right'.[54] The theme of justice was identified in the great swords of state, representing justice and mercy, one of which the king offered at the high altar.[55]

The presence of immense jewels sets a coronation above ordinary court events or even the State Opening of Parliament in the twenty-first-century setting. The public for this very rare occasion are able to witness a staggering array of gems provided over time at astounding cost.[56] Preparations for James II's coronation indicate the scale of royal finery procured from 'the Jewelhouse':

> For the king[:] two imperiall crownes sett with precious stones, the one to be called St Edwards Crowne, wherewith the king was to be crowned, and the other to putt on after the coronation, before his ma[je]sties return to Westminster Hall
>
> An orb of gold with a cross sett with pretious stones. A scepter with a cross sett with pretious stones called St Edwards
>
> A long scepter or staff of gold, with a cross upon the top, and a pike at the … of steel called St Edwards staff[.][57]

As with much of the coronation, these jewels were transparently associated with the Confessor king as we have already seen with St Edward's Crown, and we shall now consider further important objects.

St Edward's Staff

St Edward's staff has an equally important legendary status in coronation regalia. Although sometimes thought to have contained fragments of the True Cross, the standard theory behind the original staff was that it dated back to the eleventh century and the Confessor; indeed, it is possible that it is depicted in the Bayeux Tapestry, where a scene shows St Edward carrying a long staff. Holmes and Sitwell suggest that it remained at Westminster Abbey, in the fashion of walking sticks of Celtic saints, 'and presumed to have set the form of the episcopal crozier'.[58] The staff is significant in terms of sacral monarchy, precisely because it holds no actual role in a coronation service. It was carried in the coronation procession, functioning as a holy relic. This tradition, as with the cult of St Edward, was not something that one would expect to have survived England's Reformations. Nevertheless, it continued.[59]

In a remarkable account, Pepys reveals how important these associations with St Edward had been for James II. He told Arthur Charlett in 1693, that

> I have seen … a chaire … of ab[ou]t 600 yeare old, taken out of Edw[ar]d the Confessor's monument at Westm[inste]r by a workeman at the cleansieing it against K. James my unhappy maister's coronation. Who was pleased to shew it mee afterw[ar]ds, with the veneration given to reliques[.][60]

Thus, even after the Interregnum, when a new canvas was possible in designing the regalia, Charles II chose to have a replacement staff made. Indeed, Charles made it known that he sought 'a full-blooded medieval coronation'; this would involve following ancient precedent, to express 'the glamour and glory of the English monarchy'.[61]

St Edward's Spurs

> Receive these spurs, symbols of honour and courage. May you be a brave advocate for those in need.
>
> The revised wording retains the significance of courage associated with the symbol of the Spurs whilst drawing out advocacy for those in need, whether that be in the area of defence of the realm or in practical service for the most vulnerable.[62]

2023 saw the role of the spurs continue in the service. The sense of chivalry, of the world of 'knights in shining armour', had been maintained in some musical sense in the early twentieth century via the traditional English Melody arranged and harmonised by Vaughan Williams (1872–1958) of Jan Struther's (1901–1953) 'When a knight won his spurs' and in cinematic form with Disney's 1963 'The Sword in the Stone'.[63] That knightly tradition beyond the investiture with the swords is also reinforced by the presentation of 'coronation spurs', and of course the position of the King's Champion and the gauntlet at a Westminster Hall coronation banquet.[64] Evidence for the use of spurs at a Westminster coronation comes from Roger of Howden (a medieval chronicler, *d.*1201/1202). He was a clerk at the Court of Henry II (1133–1189), and his account of the coronation ornaments used for the coronation of Richard I—the lionheart king—(3 September 1189) still exists in manuscript form—held in the Medieval Manuscript Collection of the Bodleian Library (as MS. Laud Misc. 582). 'Great golden spurs' were also thought to have been 'attached' to Young King Henry's feet at his 1170 coronation—'reflecting the permeation of a strong chivalric element in the coronation rituals during the twelfth century'.[65] A world where 'English dominion on the Continent was at its peak and crusading the favoured sport of kings'.[66] As Strickland points out, the 'spurs also had a powerfully Christian meaning, for they symbolized the knight's swiftness to serve God'.[67] Something somewhat missed or not alluded to in the marginalia for Charles III's coronation in 2023 by Lambeth Palace.

As already explored, the Tudors promulgated chivalric links and saintly connections with St Edward (or at least their mythical ideas of such links). Henry VII is well known to have sought to have connected his claim to the throne to the legend of King Arthur and even named his first son Arthur.[68] Henry VIII (Henry VII's surviving second son) took on this mantle and was a jousting enthusiast. He even restored the famous 'round-table' at Winchester's ancient great hall. Regardless of whether it was a male or female sovereign, these 'knightly accoutrements were presented' as 'a contemporary description of Mary Tudor's coronation in 1554 describe[s] how the "spurs were put upon her feet"'.[69] These 'saint Edwardes sp[u]res' became a fixed part of the coronation in the '15th century … and continued to perform this function until they were dropped into the parliamentary melting pots in 1649'.[70] Elizabeth I's coronation maintained the importance of such ideas and of St Edward, with records referring to 'St Edward's staff [and] … an offering to St Edward's Shrine'.[71]

The existing gold spurs were re-created in 1661 following the Restoration of Charles II, but had later alterations (textiles replacing straps and buckles) in 1820 for George IV. Each gold spur features a Tudor rose, with gold embroidery and a velvet-covered strap. The spurs are part of the investiture element of the ceremony. In medieval and early modern times, they were worn and fastened to the monarch's feet, but in nineteenth- and twentieth-century coronations, they have been held to the ankles of the sovereign, presented, and then placed on the altar. In 2023,

> The Spurs [were] … brought forward from the altar by the Dean and handed to The Lord Great Chamberlain. The Lord Great Chamberlain approache[d] The King, presenting the regalia. The King acknowledge[d] them. The Archbishop of Canterbury [then spoke]: Receive these spurs, symbols of honour and courage. May you be a brave advocate for those in need. The spurs [were] … then returned to the altar.[72]

The right to carry the Golden Spurs is part of the Court of Claims decision-making process. In 1661 they were carried by the Earl of Pembroke and Montgomery, and from 1685 and the coronation of James II to the coronation of Queen Anne in 1714, they were held by the Yelverton family, later viscounts Longueville. Richard Yarde-Buller, 4th baron Churston carried the spurs at both the 1937 and 1953 coronations. In 2023 the Lord Great Chamberlain had the honour.[73]

St Edward's Chair and the Stone of Scone

The influence of St Edward is also evident in his so-called Coronation Chair[74] and its association with the Stone of Scone. Scone was the famous site of the Stone of Destiny or Stone of Scone, and the Moot Hill Kirk there was the ancient crowning place of the Scottish monarchs including such personages crucial to historical memory as Robert the Bruce.[75] As I have commented elsewhere, the last coronation to take place in Scotland was for Charles II at Scone in 1651,[76] although by that time, the Stone of Destiny, or Stone of Scone, had become part of the Westminster Abbey Coronation Chair.[77]

Scone's famous Stone of Destiny is a rectangular block of sandstone.[78] Yet this sandstone has a remarkable history, much of it shrouded in myth. Medieval legend considered it to have biblical origins; some thought it associated with Egypt and claimed that it had been protected and taken out of the land by the daughter of a pharaoh (rather similar to Moses's protection); others linked it to the pillow on which Jacob dreamed when he saw the angels of Bethel.[79]

Whether it had these origins or not, it was thought to have eventually arrived in Ireland and was apparently placed on the sacred Hill of Tara and was called the 'fatal stone': 'Lia-Fail', or as often referred to today, the Stone of Destiny. It was said to play a fundamental role in the authentication of true kingship, for at an Irish monarch's enthronement it would apparently groan aloud if the claimant was of true royal kingship but remain silent if he was a pretender.[80] Folklore then has it that the Stone followed a Gaelic route taken by Kenneth MacAlpin, king of Dalriada (d. 858), from Antrim to Argyll, and then to the monastery at Scone, Perthshire, in 846.[81] It was there placed upon the 'Moot Hill' that was used in the crowning of the Scottish kings. A 'moot' or 'mound' was a meeting place or ceremonial centre, sometimes a gathering of stones, a raised mound, or miniature hill, used for the inauguration of early Pictish monarchs.[82] This famous site, also referred to as the Mount of Belief, may have derived its name from Nechtan *mac* Derile (d. 732) (king of the Picts, c. 706–24; and 728–9) who had taken a keen interest in Christianity.[83] Not only did the Stone rest on this mount and represent some of the earliest origins of Scottish Christianity and kingship, but it was believed that in c. 906, 'Constantine the King [Constantine II (r. 900–943)] and Cellach the Bishop vowed that the laws and discipline of the Faith, and the rights of the Churches and the Gospels, should be kept equally as amongst the Scots'.[84]

The legend apart, the Stone played an intrinsic role as an object of veneration in the inauguration of Scottish kings such as Lulach (d. 1058), stepson of Macbeth, who was proclaimed king of Scots on it in 1057, down to 1292 and John Balliol. In addition to housing the famous Stone, Scone had also been the immemorial political centre of the 'Pictes' and Pictish kings, and evolved as the coronation site of Scottish rulers from the semi-mythical king Fergus in the eighth century, to medieval monarchs like Alexander II in 1214. Thus, it became a place of political and religious legitimisation. In 1296 Edward I of England (1239–1307) invaded Scotland and took the Stone from Scone to Westminster.[85] This marked the beginning of the Stone's place within the Coronation Chair of Westminster Abbey. Yet its long association with the Mount of Belief or Moot Hill made Scone a venerable site for the most solemn of kingly ceremonies even without the Stone. The site itself continued to be revered by monarchs in the House of Stuart, such as James I, crowned at Scone in 1424.[86] For 'James … came to Perth, and shortly after to Scone, where he was crowned king, and his wife Queene'.[87] Thus, the choice of Scone for the coronation of Charles II in 1651 had important historical, legendary, mythical, and religious significance and would add further weight to the legitimisation of Charles as a crowned sovereign in Scotland. The 'magic' and significance of the Stone was seen to work beyond Scotland described during the reign of James I of England (VI of Scotland) as having been 'borne in a chair of wood and for a perpetual honour'.[88] The use of the word 'British' is also striking in this passage by Sir George Buc, Master of the Revels:

> The other monument of **British** empire is the marble stone whereupon Jacob laid his head when he had those celestial and mystical visions mentioned in Holy Writ, which stone was brought out of Palestine into Ireland, and from thence carried into Scotland by King Kenneth, after translated to the city of Scone and used for the chair wherein the kings sat at their coronation. And out of Scotland it was brought by Edward I into England, which is witnessed by the best historians of Scotland and England.[89]

This was 1619, not 1707 or later, and here again we have the language of 'Britian' of a sense of Britishness long before the Act of Union made more palpable by the Union of the Crowns following James I (& VI)'s accession to the English throne in 1603. Buc continued that 'in this stone … the fate of the kingdom is contained … that what king of Scotland soever is lord of that stone and sovereignty possessed thereof shall be king and reign in that country where he findeth that stone, which is … prophetical … [and] accomplished in King James when he came first into England'.[90]

The Stone of Destiny has remained a key part of coronations, and in 2023 (Saturday 29 April), there was a curious service at Westminster Abbey—a religious service for a Stone—to welcome the Stone having completed a journey from the Crown Room at Edinburgh Castle to London for the coronation. Since 1996 the Stone returned and resides in Scotland (now with a new museum),[91] on the basis of returning to Westminster Abbey for coronations there. The Very Reverend Professor David Fergusson, Dean of the Chapel Royal in Scotland and Regius Professor of Divinity, University of Cambridge, said:

> Scripture recalls us to the bedrock of faith, the stones from which are hewn, the foundations upon which our lives must be built if we are to live well with one another – foundations made by God, our Creator and Sustainer. So as we mark the arrival of the Stone of Scone today, we thank God for our common purpose, for bonds of friendship, and for the rich heritage of faith.[92]

When it comes to questions of purpose, of a continuing meaning to coronations, of the relevance and use of objects and regalia, the reading of prayers and scripture in the twenty-first century for a Stone, certainly provides evidence for the endurance of such ideas. The Stone would again take a leading role within the Coronation Chair for King Charles III.

The Coronation Chair possesses its own folklore. The figure of a king, either Edward the Confessor or Edward I, was painted on the back, leading to the belief—the 'invention of tradition'—that this was St Edward the Confessor's chair. Westminster Abbey still references this link.[93] Sandford indicates why it gained that association, having been

> solemnly offered by ... King Edward the first to St Edward the Confessor, the morrow after the festival of St Botolph, anno 1297 (from whence it hath the name of St Edwards Chair).[94]

The problem with the Coronation Chair is that it is no longer as impressive as it once was. It therefore requires an imaginative effort to picture it in an early modern setting. One could be deceived into thinking that it was entirely visible on coronation day, but evidence suggests that under both Tudors and Stuarts it was covered by a substantial quantity of cloth of gold. The point, therefore, is that while now its appearance does not suggest the majesty of a Divine Right ideology, then, with such trappings, it would surely have done so.[95]

Having reviewed the history of the chair as an object, we turn to its role in the service. The Coronation Chair must be distinguished from the throne placed at the centre of the 'theatre', the intersection of nave and transept, which was used before and after the investiture with the regalia. In 1661, St Edward's chair was first located on the north side of the high altar and at the appropriate moment moved to be 'set right over against the altar'.[96] It is clear from illustrations printed by Ogilby and Sandford, especially the latter because he includes a plan and profile views,[97] that this meant a position in the sacrarium directly over the centre of the Cosmati Pavement and only about twenty feet from the altar, much closer than in modern coronations.[98] The significance of this proximity is worth pondering. As a form of relic, the chair not only emitted a form of spiritual radioactivity, but also drew power as much from its colourful past (containing the Stone of Scone) as from its presence in this sacred space. Its location, directly facing the altar, harks back to the pre-Reformation Mass in terms of the witnessing of the elevation of the host. Arguably, this setting elevated the status of both chair and altar: the chair, by being so close to the altar, was enhanced with association with grace-giving Eucharistic powers, while the altar gave spiritually by having such a deeply mystical relic opposite. A reciprocal relationship existed. This reciprocity continued in the coronation itself. For adherents of Divine Right ideology, the sovereign acquired spiritual status from being crowned in this chair, yet the chair was also imbued with added spiritual value by having the monarch crowned in it. Despite the anachronism of the reverent connection to the Confessor, this persisted, and when reflecting on James II's 1685 coronation, Sandford was content (in depicting the chair) to describe it as 'commonly called St Edwards chair'.[99]

The action at the east end of the sacrarium in the vicinity of the Coronation Chair, continued in acts of homage, as discussed in Chap. 1. These were paid to the high altar and in St Edward's Chapel, the latter located behind the high altar. The Tudors prostrated themselves at the Confessor's shrine, where it was conventional to 'offer br[ea]d and wine'.[100] Other objects either enhanced the religious sense or perpetuated the connection with St Edward. For example, and surprisingly given William III's Dutch Calvinist background, the Holy Spirit remained a prominent component in his coronation, in that we find reference to both sceptre and ivory rod with the dove.[101] Such allusions to the Holy Spirit were reinforced by this symbolism. On the second point, George I was to offer his sword to the altar, and proceeded in state to St Edward's Chapel. Hence, sovereigns of the houses of Tudor, Stuart, Orange, and Hanover all inherited and embraced this saintly mantle.[102] In the 2023 Coronation Roll, there are at least nine references to St Edward, from locations in the Abbey to objects of association.[103]

The Scottish Honours

It might be easy to assume with the extraordinary display of regalia that the crown jewels housed in the Tower of London are the oldest in the British Isles, or indeed the only regalia. Yet, as I have written about and commented elsewhere, Scotland possesses—and perhaps should in fact unsurprisingly given the Stone of Scone—an older collection, and it has now become custom for a newly crowned monarch following a Westminster Abbey coronation to visit Scotland to be presented with the Scottish Honours.[104]

Three weeks after her coronation on 2 June 1953, Elizabeth II and the then Duke of Edinburgh went to Scotland to be presented with the Honours of Scotland in Edinburgh on 24 June for a service of National Thanksgiving. King Charles III retraced these steps in 2023.

1953 was memorable for the appearance of the Honours—it was the first time in over a century that the Crown and Sceptre of Scotland were borne through the streets of Edinburgh in a procession to the High Kirk of St Giles Cathedral.[105] During the ceremony, the regalia were formally presented to Queen Elizabeth II and then returned to Edinburgh Castle. In 2023 the Crown of Scotland featured atop Queen Elizabeth II's coffin, when she lay in state at St Giles Cathedral. This tradition and connection to the honours followed on from events in July 1911, when the Scottish Sword of State had been carried before George V in connection with the dedication of the Thistle Chapel—the home of the chivalric order of the Thistle. Likewise, in 1937, George VI and Queen Elizabeth (later the Queen Mother) visited Scotland and Edinburgh for the ceremony of the keys and inspected the Honours of Scotland at Edinburgh Castle.

The Scottish Honours are the oldest regalia in the British Isles.[106] The crown, sword, and sceptre date from the late fifteenth/early sixteenth century, the reigns of James IV and James V of Scotland—respectively grandfather and father of Mary Queen of Scots. Separately to the rest of the Scottish Honours sits an ampulla last used for the coronation of Charles I in 1633.[107] The ampulla is housed in the National Museum of Scotland away from the rest of the regalia, owing to the controversy surrounding the 1633 coronation, the problematic question of anointing for Presbyterians, and the flux of the Cromwellian invasion in the 1650s.

The first monarch to use the Honours as coronation regalia was Mary Queen of Scots, crowned in 1543 at the age of just nine months.[108] Her one-year-old son, James VI of Scotland, was crowned with the Honours at Stirling Castle in 1567, and Charles I did likewise at his Scottish coronation in 1633 at the Palace of Holyroodhouse.

As already discussed, the last coronation to take place in Scotland was in 1651 for Charles II at Scone in Perthshire. He was later crowned again at Westminster Abbey in 1661 symbolising the Restoration of the monarchy. Oliver Cromwell failed to prevent Charles II's 1651 coronation,[109] but nevertheless, as with the English regalia, he sought to capture and destroy the Scottish Honours—he pursued them to Dunnottar Castle near Aberdeen but failed to take them. They were smuggled out of the castle and returned safely at the Restoration.[110]

Until the Act of Union of 1707[111]—creating the United Kingdom of Great Britain—and in the absence of a resident monarch, the Scottish Honours were taken to sittings of the Parliament in Edinburgh to signify the sovereign's presence and their consent to the passing of each Act. In 1650, for example, Charles II did not merely add the sign manual to the acts of session bringing Parliament to a close, but touched the new legislation with the royal sceptre, as a definitive blessing of his assent.[112]

After the Union, when the new United Kingdom Parliament met in London, the Honours had no ceremonial role. Mysteriously, the Honours were locked away in an old oak chest in the Crown Room at Edinburgh Castle and then seemingly forgotten.[113] In 1818, the chest was opened by none other than the famous author Sir Walter Scott[114] in the presence of the Castle Governor and, to their astonishment, there before them were the Honours. The regalia were then presented to George IV in a ceremonial visit in 1822 (following his London coronation in 1821) at the Palace of Holyroodhouse.[115] The Honours were hidden again during WWII, buried in separate locations at Edinburgh Castle in case of a Nazi invasion. In 1996, the Stone of Scone returned to Scotland and was added to the Honours Collection at Edinburgh Castle, after 700 years in Westminster Abbey.[116]

The Stone was again made part of St Edward's Chair[117] for Charles III's coronation on 6 May 2023 and was a focal point during Charles III's Scottish service of dedication at St Giles. The service of thanksgiving or dedication on 5 July 2023 involved the Honours being escorted from Edinburgh Castle to the High Kirk by a 'People's Procession' of around one hundred representatives showcasing different fields, industries, and talents from across Scotland. The service and presentation of the historic Honours will be a reminder of the monarch's role in Scotland and the older Union of Crowns of 1603.[118] It also had yet more political symbolism following Devolution and the Scottish Parliament, for 1953 there was no such settlement. Scots voted in favour of devolution during the 1997 referendum.[119] The UK Parliament then passed the Scotland Act 1998 establishing a Scottish Parliament, which opened in 1999—the first Scottish Parliament since 1707.

New Objects

In 1170, 'following the coronation, the assembled nobles and clergy led the new king in procession back to the palace, where he removed the heavy crown and put on a lighter one'.[120] In 2023, Charles III exchanged St Edward's Crown for the Imperial State Crown at the *Te Deum* towards the end of the service. Much of 2023 saw continuity in terms of the roles of objects and the types (even if remade), as was also the case in 1953.[121] During the service the Archbishop still used the Coronation Spoon of twelfth-century origin—almost certainly made for Henry II, and a medieval item of regalia surviving the destruction under the Commonwealth (that followed the execution of Charles I in 1649).[122] For a ceremony to last so long with so much continuity is remarkable. Yet, for all of the tradition, both 1953 and 2023 saw new objects emerge to add to this extraordinary collection.

In 1953, Queen Elizabeth II received a pair of 'Armills' or bracelets. This was 'a significant act of historical revivalism' for the 1661 'Armills' of Charles II 'may never have been used, and certainly played no part in a coronation from the early 18th century'.[123] Commissioning went to Garrard and Company and the coronation bracelets were gifted by the Commonwealth Nations (organised by the Commonwealth Relations Office), with 'Gold ... [and] red velvet linings' and as with the Restoration re-creations, 'made to a self-consciously "medieval" design and bestowed on the Queen by the Archbishop with the rest of the regalia'.[124] 1953 was about creating a new Elizabethan era, Gloriana II was to be ushered forth out of the wreckage of war, the Blitz, and what was still ongoing rationing. The regalia would be part of that opportunity to gleam outward from the dust and rubble.[125]

In a religious (though ecumenical) turn, 2023 saw a new Cross feature, the Cross of Wales—apparently including shards of the True Cross gifted by Pope Francis.[126] The former Archbishop of Wales, Archbishop Andrew John described it as

> a hugely significant ecumenical symbol. Taking its inspiration from the earliest roots of our Christian history, and inscribed in Welsh with the words of St David, the Cross will remind us all of the heart of our faith. It not only provides a focus of unity across our different traditions, but will also be a lasting sign of The King's respect and affection for Wales.[127]

Fig. 4.2 The Cross of Wales, Peter Powell/PA Images, Alamy

The Cross of Wales was designed by Michael Lloyd (master silversmith), in consultation with the Royal Collection, and is crafted from recycled silver bullion, from the Royal Mint at Llantrisant, a shaft of Welsh windfall timber and a stand of Welsh slate. The back of the Cross includes an inscription with reference to the last sermon of St David in Welsh: 'Byddwch lawen. Cadwch y ffydd. Gwnewch y Pethau Bychain', which translates as: 'Be joyful. Keep the faith. Do the little things' (Fig. 4.2).[128]

For the 'holy of holies' within a coronation—the anointing—2023 also saw a newly commissioned screen, gifted by the City of London Corporation and City Livery Companies (as might have occurred in the sixteenth century),[129] designed to go around the Coronation Chair, in a tradition of canopies, that go back centuries, and examples can be seen in Sandford's 1687 account of James II's coronation.[130] Thus the anointing was again kept from public eye and the television screens, as the most solemn and sacred of moments within the service. As with much of the 2023 service, the screen was made using traditional workmanship, but with 'contemporary sustainable embroidery practices' and weaving in reference to the Commonwealth throughout. The centrepiece of the design is a tree with fifty-six leaves, thus constituting the fifty-six member countries of the Commonwealth.[131]

Conclusion

Obviously, the appreciation of these objects (crown, staff, and chair) and these sacred spaces (sacrarium and St Edward's Chapel) have almost certainly varied from person to person, and will undoubtedly have changed over time, but such perceptions are impossible to document systematically. Nevertheless, the key point is that these objects and places have invariably been described in the terms discussed above—as sacred and symbolic objects, whether it be in the twelfth century or in 2023—and the probable resonances of those descriptions cannot be ignored.[132]

Even in a 2024 documentary, reflecting on the experience of '50 Canadian women who attended the late Queen Elizabeth's coronation as 17-year-olds' with '[t]welve of them' making 'a poignant return to London in 2023, where they attended a surprise tea party with [the] King' discussion centred around the crown jewels. King Charles remarked "I remember it all so well then, because I remember my sister and I had bath time in the evening … My mama used to come up at bath time wearing the crown to practise … You have to get used to how heavy [the crown] is". Light-hearted though this discussion may have been, King Charles talked of the experience as something "I've never forgotten, I can still remember it vividly".[133] These objects, therefore, continue to have a powerful resonance today and all the more when used in a coronation.

What can we make of this? Whilst the Tower of London, housing the crown jewels, receives over 3 million visitors a year,[134] a coronation takes these priceless objects from out of their safe keeping to be seen, not behind their screens but to be witnessed in an event designed and formulated for their use, and in some cases by their existence. The King's 1969 investiture as Prince of Wales saw over 200,000 people attempt a glimpse of proceedings and of his coronet in Caernarvon.[135] 2002 saw 250,000 people wait their turn to pay their respects at the lying-in-state of Queen Elizabeth, The Queen Mother—her coffin adorned with her diamond crown, including 'the Koh-i-nûr, dazzling brilliantly in the gloom of Westminster Hall'.[136] Keay argues that the

> continuing appeal and authority of royal rituals lies essentially in their ability to move the spirit. Heart-stopping historic buildings, magnificent music that lifts the soul, iridescent royal insignia and crowds of adoring spectators all combine, in the 21st century as in the 12th, to provoke a profoundly emotional response.[137]

In her view, these 'Crown Jewels, more than any other tangible objects, embody the continuity of the English appetite for royal ceremony'.[138] As we have seen with the Scottish Honours, we need to widen this argument, beyond just the English. Whether it be the monarchs of the twelfth, thirteenth, and fourteenth centuries seeking links to the Anglo-Saxons and specifically King Edward, the Confessor Saint, or Charles II's Restoration of monarchy and at the same time the regalia, but to be made anew in the old ancient tradition of the medieval, monarchs have sought value beyond their worth in the regalia. Indeed, the Cromwellian idea of melting the crown jewels down points to their resonance, even after the execution of Charles I.

Chapter 9 will present more of these findings, particularly in relation to views on monarchy and national identity, but it was striking to see in our King's College London, British Coronation Project Survey, a very high percentage of students polled selected categories linked to objects or regalia out of a possible selection for the question: 'when you think of a British Coronation, what words come to mind?' 91% of students selected crowns, 42% robes, and 20% the Stone of Destiny (or Stone of Scone) amongst responses given, contrasting with just 15% for 'Art' more generally. Thus, amongst children in 2023, the specificity of the regalia continues to have a role within the coronation, and their tangibility appears to live on within the next generation.

Notes

1. Penny Mordaunt would lose her seat at the 2024 July UK General Election. See also S. Coughlan, 24 May 2023, https://www.bbc.co.uk/news/uk-65700045, accessed 22 November 2025; A. Rhoden-Paul, 6 May 2023, https://www.bbc.co.uk/news/uk-65510506, accessed 22 November 2025.

2. S. Coughlan, 24 May 2023, https://www.bbc.co.uk/news/uk-65700045, accessed 22 November 2025; A. Rhoden-Paul, 6 May 2023, https://www.bbc.co.uk/news/uk-65510506, accessed 22 November 2025; T. Thomas, 11 May 2023, https://www.theguardian.com/politics/2023/may/11/penny-mordaunt-took-painkillers-before-sword-carrying-role-coronation, accessed 22 November 2025; N. Leake, 11 May 2023, https://www.tatler.com/article/penny-mourdant-opens-up-about-her-star-role-at-king-charles-iiis-coronation, accessed 22 November 2025; A. Syed, 6 May 2023, https://time.com/6277718/penny-mordaunt-king-charles-coronation/, accessed 22 November 2025; M. Sachdeva and E. Muir, 9 May 2023, https://www.independent.co.uk/life-style/royal-family/penny-mordaunt-who-coronation-sword-dress-b2335333.html, accessed 22 November 2025; E. Webber, 5 May 2023, https://www.politico.eu/article/my-part-in-the-pomp-meet-the-uk-minister-carrying-a-huge-sword-for-king-charles/, accessed 22 November 2025; E. Somerville, 30 May 2023, https://www.telegraph.co.uk/politics/2023/05/30/penny-mordaunt-mp-tory-members-coronation-sword-charles/, accessed 22 November 2025; L. Sleator, 11 May 2023, https://www.thetimes.com/article/penny-mordaunt-meme-sword-coronation-75h97n5g7, accessed 22 November 2025.
3. P. Wormald, 'Alfred [Ælfred] (848/9–899)', *ODNB*; https://www.ashmolean.org/alfred-jewel, accessed 22 November 2025.
4. Ditmas, 'Curtana', pp. 122–33, especially pp. 126–7.
5. Ditmas, 'Curtana', pp. 132–3. See also H. Mayr-Harting, 'Charlemagne, the Saxons, and the Imperial Coronation of 800', *The English Historical Review*, 111 (1996), pp. 1113–1133.
6. Ditmans, 'Curtana', p. 126—see N. Wright (ed.), *Historia Regum Britannie of Geoffrey of Monmouth: I Bern, Burgerbibliothek, MS 568* (Woodbridge, 1985), begun during Henry I's reign and the search of Arthur's grave at Glastonbury suggested by Henry II, though not completed until 1190; T. D. Hardy (ed.), *Rotuli Litterarum Clausarum, 1204–27* (London, 1833), I, p. 29.
7. A. D. Curry, 'King Arthur of England, count of Habsburg: the use of Arthurian imagery in Habsburg diplomacy', *Historical Research*, 96 (2023), p. 486. See also J. Whitman, 'National Icon: The Winchester Round Table and the Revelation of Authority', *Arthuriana,* 18 (2008), pp. 33–65.
8. Keay, *Crown Jewels*, p. 8 and note 1.
9. *Ibid.*, p. 8.
10. *Ibid.*, pp. 10–11.

11. BL, Harley MS 6798, fol. 87 r–v. See also M. Todd, 'England After 1558', in A. Pettegree (ed.), *The Reformation World* (London, 2000), pp. 365–86.
12. D. Chandler, and I. Beckett (eds), *The Oxford Illustrated History of the British Army* (Oxford, 1994), p. 98; R. Holmes, *Redcoat: The British Soldier in the Age of Horse and Musket* (London, 2002), p. 80. See also A. C. Thompson, *George II: King and Elector* (New Haven, Connecticut, and London, 2011).
13. Keay, *Crown Jewels*, p. 13; see BM, 1857,0715.1. The importance of the sword and the sense of identity established in the military in the Middle Ages is explored by Scales, see: L. E. Scales, 'German Militiae: War and the German Identity in the Later Middle Ages', *Past & Present*, 180 (2003), pp. 41–82.
14. Keay, *Crown Jewels*, p. 13; see also R. W. Jones, *A Cultural History of the Medieval Sword: Power, Piety and Play* (Martlesham, 2024).
15. Keay, *Crown Jewels*, pp. 126–7.
16. *Ibid.*, pp. 126–7. See also J. H. Round, *The King's Serjeants and Officers of State: With Their Coronation Services* (London, 1911), pp. 337–47.
17. Ditmas, 'Curtana', p. 122.
18. *Authorised Liturgy … Coronation Rite … Charles III*, pp. 17–21.
19. Ditmas, 'Curtana', p. 122.
20. Strickland, *Henry the Young King*, esp. Chapter 5: 'Novus Rex: The Coronation, 1170', pp. 78–94.
21. Strickland, *Henry the Young King*, pp. 84–85. See also Stubbs, *The Chronicle of the Reigns of Henry II and Richard I*, I, p. 6. On Westminster, R. D. H. Gem, 'The Romanesque Rebuilding of Westminster Abbey', *Proceedings of the Battle Conference on Anglo- Norman Studies*, 3 (1980), pp. 33–60; E. Mason, '"The site of king-making and consecration": Westminster Abbey and the Crown in the eleventh and twelfth centuries', in D. Wood (ed.), *The Church and Sovereignty c.590–1918. Essays in Honour of Michael Wilks* (Oxford, 1991), pp. 57–76.
22. TNA, E 372/16 rot. 1 m. 2d. See also Ditmas, 'Curtana', p. 124; W. H. St. John Hope, 'The King's Coronation Ornaments', *The Ancester*, I (1902), pp. 148–9; and on the workings of exchequer clerks see U. Kypta, "How to Be an Exchequer Clerk in the Twelfth Century: What the *Dialogue of the Exchequer* Is Really About," *History*, 103 (2018), pp. 199–222.
23. TNA, E 164/2 fol. 232 (Red Book of the Exchequer); M. Howell, 'Eleanor [Eleanor of Provence] (c. 1223–1291)', *ODNB*; H. Ridgeway, 'Henry III (1207–1272)', *ibid.*
24. Ditmas, 'Curtana', p. 124. See also W. Stubbs (ed.), *Chronica Magistri Rogeri de Houedene*, 4 volumes, *Rerum Britannicarum Medii Aevi*

Scriptores, 51 (London, 1868–1871), III, pp. 9–10 and Hope, 'Coronation Ornaments', pp. 148–9.

25. TNA, E 42/317; E 40/6687; see also SC 13/H 88.
26. Schramm, *Coronation*, p. 23.
27. K. B. Neuschel, 'Swords and Chivalric Culture in the High Middle Ages', in *ibid.*, *Living by the Sword: Weapons and Material Culture in France and Britain, 600–1600* (Ithaca, New York, 2020), pp. 69–70 (image from HIP/Art Resource, NY): 'Surviving images of the Emperors Otto III and Henry the Lion' show this tradition 'an hono[u]red courtier bears the ruler's sword ceremonially, while the emperor himself holds staff or scepter and other standard regalia'.
28. Strickland, *Henry the Young King*, p. 86. See also J. Luckhardt and F. Niehoff (eds), *Heinrich der Löwe und seine Zeit. Herrschaft und Repräsentation der Welfen, 1125–1235*, 3 vols (Munich, 1995), II, pp. 374–5 and p. 365 for a detailed illustration of the scabbard; W. Seipel (ed.), *A Brief Guide to the Kunsthistorisches Museum, II: Masterpieces of the Secular Treasury* (Vienna, 2008), pp. 8–9.
29. Ditmas, 'Curtana', p. 124. See also Strickland, *Henry the Young King*, p. 86: Strickland suggests it was 'probable' and that he 'bore the first sword, later identified as "Curtana" or the "sword of mercy with its blunted tip", and that he was placed by his royal rank in a position of pre-eminence between the two other sword bearers'. Strickland continues: 'As in April 1194, when King William performed this role at Richard's great crown-wearing at Winchester on the latter's return from crusade and captivity', (cf. Stubbs, *Chronica … Houedene*, III, p. 248). 'At the coronation of 1189, his brother Earl David had done so as his representative, though in this instance the central position was taken by John, count of Mortain, as the king's brother' (*ibid.*, II, p. 81). W. Scott, 'William I [known as William the Lion] (c. 1142–1214),' *ODNB*.
30. Ditmas, 'Curtana', pp. 124–5; see also Legg, *Coronation Records*, p. 51. See also Lancashire Record Office, Preston, Kenyon Papers, MS DDKE/HMC/711.
31. Strickland, *Henry the Young King*, pp. 88–9.
32. Ditmas, 'Curtana', p. 125: 'The reference is to 'duo enses, scilicet ensem Tirstrami et alium ensem de eodem regalis'—see T. D. Hardy (ed.), *Rotuli Litterarum Patentium* (London, 1835), I, p. 77*b*.
33. For more details on the 1216 Gloucester coronation see: H. Ridgeway, 'Henry III (1207–1272)', *ODNB*; BL, Cotton MS Vitellius A. XIII (an account in verse containing an illustration of the coronation); https://www.bbc.co.uk/news/uk-england-gloucestershire-33251481#:~:text=The, 24 June 2015, accessed 22 November 2025; D. A. Carpenter, 'Archbishop Langton and Magna Carta: His Contribution, His Doubts

and His Hypocrisy', *EHR*, 126 (2011), pp. 1041–65; J. Hillaby, 'A Domus Conversorum at Bristol?', *Jewish Historical Studies*, 42 (2009), pp. 1–5; J. Burden, 'Re-writing a Rite of Passage: The Peculiar Funeral of Edward II', in N. F. McDonald and W. M. Ormrod (eds), *Rites of Passage: Cultures of Transition in the Fourteenth Century* (Woodbridge, 2004), p. 20; N. Vincent, 'A Queen in Rebel London, 1215–17', in L. Clark and E. Danbury (eds), *"A Verray Parfit Praktisour": Essays Presented to Carole Rawcliffe* (Woodbridge, 2017), pp. 23–50.

34. H. Ridgeway, 'Henry III (1207–1272)', *ODNB*.
35. Ditmas, 'Curtana', p. 127; Legg, *Coronation Records*, p. 195; See also Kincaid, *Richard The Third ... Sir George Buc*, p. 48—which discusses swords in the coronation procession. According to Ditmas, 'Curtana', p. 128: 'It is unfortunate that there is no reliable illustration of the unsheathed medieval Curtana. Matthew Paris made a sketch of it in the margin of his manuscript account of the coronation of Eleanor of Provence but, alas the sword is sheathed. The earliest representation of the blade seems to be that in the *Litlyngton Missal*, presented to Westminster Abbey by Abbot Nicholas Litlyngton in 1384. This, with the *Liber Regalis* also at Westminster, records the order of the coronation service and embodies the fourth recension made at the beginning of the fourteenth century which remained in use until the coronation of James II. It was probably written and illuminated for the use of Queen Anne of Bohemia, wife of Richard II, at her coronation in 1382. The illumination shows a king enthroned, supported by an archbishop and an abbot while, on the king's left, a nobleman bears a sword'. See also L. E. Tanner, *The History of the Coronation* (London, 1952), pp. 14, 19.
36. Ditmas, 'Curtana', p. 131, see also A. Taylor, *The Glory of Regality: An Historical Treatise of the Anointing and Crowning of the Kings and Queens of England* (London, 1820), p. 312.
37. Keay, *Crown Jewels*, p. 30. See also Blair, *Crown Jewels*, II, p. 347.
38. Ditmas, 'Curtana', p. 131, see also Taylor, *The Glory of Regality*, p. 312.
39. Keay, *Crown Jewels*, p. 43.
40. M. Holmes and H. D. W. Sitwell, *The English Regalia: Their History, Custody & Display* (London, 1972), p. 4.
41. For examples, see BL, Harleian MSS 4129, fol. 13r (1661 coronation) and 6118, fol. 4r (1702 coronation).
42. BL, Stowe MS 580, fols 3r, 8r (Sir Edward Walker's conspectus). A copy of Walker's account (dated 25 May 1661) of Charles II's arrival at the Restoration and also of his 1661 coronation survives in BL, Add. MS 30195. Either that or another MS was used as the basis for Walker, *Circumstantial Account*. Further coronation material exists in other MSS

associated with Walker: BL, Add. MS 37998, Hargrave MS 497; Bodl., Carte MS 129; and SAL, MS SAL/MS/455.
43. H. D. W. Sitwell, *The Crown Jewels and other Regalia in the Tower of London* (London, 1953), p. 91.
44. Ditmas, 'Curtana', p. 122. See also Sitwell, *Crown Jewels and other Regalia*, p. 91.
45. Keay, *Crown Jewels*, p. 30. On Passau and Solingen see also: D. H. Breiding, 1 October 2022, https://www.metmuseum.org/toah/hd/make/hd_make.htm#:~:text=The%20names%20of%20Passau%20and,it%20to%20their%20own%20blades, accessed 22 November 2025.
46. D. Hurd, 'Home, Alexander Frederick [Alec] Douglas, fourteenth Earl of Home and Baron Home of the Hirsel (1903–1995)', *ODNB*.
47. S. Coughlan, 24 May 2023, https://www.bbc.co.uk/news/uk-65700045, accessed 22 November 2025; A. Rhoden-Paul, 6 May 2023, https://www.bbc.co.uk/news/uk-65510506, accessed 22 November 2025.
48. S. Coughlan, 1 March 2023, https://www.bbc.co.uk/news/uk-64798077, accessed 22 November 2025.
49. Keay, *Crown Jewels*.
50. Cook, *Britannicus*, p. 278.
51. BL, Add. MS 6286, fol. 29r.
52. *Ibid.*, Egerton MS 3350, fol. 13v.
53. *Ibid.*, Add. MS 39864, fols 76v–77r.
54. Kiryanova, 'Images', p. 25.
55. BL, Add. MS 6281, fol. 17r.
56. See Chap. 6.
57. BL, Egerton MS 3350, fol. 13v.
58. Holmes & Sitwell, *Regalia*, p. 9. The Kells Crozier in the BM is a characteristic example.
59. BL, Harleian MSS 4129, fols 3v, 5v (St Edward's Staff borne by the Lord Sandwich, 1661), 6118, fol. 8r (St Edward's Staff borne by Lord Dorset, 1702). See also Wiltshire and Swindon Archives, Chippenham, Ailesbury of Savernake Papers, MS 1300/407 (carrying St Edward's staff at the coronation of James II, 1685).
60. Bodl., MS Ballard 1, fol. 93r.
61. Keay, *Crown Jewels*, pp. 45–6.
62. *Authorised Liturgy … Coronation Rite … Charles III*, p. 18.
63. See also J. R. Watson, 'Into the Twentieth Century', in *ibid.*, *The English Hymn: A Critical and Historical Study* (Oxford, 1999), pp. 511–532. See also A. Frogley, 'Williams, Ralph Vaughan (1872–1958)', *ODNB* and N. Beauman, 'Placzek, Joyce Anstruther [pseud. Jan Struther] (1901–1953)', *ODNB*.

64. See Chap. 5.
65. Strickland, *Henry the Young King*, pp. 88–9: 'That the attachment of such spurs was not a novelty in the coronation of 1189 is suggested by Howden's statement that those used were "calcaria aurea sumpta de thesauro regis" (Stubbs, *Chronica ... Houedene*, II, p. 82), implying they were already items of regalia. A pair of finely worked gold spurs, of twelfth- century date, used in the coronation of the French kings, was kept with the royal treasure at St Denis, and survive in the Musée du Louvre (D. Gaborit-Chopin, 'Le Trésor au temps de Suger', in *Le Trésor de St Denis, les dossiers d'archéologie*, 158 (1991), p. 10). For this 'encroachment of knighthood upon kingship', see Koziol, 'England, France and the Problem of Sacrality', pp. 135–6.
66. Keay, *Crown Jewels*, p. 65. On 'Spurs' see also pp. 52–3, & p. 63.
67. Strickland, *Henry the Young King*, pp. 88–9.
68. See D. Carlson, 'King Arthur and Court Poems for the birth of Arthur Tudor in 1486', *Humanistica Lovaniensia*, 36 (1987), pp. 147–183.
69. Keay, *Crown Jewels*, p. 65. See R. Garnett (ed.), *The Accession of Queen Mary: being the contemporary narrative of Antonio de Guaras, a Spanish merchant resident in London* (London, 1892), p. 121.
70. Keay, *Crown Jewels*, p. 65. 'One paire of silver gilt spurres with buckles sett with 12 slight stones and Crimson silke strapps' values at £1. 13s. 4*d*., sent to the Mint: in O. Millar (ed.), *The Inventories and Valuations of the King's Goods, 1649–51*, Walpole Society, 43 (1970–1972), (Glasgow, 1972), p. 50.
71. BL, Egerton MS 3320, fols 16r, 17r, 22r.
72. *Authorised Liturgy ... Coronation Rite ... Charles III*, p. 18.
73. https://members.parliament.uk/member/4712/contact, Lord Carrington, accessed 22 November 2025 see https://www.coronation-roll.gov.uk/roll/, accessed 22 November 2025.
74. See also BL, Harleian MS 4129, fol. 13r (1661 coronation); W. Percival-Prescott, *The Coronation Chair. An Investigation into the History and Present Condition of the Chair* (London, 1957) and M. L. Sauerberg, 'The Coronation Chair – Revisited', *Studies in Conservation*, 50 (2005), pp. 230–3.
75. Scone Palace had come to prominence thanks to Sir David Murray, a major supporter and benefactor of James VI and I: K. Brown, 'Courtiers and Cavaliers: Service, Anglicization and Loyalty among the Royalist Nobility', in J. Morrill (ed.), *The Scottish National Covenant in its British Context 1638–51* (Edinburgh, 1990), p. 169. Sir David Murray became Lord Scone in 1606 in Parliament, and in 1608 by charter. He was later advanced to the viscountcy of Stormont in 1621 (I. Cowan and D. Easson, *Medieval Religious Houses, Scotland* (2nd edn, London, 1976), p. 98).

Out of the ruins of Scone Abbey, a considerable property was created. The 'building as now seen is almost entirely the work of the architect William Atkinson for the third Earl of Mansfield, and it took shape between 1803 and 1812' and sits as Scone Palace today. R. Welander et al., *The Stone of Destiny: Artefact and Icon,* Society of Antiquaries of Scotland, Monograph Series, 22 (Edinburgh, 2003), pp. 175–8. For more details cf. C. McKean, *The Scottish Chateau: Country Houses of Renaissance Scotland* (Stroud, 2001), pp. 209–10; and https://scone-palace.co.uk/, accessed 22 November 2025. I would like to thank in particular for their tremendous assistance: The Earl and Countess of Mansfield & Mansfield, and Sarah Adams archivist of Scone Palace.

76. Gross, '1651: The Last Coronation in Scotland': https://www.tandfonline.com/doi/full/10.1080/14629712.2021.1996947#:~:text=The%20last%20Scottish%20coronation%20occurred%20at%20Scone%20in%201651, accessed 22 November 2025. See also NRS, Kerr, GD40/2/19/1/22, fol. 1r (John Campbell, first Earl of Loudoun, Chancellor, Edinburgh, to Charles II, 16 August 1650). Cf. NRS, GD40/2/19/1/22–25: for further correspondence between John Campbell, first Earl of Loudoun and Charles II (16 August–13 September 1650). *CSP, Venice*, vol. XXVIII, 1647–52, p. 168.
77. See also, Welander et al., *Stone of Destiny*, p. 176; Cf. R. Holinshed *et al.* (eds), *The Firste Volume … Chronicles of En[gland] … Scotlande, and Ire[land] … Faithfully gathered and set forth* (London, 1571). For a detailed geological and historical analysis of the Stone of Scone, see Welander, *Stone*; and W. Rodwell, *The Coronation Chair and Stone of Scone: History, Archaeology and Conservation* (Oxford, 2013).
78. For the linguistic origins cf. *OED*. It is something of an understatement to suggest that the Stone of Destiny has not been without controversy! It is a subject that evokes widespread interest, from its authenticity and its role as incorporated in the famous Westminster Abbey Chair of St Edward the Confessor (anachronistically called after The Confessor). There have been endless debates on the proper resting place for the Stone. It has influenced monarchs down the ages; been the centre-piece for the crowning of Scottish and English monarchs; referenced in Shakespeare's Macbeth; been the subject of films such as 'Stone of Destiny' (2008) and featured most recently in the Oscar-winning 'The King's Speech' (2010); and inspired numerous folk, classical and other genres of music: For examples: Steve McDonald's 'Stone of Destiny' (2001); and John McLeod's 'Stone of Destiny' (2003). McLeod's was commissioned by Perth Symphony Orchestra and is a Symphonic Suite for orchestra in four movements: 1. Jacob's pillow—the legend begins; 2. Odyssey—a journey through time; 3. Moot hill—ghosts of ancient kings; 4. Crown trium-

phant—a coronation march. For more details of the Stone's history and significance, cf. Welander, *Stone*; and http://www.westminster-abbey.org, accessed 22 November 2025.

79. Exodus 2: 1–10 (*KJV*); 'And Jacob rose up early in the morning, and took the stone that he had put for his pillows, and set it up for a pillar, and poured oil upon the top of it. And he called the name of that place Bethel: but the name of that city was called Luz at the first. And Jacob vowed a vow, saying, "If God will be with me, and will keep me in this way that I go, and will give me bread to eat, and raiment to put on, So that I come again to my father's house in peace; then shall the LORD be my God: And this stone, which I have set for a pillar, shall be God's house: and of all that thou shalt give me I will surely give the tenth unto thee"' Genesis 28: 18–22 (*KJV*).
80. Rodwell, *The Coronation Chair and Stone of Scone*, pp. 23–6. Cf. Welander, *Stone of Destiny*, pp. 91–3.
81. Rodwell, *The Coronation Chair*, pp. 25–6.
82. S. T. Driscoll, 'Picts and Prehistory: Cultural Resource Management in Early Medieval Scotland', *World Archaeology* 30 (1998), p. 152; D. H. Caldwell and G. Ewart, 'Finlaggan and the Lordship of the Isles: An Archaeological Approach', *The Scottish Historical Review*, 72 (1993), p. 149. The *OED* has it as a hill on which a moot or assembly is held, often an important meeting location in a town or village, and later the site for churches.
83. M. O. Anderson, 'Nechtan *mac* Derile', *ODNB*; cf. N. Evans, 'Royal Succession and Kingship among the Picts', *The Innes Review*, 59 (2008), pp. 1–48; and Welander, *Stone*, pp. 102–3, 145.
84. Bute, *Scottish Coronations* (London, 1902), p. 143. See also M. O. Anderson, 'Kenneth I [Cináed *mac* Alpin, Kenneth Macalpine] king in Scotland, d. 858', *ODNB*.
85. Holinshed, *The Firste Volume*, pp. 301–2. See also, M. Brown, *The Wars of Scotland, 1214–1371* (Edinburgh, 2004), pp. 229–30; and Rodwell, *Coronation Chair*, pp. 14–16; D. Broun, 'Macbeth [Mac Bethad *mac* Findlaích] (d. 1057)', *ODNB*; G. P. Stell, 'John [John de Balliol] (c. 1248×50–1314), king of Scots', *ibid*; M. Prestwich, 'Edward I (1239–1307), king of England and lord of Ireland, and duke of Aquitaine', *ibid*.
86. See on the legend of Fergus: H. Summerson, 'Fergus I (*c*. 305BC)', *ibid*—and sometimes referred to as Fergus [called Fergus Mór] (d. 501); D. Broun, 'Malcolm I [Mael Coluim *mac* Domnaill] (d. 954), king in Scotland, *ibid*; *ibid*., 'Dubh [Duff] [Dub *mac* Coluim] (d. 966), king in Scotland', *ibid*; K. Stringer, 'Alexander II (1198–1249), king of Scots',

ibid; M. H. Brown, 'James I (1394–1437), king of Scots', *ibid*; Bute, *Scottish Coronations*, p. 143; Holinshed, *The Firste Volume*, p. 35.

87. *Ibid.*, pp. 206, 281, 385. For a pictorial impression of such a coronation at Scone, cf. The Parker Library, Cambridge, MS 171, The Scotch Chronicle (fifteenth century): 'The Chronicle was written by John Fordoun with a continuation by Walter Bower (? Bowmakar), Abbot of Inchcolm. The illumination shows Alexander III crowned at Scone (1249). The king holds a massive sceptre and is supported by an upright sword. An old man salutes him as the descendant of Gathelos, King of Athens, and Scota, Pharaoh's daughter.' Cf. BL, Hargrave MS 497, fol. 4r–v ('Scotland. Coronation of Alexander the third King of Scotland in the year 1249'); and NLS, Edinburgh, Wodrow MSS. Quarto LXXXVI (James Balfour's Annals), p. 5. See also A. Gibb, 'The Coronation of James the First, King of Scotland, and Jane Beaufort, Queen of Scotland, His Wife, 21st May, 1424', *The Scottish Antiquary* 17 (1902), pp. 1–8; and Brown, *The Wars of Scotland*, pp. 7–9.
88. Kincaid, *Richard The Third … George Buc*, p. 215.
89. *Ibid.*, p. 215. See also A. Kincaid, 'Buck [Buc], Sir George (bap. 1560, d. 1622)', *ODNB*.
90. Kincaid, *Richard The Third … George Buc*, pp. 215–6.
91. https://perthmuseum.co.uk/the-stone-of-destiny/, accessed 22 November 2025.
92. https://www.westminster-abbey.org/abbey-news/stone-of-destiny-welcomed-to-the-abbey/, 29 April 2023, accessed 22 November 2025.
93. https://www.westminster-abbey.org/history/explore-our-history/the-coronation-chair/#:~:text=Origins%20and%20decoration,of%20the%20Abbot%20of%20Westminster, accessed 22 November 2025. For the interesting afterlife of George I's throne, see W. Burchard and S. Edwards, 'A Very Royal Perquisite: The Eventful Life of George I's Coronation Throne', *Furniture History Society Newsletter*, No. 195 (August 2014), pp. 5–9; and A. Bowett, 'George I's Coronation Throne', *Apollo*, CLXI (2005), pp. 42–7.
94. Sandford, *History*, p. 39.
95. For eighteenth–nineteenth-century visual interpretations, see also BL, Add. MS 42044 and LMA, SC/PZ/WE/01/2904. M. Hayward, 'William Green, Coffer-Maker to Henry VIII, Edward VI and Mary I', *Furniture History*, 36 (2000), pp. 8–9; Monod, *Power of Kings*, pp. 197–8.
96. Ogilby, *Entertainment*, pp. 175, 170.
97. Sandford, *History*, pp. 36b, 80b–c, f–g.
98. In 1685 the chair is also described as being placed 'against the altar', while a 'chaire and traverse [were placed] within St Edwards Chappell':

BL, Egerton MS 3350, fol. 12r. A traverse, in this context, meant a temporary closet.

99. Sandford, *History*, pp. 36b–c, 39.
100. BL, Add. MS 6113, fol. 4v.
101. *Ibid.*, Add. MS 31043, fol. 75v.
102. *Ibid.*, Add. MS 6281, fols 17r, 22r.
103. https://www.coronationroll.gov.uk/roll/, accessed 22 November 2025.
104. G. Gross, 4 July 2023. https://www.telegraph.co.uk/royal-family/2023/07/04/king-charles-scottish-honours-coronation-st-giles-cathedral/, accessed 22 November 2025.
105. C. Tabraham, *The Honours of Scotland: The Story of the Scottish Crown Jewels & The Stone of Destiny* (Edinburgh, 2019), p. 102; See also https://www.royal.uk/honours-scotland, accessed 22 November 2025; https://www.stgilescathedral.org.uk/, accessed 22 November 2025.
106. https://www.edinburghcastle.scot/see-and-do/highlights/honours-of-scotland, accessed 22 November 2025. See also NLS, MSS 2051 (Barras Papers), and 2052 (Regalia Papers); and J. J. Reid, 'The Scottish Regalia, Anciently Styled the Honours of Scotland', *Proceedings of the Society of Antiquaries of Scotland*, 24 (1889–90), pp. 18–48.
107. https://www.nms.ac.uk/discover-catalogue/anointed-with-oil-the-coronation-ampulla-of-charles-i#:~:text=The%20ampulla%20held%20the%20oil,Queen%20of%20Scots%2C%20in%201543, accessed 22 November 2025. See also: NRS, MS CH12/12/1019, p. 6; Wordsworth, *Coronation.*
108. J. Goodare, 'Mary [Mary Stewart] (1542–1587)', *ODNB.*
109. NRS, Kerr, GD40/2/19/1/22, fol. 1r (John Campbell, first Earl of Loudoun, Chancellor, Edinburgh, to Charles II, 16 August 1650). Cf. NRS, GD40/2/19/1/22–25: for further correspondence between John Campbell, first Earl of Loudoun and Charles II (16 August–13 September 1650). See also *CSP, Venice*, vol. XXVIII, 1647–1652, p. 168.
110. Tabraham, *The Honours of Scotland*, pp. 75–82.
111. https://www.parliament.uk/about/living-heritage/evolutionofparliament/legislativescrutiny/act-of-union-1707/, accessed 22 November 2025.
112. NRS, Minutes of Parliament, PA3/2, fol. 86r, cf. Brown, *Records,* M1650/11/34. See also NRS, PA7/23/2/76, fol. 1r (28 December 1650), draft coronation invitation or summons to the Earl of Erroll, Great Constable, to attend the coronation on 1 January 1651.
113. Tabraham, *Honours of Scotland*, pp. 91–3; see also https://www.edinburghcastle.scot/, accessed 22 November 2025.
114. D. Hewitt, 'Scott, Sir Walter (1771–1832)', *ODNB.*

115. Tabraham, *Honours of Scotland*, pp. 93–101; C. Hibbert, 'George IV (1762–1830),' *ODNB*. See also J. Prebble, *The King's Jaunt: George IV in Scotland, August 1822* (Edinburgh, 2000); R. Withington, 'Scott's Contribution to Pageantic Development: A Note on the Visit of George IV to Edinburgh in 1822', *Studies in Philology*, 17 (1920), pp. 121–25.
116. Tabraham, *Honours of Scotland*, pp. 101–102; E. Quigley, 27 November 2021, https://www.bbc.co.uk/news/uk-scotland-59394186, accessed 22 November 2025.
117. https://www.westminster-abbey.org/abbey-news/stone-of-destiny-welcomed-to-the-abbey, 29 April 2023, accessed 22 November 2025.
118. https://www.parliament.uk/about/living-heritage/evolutionofparliament/legislativescrutiny/act-of-union-1707/overview/union-of-the-crowns/, accessed 22 November 2025.
119. https://www.parliament.scot/about/history-of-the-scottish-parliament/the-path-to-devolution, accessed 22 November 2025. See also Tabraham, *Honours of Scotland*, p. 106.
120. Strickland, *Henry the Young King*, pp. 89–90.
121. https://www.coronationroll.gov.uk/roll/, accessed 22 November 2025.
122. Keay, *Crown Jewels*, pp. 22–3.
123. *Ibid*., p. 183.
124. *Ibid*.
125. J. Richards, 'The coronation of Queen Elizabeth II and film', *Court Historian*, 9 (2004), pp. 69–79; Keay, *Crown Jewels*, pp. 185–6.
126. https://www.vatican.va/content/francesco/en.html, accessed 22 November 2025.
127. https://www.cbcew.org.uk/archbishop-stack-cross-of-wales-presentation/, 26 January 2024, accessed 22 November 2025. See also https://www.royalmint.com/king-charles-iii/the-cross-of-wales/, accessed 22 November 2025; S. Coughlan, 19 April 2023, https://www.bbc.co.uk/news/uk-64856842, accessed 22 November 2025; https://www.churchinwales.org.uk/en/news-and-events/cross-of-wales-kings-gift-to-church-to-be-officially-received/, 22 January 2024, accessed 22 November 2025.
128. https://www.cbcew.org.uk/archbishop-stack-cross-of-wales-presentation/, 26 January 2024, accessed 22 November 2025.
129. See for example, Corporation of London Records, COL/SD/01/002 (Accounts of money subscribed by companies and bills of expenses for coronation of Charles II); For the 1953 coronation see *ibid*., COL/AC/13/004/10; see also M. C. Wren, 'The Chamber of London in 1633', *The Economic History Review*, 2nd Series, I (1948), pp. 46–53; and S. Bonnett, *The City and the Coronation … Compiled Largely from Material in the Corporation's Records Office* (London, 1953).

130. See image: 'The barons of the Cinque Ports holding the canopy over James II, 1685' (Sandford, *History*, no. 18).
131. See: https://www.royal.uk/news-and-activity/2023-04-29/the-anointing-screen, 29 April 2023, accessed 22 November 2025; https://www.coronationroll.gov.uk/further_info/anointing-screen/, accessed 22 November 2025; https://royal-needlework.org.uk/embroidered-anointing-screen/, 29 April 2023, accessed 22 November 2025.
132. Sandford, *History*, pp. 36b–c, 39.
133. B. Hatton and S. Coughlan, 9 December 2024, https://www.bbc.co.uk/news/articles/cd75d47n34do, accessed 22 November 2024.
134. https://www.hrp.org.uk/tower-of-london/history-and-stories/the-story-of-the-tower-of-london/#gs.h01nm3, accessed 22 November 2025.
135. Keay, *Crown Jewels*, p. 186 (his coronet made for the occasion by the architect and goldsmith Louis Osman, see also C. Black, 21 November 2024, https://www.bbc.co.uk/news/articles/c9dl3v522xdo, accessed 22 November 2025.
136. Keay, *Crown Jewels*, p. 186, see also: A. Anand, 20 April 2016, https://www.bbc.co.uk/news/world-asia-india-36095025, accessed 22 November 2025; D. C. Kinsey, Koh-i-Noor: Empire, Diamonds, and the Performance of British Material Culture,' *Journal of British Studies*, 48 (2009), pp. 391–419; B. P. Dean, "Thoreau and 'The Celebrated Koh-i-Noor Diamond,'" *The Thoreau Society Bulletin*, 242 (2003), pp. 6–7.
137. Keay, *Crown Jewels*, p. 186, see also L. Miall (ed.), *Richard Dimbleby, Broadcaster, by his Colleagues* (London, 1966).
138. Keay, *Crown Jewels*, p. 186.

PART III

Senses & Expenditure

CHAPTER 5

Banqueting: Food and Wine

As mentioned in the introduction with reference to the *Economist*, there was an unfounded view that Britain is celebrating royal and jubilee occasions with less fervour than in the past.[1] Street parties up and down the land, along with substantive viewing figures across multiple media are a case in point. What this alludes to is the link between a coronation at Westminster Abbey and wider public celebration and within that, the feasting and libation enjoyed by many down the ages.

Elizabeth II's coronation menu provided the nation with a new dish, that of 'Coronation Chicken', and there were celebratory luncheons at the guildhall and two coronation banquets in the ballroom at Buckingham Palace on 3 and 4 June 1953.[2] Of all the legacies of the 1953 coronation celebrations, one of the most lasting (and perhaps surprising to those at the time) was the invention of that new dish, and a luxury at the time given the legacy of rationing, and the price of chicken.[3] We are yet to see whether the 'Coronation Quiche' of 2023 will endure so ubiquitously.[4] Yet, 'Coronation Chicken' points to the very heart of a coronation and the wider celebrations that accompany it. Such an event is far **more** than a Westminster Abbey service, with all the pomp and grandeur. For many centuries it was matched by a coronation banquet, at times so spectacular, even great diarists for the ages, were lost for words. This central Westminster Hall banquet was then matched by similar celebrations up and down the country, leading to what we might now term a 'street party' celebration. Indeed, we have become accustomed to seeing the Union Jack waved

G. W. C. Gross, *Crown and People*,
https://doi.org/10.1007/978-3-032-20786-9_5

along the Mall in recent years—such scenes of celebration have become familiar parts of our national way of commemorating great events, including coronations and Jubilees amongst others. The parties often mean music, bunting, picnics, accompanied by plenty of wine and beer, fireworks and bonfires, captured in photographs with friends and neighbours. Yet for all of the contemporary feel, the UK's obsession with street parties is not a recent phenomenon. It might be thought that such a tradition emerged with Queen Victoria's Jubilee celebrations and then from the coronation of Edward VII in 1902 onwards—yet street parties have a much older history going back to the medieval and early modern eras.[5] Records from the British Library for Anne Boleyn's 1533 coronation reveal a veritable overflowing of wine for the populace in the City of London, 'at the great conduit in Cheap, a fountain ran continuously, at one end white wine, the other claret, all the afternoon'.[6]

These metropolitan festivities were accompanied by nationwide celebrations beyond the Westminster bubble. Provincial celebrations were widespread, and the country at large remembered coronation occasions regardless of distance from the capital. In Nottingham, Common Council minutes evidence coronation preparations for Charles I, 'bells shalbe ronge att everie churche, and bonfires made in the streets' in 1626.[7] For Charles II's coronation in 1661—records show '10 shillings' being spent on 'payments for ringers … and flags for coronation day' in Titchfield, Nottinghamshire, with similar celebrations up and down the land. In 1714, a hefty £9 was spent in Thornbury, Gloucestershire for 'ale att the coronation of King George I'.[8]

Early newspaper reports provide yet more evidence for this street party tradition. *The London Gazette* (founded in 1665 and we should note—effectively a Crown paper) recorded that in Nottingham for James II's 1685 coronation the day was observed with a military march, and a mayoral parade, which was accompanied with 'acclamations of long live King James the Second, and all expressions of joy'. Not only was the town hall arranged for loyal toasts but so too

> about all the crosses there was planted vessels of ale that the common sort might drink the king and queens healths, which they did heartily. There were … tables furnished for all commers. The day was spent in musick and feasting, and the night in ringing of bells, bonfires, and fireworks, the town not sparing for any charge or pains to express their loyalty and satisfaction to be governed by so glorious a monarch.[9]

We have excellent detail on James II's coronation banquet, for it was meticulously recorded by Francis Sandford, from seating plan to the number of dishes (a staggering 1445). The first course included forty-six dishes of hot meat, presented in a procession of seventy-three persons, including three officers on horseback. [10] The lavish nature of the occasion and general merriment was felt far beyond Westminster, as records from the city of Bristol reveal.[11]

Although celebrations occurred throughout the kingdom, even on these national occasions wealth and status might determine the extent of participation. The division between rich and poor, in urban areas, has been explored by George Tresidder in a detailed study of elite hegemony and local relations in connection with coronation day festivities. One problem with this approach is that document survival is inherently elitist, in terms of private individuals and institutions. Whilst we therefore have reservations about aspects of his case, evidence from Nottingham celebrations for Queen Anne's coronation in 1702 do show that gradually 'during the late seventeenth and early eighteenth centuries, coronation celebrations communicated the dominance of the Corporation, the gentry, and the economic magnate in the urban hierarchy'.[12] Nevertheless, although it may point towards the main payers for these events (corporations for instance), in terms of substantive sums that does not take away from all members of various communities participating in celebrations regardless of their financial positions. Receipts found in Shakespeare Centre Library and Archive in Stratford-upon-Avon demonstrate people spending £1 12s. 6d. on 'beer and tobacco' for Queen Anne's coronation in 1702—an incredibly significant figure at that time, amounting to about forty days of wages for an average labourer, and was thus sponsored by the town council and leading members of the community.[13] Yet, this was an example of the early modern 'street party'; in Stratford-upon-Avon rich and poor both celebrated alike, even if the main financial contribution had come from those with the broadest shoulders, an insight into the social profile of the time.

The history of street parties show that formal and informal parties have always coexisted and have a central place in those celebrating these royal events—evidenced by TV star Barbara Windsor being appointed 'street party ambassador' during the Diamond Jubilee celebrations in 2012.[14] Charles III's coronation celebrations were no different and saw people across the United Kingdom 'share food and fun together' during 'Coronation Big Lunches'—10 million as part of the Eden Communities Project.[15]

Thus, we have at the heart of the magnificence of a coronation, the tradition of a sumptuous feast too, with similar events up and down the land. By applying a 'follow the money' approach we are able to see the extent of pattern, revealing a connection to the State from as early as the Tudors, far in advance of any modern sense of 'national identity'. No aspect of a coronation, whether central or local, was cost-free. Indeed, the costs were huge, especially for the coronation banquet. Who was spending the money, why funds were spent in a certain way, and why they were perhaps spent differently from one coronation to another are questions leading to some very interesting conclusions, which are indicative of wider changes during the tumultuous history of the British Isles. This area is all the more intriguing because of a remarkable coincidence: the enormous cost of coronations increased at the same time as 'the birth of the tax state' during the seventeenth century.[16] This coincidence itself raises further questions. Did, for example, the taxpayer voice concerns as to the substantial sums involved? If the organisers got it right, then the public were happy. If, however, they got it wrong then huge disquiet could be raised. It is thus, not as simple as the public expecting a cost-efficient event. Whilst the 1821 coronation of George IV was both spectacularly expensive, lavish and at times wasteful, it was also seen to be so, whilst the absence of spending for 1831 for William IV had the event disparaged as the 'penny coronation'.[17] James II was aware of the extraordinary cost of coronations and abolished the traditional grand procession in an effort to be seen as 'frugal and cautious, and no great admirer of outward pomp and popularity'.[18] According to Edie, James II estimated savings of £60,000.[19] However, this sum was soon spent on jewels for his consort, Mary of Modena. Not only did the king fail to harness the public relations opportunities of coming face-to-face with his people in the procession, but his efforts at parsimony failed too: lavish spending on the regalia in fact dramatically escalated overall expenditure. The original draft accounts show that Richard de Beauvoir, the goldsmith, was required to make a new diadem at prodigious cost, and the new total for crown jewels can be put somewhere in the region of £100,000 (British Library records have it as £100,650; whilst Sandford puts the total at £111,900).[20] Indeed, in many cases the absence of spending could frustrate the public as much as the excess. The occasion had to be right, just as any major event in the present, from Olympic opening ceremonies to festivals around the world.

From seventeenth-century diaries to the present, people cared and continue to care about these events. We cannot look into people's minds, but we can read what they have written (and what was spent) and study the statistics on viewing figures for royal spectacle. The pictures of Green Park and parks up and down the land and trees around the country decorated with flowers and other tokens of respect in September of 2022 showed that a monarch (in Queen Elizabeth II) in the twenty-first century meant something very profound to people, not forgetting those that queued for hours for the Lying-in-State. The 2023 coronation saw the Mall heaving with those hoping to get the best spots for the occasion days before the event.[21] So too, as there has always been—2023 saw protesters and those not in favour of such monarchical events making their voices heard. It is often forgotten that in 1714 there were major riots following the coronation of George I—'not in my name' is not a new phrase.[22]

The street-party style commemorations of 2016 for the Queen's ninetieth birthday and 2022 Jubilee celebrations would not have been so far removed from such celebrations in the seventeenth and early eighteenth centuries. Newspapers undoubtedly played their parts in creating publicity. In this instance, they tell us more of what was going on in the country and, indeed, from a crown position, what they hoped was happening and what they wanted readers to hear. Bonfires and bells were certainly fitting and were part of beacon lighting for the 2022 Platinum Jubilee celebrations for Queen Elizabeth II. For Charles III in 2023, it was 'ring for a King'.[23]

In 1613, James I spent a sum of £2880 (hundreds of thousands in today's money and nearly 60,000 days' worth of skilled labour) on fireworks alone for the marriage of Elizabeth Stuart.[24] Coronations follow this pattern, indeed they are the summit of magnificence—as the most important royal event of all. Most importantly, the 'atmosphere' of these events evoked wonder and mystery captured in accounts and first-hand reports of people's experiences, and it always seems to be an air of splendour, clear in modern accounts, especially in those of Elizabeth II's coronation in 1953: 'The procession was magnificent. The colour and pageantry cannot be described. Uniforms superb and resplendent'.[25] This was also true of the magnificence felt by Mary Countess Cowper at the coronation of George I in 1714, 'I own I was never so affected with joy in all my life; it brought tears into my eyes'.[26] And not to leave other famous diaries out—Pepys in his 1661 recollections of Charles II's Restoration coronation echo similar themes and are as near as one gets to evidence of impact: 'Now, after all this, I can say that, besides the pleasure of the sight of these glorious things, I may now shut my eyes against any other objects, nor for the future trouble myself to see things of state and show, as being sure never to see the like again in this world (of course he did in 1685 as a baron of the Cinque Port for James II's coronation)'.[27] John Evelyn was so enamoured with Charles II's crowning that he wrote a 'Panegyric' for the day, presenting it in the Privy Chamber to the king, 'which he was pleased to accept most graciously'. London's high society was delighted with proceedings and continued to party—Evelyn attended the marquess of Ormond's 'magnificent feast' the day after the coronation. The impact of the occasion seems to have permeated to many Londoners, for on 1 May, over a week after the main event, Evelyn reported that he 'went to Hyde Park to take the air, where was his majesty and an innumerable appearance of gallants and rich coaches, being now a time of universal festivity and joy'.[28]

Magnificence is a continuous theme. This was a day of impressive proportions, in costume, regalia, and personnel. Yet what of celebrations out of London? Are these new—was it always the case, long before a mechanised state? Was there a sense of community unified by allegiance to the crown, perhaps before historians have previously thought?

The Westminster Abbey coronation and metropolitan festivities were accompanied by nationwide celebrations. After the Restoration, numerous

Fig. 5.1 At the banquet following the coronation of Henry the Young King in 1170, Henry II serves his son at the table, from an Anglo-Norman verse, *Life of Thomas Becket*, *c.*1220–1240. British Library/Alamy

Irish corporations 'enthusiastically commemorated the anniversaries of both the coronation and the Restoration each year, providing alcohol for the local inhabitants and encouraging the construction of bonfires'.[29]

How do we know these things? Diaries as already cited, newspapers and written accounts—correspondence, printed coronation sermons all reveal the extent of interest and impact beyond Westminster.

Coronation sermons (see Chap. 2) were printed and distributed, and became publications of interest and value, like a borrowable present and the luxury of exotic tea in the early eighteenth century. On 1 May 1702, Sir Thomas Rawlinson wrote to John Seeley in London:

> I have here sent you some Bohea tea (an oolong tea, roughly equivalent to Lapsang Souchong), as a present which I desire your acceptance, I know itt to be good and very wholsome, and the sermon preached att the coronation of Queen Anne which you may lend, butt not to give it away, but to keep it.[30]

Moving from tea to further refreshment in food and wine. For centuries, from the Anglo-Saxons to the Westminster Abbey coronations of 1066 onward, wine has been a prominent feature of British coronations—an ever present element.[31] For one, it has been part of the sacramental religious side of the ceremony (as the accompanying element to the bread—the bread and the wine), featuring before the Reformation in the Mass, and then later in the Eucharist or Holy Communion of a Protestant Church of England tradition. Secondly, it has been at the core of royal banquet or feast, and wider festivities that followed the coronation ceremony. For example, for Henry the Younger on 14 June 1170, the carafe of wine was a focal point of the coronation banquet.[32] In addition, both at home and abroad, wine has also been consumed—in considerable quantities—in celebrations connected with coronations.

Detailed accounts survive for Henry IV's (Bolingbroke/Lancaster) coronation banquet of 1399—and show how significant the occasion was not just for feasting and celebrating, but for diplomacy and consolidating Henry's power.[33] His coronation was held in immensely tense conditions, following his coup to overthrow Richard II (only days earlier). Given the dramatic events and delicate state of political affairs, there was similar concern that Henry might himself be overthrown too. Thus, the coronation and accompanying banquet had to run smoothly and impress all segments of society. At the same time Henry IV had to balance England's delicate relationship with France. In essence the coronation had to cement his leadership, whilst not causing a civil or foreign war, and yet also show the power of the English crown reinstated—quite a PR exercise! The date for the coronation was chosen quite deliberately—13 October—as the feast of St Edward the Confessor—the most important of saintly patrons for English monarchs (as discussed in Chap. 1).[34] The seating plan for his banquet was carefully constructed to consolidate Henry's relationships with key subjects—those who had helped him in rebellion against Richard II and those whom he believed would be important for maintaining his hold on power.[35] As became customary, Henry was seated with his family and key members of the church on an elevated dais looking down on the rest of the guests, thus emphasising power both politically and religiously. For this banquet, the aim was not a finally balanced menu, but rather tables adorned to impress the gathered audience. The fare included soups, wild boar, venison, capons, cygnets, sturgeon, pheasants, and heron amongst other boiled, roasted, and stuffed meats. The banquet took the form of three courses of these remarkable offerings, each accompanied by a 'sotelte' or subtlety, which is a decoratively carved sugar sculpture often in the form of religious figures—whether saints, angels, or other such iconography. The use of so much sugar was also a sign of tremendous wealth, for sugar was a luxury in medieval England, as with salt and spices more generally.[36]

Not only did the coronation banquet filter outward an outpouring of celebration and national festivity, but careful analysis of the difference between occasions reveals differing emphases, whether political, religious, and so too the strength or weakness of succession. An example would be the comparison of the coronations of Catherine of Valois (23 February 1421) and her son Henry VI (6 November 1429, 16 December 1431—English and French coronations) taking place within eleven years of each other.[37] From the menus, and notably the 'soteltes'[38] (elaborate sugar sculptures) accompanying each course we see entirely different settings for the power of crown and the priorities they sought to push forward. The food served at the banquets was hugely symbolic with heraldic imagery and the aim of conveying monarchical ideas of queenship and kingship. The menu has been preserved to us, translated from the French into English and digitised, and now held in the British Library including a dazzling array of medieval delicacies and an extravaganza of game.[39] Both banquets served three courses of food at levels any gourmand would have found exceptional.[40] The marriage between Henry V and Catherine had been part of Anglo-French diplomacy for many years, culminating in the

Treaty of Troyes, signed on 21 May 1420, which agreed upon the succession of Henry V and his heirs after Charles VI's death and the disinheritance of the dauphin Charles.[41] Nevertheless, Catherine's coronation on 23 February 1421 was a celebration of Catherine in her own right as an English queen consort. Henry V was absent 'in order not to detract from Catherine's glory on that day'.[42] The menu for the coronation banquet served as an endorsement of Anglo-queenship showing the political potency of food and wine. For at the same time the seating plan was carefully arranged given the ongoing war (Hundred Years') and the position of the dauphin. In 2004 with relations difficult between President Chirac and Prime Minister Tony Blair, and as with so many of her state banquets and dinners, Queen Elizabeth II would politicise the menu and format of entertainment in the politest form possible.[43] Dishes in Catherine's banquet consisted mainly of fish and shellfish, including 'troute', 'grete crabys', and 'lampryns'. Whilst some attribute this to the fact that Catherine's coronation occurred during Lent, seafood was also seen as a more feminine food at that time, meaning that the dishes served could be seen as a way to illustrate ideas of queenship.[44] Indeed, the coronation banquet of Elizabeth of York on 25 November 1497 also consisted mainly of seafood and poultry, compared to Henry IV's which contained a considerable quantity of red meat.[45] The design of the food itself was also rich with royal imagery. The first course included a 'lech lumbarde' (a sweet, jellied dish) displaying the 'impaled arms of Henry and Catherine, together with the Lancastrian collar of esses badge popularized by Henry IV, and the Valois golden broom-pod badge of Charles VI'.[46] The presentation of the Houses of Lancaster and Valois being intertwined, both in terms of Henry and Catherine's marriage and its inclusion of precedence (in displaying the badges of Henry IV and Charles IV), conveys a sense of dynastic security that refers to the Treaty of Troyes and its agreement that the son of Henry and Catherine will be heir to both the English and French thrones. Whilst this ignores the uncertainty surrounding the dauphin's claim to the French throne, it is interesting how Catherine's banquet seems to be more transparent in its portrayal of the agreement being between the royal houses, compared to Henry VI's banquet with an emphasis on the dual imagery of St George and St Denis (third-century saints) and St Edward and St Louis (semi-mythical kings of England and France).[47] Henry VI's coronation banquets sought to assert a dominance (in some respects imperial) over England and France, again with the use of menu. In the context of his rival Charles VII's coronation as King of

France on 17 July in Reims in 1429, the opulence of the feast following Henry's English coronation and the extravagance of its imagery can be seen as an attempt for young seven-year-old Henry to claim legitimacy over the French throne.[48] The 'soteltes', accompanying each course also involved commissioned verses by Lydgate, to add to the polemic of the coronation banquet.[49] Henry's French coronation banquet, which took place in Paris rather than Reims, was heavily criticised by French sources for its disorganisation. His English coronation banquet was therefore critical in driving forward the political agenda of two-state rule. Catherine's banquet, by contrast seems to represent the driving forward of medieval English queenship.

Henry VI's English coronation banquet included 'flampayne [pork pie] poudered with lepardis and flour de lices of golde'.[50] This 'conspicuous comingling of English leopards and French lilies' further asserts Henry VI's bi-national heritage and his claim to both thrones.[51] Additionally, images such as 'a redde lech with lions corven theryn of white', 'a leparde of dole sittyng theryn', and 'artelop of redde corven theryn, a crowne about his neck with a cheyne of golde' are equally heraldic, displaying both extravagance and dynastic superiority.[52]

By contrast, the food served at Henry VI's French coronation banquet in 1431 was received negatively. Whilst the banquet is recorded in less detail, it seems like the messages of the dual monarchy had a weaker effect. Whilst the chronicler of the Brut records that the meal contained 'all delicacye of metes and drynkes þat myght be ordeyned', the comment from Bourgeois of Paris', that the food had been cooked three days prior to the feast, implies a lack of English control and experience in French lands.[53] Whilst this source only records one chronicler's opinion, there seems to be a sense of dissatisfaction with the English monarchy in Paris. This is reflected in England's weakening hold of France in the ongoing war. Whilst the execution of Joan of Arc on 30 May 1431 was significant in raising English spirits, the ongoing disputes between Bedford and Beaufort, as well as the influence of Charles VII's coronation which marked him as the legitimate king two years earlier, marked a significant reversal of English fortunes that can be seen in Henry VI's French coronation banquet.[54]

The importance of food choices or 'refreshments' continued to matter from dynasty to dynasty.[55] As Sybil Jack has argued for James I, following the homage and communion service, 'the king changed his clothes and put on a different crown to return in procession bearing the sceptre to the palace and the banquet. The importance to the ritual of what the king ate must not be underplayed, for it represented spiritual food and the symbolism of each food was often discussed in medical, herbal and other texts relating to health'.[56]

Turning from the food, it is worth also considering the consumption of drink, and particularly wine at coronation banquets and wider celebrations and street parties, and what that meant socially, politically, and religiously. The following discussion will deal with wine by section, focussing on Champagne, Rhenish or Riesling, Claret, and Sauternes.

Champagne

When one thinks of great events, of celebrations, royalty, pomp, and ceremony—a bottle of bubbles or two (!) are never far away and coronations have had champagne at the very heart of the drinking experience. Appropriately, champagne originates from Reims in France, the crowning place of French kings and is therefore perhaps the most suitable 'ointment' for feasting.[57] Traditionally, the coronation banquet took place in Westminster Hall following the coronation ceremony in Westminster Abbey.[58] Though on occasion plague would prevent such gatherings as was the case for Charles I in 1626, saving the monarch a considerable sum in feasting, but in the eyes of many, turning the coronation occasion into a private Westminster Abbey event rather than a spectacle to be seen by the wider populace.[59] Westminster Hall is the oldest building connected with the Palace of Westminster and has played a major role in British history as the home to the legal courts of the country before the Royal Courts of Justice—hosting famous trials and speeches, along with sumptuous feasts.[60] In recent history it has been the focal point for the lying-in-state of monarchs, as seen for the late Queen Elizabeth II. The last great Westminster Hall banquet was in 1821 for George IV.[61] The lavish nature of the occasion did not win the monarch much favour with the public and this ancient event was discontinued in the traditional setting of Westminster Hall, a tradition that had begun in 1189 with Richard I 'the Lionheart'.[62] Strickland argues for an earlier banquet in 1170 for Young King Henry, and '[a]n illustrated Anglo-Norman poem on the life of Becket, composed *c.*1220–1240, depicts both the Young King's coronation and the ensuing banquet, at which Henry II offers a cup to his son'.[63] On any view the concept of a coronation followed by a feast was of long standing and well-developed in the medieval era. Banquets continued in the modern era (post 1821), but at Buckingham Palace, and on a smaller scale than at Westminster Hall. Not all such traditions have continued. From as early as Edward III's coronation in 1327[64] to 1821, the mayor of Oxford was given the role of Assistant Butler at the coronation banquet. This service was no longer required when William IV dispensed with the Westminster Hall occasion, but the mayor continued to be invited to the coronation as a perquisite of the Oxford role, but this ended in 2023.[65]

George IV was adamant that his coronation be recorded for posterity in written form and we have detailed records, not only for the banquet but for the entire proceedings and costumes too.[66] The hall setting inspired furnishings that took on a gothic theme with galleries surrounding the main hall stage. The Royal platform was designed by Fredrick Westmacott, whilst John Russel charged £752 for the canopy, chair of state, and six elbow chairs. It was little wonder that the entire cost came to £238,000.[67] George IV was also hugely influenced by France and French style, with Andre-Charles Boulle chandeliers featuring prominently. Not all went to plan (and more will be covered in Chap. 8) for a state of confusion and panic followed after the populace 'in a joyous mood' tried to force their way into the kitchen where the coronation plate had been stored for 'safety'. Soldiers had to be called in to restore order and the intruders kept at bay.[68]

In 1902, Edward VII's ill health delayed the coronation from 26 June to 9 August, following a pre-coronation feast that was thought to be so lavish (!) that it may have brought on the king's illness. On 9 August, feasting took place in Buckingham Palace, and whilst much of his banquet had long since been given to charity (2500 quails had been given to the poor in Whitechapel)[69] he did not go without, and it was said that there was still enough wine and champagne to float an entire fleet of the battleships of the Royal Navy![70]

What of the champagne? Champagne was at the heart of Edward VII's coronation banquet feasts in 1902, a sovereign with a passionate interest in Parisian custom, indeed everything French. The epicurean monarch made sure his guests enjoyed two options: a Mumm 1892 and a Pommery 1893. Moving to the late Queen's coronation in 1953, and possibly with Sir Winston Churchill's enthusiastic support, the assembled enjoyed Pol Roger's 1934 vintage.[71] Churchill's hand seems very likely here. Following the liberation of France, Churchill was served Pol Roger 1928 in Paris. According to his son, Randolph, his father bought up all of the 1928 he could get his hands on and when that ran out, drank his plentiful supply

Fig. 5.2 'His Majesty King Edward VII in full coronation robes'. From the painting by S. Pegg, featured in *The Illustrated London News and Sketch Ltd*, 'Record of the Coronation Ceremony', 1902 (from the British Library archive)

of 1934 until his death. Elizabeth II's second reception in 1953 also included a Krug 1945 option.[72] These then were the champagnes of the coronation feast celebrations for Edward VII and Elizabeth II—one, a classic indulgent display of consumption and excess, the other, the attempt to create a new Elizabethan age on the back of the Festival of Britain.[73] For Elizabeth II it is better to talk of 'banquets' for she required two separate banquets to accommodate over 8000 guests, including heads of state, commonwealth representatives, and the wider royal family. The main ballroom and state dining room of Buckingham Palace played host, with the Queen's rectangular table at the centre of the room surrounded by circular tables (note again the wedding analogy, for such a similar format is not unusual at wedding receptions). The floral decorations were arranged (as ordered by Elizabeth II) to ensure that both she and Prince Philip would be visible to all of the guests attending.[74]

Rhenish Wines

Whilst we have begun in the more typical drinking order of recent times, we now turn our attention further back in history to Hock or Rhenish wines. These examples today would likely be classified under the label of Riesling. The name 'hock' even gave rise to wine glasses specifically named after such wine. Hock is the traditional generic English term for (white) Rhenish wines from the Rhine regions of Germany in general.[75] It is a contraction of Hochheim on the river Main just west of Frankfurt. Whilst Riesling is one of the most divisive of grapes and wines—a 'marmite' wine, dividing opinion in the twenty-first century, our royal forbears had no such difficulty in placing Hock wines firmly within a coronation context.[76] One of the most recorded of early coronation celebrations was that of Anne Boleyn in 1533 and unique in an English context in being the independent crowning of a Queen Consort.[77] Whilst one might have anticipated a strong Rhenish wine presence to the Tudor court for the arrival of the German Anne of Cleves in 1540, Anne Boleyn had no such Germanic links. Indeed, she is well known for her time at the French court. Nevertheless, her coronation saw a veritable overflowing of German wines, indicating a general availability and popularity in England. Verses survive referencing Anne Boleyn's coronation procession[78] as well as a remarkable description of wine fountains from the City of London in 1533 for the festivities:

> At Gracechurch Corner was erected 'the Mount Parnassus, with the fountain of Helicon'. It was formed of white marble. 'Four streams rose on … high and met in a cup above the fountain which ran copiously till night with Rhenish wine. At the great Conduit in Cheap, a fountain ran continuously, at one end white wine, the other claret, all the afternoon'.[79]

Tastes vary, it was not so much that people drank wine or beer—the grape or the grain—but rather, that early modern citizens of Tudor London consumed substantive quantities of both.

Mary Tudor's coronation is all the more extraordinary given she was part of the only successful rebellion of the Tudor age. Her banquet was carried out as per tradition in Westminster Hall, with the Earl of Worcester as her carver.[80] However, even by Henry IV or Richard III's standards she seems to have sought to match her late father, Henry VIII's efforts 'greater than any Caesar had known'[81] for 7112 dishes are recorded as being served, with Mary receiving 312; 4900 dishes are recorded as 'waste' and then distributed amongst the people of London. Henry VIII's coronation extravaganza had been seen to herald in for many a new age of expectation and promise, highlighted by Thomas More's composition of a suite of coronation poems in celebration (Fig. 5.3).[82] For it was not only coins or medals, or poetic verse, but also food that would be given to those present and those in need at such occasions. Such acts were of course excellent public relations opportunities for a new monarch and continued under Elizabeth I.[83]

Rhenish wines remained firmly in vogue in the Stuart world of the seventeenth century (and would remain a feature of coronation banquets into the eighteenth and nineteenth centuries, with 'hock' in abundance for George IV's 1821 Westminster Hall coronation banquet).[84] Robert Spencer, the 2nd Earl of Sunderland's wine cellar records of 1666 included 6% of Rhenish wine, and this made up an even larger percentage of his white wine collection.[85] In total over half of his wines were French, but a reasonable percentage came from Germany. The diarist Samuel Pepys watched and recorded in detail the Restoration coronation of Charles II in 1661 and was a baron of the cinque ports for the coronation of James II in 1685. His actions on coronation day, 23 April 1685, are recorded in Sandford's depictions of key figures of the event—Pepys is seen carrying the canopy over the king in the royal procession.[86] His diaries include at least twenty-nine entries related to Rhenish wine (or perhaps more importantly a Rhenish wine tavern or shop!). By contrast, claret only makes

Fig. 5.3 Extract from Sir Thomas More's poems on the coronation of King Henry VIII and Queen Katherine of Aragon, 1509 (from the British Library archive, Cotton Titus D.IV, fol.12v)

thirteen entries. In all, he has 335 entries devoted to wine. It seems that Pepys had a passion for another marmite item, that of the 'anchovy' as a food to be paired with his German wine drinking sessions:

> Thence with my cozen Roger Pepys, it being term time, we took him out of the Hall to Priors, the Rhenish wine-house, and there had a pint or two of wine and a dish of anchovies, and bespoke three or four dozen bottles of wine for him against his wedding. (3 February 1659/1660)[87]

The diarist John Evelyn recorded a similar interest in wine and the frequenting of the same Rhenish wine shop on Cannon Row in the City of Westminster in the 1660s.[88] Digressing briefly, but in the context of trade and commerce of which wine was a vital import in the early modern era when water was not safe to drink, we turn briefly, to how a coronation united these two great cities of London. Whilst today London is an all-encompassing term, in the medieval and early modern eras, there was a clear distinction between the City of London and Westminster and this was important in the context of a coronation. Many readers familiar with Trafalgar Square will know of the nearby church—St Martin-in-the-Fields. That church was quite literally in a field and sheep safely grazed what is now the square. The two cities were thus independently arranged, but in a coronation, a procession would take place of the monarch travelling from the City of London (the Tower of London) to Whitehall and the Palace of Westminster. A coronation thus metaphorically bridged these two cities and in so doing joined together both politics and trade under one ceremonial crowning.

During the late 1670s and 1680s Parliament passed various embargos on French wines and goods during a time of increasing conflict with France. Nominally it was a success and drove customers to Italian, German, Spanish, and Portuguese wines. This also helped to promote Rhenish varieties, and enthusiasm for such wines increased. That said new research reveals that cunning English merchants circumnavigated the embargo, by buying French wines via Italian, Spanish, Portuguese, and German brokers.[89] It is also now known, that wine being imported from Portugal under a Portuguese origin vastly outweighed the quantity of wine being produced in Portugal, and also encouraged 'false declarations'.[90] Burgundy and claret thus arrived, just under different country labels. Indeed, it is possible to argue that the embargo simply drove up French wine prices but it did little to change English tastes. Thus highlighting the law of unintended consequences.

James II's coronation banquet in 1685 was a *tour de force* and his table alone was presented with over 600 dishes and copious quantities of libation followed, not least French and German wines.[91] With the arrival of the Hanoverians, formally as the new royal House in 1714 with George I, German wines remained a theme in royal cellars and acquired something of a royal blessing. An account charge from the Royal Collection archives reveals a charge of 322 pounds for his royal highness George I for twenty-two aums of Rhenish wine.[92] George III continued this custom with 'claret and hock (Rhenish wine) at his own table'.[93] An aum was originally a liquid measure used in Germany and the Low Countries which varied in different places from about thirty to forty-four imperial gallons (136 to 200 litres). In South Africa, it apparently still features to this day, as a measurement amongst certain vintners and vineyards. To give an idea of scale for these feasts, George II's coronation banquet in 1727 was lit by over 2000 wax candles!

Royal tastes influenced courtiers. For instance, the Earl of Sunderland's 1666 wine cellar reflected Charles II's interests and the fashionable tastes of the 'Sun King' Louis XIV of France. Similarly, under George II, the duke of Newcastle acquired a passion for German wines.[94] In 1748 George II sent his advisor the 1st duke of Newcastle to Hanover to develop better how the two dominions would work together. Newcastle not only worked on his political brief, but in so doing, developed an affection for the local wines and surviving letters record his request on his return to England to have wine shipped over.[95]

With Queen Victoria's marriage to Prince Albert of Saxe-Coburg and Gotha in 1840, the United Kingdom has enjoyed a familial yet complicated relationship with Germany that is often difficult to understand.[96] The same can probably be said about its relationship to German wines in the last two centuries. Some English consumers, prized Rhenish white wines in the 1830s precisely for their purity, lack of adulteration, and relative dryness and decried port for its excess of sweetness and spirit, but such perceptions were probably eroded later in the century. During the First World War with sugar rationing, the British wine consumer may have lost their affection for dry wines. Some even liked those with more age and one German wine was colloquially known as 'old hock'. Yet, Riesling wines were a consistent feature at Royal banquet's in Victorian and Edwardian England. Whilst Queen Victoria and Prince Albert 'enjoyed sherry' perhaps more than 'any other wine', her cellars nevertheless 'contained a startling range of wines'.[97] Edward VII's 1902 coronation saw a Hock, Marcobrunner Cabinet, and jumping forward to 1953, Queen Elizabeth II continued this tradition, with a Johannisberger Erntebringer Riesling 1949 being made available to her guests.[98] Both entries are somewhat surprising. Edward VII adored all things French, and disliked much of the German culture of his Mother's court; and the 1953 coronation was just a few years on from the Second World War. Given that rationing was in the process of ending and London still bore many of the hallmarks of the Blitz it is striking that this polarising wine still featured and perhaps goes to show that tastes and fashions often transcend politics.

Turning to the Commonwealth, for the coronation of Elizabeth II, celebrations took place across the globe from Canada to the Antipodes, and Australian Riesling played a part in the festivities. In 1953 HMS Sydney brought to London a special contingent of Anzac troops (that had won VCs) to be in the traditional coronation procession; and to take part in a Coronation Naval Review.[99] Whilst Great Britain had street parties, so too did the nations of the Commonwealth, and great dinner menus too. Singapore held a whole week of celebration.[100] Records from a dinner of dignitaries in Canberra, Australia, shows the consumption of a special banquet including: Consomme royale; lobster; roast turkey and ham; asparagus; and strawberries—and as to Riesling or Hock we have two mentions. A Riesling Yalumba Carte d'or and a Buring's Old crusty Hock, private bin.[101] The Queen would also be the first British sovereign to visit Australia in 1954. The crowning banquet of her tour would include a Riesling, this time of the Lindemann Cawarra stable.[102]

Claret

The British affection for claret is well-known, and the wine has been part of coronation banquets for centuries. British royal connections with claret goes back to the medieval age, and it is indeed the Anglicised term for Bordeaux wine. In one of King John's (1167–1216)[103] better moves, in his coronation year of 1199, he gave St Emilion a royal charter in exchange for rights to the coveted local wines there. Whilst it will take a lot to improve King John's reputation, this was not a bad move!

How it was drunk and in what manner varied to different levels of appreciation. On the night of Charles II's Restoration coronation on St George's Day 1661, Samuel Pepys and his retinue (as he recorded) 'drank

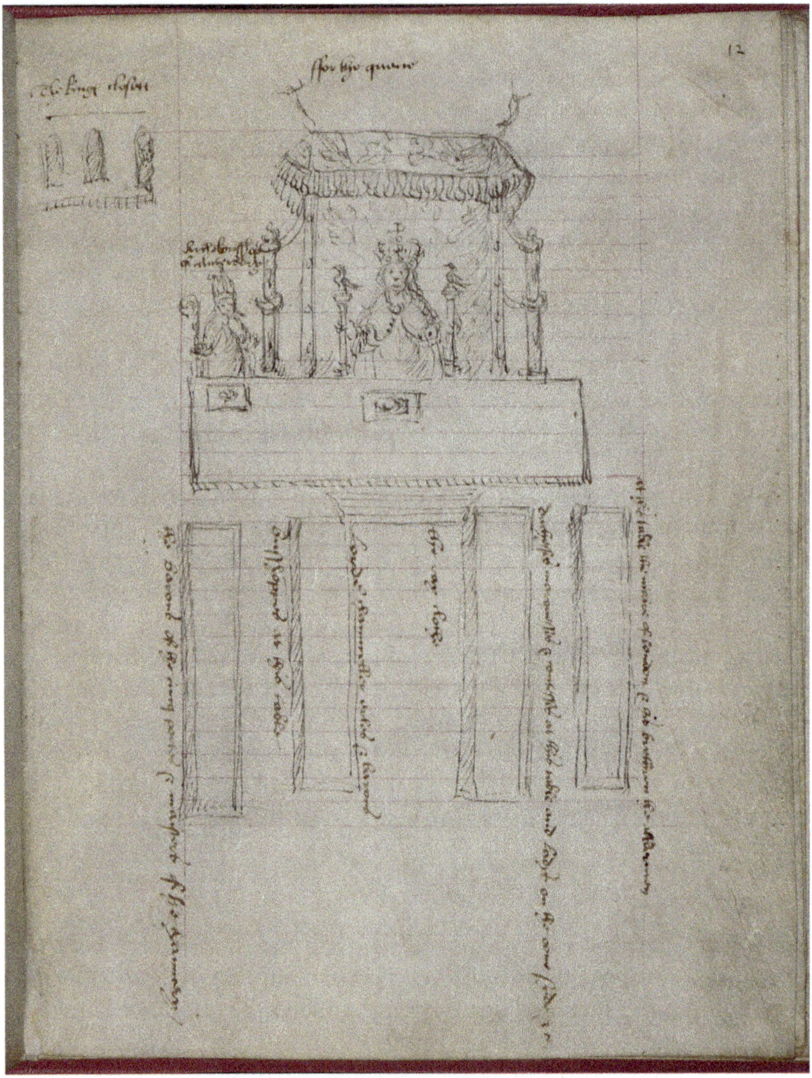

Fig. 5.4 Sketch of Queen Anne Boleyn, seated under a canopy, crowned, with sceptres in each hand; the Archbishop of Canterbury on her right. Below, a plan for the queen's coronation banquet in Westminster Hall, 1 June 1533 (from the British Library archive, Harley 41, fol. 12)

the King's health and nothing else, till one of the gentlemen fell down stark drunk and there lay speweing'.[104] Wine fountains for the general populace to enjoy have already been mentioned in the context of Anne Boleyn's coronation in 1533, yet the concept was nothing new. In 1308 for the coronation of Edward II (1284–1327), a fountain in one of the domestic halls spouted red and white wine (!) and a spiced drink known as pimento.[105] The red wine was almost certainly claret.

During the seventeenth and eighteenth centuries, claret became highly politicised—a bastion of Tory sympathy, but dangerously French and Jacobite for Whigs who favoured the wines of Portugal. By the 1680s and increasing conflict with France, pressure grew to boycott or embargo French wine sales more permanently, and this culminated in the Methuen Treaty of 1703.[106] Unsurprisingly, the price of wine went up. Between 1661 and 1685, the price of French-wine had more than doubled. Yet we still wanted more and England's love affair with French wine endured. For all of the partisan battle lines, in general the love of French wine dominated over one's political pallet.

Returning to the 2nd Earl of Sunderland's wine cellar of 1666, over half of his 635 bottles of wine were of French origin, and claret dominated at 191 bottles recorded.[107] Yet it was not until Queen Anne's reign that 'luxury claret' truly arrived at scale 'on the English market'.[108] Quantity was perhaps as important as quality in the early modern period as already referenced for James II's 1685 coronation banquet—which was of such scale that it attracted and generated illustrations and prints, that were published internationally, as can be seen in an Italian account of James II's 1685 coronation, which was produced in Bologna and Naples.[109] News of the spectacular coronation banquets, which included over a thousand dishes in 1685, from 'salletting' to 'sweet meats', also spread extensively in the form of receipts.[110] The royal chef, Patrick Lamb, published a recipe book of royal cookery in 1710.[111] In addition to place-settings, it details receipts from jellies to fricassee of chickens and 'crawfish or lobster soupe'—this was most certainly the art and wealth of gluttony.[112]

Edward VII concluded the entrée section of his 1902 coronation banquet in a more delicate manner, with truffles and brandy sauce, accompanied by an offering of Château d'Issan, thereby paying homage to an ancient connection of that fine estate to the medieval English royal family. Château d'Issan was served at the wedding of Eleanor of Aquitaine to King Henry II in 1152.[113] Jumping forward to 1953, claret endured, for Elizabeth II's lucky guests were treated to a first growth—a Château Lafite

1934.[114] This echoed Queen Victoria's enthusiasm for the Lafite label, that had been so prevalent in her private cellar, '16 hogsheads of [the] 1834' vintage.[115]

Sauternes

Sauternes have long graced the dinner tables of monarchs and given their production involves 'noble rot' there could be little more appropriate for a sovereign. It is perhaps far from surprising that a wine as prestigious as Château d'Yquem (vintage 1928) featured at Elizabeth II's coronation banquet in 1953.[116] The royal pallet for something sweet was nothing new as will be covered below.[117] If you were interested in a bottle of the '28', a certain wine shop just off Berkley square (London) is retailing a bottle for just over £4800 pounds.

Shakespeare echoing heraldic accounts of Richard III's (1452–1485) coronation shows such interest in sweet wines was present there. This chapter is not an attempt at reputational improvement for our lesser-loved monarchs—King John and Richard III (1452–1485)—but they both clearly knew a thing or two about wine. Richard III made sure at his coronation banquet that he was served by the lord mayor a sweet wine of refinement. At his 1483 coronation feast, he enjoyed his peacocks, partridges, venison bake, capons, and custards with a plenitude of red wine, but more importantly in the context of sweet wine, there was also much consuming of Malmsey Madeira being served to the king and queen (Anne Neville) 'sweet wyne' in a gold cup.[118] Shakespeare echoing the ubiquitous nature of sweet wine at this time, recounts the tradition that Richard's brother, the duke of Clarence, was drowned in a butt of Malmsey. Shakespearean references to sweet wines of France, Portugal, and the Canary Islands also feature in plays from *Love's Labour Lost* to *Twelfth Night* and *The Merry Wives of Windsor*.

Richard III's coronation banquet not only included a vast array of dishes and produce, but the scale is noteworthy too—with nearly 3000 guests in attendance and the timing so extraordinary, beginning at something like four in the afternoon and failing to reach a third course as the meal ran on into the night as to be abandoned.[119] To cater for such capacity, the figures for provisioning are again striking: 218 pigs, 156 deer of varying type, 148 peacocks, 140 sheep, 100 calves, and 30 bulls. Not forgetting 16 pounds of powdered ginger, 150 pounds of almonds, and plentiful sugar. As was customary, the 'King's Champion' rode into the hall to ask if anyone who thought themselves worthy of challenging the monarch to the throne, to a duel.[120]

Returning to Samuel Pepys, he mentions that on the back of what was clearly a very trying day with workmen and his wife being ill, the 9 May 1661, not many days after the coronation festivities of St George's Day, 23 April (for Charles II), he made up for it by enjoying in the Swan Tavern on King Street in Westminster, a 'tankard of white wine and sugar'.[121] This represented the tastes of the day and matches the wine records of the 2nd Earl of Sunderland's 1666 cellar, that contained a good proportion of sweet wines, Cyprus, Madeira, and Mountain wines. Approximately a sixth of his cellar was designated to wines of such a nature.[122]

The Victorian court enjoyed tremendous quantities of sauternes and it was a set accompaniment to royal dinners at Buckingham Palace, as proscribed by the head chef Charles Francatelli (in service at Buckingham Palace in the 1840s). Francatelli would serve Chablis or Sauternes as an accompaniment to oysters, with sherries for soups.[123]

In the twentieth century fortified wines and sauternes found themselves as part of coronation cocktails, from the Brooklyn Coronation for George VI in 1937 to a Sauternes Cobbler (a mixture of sauternes, with ice or soda, an orange slice, syrup, and seasonal berries). Even in the world of grape vines, there is a coronation grape grown in Canada—a table grape popular for the sweetness generated.[124]

Beyond Westminster

> One not only drinks the wine, one smells it, observes it, tastes it, sips it and ... one talks about it.

Edward VII (1841–1910) with all his epicurean tastes revelled in everything food and wine, as this marvellous quotation attributed to the hedonistic monarch illustrates he was a true lover of wine, a Dionysus or Bacchus of a monarch.[125] Yet, what of those beyond Westminster? How did the wider country celebrate with wine and beer?

An array of records from archives across the UK demonstrate a street party tradition going back centuries and accompanied by suitably generous quantities of food and drink. The city chamberlain and Common Council in Bristol were responsible for much of the expenditure for the 1685 celebrations for James II's coronation; they paid for 'two hogshead[s] of claret costing £11 5*s*. [in order] that the four conduits should run (!)

with wine'.[126] In All Saints parish Bristol, 12*s.* 6*d.* was spent on ringing 'the day the queen was crowned upon' and this was accompanied by expenditure of 4*d.* for 'carrying the wine' that was to be consumed.[127] For the coronation of Queen Anne in 1702, receipts demonstrate people spending £1 12*s.* 6*d.* on 'beer and tobacco'—the early modern 'street party'—in Stratford-upon-Avon for rich and poor alike. Such celebrations were witnessed in different parts of the realm. For instance, the City of Chester Assembly organised coronation day celebrations for Britain's new Hanoverian dynasty in 1714.[128] For George I, the Corporation of Bristol spent at least £55 on 'rejoycing this day', which included 10*s.* for '2 trumpeters' and 2*s.* 8*d.* for eight 'drinking horn[es]', and 'beer at 10*s.*'; these 'sundry disbursement[s]' clearly put music and alcohol at the heart of the jollity, along with 'cheese [at] 5*s.*' and 'tobacco [at] 4*s.*'.[129] Correspondence surviving from even very small villages such as Coxwold in North Yorkshire highlight the far-reaching nature of this tradition, for example, for George III's accession the community gathered for a roasted Scotch Ox and drink and then again for his 1761 coronation, they shared more beef and barrels of ale, along with accompanying bell ringing, bonfires, and a ball.[130] The bell-ringing tradition continued long after the event itself, for instance, in 1723 in the Parish of Hartfield in East Sussex, 'half a crowne' was spent to remember and celebrate the 'Restoration', 'Queen Anne's accession to the Crowne', 'King George's Cro[w]nation', and 'Gunpowder Treason'.[131] In Nottingham, Common Council minutes evidence coronation preparations. On 27 January 1626, it agreed that 'bells shalbe ronge att everie churche, and bonfires made in the streets, to shewe the people's rejoycinge on the day of the king's corona[t]ion'.[132] Charles II's 1661 coronation saw similar celebrations as far afield as Ireland, to Leith, Edinburgh, Cambridge, Cornwall, and Weymouth.[133] Such events emulated medieval feasts, as the eleventh-century depiction from a Psalter shows, with a heavily laden table of food and the presence of wine cups or goblets for the occasion.[134] We know from Samuel Pepys that London beyond Westminster was overflowing with celebrations for the Restoration procession and coronation of Charles II. Pepys for the afternoon of the procession took up a vantage point in a house in Cornhill (the street running between Bank Junction and Leadenhall Street in the City of London) and was joined by his wife and colleagues from the Navy Office. They had 'wine and good cake, and saw the show very well'. This was a spectacle not to be missed.[135] We find the same picture for Anne's coronation: on 14 April 1702, shops were searched 'for silk convenient to make 2 banners … [and to]

prepare … [for] the corona[t]ion'. However, on this occasion, when the solemnity was over,

> there [was to] be a treat of wyne provided att th[e] hall for the better sort of people to drink the queens health and likewise an hogshead of ale for the poore. And that M[aste]r Chamberlain do prepare one dozen and one halfe bottles of canary, 3 dozen of whitewine and 3 dozen of claret for the purposes of the aforesaid and likewise halfe an hogshead of ale for the town officers, constables, halberdmen … and 5 dozen of French rolls and ten dozen of white bread.[136]

Street parties are thus nothing new. Records from Port Talbot, Swansea, and Neath show this continuity from bell ringing for Charles I to banquets and artillery fire in 1821, fireworks and feasting in 1831, to decorations, tea, and bunting for Edward VII, George V, and George VI—impressive in scale and ubiquity.[137] In the Quantocks, beef, plum pudding, and drinks, to be enjoyed on long tables, saw the local community gather for Queen Victoria's coronation in 1838, with sporting entertainment and a bonfire to end proceedings.[138] At the dawn of the twentieth century, celebrations for Edward VII's coronation were extensive with bands, music hall performances across the land (and wider empire), fêtes, teas, and copious wine and beer.[139] A similar pattern can be seen in 1953, for example in Newbury a coronation carnival took place, and in Wantage, there featured a whole programme of events, from the roasting of an Ox and accompanying refreshment, to bunting, dancing, fancy dress, and a torch light procession.[140] This pattern of food and wine featuring as part of coronation festivities both within the Westminster solemnities and beyond was widespread and age-old. It was not so much that people drank the grape or the grain, but rather the quantities and the types that have evolved.

Conclusion

Monarchy, food, and wine have thus been entwined for centuries, from the subtlety, to the invention of a new dish, from the aperitif to the digestif, they have shaped fashionable tastes and secured the warrants for progress in the next exciting venture. In the world of wine, these days English sparkling wines are just as likely to feature at Buckingham Palace and Clarence House as a (French) Champagne, and indeed Camel Valley is a royal warrant holder.[141] For example at the state banquet for the Emir of Qatar on 3 December 2024, the wines included the English sparkling

Fig. 5.5 Coronation street party for the Coronation of King Charles III in Thaxted, Essex, UK, 2023, including Morris Men in the town street. Photograph Brian Harris/Alamy News

wine Chapel Down Reserve 2018 (and the tradition of claret continued with a Château Lynch-Bages, Pauillac 2000).[142]

Why does this all matter? It matters, precisely because the public have felt part of proceedings and have created their own celebrations across the land. In 1661, Pepys not only provides us with an account of the coronation service, but also of the Westminster Hall banquet. Pepys noted the enormous crowd lining the streets outside:

> I went out a little while before the king had done all his ceremonies, and went round the Abbey to Westminster Hall, all the way within rayless, and 10,000 people, with the ground covered with blue cloth; and scaffolds all the way.[143]

Celia Fiennes's description of the city of Bath's coronation day celebrations for Queen Anne's 23 April 1702 Westminster Abbey ceremony continues this theme. With the arrival of the procession for a service at Bath Abbey, 'the granadeers salute[d] them just as they enter[ed] the abby with a volley of shott' and, emulating Westminster Abbey practice, they heard 'a sermon'. The departing march from Bath Abbey was marked by 'artillery salutes [and] ... another volley', as it returned 'to [the] Guild Hall where [there was] ... a sumptuous feast with musick and danceing'.[144]

In 2023, with '40 communities' applying for permission, Cornwall Council approved dozens of street parties (requiring road closures) in order to celebrate the monarch's coronation.[145] From the medieval to the present, the time immemorial nature of the gathering together to celebrate such occasions thus continues.

Notes

1. See https://www.economist.com/britain/2022/05/26/britain-celebrates-a-jubilee-again, 26 May 2022, accessed 22 November 2025: 'The Platinum Jubilee: Land of hops and glory'—the argument being that 'Britain is celebrating jubilees more often, but less confidently'.
2. https://www.rct.uk/collection/themes/exhibitions/the-queens-coronation-1953/buckingham-palace/coronation-banquets, accessed 2 September 2023.
3. H. Tucker, 1 May 2023, https://www.bbc.com/travel/article/20230430-coronation-chicken-the-story-behind-the-royal-dish, accessed 22 November 2024.
4. https://www.royal.uk/the-coronation-quiche, accessed 18 October 2023.
5. https://www.rct.uk/collection/themes/Trails/royal-jubilees/queen-victoria, accessed 22 November 2025.
6. BL, Harley MS 41, fol. 21r; and G. Kipling, "'He that Saw It Would Not Believe It:' Anne Boleyn's Royal Entry into London," in Alexandra F. Johnston and Wim Hüsken (eds), *Civic Ritual and Drama* (Amsterdam - Atlanta, 1997), pp. 39–80.
7. Nottinghamshire Record Office, Nottingham, MS CA 3400, fol. 50r–v.
8. Notts. RO, MS DD/5P/7 (iii); BL, Add. MS 6308, p. 35; Gloucestershire Archives, Gloucester, MS D688/2 ('pd. for ale att the coronation of King George', £9, Thornbury, 20 October 1714).
9. *TLG*, 30 April–4 May 1685 (No. 2030), p. 2.
10. CA, MS 'Coronations – Charles II/ James II/William & Mary', Item [28] has it as 1134; Sandford, *History*, pp. 114–5. See also TNA, LS 9: Lord Steward's Department, Kitchen Books, LS 9/49 (bill of fare for coronation, 23 April 1685); E. Handlin, https://library.brown.edu/readingritual/handlin_jamesII.html, accessed 22 November 2025 and https://www.parliament.uk/about/living-heritage/building/palace/

westminsterhall/other-uses/spectacular-coronation/, accessed 22 November 2025.

11. Anon., 'Records of Coronation Celebrations in a Provincial Town', twentieth century [unpublished typescript notes at Bristol Record Office, no call-number] 8/91; Bristol Record Office, MS P/AS/Chw/3 (b), fol. 12r; See also E. Perry, 'Gift Plate from Westminster Hall Coronation Banquets', *Apollo*, LVII (1953), pp. 198–200; and C. Oman, 'Restoration Silver at the Royal Academy', *The Burlington Magazine*, 103 (February 1961), pp. 44–7.
12. G. A. Tresidder, 'Coronation Day Celebrations in English Towns, 1685–1821: Elite Hegemony and Local Relations on a Ceremonial Occasion', *British Journal for Eighteenth Century Studies*, 15 (1992), pp. 1–16.
13. For 1714 and 1727 urban celebrations see for example Perth and Kinross District Archive, Perth, Burgh Records, MS B59/33/6.
14. https://www.standard.co.uk/hp/front/boris-johnson-makes-barbara-windsor-capitals-street-party-queen-6575673.html, 12 April 2012, accessed 22 May 2025; https://www.nottinghamshire.gov.uk/council-and-democracy/get-involved/kings-coronation/the-coronation-big-lunch, accessed 22 November 2025; https://www.edenprojectcommunities.com/big-lunch/the-big-lunch-through-history, accessed 22 November 2025.
15. https://www.royal.uk/coronation-weekend-plans-announced, 21 January 2023, accessed 22 November 2025.
16. Braddick, *Taxation*, p. 298. Cf. Braddick, *Nerves of State*, and Brewer, *Sinews*.
17. See LPL, MS 1083b: Service for George III, revised for William IV. Archbishop Howley noted that William IV's service 'was printed from this copy: but some farther alterations were introduced as it passed through the press'; *TLG*, 13 September 1831, Issue 18848, pp. 1861–1875: https://www.thegazette.co.uk/London/issue/18848/page/1861, accessed 22 November 2025; Victoria and Albert Museum, London, National Art Library, 38041016058729 (R. Hyde, Paper Peepshows. The Jacqueline and Jonathan Gestetner Collection (Woodbridge: The Antique Collectors' Club, 2015), cat. 224 (The Coronation in the Abbey of St Peter's Westminster, of His Majesty King William IVth and Queen Adelaide, Essex, C., ca.1831); London Museum, A16163 (G. Cattermole, 'Coronation Procession of King William IV and Queen Adelaide' (1831); NRS, Kennedy Papers, MS GD25/9/30/2. See also: D. Torrance, 'The coronation: History and ceremonial', *Parliamentary Research Briefing*, Number CBP9412 (2023), p. 15 (n.) 42; J. Van Der Kiste, *William IV: The Last Hanoverian King of Britain*

(Barnsley, 2022), pp. 122–6; S. Poole, 'Collins in Context: William IV, Affability and the Reform Crisis, 1830–37' in *ibid.*, *The Politics of Regicide in England, 1760–1850: Troublesome Subjects* (Manchester, 2000), pp. 163–4; C. Shenton, *Mr Barry's War: Rebuilding the Houses of Parliament After the Great Fire of 1834* (Oxford, 2016), pp. 83–84; I. Ward, *Writing the Victorian Constitution* (Cham, Switzerland, 2018), pp. 1–2.

18. Edie, 'Public Face', p. 318. See also L. Echard, *The History of England. From the First Entrance of Julius Caesar and the Romans, to the End of the Reign of King James the First. Containing the Space of 1678 Years*, 3 volumes (1st edition, London, 1707; 2nd edition, London, 1718), III, p. 734.
19. Edie, 'Public Face', p. 318.
20. BL, Add. MS 17019, fol. 43r–v; Sandford, *History*, p. 42.
21. https://www.bbc.co.uk/news/uk-62872323#:~:text=People%20were%20told%20not%20to,to%20know%20about%20the%20queue, 19 September 2022, accessed 22 November 2025; A. Stewart, 6 May 2023, https://www.bbc.co.uk/news/uk-northern-ireland-65461480, accessed 22 November 2025; https://www.bbc.co.uk/news/av/uk-65498600, 5 May 2023, accessed 24 November 2025.
22. https://www.bbc.co.uk/news/uk-65507435, 5 May 2023, accessed 22 November 2025; J. D. Oates, 'Jacobitism and Popular Disturbances in Northern England, 1714–1719', *Northern History*, XLI (2004), p. 111: quoting Anon., *The History of all the Mobs, Tumults and Insurrections in Great Britain* (1715), p. 53.
23. Cressy shows, regarding the Stuart calendar, just how prevalent this custom of celebration and commemoration was, see Cressy, *Bonfires*, *passim*. For 2023 see for examples: B. Jackson (BBC Radio Leicester), 5 April 2023, https://www.bbc.co.uk/programmes/p0ffl hj6, accessed 22 November 2025; J. Bostock (BBC Radio Leicester), 7 May 2023, https://www.bbc.co.uk/programmes/p0fly8z0, accessed 22 November 2025; M. Bailey (Radio Newcastle) & J. Lonsdale, https://www.bbc.co.uk/sounds/play/p0fl2s3z, accessed 22 November 2025. On newspapers see H. Barker, *Newspapers, Politics and English Society, 1695–1855* (Harlow, 2000), *passim*.
24. I. W. Archer, 'City and Court Connected: The Material Dimensions of Royal Ceremonial, ca.1480–1625', *The Huntington Library Quarterly*, 71 (2008), pp. 165–6. See also BL, Add. MS 58833, fol. 18v.
25. M. Bloch (abridged and introduced), *James Lees-Milne: Diaries, 1942–54* (London, 2006), p. 453.
26. Anon. (ed.), *Diary of Mary Countess Cowper, Lady of the Bedchamber to the Princess of Wales, 1714–1720* (London, 1864), pp. 3–5.

27. Latham & Matthews, *Pepys*, II, pp. 81–88.
28. E. S. de Beer, *Evelyn*, III, pp. 249–50; J. Evelyn, *A Panegyric to Charles the Second, Presented to His Majestie … the Day of His Coronation …* (London, [1661]).
29. Harris, *Restoration*, pp. 94–5; Irish Manuscripts Commission: S. Pender (ed.), *Council Book of the Corporation of Waterford, 1662–1700, Together with Nine Documents of 1580–82* (Dublin, 1964), pp. 42, 46; R. Caulfield (ed.), *The Council Book of the Corporation of Youghall, from 1610 … to 1800* (Guildford, 1878), pp. 326, 334–5, 338, 346. See also Herefordshire Record Office, Hereford, MS BG11/17/5/75 (bonfires celebrating coronation of William III and Mary II, 1689).
30. Bodl., MS Rawl. Letters 63, fol. 12r (Bohea tea is an oolong tea, roughly equivalent to Lapsang Souchong).
31. Across the UK, see also: Gross, '1651: The Last Coronation in Scotland': https://www.tandfonline.com/doi/full/10.1080/14629712.2021.1996947#:~:text=The%20last%20Scottish%20coronation%20occurred%20at%20Scone%20in%201651, accessed 22 November 2025.
32. Strickland, *Henry the Young King*, pp. 90–100 and see cover illustration. See also his reference, p. 90 of F. Madden (ed.), *Matthaei Parisiensis monachi sancti Albani, Historia Anglorum*, 3 vols, Rolls Series (London, 1865–1869), I, pp. 352–3.
33. A. Brown & H. Summerson, 'Henry IV [known as Henry Bolingbroke] (1367–1413),' *ODNB.*
34. https://www.westminster-abbey.org/worship-music/services-times/edwardtide/, accessed 22 November 2025; https://www.westminster-abbey.org/abbey-commemorations/royals/edward-the-confessor-and-edith/, accessed 22 November 2025; https://www.stgeorges-windsor.org/news/edward-the-confessor/, accessed 22 November 2025.
35. A. Tuck, 'Richard II (1367–1400)', *ODNB.*
36. On Henry IV's Coronation Banquet 1399, see: R. J. Mitchell, *The Medieval Feast: The story of the coronation banquet of King Henry IV in Westminster Hall, 13th October, 1399* (London, 1958); L. B. Mitchell, 'The Coronation of Henry IV,' *Social Science*, 6 (1931), pp. 130–33; and G. Bray (ed.), *The Reign of Henry IV (1399–1413): Records of Convocation* (Woodbridge, 2023), pp. 69–86. See also C. Helstosky (ed.), *The Routledge History of Food* (London, 2015); and C. M. Woolgar, *et al.* (eds), *Food in Medieval England: Diet and Nutrition* (Oxford, 2006).
37. R. Griffiths, 'Henry VI (1421–1471)', *ODNB.*
38. C. Sponsler (ed.), John Lydgate, "Soteltes at the Coronation Banquet of Henry VI," *Mummings and Entertainments,* (Kalamazoo, Michigan, 2010), see also https://metseditions.org/read/7PVQMQqHB4eI4wZmsR2WWS2QR65rjZb, accessed 22 November 2025.

39. https://blogs.bl.uk/digitisedmanuscripts/2023/05/the-coronation-banquet-of-henry-vi.html, accessed 20 November 2023—see BL, Egerton MS 1995, fols. 176v–177r. See also J. A. Mitchell, "Queen Katherine and The Secret of Lydgate's 'Temple of Glas.'" *Medium Ævum*, 77, (2008), p. 68.
40. H. Blatt, "Reading Materially: John Lydgate's 'Soteltes for the Coronation Banquet of Henry VI,'" in H. Blatt, *Participatory Reading in Late-Medieval England* (Manchester, 2018), pp. 105–27.
41. M. Jones, 'Catherine [Catherine of Valois] (1401–1437)', *ODNB.*
42. *Ibid.*
43. S. Bates, 19 November 2004, https://www.theguardian.com/uk/2004/nov/19/politics.france, accessed 22 November 2025; N. Reynolds, 19 November 2004, https://www.telegraph.co.uk/news/uknews/1476967/President-Chirac-faces-the-musical.html, accessed 22 November 2024; K. Willsher, 25 May 2024, https://www.theguardian.com/world/article/2024/may/25/history-is-written-at-the-dining-table-what-4000-menus-tells-us-about-royals-politicians-and-society, accessed 22 November 2025.
44. J. F. Burden, *Rituals of Royalty: Prescription, Politics and Practice in English Coronation and Royal Funeral Rituals c. 1327 to c.1485*, (York Ph.D. thesis, 1999), p. 199: https://etheses.whiterose.ac.uk/2497/1/DX212138.pdf, accessed 23 October 2024. See also E. Barker, "The Coronation and Banquet of Henry IV" (University of Wisconsin unpublished paper): https://dc.uwm.edu/cgi/viewcontent.cgi?article=1064&context=rsso, accessed 23 October 2024.
45. J. Leland and T. Hearn (eds.), *Antiquarii De rebus Britannicis Collectanea* (London, 1774), IV, pp. 226–7. See also E. Barker, "The Coronation and Banquet of Henry IV" (University of Wisconsin unpublished paper): https://dc.uwm.edu/cgi/viewcontent.cgi?article=1064&context=rsso, accessed 23 October 2024.
46. Burden, *Rituals of Royalty*, p. 199.
47. Lydgate, "Soteltes at the Coronation Banquet of Henry VI," see also https://metseditions.org/read/7PVQMQqHB4eI4wZmsR2WWS2QR65rjZb, accessed 22 November 2025.
48. BL, Cotton MS Julius E IV/3, fol. 23v (for depiction of the coronation); https://www.nationaltrustcollections.org.uk/object/557886, accessed 22 November 2025; https://forteressechinon.fr/en/discover-fortress/its-great-characters/charles-vii, accessed 22 November 2025; see also M. Clermont-Ferrand, 'Joan of Arc and the English Chroniclers: Monstrous Presence and Problematic Absence in *The Chronicle of London, The Chronicle of William of Worcester*, and *An English Chronicle 1377–1461.*' *The Medieval Chronicle*, 7 (2011), pp. 151–66.

49. Lydgate, "Soteltes at the Coronation Banquet of Henry VI," see also https://metseditions.org/read/7PVQMQqHB4eI4wZmsR2WWS2QR65rjZb, accessed 22 November 2025.
50. *Ibid.* See also BL, Egerton MS 1995, fols 176v–177r.
51. R. Epstein, 'Eating their words: food and text in the coronation banquet of Henry VI,' *Journal of Medieval and Early Modern Studies*, 36 (2006), pp. 370–2.
52. *Ibid.* See also: K. Will, 'When is a Panther not a Panther? Representing Animals in Early Modern English Heraldry', *Early Modern Culture*, 11 (2016), pp. 78–98.
53. F. W. D. Brie, (ed.), *The Brut, or The chronicles of England. Edited from Ms. Raw. B171, Bodleian Library, &c.,* ... (London, 1906–8), p. 461: https://quod.lib.umich.edu/c/cme/APG1531/1:2.9?rgn=div2;view=fulltext, accessed 22 November 2025; B. Wolffe, *Henry VI* (New Haven, Connecticut), pp. 61–62.
54. On Joan of Arc in this context see G. Williams, 'Manipulation and the Maid: Joan of Arc and the Siege of Orléans', *Medieval Warfare*, 4 (2014), pp. 25–32; Clermont-Ferrand, 'Joan of Arc'.
55. Doran, *Tudor to Stuart*, p. 142.
56. Jack, 'Coronation of James I', p. 88.
57. For more details see Jackson, *Vive le Roi!*.
58. https://ukparliament.shorthandstories.com/spectacle-ceremony/index.html, accessed 22 November 2025.
59. P. Hunneyball, https://historyofparliament.com/2023/05/11/1626-coronation-charles-i/, accessed 22 November 2025.
60. https://www.parliament.uk/about/living-heritage/building/palace/westminsterhall/, accessed 22 November 2025.
61. https://www.parliament.uk/about/living-heritage/building/palace/westminsterhall/other-uses/coronation-banquets/, accessed 22 November 2025.
62. https://assets-learning.parliament.uk/uploads/2023/05/Coronation-Timeline.pdf, accessed 22 November 2025; https://www.parliament.uk/about/living-heritage/building/palace/westminsterhall/other-uses/coronation-banquets/#:~:text=From%201189%20to%201821%2C%20Westminster,Richard%20the%20Lionheart%20in%201189, accessed 22 November 2025; J. Gillingham, 'Richard I [called Richard Coeur de Lion, Richard the Lionheart] (1157–1199),' *ODNB.*
63. Strickland, *Henry the Young King*, p. 90, referencing Madden, *Matthaei Parisiensis monachi sancti Albani, Historia Anglorum*, I, 352–3. See also F. Barlow, 'Becket, Thomas [St Thomas of Canterbury, Thomas of London] (1120?–1170)', *ODNB.*
64. W. Ormrod, 'Edward III (1312–1377)', *ODNB.*

65. https://www.oxfordhistory.org.uk/mayors/government/coronation.html, accessed 22 November 2025; see also R. Thomson, *A Faithful Account of the Processions and Ceremonies Observed in the Coronation of the Kings and Queens of England; Exemplified in that of … King George the Third and Queen Charlotte …* (London, 1820), pp. 15–20.
66. https://www.rct.uk/collection/1005090/ceremonial-of-the-coronation-of-his-most-sacred-majesty-king-george-the-fourth, accessed 22 November 2025. See also Eton College, Aq.1.1.2.
67. Strong, *Coronation*, p. 372.
68. G. de Bellaigue, 'A Royal Mise-en-Scène: George IV's Coronation Banquet,' *Furniture History*, 29 (1993), p. 181.
69. https://www.rct.uk/collection/2301735/the-kings-coronation-dinner-to-the-people-5-july-1902, accessed 22 November 2025.
70. https://www.rct.uk/collection/2301735, accessed 22 November 2025; see also https://www.nationaltrustcollections.org.uk/object/772308, accessed 22 November 2025.
71. https://www.royal.uk/royal-archives-coronation, accessed 22 November 2025.
72. H. Tucker, 1 May 2023, https://www.bbc.com/travel/article/20230430-coronation-chicken-the-story-behind-the-royal-dish, accessed 22 November 2024.
73. https://www.vam.ac.uk/articles/the-festival-of-britain, accessed 22 November 2025.
74. https://www.bbc.co.uk/news/uk-23265716, 12 July 2013, accessed 22 November 2025; https://www.rct.uk/sites/default/files/null/Fact%20Sheet_The%20Coronation%20Banquet.pdf, accessed 1 October 2024; https://www.bibelotslondon.com/antique-coronation-banquet-menu-buckingham-palace-hosted-by-queen-elizabeth-ii-6037-p.asp, accessed 2 October 2024.
75. *OED.*
76. To show just how divisive Riesling is, one need merely turn to a favoured search engine. A basic search reveals not far off 23 million hits for Riesling. If you go further and include the word 'hate', you end up with not far shy of 2 million. Hate is a strong word to generate nearly 10% of Riesling entries. When one does the same association for claret, the search engine will suggest you might have got it wrong! Needless to say our ancestors did not feel the same way and Rhenish wines did not carry such harsh criticism.
77. As commented on elsewhere (and reproduced here) this was a hugely significant coronation, providing evidence for the banquet and street party tradition of the early modern world. See also G. W. C. Gross, 'https://subscribe.worldoffinewine.com/product/issue80-june-2023/'

(accessed 23 November 2025), in *The World of Fine Wine*, Issue 80 (June) (2023), pp. 134–41. This article contributed to many of the ideas expanded on in this chapter.

78. BL, Royal MS 18 A. LXIV. See also E. Ives, 'Anne [Anne Boleyn] (c. 1500–1536)', *ODNB*.
79. R. V. French, *Nineteen Centuries of Drink in England: A History* (2nd edition, 1884–90, London), pp. 134–5; J. G. Nichols (introductory remarks), *London pageants, I. Accounts of fifty-five Royal Processions and Entertainments in the City of London; chiefly extracted from contemporary writers. II. A bibliographical list of Lord Mayors' pageants* (London, 1831), pp. 41–2; BL, Harley MS 41; and Kipling, "'He that Saw It Would Not Believe It:' Anne Boleyn's Royal Entry into London".
80. W. Robinson, 'Somerset, William, third Earl of Worcester (1526/7–1589)', *ODNB*; J. Edwards, *Mary I: England's Catholic Queen* (London, 2011), pp. 123–34. See also A. Hunt, "'What art thou, thou idol ceremony?': Tudor coronations and literary representations, 1509–1559', PhD thesis, Birbeck, University of London (2005); A. Samson, 'The marriage of Philip of Habsburg and Mary Tudor and anti-Spanish sentiment in England: political economies and culture 1553–1557', PhD thesis, Queen Mary, University of London, (1999), pp. 54–67.
81. Scarisbrick, *Henry VIII*, p. 18.
82. BL, Cotton MS Titus D. IV (Thomas More's coronation suite for Henry VIII, 1509). See also S. House, 'More, Sir Thomas [St Thomas More] (1478–1535),' *ODNB*.
83. *CSP, Venice*, 7: 1558–1580, pp. 11–19.
84. https://www.british-history.ac.uk/old-new-london/vol3/pp544-560, accessed 22 November 2025.
85. C. Ludington, *The Politics of Wine in Britain* (London, 2013), pp. 22–4.
86. Sandford, *History*, pp. 79–81 (reference on page 79, images unpaginated); and see Introduction chapter above.
87. https://www.pepysdiary.com/diary/1660/02/03/, accessed 22 November 2025.
88. E. S. de Beer (ed.), *Evelyn*.
89. Ludington, *The Politics of Wine in Britain*, pp. 31–4.
90. *Ibid.*, p. 45.
91. CA, MS 'Coronations – Charles II/ James II/William & Mary', Item [28]. See also Sandford, *History*, pp. 110–5.
92. The Royal Collection Archives, Windsor, GEO/ADD/1/39.
93. Ludington, *The Politics of Wine in Britain*, p. 144.
94. *Ibid.*, pp. 22–26.
95. See for example BL, Add MS 32717, fol. 212.

96. H. Matthew & K. Reynolds, 'Victoria (1819–1901)', *ODNB*; S. Weintraub, 'Albert [Prince Albert of Saxe-Coburg and Gotha] (1819–1861)', *ibid.*
97. Ludington, *Politics of Wine*, pp. 232–33.
98. https://www.royal.uk/royal-archives-coronation, accessed 22 November 2025.
99. https://www.toronto.ca/explore-enjoy/history-art-culture/online-exhibits/web-exhibits/web-exhibits-culture-people/toronto-remembers-the-coronation-of-elizabeth-ii/, accessed 22 November 2025; https://www.navy.gov.au/hmas-sydney-iii, accessed 22 November 2025.
100. https://www.nlb.gov.sg/main/article-detail?cmsuuid=12d4e7ff-b08f-4372-864b-a5a1a84b7c64, accessed 22 November 2025.
101. National Archives Australia: A3522, 8/33; and A462, 821/1/119.
102. https://www.records.nsw.gov.au/image/NRS12160%5B4_8533-3%5D_003, accessed 22 November 2025 & https://www.navy.gov.au/history/feature-histories/ships-named-anzac, accessed 22 November 2025.
103. J. Gillingham, 'John (1167–1216)', *ODNB*.
104. https://www.pepysdiary.com/diary/1661/04/23/, accessed 22 November 2025; for 1651 see also Gross, '1651: The Last Coronation in Scotland': https://www.tandfonline.com/doi/full/10.1080/14629712.2021.1996947#:~:text=The%20last%20Scottish%20coronation%20occurred%20at%20Scone%20in%201651, accessed 22 November 2025.
105. BL, Harley MS 2901; see also R. A. Brown, H. M. Colvin & A. J. Taylor, *The History of the King's Works, The Middle Ages* (London, 1963), Vol. I, pp. 506–7. See also J. Phillips, 'Edward II [Edward of Caernarfon] (1284–1327)', *ODNB*.
106. Ludington, *Politics of Wine*, pp. 2–3.
107. *Ibid.*, pp. 22–4.
108. Ludington, *Politics of Wine*, p. 83.
109. FSL, D 219 I8 no. 1.
110. CA, MS 'Coronations – Charles II/ James II/William & Mary', Item [28].
111. P. Lamb, *Royal Cookery; or, The Complete Court-Cook. Containing the Choicest Receipts in all the Particular Branches of Cookery, Now in Use in the Queen's Palaces of St James's, Kensington, Hampton-Court, and Windsor. With Near Forty Figures (Curiously Engraven)* (London, 1710).
112. *Ibid.*, pp. 17–18. See also http://foodhistorjottings.blogspot.co.uk/2012_04_01_archive.html, 28 April 2012, accessed 23 November 2025. For a contemporary update to royal recipes, see T. Parker Bowles, *Cooking and the Crown: Royal Recipes from Queen Victoria to King Charles III* (London, 2024).

113. J. Martindale, 'Eleanor [Eleanor of Aquitaine], suo jure duchess of Aquitaine (c. 1122–1204)', *ODNB*; and T. Keefe, 'Henry II (1133–1189)', *ibid.*
114. You can still purchase a bottle of Château Lafite 1934, retailing at *c.*£1,800.
115. Ludington, *Politics of Wine*, pp. 232–3: 'approximately 4,032 bottles'.
116. https://www.royal.uk/royal-archives-coronation, accessed 23 November 2025.
117. Another oft mentioned wine of royal reputation is that of Royal Tokaji—a wine for Hungarian princes and ultimately reserved by the 1900s for the Imperial Austro-Hungarian household.
118. Sutton and Hammond, *Richard III*, p. 281; See also BL, Add. MS 45716A, fols, 71–78 and Kincaid, *Richard The Third ... George Buc*, pp. 49–50.
119. Sutton and Hammond, *Richard III*, pp. 281–2.
120. *Ibid.*, pp. 286–7.
121. https://www.pepysdiary.com/diary/1661/05/09/, accessed 23 November 2025.
122. Ludington, *Politics of Wine*, pp. 23–4.
123. C. Oliver, *Dinner at Buckingham Palace: Secrets & Recipes from the reign of Queen Victoria to Queen Elizabeth II* (London, 2003). Charles Francatelli was portrayed in the Television series *Victoria* (2016–2019).
124. https://www.rhs.org.uk/plants/372820/vitis-sovereign-coronation-(b-s)/details, accessed 23 November 2025.
125. See also FSL, MS Y.c.573 (ode for the coronation of Edward VII).
126. Anon., 'Records of Coronation Celebrations in a Provincial Town', twentieth century [unpublished typescript notes at Bristol Record Office, no call-number] 8/91. See *OED* for definition: 'A hogshead of wine was originally fixed at 63 wine gallons, and is now fixed at 52½ imperial gallons (approx. 238.67 litres), or 63 US gallons (approx. 238.48 litres). A hogshead of beer is fixed at 54 imperial gallons (approx. 245.49 litres or 64.85 US gallons)'.
127. BRO, MS P/AS/Chw/3 (b), fol. 12r.
128. Shakespeare Centre Library and Archive, Stratford-upon-Avon, MSS BRU/5/3/142, BRU/5/4/163 and BRU/5/4/193 ('Money spent on coronation day' continued for George I's reign) & Cheshire Record Office, Chester, MS ZA/B/3/219, fol. 219r.
129. BRO, MS F/AC/Box/19/1.
130. https://www.laurencesternetrust.org.uk/sterne/life-and-times/sterne-in-coxwold-letters/, accessed 23 November 2025. See also M. New, 'Sterne, Laurence (1713–1768)', *ODNB*.
131. ESRO, MS PAR 360/30/1/1.

132. Notts. RO., MS CA 3400, fol. 50r–v.
133. BL, Add. MS 6308, p. 35; Cornwall Record Office, Truro MS J/1/1959.
134. BL, Cotton MS Tiberius C VI, f. 5v.
135. https://www.pepysdiary.com/diary/1661/04/22/, accessed 23 November 2025.
136. Notts. RO., MS CA 3469, fol. 22r.
137. https://www.swansea.gov.uk/article/22308/How-we-celebrated-the-coronation-in-times-gone-by, accessed 23 November 2025.
138. https://swheritage.org.uk/news/celebrations/.
139. K. Howells, 18 April 2023, https://blog.nationalarchives.gov.uk/celebrating-the-coronation-of-edward-vii/#return-note-61427-2, accessed 23 November 2025.
140. Royal Berkshire Archives, N/D52/1/12–13 and D/EX2547/4/5/12.
141. https://www.fruitandvine.co.uk/cornwall-vineyard-receives-royal-warrant/, accessed 24 November 2025; https://www.royalwarrant.org/company/camel-valley, accessed 23 November 2025.
142. S. Coughlan, 3 December 2024, https://www.bbc.co.uk/news/articles/c791wr2e7nyo, accessed 23 November 2025. I am indebted to the kind support and guidance of Simon Field MW and Rebecca Lamont, with whom I have joined forces for a series of history and wine talks, see https://www.therlws.com/grand-cru-events, accessed 10 October 2024.
143. Latham & Matthews, *Pepys*, II pp. 81–8 (22–3 April 1661).
144. Morris, *Fiennes*, pp. 22–3. See also D. Hey, 'Fiennes, Celia (1662–1741)', *ODNB*.
145. https://www.cornwalllive.com/news/cornwall-news/cornwall-set-celebrate-coronation-king-8341068, 11 April 2023, accessed 22 November 2025.

CHAPTER 6

Coronation Cost, Bonfires, Bells, and Fireworks

The 2023 coronation of Charles III, cost the UK taxpayer an estimated £72 million pounds, under half of the cost of Elizabeth II's funeral and national mourning arrangements in 2022.[1] There is some discrepancy between the costs of Elizabeth II's coronation in 1953, in today's money, it was roughly £50 million, but the scale was larger than 2023 (including a Naval Review). Even with the excellent currency converter of the national archives, with inflation, and so too decimalisation changes and purchasing power, the events, scale, and cost were comparatively larger in 1953, than in 2023, but it remains very hard to compare financially.[2] Nevertheless, the cost of the 2023 coronation was considerable, although not out of line with hosting a major sporting event and indeed the costs in the below table do not include money generated in tourism, hospitality, media, literary and other output, memorabilia and merchandise sales, for examples. The 2019 ICC Cricket World Cup for instance was seen as a significant net benefit to cities across the UK hosting fixtures.[3] Such analysis has yet to be completed for the benefits to the country economically for a coronation, and because of the scale and reach of a coronation (both at home and abroad) it is exceptionally hard to quantify (Table 6.1).

Yet, why does cost matter? Why should we look beyond the confines of the Westminster Abbey ceremony? Skinner's influential article has shaped much of political thought on the power of monarchy, where he indicates how the authoritative impersonal State (as delineated by Hobbes) resulted

G. W. C. Gross, *Crown and People*,
https://doi.org/10.1007/978-3-032-20786-9_6

Table 6.1 Coronation Cost, 1902–2023

Coronation	*Cost*
Edward VII (1902)	£193,000
George V (1911)	£185,000
George VI (1937)	£454,000
Elizabeth II (1953)	£912,000–£1.5 million
Elizabeth II Funeral & national mourning (2022)	£162 million
Charles III (2023)	£72 million

from the conceptual disengagement of the State firstly from rulers and secondly from the whole of society (or community) over which power was exercised. Skinner asserts that

> among the assumptions that suffered displacement, the most important was … that sovereignty is conceptually connected with display, that majesty serves in itself as an ordering force … One outcome of distinguishing the authority of the State from that of its agents was thus to sever a time-honoured connection between the presence of majesty and the exercise of majestic powers. Displays of stateliness eventually came to be seen as mere 'shows' or 'trappings' of power, not as features intrinsic to the workings of power itself.[4]

Whilst much in his essay is persuasive, his argument fails to account for the continuing potency of the monarch, long into the eighteenth century in Britain, and indeed to the present, or for the massive investment in coronations. This potency inhered in the royal prerogative is significantly still in existence, but by custom now considerably neglected. Perhaps more powerful still is what we might refer to as 'soft power', whether that be State visits, Commonwealth meetings, COP conference speeches, royal warrants, and royal tours, the monarchy continues to contribute to national and global discussion and can shape tastes even in the twenty-first century.

Introduction

A coronation was designed for magnificence, displaying the most fashionable jewels and robes and involving music, fireworks, feasting, and other entertainments; it came at tremendous cost. This chapter indicates the

Fig. 6.1 Coronation Naval Fleet Review programme at Spithead, Portsmouth, for Queen Elizabeth II, 1953, Alamy

scale of the financial burden for Crown and State. A comparison will be drawn with civic festivities countrywide. Ever since this project's inception, a major aim has been to 'follow the money'; by investigating finances, one may perceive just how extensive coronation celebrations were. The point of this approach is to see whether or not the examination of either unknown or underused sources yields new insights into the wide-reaching nature of a coronation.

It is a matter of assessing a coronation in terms of 'ripples', spreading away from Westminster Abbey, the Court, and the capital. The findings are fascinating: by bringing together a range of dispersed sources, we are able to contextualise coronation expenses, and to begin properly to grasp the enormous cost of such occasions, particularly in the seventeenth century.

A problem that was immediately apparent, when comparing primary and secondary sources, was an absence of detailed information on coronation expenditure; where available, figures given by earlier historians do not always appear to correspond with archival evidence. This chapter will outline what has been said and will then, as far as possible, provide much more comprehensive data. Such fact-finding is extremely important because the historiography consists of several interpretations based upon previous figures. One of the major arguments has been that expenditure allegedly declined, causing later seventeenth-century coronations to be very different to the lavish displays under the Tudors and early Stuarts. Moreover, this supposed reduction is taken to indicate declining royal power and even the end of the monarch's divine or semi-divine status.

In correcting old figures and filling gaps, this chapter builds upon a wide array of primary sources, such as (at the National Archives) the records of the King's Works and the accounts of the lord chamberlain's department, heraldic records held in the College of Arms and State Papers and miscellaneous manuscripts found in archives across the United Kingdom and in the United States of America. It has not been possible to ascertain precise figures for each coronation, as some documents do not survive, or may be undiscovered, being either misplaced or uncatalogued in sizeable collections, such as those at the College of Arms. To pursue every kind of source exhaustively for each coronation would be beyond the scope of one book. However, further work is planned. For now, this chapter will move into uncharted waters, and provide, in some cases, the first estimates relating to coronations, taking 1661–1714 as particular case studies. That they are estimates should, of course, be stressed, even if they are well informed by primary sources. Nevertheless, approximations are necessary, and their status is no reason for avoiding exploration of this field, for this chapter argues that historians have overlooked cost and therefore significant aspects of coronations; that significance is brought out by a 'follow the money approach'.

Having compared these coronations, some important arguments may be advanced, the most crucial being that coronation expenditure remained considerable in the period 1660–1714. Inflation needs to be taken into account, but, even with rising prices, the costs were huge.[5] They did not decline, as has been argued, and in an age of The National Debt[6] and the Civil List[7]—a nation and a monarch 'strapped for cash'—coronations escaped what might have been serious cuts. It is thus clear that a coronation must have retained tremendous significance. What was this significance? Legitimacy, sacerdotalism, providentialism, continuity, the dawn of empire—all these features can be addressed, and have been examined elsewhere in this book; certainly, the coronation tradition in Britain did not come cheaply.

The first part of this chapter will examine the historiography, the figures given to date, and the question of coronation financing overall. We shall then move to a case-by-case format, in which tables covering each coronation will be analysed sequentially. This approach may seem rather plodding, overly chronological, yet it was exactly the process that the heralds and the Privy Council adopted. There is specific precedent from 1603 and 1689 that outlay was to match that for the previous coronation. For example, Edward Somerset, Earl of Worcester, master of the horse, was to be given 'all such allowance against his majesty's entry into London [1603], as was allowed unto the master of the horse at the coronation of Elizabeth [I]'.[8] The exceptions to this chorological approach are the Scottish coronations of Charles I and Charles II. Charles I's 1633 coronation will frequently be cited. However, Charles II's 1651 coronation, despite falling marginally outside the main focus of study, will be examined in detail at the end of part I as a significant anomaly. We will for the first time provide an estimate for the cost of this coronation and will reveal that 1651 was far from the drab affair that has been suggested.[9] This conclusion, matched by an article in The Court Historian challenges previous assumptions concerning the alleged lack of pomp and circumstance and Charles's supposed dislike for the occasion.[10]

The second section of this chapter deals with coronation 'longevity': the widespread nature of celebrations across the realm, the costs involved, and the 'impact' of monarchical ceremonial far beyond Westminster.

Part I: Historiography of Coronation Expenditure

Historiography

Coronation expenditure has been considerably under-researched. For example, Madway's detailed inquiry into Charles II's coronation ignores cost, although the essay is entitled 'The Most Conspicuous Solemnity', while Schwoerer's coverage of William and Mary's coronation also neglects this facet.[11] These omissions are perhaps understandable: scholarly contributions often take into account just one reign or coronation, as in these cases, and figures by themselves (although sizeable) do not indicate significance without some comparison. Furthermore, investigating costs is time-consuming and it can be challenging to reach precise figures. Nevertheless, the effort can be rewarding, for it is only when assembling a sequence of estimates that relative scales, and therefore trends, begin to emerge.

Figures occasionally appear in passing in some of the secondary literature, and these will be considered below, but there is no sustained focus on coronation expenditure. On Mary I and Elizabeth I, Hoak writes that working out 'the whole cost of a coronation remains elusive'. Nevertheless, he discusses some of the expenditure involved and provides an estimate of £20,000 for 1558/1559.[12] Jenny Uglow and Sharpe, for example, both mention costs for Charles II's 1661 coronation.[13] John Adamson and Smith refer to costs in extremely broad time-frames, namely for the Tudor, Stuart, and Hanoverian Courts. However, these glances are purely incidental and not part of a detailed attempt to analyse costs, such as would necessitate presenting a breakdown of figures.[14] Keay's thorough work on the crown jewels provides information on prices, and is generally an invaluable starting point for appreciating the lavish nature of these royal diadems, but does little to relate those costs to outlay on the coronation in total.[15] Only two publications look below the surface, tabulating expenditure specifically and discussing it: those by Ian Archer and Strong. These contributions will be discussed below, starting with the former.

Archer's work offers a very useful insight into the way in which the City of London (governed by its corporation)[16] interrelated with Westminster for royal events in the Tudor and early Stuart periods. He shows how 'the city's apparently separate spaces were connected' and notes 'the complex web of interdependency' characterising the London economy. In addition, this era saw 'the City playing an increasing role in the machinery of royal credit'.[17] Archer's essay reminds one that it was not only the rich and famous who gathered for such occasions, but 'Londoners' too, arguing that they 'were unusual among the king's subjects of non-aristocratic or non-courtly rank in being included in the coronation … processions'. Indeed, 'the royal progress through the City … underscored the reciprocal ties of Crown and City'.[18] This fact is important, in that ordinary British subjects were (at their own liberty) considerably more involved in these years, at the accession to the Crown, than their equivalents in the more provincial far-away coronations of French kings at Reims, or later in the seclusion of Court ritual in Versailles. Provincial trades and, importantly, those of the capital were 'directly benefited', rather than 'a specialist group segregated from City tradesmen'—this situation contrasted with Court life in Madrid under Philip II.[19] Moving beyond Archer, this chapter argues that although not directly present, citizens other than Londoners celebrated, benefited from, and felt part of the crowning of new monarchs. In the Abbey, it was not only the lord mayor and aldermen of London who participated, but also those of Oxford.[20] Later in this chapter, we shall examine parallel festivities elsewhere. The present discussion will also indicate that although Archer is right in that Londoners' loyalty 'was underscored by an appreciation of the economic benefits of the demand of courtly ceremony … brought into focus in accession years', other factors—most notably Jacobitism and the fear of Roman Catholicism—played equally vital roles in ensuring the continuity of coronations and in fostering public appreciation both of them and of the Court.[21]

Archer highlights how lavish a coronation was: in 1603, royal robes 'alone cost about the same as the City's pageants'—a grand total of £4168.[22] Such was the occasion's importance that the Crown left no expense spared. Archer's research partly makes up for the previous lack of 'attention [that] has been paid to the material conditions of royal ceremonial'.[23] Nevertheless, his study ends in 1625 and provides less detail on coronation expenditure than it does for royal funerals, listing only one total figure concerning costs for a series of 'selected royal coronations, 1483–1604' (Table 6.2):

Table 6.2 Ian Archer's calculations of coronation costs, 1483–1604

Sovereign	*Year*	*Total cost (£)*
Richard III	1483	3125
Henry VII	1485	1507
Henry VIII	1509	8034 +
Edward VI	1546/1547	7116
Elizabeth I	1558/1559	16,742 [20,000][a]
James I	1603–1604	36,145

[a]Hoak, 'Transformation', p. 124

The problem with Archer's table is that, without a breakdown of components, it is unclear to what these figures precisely relate. Only with James I, does he indicate that the statistic covers the 'cost of the coronation and the entry ... combined; ... [the] events ... [being] held separately because of the plague'.[24] Archer later goes on to explain

> that the figures given are minima. In the case of the coronations, first, the costs in the accounts [those of the lord chamberlain's department in TNA] cover only the ceremonies pertaining to the entry and the crowning itself and exclude the banquet, tournaments, and masques that followed. In addition, many of the noble participants were responsible for their own attire or that of their retinues.[25]

He notes that such accounts 'do not tell us about the spending on jewellery'.[26] In terms of working out a total cost, this is a substantial omission, for we shall see in due course—particularly for the coronations of Charles II and James II—that this was often colossal. Whilst these figures therefore afford some initial perspective on coronation expenditure, they are far from adequate. A fuller picture is needed in order to grasp the true scale.

Archer draws attention to the magnitude of financial commitment involved in accession years, for coronations followed normally expensive funerals, 'meaning very large additional wardrobe expenditures ... £16,500 in 1509, £24,600 in 1558–1559, £53,573 in 1603–1604'.[27] Ordinarily, Wardrobe outgoings might amount to between '£6,000 ... [and] £9,500 *per annum*' at the beginning and end of Elizabeth's reign, rising to '£30,000 *per annum* in the early years of James I'.[28] According to Archer, the 'expenditure on the funeral, coronation, and entry of 1603–1604 was not far off the total yield of direct taxation for the entire country in that year (£67,000)'.[29] It is clear, therefore, that coronations involved an enormous outlay that (military expenses apart) was almost unique in any reign. One exception, but also involving ceremonial activities, was the royal wedding of the elector palatine of the Rhine and princess Elizabeth Stuart in 1613, costing '£93,294 ... including £2,880 for fireworks on the Thames and another £4,800 for a naval fight on the river'.[30] If royal marriages were obviously exceptional events, then the funerals of the social elite, and other regular festivities, may offer useful points of comparison. Apropos of such occasions, Archer writes that

> aristocratic funerals in the later sixteenth century cost up to £3,000, more usually around £1,000. The biggest event the City put on, the lord mayor's show, cost about £750–£1,000 each year.[31]

Coronation figures, when contextualised vis-à-vis aristocratic funerals and the lord mayor's show, indicate the colossal scale involved. When one considers 'that the expenditure revealed in the royal accounts is only a fraction of the spending actually generated, because of the amount of individual spending by the Court elite that royal ceremonial stimulated', it becomes obvious that coronations were on a completely different plane to everything else.[32]

Although Strong's book begins with medieval coronations, his analysis of costs focuses on the eighteenth and nineteenth centuries. That examination constitutes a useful starting point and is the first attempt to assess expenditure comparatively. However, as with Archer's tables it is not clear how Strong reaches his figures, or, indeed, what their significance is. As we have noted, there are major difficulties in establishing true coronation costs. With the increasing role of the British State, this is made all the more difficult. One problematic consequence is that if an historian has not defined 'cost', whether just building works or everything, then the statistics for outlay appear insubstantial. In such circumstances, it might readily be argued that a particular coronation was a quiet affair, lacking the pomp and ceremony of previous occasions. Covering the coronations from George I to Queen Victoria, Chapter 8 of Strong's *Coronation* is entitled 'Insubstantial Pageants',[33] and this interpretation owes much to his assessment of the expense of those events. He rightly treats the coronation of George IV as exceptional, but his figures are undefined. It is unclear as to whether or not the figures cited constitute his totals (and not those found in any source) and we can only assume that he means the entire cost, for no subsequent breakdown is given; his categories are the Office of Works; the banquet; jewels and plate; and uniforms, costumes, robes, and mantles. It is well known that George IV's coronation was an extravagant

Fig. 6.2 The Coronation Banquet for George IV, 1821, by George Jones (1786–1869) RCIN 404463—Royal Collection/Alamy

occasion, but the increase from £9430 for George III's coronation to £238,000 for George IV's should have raised serious questions—this is a leap of nearly twenty-five times the earlier sum (Fig. 6.2). On the basis of my research, a more accurate set of figures can be compiled. These

Table 6.3 Roy Strong's calculations of coronation expenditure, 1714–1838[a]

Coronation and date	*Year*	*Total cost (£)*
George I	1714	7287
George II	1727	8720
George III	1761	9430
George IV	1821	238,000
William IV	1831	43,159
Victoria	1838	69,421

[a]Strong, *Coronation*, p. 372

findings do not underestimate the extraordinary expense of 1821: it was almost certainly four times the cost of any conventional coronation. Nevertheless, these more accurate estimates allow us to dispel the idea that by the time we reach George I's coronation in 1714 'the severance from … medieval tradition was complete'[34] and that, in financial terms, there really was 'a reaction against the overbearing ceremonial of the Baroque era' (Table 6.3).[35]

The works of Archer and Strong are useful as a series of benchmarks, yet their combined coverage still leaves a gap between the coronations of James I and George I. This chapter fills that void.

For the second part of this chapter, the historiography is broader than that for the first, particularly in terms of celebrations. Cressy has shown the growing list of subjects for commemoration in the Elizabethan and Stuart calendars.[36] The research for this book reveals that the list continued to grow after the Restoration. Churchwardens' accounts disclose much of this organised celebration, as discussed in Hutton's book, which states that eighty-one parishes in his England-wide sample commemorated Charles II's coronation, though unhelpfully he does not identify which parishes or quote what the entries record.[37] This chapter builds upon his analysis and demonstrates that, regarding homage and celebration, parishes were doing much the same in 1714 as in 1661. Church bells continued to ring for the crowning of a new monarch and in memory of 'crownation day'.[38]

Charles II, 1661

Charles II's return from exile in 1660 heralded grandiose ceremonies, planned in great detail by Garter King of Arms, Sir Edward Walker; they are illustrated in Ogilby's famous prints.[39] 'Legacy' was to be a major factor in the opulence and duration of these occasions. The Restoration called for celebration, and the monarchy needed to be held up so as to secure its survival. These imperatives came at tremendous cost. Yet, as Table 6.4 shows, this book estimates the true cost as substantially more than historians have previously stated. One of the reasons for this greater expense was that government borrowing was so high. According to Nichols:

> during Charles II's reign, over twelve per cent of the government's receipts were loans paid directly into the Exchequer and, during some years, loans made up as much as one-third of the total receipts.[40]

When one considers that the 'total cash on hand in the Exchequer on June 30, 1660 was a paltry £141 7*s.* 11*d.*', then the detailed figures to be presented below really underline the necessity for a coronation, for nothing else but a true need could have justified the massive burden on a badly impoverished Crown. The only way that Charles II could cope was to rely on the City of London. In return for the removal of the republic's standing army, the City 'agreed to loan Charles £100,000'.[41] Later, the East India Company would in addition help support the king, particularly over the costs of the Second Dutch War: 'during 1666 and 1667, the company loaned a total of £120,000'.[42]

Fraser puts total cost of Charles II's coronation as over £30,000[43]; Strong calculates it as £31,798.[44] However, these figures seem defective, when allowance is made for the City of London's loan, the great pre-coronation procession and the re-making of the regalia, which, incidentally, was important enough to merit commemoration in an oil painting, presumably commissioned by the Crown.[45] These statistics also seem considerably at odds with the rumours of what various members of the elite had lavished on their wardrobes. It was claimed that the 2nd duke of

Table 6.4 Previous and revised estimates of coronation expenditure, 1661

Fraser	*Strong*	*This book*
£30,000[a]	£31,798[b]	£130,000

[a]Fraser, *Charles II*, pp. 198–9. See also J. H. Plumb and H. Wheldon, *Royal Heritage: The Story of Britain's Royal Builders and Collectors* (London, 1977), p. 128

[b]Strong, *Coronation*, p. 350, citing Blair, *Jewels*, I pp. 389–91

Buckingham spent roughly that figure (£30,000) on clothes for himself and his staff. Adamson and Hutton both give that example. It was said of Lord Clarendon that he 'shone like a diamond, and an onlooker wondered how many ostrich feathers could have been found in England'.[46] These are insights into the luxury being flaunted, although the figures are almost certainly exaggerations; nevertheless, they make one question whether or not the total **public** cost of the entire coronation could really have been the same as (or anywhere close to) the clothing bills of two powerful courtiers. To give some idea of what this figure meant in real terms, a sum of £30,000 amounted to approximately the consolidated income of a successful knight for ten years. As can be seen in Ogilby's illustrated account,[47] London was transformed for the procession, but this scene-setting came at a substantial cost to the City: 'the aldermen and companies paid £10,000 for four triumphal arches a hundred feet high' in homage to Roman classical tradition.[48] This would have left only around £20,000 for the remaining coronation expenses, based on statistics given by Fraser and Strong. Again, this scenario does not work proportionally or seem remotely correct. When one takes into account that it was said that James II in 1685 had saved £60,000 on the expense of a procession that would have matched his late brother's cavalcade, then the figures really do not add up.[49] Even with the lapse of twenty-four years, and allowing for inflation, this was still a very sizeable figure; the totals given for Charles II's expenses simply fail to correlate.

In examining the cost of the new crown jewels, it becomes clear that the received figure of approximately £30,000 cannot possibly be the overall public expenditure on the entire coronation. Strong, using Blair, has the total cost of Charles II's coronation as £31,798 9*s.* 11*d.*, 'of which [£]12,050 3*s.* 5*d.* appertained to the remaking of the regalia'.[50] The trouble is that the actual figure was around £18,000 more than that. During the Commonwealth, we should recall that the ancient crown jewels had been destroyed. One of the substantial problems for the Restoration regime was to make this old regalia anew, particularly the solid gold St Edward's Crown. The task was given to Sir Robert Vyner, goldsmith and city banker, who would later be elevated to a baronetcy and serve as lord mayor of London, working under the supervision of the master of the wardrobe, the Earl of Sandwich, and the master of the Jewel House, Sir Gilbert Talbot.[51] Historians have given various estimates for the cost of the new regalia made at this time, all centring around £30,000. Uglow provides a figure of £30,000[52]; Lenman does likewise[53]; and Edie, following Purey-Cust, lists a more precise number of £31,978 9*s.* 11*d.*,[54] which had already been derived from primary sources by Robert Cole, in a letter to Sir Henry Ellis in 1841.[55] It is possible that Strong has used this figure (or almost exactly this figure) as the total cost of the coronation, whereas it relates only to the cost of the crown jewels. Importantly, this total of £31,978 9*s.* 11*d.*[56] has recently been confirmed in Barclay's article on St Edward's Crown, which reveals that Vyner was not fully reimbursed until July 1662.[57]

Where does this discovery leave us? Charles II's coronation left no expense spared.[58] To put *c.*£30,000 further into context, John Denham, surveyor general of the Kings Works, was advanced £1000 (on 3 April 1661) merely 'for building of a throne and other necessary works'.[59] Therefore, the Fraser-Strong figure simply cannot have accounted for everything. Thus, a more realistic grand total must rest on a combination of the amounts ascertainable for key elements, as indicated in the following table (Table 6.5).

Is this new estimate reasonable? How does it relate to previous coronations? When set against Archer's total of £36,145 for James I's coronation, a figure of over three times that much would not seem improbable, given the time-lapse and level of magnificence called for in 1661.[60] Archer even explains that his estimate is based on a combination of 'the coronation and the entry' in 1603, despite the fact that 'these events were held separately because of plague'.[61] The cost borne by the City of London was

Table 6.5 Charles II, coronation expenditure, 1661

Category of expenditure	*Cost (£, in round figures)*
Works, banquet, and wardrobe	£30,000 (of which coronation banquet provisions cost £1290, 15*s.*, 7*d. ob.*, according to Sandford;[a] (excluding wages))
City of London costs	£10,000+[b]
Procession	£60,000 (needs adjustment for inflation and backdating 24 years)[c]
Crown jewels	£30,000[d] (from parliamentary grant of £70,000 towards coronation expenses, including jewels for the crown)[e]
Total	£130,000

[a]Sandford, *History*, p. 6. See also TNA, Work 3/1, fols 1r–9r
[b]Uglow, *Gambling Man*, p. 113
[c]Edie, 'Public Face', p. 318
[d]TNA, LC 5/107, fols 79v–80v; *ibid.*, T 51/3, pp. 321, 330; *ibid.*, E 403/1761, fol. 58r–v; BL, Add. MS 44915, fols 3r–4v
[e]Anon. (ed.), *Journals of the House of Lords* (London, 1767–), 8, pp. 209–13 (17 December 1660)

tremendous and details of that expenditure can be seen in the Corporation of London records. We know that, from the spring of 1603, the Common Council organised a committee to establish 'the beste and fyttest meanes to be performed by this citie' for James I's arrival for his coronation. The members began by 'assess[ing] the guilds for [£]2,500[,] … later assessments in July 1603, February 1604, and May 1604, brought the total sum to £4,100, a generous amount even if all of it did not go specifically to the construction of pageant devices'.[62] Proportionally, these figures would roughly fit an expenditure rise from 1603 to 1661 of two to three times. The City's costs in 1661 amounted to over £10,000.[63] Crucially, this was a price that, for many, had the desired impact: it bedazzled onlookers with the grandeur of majesty, for here was the reinstitution of worldly power at its zenith. Pepys recorded his impression of the coronation cavalcade: 'so glorious was the show with gold and silver, that we were not able to look at it – our eyes at last being so much overcome'.[64] Another source noted that 'the City … was at a very great expence' for such diadems and show.[65] For all concerned, the 1661 outlay was tremendous, but not utterly inconsistent with the Corporation's expenditure for earlier Stuart coronations. We may conclude, therefore, that 1661 was unprecedented in scale, not least because plague, which had caused reductions in 1603 and 1626, was not a factor. Whilst Charles II's Westminster Abbey coronation was enormously expensive, it also came close to benchmark figures for previous occasions, allowing for inflation. Significantly, it was considerably dearer than has been appreciated in modern scholarship. The revised total helps to put into perspective statistics that can be generated for following coronations and enables us to assess the arguments insisting on declining coronation expenditure.

James II, 1685

Given the political flux preceding James II's accession, particularly the Exclusion Crisis, and that which followed, in Monmouth's Rebellion, one might expect his coronation to have been fully investigated by historians. It is surprising, therefore, to find that this is not the case; although we have Sandford's account, and Edie's discussion, finances remain obscure.[66]

As we have seen above, the 1661 coronation was both colossal and opulent. Yet this book can reveal that James II's crowning was nearly as expensive as his brother's, in this instance because of the immense outlay on jewels. 1685 saw considerable planning too:

> warrants [were] … directed to the severall offices to provide all things for the coronation … Jewellhouse, Greate Wardrobe, surveyor of the Workes, master of the Roabes, groome of the Stole to the king, Mint, master of the Ordinance … [and even] ticket[ing].[67]

James II was aware of the extraordinary cost of coronations and abolished the traditional grand procession in an effort to be seen as 'frugal and cautious, and no great admirer of outward pomp and popularity'.[68] According to Edie, James II estimated savings of £60,000.[69] However, this sum was soon spent on jewels for his consort, Mary of Modena. Not only did the king fail to harness the public relations opportunities of coming face-to-face with his people in the procession, but his efforts at parsimony failed too: lavish spending on the regalia in fact dramatically escalated overall expenditure. The original draft accounts show that Richard de Beauvoir, the goldsmith, was required to make a new diadem at prodigious cost, as Table 6.6 reveals.[70] Sums for the component diamonds alone are staggering. They are significantly higher than the figure of '£530 worth of precious stones' recorded by Jones (Fig. 6.3).[71]

In seeing where James spent his money, we witness his poor decision-making. He failed to capitalise on the political honeymoon accorded to most new sovereigns. His distance from the people would win him no favours when the time came for a stand against William of Orange. He laid out what he presumably supposed would secure a lasting legacy, namely a glittering addition to the regalia, but his political acumen was deficient in the short term. Subjects expect to see jewels, yet they also long to see their

Table 6.6 James II, new crown jewel costs, 1685

Item of expenditure	*Cost (£)*
'Diamonds in the cro[w]ne: 4 in the bands'	40,000
'Two [diamonds] in the cen[tr]e'	10,000
'20 [?10] [diamonds] in the c[i]rkell'	30,000
'4 gr[e]ait h[e]arts [rubies?]'	6000
'8 more [diamonds] in the flower jew[el]lery'	4000
'Pairses [pearls]'	2500
'All the diamonds in the 5 cro[w]nes & globe amounds'	8150
Total (discrepancy between surviving accounts)	100,650[a]
	111,900[b]

[a]BL, Add. MS 17019, fol. 43r–v
[b]Sandford, *History*, p. 42

Fig. 6.3 The crown of Mary of Modena, Modified after 1685, Royal Collection Trust

monarch; James II failed to grasp the balance—he was out of touch over the ingredients for a successful coronation. Taking all known costs of James II's coronation together, verified by important sources at the College of Arms, the final figure is significant, on a par with 1661, as Table 6.7 discloses.

The conclusion is clear: coronation expenditure did not diminish under the later Stuarts; if anything, Charles I's sons spent more money proportionally than either their father or grandfather. Would this continue with the arrival of William of Orange and partial dynastic change?

William III and Mary II, 1689

William and Mary were crowned in extremely unusual circumstances, in that their predecessor was still alive, and had not personally abdicated his responsibilities nor, in the eyes of many, abandoned his Coronation Oath. Getting through the formalities would be all the more important at a time of questionable legitimacy for the new joint rulers. Therefore, the heralds were busy making proclamations and organising ceremonies, including that concerning the creation of peers, for it was necessary to bolster

Table 6.7 James II, coronation costs, 1685

Category of expenditure	*Cost (£)*[a]
Works	1670 0*s.* 7*d.* (College of Arms) 1181[b] (Strong)
Great Wardrobe	4553 9*s.* 4*d.* (College of Arms) 4533[c] (Strong)
Queen consort's crown	100,650[d] 111,900[e]
Liveries for guards	2200 (College of Arms)
Watermen's liveries	315 10*s.* 0*d.* (College of Arms)
Liveries for stables and footmen	1608 4*s.* 0*d.* (College of Arms)
Coronation banquet	No figure, but banquet provisions for Charles II amounted to 1290 15*s.* 7*d.* *ob.*, according to Sandford;[f] this figure excludes wages[g]
Total	£120,000 approximately

[a]Costs from CA come from MS 'Coronations – Charles II/ James II/William & Mary', Item [48], pp. 1–2
[b]Strong, *Coronation*, p. 350. See also H. M. Colvin, *The History of the King's Works*, 6 volumes (London, 1963–1982), V p. 454
[c]Strong, *Coronation*, p. 350. See also Arundel Castle, MSS GI/99–105
[d]See Table 6.6 above
[e]Sandford, *History*, p. 42
[f]*Ibid.*, p. 6
[g]See also CA, MS 'Coronations – Charles II/ James II/William & Mary', Item [28] ('The number of dishes for their ma[jestie]s table at the corona[ti]on dinner, 23 April 1685' was 1134); Sandford, *History*, p. 115, recording that a staggering 1445 dishes were served

support. These expenses were not inconsiderable, as the following tables indicate.

Such costs (over £550) show how a coronation meant expenditure far wider than simply for its staging. Beyond the ceremony itself, costs were incurred on things ranging from proclamations and the production of coins and medals, right down to robes, not forgetting commemorative literature.

It is well known that William was not keen on overtly ritualised occasions, yet his coronation emulated the trappings of its Stuart forerunners; the cost was still significant. Indeed, only four years on from James II's coronation, the planners in 1689 looked to match those expenses as a means of economy. For example, the lord steward, preparing his estimate for the coronation banquet, envisaged 'the same number of tables as at the last coronation[,] but more proper and not exceeding in the expense'.[72] As we concluded above, James II's coronation was tremendously expensive, although that fact has been neglected hitherto; it is therefore significant that William and Mary's coronation sought to parallel 1685 costs. Indeed, we are fortunate to have a report, written by Sir Christopher Wren, that takes into account a rise in costs:

> S[i]r Chr[istopher] Wren hath delivered a report that the exact charge of all the work done by his office at the last coronation, for fitting and preparing Westm[inste]r Hall for the dinner with galleries, taking down and setting up the Courts of Justice, the throne and scaffolds in Westm[inste]r Abbey, rayling the streets … amount to £1670 0*s*. 7*d*. … and in regard that timber and boards are now dearer one 5th part, this charge may be £1800 to be done by lord chamberlains warr[an]t.[73]

One reason for the considerable additional expense was that Mary was to be crowned queen in her own right, albeit in practice subordinate to her husband. This situation necessitated the creation of an extra set of regalia and, of course, there was need for another coronation chair.[74] Yet again, the crown jewels were intended to add opulence, but at a price. Although the precise figures for these gems are unknown, the jeweller's charge for attending to the regalia was tremendous:

> The master of the Jewell House … certifies that the jewellers charge, for making … the jewels, for adorning this regalia will come to £3,702 … To which must be added for the queen an orb of gold, adorn[ing] the kings, and a scepter adorned as the kings[.][75]

Considering this figure excludes the banquet's true cost and, indeed, the procession, then the sum is almost certainly above £30,000. The regalia figure may also need revising with further research. Thus, it is clear that the coronation again came at vast cost. For William III, this cost is significant. A coronation was worth this expenditure and (for the monarchs) the endurance because it cemented their positions in a revolutionary epoch. William and Mary could not afford to omit this crowning occasion, and these figures reveal that, far from cutting back, they permitted a full and expensive ceremony in line with others of this period.

Queen Anne, 1702

Nothing suggests that spending declined with Anne's accession, nor indeed that her coronation was any less luxurious. In fact, the 1702 crowning saw significant spending on jewels and the concluding banquet. The Crown borrowed jewels valued at over £171,000 at a rate of 4%, almost certainly a 'charge made by Sir Richard Hoare, the goldsmith-banker, [who was involved in] … the hire of some silver plates for the queen's banquet'.[76] A comparison with the 1821 extravaganza puts Anne's loan into perspective: for George IV's coronation, the 'charge for the loan of gems from the Court goldsmiths, Rundell, Bridge and Rundell, was ten per cent. Everything [was] … replaced, remade as closely as possible to the old patterns'.[77] George IV's coronation was notable for conspicuous consumption: a new crown setting required an 'unprecedented' quantity of jewels: 'a total of 12,532 diamonds'.[78] Despite falling short of this magnitude, Anne's coronation was nevertheless expensive, as Table 6.10 reveals.

These figures require further discussion if their significance is to become apparent. £12,000 had been awarded from the Civil List, which was to be divided: £3000 for William III's funeral and £9000 for Anne's coronation. This is one of the earliest examples of linkage with the Civil List. Amongst the first directions made with Anne's forthcoming ceremony in mind was the grant (1 April 1702) of £1500 a week to the master of the Great Wardrobe.[79] Research into the ensuing costs reveals not only aspects of the planning process, but also the timescale for fulfilment of orders by employees and its suppliers. The pressures could be considerable. This scenario is best illustrated by the case of the crown jewels. The main difference between the huge figures for the coronations of Charles II and James II and the lesser totals for William and Mary, Anne and George I was the absence of formidable spending on jewels. Whereas Charles II and James II had had pieces either re-created or fashioned from scratch, the later monarchs sought to hire additional items, indulging in minor expenditure. It is certainly true that William and Mary required more regalia for their joint coronation, but they did not seek to spend beyond that need. The budget of Anne's goldsmith, Charles Shales, was £10,000—a significant figure, but hardly extortionate by earlier standards.[80] The Treasury warrant here was issued on 12 April 1702 and actioned on 14 April.[81114] Depending on precisely when he received the order, Shales had no more than 9–10 days in which to prepare, for Anne's coronation was scheduled for 23 April. The accounts of C[harles] Godfrey, master of the Jewel House, record items for that coronation, as well as for William III's funeral—a total of £14,132 15*s.* 0*d.* This covered work to

> boil, loan and repair ... white plate for the king's funeral[:] 3 sconces and 2 large branches, in all 11,329 ounces [at a cost of] £231 12*s*. 3*d*.; and [to] adorn ... 2 several crowns for her majesty's use at the Parliament House and for the loan of diamonds for the same [at a total cost of] £920 ... and [to] adorn ... with diamonds and jewels the Crown of State, circlet, St. Edward's Crown, orb and sceptre and for a ruby ring for her majesty to wear at her coronation [at a total cost of] £1264 10*s*. 0*d*.[82]

In traditional circumstances, when a coronation quickly succeeded a funeral, the combined costs, as here, took a heavy toll on Crown and State finances. In 1626, Charles I had planned a lavish funeral for James I, costing (according to Sharpe) approximately £50,000. His coronation coming only weeks after that event must have been devastating for the already 'depleted state of the royal coffers'.[83] In 1714, the total outlay on Anne's funeral was estimated to be £20,599 4*s*. 3*d*. *ob*. *qu*. When one adds this total to that relating to George I's coronation, one ends up with a gigantic gap in the revenue.[84]

The traditional concluding banquet was, of course, another major drain on resources.

Sir Benjamin Bathurst, tasked with arranging the 'coronation dinner', had at his disposal £10,000 under an order given on 18 April 1702.[85] In terms of finances, this gave him under a week for preparations. Additionally he received a further £3000 to be 'on account [for the] provisions' for the banquet.[86] These disbursements indicate that Anne's coronation dinner was every bit as expensive as the previous three. Clearly, coronation festivities were not in decline.

Calculating a figure for Anne's coronation is complicated by the fact that some component sums are missing. Strong gives the cost of infrastructure works as £4677. However, a breakdown is lacking and the figure may not include works associated with the pre-coronation procession.[87] We also do not have details of the costs borne by the City of London or the Corporation's grant to the Crown, or indeed the outlay on music and further festivities. On this basis, and in view of recorded spending, it is likely that the 1702 coronation cost a minimum of £50,000. If a complete overhaul of the crown jewels had been needed, then it is easy to see how that extra burden would have brought the 1702 total within reach of those achieved in 1661 and 1685.

George I, 1714

George I's coronation of 1714 is the first one to appear in Strong's table. His total seemingly indicates a substantial decline from the heady days of opulent Stuart ceremonial to an austerity perhaps characteristic of the Hanoverian Court. Yet this figure is consistent with what we have found for Anne's coronation. Moreover, it is wholly at odds with an important estimate for George I's coronation charges that has been discovered (hitherto unknown) in the New York Public Library.

How do we explain £50,235 37s. 2*d.*? Although we do not have all the figures, the picture (see Table 6.12) is one that confirms a sum in excess of £50,000, in fact nearer £65,000 and is in line with the totals ascertainable for earlier coronations, excluding the making of expensive new regalia.

These figures are particularly interesting because they reveal the sweeping nature of coronation costs, and something of the social impact. From gardeners to tailors, from musicians to apothecaries—a coronation brought employment to a vast array of people, belonging to hugely differing branches of early modern society; a striking number of luxury objects were involved. 'Sundry tradesmen' were mobilised in general preparations, whilst specialists were commissioned to undertake skilled work, such as attending to robes. For example, T. Pembroke, administrator to Jacob Whiddon, had the task of providing the 'lining and edging [for] the great purple coronation robe and for ermine for the crimson coronation robe'; these were then worked on by Robert Graham, tailor. The king was even supplied with 'gold fringe gloves' for coronation day. The cost of such tailoring totalled just under £2500.[88] This expenditure was authorised by William, 1st Earl Cadogan, master of the robes, and issued out of the Declared Accounts of the Civil List. In the Abbey, specialised construction work was executed under the direction of Charles Dartiquenave, paymaster of the works and buildings. John Hopson, master joiner, was given the responsibility of repairing the Coronation Chair and making a 'wainscott pedistall pulpit'. Outside, John Dear was required to repair Cotton Garden after the coronation.[89] With the approval of John, 2nd duke of Montagu, keeper of the Great Wardrobe, Nathanial William, serjeant furrier, was entrusted with the job of making sure that the Abbey was aired and cleaned. The coronation banquet was as lavish as former feasts, consuming £3,740 6*s.* 5*d. qu.* 'for victuals'.[90] The composer William Croft was commissioned (at a cost of £42) to provide the coronation music, as well as that for a thanksgiving service to be held at St Paul's Cathedral.[91]

Even sumptuous wall-hangings were brought from Hampton Court to adorn part of the Westminster Abbey fabric, costing £46 8*s*. 6*d*.[92] Perhaps the most unusual entry in these Exchequer accounts is that of the apothecaries in ordinary—James Chase and Daniel Malthus—who for £206 provided the anointing oil: 'a very large composition of rich, essentiall, chymical, odoriferous oyles, balsams and spirits highly perfumed'.[93] Finally, commemorative pieces were required. For instance, Samuel Stebbing, Somerset Herald, was commissioned to produce five manuscript books recording proceedings: one each for George I, the Prince of Wales, the Princess of Wales, the archbishop of Canterbury, and the dean of Westminster; in tribute to the Coronation Oath's importance it was stipulated that, that was to be particularly engrossed.[94] Some of these expenses were not coronation related, also covering other necessities, such as addressing tasks left over from Anne's Lying-in-State and funeral. In other cases, outlay was for jobs that had to be undertaken anyway in connection with the sitting of Parliament.[95] Nevertheless, these complications aside, each task had to be paid for, much of the money coming directly from the Civil List, granted by Parliament.

To conclude: all parts of the State were gathered together to make this event, or rather complex of events, remarkable. Various Crown officers and their roles, together with countless expensive bespoke objects, all contributed to this grandest of State occasions. Thus, coronation magnificence exhibited to the world both the power and wealth of the new sovereign, besides the status of those taking part, even if much of the pomp and circumstance was based upon loans, or the riches of the City of London. Despite the fact that aspects of coronation outlay remain to be clarified, it is already obvious that the topic highlights the transition of government finance from the pre-1688 situation to a very different one after: it 'was no longer solely the king's responsibility'. Parliament would henceforth share the burden; post-1694, 'the creation of the Bank of England centralized and handled the bulk of the credit operation' of the State. Therefore, what we find from investigating coronation expenditure is the transformation to a system of 'modern government credit, … root[ed] in the reign of Charles II' and the constitutional changes of the Glorious Revolution, which resulted in government finances becoming 'the responsibility of the nation'.[96] A coronation that had already become a national event constitutionally, politically, and religiously was by 1714 also a national occurrence in financial terms—paid for by the British people. Furthermore, and crucially, here was an event that was anything but in decline; the indulgence in conspicuous consumption continued well into 1727, for 'George II's coronation was an especially lavish affair'.[97] We apparently possess first-hand evidence to support that contention: according to Evelyn, it was 'the finest coronation that ever was in England and consequently one of the finest sights in the world'.[98]

Charles II, 1651, 'An Anomaly?'

It might be assumed that, in judging the costs of the coronations of 1661–1714, the baseline is represented by that of 1626 (with or without 1633). However, there was a coronation much closer to the period covered by this book, namely that at Scone in 1651, which provides useful comparison. This exercise is all the more valuable because Charles II's Scottish coronation has either been completely forgotten or become the subject of distorted interpretations. It has long been suggested that this coronation was a hastily arranged affair, 'verg[ing] on the humiliating',[99] involving little pomp, and thus minimal cost. Furthermore, historians have argued that Charles both 'resent[ed]'[100] this coronation and could not have found it to 'have been very joyful'.[101] Yet Clarendon commented that it 'passed with great solemnity and magnificence, all men making show of joy, and being united to serve his majesty'.[102] Thorough archival research by the present writer has revealed substantial material unused by previous scholars. These new manuscripts allow us to assess this disparity, particularly in relation to cost.[103]

Although we do not have all relevant figures, much documentation being lost due to the widespread flux of the late 1640s and early 1650s, there are nevertheless enough sources to indicate that this was an event, in expenditure terms, on a par with earlier Stuart coronations. One key new source concerns post-Restoration retrospective taxation granted by the Scottish Parliament. This taxation was imposed on the Scottish regions in order to recoup costs for 1651 based on an Act of Parliament (12 July 1661). That manoeuvre was necessary because the sums normally collected 'according to the monthly roll of maintenance for shires 6 August 1649' had ceased with the political upheaval of 1649–1651.[104] Of course, individuals had also incurred expense. For instance, the Earl of Kinghorne had paid £26 4*s*. 4*d*. on 14 March 1650/1651 for 'ma[i]ntenance [costs for the] coronation'.[105] Table 6.13 shows the sums raised under the 1661 Act for the months March and June 1651 for the king's maintenance in Scotland.

These are significant figures, but such maintenance allowances for Charles II in Scotland, or rather the debts relating to them, should be understood in conjunction with other sources. For instance, the February accounts of Scone Palace dealing with January expenditure, and therefore coronation month, detail two exceptionally large figures of £3380 and £4420.[106] The magnitude here fosters an impression more consistent with Clarendon's description than with modern historians' arguments. It is increasingly clear, therefore, that Charles's brief time in Scotland (June 1650–August 1651) involved considerable disbursements. His coronation, far from being drab, did not lack traditional pomp and ceremony, allowing, nevertheless, for the tastes of his presbyterian, covenanting allies. Charles's coronation required a degree of magnificence and solemnity in order for it to function as a beacon to supporters, the undecided and the opposition alike. Nothing less would do. Thus, Charles wore a robe of a richness befitting such an occasion and his train-bearers were not assorted nobodies, but rather peers' sons. Like his ancestors, he sat in the Scone kirk on the throne under a canopy of crimson velvet—hardly, therefore, an ephemeral or cheap item. On his return to the palace, the banquet illustrated a taste for luxury: royal Household books show a substantially increased food order, including 'twenty-two salmon, a total of ten calves' heads, vast numbers of partridges and meat'.[107] Naturally, such splendid fare was not to be eaten without suitable tableware, and the accounts reveal that damask napkins embroidered with 'CR' and expensive cloth from Holland were also obtained in readiness for the great day.[108] Newly discovered manuscripts in the Scone Palace Archives disclose similar entries for generous food orders. Amongst further purchases relating to Charles's Scone sojourn and coronation were 'linning … of Holland cloath', as well as 'silk … buttons [and] ribbons'.[109] A horse was procured for £280, possibly intended for the king himself.[110] Expenditure totals for January–March are utterly disproportionate to those for other months, which reached hundreds rather than thousands. What conclusion can we draw? Keay suggests that the 'traditional days of fasting and prayer before a coronation' were displeasing for Charles as they 'were turned into opportunities for the Scots to enumerate the wrongs of his father and grandfather'.[111] Yet the evidence for provisioning at Scone does not suggest that Charles allowed anyone to dampen his spirits! This coronation was thus far from cheap and must have been near crippling for Scone's owner, Lord Stormont, even taking into consideration whatever small assistance Charles had to offer. A 'follow the money' approach therefore allows us to revise the received historiography: the 1651 coronation was not hugely anomalous and may well have constituted, in the king's mind, the benchmark against which to measure investment in his 1661 Westminster Abbey coronation.

Coronation Expenditure in Context

To put these sizeable figures into perspective, it is useful to end this section with non-coronation comparators. Hence Table 6.14 presents costs (either estimated or actual) relating to a wide range of matters, both civil and military.

If one compares these figures with those of total coronation expenses given in Tables 6.6, 6.7, 6.8, 6.9, 6.10, 6.11, 6.12, and 6.13., it is clear that, coronations apart, only military expenditure and Elizabeth Stuart's marriage cost the Crown and State more. Indeed, her nuptials 'cost the Exchequer ... almost an entire year's worth of the Crown's landed income [!]'.[112] Adamson suggests that this kind of spending on royal ceremonial was designed 'to create an impression of the royal household as a place of almost super-human opulence – and at an equally prodigious cost'.[113] The extent of disbursements, in relation to general expenditure, highlights 'the importance attached to such ostentation ... in sustaining the prestige and authority of the royal house'.[114] Outlay on armies and navies reached an entirely new level, far above even royal ceremonial. Funerals were also expensive, but not in the same league as coronations. In view of the frequency with which military spending was required in these tumultuous years, it is perhaps all the more notable that coronations continued to occur so magnificently. After all, the main pieces of Charles II's new regalia cost above £13,000—the equivalent of three new fully fitted warships.[115] In an era of growing demands on the public purse, these comparisons are strong indicators of the importance of coronations, religiously, politically, and socially. As vehicles for enhancing monarchical and national prestige, they were simply too valuable to cut. The situation was no different in 2023. Approximately £50 million was spent on Charles III's coronation by the Department for Culture, Media and Sport (DCMS) and in contrast to the early modern world (an age before police in the manner of today) £22 million by the Home Office for policing the occasion. Whilst the length of the service, the absence of a Naval Review,[116] and the number of guests were significantly less than in 1953, the cost was still considerable at a time of a cost of living crisis and was widely reported

Table 6.8 William III and Mary II, coronation expenditure, 1689

Account 1[a]	
Coronation fees due to M[aste]r May[,] Chest[e]r Herald[:]	
	The king's corona[t]ion fee and assuming his stall at Windsor £8 2*s.* 0*d.*
	Creation of 16 noblemen £4 12*s.* 7*d.*
	Scarlet robes at coronation £10 11*s.* 4*d.*
Total	£23 5*s.* 11*d.*
Account 2[b]	
Coronation officers of the arms fees[:]	
	Kings warrant £3 10*s.* 0*d.*
	Stamp £0 5*s.* 0*d.*
	Warrant £1 10*s.* 0*d.*
	Order £0 12*s.* 6*d.*
Total	£5 17*s.* 6*d.*
Account 3[c]	
Heralds notes, 8 May 1689	
For proclaiming their ma[jes]ties	£40
Coronation of the king	£100
Coronation of the queen	£100
Scarlet robes	£167
Assuming the seat as sovereign of the Order [of the Garter?]	£40
Total	£447
Account 4[d]	
M[aste]r King's charges for William and Mary coronation, account of the ceremonial	£100
Grand total	£552 17*s.* 6*d.*

[a]CA, MS 'Coronations – Charles II/ James II/William & Mary', Item [53]
[b]Ibid
[c]*Ibid.*, Item [54]
[d]*Ibid.*, Item [59]

to be a concern.[117] Nevertheless, the reasons above trumped the cost—and as covered in reference to the Coronation Oath(s), and the wider sense of the seeing out or playing out of the British Constitution, the event was a marker for soft power both here and abroad, making clear what Britain stands for, with 'justice' and 'mercy' at the heart of the ceremony in oath and objects.[118]

Table 6.9 Some costs associated with the coronation of William III and Mary II, 1689

Subject of expenditure	*Source and amount*		
	Sandford	Strong	New research in College of Arms
Works		£2240[a]	£1800 (Sir Christopher Wren report)[b]
Great wardrobe		£9758[c]	
Liveries for yeomen of the guard (Earl marshal's office)			£2200[d]
Liveries for stables and footmen			£1608 4*s.* 0*d.*[e]
Liveries for watermen			£315 10*s.* 0*d.*[f]
Banquet (excluding wages)	Coronation banquet provisions amounted to £1,290 15*s.* 7*d. ob.*, according to Sandford[g]		
Regalia			£3702[h]
Mint/Gold medal making			1200 silver medals and 200 of gold; no cost listed; £1000 roughly in value at previous coronation for same number. So assume £1000+
Totals	£1290 15*s.* 7*s.*	£11,998	£10,625 14*s.* 0*d.*
Grand total	£23,000 (including Strong figures)		

[a]Strong, *Coronation*, p. 350. See also Colvin, *King's Works*, V p. 454
[b]CA, MS 'Coronations – Charles II/ James II/William & Mary', Item [48], p. 1. See also TNA, Work 3/1, fol. 9r
[c]Strong, *Coronation*, p. 350
[d]CA, MS 'Coronations – Charles II/ James II/William & Mary', Item [48], pp. 1–2
[e]*Ibid*
[f]*Ibid.*, p. 2
[g]Sandford, *History*, p. 6
[h]*Ibid*

Table 6.10 Queen Anne, coronation costs, 1702

Items	*Estimate (£)*
Wardrobe	9000[a]
Jewels	10,000[b]
Banquet and household expenses	10,000[c]
Further banquet expenses	3000[d]
4% interest charge for jewel loan	6840[e]
Procession, other festivities, and music	Not yet found
Other works expenses	4677[f]
Total	43,517
Grand total (when including further expenditure not listed above)	50,000+

[a]W. A. Shaw, *et al.* (eds), *Calendar of Treasury Books … Preserved in The Public Record* Office, 32 volumes in 64 parts (London, 1904–1957), XVII pp. 180–90. See also Strong, *Coronation*, p. 350 (figure of £8828)

[b]R. P. Mahaffy, et al. (eds), Calendar of State Papers, Domestic Series, of the Reign of Anne, Preserved in the Public Record Office, 4 volumes (London, 1916–2006), I p. 27

[c]Ibid

[d]Shaw, *Treasury Books*, XVII pp. 191–203

[e]Jones, 'Coronation Plate', p. 246

[f]Strong, *Coronation*, p. 350. See also Colvin, *King's Works*, V p. 454

Table 6.11 Cost calculations for George I's coronation, 1714

Strong	*Gross: Revised figure*
£7287[a]	£50,235 37*s.* 2*d.*[b]

[a]Strong, *Coronation*, p. 372

[b]NYPL, MS 1214, Vol. I fol. 345r

Part II: Longevity, Celebration, and Reportage

Queen Victoria wrote in her diary of her dinner post-coronation (1838) and of the celebrations taking place in Green Park after, for she stayed

> in the drawing-room till 20 minutes past 11, but remained till 12 o'clock on Mamma's balcony looking at the fireworks in Green Park, which were quite beautiful.[119]

Table 6.12 George I, coronation expenditure, 1714

Item	*Amounts (£)*
Account of the coronation, 'engrossing'[a]	5[b]
Anointing oil	206[c]
Cofferer of the Household	3740 6*s.* 5*d.* *qu.*[d]
Coronation Chair (master joiner)	38 1*s.* 6*d.*[e]
Cotton Garden	50[f]
Charge of coronation as connected with the Jewel House	14,850[g]
Heraldic 'engrossing' work	36 12*s.* 6*d.*[h]
Housekeeper of Westminster Abbey	82 6*s.* 8*d.*[i]
Miscellaneous, including robes (sundry tradesmen)	2100[j]
Music (William Croft)	42[k]
Serjeant furrier	16 13*s.* 4*d.*[l]
Tailor	389[m]
Wardrobe (payments and allowances)	26,349 9*s.* 2*d.*[n]
Wardrobe (Thomas Williams)	46 8*s.* 6*d.*[o]
Works and repairs for funeral and coronation expenses	17,128 2*s.* 10*d.*[p]
Total	65,000+

[a]This could be the production of the Coronation Roll for deposit in Chancery
[b]TNA, E 351/3140. See also *ibid.*, AO 1/2368/146
[c]*Ibid.*, E 351/567. See also *ibid.*, AO 1/410/151
[d]*Ibid.*, E 351/1874
[e]*Ibid.*, E 351/3319. See also *ibid.*, AO 1/2448/148
[f]*Ibid*
[g]J. Redington and W. A. Shaw (eds), *Calendar of Treasury Papers Preserved in Her Majesty's Public Record Office*, 6 volumes (London, 1868–1897), V pp. 28–9 (29 November 1714)
[h]TNA, E 351/3140. See also *ibid.*, AO 1/2368/146
[i]*Ibid.*, E 351/567. See also *ibid.*, AO 1/410/151
[j]*Ibid.*, E 351/2847. See also *ibid.*, AO 1/2055/40
[k]*Ibid.*, E 351/567. See also *ibid.*, AO 1/410/151. See also B. M. Zon, 'Croft, William (*bap.* 1678, *d.* 1727)', *ODNB* and Range, *Music*, pp. 126–7
[l]TNA, E 351/3140. See also *ibid.*, AO 1/2368/146
[m]*Ibid.*, E 351/2847. See also *ibid.*, AO 1/2055/40
[n]*Ibid.*, E 351/3140. See also *ibid.*, AO 1/2368/146
[o]*Ibid.*, E 351/567. See also *ibid.*, AO 1/410/151
[p]*Ibid.*, E 351/3319. See also *ibid.*, AO 1/2448/148

Table 6.13 King's maintenance in Scotland, under 1661 Act of Parliament for 1650–1651

Area	*Region (£)*
Southern Scotland	67,125 7*s.* 5*d.*[a]
Highlands and Islands	£79,698 15*s.* 9*d.*[b]
Other regions (unspecified)	£6384 (with several unspecified exemptions)[c]
Other regions (unspecified)	£82,022 8*s.* 9*d.* (with several unspecified exemptions)[d]

[a]NAS, MS E67/2/5
[b]*Ibid.*, MS E67/2/8
[c]*Ibid.*, MS E67/2/6.
[d]*Ibid.*, MS E67/2/7

Introduction

The second half of this chapter will show that long before the mechanised state (and continuing) Britain celebrated across counties, towns, villages, and burghs. If drinking a toast to the sovereign is indicative of support, then the Crown enjoyed widespread approbation. Britain acted as a nation on coronation day, decades before the Act of Union. Multiple factors contributed to this scenario, but it was chiefly affection for the new monarch and the institution of monarchy, and fear of a rival dynasty and Roman Catholicism, that united much of the populace.

We might also refer to this chapter as dealing with coronation 'longevity': the widespread nature of celebrations across the realm, and the costs of holding them. In 2023, as in 1661, and indeed before the Restoration, different parts of the country, and in the eighteenth and nineteenth centuries—of the growing empire—paid homage to the newly crowned monarch, just as the social elite were doing so in Westminster Abbey and in the processions and other festivities of the metropolis. For those in the provinces, sacral monarchy lived on and was remembered in the calendar with bell-ringing and rejoicing. More particularly, this section looks at the afterlife of coronations, in the prolongation of expenditure and the reportage of events, seen in letters, diaries, and newspapers. In probing both pomp and circumstance and the way in which it was reported, the chapter shall uncover something of the social dimension of coronations: not only the celebrations themselves, but also their impact on individuals and organisations, often far removed from the political centre.

Table 6.14 Non-coronation cost comparators, 1613–1693

Reason for Expenditure	*Cost(£)*
(i) Marriages and funerals	
Marriage of Elizabeth Stuart, 1613	93,294[a]
Funeral of Queen Mother, Henrietta Maria, 1669	24,752[b]
(ii) Military expenses, 1625–1626[c]	
Support for king of Denmark	30,000 a month
Support for count Mansfeld's continental operations	20,000 a month
Support for Dutch states	9000 a month
Single 200 ton, 120 manned warships	400 a month
The *Vanguard* (six months' service, excluding wages for crew of 230 men and gunners)	3000 (in excess of this figure, just for preparation)
Putting fleet into action, 1625	170,000 (in excess of this figure, which also included £65,000 for sailors' wages)
Estimate to Privy Council in 1626 to maintain offensive and defensive war; also listed by parliamentarian Ferdinando Fairfax in correspondence with his father[d]	1,000,000 (at least) a year
Financial arrears for naval expenditure, December 1627	250,000 (in excess)[e]
(iii) Public Revenue, 5 November 1688–Michaelmas 1693, Military Receipts and Payments[f]	
Army	5,948,902 16*s.* 9[7?]*d. ob.*
Navy	3,126,037 8*s.* 0*d. qu.*
Ordnance	674,493 17*s.* 6*d. ob.*
Total for (iii)	9,749,434 2*s.* 2*d. qu.*

[a]Archer, 'Material Dimensions', pp. 165–6. See also BL, Add. MS 58833, fol. 18v
[b]CLO, MS 115 [App. I]
[c]Cressy, *Charles I*, p. 129
[d]Ibid.; G. W. Johnson (ed.), The Fairfax Correspondence. Memoirs of the Reign of Charles the First, 2 volumes (London, 1848) Johnson, Fairfax Correspondence, I, pp. 25–6
[e]Cressy, *Charles I*, p. 129
[f]CLO, MS 147 Part 1, p. 30

Longevity

Coronations had long-range preparation costs and immediate expenses, such as £1000 given to John Denham, surveyor general of the King's Works, a month before Charles II's 1661 crowning.[120] However, they also generated costs that could develop into debts and therefore brought creditors into the frame too. These events, financially speaking, had a substantial afterlife, often remaining 'on the books' into subsequent years. For

James I's coronation, £6000 was paid to creditors for wardrobe expenses on 4 May 1604,[121] roughly eight months after the event; Lord Oxford would only receive his coronation fee of £200 on 22 May.[122] The pattern of late payment would continue over the period 1661–1714. For example, 'serjeant trumpetter' John Shire, and 'the rest of his majesty's trumpetters', had to put in a special post-coronation petition in 1714 in the hope of receiving their 'sum of ten pounds; and also the sum of sixty six pounds and three shillings and four pence'.[123] Crown and State finances functioned on a system of credit. Vast coronation expenditure thus had to be managed within that culture—another indication of how far-reaching the ramifications of coronations were.

We should recall that expenditure, for private individuals and institutions, began to accrue before a coronation, in terms of costs involved in applying to the Court of Claims for the right to perform certain offices, and that fees and perquisites were often paid late. Even State servants suffered delays. For instance, on 26 August 1661, four months after the coronation, Thomas Townsend, clerk of the Great Wardrobe, told Lord Sandwich that he had

> solicited both the lord treasurer, and the chancellor of the Exchequer for moneys to satisfy the creditors of the Wardrobe, but hitherto in vain. [And that he had] [p]rocured the king's attention to the matter by means of the lord chamberlain, but still has little hope of any money until after Michaelmas. Out of the order for £6,000 upon the coronation account, [we] ha[ve] received as yet only £2,505.[124]

It is clear that this Wardrobe account would not be settled until well into 1662. It was also not unknown for claims for fees to be dismissed altogether, as was the case for the Earl of Lindsey in 1689, who complained to Lord Danby of William III's rejection of his request for payment of coronation fees.[125] Incidentally, but importantly, these figures also verify the argument advanced earlier in this chapter, namely that coronation costs must have been far higher than those suggested by Strong. It would be very surprising indeed if the outlay for George I's coronation was only £1287 more than the sum covered by a single payment to creditors for Wardrobe expenses regarding the 1603 coronation.

Given an impoverished Crown and the likelihood of coronation debts, earlier kings had resorted to money-making expedients. Charles I notoriously attempted to recoup money by imposing fines on individuals for failing to accept knighthoods at his 1626 coronation. This practice was known as Distraint of Knighthood. Research for this book has uncovered several Yorkshire receipts for these fines. For example Samuel Clough of Halifax paid his '10 pound … fine for not receaving the order of knighthood at his ma[jes]t[ie]s coronation' as late as 23 September 1630[126]; Francis Popelay of Gommersall finally relieved his debt of £10 that same day[127]; and Miles Dodson of Kirkby Overblow discharged his £15 11*s.* 11*d.* fine on 25 September.[128] As late as 4 December 1630, John Ogle of Causey Park finally settled his debt for similarly refusing a knighthood.[129] These figures are small, but the total funds raised were substantial. Leonard's detailed study found that by the end of June 1630 £11,767 had been extracted from 728 men in this way. He concludes that 'in a sense Charles I's knighthood business could be deemed a success. Between 1625 and 1635 it was the largest single source of extraordinary revenue apart from the sale of Crown lands, the five subsidies of 1628 and (by a slight margin) the loan at the rate of five subsidies'. He records that £173,537 had been gathered by Easter 1635.[130] Here again, the afterlife of a coronation was long indeed, both for those fined and for the commissioners under Wentworth (Sir Thomas, 1st Earl of Strafford) who had to pursue debtors.[131]

More Indirect Costs: Robes and Liveries

As just noted, there could be indirect costs that might affect many people. Such costs are easily forgotten. Another category, also easily neglected, involved outlay on robes and liveries, something that ended in 2023 with peerage no longer invited en masse as in days of yore.[132] For those courtiers attending the coronation, and especially those raised to new levels, being furnished with correct attire was clearly important. For example, Sir Horace Townshend, elevated to a barony (1660/1661), incurred expenses for the 'preparation of robes' for the coronation and for parliamentary use—there were two distinct sets.[133] Lord Hatton spent £12 alone on his coronation robes.[134] These were exceptionally lavish in order to highlight the wearers' elite status: Lord Leigh of Stoneleigh spent £25 on 16 April 1685 'in respect for ermine for a coronation robe, 15*s.* for making a cap and tassel and £2 for making a robe'.[135] These were not insignificant sums. Expenses also included the costs of equipping staff. For liveries for his footmen at the 1661 coronation, the Earl of Southampton paid £8 15*s.*

Fig. 6.4 Lithograph with hand-colouring: view of Trafalgar Square, looking towards the National Gallery, during Queen Victoria's coronation procession; crowds of people stand and cheer at a royal carriage drawn by eight white horses followed by soldiers on horseback, 1838 (The British Museum Images)

0*d.*[136] In many cases, costume expenses were accounted for in the following year. We see this in the case of Fergus Kennedy, factor to the Earl of Cassillis: relevant expenditure is recorded in the 1634 accounts for the 1633 Edinburgh coronation. It is important, therefore, for historians not to restrict themselves to coronation years alone.[137]

Coronation Ticketing

Coronations were 'must see' events, but, beyond invited guests, it was difficult to gain access to the Abbey. As early as James II's coronation, one needed entry tickets.[138] However, this did not stop 'curiosity': either discussion about admission or attempts to find a way to gain a view, as recorded in the following exchange, which indicates Bernard's keenness to witness this grandest of occasions:

> As to your query; it wil[l] be very difficult to gett a place in the abby, so as to see with any kind of advantage the ceremony of anointing [and] crowning ... the gallery ... boxes ... the theater being allotted for for[e]ign ministers, the lords [and] ladyes [and] other persons concerned in the solemnity, [and] the other scaffolds [and] the corridere, ... along the church being taken up already ...[,] but little to bee seen at that distance. But most agree that the procession will bee best seen in the street, w[i]ch will bee the most glorious part of the shew, ... affect to bee present at, rather than bee in the church or hall.[139]

As Smith explains, the best spot for observing the procession was the street, as in modern times. In the end, Bernard could not attend the coronation, but Smith did and in a letter from London of 30 April 1685 recounted that Bernard 'would not have repented of [his] journey'.[140] Places to view 'the proceedings at the coronation from Westminster Hall to the Abbey and thence to the hall again to dinner' could cost as much as 8*s.* in 1685, but that was worth it, for, according to Andrew Allam, 'the sight was splendid and great'.[141] Such was the commemorative and sentimental value of coronation tickets that they were evidently treasured and still survive, such as the heavily embossed version for George IV's 1821 coronation and examples from Queen Victoria's 1838 coronation are also extant.[142]

Firework Celebrations

Music is often associated with coronations—all the more so after 1727, given the success of Handel's *Zadok the Priest*; Range calls it a 'concert coronation'.[143] But apart from music, the most spectacular feature to jolt the public 'senses' was the enormous firework display that had become traditional, as was the case in 1838 for Queen Victoria. There is also some evidence for local displays, such as records for the purchase of saltpetre in 1684/1685.[144] Fireworks were not unique to coronations: James I spent £2880 alone for Thames fireworks for Elizabeth Stuart's marriage in 1613.[145] Yet, how did these pyrotechnics have an impact, if, as we all know, fireworks are so evanescent, lasting for seconds or minutes, and in events not many hours from beginning to end? There are two main reasons. Firstly, coronation firework displays were on another level: surpassing anything normally seen by the public: in 1661, the coronation and the fireworks the day after were of a 'sumptuousness ... [that] exceeded the glory of what hath passed of the like kind in France'.[146] Secondly, they had an afterlife in print, with images reproduced in official accounts. Examples include Sandford's detailed record of James II's coronation and Romeyn de Hooghe's Dutch print of the accession of William and Mary, published in London, Hamburg, and the Netherlands in 1689. There is also a print showing firework celebrations held in The Hague for William III's accession.[147] These massive displays were not to be missed—they were certainly worth the journey to London, as viscount Mountjoy reported to the duke of Ormond in anticipation of the event on 15 April 1685: one should come 'to see the coronation w[i]th all the fireworks'.[148] Such was the impact of these particular coronations that Elizabeth I of Russia was to have a similar display at her coronation in 1742; it is reproduced in the same fashion as the British occasions.[149] In that regard, Britain was something of a trendsetter for these magnificent sky illuminations, and later 'festival or fête books'.[150]

Provincial Celebration: 'The Ripple Effect'

The Westminster Abbey coronation and metropolitan festivities were accompanied by nationwide celebrations. Harris has highlighted how, after the Restoration, numerous Irish corporations 'enthusiastically commemorated the anniversaries of both the coronation and the Restoration each year, providing alcohol for the local inhabitants and encouraging the construction of bonfires'.[151] Cressy shows, regarding the Stuart calendar, just how prevalent this custom of celebration and commemoration was.[152] Ralph and Tresidder have independently looked at aspects of this localism, but with a narrow focus: either on the records themselves, or from a municipal perspective beginning in 1685, not 1661.[153] This Chapter builds on those foundations, with a broader aim of analysing provincial celebration more widely and, in so doing, showing that the country at large remembered these occasions regardless of their distance from the metropolis.

In Oxford, in 1685, the 'coronation was celebrated … with great solemnity, both at St Mary's [and at] the Theatre; Dr Hall [master of Pembroke College, later bishop of Bristol] was appointed to preach, who gave … a very excellent sermon, upon Rom. 13:5'.[154] In 1689, Bath commemorated William and Mary's coronation, memorialised in prints.[155] Receipts demonstrate people spending £1 12*s.* 6*d.* on 'beer and tobacco'—the early modern 'street party'—in Stratford-upon-Avon for Anne's coronation; here, rich and poor both celebrated, an insight into the social profile, which, as we see below, has been investigated by Tresidder.[156] Such celebrations were witnessed in different parts of the realm. For instance, the City of Chester Assembly organised coronation day celebrations for Britain's new Hanoverian dynasty in 1714.[157]

In Nottingham, common council minutes evidence coronation preparations. On 27 January 1626, it agreed that 'bells shalbe ronge att everie churche, and bonfires made in the streets, to shewe the people's rejoycinge on the day of the king's corona[t]ion'.[158] We find the same picture for Anne's coronation: on 14 April 1702, shops were searched 'for silk convenient to make 2 banners ... [and to] prepare ... [for] the corona[t]ion'. However, on this occasion, when the solemnity was over,

> there [was to] be a treat of wyne provided att th[e] hall for the better sort of people to drink the queens health and likewise an hogshead of ale for the poore. And that M[aste]r Chamberlain do prepare one dozen and one halfe bottles of canary, 3 dozen of whitewine and 3 dozen of claret for the purposes of the aforesaid and likewise halfe an hogshead of ale for the town officers, constables, halberdmen ... and 5 dozen of French rolls and ten dozen of white bread.[159]

Although celebrations occurred throughout the kingdom, even on these national occasions wealth and status might determine the extent of participation. The division between rich and poor, in urban areas, has been explored by Tresidder in a detailed study of elite hegemony and local relations in connection with coronation day festivities. Although one has reservations about aspects of his case, which cannot be explored here, the foregoing Nottingham example from 1702 neatly fits his thesis, namely that gradually 'during the late seventeenth and early eighteenth centuries, coronation celebrations communicated the dominance of the Corporation, the gentry, and the economic magnate in the urban hierarchy'.[160]

One of the best known accounts of local coronation celebrations was that for Bath, recorded by Celia Fiennes (1662–1741). She visited that city in 1687, or possibly earlier, but her description of these festivities dates from the celebrations on 23 April 1702. Fiennes highlighted the fact that the mayor and 'officers[,] masters and wardens'—in other words, the mercantile elite—organised a grand march; she particularly noted the important role of women in the procession. With leading Bath figures away at the Westminster coronation, municipal officials took charge, temporarily elevated to senior posts. Fiennes shows how colourful such a display must have been for contemporaries, perhaps not unlike the Notting Hill Carnival of today. For example, there were 'flag[s,] ... plummes of feathers[,] ... young men ... with ... ribons in their hatts; [women] with ... wastecoate[s of] gold lace ... peticoates [of] silk ... [and] ribons' a plenty.[161] People carried items bearing the 'inscription, God save Queen Ann'.[162] Imitating metropolitan proceedings, 'two maides [carried] two sceptres gilt, next them two more that bore the crown between them, which was gilt also ... followed ... [by] the troupe'.[163] The procession was supplied with 'all sorts of pretious stones [from] the Jewellers shops', resulting in the replica crown being 'very rich in pearles'.[164] The whole community seems to have been involved in this celebration with more people following: 'their number was also about 100 ... next after followed all the young men of the town form'd into a company of granadeers with their proper officers ... red cap ... scarlet ... their number was about 30'.[165] Then, consistent with English tradition, came 'four couple of maurice dancers'.[166] A coronation celebration Bath-style had 'danceing all the way' and a sense of folklore; at the same time, it also had official local religious and city legitimisation in the presence of 'the clergy ... M[aste]r Major [Mayor] ... the Corporation, aldermen [dressed] ... in their scarlet gowns and [the] com[m]on councill in their gowns' too.[167] The proceedings, like those in the capital, were accompanied by sound-effects: 'drums of all sort[s] [and] of musick both wind and stringed instruments'; artillery noise emanating from 'two blunderbusses' was also audible.[168] With the arrival of the procession for a service at Bath Abbey, 'the granadeers salute[d] them just as they enter[ed] the abby with a volley of shott' and, emulating Westminster Abbey practice, they heard 'a sermon'.[169] The departing march from Bath Abbey was marked by 'artillery salutes [and] ... another volley, as it returned 'to [the] Guild Hall where [there was] ... a sumptuous feast with musick and danceing'.[170] This banquet concluded the day's formal ceremonies. Everyone had played their part. Some would have had better positions than others, and we have seen that there were clearly defined processional roles; nevertheless, the event was not solely intended for the elite.

Such scenes were paralleled in other parts of the country. For example, in Bristol, which had a long history of laying on coronation celebrations.[171] Records of Common Council meetings 1670–1722 reveal considerable outlay in these commemorations. Moreover, one entry refers to James II as 'the kings most excellent ma[jes]tie ... by the grace of God[,] king of Great Brittain[,] France and Ireland'. Is this evidence of diligent copying of some document giving the new royal style or does it indicate a stronger sense of **British** nationhood at a comparatively early date? It is hard to tell. Perhaps 'Defender of the Faith' had also been added more in hope than anything else.[172] Local celebrations such as Bristol's highlight the aspirations and fears harboured by people living far beyond Westminster; there was considerable concern over James II's Roman Catholicism. The Common Council and city chamberlain were responsible for much of the expenditure. In 1685, for James II's coronation, they paid for 'two hogshead of claret costing £11 5*s.* [in order] that the four conduits should run with wine'.[173] In 1702, they spent £12 11*s.* 11*d.* with the intention 'that the day be observed in this city with the utmost pomp, splendour and solemnity'; as in London, children represented institutions, and here the boys of Queen Elizabeth's Hospital processed in their 'blue gowns and coats'.[174] For George I, the Corporation of Bristol made a 'humble address [for his] happy accession to the Brittish throne [and the] many nationall blessings' that they felt this brought.[175] In 1714, an impressive £55 was spent on 'rejoycing this day', combining musical entertainment, food, beer, and tobacco.[176] Artillery fire, like church bells, advertised celebrations, and £19 11*s.* 4*d.* was spent on 'fireing the guns at the king's coronation'; £2 6*s.* 6*d.* was also spent 'on fireing the guns' on Brandon Hill.[177] One didn't just wish to celebrate the occasion: one also wished to tell the whole region that celebrations were in order. Evidently, rejoicing was widespread. George IV's coronation in 1821 would see similar such celebrations in Leeds, with 'free beer and food for workers as well as gun salutes, decorated public buildings, ringing church bells and parades through the city … [with] the real highlight of the day … as … Volunteers marched out of town together with regular troops stationed in the city. Under the eyes of about twenty thousand people, the troops celebrated the occasion … with the presentation of flags and standards …[.]'[178]

Churchwardens' accounts reveal local commemoration at parochial level. In Titchfield, Nottinghamshire, 10*s.* was spent on 'payments for ringers … and flags for coronation day' in 1661.[179] In Nottingham, in the parish church of St Mary, the sexton, John Elliot, was given 'the sume of tenn *s.* for ringing on the coronation day' of Queen Anne in 1702.[180] In All Saints parish Bristol, 12*s.* 6*d.* was spent on ringing 'the day the queen was crowned upon' and this was accompanied by expenditure of 4*d.* for 'carrying the wine' that was to be consumed.[181] Such coronation-related payments often exceeded those for proclaiming the accession of a monarch, for instance in 1702, All Saints parish Bristol spent 8*s* and in 1714 just 6*s* for ringing in the accession of Queen Anne and George I, respectively—in both cases less than that for the coronation of Queen Anne in 1702.[182] Charles II's birthday became synonymous with his Restoration and 29 May continued to be celebrated into the eighteenth century: in Christ Church Bristol, for example, 15*s*. was spent on bell-ringing.[183] In Sussex, Horsham parish 'payd the ringers on coronation [day] – 12*s*.' in 1703, the year after Anne's St George's Day crowning; the date had become a fixture in the national calendar, a continuation of the Elizabethan and Stuart tradition of remembering 'crownation' days.[184] To put this payment into context, it was matched in Horsham for Anne's birthday, but exceeded by payment for the 'ringers for [the] Gunpowder Plot … [of] £1 [and] 10*s*.'.[185] Protestant sensibilities concerning the memorialisation of 5 November made that perhaps the only event to weigh (for some) more heavily than crownation day, at least in this locality. The tradition of parochial coronation celebration was as evident in 1714 as it had been in 1661. Thornbury (Gloucestershire) spent £9 on 'ale att the coronation of King George', an indication of considerable rejoicing.[186] Christ Church Bristol marked nearly all the formal royal occasions of 1714: on 3 August, the churchwardens 'paid for ringing when King George was proclaimed'; on 7 August, 12*s*. for 'tolling the bell when the Queen [Anne] was buried'; on 18 September, 12*s*. 6*d*. for the 'king's landing'; and 15*s*. for George I's coronation on 20 October (the same payment as for ringing on 5 November).[187] For George I's reign, St Peter the Less in Chichester paid 2*s*. for 'ringing when his ma[jes]tie was proclemed', and '£1 3*s*. … on crownation day'.[188] In this case, the disbursement exceeded the '2*s*. p[ai]d for the ringing [in remembrance of the] Gunpowder Plot'.[189] These payments continued the following year, if slightly reduced: on 3 August, '2*s*. … [were] paid for the ringing on King Georges proclamation day'; on 20 October, 2*s*. 6*d*. were paid to ringers for the coronation day; and 2*s*. 1*d*. were paid for bell-ringing to commemorate 5 November.[190] What conclusion can be drawn from these examples? The nationwide church bell-ringing 'helped to make these … celebratory dates … both musical and memorable'; in this way, the pealing of bells became politicised, either actually or potentially, as a tool of the establishment.[191] Bell-ringing, once used to announce saints' days, assumed new meaning in sounding for 'England's monarchs and their moments of remarkable deliverance', a custom that was taken up with increased vigour for Elizabeth I.[192] Nevertheless, one should be careful before seeing these as a secularising development. With pervasive beliefs in providentialism and the Divine

Right of Kings, parishes saw these days as holy ones for the queen—each was 'a quasi-religious occasion'.[193] Commemorative bell-ringing in general, and not for Elizabeth I in particular, did not end in 1714, for the bells continued to peal in the 1710s and beyond.[194] Such was the national significance of crownation day, both politically and religiously, that it was even cited in formal documents and in surprising contexts. For example, in Norwich a legal document connected with a prosecution, issued on 23 October 1718, referenced a recent felony as having taken place on crownation day.[195]

Whilst it would be impossible in a single volume to tackle Commonwealth and Empire celebrations for the history of British coronations—the scale and number would be too vast to include here—it is worth noting various important events of 1911 and 1924 in terms of occasions in which the coronation (and associated celebrations) echoed outwards both here and abroad. 1911, which had seen George V's coronation on 22 June at Westminster Abbey, was followed by the 'so-called Coronation Durbar' in India in December of that year, 'the only time that … [a British] empress or emperor' made such a journey to the Raj.[196] Yet, similar efforts were made to extend the reach of the celebrations. George V was 'the only reigning British emperor to visit his Empire' and as such the Durbar, in 'Mughal style' had 'great symbolic importance and a special crown was made [for] the occasion, the Imperial crown of India … of gold and silver and covered in diamonds, rubies, emeralds and sapphires'.[197] Whilst efforts to cement British rule in India were at the forefront of these plans, back home an equally important task was at hand, for the 'king-emperor's subjects … were invited to a show designed to educate them about the empire', the Festival of Empire in London.[198] The exhibition took place between 12 May 1911 and 28 October 1911, 'in and around Paxton's Crystal Palace, which had been moved from Hyde Park and erected in an enlarged form in Sydenham in Kent in 1854'.[199] Visitors could travel 'for a mile and a half on an electric train called the All Red Tour, the name picking up on the "All Red Line", the common designation for the telegraph that linked all the territories of the British Empire', thus taking in a 'landscape' from Canada to New Zealand.[200] In 1924, this educational mission continued with the Wembley 'British Empire Exhibition' and 'Pageant of Empire'—again part of a plan to 'convince the British people of their mission' to continue to rule across much of the world.[201] It opened (as with many a coronation) on St George's Day 1924 and was extended until the conclusion of October in 1925. In that time, '[t]wenty-seven million people visited the exhibition'.[202] In Watanabe-O'Kelly and Simonelli's view, from 'the latter part of the nineteenth century and … after World War I, the concept of a commonwealth began to be promoted as a way of redefining the notion of empire'.[203] Here again, we see the reach of a coronation and in turn a new positioning in terms of the creation of the commonwealth and Britain's role in the world.

Reportage

As we saw in Chap. 2, coronation sermons publicised a distinct agenda, while this chapter has shown that coins and medals spread the monarch's image. Coronations were also an opportunity to be seen in the flesh: a fact worth reporting. We turn, therefore, to the important subject of reportage. Coronation spending was a public statement of the magnitude of a State's resources, of its strength, of its religious zeal, of its diplomatic intentions, and of its claims to dominion. These things also merited wider notice. Official accounts, diplomatic dispatches, newspapers, letters and prints, and diaries largely made up the reportage of such events, and these categories will be discussed in turn.

Official Accounts and Spin-Offs

Coronation sermons as discussed in Chap. 2 were printed and distributed, and became publications of interest and value, like a borrowable present and the luxury of exotic tea in the early eighteenth century. On 1 May 1702, Sir Thomas Rawlinson wrote to John Seeley in London:

> I have here sent you some Bohea tea, as a present which I desire your acceptance, I know itt to be good and very wholsome, and the sermon preached att the coronation of Queen Anne which you may lend, butt not to give it away, but to keep it.[204]

Beyond sermons, however, important official publications commemorated the occasion. These are particularly significant because the monarch was often directly involved in overseeing the creation of these texts. They therefore tell us something of Crown priorities in terms of what a coronation was designed to present for public consumption, in terms of image and message. In the Introduction, the works of Ogilby, Sandford, and Walker were discussed. It is unnecessary to retrace those steps, but concentrating on Ogilby, several key points can be made.

One, in order to generate the 'official' publication, Ogilby petitioned Charles II in March 1661, roughly a month before the coronation. He sought the 'priviledge' so as 'to prevent the false relations, which, if not prohibited, wilbe made of it, to the disadvantage of so great a solemnity, [and] the prejudice of your pet[ison]ers design therein, w[hi]ch is only to represent it to the world suitably to [th]e greatnesse thereof'. Ogilby was anxious to acquire a monopoly.[205] Two, Charles II instituted a censorship, whereby the 'Garter Principal King of Armes' was to review Ogilby's efforts. This was not an option, but rather a command:

> Our expresse will … is that you do not print or publish the said proceedings and ceremony or any part thereof, until the same has been viewed[,] corrected and approved by him the said S[i]r Edward Walker[.][206]

Therefore, not only does this evidence a censorship protocol, but it also reveals the Crown's anxiety that people encounter an approved version of the ceremony. By implication, Ogilby's was a mouth-piece for the restored monarchy: with an emphasis on regality, on imperialism, on magnificence, and above all, on Crown power. Three, once happy with Ogilby's work, Charles reinforced his monopoly rights in a license of 25 May 1665, three years after publication. This copyright set out to

> prohibit, and forbid all our subjects to reprint the said books in any volumes, or any of them; or to copy or counterfeit any the sculptures or ingravements therein, within the term of fifteen years.[207]

The order was under the sign manual, indicating the king's direct involvement. It also shows that Ogilby's work was still perceived by both writer and Crown as important enough to protect for such a long period. The coronation in this official publication lived on, long after 23 April 1661.

Official accounts were extremely important in setting out royal priorities, but they make up a small percentage of coronation reportage. Indeed, it is in other media, that we gain a wider sense of what a coronation meant to those beyond the Crown. Initially, we turn to those diplomats and foreign dignitaries who perhaps reported their eye-witness impressions.

Diplomatic Dispatches

Most published calendars of foreign State Papers do not go as late as would help with this type of research and manuscript dispatches reveal yet further material to explore in due course, though that in itself would be a volume too.[208] In the meantime, it is important to note the extent of foreign representation and therefore the **potential** number of descriptions, of which some unknown proportion might be presumed extant. Valuable insights come from two sources: Ogilby's, *Entertainment* (1662), and the Calendar of Treasury Books for April 1685, where one item (27 April) lists foreign dignitaries to whom coronation medals were to be distributed. Information drawn from various sources is given in Table 6.15.

The rising number of representatives, and from a larger range of countries, is especially notable. Britain's role on the European stage, and indeed worldwide, had changed radically by 1714. Consequently, the importance of diplomatic representation had grown correspondingly. Coronations, in short, were becoming more internationalist.

As a foretaste of what might be discovered upon further investigation, there is a valuable report submitted by a Venetian representative on Charles II's coronation in 1661.[209] It is useful because it discloses what he thought most important to record for the benefit of his masters in Venice, namely that the coronation was:

> so desired by his [Charles II's] subjects, with all possible splendour and decorum, no one sparing his money to make it exceptional and memorable for ages to come, and it was certainly the most conspicuous solemnity that has ever been seen in this realm.[210]

He went on to say, that the metropolis was 'decorated in the most delightful manner', with several triumphal arches, which had taken months to create. There was much music and bonfire-making: 'abundant evidence of rejoicing and consolation'. He observed the extent to which the realm was represented in the Abbey, in the shape of peers, judges, and magistrates. Most significantly, Charles was 'consecrated and crowned', which reinforces Chap. 5's argument about quasi-sacerdotalism. Other foreign representatives were noted too, as well as the concluding distribution of coronation medals. In terms of measuring impact, one report is obviously not conclusive, but the Venetian representative went out of his way to record that all transpired to 'great satisfaction of the people'. The king also held audiences with diplomats. Finally, he estimates the far from inconsiderable expenditure of these foreign dignitaries. For example, 'the Spanish ambassador ... must have spent over [£]3000'. However, he himself disbursed '[£]215 ... in accordance with the Senate's instructions'.[211] A

Table 6.15 Diplomatic representation (States rather than individuals) at the coronations of Charles II, James II, and George I

State	*1661*[a]	*1685*[b]	*1714*[c]
Brandenburg	*	*	
Cologne		*	
Denmark	*	*	*
Florence		*	
France	*	*	*
'Genova'	*	*	*
Hamburg	*		
Hanover		*	
Hesse Homberg	*	*	
Holland		*	*
Holstein			*
Holy Roman Emperor			*
Modena		*	*
Nassau	*	*	
Neuburg		*	
Orleans	*		
Palatine [Rhine Palatinate][d]	*		*
Parma			*
Poland			*
Portugal	*	*	*
Prussia			*
Russia			*
Savoy		*	
'Saxe'		*	*
Sicily			*
Spain	*	*	*
States of the Dutch Republic			*
Sweden	*	*	*
'Treves'		*	
Tripoli (part of Ottoman Empire)			*
Tuscany			*
Venice	*	*	*
Total	13	19	21

[a]Ogilby, *Entertainment* (1662), p. 175
[b]Shaw, *Treasury Books*, VIII pp. 135–59 (27 April 1685)
[c]*Ibid.*, XXIX pp. 730–42 (12–15 September 1715). It should be noted that this information is from several months after the coronation and relates to medals to be distributed to those foreign dignitaries present at the coronation. This raises an interesting question. It could be that although some medals were produced for the 1714 coronation, they may not have been distributed to ambassadors at that time. There were anxieties over the quality of medals, so that may have been the reason. If they were definitely distributed in 1714, then it is hard to explain why another round was made only eleven months later
[d]Probably Rhine Palatinate because of the family connection with James I's daughter Elizabeth (the Winter Queen) who married the elector of the Rhine

dispatch of 28 May shows that the Senate was satisfied with his report and provided generous reimbursement:

> To relieve him of the expenses in connection with this ceremony they have decided to give him a present of 500 ducats.[212]

Although highlights will have varied from person to person, this evidence at least hints at what might be available in this class of record. It is certainly clear that a coronation was a 'must see' spectacular, perceived by some to have a quasi-sacerdotal dimension.

Newspapers

Newspaper material has been used throughout this book. During the late sixteenth and seventeenth centuries it is 'widely accepted [by historians] that the amount of published information about politics and current affairs was progressively increasing'.[213] One question here is to what extent newspapers covered coronations and disseminated news about them. *The London Gazette*, *Mercurius Publicus*, and the *Evening Post* all contributed to coronation reportage. Indeed, it seems clear that public interest fuelled the expansion of print culture. As Ian Atherton states in a remarkable example,

> even imprisonment in a foreign land could not dull the appetite for news: English prisoners-of-war in 1666 had *The London Gazette* smuggled into their Rotterdam gaol as beer-bottle stoppers.[214]

The London Gazette (founded in 1665) was effectively a Crown organ and, as discussed elsewhere in this book, noted the forthcoming coronation date, meetings of the Court of Claims, and even the oath texts for William III and Mary II. Following each coronation, it reported the details: the account of James II's coronation emerged within days.[215] However, the practice was to stress the order of events, rather than personal perceptions. What is more interesting on the other hand are accounts of local celebrations.[216] These notices clearly gave readers a more extensive sense of what was going on beyond their immediate locality than almost anything else could have done. For instance, *The London Gazette* issue of 30 April 1685 noted that in Nottingham 'the 23 instant being the day of their majesties royal coronation, was observed here as followeth': with a military march, a mayoral parade, which was accompanied with 'acclamations of long live

King James the Second, and all expressions of joy'. Not only was the town hall arranged for loyal toasts, but so too

> about all the crosses there was planted vessels of ale that the common sort might drink the king and queens healths, which they did heartily. There were … tables furnished for all commers. The day was spent in musick and feasting, and the night in ringing of bells, bonfires, and fireworks, the town not sparing for any charge or pains to express their loyalty and satisfaction to be governed by so glorious a monarch.[217]

The street-party style commemorations of 2016 for the Queen's ninetieth birthday would not have been so far removed from such celebrations in the seventeenth and early eighteenth centuries. Newspapers undoubtedly played their parts in creating publicity. In this instance, they tell us more of what was going on in the country and, indeed, from a crown position, what they hoped was happening and what they wanted readers to hear. Bonfires and bells were certainly fitting. With wider mass media and an empire to feed on news, the nineteenth and twentieth centuries saw illustrated editions and mass publications covering the coronation. At accession, Queen Victoria appeared as such a '[y]oung, female, attractive, [and] politically innocent' monarch, so 'far removed from the excesses of her aged Hanoverian uncles' that numerous 'poems, prints and street ballads were produced, all effusively idealising Victoria'. Perhaps of all 'the most striking elements of the sentiment around Victoria in the first years of her reign was the way in which it was conceived of as being driven by the growth of a commercially orientated print and visual culture'.[218] In 1937, the *Illustrated London News* 'produced the lavish folio-size Coronation Record Number, costing five shillings and containing both colour and black and white photographs' for George VI. A similar version was made for Elizabeth II in 1953.[219]

Given the volume of material available, these can only be preliminary findings.[220] Nevertheless, what has been examined here shows the development and later proliferation of media, not just reporting news, but driving the agenda, in part politically, in part financially. This aspect is made all the more interesting by the fact that the system was hardly unique to Britain and began as early as the seventeenth century: for instance, the coronation of the duke of Braganza in 1640 as John IV of Portugal received significant coverage.[221]

Letters and Prints

The magnificence of coronations naturally provoked extensive letter writing. For example, Thomas Mason wrote to John Peirson on 20 March 1660/1661 of the 'great prepirations for his ma[jes]t[i]es coronatio[n]'.[222] Different parts of the realm were touched by the event: Henry Gascoigne in Dublin received news of the 'proceeding at the coronation' the following day, 24 April 1685.[223] In 1702, Sir Thomas Rawlinson wrote to Master Townson, in London, that 'her majest[y Queen Anne] is to be crown[e]d the 23 [of April] ... and great preperations are macking ... his majestie [the late William III] was buried ... Sunday night last, att Westminster Abey'.[224] Alongside other records, letters provide invaluable coronation information, underlining eager expectations:

> Great preparations are making at Westminster ... St George's Day [and] ... prayers [and] sermons are performed in K[ing] Henry the Eig[ths] chappele [and] ... the heralds ha[ve] their scheme ordered.[225]

So said Thomas Smith in a letter to Edward Bernard of 28 March 1685. Coronations were events that commanded public attention, both at home and abroad. Much more than a mere accession proclamation, they marked out the inauguration of a new reign, potentially advertising a fresh approach, in some cases that of a different dynasty. The arrival of a new monarch generated considerable international correspondence, as can be seen with William III and the Earl of Portland.[226] Foreign officials, statesmen, and royal figures were equally soaked up in the drama, all wishing to have their say. Some literature consists of standardised letters of 'congratulation' from other countries, such as the Republic of Geneva.[227] In a letter of 24 March 1684/1685, Laura, duchess of Modena (in Rome) corresponded with Sir Richard Bulstrode (British agent, later resident ambassador in Brussels), discussing the forthcoming coronation, the state of European affairs, religious devotion, and the prodigy of God in relation to her daughter and son-in-law.[228] Not only does this evidence show the spread of coronation-related news, but it also shows an awareness of political and religious implications too.[229] In this instance, if the Whigs were worried about James II's Roman Catholicism, then they had real cause for concern. Furthermore, whilst preparations were in hand, there was little hope of an alternative, given that one potential royal rival, the duke of Monmouth, was 'forbid coming to the Hague' so as to join forces with William of Orange, another potential claimant.[230] In 1702, Queen Anne's safe accession and coronation came at a time of European military conflict in the War of the Spanish Succession (1701–1714). Her coronation was designed to project English stability, and to stress the need for 'the preservation of the balance of Europe'.[231] George I's accession came against the backdrop of 'very great ... publick debts' and the existence of a real opponent in the shape of James Edward Stuart, the Old Pretender, and Jacobite plans for an imminent rebellion.[232] His coronation followed in the context of a series of tremendous military successes under Queen Anne, and growing imperial trade. It was therefore all the more important as a means of emphasising his legitimacy internationally; the ends were significant enough to justify the means.

These points were reinforced in George I's speech to both Houses of Parliament on 21 March 1714/1715, when he declared that this was the 'throne of [his] ancestors', of the 'Protestant succession'. He highlighted the 'unparallel'd successes of [recent] war' and 'the security and trade' that this had given 'Great Britain' and 'the nation' embodied in '[t]he established constitution in Church and State'.[233] Such news reached as far away as the Tuscan colony of Leghorn (Livorno), a fact noted by Hendriks, who writes that:

> The English colony at Leghorn in November, 1714, seems to have had amongst its number someone quite equal to a poet laureate in ability to give expression to joyful aspirations, and to glorifications, on the advent of a new British reigning house. I may add that my copy, probably unique, is printed on fine red satin, with well-displayed headings in capitals ... [The poem ends with the line] Giorgio il Grande Viva, Viva.[234]

A coronation was manifestly an opportunity to be seen and to represent a community, school, or town. For instance, the supporters to Mary of Modena, the 'boys of London and Winchester', were noticed by Andrew Allam when writing to Anthony Wood recounting what a 'splendid and great' occasion it had been.[235]

As prints, illustrations of coronations travelled widely, and were published internationally, as can be seen in an Italian account of James II's 1685 coronation, which was produced in Bologna and Naples.[236] News of the spectacular coronation banquets, which included over a thousand dishes in 1685, from 'salletting' to 'sweet meats', also spread extensively in the form of receipts.[237] Patrick Lamb, the royal chef, published a recipe book of royal cookery in 1710.[238] Besides place settings, it details receipts from jellies to fricassee of chicken and 'crawfish or lobster soupe'—this was most certainly the art and wealth of gluttony.[239]

Diaries

Diaries are an exceptionally important addition to coronation reportage. The crucial question is what did those writing them think worth recording? Eye-witness testimony by its very nature has to be selective, so the selection indicates perceived significance. Nevertheless, there are two aspects here, for it is not just what diarists chose to describe, but also how they do it that matters, i.e. what (if any) are their reflections on their descriptions. In this section, we shall analyse sequentially four diaries: those of Pepys; Evelyn; Lord Burlington and Cork; and Mary, Countess Cowper.[240]

We have already encountered Pepys as a coronation participant: he was a Cinque Port's representative in 1685. However, much better known is his account of impressions at the 1661 coronation of Charles II. For the pre-coronation cavalcade, he rose 'earely and made myself as fine as I could, and put on my velvet coat, the first day that I put it on, though made half a year ago'. In other words, this was a special occasion worthy of the best finery:

> It is impossible to relate the glory of this day, expressed in the clothes of them that rid, and their horses and horses clothes … embroidery and diamonds were ordinary among them.

Later that day, he took up a vantage point in a house in Cornhill (the street running between Bank junction and Leadenhall Street in the City of London) and was joined by his wife and colleagues from the Navy Office. They had 'wine and good cake, and saw the show very well'. This was a spectacle not to be missed.[241] For coronation day itself, Pepys provided a considerably longer diary entry. It is worth quoting extensively because of the remarkable view of Abbey proceedings that he (supposedly) enjoyed, possibly from the triforium.[242]

> [At] about 4[am] I rose and got to the Abbey, where I followed Sir J. Denham, the surveyor, with some company that he was leading in. And with much ado, by the favour of M[aste]r Cooper … did get up into a great scaffold across the north end of the Abbey, where with a great deal of patience I sat from past 4 till 11 before the king came in. And a great plea-

> sure it was to see the Abbey raised in the middle, all covered with red, and a throne (that is a chair) and footstool on the top of it; and all the officers of all kinds, so much as the very fidlers, in red vests.[243]

What we gain from this is the palpable sense of high expectations, akin to a supporter arriving early before a cup match final. Yet this is something more. Pepys arrived hours early, simply to have the opportunity of seeing his monarch crowned. In his eyes this was undoubtedly a 'must see' event. We also learn of the different aspects of the occasion, with various officials, surveyors to music makers, all coming together to make the day happen. Finally, after such a long wait the day proper began:

> At last comes in the dean and prebends of Westminster, with the bishops (many of them in cloth of gold copes), and after them the nobility, all in their Parliament robes, which was a most magnificent sight. Then ... the king with a scepter (carried by my Lord Sandwich) and sword and mond before him, and the crown too.[244]

Magnificence is a continuous theme throughout all our select diaries. This was a day of impressive proportions, in costume, regalia, and personnel. It must also be remembered that, for all those who had lived through the Civil Wars, Regicide, and the Commonwealth, this day cannot but have made a powerful impression. It completely confirmed the Restoration. Eventually, the monarch came into Pepys's view and he saw the ceremony played out, noting the following moments:

> The king in his robes [entered], bare-headed, which was very fine. And after all had placed themselves, there was a sermon and the service; and then in the Quire at the high altar, the king passed through all the ceremonies of the coronacon, which to my great grief I and most in the Abbey could not see. The crown being put upon his head, a great shout begun, and he came forth to the throne, and there passed more ceremonies: as taking the oath, and having things read to him by the bishop; and his lords (who put on their caps as soon as the king put on his crown) and bishops come, and kneeled before him. And three times the King at Arms went to the three open places on the scaffold, and proclaimed, that if any one could show any reason why Charles Stewart should not be king of England, that now he should come and speak. And a general pardon also was read by the lord chancellor, and meddalls flung up and down by my Lord Cornwallis, of silver, but I could not come by any.[245]

Two points stand out: Pepys's feelings at seeing his sovereign and the fact that the sermon is mentioned distinctly. This underlines the argument in Chap. 2 that the sermon was important in its own right and was not simply subsumed in the rest of the service. Moreover, the acclamation and rejoicing for the crowned monarch is emphasised, as is the central importance of the oath. What is intriguing is the wedding-like question as to whether or not anyone objects to the king as sovereign. Perhaps Pepys has merged this idea with the acclamation, for the recognition is not put in this way. What can we conclude? Arguably, it underlines the real contractual character that people recognised (or at least Pepys did) in a coronation. There was a legitimate sense that those present were consenting to this new monarch; it was not a fait accompli. Not only do we have an account of the coronation service, but also of the Westminster Hall banquet. Pepys noted the enormous crowd lining the streets outside:

> I went out a little while before the king had done all his ceremonies, and went round the Abbey to Westminster Hall, all the way within rayless, and 10,000 people, with the ground covered with blue cloth; and scaffolds all the way.[246]

Without duplicating what is quoted from the diary of Richard Boyle, 1st Earl of Burlington and 2nd Earl of Cork (1612–1698), Pepys's entry corroborates his in terms of the champion's challenge and the monarch drinking from the gold cup, which becomes the champion's perquisite. Pepys adds slightly more detail on the important people involved at the banquet: the Knights of the Bath carrying the first course to the king; the heralds taking part in 'fine ceremonies … leading up people before him, and bowing'—introducing people therefore to the sovereign; and the duke of Albemarle 'going to the kitchin and eat[ing] a bit of the first dish that was to go to the king's table'. Thus nothing was to be left to chance for the monarch's safety.[247] Pepys's concluding remarks at the end of such a long day are as near as one gets to evidence of impact:

> Now, after all this, I can say that, besides the pleasure of the sight of these glorious things, I may now shut my eyes against any other objects, nor for the future trouble myself to see things of state and show, as being sure never to see the like again in this world.[248]

Evelyn's diaries are also famous. However, it is easily forgotten that so enamoured was he with Charles II's crowning that he wrote a 'Panegyric' for the day, presenting it in the Privy Chamber to the king, 'which he was pleased to accept most graciously'. London's high society was delighted with proceedings and continued to party—Evelyn attended the marquess of Ormond's 'magnificent feast' the day after the coronation. The impact of the occasion seems to have permeated to many Londoners, for on 1 May, over a week after the main event, Evelyn reported that he 'went to Hyde Park to take the air, where was his majesty and an innumerable appearance of gallants and rich coaches, being now a time of universal festivity and joy'.[249]

Whilst these two diaries are standard works and confirm what the Venetian agent reported about the sumptuousness of events, other diaries yield further insights, especially about politics and wider impact, even if written by members of the social elite. Although this is a far cry from representativeness, in this case that is all to the good, for aristocratic authors were likely to have enjoyed a seat in the Abbey itself. Richard Boyle's neglected diary is a particularly good example for it covers the entire programme. Cork describes the sight of those assembled at the Tower of London on 22 April 1661 as

> the most splendid that has been, I thinke seen in Christendome … exce[e]d[ing] much the king of Frances entrance into Paris. My L[or]d Northumberl[an]d was that day l[or]d high constable, duke of Ormond l[or]d high steward, and ea[rl] of Suffolke l[or]d marshall, who carried the sword. The guards of horse marcht part in the front, and the other in the reare. The pensioners went on foote at each side by the king and the master of the horse led the kings hedde horse.
>
> The cittye stood in armes all the way wee past to Whitehall.

This passage highlights the significance of office-holding and the need to impress in a European context. Britain and London are compared to the age-old nemesis of France and Paris. Cork clearly appreciated who had been favoured with coronation positions. His entry for St George's Day is worth quoting in full, given the rare depiction of pre-coronation Westminster Hall proceedings, as well as the important role of homage within the service.

> At seven a clock wee all attended at the Painted Chamber where wee put on our robes, and all the barons had by the kings allowance libertye to weare velvet caps as the earles did, but without earles coronets but wee all wore a gold lace, and shall have permission to weare a coronet lesse than the viscounts. [A]bout nine of the clock all the peeres went in order as they had ridden the day before into Westminster Hall, where at the upper end the king seated himselfe untill the deane of Westminster the canons and the bushops attended him with the regalia which were upon a table delivred by the deane of Westminster to his ma[jes]ty who thus did distribute them. [A] scepter was given too my L[or]d Sandwich to carrye, the spurres to the ea[rl] of Pembroke a sword without a point drawne to the ea[rl] of Oxford. [A]nother to the ea[rl] of Darbye drawne with a point a 3d with a point & drawne to the ea[rl] of Shrewsberye, a second sceptre set w[i]th diamonds to the ea[rl] of Bedford. [A] 3d to the du[ke] of Albemarle with a dove on the top: The globe to the du[ke] of Bucking[h]am and the crowne richly set with jewells to the du[ke] of Ormond the anointing oyle to the bushop of London and the cover to the bushop of Exeter then wee all went two and two lords into Westminster thorogh the guards and there the king was crownd in the old marble chaire by the arch-bushop of Canterberye, which ceremonye I saw standing just by the chaire, after all the bushops kist the kings cheeke and of all the degrees of peers did the like, for everye degree, then everye peer put his hand upon the kings crowne, and all declared owning the king for king of England, and adhering to him.

What an impact the gold lace, coronets, and regalia must have had on onlookers, together with the peerage in their finery. Cork also noticed post-coronation events:

> The ceremony[s] ended wee returned to Westminster Hall, where the king dined and all the Lords at another table, the kings second course was ushered in by the l[or]ds high constable steward and marshall all on horseback and afterwards they brought in the kings champion Dimock … on horseback who threw downe his gantelet, chalenging any that denied the title of the king to [be] undoubted, That performed he advanced neer the king his launce being carried before him … his ma[jes]ty having drunke in a cup of gold, did send it to him who after hee had pledged him has the cup as a reward: The dinner ended, it lightned and thundred excessively[.][250]

This account assembles many of the different elements analysed in this book. The gold cup is a perquisite, again noteworthy to contemporaries, and in the closing remarks we have yet more evidence of the perceived power of the elements. There is nothing more for 24 April, for the Earl had clearly enjoyed himself too much: 'being tired with the two former days attendance[,] I kept my house all this day'.[251] His point about the changing weather is particularly interesting: the shift from pleasant conditions for most of the events to a stormy evening. The early modern *mentalité* interpreted these circumstances very differently: everything was viewed in terms of God's judgement on the world. We have another example from later in the period: for Queen Anne's 1702 coronation, the 'brightness of the day contributed to the splendo[u]r of the cavalcade and shewe that heaven smiled upon the placing of the crown of her ancestors on her royall head whom god grant long to wear it'.[252]

The reader is also fortunate to have a diary offering a female perspective: that of Mary, Countess Cowper (1685–1724), perhaps the most interesting of all.[253] Cowper began her famous diary shortly after George I's accession. She became a lady of the bedchamber to the Princess of Wales, affording almost unrivalled access at Court. Her account of the 1714 coronation emphasises the importance of religion, and the political imperative of legitimisation, given the Jacobite threat. In rather haphazard circumstances, with various ladies jostling for position, she felt that she had

> got … the best place in the Abbey, for I saw all the ceremony, which few besides did, and I own I never was so affected with joy in all my life; it brought tears into my eyes, and I hope I shall never forget the blessing of seeing our holy religion thus preserved, as well as our liberties and properties.[254]

She finishes with particularly striking lines on Jacobite sympathisers:

> One may easily conclude this was not a day of real joy to the Jacobites. However, they were all there, looking as cheerful as they could, but very peevish with everybody that spoke to them.[255]

What does this tell us? It is an amazing insight into the make-up of the Abbey congregation. It is surprising that such people were present, but, given the comprehensiveness of a coronation, it was hard for a courtier to actively avoid attendance. Furthermore, a coronation was a chance to unite those across the political spectrum, in an effort to bind the nation together at the beginning of a new reign.

From these instances, it is clear that, for those present, coronations were events of immense grandeur and religious significance, making an immediate and lasting impact. From costumes to feasting—whether formal Court events or the informality of street parties—this was a truly noteworthy occasion that made (at least on these writers) a substantial impression. Just as importantly in 1714, as it had been in 1661, there was a crucial political message too. For Cowper, the coronation instilled and cemented a Whig ideology: of the rights of citizens against arbitrary rule, and of Anglicanism against Roman Catholicism. This was not ceremonialism for ceremonialism's sake.

Conclusion

One of the most difficult tasks in preparing this chapter was piecing together estimated figures for coronation expenditure. Having done that in Part I, and shown the spending across all five coronations of 1661–1714, we can safely conclude that this was an event (or rather complex of events) that mattered enormously to both Crown and State—a fact insufficiently recognised by previous historians, who have based their interpretations on wildly inaccurate figures. These coronations did not see a decline in spending and, by extension, in importance. No doubt there were many other pressing demands on the public purse, especially militarily, yet these caused no diminution in funding for coronations. They were too important not to be seen as a sound investment. But what was this popular dimension? In Part II, we examined local celebrations, which were widespread, and a coronation's impact, both financially and as measured by reportage. Support for a new monarch was considerable. Strong argues that 'by 1702, what had begun as a ritual in Westminster Abbey was **well on the way** to becoming a day of national rejoicing'.[256] This chapter has demonstrated that coronation celebrations were **already** days of national rejoicing long before 1702: as Fiennes wrote, inter alia, it was 'bonfires as usual' that brought to a close the Bath rejoicings.[257] The crucial change that had occurred in the period covered by this book is that, by 1714, coronations had become days massively financed by the nation too.

Notes

1. Strong, *Coronation*, p. 458 see also https://www.nytimes.com/2003/03/11/opinion/IHT-1953coronation-costly-for-uk-in-our-pages100-75-and-50-years-ago.html, 11 March 2003, accessed 23 November 2025; see also J. Howard, 21-22 November 2024, https://www.bbc.co.uk/news/articles/c04lyddv2p5o, accessed 23 November 2025; C. Adams, 18 May 2023, https://www.bbc.co.uk/news/uk-65636772#:~:text=Local%20News-,Queen%20Elizabeth%20II%3A%20Funeral%20and%2010%20days,mourning%20cost%20government%20%C2%A3162m&text=Queen%20Elizabeth%20II's%20funeral%20and,11%20days%20after%20her%20death, accessed 23 November 2025.
2. https://www.nationalarchives.gov.uk/currency-converter, accessed 23 November 2025.
3. S. Carp, 4 March 2020, https://www.sportspro.com/news/2019-cricket-world-cup-uk-economy-impact-england-wales/, accessed 23 November 2025; B. Avison, 4 March 2020, https://www.hostcity.com/news/city-development/economic-impact-cricket-world-cup-2019-revealed, accessed 23 November 2025.
4. Skinner, 'The State', pp. 125–6.
5. It is extremely hard to calculate inflation during this period and to establish modern equivalents for early modern sums. This problem is made all the more difficult for coronations because we are not dealing with everyday items or expenses. For helpful works on inflation, see E. H. Phelps Brown and S. V. Hopkins, 'Seven Centuries of the Prices of Consumables, Compared with Builders' Wage-Rates', *Economica*, XXIII (1956), pp. 296–314; Phelps Brown, 'Gregory King's Notebook and the Phelps Brown-Hopkins Price Index', *The Economic History Review*, XLIII (1990), pp. 99–103. For an online mechanism for inflation calculations, see https://www.bankofengland.co.uk/monetary-policy/inflation/inflation-calculator, accessed 22 November 2025; and https://www.nationalarchives.gov.uk/currency-converter/, accessed 23 November 2025.
6. G. O. Nichols, 'English Government Borrowing, 1660–1688', *Journal of British Studies*, 10 (1971), pp. 83–104.
7. E. A. Reitan, 'From Revenue to Civil List, 1689–1702: The Revolution Settlement and the "Mixed and Balanced" Constitution', *The Historical Journal*, XIII (1970), pp. 571–88; *Ibid.*, 'The Civil List in Eighteenth-Century British Politics: Parliamentary Supremacy versus the Independence of the Crown, *The Historical Journal*, IX (1966), pp. 318–37; FSL, MS X.d.30 (43).

8. FSL, MS X.d.30 (43).
9. See particularly Keay, *Monarch*, and M. Lee, Jr., *The 'Inevitable' Union and Other Essays on Early Modern Scotland* (East Linton, 2003).
10. Gross, '1651: The Last Coronation in Scotland': https://www.tandfonline.com/doi/full/10.1080/14629712.2021.1996947#:~:text=The%20last%20Scottish%20coronation%20occurred%20at%20Scone%20in%201651, accessed 22 November 2025.
11. Madway, '"Solemnity"'; Schwoerer, 'Coronation'.
12. Hoak, 'Transformation', p. 124.
13. Uglow, *Gambling Man*, pp. 113–15; K. Sharpe, *Rebranding Rule: Images of Restoration and Revolution Monarchy, 1660–1714* (New Haven, Connecticut, 2013), p. 104. See also Sharpe, *Image Wars*, p. 232 (funeral costs of Elizabeth I and James I).
14. Adamson, 'Kingdoms', pp. 100–2; Smith, *Georgian Monarchy*, pp. 100, 106. Keay, *Crown Jewels*, p. 46.
15. Keay, Crown Jewels, p. 46.
16. On City of London finance, see Wren, 'London'.
17. Archer, 'Material Dimensions', p. 158.
18. *Ibid.*, p. 178.
19. *Ibid.*, pp. 175–6.
20. https://www.oxfordhistory.org.uk/mayors/government/coronation.html, accessed 22 November 2025. See also M. Toynbee, 'The City of Oxford and the Restoration of 1660', *Oxoniensia*, XXV (1961 for 1960), pp. 73–95; and [W. Robinson], *Collections Relative to Claims at the Coronations of Several of the Kings of England, Beginning with Richard II* (London, 1820), p. 74. Cf. Oxfordshire History Centre, Oxford, MS C/FC/1/A1/03, fol. 272r.
21. Archer, 'Material Dimensions', p. 179.
22. *Ibid.*, p. 160.
23. *Ibid.*, p. 159. See his tables on p. 161.
24. Archer, 'Material Dimensions', p. 161.
25. *Ibid.*, p. 164.
26. *Ibid.*, p. 165.
27. *Ibid.*
28. *Ibid.*
29. *Ibid.* See also Archer, 'Taxation'; and R. Schofield, 'Taxation and the Political Limits of the Tudor State', in C. Cross *et al.* (eds), *Law and Government Under the Tudors: Essays Presented to Sir Geoffrey Elton Regius Professor of Modern History in the University of Cambridge on the Occasion of his Retirement* (Cambridge, 1988), p. 232. See also BL, Add. MS 34321.

30. Archer, 'Material Dimensions', pp. 165–6. See also BL, Add. MS 58833, fol. 18v.
31. Archer, 'Material Dimensions', p. 166. For funerals, see L. Stone, *The Crisis of the Aristocracy, 1558–1641* (original edition, Oxford, 1965), pp. 784–5; R. Houlbrooke, *Death, Religion, and the Family in England, 1480–1750* (Oxford, 1998), pp. 261–3, 267–9; Cressy, *Ritual*, pp. 438–43; and P. S. Fritz, 'The Trade in Death: The Royal Funerals in England, 1685–1830', *Eighteenth-Century Studies*, 15 (1982), pp. 291–316. For the Lord Mayor's Show, see R. T. D. Sayle (ed.), *Lord Mayors' Pageants of the Merchant Taylors' Company in the 15th, 16th & 17th Centuries* (privately published, Reading, 1931), pp. 61–9; J. Robertson and D. J. Gordon (eds), *A Calendar of Dramatic Records in the Books of the Livery Companies of London, 1485–1640*, Malone Society Collections, III (London, 1954), pp. 61–8.
32. Archer, 'Material Dimensions', p. 174.
33. Strong, *Coronation*, pp. 353–419.
34. *Ibid.*, p. 372.
35. *Ibid.*, p. 371.
36. Cressy, *Bonfires*, *passim*.
37. Hutton, *Merry England*, p. 251.
38. C. Marsh, *Music and Society in Early Modern England* (Cambridge, 2010), pp. 480–1. See especially Cressy, *Bonfires*, pp. 50–66.
39. Ogilby, *Entertainment*, and Walker, *Circumstantial Account*. See also Ogilby, *Relation*.
40. Nichols, 'Borrowing', p. 83.
41. *Ibid.*, p. 89. See also TNA, SP 38/20 and SP 44/3, fol. 40r–v.
42. Nichols, 'Borrowing', p. 85.
43. Fraser, *Charles II*, pp. 198–9. See also Plumb & Wheldon, *Heritage*, p. 128.
44. Strong, *Coronation*, p. 350, citing Blair, *Jewels*, I pp. 389–91.
45. https://www.royalcollection.org.uk/collection/404951/charles-ii-1630-1685, accessed 23 November 2025.
46. Hutton, *Charles the Second*, p. 165. See also Adamson, 'Kingdoms', p. 101.
47. Ogilby, *Entertainment*.
48. Uglow, *Gambling Man*, p. 113.
49. Edie, 'Public Face', p. 318. See also Echard, *History*, III p. 734.
50. Strong, *Coronation*, p. 350, citing Blair, *Jewels*, I pp. 389–91.
51. Lenman, 'Exiled Stuarts', p. 187. See also Blair, *Jewels*, *passim*. See also Uglow, *Gambling Man*, p. 115; and H. D. W. Sitwell, 'The Jewel House and the Royal Goldsmiths', *The Archaeological Journal*, 117 (1960), pp. 131–55. On Sir Robert Vyner, see also NAL, V&A, English Non-Illuminated MSS 20, 25, 26; and Glamorgan Record Office, Cardiff, MS DCL/2/86.

52. *Ibid.* See also Legg, *Coronation Records*, pp. 283–96; Strong, *Coronation*; and Keay, *Monarch*, p. 5, noting that the crown is still used for coronations.
53. Lenman, 'Exiled Stuarts', p. 187.
54. Edie, 'Public Face', p. 313 (n. 10); BL, Stowe MS 580, fol. 5v; *ibid.*, Add. MS 37998, fol. 101r–v; A. P., *Coronations: Their Rise and Development in England* (Leeds, 1911), p. 42.
55. R. Cole (ed.), 'Particulars Relative to that Portion of the Regalia of England which was Made for the Coronation of King Charles the Second,' *Archaeologia*, 29 (1842), pp. 262–6.
56. TNA, LC 5/107, fols 79v–80v; *ibid.*, T 51/3, pp. 321, 330; *ibid.*, E 403/1761, fol. 58r–v; BL, Add. MS 44915, fols 3r–4v. See also printed format in Cole, 'Regalia'.
57. A. Barclay, 'The 1661 St Edward's Crown – Refurbished, Recycled or Replaced?', *The Court Historian*, 13 (2008), pp. 162–3.
58. Cf. Backscheider, *Spectacular Politics*, pp. 5, 13.
59. PML, MA Unassigned, Rulers of England Box 10, Charles II, Part 3, no 9.
60. Archer, 'Material Dimensions', p. 161.
61. *Ibid.*
62. D. Bergeron, *English Civic Pageantry, 1558–1642* (London, 1971), p. 73.
63. The Clothworkers' Company, Clothworkers' Hall, London, MS CL/B/1/9, fol. 168r–v.
64. Latham & Matthews, *Pepys*, II p. 83 (22 April 1661).
65. Uglow, *Gambling Man*, p. 113.
66. Sandford, *History*; Edie, 'Public Face'.
67. BL, Egerton MS 3350, fol. 11v.
68. Edie, 'Public Face', p. 318. See also Echard, *History*, III p. 734.
69. Edie, 'Public Face', p. 318.
70. BL, Add. MS 17019, fol. 43r–v.
71. E. A. Jones, 'Some Coronation Plate', *The Burlington Magazine*, 70 (1937), p. 246.
72. *Ibid.*, Item [48], p. 1 (Report to the sovereigns concerning coronation, William and Mary, 1689).
73. *Ibid.* See also TNA, Work 3/1, fol. 9r. For 1702 and instructions to Sir Christopher Wren see SAL, MS SAL/MS/444/3.
74. L. G. Schwoerer, 'Images of Queen Mary II, 1689–1694', *Renaissance Quarterly*, 42 (1989), pp. 717–48, reprinted in G. J. Schochet *et al.* (eds), *Restoration, Ideology, and Revolution*, The Folger Institute Center for the History of British Political Thought Proceedings, 4 (Washington DC, 1990), pp. 426–7 and Schwoerer, 'Coronation', p. 117.

75. CA, MS 'Coronations – Charles II/ James II/William & Mary', Item [48], p. 2.
76. Jones, 'Coronation Plate', p. 246.
77. *Ibid.*
78. Black, *Hanoverians*, p. 159.
79. Shaw, *Treasury Books*, XVII pp. 180–90.
80. TNA, SP 34/1/15, fol. 19r–v.
81. *CSP, Anne*, I, p. 27.
82. Shaw, *Treasury Books*, XVII pp. 191–203.
83. Sharpe, *Image Wars*, p. 232.
84. New York Public Library, New York, USA, MS 1214, Vol. I fol. 345r.
85. TNA, SP 34/1/16, fol. 20r–v. *CSP, Anne*, I p. 27; PML, MS Unassigned, Rulers of England Box 11B, Anne, no. 4.
86. Shaw, *Treasury Books*, XVII pp. 191–203.
87. Strong, *Coronation*, p. 350. See also Colvin, *King's Works*, V p. 454.
88. *Ibid.*, E 351/2847. See also *ibid.*, AO 1/2055/40.
89. *Ibid.*, E 351/3319. See also *ibid.*, AO 1/2448/148. Cotton's Gardens were named after Sir Robert Cotton, founder of the Cotton Library, and belonged to his family home, which lay in (or close to) the precincts of the Old Palace of Westminster: W. Thornbury and E. Walford, 'The Royal Palace of Westminster', *Old and New London: A Narrative of its History, its People, and its Places*, 6 vols ([London], 1873–1878), III pp. 491–502.
90. TNA, E 351/1874.
91. *Ibid.*, E 351/567. See also *ibid.*, AO 1/410/151. See also B. M. Zon, 'Croft, William (*bap.* 1678, *d.* 1727)', *ODNB* and Range, *Music*, pp. 126–7.
92. TNA, E 351/567. See also *ibid.*, AO 1/410/151.
93. *Ibid.*
94. *Ibid.*, E 351/3140. See also *ibid.*, AO 1/2368/146 and C 57/9.
95. TNA, E 351/567 (charges of John Incledon, housekeeper of Westminster Palace, for coronation preparations during Queen Anne's Lying-in-State). See also *ibid.*, AO 1/410/151.
96. Nichols, 'Borrowing', p. 104.
97. Smith, *Georgian Monarchy*, p. 100. See also TNA, PC 2/90/61, 70, 82–4, 88, 93–112; N. Sykes, *William Wake, Archbishop of Canterbury, 1657–1737*, 2 vols (Cambridge, 1957), II, pp. 186–7.
98. John Evelyn to his brother, 26 October 1727: formerly BL, SJE 10, possibly now in *ibid.*, Add. MS 78471, though seemingly misplaced.
99. J. Morrill, *'Uneasy Lies the Head that Wears a Crown': Dynastic Crises in Tudor and Stewart Britain 1504–1746* (Reading, 2005), p. 31. For a full exposition of the 'resentment' thesis, see Lee, *'Inevitable' Union.*

100. Harris, *Revolution*, p. 44.
101. Keay, *Monarch*, pp. 46–7.
102. W. D. Macray (ed.), *The History of the Rebellion and Civil Wars in England Begun in the Year 1641, by Edward, Earl of Clarendon*, 6 volumes (Oxford, 1888), V p. 172.
103. Further research is projected in order to paint the full picture.
104. NRS, MS E67/2/5. See also *ibid.*, MS E67/2/1 (Robert Russel's charge of the two months' maintenance in southern Scotland imposed by Act of Parliament for the king's use, 1651).
105. GC, Box 59/3/11. See also *ibid.*, Box 59/5/23 (October 1651: retrospective discharge for the coronation and for 'his lord[ships] maintenance').
106. Scone Palace, Perth, Vol. 1 fol. 24r.
107. NRS, GD150/2949.
108. *Ibid.*, MS E31/19, fol. 32r–v.
109. ScP, Bundle 268, fols 1r–3v (Such items were expensive, amounting to '149 sh[illings]').
110. For further costs, see *ibid.*, Vol. 1 nos 12–28 [fols 10r–22r].
111. Keay, *Monarch*, p. 57.
112. Adamson, 'Kingdoms', pp. 100–1. See also R. W. Hoyle, 'Introduction: Aspects of the Crown's Estate, *c.*1558–1640', in R. W. Hoyle (ed.), *The Estates of the English Crown, 1558–1640* (Cambridge, 1992), pp. 10–11 (Table 1:1).
113. Adamson, 'Kingdoms', p. 100.
114. *Ibid.*
115. Latham & Matthews, *Pepys*, V p. 75 (n. 5) (4 March 1663/1664). See also C. D. Chandaman, *The English Public Revenue: 1660 –1688* (Oxford, 1975).
116. V. Low, 13 February 2023, https://www.thetimes.com/article/kings-fleet-wont-sail-to-mark-coronation-n76j7rl8m, accessed 23 November 2025.
117. See for examples: T. Welsh and A. Foster, https://www.bbc.co.uk/news/uk-england-london-65476887, accessed 23 November 2025; I. Kottasová, 2 May 2023, https://edition.cnn.com/2023/05/02/business/cost-of-living-doncaster-coronation-gbr-cmd-intl/index.html, accessed 23 November 2025; I. McRae, 3 May 2023, https://www.big-issue.com/news/social-justice/how-much-kings-coronation-cost/, accessed 23 November 2025.
118. See Chaps. 3 and 4 above.
119. Queen Victoria diary: Thursday 28 June 1838 entry (http://www.queenvictoriasjournals.org/, accessed 23 November 2025). See also Public Record Office of Northern Ireland, Belfast, MS D638 /

MIC573/19 (celebrations also included a coronation ball at Apsley House hosted by the Duke of Wellington); cf. V&A, MS WM.1-2003 (invitation to Lord and Lady Boyle from the first Duke of Wellington to a Coronation Ball at Apsley House on 28 June 1838).
120. PML, MS Unassigned, Rulers of England Box 10, Charles II, Part 3, no 9.
121. The William Salt Library, Stafford, S.MS. 169/14.
122. *Ibid.*, S.MS. 169/24.
123. BL, Add. MS 31043, fol. 135r–v. See also W. H. Husk, *An Account of the Musical Celebrations on St Cecilia's Day in the Sixteenth, Seventeenth, and Eighteenth Centuries. To Which Is Appended A Collection Of Odes On St. Cecilia's Day* (London, 1857), pp. 28 (n), 47.
124. Bodl., MS Carte 73, fols 583r–584v.
125. Historical Manuscripts Commission: *Eleventh Report*, Appendix, Part VII: The Manuscripts of the Duke of Leeds, The Bridgewater Trust, Reading Corporation, The Inner Temple, &c. (London, 1888), p. 35.
126. PML, MA Unassigned, Misc English.
127. FSL, MS X.d.428 (164).
128. *Ibid.*
129. Northumberland Archives, Woodhorn, MS ZBR/38.
130. H. H. Leonard, 'Distraint of Knighthood: The Last Phase, 1625–41', *History*, 63 (1978), pp. 23–37.
131. FSL, MS X.d.428 (164). See also NAW, MSS ZBR/38 and SANT/BEQ/4/12/97/A.
132. See for examples: T. Diver, 1 April 2023, https://www.telegraph.co.uk/royal-family/2023/04/01/dress-down-coronation-peers-coronets-palace-king-charles/, accessed 23 November 2025; V. Ward and T. Diver, 10 February 2023, https://www.telegraph.co.uk/royal-family/2023/02/10/peers-uk-ministers-lobbying-attend-king-charles-coronation/, accessed 23 November 2025.
133. Norfolk Record Office, MS MC 1601/1640 862X8.
134. Northants. RO, MS 2647 (for 1661).
135. SCLA, MS DR18/5/811.
136. Notts. RO, MS DD/5P/7/1.
137. NRS, MS GD25/9/13.
138. BL, Egerton MS 3350, fols 11v, 17r.
139. Bodl., MS Smith 57, fol. 39r (Thomas Smith to Edward Bernard, London, 9 April 1685).
140. *Ibid.*, fol. 41r.
141. *Ibid.*, MS Wood F.39, fol. 41r–v.
142. WSL, MS M.534; see also FSL, MS Y.d.353 (ticket for admission to the royal box for George IV's 1821 coronation). NLI, Headfort Papers, MS

49,034/2 (Admission ticket to Westminster Abbey for the 1838 coronation of Queen Victoria).
143. Range, *Music*, p. 129. See also D. Burrows, 'Handel and the 1727 Coronation', *The Musical Times*, 118 (1977), pp. 469–73.
144. Staff. RO, MS D742/M/1/60.
145. Archer, 'Material Dimensions', pp. 165–6. See also BL, Add. MS 58833, fol. 18v.
146. Harris, *Restoration*, p. 69.
147. For more details on coronations and fireworks, see S. Boorsch, 'Fireworks!: Four Centuries of Pyrotechnics in Prints & Drawings', *The Metropolitan Museum of Art Bulletin*, New Series, 58 (2000), pp. 3–52. See also FSL, Art Vol.d105no.41, fols 14r–v, 39r, 63r.
148. Bodl., MS Carte 217, fol. 137r (Sir William Stewart, 1st viscount Mountjoy, to James Butler, 1st duke of Ormond, Dublin, 15 April 1685). See also S. Werrett, *Fireworks: Pyrotechnic Arts and Sciences in European History* (Chicago, Illinois, 2010), *passim*.
149. Eton College, BRXYZ-R BK.1.5.
150. Boorsch, 'Fireworks!', p. 4.
151. Harris, *Restoration*, pp. 94–5; Pender, *Waterford*, pp. 42, 46; Caulfield, *Youghall*, pp. 326, 334–5, 338, 346.
152. Cressy, *Bonfires*, *passim*.
153. E. Ralph, 'Records of Coronation Celebrations in a Provincial Town', *Bulletin of the Society of Local Archivists*, 13 (1954), pp. 17–21; Tresidder, 'Celebrations'.
154. Bodl., MS Eng. Letters e. 29, fol. 8r.
155. FSL, Art Vol.d105no.41, fol. 38r.
156. SCLA, MSS BRU5/3/142, BRU5/4 ('Money spent on coronation day' continued for George I's reign).
157. CRO, MS ZA/B/3/219, fol. 219r.
158. Notts. RO, MS CA 3400, fol. 50r–v.
159. *Ibid.*, MS CA 3469, fol. 22r.
160. Tresidder, 'Celebrations'. One problem with this approach is that document survival is inherently elitist, in terms of private individuals and institutions.
161. Morris, *Fiennes*, p. 21. See also D. Hey, 'Fiennes, Celia (1662–1741)', *ODNB*.
162. Morris, *Fiennes*, p. 21.
163. *Ibid.*
164. *Ibid.*, p. 22.
165. *Ibid.*
166. *Ibid.*
167. *Ibid.*

168. *Ibid.*, p. 23.
169. *Ibid.*
170. *Ibid.*
171. Anon., 'Records of Coronation Celebrations in a Provincial Town', 20th century [unpublished typescript notes at BRO, no call-number] 8/91.
172. BRO, MS M/BCC/CCP/1/7, fol. 213r–v.
173. Anon., 'Records of Coronation Celebrations in a Provincial Town', 20th century [unpublished typescript notes at BRO, no call-number] 8/91.
174. *Ibid.*; BRO, M/BCC/CCP/1/8, fol. 236r.
175. *Ibid.*, MS M/BCC/CCP/1/9, fol. 357r.
176. *Ibid.*, MS F/AC/Box/19/1.
177. *Ibid.*
178. J. Neuheiser, *Crown, Church and Constitution: Popular Conservatism in England, 1815–1867* (Oxford, 2016), p. 47.
179. Notts. RO, MS DD/5P/7 (iii).
180. *Ibid.*, MS 1799 (27 April 1702).
181. BRO, MS P/AS/Chw/3(b), fol. 12r.
182. *Ibid.*
183. BRO, MSS P/xch/Chw/1(c), fols 160r–162v, P/xch/Chw/1(d), fol. [14r–v].
184. WSRO, MS Par 106/9/1, fol. 119v. See also Cressy, *Bonfires*, pp. 50–66.
185. WSRO, MS Par 106/9/1, fol. 119v.
186. GA, MS 688/2 (20 October 1714).
187. BRO, P/xch/Chw/1(d), fol. [14r–v].
188. WSRO, MS PAR/45/8/1, fol. 3r–v.
189. *Ibid.*
190. *Ibid.*, fol. 50r.
191. Marsh, *Music*, p. 480.
192. *Ibid.* See especially Cressy, *Bonfires*, p. 54.
193. Marsh, *Music*, p. 481.
194. Smith, *Georgian Monarchy*, pp. 144–6 (1710s: Taplow and Clifton Reynes in Buckinghamshire; in 1727: Bury St Edmunds and Hawstead in Suffolk and Orton Waterville in Cambridgeshire).
195. Norf. RO, NCR Case 6a/4/86.
196. H. Watanabe-O'Kelly, *Projecting Imperial Power: New Nineteenth-Century Emperors and the Public Sphere* (Oxford, 2021), pp. 237–8.
197. *Ibid.*; See also https://www.rct.uk/collection/31706/the-imperial-crown-of-india, accessed 23 November 2025.
198. Watanabe-O'Kelly, *Projecting Imperial Power*, p. 242; see also J. Auerbach, 'Empire under Glass: The British Empire and the Crystal Palace, 1851–1911', in *Exhibiting the Empire. Cultures of Display and the British*

Empire, edited by John McAleer and John M. MacKenzie (Manchester, 2015), pp. 142–67.

199. Watanabe-O'Kelly, *Projecting Imperial Power*, p. 242; see also A. Hassam, 'Portable iron structures and uncertain colonial spaces at the Sydenham Cystal Palace', in *Imperial Cities. Landscape, Display and Identity*, edited by Felix Driver and David Gilbert (Manchester, 1999), pp. 174–93; *Indian Court. Festival of Empire 1911. Guide Book and Catalogue* (London, 1911), p. x.
200. Watanabe-O'Kelly, *Projecting Imperial Power*, p. 242.
201. *Ibid.*, p. 248.
202. *Ibid.*
203. *Ibid.*, p. 249; see also D. Simonelli, '"[L]aughing nations of happy children who have never grown up": Race, the Concept of Commonwealth and the 1924–5 British Empire Exhibition', *Journal of Colonialism and Colonial History*, 10 (2009), pp. 23–46; N. Ghuman, 'Elgar's *Pageant of Empire*, 1924: An imperial leitmotif', in *Exhibition the Empire. Cultures of Display and the British Empire*, edited by John McAleer and John M. MacKenzie (Manchester, 2015), pp. 220–56; *The Times,* Exhibition Supplement, 23 April 1924.
204. Bodl., MS Rawl. Letters 63, fol. 12r (Bohea tea is an oolong tea, roughly equivalent to Lapsang Souchong).
205. TNA, SP 29/33/73, fol. 127r–v.
206. M. A. E. Green (ed.), *Calendar of State Papers, Domestic Series, of the Reign of Charles II, 1660–1661, Preserved in the State Paper Department of Her Majesty's Public Record Office* (London, 1860), p. 606.
207. *CSP, Domestic, 1664–5*, p. 384.
208. Foreign (specifically diplomatic) interest was increasingly widespread in this period and would continue. For instance, the correspondence of Andrew Stevenson, American ambassador to Britain at the time of Queen Victoria's coronation in 1838, reveals much interest in the coronation—material hitherto not exploited by historians of this subject: Library of Congress, Washington DC, USA, Stevenson Papers: Box 8, fols 27102r–27103v (Anna M. Beneld to Andrew Stevenson, [June? 1838], referring to excitement about the coronation and to the Caledonian Ball), 27077r–27078v (Francis S. O. Smith to same, 19 June 1838, referring to Americans asking Stevenson for help in obtaining coronation tickets), 27054r–27055v (J. Watson Webb to same, 9 June 1838, wishing to obtain a seat at the coronation) and 27042r–27043v (Emma Woolnoth to same, 2 June 1838, referring to a coronation print).
209. *CSP Venice*, XXXII item 340 (6 May 1661).
210. *Ibid.*
211. *Ibid.*
212. *Ibid.*, item 351 (28 May 1661).

213. A. Fox, 'Rumour, News and Popular Political Opinion in Elizabethan and Early Stuart England', *The Historical Journal*, 40 (1997), p. 597.
214. I. Atherton, 'The Itch Grown a Disease: Manuscript Transmission of News in the Seventeenth Century', in J. Raymond (ed.), *News, Newspapers, and Society in Early Modern Britain* (London, 1999), p. 39.
215. *TLG*, 23–7 April 1685 (No. 2028), p. 1. Cf. *Kingdomes Intelligencer*, 29 April–6 May 1661 (No. 18), pp. 254–6.
216. Examples of local celebrations and reportage: *Mercurius Publicus*, 8 April–9 May 1661 (Nos 16– 18), pp. 241–4, 257–70, 281–4; *TLG*, 27–30 April 1685 (No. 2029), p. 2 and *ibid.*, 11–14 May 1685 (No. 2033), p. 2 and *ibid.*, 30 April–4 May 1702 (No. 3806), p. 3; *Evening Post*, 14–17 October 1727, pp. 2–3; *Gloucester Journal*, 24 October 1727, p. 2. For later celebrations (George IV, 1821), see also *Manchester Guardian*, 24 July 1821, pp. 1–2 and *The Times* (24 July 1821), p. 3.
217. *TLG*, 30 April–4 May 1685 (No. 2030), p. 2.
218. J. Plunkett, 'Of Hype and Type: The Media Making of Queen Victoria 1837–1845', *Critical Survey*, 13 (2001), p. 7.
219. Watanabe-O'Kelly, *Projecting Imperial Power*, p. 253; For an extant copy see Yale Center for British Art, Folio A 2015 1e, 'The Illustrated London News Coronation Ceremony Number: EIIR'.
220. Snyder did significant work on newspaper circulation for Queen Anne's reign; this was sizeable with *c.*10,000 copies of each issue alone of *TLG* from 1705–1707: H. L. Snyder, 'The Circulation of Newspapers in the Reign of Queen Anne', *The Library*, 5th Series, XXIII (1968), pp. 226–9 (App. B).
221. FSL, MS W.b.132 (147) no. 1, fol. 189r–v.
222. Bodl., MS Rawl. Letters 108, fol. 85r.
223. *Ibid.*, MS Carte 217, fols 140r–v.
224. *Ibid.*, MS Rawl. Letters 63, fol. 11r.
225. *Ibid.*, MS Smith 57, fol. 37r.
226. BL, Egerton MS 3336, fols 26r–28v (1689).
227. Bodl., MS Smith 57, fol. 39v (Thomas Smith to Edward Bernard, London, 9 April 1685: reporting that representatives of the Republic of Geneva wrote to his majesty with the superscription 'au Roy dela grand Bretaigne').
228. PML, MA Unassigned, Rulers of England Box 10, James II, Family, No. 50.
229. Such communication was, of course, not unique to Court news. For communication as far apart as Scone near Perth, Scotland, and Windsor, on the news of the queen's birthday, see ScP, Box 74, Bundle 3.
230. Bodl., MS Smith 57, fol. 35r (Thomas Smith to Edward Bernard, London, 10 March 1684/1685).

231. BL, Add. MS 70285, fol. 1r (draft of speeches from the throne, in the hand of Sidney Godolphin, 1st Earl of Godolphin, 1702, lord high treasurer). See also R. A. Sundstrom, 'Godolphin, Sidney, 1st Earl of Godolphin (1645–1712)', *ODNB*.
232. BL, Add. MS 47087, fol. 92r.
233. *Ibid.*, Add. MS 47087, fol. 92r–v. See also *ibid.*, Add. MS 31043, fols 78r–79v.
234. F. Hendriks, 'George I: Coronation Celebration at Leghorn, 1714', *Notes and Queries*, 9th Series, X (1902), p. 405.
235. Bodl., MS Wood F. 39, fol. 41r–v.
236. FSL, MS D 219 18 no. 1.
237. CA, MS 'Coronations – Charles II/ James II/William & Mary', Item [28]. [310]
238. Lamb, *Cookery*.
239. *Ibid.*, pp. 17–18. See also http://foodhistorjottings.blogspot.co.uk/2012_04_01_archive.html.
240. Within the Royal context see R. Doebner (ed.), *Memoirs of Mary, Queen of England, 1689–1693, Together with her Letters and those of King James II. and William III. to the Electress Sophia of Hanover* (Leipzig, 1886).
241. Latham & Matthews, *Pepys*, II pp. 81–8 (22–3 April 1661).
242. The triforium is a gallery/balcony area seventy feet above ground with a remarkable view of the abbey and of the Palace of Westminster: https://www.westminster-abbey.org/visit-us/plan-your-visit/the-queens-diamond-jubilee-galleries (triforium), accessed 23 November 2025.
243. Latham & Matthews, *Pepys*, II pp. 81–8 (22–3 April 1661).
244. *Ibid.*
245. *Ibid.*
246. *Ibid.*
247. *Ibid.*
248. *Ibid.*
249. de Beer, *Evelyn*, III, pp. 249–50; Evelyn, *Panegyric*.
250. CHD, MS 29 (23–4 April 1661). On Cork, see T. Barnard, 'Boyle, Richard, 1st Earl of Burlington and 2nd Earl of Cork (1612–1698)', *ODNB*.
251. CHD, MS 29 (23–4 April 1661).
252. GC, NRAS885/1/Box 70/Folder 1/Bundle 3 (side 2 of 1 document: London, letter of 23 April).
253. A. Kugler, 'Cowper, Mary, Countess Cowper (1685–1724)', *ODNB*.
254. Anon. (ed.), *Diary of Mary Countess Cowper, Lady of the Bedchamber to the Princess of Wales, 1714–1720* (London, 1864), pp. 3–5.
255. *Ibid.*, p. 5.
256. Strong, *Coronation*, p. 349 (my emphases).
257. Morris, *Fiennes*, p. 23.

PART IV

Material Remembrance & Responses

CHAPTER 7

An Afterlife in Coins and Medals

Coronations involve more than the great symbols of regal power—the regalia and St Edward's Chair—so prominent within the Abbey service. To see how monarchical magnificence and influence rippled outwards, to see the impact of these events upon communities up and down the country, one should look at other items of material culture— and this includes medals, coins, and currency. The work of Sharpe, Edie, Hone (and in more antiquarian form Edward Hawkins *et al*) are cases in point. A coronation was not just 'solemn ritual and ceremony'—it was usually accompanied by 'public rejoicing and festivity', and monarchs were aware of this fact; these were 'public ceremonies', to be celebrated nationwide, but also to be shown to 'foreign dignitaries ... [and] ambassadors'.[1] As Hone has argued the sermon, coins and medals[2] had an afterlife long after the great occasion and were thus 'of particular importance because [they] ... had a continued existence beyond the ceremony ... [including] a diplomatic function'.[3] As Sharpe has argued, whether it was the Henrician or Elizabethan emphasis on 'personality' and 'image', or with the 'civil war and revolution, the contest for representation and support still involved a struggle to claim and appropriate, as well as contest, the vocabularies and signs of authority that had underpinned monarchy and successions of kings'.[4] In each instance, 'memories of predecessors—the Virgin Queen for James I, for example—bequeathed expectations and hopes which perforce helped to form the script of a new monarch's self-representation'.[5]

G. W. C. Gross, *Crown and People*,
https://doi.org/10.1007/978-3-032-20786-9_7

The same was true for Queen Victoria's early reign, as John Plunkett has argued 'her accession ended the long and uninspiring affiliation [perhaps overly harsh] with the throne by the sons of George III', and she 'basked in the tangible freshness of a revivified royal populism'.[6] In essence these elements, allowed and helped to encourage or foster the continuing commemoration of the event, and in the case of battles over legitimacy made such work essential. Much of this was done in calendar form in the early modern world, as explored by Cressy,[7] but currency was if anything a more ubiquitous opportunity to utilise. From ancient times, most notably the Romans, emperors and monarchs have featured on currency. So too in the early modern world, during our brief period of a republic, the Lord Protector, Oliver Cromwell, featured on our coinage, Great Seal, and in official medals in the 1650s.[8]

Writing a decade before the 2023 coronation Sharpe argued that

> Doubtless when the time comes for Charles III to succeed to the throne, histories, images and films of Charles I will appear in proliferation. We can be fairly confident that they will be deployed, appropriated and contested—by the advocates of a republic as well as the friends of monarchy.[9]

It is certainly the case that Charles III has been quick to stamp his mark on the coinage, but perhaps not as Sharpe imagined, in the sense, that the emphasis has been on the King's interests and goals for the planet with conservation, rather more than a direct image of the monarch. A new set of coins feature flora and fauna of endangered species from across the United Kingdom, including the oak tree leaf (of Charles II fame) to the red squirrel and capercaillie amongst others.[10]

From trade at home to merchants abroad, the image and fame of a monarch could be advanced by currency. Coronation coins or medals were struck for the major event to spread the news of the occasion, the image of the new monarch and in the gifting of funds to enrich (quite literally!) support. This also helped spread news and knowledge of their country abroad. Elizabeth II's image, for instance, was also used on coinage in many Commonwealth countries. Queen Victoria's profile had of course featured across many parts of the British Empire—thus, the coinage along with the telegram, connected people of many of the different time zones of the world. It is thought that Athelstan (d.939) is the first English king to be depicted wearing a circlet or crown on his coinage. In time the accuracy of the depiction improved, so the likeness mattered. This was important for the monarch's subjects, particularly in an age before print, and remaining even after, for the coinage was likely the only image of a king or queen, that a subject was likely to see in their lifetimes.

The coinage (and coinage globally) has always had propaganda influence both at home and abroad. The coat of arms of the dynasty would also be present showing as with the Tudors and then Stuarts their dominance over the British Isles. In Tudor times, for instance, Henry VIII sought to promote his personal image as well as the power of the crown with his coinage. Yet, he was perennially short of funds and in the 1540s had to turn to debasing the coinage. This involved combing the precious metal content of a coin with a more common base metal, whilst retaining the same face value of each coin. In essence, the result involved more coins but with reduced quality, being struck from the same quantity of precious metal. However, the coins were struck with copper, with just a thin layer of silver applied to make the appearance more acceptable. With time, the layer wore away, especially around Henry VIII's nose, resulting in a red colour of copper emerging from underneath, thus giving Henry the unfortunate nickname 'Old Coppernose'.[11] This debasement aside, coronation medals tended to be of tremendous quality and were made at great expense, matching the wider spending for such successional junctures.

The generosity of the monarch was also unveiled following the enthronement and at the point of homage. At this point, 'the Treasurer of the King's Household, accompanied by the Lord Keeper of the Great Seal, went in turn to each of the four corners of the dais or platform on which the throne was set, tossing out specially minted coronation medals to the assembled spectators'.[12] These were made of gold for the most important dignitaries, but also of silver and bronze too. The diarist, John Evelyn records that all members of Parliament received medals in 1689, worth a considerable 45 shillings each.[13]

Whilst medieval monarchs distributed money with the tradition of touch coins and the King's Evil and may well have given coins at their coronations too, the first specifically made coronation medal belongs to the reign of Edward VI—and examples can be found in the National Maritime Museum, Greenwich, and in the British Museum.[14] The obverse of the young king's coin presents a text, not unlike the Supremacy coin of Henry VIII (Figs. 7.1 and 7.2).[15]

Coronation medals were widely distributed during and after an early modern coronation. Ownership went far beyond the elite. For numismatic expertise, Hawkins's work remains the most comprehensive

Fig. 7.1 Coronation Medal, Edward VI, 1546/1567 (The British Museum Images, G3,EM.1)

Fig. 7.2 Supremacy Medal, Henry VIII, 1545 (The British Museum Images, M.6802)

encyclopaedia[16] This catalogue has been especially helpful when analysing finds such as the coins held in Oriel College, Oxford.[17] There are seventeen medals depicting English monarchs from Edward the Confessor to Charles I. They are stored in a silver casket, the lid of which shows Charles in profile. Although these items were not created directly in relation to a coronation, they are important because they appear to be Civil War propaganda pieces, and they underline the point (which was emphasised within a coronation) of monarchical continuity, traced back to Edward the Confessor. A similar set belongs to the Royal Collection. An important element of this project has been to explore the distribution of coronation coins as propaganda pieces.[18] How far did they really reach in terms of the wider populace and were they considered as more than souvenirs? Were they produced by one central Royal Mint or did clandestine mints exist? Did they take on any spiritual value as icons? If having a crowned head on a coin of mass distribution really influenced the public, in the context of battling for political authority and legitimacy, then the coronation of a ruler becomes far more significant. It is argued that these coins and medals were essential items in the legitimisation of a new regime.

Coins are amongst the oldest forms of royal advertising; this was one of the few ways in which lay subjects resident distantly would see a projection of the face(s) of the monarch(s). A coronation involved and continues to involve the production of celebratory medals and coins, utilising the Royal Mint. Indeed, in the present, our currency, from denominations, weights, and style are still determined by the Royal Mint (with over a 1000 years of history), and Royal Prerogative as set out in the Parliamentary Coinage Act 1971 (and updated 2011). Monarchs featured on the coinage, but it was not until the twentieth century that the image of a monarch on all Pound Sterling banknotes began. In the 1960s, Queen Elizabeth II was the first monarch to have her portrait on all of the Bank of England's banknotes. Uniquely, therefore, in the reign of Charles III, this is the first time that the Bank of England has had to change the monarch on banknotes.[19]

Whilst not unique to Britain, for records in the Scottish National Archives reveal Danish medals too, medal issues in the early modern world were made for loyal supporters, but also for the wider public.[20] For Charles I's grand entry into London before his 1626 coronation, coins were minted at a cost of £150.[21] In 1633, for Charles I's Scottish coronation, we have accounts of the post-coronation distribution of special coins, 'struck on purpose for this solemnity', for the general public[22]:

> And immediately after his ma[jes]tie begnde [*sic*] to marche from the stage, … pi[e]ces of gold and silver coyness for the purpois of … [giving] to the weal … [were spread] among the people … This coyne had the ings face on the one syde, in his coronation robes with this circumscriptione, carolnis dei gratia scotia, angl: fran: & hyb: rex. Coronat. 18 Junij 1633. And on the rewersse a thissell … hinc nostra crenere rosa.[23]

Extensive analysis of coronation medals exists in the work of Hawkins *et al*, but further points can be made.

One, not only were these items often of exceptional quality, but they also ranged in style. It is therefore important to distinguish, as Hawkins does, between official medals, distributed at the coronation, and copies resulting from private or overseas enterprise. For Charles II's coronation, an official 'coronation medal [was] struck for distribution among the spectators … engraved by Thomas Simon' which 'has never been surpassed for minuteness and delicacy of work'.[24] Simon was remunerated with the sizeable sum of £110 for his work. Cast in gold and silver, it replicated the message of his coronation sermon as the arrival of stability, of peace, and of Restoration. Above the monarch hovers an angel of peace accompanied with laurel branch and at the same time placing a crown on Charles's head. The motto 'EVERSO. MISSUS. SUCCURRERE. SECLO. … variously translated as "Sent to save a sinking ship" or "Sent to support a fallen age", XXIII. APR. 1661' is almost Burkean.[25] Eight designs of coronation medal were made and two memorial coins. These 'coronation memorial small medalet[s]' were 'struck probably for sale in the streets at the time of the coronation' and therefore indicate the existence of a market for such items. Coronation memorabilia was therefore significant for contemporaries.[26] Such production would continue long after the Restoration. In 1714, for example, 'a bad imitation of the coronation medal … [was] executed for distribution among the populace'.[27] James II's coin by John Roettier was produced in gold, silver, and copper (or possibly bronze) — and 300 gold and 1200 silver medals were distributed at the Abbey service. They emphasised the monarch's naval career as Lord High Admiral, and his interest in imperial power by divine right—for the legend reads from a military crown to an imperial one, and whereas Charles II's crown was presented by an angel of peace, James receives his from a 'stark figure' and thus 'the effect is austere and severe, evoking not the happy workings of Providence, but the abstract principle of authority and right'.[28]

Two, eight medal types were produced on average for the coronations 1661–1714, but William and Mary's is anomalous. Significantly, at least twenty-eight others beyond the official medal were cast, including several overseas: at The Hague and in Nuremberg. Of all the accessions in the seventeenth and eighteenth centuries, arguably 1689 was the most complex, in that the preceding head of state was still alive. It would appear therefore that medals played a part in the battle to legitimise the Glorious Revolution as also seen in the setting. Describing Item 39, Hawkins explains that the meaning of their succession can be discerned from these coins, 'emblematical of Great Britain', for William and Mary are presented as

> the orange and the rose, with the four sceptres of England, France, Scotland and Ireland united under one crown, and supported upon the laws of England, and the Bible, thus provid[ing] for the security of the kingdom and the happiness of the people. The Eye of Providence indicates the only source of such a happy combination [in this pairing].[29]

By contrast, the obverse has James as the 'fallen oak', whilst William is the 'flourishing orange-tree'.[30] Not all the coins for the coronation of William and Mary met with public approval. Roettier also designed a 1689 coronation medal, cast in gold, lead, and silver. The obverse presents William and Mary 'conjoined' but was relatively uncontroversial, however, the reverse has the rather depressing motto of "lest the whole be lost" accompanied by a mythological scene with Jove throwing a thunderbolt against Phaeton, who thus falls from his chariot to a flaming earth beneath. Evelyn described the medal as 'very mean'.[31] The idea was that Phaeton portrayed James II and had thus been cast aside as a failed ruler, therefore highlighting the deliverance and legitimacy of the Glorious Revolution and the reason for this new era and the need for new authority. However, another interpretation might have seen this as William and Mary usurping the throne and thus facing the potential wrath or anger of the almighty. A letter at the time reveals deep concern as to the multiple readings of this scene, given also that Tullia of 'classical history had driven her chariot over the body of her dethroned father'.[32] Roettier might have been better to have used other themes also used at the time and produced, including the Dutch orange tree intertwined with the English rose. One writer makes it very clear that Roettier had missed the mark (in their view):

I wish the author had either consulted books or men, for a more significant and unexceptional emblem. [The writer goes on …] If you know the person, advise him to get himself included in the Act of Indemnity; it being a crime equal to counterfeiting the king's coin, to contrive a coronation emblem that gives such occasion of censure and reflection to malcontents and maligners of King William, our present Phoebus, and from whom we expect a wonderful deliverance.[33]

On occasion as in this instance, the setting did not work or was open to more interpretation than intended. In an earlier age, Oliver Cromwell and the Protectorate had looked to legitimise the Commonwealth's position in coins of 1656, and also in a memorial medal of 1658, strikingly similar to a coronation medal.[34] In many ways they had reappropriated the Royal Mint to quite literally stamp their authority on the country whilst also utilising the crown jewels which were 'dropped into the Mint melting pots'. In so doing, they sent

> the queen's crown, Edward VI's crown, the orb, two sceptres and the coronation bracelets. The liquid gold was then pressed into hundreds of small blank discs. Sandwiched between engraved metal dies and struck by the mintmen's hammers, the once-hallowed gold became money, emblazoned with the simple words 'The Commonwealth of England'.[35]

In this battle for legitimacy, during Charles II's attempt to regain power in 1650–1651 and his Scone coronation, coins and medals were created (in addition to printed material). Despite the complexities, and with the Commonwealth invasion force hard on his heels, there was still time for coronation medals to be produced for propaganda purposes. Indeed, the language deployed here would not suggest that Charles II was in any way embarrassed by that coronation, as with the received wisdom discussed in Chap. 6. Charles is styled 'King of Scotland, England, France, and Ireland, Defender of the Faith, crowned at Scone, 1 Jan. 1651' and his motto (that of the Order of the Thistle) is the exceptionally menacing: 'no one shall provoke me with impunity' (Figs. 7.3 and 7.4).[36]

Three, the political value of coins was to be seen in both words and images. George I is not only coupled with St George, but also accompanied by the inscription 'FIDEI DEFENSOR ET AEQVI'.[37] His inheritance is to support Protestantism and to uphold justice, in contrast to Jacobite Roman Catholicism and the fear of arbitrary rule.

Fig. 7.3 Coronation Medal, Charles II, 1651 (The British Museum Images, BNK, EngM.77)

Four, by 1714 we see a shift from coins produced for distribution to coronation spectators to an 'official medal struck for distribution amongst the officers of State and spectators'.[38] Hence, the system had developed a protocol. When one looks at the increased number of officials by 1714, including foreign representatives such as ambassadors, this would seem to underline a more formalised structure that was catering to the politics of Britain on the European stage. Foreign dignitaries were to be reminded of the event with a formal token.

Five, as has been mentioned, besides domestic production, coins were additionally struck as far away as Nuremberg. The event's reach is thus significant.

Six, the quality of the likeness of coronation medals and the wider coinage has considerably improved and so too a pattern of positioning evolved. From the reign of Charles II, a tradition emerged whereby the monarch represented on the coinage faced in the opposite direction to their immediate predecessor. Notably, the exception to this was Edward VIII of abdication fame and the uncrowned British monarch of the twentieth century. Edward's image by convention, should have faced right, yet his designs faced left, out of personal preference. His brother and successor George VI restored the custom, with his portrait facing left as if Edward VIII's had faced right.[39]

The True Manner of the Crowning of Charles the Second King of *Scotland*, on the First day of *January*, 1650. Together with a Description of his Life, and Throne; *And a cleare view of his Court and Counsell.*

The Manner of Crowning *CHARLES* the Second King of *Scotland*.

The Oath sworn by *CHARLES* the *Second*, King of Scotland, at his Coronation, 1 Jan. 1650.

A Speech made by *CHARLES* the Second, King of Scotland at his Coronation on 1 January 1650.

The Ministers Speech at the tendring of the Crown to the King.

A Description of the Life and Throne, and a cleare view of the Court and Councel of Charles the Second King of Scotland.

FINIS.

Published by Authority.

London Printed by *Robert Ibbitson*, 1651.

Fig. 7.4 *The True Manner of the Crowning of Charles the Second King of Scotland, on the first day of January, 1650[/51]* (London, 1651) (from the British Library archive, 699.f.15 (81))

Seven, as has been argued throughout this book, a coronation was a prime opportunity to publicise priorities, setting out one's stall for the new reign. In each case, the monarch gave approval to, or actively chose the intended image to symbolize their rule. The medal was not just for those lucky recipients in the Abbey, but for the many beyond that may see the design in print or to see one of the originals themselves. Thus, these medals and their accompanying message or motif went out and circulated far and away from the original Westminster starting point, as with any copy of the coronation sermon. This can be seen in the imagery, and accentuated by the words used, for example, in Queen Anne's official coronation coin, by John Croker, and the master of the mint Isaac Newton, cast in bronze, gold and silver.[40] Queen Anne had given very little time for preparation for the coronation—she acceded to the throne on 8 March 1702 and picked the following month and St George's Day, 23 April for the date. Hone's work has brought to light the role of the famous Sir Isaac Newton, in his capacity as Master of the Mint.[41] The Master was not happy with the time provided, and he 'complained to Sidney Godolphin, Lord High Treasurer, that the time allotted for making medals was "very short"'.[42] The queen is presented as 'Pallas, hurl[ing] thunder against a doubleheaded and four-armed monster, holding clubs and stones, and whose lower limbs terminate[d] in snakes'. She is described as 'the vice-regent of the thunderer' taking on the monster of France, 'identified in Newton's notes and reports in the newspapers as a "gyant" —and 'probably thinking of the Gigantomachia: that is the war between the classical pantheon and the Giants, a motif that had previously featured on a medal for the accession of Charles II, engraved by George Bower'.[43] Newton also saw this monster as 'emblematic of "any Enemy with which Her Maj^{t}y hath or may have War": in this case, the double Catholic threat posed by Louis XIV and James Francis Edward, the two faces of the [gyant]'.[44] The monster of France was a trope long used and would reappear beyond Louis XIV to that of Napoleon.[45] Here, Edie and Hone differ somewhat. Edie argues that the 'mythic allusion' of Pallas, 'diminished' or 'lessened her personal authority' and that '[i]t was apparently not enough that Anne should be portrayed as herself, as Charles II had been, or by an emblem, as had James II'. In Edie's view, 'it is remarkable that Queen Anne approved the design', whilst acknowledging that unlike her predecessors she did not have to 'declare her authority' in the same way, for her succession was not as disputed.[46] Her role, by contrast, was to cement obedience from her subjects to the crown and state and then to edify their determination to continue war with France and the Sun King. As discussed, Sharp's coronation sermon did much of this in his calling to the congregation (and in print) beyond, and her medal illustrated the point. 'The "sinews of power," as John Brewer has put it, were not hers to exercise, only to spur.'[47] Hone takes the view that Anne's medal alluded to William's reign, as the 'obverse … was based on a portrait by Sir Godfrey Kneller, William's preferred court painter'[48] and 'the mythic genealogy' also connected their two coronation medals. Anne's motto as 'vicegerent of the thunderer' in Newton's mind also "relates to the last Coronation medal [for] … 'the Thunder signifys War, & that King was a Warriour all his life-time"[49] for 'her Majesty continues the Scene of the last Reign'.[50]

In Whig and Tory politics, Anne's medal divided opinion. 'Opportunistic Whig panegyrists such as John Hughes and John Dennis, for instance, used the medal to fashion Anne as William *redivivus*: Hughes writing that Anne "*shall supply the Thunderers Place*" and go to war against "the Giants impious Race"'.[51] According to Hone, 'Tory writers pointedly omitted to mention the medal in any of their many succession panegyrics, suggesting that Whig interpretations of its symbolism had become entrenched'.[52] Newton's hand may well be at play here, for he was a 'committed Whig and occasional MP' too, thus 'it should not surprise us if he attempted to smuggle a partisan message into the design'.[53] Another reason for the choice of medal design was for beyond the seas too—it was to remind allies of England's resolve to pursue the war—the new ruler would not be changing tack.[54] As Richard Holmes has commented,

'Marlborough … left London for the Hauge on 14 March 1702 … to reassure the members of the Grand Alliance that England was steadfast in her commitment. The previous summer William [III], conscious of his own failing health, had chosen Marlborough to command the twelve battalions sent to the Low countries and made him ambassador to the Dutch Republic'.

Anne continued this royal favour by making him 'a Knight of the Garter immediately after her succession, and went on to appoint him captain general of her army and master general of the ordnance'.[55] Royal Mint accounts reveal the production of 1200 silver medals for the wider congregation, 518 medals for Parliamentarians, and a further '40 Medals of Gold … for foreign Ministers & Persons of quality'. (Fig. 7.5)[56]

These glorious medals 'distributed by the treasurer of the Household at the coronation' show how her strategy was to continue Williamite policy in combating French power and is 'typified by Pallas wielding the bolts of

Fig. 7.5 Coronation Medal, Queen Anne, 1702 (The British Museum Images, G3,EM.39)

Jove'.[57] Why is this so important? It is hugely significant because, in terms of impact, at least four unofficial versions were made of Queen Anne's approved coin, as 'medalets or jetons issued for sale in the street'.[58] The medal was carrying on a message of the position of the crown, regardless of the reality of Anne's health or ability to wage a war against Louis XIV's France in any personal capacity—Anne was too ill to even walk to her coronation in the procession. Yet, that did not matter, the message was all important for the new reign.

The cost of medal production was significant; here we can improve upon Hawkins *et al.* Treasury Books (entry of 21 April 1685) have James II ordering more medals, with some to be given to foreign representatives. The king's direct intervention is clear:

> It is the king's pleasure that there be provided against the coronation 100 gold medals of the king and 50 gold medals of the queen more than have been directed to be provided.[59]

We know that William and Mary dramatically increased this figure, arguably another sign of the propaganda campaign and the important role that coins were perceived to play in it. According to a copy of a Privy Council register entry (12 March 1688/1689),

> His majesty ... is ... pleased to order that the master of his ma[jes]tys Mint do cause, to be made ... the number of three [probably originally 'two'] hundred medals of gold and the number of twelve hundred medals of silver of the king and queens ma[jes]ty according to a pattern chosen by her ma[jes]ty and delivered to her, the value of each of the medals of gold and silver to be the same as at the last coronation.[60]

This was a very important rise in medal production; although the number was to increase dramatically, quality was to be consistent with that in 1685. Of note is Mary II's crucial role in choosing medal designs. Joint monarchy is evident at least in coronation preparations, as this council evidence demonstrates. In Hone's view, 1702 saw the 'expanding [of] the coronation's audience through improved infrastructure and distributing tokens', yet this somewhat underplays the changes that had already taken place in previous coronations, not to mention the considerable public interest and audiences for Tudor coronations. The distinction perhaps was England's developing empire and trading links across the globe by the time of Anne's reign. The distribution of coronation medals to foreign dignitaries was not new, but it remained hugely important in spreading the message of Anne's constitutional role and priorities in continuing the struggle with France.[61] Coronation planners were thus building on age-old established customs and then modifying them for effective use in the context of their times.[62] By the turn of the twentieth century, this had widened further, and turned to voluntary, charitable, and service personnel presentations, from those of the St John's Ambulance services, to members of the armed forces as well as school children.[63] Another sign of the move to a 'welfare monarchy' in the modern era.[64] Though continuity should be noted again for the voluntary sector had been a key part of proceedings for centuries as almoners and 'pensioners' had been present in coronations and coronation celebrations in the medieval and early modern era, as proscribed by the *Liber Regalis* and as Richard Boyle, 1st Earl of Burlington and 2nd Earl of Cork records in his neglected diary of 1661.[65]

Eight, and of crucial importance: coins survived as reminders of coronations past and (ultimately) as collectors' pieces, and they continued to be made right up to the present era. Around 400,000 Coronation Medals were issued for the 2023 Coronation, being presented to those that supported the ceremony from police officers to military staff, St John Ambulance personnel, choristers, and others serving in the service. In addition, they were also given to members of the armed services, the police, fire, and emergency services—to those that had given a full five calendar years of service. Furthermore, Victoria Cross and George Cross medal holders also received medals.[66] The reach of the 400,000 when you think of the families involved and the generations that will retain and keep these medals shows the extended arm of a coronation service, far beyond the walls of Westminster Abbey. A coronation's afterlife can be seen in these items. For example, existing receipts indicate the distribution of 'gold coronation meda[ls]' for George I's 1714 crowning to the Earl of Cholmondeley.[67] Such items became treasured heirlooms, as can be seen from Scott family papers, which include reference to 'coronation pieces of Charles I'[68] and from an inventory of royal coins spanning the period from Edward IV to Queen Victoria.[69]

Coronation medals continued throughout the Georgian era. For George IV in 1821, the work of Benedetto Pistrucci (1784–1855) would feature (an Italian medallist and his work of St George and the Dragon still features on coinage to this day), and indeed his work would be the design in 1838 for Queen Victoria's Coronation medal.[70] The imagery of George IV's coin continues the classical theme, with three women dressed in Greco-Roman robes swearing allegiance to the new monarch as representatives of England, Ireland, and Scotland. William IV's by contrast introduced a new concept and that of the medal featuring the king crowned, on one side, and his consort, Queen Adelaide shown, on the other. Queen Victoria's coin, has Britannia featuring, thus bringing into play an increasingly imperial theme with the burgeoning British Empire.[71] By 1902, coronation medals were being produced as far away as Australia by the Stokes & Sons Mint.[72] In Victoria (Australia), medals were awarded to school children as part of very considerable celebrations, with over 40 coins produced across the entire country.[73] In many instances, the medals were produced with the original coronation date of 26 June as production of coins had continued ahead, but the below example has the correct rearranged date of 9 August 1902 (Fig. 7.6).[74]

This pattern of commemorative medals would be continued in 1911 in Western Australia for King George V and Queen Mary as the images (Fig. 7.7) highlight.

In 1953, thirty-seven medals for Queen Elizabeth II were engraved by royal command with the words 'MOUNT EVEREST EXHIBITION' to commemorate and to present to (Sir) Edmund Hillary and Sherpa Tenzing Norgay and their team, following their successful ascent as part of the British expedition to climb Everest on 29 May 1953.[75]

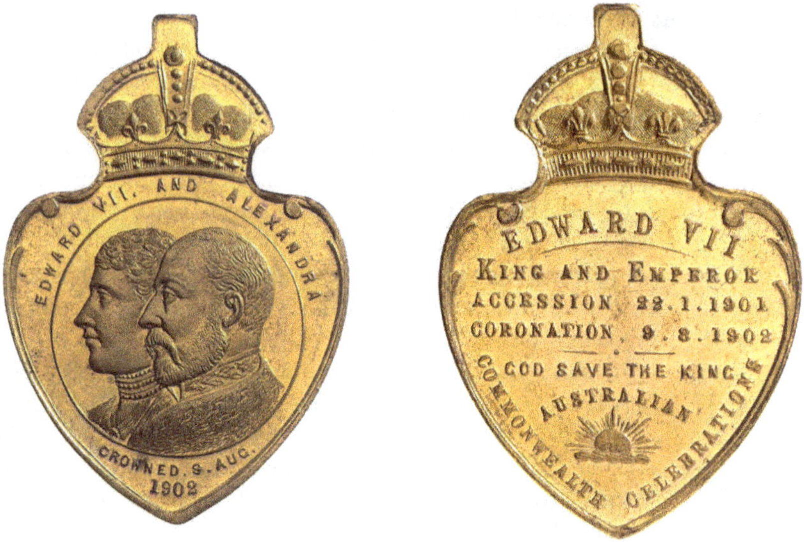

Fig. 7.6 Coronation medal for Edward VII & Queen Alexandra, 1902 (Source: Museums Victoria, Australia; Photographer: Jon Augier; https://collections.museumsvictoria.com.au/items/53017)

One final question needs to be discussed: Why do coronation coins matter or rather how do they show a sense of connection to the crown, nation, and wider commonwealth?

These objects are noteworthy for their value. For instance, Spink of London record numerous sales of coronation coins, with some fetching in excess of £1,000.[76] Yet, there is more than material gain to a coronation medal. Images from the archives speak of pride in wearing such medals. One such example can be seen from the Australian War Memorial collection, where six of men of the coronation corps for 1902 are photographed on their return voyage to Australia having taken part in the coronation parade for Edward VII. Each member wears his medal for service in the Boer War as well as their coronation medal.[77] Yet, we can go further given the existence of coronation medals in the 'present' and how receivers have reflected on being recipients of such medals tells us much. Chief Fire Officer John Roberts reported on 5 May 2023, on behalf of The West Yorkshire Fire & Rescue Service, that

Fig. 7.7 Coronation medal for King George V & Queen Mary, 1911 (Source: Museums Victoria; Photographer: Jennifer McNair; https://collections.museumsvictoria.com.au/items/1098726)

> We are proud to serve our communities … here in West Yorkshire. We were delighted to be thanked with the Jubilee medal last year, bestowed upon us by Her late Majesty, Queen Elizabeth II, so to be honoured again in this way is very humbling. On behalf of West Yorkshire Fire and Rescue Service, I wish Their Majesties all the best in their reign.[78]

On 30 July 2024, (having received their medal) Magpas Air Ambulance Critical Care Paramedic and Clinical Operations Manager, Andy Smith, stated

> It was an honour to be awarded this medal alongside so many of my clinical team members, celebrating this momentous historical occasion together and the work we do in the East of England.

The CEO of Magpas Air Ambulance, Daryl Brown MBE DL went further:

> We are so happy to see our amazing doctors, paramedics and pilots included in The King & Queen's Coronation medals distribution, and we are very thankful to The Deputy Lord Lieutenant for awarding the medals in person on behalf of His Majesty The King. The recipients of the medal are a rare and wholly deserving type of person and we are delighted to have over 30 of these exceptional individuals qualify in their time with Magpas Air Ambulance.

Part of the impact of such a medal is for morale, but that can only work if people feel a sense of pride or connection to such an honour. This is further noted by Darly Brown:

> These clinicians selflessly serve our communities, treating patients in extreme life-threatening emergencies, 24/7. We hope they will provide the team with a welcome boost as they continue to save lives around the clock this summer.[79]

Whilst not the coronation medal, a few final words should be added on the new coinage for Charles III's reign. For the first time in over 40 years, we have a new face on our pound coins as King Charles III's £1 coins entered circulation in 2024.[80] There is continuity in the style of imagery, format, and the continuing reference to 'F.D.' —*Fidei Defensor*—'Defender of the Faith', the title bestowed to Henry VIII, but that has remained even after his renunciation of Roman obedience and ever since. Yet, the influence and mark of King Charles III on the coinage is for all to see in a new knowing appropriation of the coins with references to nature and enunciated further by the BBC to millions around the world in articles and coverage more generally.[81] This follows his environmental concerns (and lifelong campaigning) showcased in the coronation in 2023. The monarch as per the Parliamentary Coinage Act of 1971 (and updated 2011) may make changes to design.[82] Images and coins are powerful, as we have seen, and able to reach people far beyond the classic centres of power. This is a tribute to his longstanding environmental and climate interests and with a hope that children and adults will, as they use the coinage, think about nature and the endangered wildlife and habitat around them, from puffins, to bees, salmon, and other flora and fauna of the British Isles. Thus, an ancient custom endures, but with fresh priorities.

Notes

1. Edie, 'Public Face', p. 311.
2. In the literature, the words coin, medal and token are used interchangeably.
3. Hone, 'The Last Stuart Coronation', p. 132.
4. Sharpe, *Image Wars*, pp. 5–8. See also B. J. Cook, 'Stampt with your own *Image*': Numismatic Dimension of Two Stuart Successions', in P. Kewes and A. McRae (eds), *Stuart Succession Literature: Moments and Transformations* (Oxford, 2019), pp. 303–18; Sharpe, *Rebranding Rule.*
5. Sharpe, *Reading Authority*, p. 154.
6. Plunkett, 'Of Hype and Type', p. 7.
7. See Cressy, *Bonfires*, *passim*.
8. See Sharpe, *Image Wars*, pp. 439–440, 506–509.
9. Sharpe, *Reading Authority*, p. 171.
10. https://www.royalmintmuseum.org.uk/learning/teaching-resources-7-11/wildlife/, accessed 23 November 2025; https://www.royalmint.com/aboutus/press-centre/the-royal-mint-unveils-new-coins-of-the-nation/, 12 October 2023, accessed 23 November 2025.
11. https://www.royalmint.com/aboutus/press-centre/the-royal-mint-unveils-remastered-henry-viii-coin-as-part-of-popular-british-monarchs-collection/#:~:text=This%20layer%20eventually%20wore%20away,nickname%2C%20'Old%20Coppernose, accessed 23 November 2025 see also https://www.bbc.co.uk/newsround/64451239, 1 February 2023, accessed 23 November 2025.
12. Edie, 'Public Face', p. 312.
13. de Beer, *Evelyn*, IV, p. 633. See also Purey-Cust, *Coronations*, p. 58.
14. See National Maritime Museum, Greenwich, London, Caird Collection, MEC1108; BM, G3, EM.1. For the coronation medals of Edward VI, Elizabeth, James I, and Charles I, see Hawkins, *Medallic Illustrations*, I, plates III, VI, XIV, and XX. See also J. Pinkerton, *The Medallic History of England to the Revolution: with forty plates* (London, 1790), plate IV.
15. See NMM, Greenwich, MEC1107 (and also BM, G3,EM.1 (1546/1547) Coronation Medal). Elizabeth I's coin had the young queen represented by a phoenix and for James I in 1603, he is crowned by a lion. See also: https://hunterian.blog/coronation-coins-and-medals/, 4 May 2023, accessed 23 November 2025.

16. Hawkins, *Medallic Illustrations*.
17. OCA, AH 5 D1: undated [mid-seventeenth-century] cast silver medals, workshop of Simon van de Passe.
18. Because of the scale of the task, the widespread distribution of items, many in private collections, this is a preliminary enquiry, pending further investigation later.
19. S. Coughlan, 9 April 2024, https://www.bbc.co.uk/news/uk-68769481, accessed 23 November 2025; https://www.bankofengland.co.uk/news/2022/december/king-charles-iii-banknotes-unveiled, 20 December 2022, accessed 23 November 2025.
20. This was not unique to Britain: see NRS, MS GD477/358/16 (details on gold coronation piece of Charles I, and one of silver, and one of the king of Denmark).
21. WSL, S.MS 164/7, pp. 39, 43.
22. NRS, MS CH12/12/1019, p. 6.
23. NLS, Adv. MS 33.2.26, fol. 42v.
24. Hawkins, *Medallic Illustrations*, I, pp. 472, 476–7. See also BM, M.7477 (coronation medal, Charles II).
25. Edie, 'Public Face', pp. 316–8. See also T. C. Banks, *An Historical and Critical Account of the Institution of the Coronation Ceremony; its Indispensability; the High and Official Services of the Day; the Origin of Inunction* (London, 1830), p. 149, and Hawkins, *Medallic Illustrations*, I, p. 472. On Burke, see also E. Jones, 'Conservatism, Edmund Burke, and the Invention of a Political Tradition, *c.* 1885–1914', *The Historical Journal*, 58 (2015), pp. 1115–39.
26. Hawkins, *Medallic Illustrations*, I, pp. 472, 476–7. See also BM, M.7477 (coronation medal, Charles II).
27. Hawkins, *Medallic Illustrations*, II, pp. 424–5.
28. Wordworth, *Coronation*, p. 46 n. 6; Edie, 'Public Face', p. 320; Banks, *Historical Account*, p. 149; Hawkins, *Medallic Illustrations*, I, p. 605; see also *ibid.*, *Medallic Illustrations*, II, plate LXII; J. Evelyn, *Numismata. A Discourse of Medals, Ancient and Modern* … (London, 1697), p. 148.
29. Hawkins, *Medallic Illustrations*, I, pp. 668–9. See also BM, M.7742 (coronation medal, William III and Mary II, 1689) and importantly the inscription, as a further example of this attempt to legitimise: 'Their majesties crowned, the papacy ejected, tyranny expelled, Britain is happy'.
30. *Ibid.*
31. Edie, 'Public Face', p. 324; de Beer, *Evelyn Diary*, IV, p. 63. See also Banks, *Historical Account*, p. 150; Hawkins, *Medallic Illustrations*, I, pp. 662–3.
32. Edie, 'Public Face', p. 324.

33. "A Letter from a Gentleman in the Country to his Correspondent in the City, Concerning the Coronation Medal, distributed April 11th, 1689," in W. Scott (arr.), *A Collection of Scare and Valuable Tracts, on the most interesting and entertaining subjects: But chiefly such as Relate to the History and Constitution of these Kingdoms. Selected from an Infinite Number in Print and Manuscript, in the Royal, Cotton, Sion, and other Public, as well as Private, Libraries, Particularly that of the Late Lord Somers* (London, 1809–1815), X, pp. 209–11. The "Letter" may have been circulated in manuscript form; there is no evidence that it was printed before 1813.
34. See BM, E.3442 and *ibid.*, M.7396.
35. Keay, *Crown Jewels*, p. 43.
36. BM, M.7336 (coronation medal, Charles II, 1651). An interesting collection of Civil War propaganda medals exist as OCA, AH 5 D1.
37. Hawkins, *Medallic Illustrations*, II, p. 425.
38. *Ibid.*, II, p. 424.
39. Shawcross, *The Queen Mother*, p. 230. See also 'The Abdication Crisis' in Williamson and Baldwin, *Baldwin Papers*, pp. 387–425.
40. Hone, 'The Last Stuart Coronation', p. 141; Edie, 'Public Face', p. 325. See also Banks, *Historical Account*, p. 151; cf. *The History of the Life and Reign of her Late Majesty Queen Anne: Wherein all the Transactions of that Memorable Reign Are faithfully Compil'd from the Best authorities, and Impartially Related* (London, 1740).
41. Hone, 'The Last Stuart Coronation', p. 134; https://www.royalmintmuseum.org.uk/journal/people/isaac-newton/, accessed 20 August 2024.
42. Hone, 'The Last Stuart Coronation', p. 134 quoting H. W. Turnbull, *et al.* (eds), The *Correspondence of Isaac Newton*, 7 volumes (Cambridge, 1959–1977), IV, p. 384.
43. Hone, 'The Last Stuart Coronation', p. 141: Hone argues that scholars have erred in identifying the monster as a 'hydra'. The misinterpretation stems from Abel Boyer, writing two decades later in A. Boyer, *The History of the Life & Reign of Queen Anne. Illustrated with all the medals struck in this reign, ... and other useful ... cuts. To which is added, an appendix ...* (London, 1722), p. 718. See also J. Hone, 'Isaac Newton and the Medals for Queen Anne', *Huntington Library Quarterly*, 79 (2016), 119–48; R. S. Westfall, *Never at Rest: A Biography of Isaac Newton* (Cambridge, 1980), pp. 621–3; Sir John Craig, *Newton at the Mint* (Cambridge, 1946). For Newton's take on the Gigantomachia, see J. Z. Buchwald and M. Feingold, *Newton and the Origin of Civilization* (New Haven, Connecticut, 2012), p. 379.
44. Hone, 'The Last Stuart Coronation', at p. 141. See TNA, Mint 19/3, fol. 289r.

45. W. Hauptman, "'The Blood-Stained Brush': David and the British circa 1802." *The British Art Journal*, 10 (2009), pp. 78–97; H. Peyre, 'Napoleon: Devil, Poet, Saint.' *Yale French Studies*, 26 (1960), pp. 21–31; E. Bertram and Robert E. Norton (eds), 'Napoleon', in E. Bertram and Robert E. Norton (eds), *Nietzsche: Attempt at a Mythology* (Champaign, Illinois, 2009), pp. 171–82; see also A. Roberts, *Napoleon the Great* (London, 2016).
46. Edie, 'Public Face', pp. 326–8. Of course Jacobites did dispute Anne's succession recognising James II's son as the true successor in September 1701 at the death of James II. Scotland did see Jacobite developments following William III's death, but this had more to do with a potential political Union between England and Scotland, than Anne's succession. Her position as a Stuart was all important.
47. Edie, 'Public Face', p. 328 quoting Brewer, *Sinews*, chapters 5 and 8.
48. Hone, 'The Last Stuart Coronation', p. 141; The portrait is number 46 in J. D. Stewart's *catalogue raisonné* of Kneller's works: *Sir Godfrey Kneller and the English Baroque Portrait* (Oxford, 1983), p. 91. See also *The Post Man*, 951 (4 April 1702).
49. Hone, 'The Last Stuart Coronation', p. 141. See TNA, Mint 19/3, fol. 289r, Cf. I. Newton, *The Chronology of Ancient Kingdoms Amended* (London, 1722), p. 226.
50. TNA, Mint 19/3, fol. 289r.
51. Hone, 'The Last Stuart Coronation', p. 142 quoting J. Hughes, *The House of Nassau: A Pindarick Ode* (London, 1702), p. 12; see J. Dennis, *The Monument: A Poem Sacred to the Immortal Memory of the Best and Greatest of Kings, William the Third* (London, 1702), pp. 9–10.
52. Hone, 'The Last Stuart Coronation', p. 142. As Hone reports the 'only record of the Tory response comes from Oxford, where the Vice Chancellor–a Tory high-flyer named Roger Mander–prohibited a student from reading "a copy of Verses upon the Inscription on the Medal, at Her Majesties Coronation, *VICEM GERIT ILLA TONANTIS*". See R. West, *The True Character of a Church-Man, Shewing the False Pretence to That Name. Together With the Character of a Low Church-Man Drawn in Answer to It, With Remarks* (London, 1702), p. 40. On Anne's Tory succession panegyrics, see J. Hone, 'Politicising Praise: Panegyric and the Accession of Queen Anne', *Journal for Eighteenth-Century Studies*, 37 (2014), pp. 147–57.
53. Hone, 'The Last Stuart Coronation', p. 142.
54. See also J. Hone, 'Isaac Newton and the Medals for Queen Anne', pp. 130–1. Hone argues that an undated medal, also from Queen Anne's reign, referred to as the 'Palladium', may well be another coronation medal, designed by Newton, with the monarch again depicted as Pallas,

with the theme of Troy of Homer's *The Iliad*, and Athene – the crucial God – on which security was relied on. The link to the European alliance against France would have been obvious to diplomats. See also J. H. Lochner, *Samlung Merkwürdiger Medaillen* (Nuremberg, 1744), cited and translated in David Pickup, 'John Croker and the Alehorne Manuscript', *The Medal*, 20 (1992), 19–31.

55. R. Holmes, *Marlborough: Britain's Greatest General* (London, 2009), p. 195.
56. TNA, Mint 19/3, fol. 336r. The 518 gold medals for the House of Commons were only 'made afterwards' – a typical case of insufficient funding at a time of immense spending for the wider coronation (fol. 332r). The Speaker of the House of Commons, received the medals the following month, on 9 May: BL, Add. MS 70020, fol. 179r. See also F. Heal, *The Power of Gifts: Gift Exchange in Early Modern England* (Oxford, 2014), p. 175; L. Kreitzer, 'Paying Gold with Chocolate: Thomas Simon and a Gift for the Swedish Ambassador in 1656', *The Medal*, 64 (2014), pp. 10–15.
57. Hawkins, *Medallic Illustrations*, II, p. 228.
58. *Ibid.*, II, p. 229. Charles I's 1626 coronation medal by Nicholas Briot also included a militaristic emblem, representing his wish to continue war with Spain. In that instance the motif was of a mailed arm and hand with sword.
59. Shaw, *Treasury Books*, VIII, pp. 135–59 (21 April 1685).
60. BL, Add. MS 38861, fol. 52r.
61. Hone, 'The Last Stuart Coronation', p. 145.
62. See for example The Huntarian Numismatics collection of Coronation coins going back to Edward VI at The Huntarian Museum and Art Gallery, at The University of Glasgow, GLAHM:38005.
63. For example, see: The Museum of the Order of St John, London, LDOSJ:44 (https://museumstjohn.org.uk/collections/king-edward-vii-coronation-medal-king-george-v-coronation-medal-and-service-medal-with-bars-awarded-to-mrs-e-denchfield/, accessed 1 August 2024); and https://royalleicestershireregiment.org.uk/archive/medals-list-honours/commemorative-medals/230151-king-edward-vii-coronation-medal?#:~:text=This%20medal%2C%20designed%20by%20Emil,officers%20involved%20in%20the%20celebrations, accessed 23 November 2025; and Falkirk Council Collections, 1982-095-001 (1911 George V coronation medal distributed to all the children in Falkirk schools (https://collections.falkirk.gov.uk/objects/6540/medal-commemorative-coronation-george-v, accessed 23 November 2025). See also F. C. Eeles, *The English Coronation Service. Its History and Teaching. With the Coronation Services of King Charles I. and of Queen Victoria* (Oxford, 1902).

64. See for examples F. Prochaska, *Royal Bounty: The Making of a Welfare Monarchy* (New Haven, Connecticut, 1995); D. Cannadine, "Welfare Monarchy" in *ibid.*, *History in Our Time* (New Haven, Connecticut, 1998), pp. 25–32; E. Owens, *The Family Firm: Monarchy, Mass Media and the British Public, 1932–53* (London, 2019), pp. 133–98; and J. Ridley, *George V: Never a Dull Moment* (London, 2021).
65. See Legg, '*Liber Regalis*', p. 114 and CHD, MS 29 (23–4 April 1661). On Cork, see T. Barnard, 'Boyle, Richard, 1st Earl of Burlington and 2nd Earl of Cork (1612–1698)', *ODNB*. Richard Boyle's diary is a particularly good example for it covers the entire programme for Charles II's procession and coronation celebrations.
66. See: https://www.gov.uk/guidance/medals-campaigns-descriptions-and-eligibility#:~:text=On%205%20May%202023%2C%20the,expected%20total%20of%20400%2C000%20recipients, accessed 23 November 2025. See also https://www.thegazette.co.uk/all-notices/content/104168, accessed 23 November 2025; and https://www.raf.mod.uk/our-organisation/stations/raf-cosford/news/coronation-medals-presented-to-our-personnel/, 29 March 2024 accessed 23 November 2025.
67. CRO, MS DCH/K/15.
68. NRS, GD477/358.
69. The John Rylands Library, Manchester, MS EGR4/1/12/10.
70. See also PRONI, MS D207/73/277.
71. RCIN 443368 (Queen Victoria Coronation Medal); see also https://www.royalmintmuseum.org.uk/journal/curators-corner/crowned/medals/, accessed 23 November 2025 & https://www.nam.ac.uk/explore/coronation-medals, accessed 23 November 2025.
72. https://en.numista.com/catalogue/mint.php?id=5136, accessed 22 November 2025.
73. Museums Victoria, Australia collection, 33092 (Coronation medal of King Edward VII & Queen Alexandra, 1902).
74. See for example https://collections.museumsvictoria.com.au/items/75743, accessed 22 November 2025.
75. https://www.nationalgeographic.com/adventure/article/sir-edmund-hillary-tenzing-norgay-1953, 3 March 2013, accessed 22 November 2025.
76. For images and more details on coronation coins in gold and silver see Spink website.
77. The Australian War Memorial, Canberra, A04831 (South Africa, 1899–1902, Boer War) Black & white – Film polyester negative photograph (https://www.awm.gov.au/collection/C728, accessed 22 November 2025). Such records can be found across the Commonwealth, for Canada see for examples: https://tankmuseum.ca/blog-post/the-ontario-regiment-and-the-coronations/, accessed 1 August 2024 and

https://recherche-collection-search.bac-lac.gc.ca/eng/home/record?idnumber=2854828&app=fonandcol&q=KLEIN, accessed 26 August 2024.
78. https://www.westyorksfire.gov.uk/news/coronation-medal-go-front-line-emergency-service-workers-fire-service, 5 May 2023, accessed 23 November 2025.
79. https://magpas.org.uk/a-token-of-thanks-clinicians-receive-the-coronation-medal/, 30 July 2024, accessed 23 November 2025.
80. N. Nanji, 20 August 2024, https://www.bbc.co.uk/news/articles/c3ejnv74dwno, accessed 23 November 2025.
81. N. Nanji, 20 August 2024, https://www.bbc.co.uk/news/articles/c3ejnv74dwno, accessed 23 November 2025; K. Peachey, 13 October 2023, https://www.bbc.co.uk/news/business-67091137, accessed 23 November 2025.
82. https://www.legislation.gov.uk/ukpga/1971/24, accessed 23 November 2025.

CHAPTER 8

Gaffes, Incidents, and Critiques

'Stuff happens!'. It certainly does. And coronations are not without their tally of amusing mistakes and disasters. Was it a good idea to put what were presumably fancy new shoes on the ten-year-old Richard II for his coronation in 1377? As he was being carried shoulder-high back to Westminster Hall afterwards, one fell off and was lost. Only just over half the peerage obeyed the summons to attend the coronations of William III and Mary II in 1689.[1] The famous Gold State Coach (used during the 2023 proceedings) was commissioned for the coronation of George III in 1761, but was not ready for the occasion and has remained one of the most purportedly uncomfortable carriages to travel in the world over, described by William IV as being worse than journeying at sea and by the late Queen Elizabeth II as 'horrible' and 'not meant for travelling in at all'.[2] Queen Caroline, consort of George IV, was notoriously denied entrance to Westminster Abbey when she sought to gatecrash her estranged husband's coronation in 1821.[3] The ensuing banquet was something of a trial for those peers' wives sitting in the Hall's galleries because nobody had thought to protect them from the hot wax dripping from candles burning in the massive chandeliers. Queen Victoria's coronation was so inadequately rehearsed that there were several hitches. She wrote that the Archbishop of Canterbury '**ought** to have delivered the Orb to me, but I had already got it, and he (as usual) was **so** confused … and knew nothing'.[4] At one point, two pages of the service book were accidentally turned over at once, with the

G. W. C. Gross, *Crown and People*,
https://doi.org/10.1007/978-3-032-20786-9_8

result that the Bishop of Bath and Wells instructed her to go to St Edward's Chapel, from which she hastily had to be retrieved. Worse: the aged primate jammed the Coronation Ring on to the wrong finger, and it could only be removed later with considerable pain. At the Homage, the elderly Lord Rolle tripped as he was ascending the steps to the throne and tumbled down, as Queen Victoria recorded in her diary, 'Poor old Lord Rolle, who is 82 and dreadfully infirm, in attempting to ascend the steps, fell and rolled quite down, but was not the least hurt; when he attempted to reascend them I got up and advanced to the end of the steps, in order to prevent another fall [...]'. A moment further immortalized by John Martin's great painting of 1839.[5]

When it comes to the regalia, it is not easy to tell which is front and back of St Edward's Crown. A solution to the problem was found in 1937: a small thread was attached to the rear as a marker. Unfortunately, somebody removed it before the ceremony began, not being aware of its purpose. Consequently, Archbishop Lang was non-plussed at the supreme moment, and can be seen on film turning the crown round and round in a vain attempt to find the thread, before finally lowering it on to George VI's head. Queen Elizabeth II, who was present, remarked in a (2018) documentary that her father was not at all amused by that slip-up.[6] Such stories shed valuable light on coronation preparations. The British may enjoy a reputation for brilliance in planning grand ceremonial down to a 't', but there was (and is) always room for the unpredictable and impact of local and global events. Harold Macmillan's phrase of 'events, dear boy, events' could not be more appropriate.[7] This chapter highlights just some of those moments[8] at the same time, also drawing attention to times when a coronation was criticised or came at a time of less-than popular approval. Why does this also matter? It is significant because it might be easy amongst all the ceremonial, pomp, and pageantry to imagine that coronations have or had some kind of universal approval and that criticism or republicanism might be something new—but this is anything but the case, as this chapter will reveal. Praise but also critique of royal ceremonial and of monarchy have been part and parcel of our nation's story, from some of the earliest recorded occasions. Turning to the Medieval, we have instances of extraordinary brutality and of atrocities that belie many of the assumptions of coronation events.

William the Conqueror

William the Conqueror's coronation on Christmas Day in 1066, just a few months after his victory at the Battle of Hastings was marred by a bizarre incident. The guards outside the cathedral mistook the cheers of acclamation for a riot—so they immediately set fire to the surrounding buildings—'[n]othing could illuminate better the true character of William's accession to kingship than this tale of heavy security' or heavy-handiness and brutality.[9] For Douglas, this was a 'portentous event' and whilst it caused 'alarm and confusion' and of course destruction beyond, 'nothing … could impair the legal consequence of what had taken place. Duke William of Normandy was now king of the English'. Whilst the event was far from what had been planned (an early example of how this set-piece occasion can and could go wrong), the legitimisation, the stamping of authority on his conquered land, that this coronation gave William, was significantly more important than the brutal blundering of the new King's guards.[10] Although the heavy-handed and brutal nature of William's guards alluded to the nature of his rule, his coronation was an essential part in the battle of legitimacy for the English throne. Harold had rushed to be crowned following Edward the Confessor's death, so there is little doubt that contemporaries valued this important ceremony. Whether it took place at Westminster Abbey or not remains open to debate, but as Douglas argues, it is thought that 'Godwineson [Harold Godwinson],[11] having obtained the support of a group of English magnates who were in London, had himself crowned as king … by Aldred, archbishop of York, in the Confessor's new Abbey of Saint Peter of Westminster'.[12] It is also asserted that 'Harold had the full support of England's religious elite'.[13] Thus, it was crucial that William lay claim to this authoritative legal and religious position. Whilst it is thought that he had some form of 'second coronation' in 1070 linked to the visitation of 'three papal legates', his 1066 coronation 'remained the basis of his kingly authority'.[14]

Richard I

The legacy and impact of Richard I's coronation saw one of the darkest moments in English history triggered by such ceremonial. Richard I or Richard Coeur de Lion—was crowned and anointed at Westminster Abbey on 3 September 1189. Roger of Howden's[ ][15] account provides us with one of the earliest expositions on an English coronation. Yet, far from being a day of universal rejoicing up and down the land for the Lionheart king, it saw what in modern terms would be described as a pogrom—Westminster and City of London gave way to 'anti-Jewish riots', and these continued to spread northward in February and March of 1190, culminating in a widespread massacre of the Jewish population in York.[16] Ralph de Diceto 'an eyewitness and participant in the coronation ceremony … [wrote] "the peace of the Jews, which they had always maintained since antiquity [in England], had been severed".[17] In some accounts, the day is seen as linked in some way astrologically to being an 'Egyptian' one, possibly in reference to the Old Testament struggles, exile and captivity of the Jewish people:

> Thus, at the coronation of Richard Coeur de Lion, September 3, 1189—a day which had been marked by astrologers as an "Egyptian day," or one of evil omen—not only did numerous such evil portents appear as bats "inconveniently circling in the same tracks, and especially round the king's throne," bells pealing at unusual hours and without human aid, and similar dreadful signs, but, what was of more consequence, there took place a terrible massacre of the Jews, which we of the present day can hardly comprehend.[18]
> Richard … was consecrated king … on the third day … of September, a day which, from the ancient superstition of the Gentiles, is called Evil, or Egyptian, as if it had been a kind of presage of the event which occurred to the Jews, and to be Egyptian rather than English; since England, in which their fathers had been happy and respected under the preceding king, was suddenly changed against them, by the judgment of God, into a kind of Egypt where their fathers had suffered hard things[.][19]

Roger of Howden and William of Newburgh[20] provide us with the 'grim details' in Latin accounts, whilst in Hebrew we have a text from Ephraim of Bonn's (poet and chronicler).[21] It seems that the entire proceedings rested on a misunderstanding, rather like the ensuing violence following the acclamation at William the Conqueror's 1066 Christmas Day coronation. An important delegation of eminent Jews sought to give thanks and homage at Richard's coronation, but their efforts to attend were seen as suspicious and a danger to the proceedings, and they were thus set upon in 'chaotic' and unseemly 'attacks'. This violence then spread further across the cities of London, and from 'King's Lynn and Norwich to [Lincoln], Stamford, [and] Bury', and would ultimately result in the tragedy of York, the following spring.[22] Marcus and Saperstein conclude that the savagery in York was encouraged by 'a band of unscrupulous nobles' in an effort 'to wipe out the Jewish community to whom ... [they] ... were heavily indebted. The plot succeeded, the community was destroyed, and, for the time being at least, the nobles were free of their creditors'. Perhaps the background of the Third Crusade (1189–1191) fuelled 'the religious zeal of the English people' and encouraged such actions.[23] Blurton also draws attention to the fall of Jerusalem 'to Saladin' in 1187 as contextual background, and with 'that disaster [in mind] ... it may have been no longer enough to think about the way in which individual Christian bodies might be threatened by the continued presence of Jews in Christian society, rather the health of the entire Christian body politic may have seemed to demand the more immediate concern'.[24] In summary, far from bringing in an age of peace and prosperity amongst **all** his peoples, Richard I's coronation ushered in a time of devastation for his Jewish population and a hundred years later (under Edward I),[25] they would be formally expelled from England, not to return until their readmittance under Oliver Cromwell's rule in the 1650s.[26]

Charles I

Turning from the Medieval to the Early Modern, and Charles I's coronation—we see something of what would become part of his reign, in money collecting *via* legal, yet somewhat unsavoury or unpopular moves.[27] Given an impoverished Crown and the likelihood of coronation debts, Charles I had resorted to money-making expedients. As discussed in Chap. 6, Charles I used the disreputable practice of fining individuals for failing to accept knighthoods (the Distraint of Knighthood).[28] This was hardly a good omen for the rest of his reign.

James II

Much has been written about the success of Charles II's Restoration coronation (and covered in this book), in terms of contemporary support and interest. James II's coronation appeared to have been received with similar feelings, heralded as a success, yet after his demise, contemporaries began to reflect on what seemed like pointers from the coronation of potential problems ahead. The coronation of James II and his queen Mary of Modena took place on 23rd April 1685 (again St George's Day). Francis Sandford wrote a history of this coronation which included the names of all those who walked in the processions from Westminster Hall to the

Abbey and extensive engravings of both the procession and ceremony. Once James was in exile, following the Glorious Revolution of 1688/1689 and the takeover of William III and Mary II (James's daughter), it was remembered that during the coronation of 1685 the crown appeared in danger of falling off his head and at the moment of the crowning, the Royal Standard (at the Tower of London) was torn by the wind. Writers were quick to pick up on a potential scriptural allegory. For example, one writer's musings in January 1710/1711 shows how, with hindsight, James II's end could be foretold from his crowning:

> Melancholick reflections for an hour, or two … made me call to my mind the story of Bernini, and his bust, burnt in Whitehall. It made me also call to mind the omens that happened at the coronation of his son James II. W[hi]ch I saw … the tottering of his crown upon his head, the broken canopy over it, and the flag hanging upon the white tower over[h]a[n]g[ing] my door, when I came home from the coronation. It was torn by the wind at the same time the signal was given to the Tower that he was crown'd: I put no great stresse upon omens, but I cannot despise them; most of them, I believe, come by chance, but some from superiour intel[l]ectual agents, especially those, w[i]ch regard the fate of kings, and nations[.][29]

The biblical allusions are clear with the torn flag being seen as the 'curtain of the temple [being] torn in two' (Mark 15:38) following Christ's crucifixion. The comparison with the holy nature of the sovereign is obvious, together with the providential conclusion that such omens are the work of a higher being. From signs or bad omens of things to come, we turn to widespread rioting and discontent in 1714 and the Hanoverian arrival.

George I: Riots

> AN ANONYMOUS CONTEMPORARY observed 'Since the Reign of King George [I], which has not continued much above a year, there has been more riots and insurrections in Great Britain than have happened since the Conquest'.[30]

In a contemporary age, when questions are often raised on the popularity of monarchy or presidential systems, and in a world of almost instantaneous polls, it is sometimes easy to imagine that widespread protests and disagreement over accessions and ceremonies of power are new. They are not. As Oates points out, the above account was an 'exaggeration', but the accession to the throne of the Hanoverian George I, in 1714, did not go ahead with universal acclaim in Britain, there was much discontent and the number of riots and 'geographical spread was significant'.[31] Northern England, for example, saw 'disturbances' between the years '1714–1719' in 'Chester, Manchester, Oldham, Liverpool, Leeds, Warrington, Newcastle, Sheffield, Pontefract, Halifax, and York'.[32] Yes, it is true that this was in a world of Jacobitism with an alternative claimant to the throne, from James the Old Pretender, to Charles, the Young Pretender (Bonnie Prince Charlie),[33] but there have been so many moments in the history of accession to the English and later British throne involving potential alternative claims to the actual monarch, that this was just one of those instances that saw a multitude of discontent in what was an age of division and of polarisation.[34] Again—words that are bandied about as if they are something new—but for the years 1714–1722 it is thought that 'fifty-seven ... Jacobite disturbances [took place] in England, many in the south west and the Midlands'.[35] Perhaps unsurprisingly many of the dates of such uprisings can be linked to important moments in the political calendar, from the coronation of George I, to the anniversary of Charles II's Restoration and James Francis Stuart's birthday of 10 June. The politics of calendar lived on long after the Tudors and Stuarts.[36] Whether, as with more modern-day riots, these were for particular political (or at that time dynastic reasons) or socio-economic, or indeed religious reasons, is hard to absolutely pinpoint—a combination of all these factors is perhaps the best explanation, and in some cases may very well have had local trigger points, unrelated to national issues. As Oates highlights, '[c]ontemporaries were uncertain how far dynastic concerns were paramount in these riots. Abel Boyer, the writer and lexicographer, certainly thought they were of crucial significance', writing

> The Truth is; the Tories and Jacobites reserved the Demonstrations both of their Joy and Insolence for the next Day, which being the Anniversary of the Restoration of the Royal Family, they celebrated it in the most extraordinary manner, not only out of compliment to the former, but rather with the fond wishes and hopes of a future Restoration.[37]

Sometimes such discontent was fuelled by ongoing Whig and Tory factionalism or in response to *possibly* insensitive Whig celebrations, for instance, 'The Corporation of Liverpool made very public demonstrations of joy when it learnt that the King [George I] had arrived safely in

England', with bells, flags, bonfires, and cannon fire. In other locations, Tory rioting was in response to knowledge simply of the London Westminster Abbey event and George I's accession. *The Flying Post* recounts 'A Jacobite took a drink offered by the Whigs, but would not drink to King George, and then one of the Whigs threw a pot of ale at him'.[38] In York, the City Corporation there had to call for a stop to disturbances taking place both night and day, following George I's coronation.[39] In the end, the considerable discontent, led to legislation—and the origins of a phrase still in use to this day of 'reading the riot act'—allowing local authorities to order illegally assembled groups of more than twelve people to disperse. The accession of George I and associated coronation can be seen as a contributing factor, and firmly part of the background to the Riot Act.[40]

Hanoverian Splendour and Mishaps Combined

The Georgian era would see yet more mishaps and embarrassing public spectacle. Handel's most famous coronation anthem 'Zadok the Priest', composed for George II's[41] coronation in 1727 was not even performed at the right moment. Lambeth Palace Library hold the intriguing records of MS 1079b—Archbishop Wake's[42] service notes—which record that through 'negligence' on the part 'of the choir of Westminster' an anthem was not even sung, and 'Zadok the Priest' ended up featuring at the moment the *Veni creator spiritus* should have been produced.[43] George III's[44] coronation in 1761 went on for such a long time, that many of the audience assembled in Westminster Abbey, began to eat (!) during the coronation sermon of Robert Drummond, archbishop of York.[45] George III was knowledgeable of the order of service and must have been frustrated (although he did not show it) of the inefficiency of the officiating heralds. Strong, quoting a letter from Catherine Talbot of 22 September 1761 (the day of the coronation), highlights how the king "had much patience and good humour in bearing their numerous mistakes, and stupidities, as quickness and attention in setting them right". Worse followed for Queen Charlotte, for at the end of proceedings she found 'the Duke of Newcastle making use of her retiring chamber'. According to James Henning, the entire occasion was "confusion, irregularity, and disorder"; and the Deputy Earl Marshall, the Earl of Effingham, admitted "it was true; there had been great neglect in that office".[46] Roberts summarises the event as a classic mix of 'splendour with farce'—but it did include in the audience on a more notable and impressive level, Benjamin Franklin, the then British royalist supporter (over fears of French claims to Canada and in turn the American colonies).[47] As I have commented elsewhere, George IV's coronation saw yet further blunders, with Queen Caroline's (the king's estranged wife) efforts to gatecrash the coronation, as well as a banqueting nightmare for the peers' wives (see above). Queen Caroline was 'humiliated by being refused entry' and 'less than a fortnight after the coronation she was taken ill at the theatre, and after a short but painful illness she died, apparently of an intestinal obstruction, on 7 August 1821'.[48] Queen Caroline's 'exclusion … from the Coronation both symbolically and literally provided a figure of maligned womanhood'.[49] In response to the lavish spending, scandal, and gargantuan nature of George IV's coronation, William IV[50] sought to pare back the entire occasion for his 1831 ceremony, but this misfired with some of the public, and was thought of as the 'penny coronation' or 'Half-Crownation'. William also dispensed with the Coronation Banquet at Westminster Hall. Nevertheless, the revised setting for his Coronation Procession in Gold State Coach—set a pattern for later coronations—as captured in watercolour by George Cattermole.[51] See below an illustrated example of the procession for George IV's coronation (Fig. 8.1).

From Queen Victoria to 2023

As already discussed, Queen Victoria's coronation of 1838 was littered with mistakes, blunders, and a deal of pain for the young Queen's finger. Edward VII's coronation of 1902, may well have heralded in a new age, but it did not go without error or amusement. As the *Church Times* reported, The Archbishop of Canterbury, Frederick Temple although 'infirm'[52] presided over the service but 'a painful incident … ensued' when it came to the homage. For

> [t]he aged Primate … tried in vain to struggle to his feet to give the kiss on the monarch's left cheek. The King strenuously assisted him with both hands; at last with the aid of the Bishops of Winchester and Bath and Wells (the last-named being motioned by the King as one of his supporters to assist) the Primate was led off with difficulty to the north of the altar [.][53]

In 2023, Prince George's attendance at the coronation made him the first future king to attend his grandfather's coronation, since Edward VIII[54]

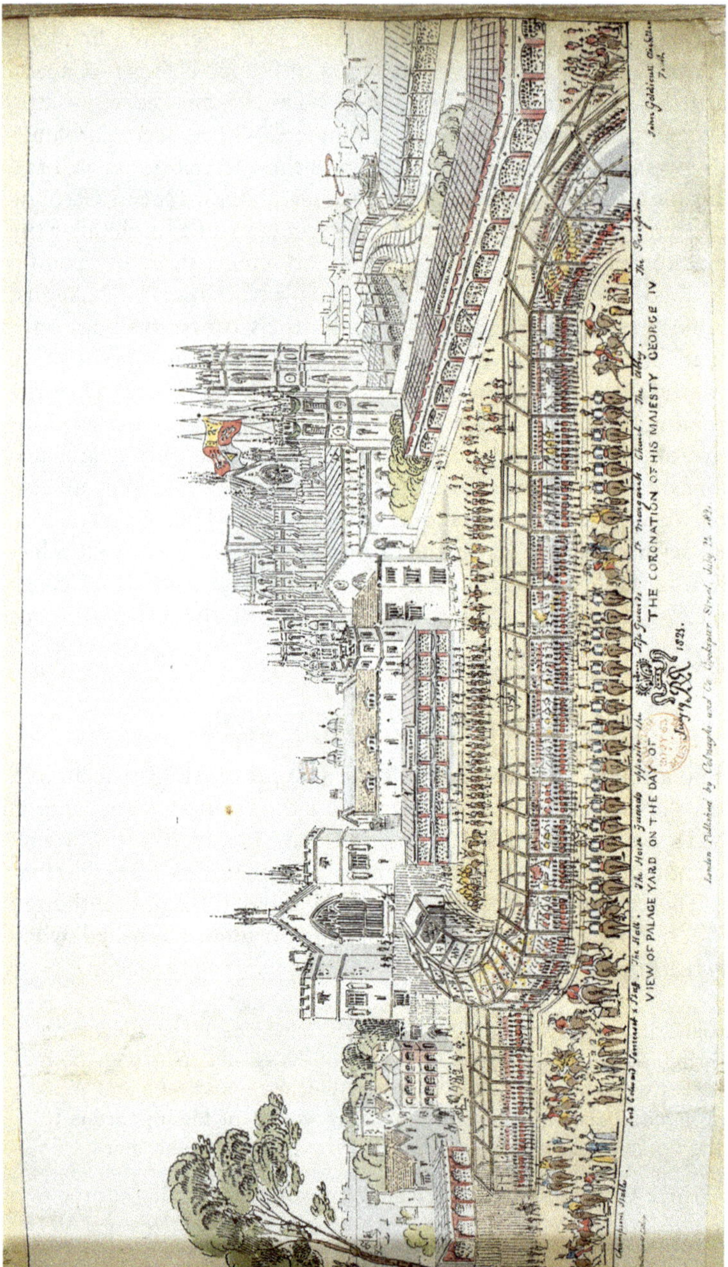

Fig. 8.1 View of the palace yard on the day of the coronation of his majesty George IV in 1821 from A Collection of 226 Engravings, etc., illustrating London and Environs, [London] 1825 (from the British Library archive, Maps.C.18.d.6. (46))

and George VI[55] at the turn of the twentieth century. It was said in 1902 that the grandchildren whispered and fidgeted a great deal, but watched 'in awe' as their father paid homage to their grandfather—the newly crowned Edward VII. It was reported that one of their great-aunts dropped an order of service over the edge of the box into a large gold vessel below creating a 'deafening clatter' which gave the grandchildren the giggles (!)—only to be stopped by a stern rebuke from the Prince of Wales (later George V).[56] George V would also record his experience of the day in his diary as 'Dear Papa & Mama's Coronation Day'—a day 'never to be forgotten'.[57] Yet, the 1902 occasion, very nearly didn't happen, with King Edward VII struck down with appendicitis, it had to be delayed. As already discussed, the Edwardian feast for the Coronation Banquet was distributed to those in need in London, including a vast quantity of quail.[58] This was not the first incident of coronation delay, for throughout history, they have been prone to such unforeseen events. In the early modern era, both the coronations of James I and Charles I (1603 and 1626) had been impacted by plague. In 1603, London had been suffering from a plague epidemic, and indeed James I had issued a proclamation announcing a cut-down version of the normal celebrations. Plague also affected Charles I's coronation in February 1626.[59]

A Pointed Break with Tradition

The abdication crisis of 1936 needs no further retelling here, but it was very pointed that the dowager Queen Mary[60] chose to attend the coronation of her son George VI in 1937. This was a break with tradition. Formerly Queens dowager were not present at coronations of their successors. In June 1911, the dowager Queen Alexandra remained at Sandringham. The obvious explanation of this break with tradition was to give a public sign—Queen Mary's—of support for George VI following the abdication of her elder son Edward VIII.[61]

The Churchills

As a more than interesting aside in this chapter of gaffes, critiques, and surprising incidents, overseeing, 1911, 1937, and 1953, were none other than Winston Churchill and his wife Clementine—present at all three coronations. In 1911, George V showed great 'thoughtfulness and solicitude' by making special provision for Clementine, recently a new mother. On hearing that Clementine Churchill would not be able to attend for she could not 'have left her precious new baby so long unsustained' given the length of a coronation, George V spared no effort in making it possible in the most comfortable of manners available. Her daughter Mary records

> A royal brougham called for her at her house and drove her to Westminster Abbey, so that she arrived at the latest possible moment; she watched the ceremony until after the actual crowning of the King, then slipped discreetly away and was driven home to the hungering Randolph.[62]

Foreign Comparison and 2023

Given the litany of coronation mistakes presented in the previous pages, it might be easy to imagine this was something bespoke to the Westminster Abbey service, but that is far from the case. Carefully staged ceremonies and celebrations could go spectacularly wrong in any age, and any country, as it did at Nicholas II's coronation in 1896, with the disastrous Khodynskoe Field massacre—in which over a thousand Russians gathering for a popular feast in honour of the new Tsar, died in a mass stampede. Far from showing order, the coronation celebrations highlighted a 'regime bereft of control'.[63] As one member of the Russian Bulletin put it, 'this is a bad omen. Nothing good will come of this tsar's reign'.[64] The perceived success of a coronation and the accompanying celebrations made dramatic impressions on those who witnessed them. From the beginning, the perception of Nicholas II's regime was tarnished by an ill-fated sense of disaster. For all of the disaster of 1896 in Moscow, to this chapter that has seen the dreadful massacres and violence of 1066 and 1189 in England, and from the riots of 1714 across Britain, to attempted gatecrashing, and tumbling peers, most coronations put on displays of the utmost grandeur that left spectators in awe. Nevertheless, the key point here is that they have not been 'uneventful' beyond the ceremonial and have not been uniformly received or equally successful across different eras and dynasties. Creating a legacy that survives the immediacy of the occasion is a tremendous challenge as James II discovered—and with the complexities of managing public mood—to overspend in George IV's case can lead to criticism, just as much as to underspend in 1831. A balance that chimes with the public mood is no simple task as we shall explore in the following chapter with the reception of 6 May 2023. We end this chapter with one of the more problematic and controversial moments of 2023, a proposed 'Homage of the People'. The idea as an 'innovation' was raised a number of days in advance of the coronation, to update the service by replacing the homage by the peerage, with members of the public 'pledging allegiance' to King Charles III. The liturgy and accompanying commentary published by Lambeth Palace states:

> [Liturgy]
> All:
> I swear that I will pay true allegiance
> to your Majesty, and to your heirs and
> successors according to law. So help me God.
>
> [Commentary]
> This is a new and significant moment in the
> tradition of the Coronation. Never before in our
> history have the general public been offered
> such an opportunity to join with national figures
> in declaring their allegiance to a new Sovereign.[65]

A backlash to the idea immediately ensued, with discontent from across the political spectrum, with some labelling the idea 'offensive' and others 'tone deaf'.[66] It later emerged following a Jonathan Dimbleby interview[67] and various public comments from Lambeth Palace that the proposal had stemmed, not from the monarch, but from the then Archbishop of Canterbury, Justin Welby, and his team. Dimbleby in a BBC Radio 4 Today programme discussion stressed that he felt the sovereign would find such a concept 'abhorrent' and the last thing his 'close friend' King Charles would want, would be to be 'revered'. Many saw the concept as wholly un-British and rather something out of an American tradition of pledging allegiance to the flag, leaving members of the public uncomfortable with this rather forced idea of swearing allegiance to the King. The Archbishop of Canterbury, having misjudged the mood, was forced to refer to the whole idea as 'voluntary', and an 'invitation' not a 'command'. The Dimbleby interview the day before the coronation made the situation much easier for the Monarch and the magnificence of the actual day overshadowed the drama of the allegiance incident or proposal. However, it showed yet again, how even with the best arranged plans, mishaps continue into the twenty-first century, though as in this case, and in so many of the other examples presented in this chapter, not personally caused by or at the hands necessarily of the monarch.[68]

Notes

1. See for example summons: Staff. RO, MS D(W)1778/I/i/1798.
2. https://www.coronationroll.gov.uk/further_info/gold-state-coach/, accessed 23 November 2025; *The Coronation* (BBC, 2018) – Television documentary with Alastair Bruce made to commemorate the Sapphire Jubilee of Elizabeth II, the 65th anniversary of the coronation of Elizabeth II; See also M. Kite and Roy. Thomson, *Conservation of Leather and Related Materials* (Burlington, Massachusetts, 2006), pp. 265–7 (documents restoration and discomfort from the construction); W. Seymour, *Sovereign Legacy: An Historical Guide to the British Monarchy* (London, 1980), p. 273; G. A. Thrupp, *The History of Coaches* (London, 1877), p. 63. The Gold State Coach was designed by Sir William Chambers and built in the London workshops of Samuel Butler in 1762. On 6 May 2023, the King and Queen travelled to the Abbey from Buckingham Palace in the newest of the royal carriages –the Diamond Jubilee State Coach, first used in 2014. The King's Procession was observed by thousands of spectators as it followed the 1.3-mile (2.1km) route down the Mall to Trafalgar Square through Admiralty Arch, along Whitehall and Parliament Street to Parliament Square, bringing the King and Queen Consort to Westminster Abbey. Following the Service, their Majesties returned to Buckingham Palace in the Gold State Coach, used at every coronation since 1831, along the same route in reverse. The Royal family then greeted the crowds from the balcony, thus concluding the Coronation Day.
3. See T. W. Laqueur, 'The Queen Caroline Affair: Politics as Art in the Reign of George IV', *The Journal of Modern History*, 54, (1982), pp. 417–66; T. Fulford, 'Cobbett, Coleridge and the Queen Caroline Affair', *Studies in Romanticism*, 37 (1998), pp. 523–43; K. Cockin, 'Queen Caroline's Pains and Penalties: Silence and Speech in the Dramatic Art of British Women's Suffrage', *Law and Literature*, 24 (2012), pp. 40–58. See also Neuheiser, *Crown, Church and Constitution*, p. 54.
4. A. C. Benson and Viscount Esher (eds), *The Letters of Queen Victoria: A Selection from Her Majesty's Correspondence Between the Years 1837 and 1861*, 3 volumes (London, 1907), I, p. 156 (her emphases). Queen Victoria's diary entries are now available *via* digitisation at: (http://www.queenvictoriasjournals.org/, accessed 23 November 2025). Her coronation entries are fascinating.
5. https://www.tate.org.uk/art/artworks/martin-the-coronation-of-queen-victoria-n05753, accessed 23 November 2025. See www.queenvictoriasjournals.org (accessed 23 November 2025) for her coronation day Thursday 28 June 1838.

6. *The Coronation* (BBC, 2018) – Television documentary with Alastair Bruce made to commemorate the Sapphire Jubilee of Elizabeth II, the 65th anniversary of the coronation of Elizabeth II.
7. A. King and I. Crewe, *The Blunders of our Governments* (London, 2013), pp. 277–9.
8. An entire monograph could be filled with such incidents, those presented here are a selection to provide a flavour from across the centuries, with some well know examples and others less so.
9. Bates, *William the Conqueror*, p. 256. See also G. Garnett, *The Norman Conquest: A Very Short Introduction* (Oxford, 2009), pp. 20–25; and S. G. 'Westminster Abbey', *The Aldine*, 8 (1877), p. 285.
10. Douglas, 'The Conquest of England January 1066–March 1067', p. 207. See also Cole, *The Norman Conquest*, pp. 201–2.
11. R. Fleming, 'Harold II [Harold Godwineson] (1022/3?–1066)', *ODNB*.
12. Douglas, 'The Conquest of England January 1066–March 1067', p. 182; see also Cole, *The Norman Conquest*, p. 110.
13. Bates, *William the Conqueror*, p. 216.
14. *Ibid.*, pp. 334–6.
15. D. Corner, 'Howden [Hoveden], Roger of (d. 1201/2)', *ODNB*. Stubbs, *Chronica Magistri Rogeri de Houedene*; H. T. Riley (ed.), *The Annals of Roger de Hoveden: Comprising the History of England and of other Countries of Europe from A.D. 732 to A.D. 1201*, 2 volumes (London, 1853); See also J. Gillingham, 'Two Yorkshire Historians Compared: Roger of Howden and William of Newburgh', *Haskins Society Journal* 12 (2002), 15–37.
16. J. Gillingham, 'Richard I [called Richard Coeur de Lion, Richard the Lionheart] (1157–1199)', *ODNB*.
17. H. Blurton, 'Egyptian Days: From Passion to Exodus in the Representation of Twelfth-Century Jewish-Christian Relations', in S. R. Jones and S. Watson (eds), *Christians and Jews in Angevin England: The York Massacre of 1190* (Woodbridge, 2013), pp. 222–3 – quoting 'pax Judaeorum, quam ab antiquis temporibus semper obtinuerant, ab alienigenis interrum pitur', Stubbs, Diceto, *Historical Works* II, p. 69.
18. See also S. G. 'Westminster Abbey', p. 285.
19. Blurton, 'Egyptian Days', p. 222. Blurton here is quoting/translating from: William of Newburgh, 'Historia Rerum Anglicarum', in R. Howlett (ed.), *Chronicles of the Reigns of Stephen, Henry II and Richard I*, 4 vols., RS 82 (London, 1884–1889), I–II; J. Stevenson (trans.), William of Newburgh, 'Historia Rerum Anglicarum', in *The Church Historians of England*, 5 vols. (London, 1853–1858), IV, pt. 2, pp. 397–672.
20. J. Taylor, 'Newburgh, William of (b. 1135/6, d. in or after 1198)', *ODNB*.
21. https://www.oxfordreference.com/display/10.1093/oi/authority.20110803095754366, accessed 23 November 2025.

22. R. Nisse, 'Josephus, Jerusalem, and the Martyrs of Medieval England', in R. Nisse, *Jacob's Shipwreck: Diaspora, Translation, and Jewish-Christian Relations in Medieval England* (Ithaca, New York, 2017), p. 42. See also Blurton, 'Egyptian Days', p. 223.
23. J. R. Marcus and M. Saperstein (eds), 'The York Riots 1190', in J. R. Marcus and M. Saperstein (eds), *The Jews in Christian Europe: A Source Book, 315–1791* (Pittsburgh, Pennsylvania, 2015), pp. 103–8, at p. 103. See also R. B. Dobson, *The Jews of Medieval York and the Massacre of March 1190* (York, 1974); J. D. Hosler, 'Henry II, William of Newburgh, and the Development of English Anti-Judaism', in *Christian Attitudes Toward the Jews in the Middle Ages: A Casebook*, ed. M. Frassetto (New York, New York, 2007), pp. 167–82; and S. L. Einbinder, *Beautiful Death: Jewish Poetry and Martyrdom in Medieval France* (Princeton, New Jersey 2002).
24. Blurton, 'Egyptian Days', p. 237. See also Sebag Montefiore, *Jerusalem*, pp. 247–56.
25. M. Prestwich, 'Edward I (1239–1307)', *ODNB*.
26. J. Morrill, 'Cromwell, Oliver (1599–1658)', *ODNB*.
27. Cressy, *Charles I*, pp. 103–11.
28. See Leonard, 'Distraint of Knighthood: The Last Phase, 1625–41', pp. 23–37; and M. R. Powicke, 'Distraint of Knighthood and Military Obligation under Henry III', *Speculum*, 25 (1950), pp. 457–70.
29. Bodl., MS Ballard 12, fol. 186r–v.
30. Oates, 'Jacobitism and Popular Disturbances in Northern England, 1714–1719', p. 111: quoting Anon., *The History of all the Mobs, Tumults and Insurrections in Great Britain* (1715), p. 53.
31. Oates, 'Jacobitism and Popular Disturbances in Northern England, 1714–1719', p. 111. See also W. A. Speck, *Stability and Strife, England, 1714–1760* (1977), pp. 169–70.
32. Oates, 'Jacobitism and Popular Disturbances in Northern England, 1714–1719', pp. 111–2.
33. E. Gregg, 'James Francis Edward [James Francis Edward Stuart; styled James; known as Chevalier de St George, the Pretender, the Old Pretender] (1688–1766)', *ODNB*; M. Pittock, 'Charles Edward [Charles Edward Stuart; styled Charles; known as the Young Pretender, Bonnie Prince Charlie] (1720–1788)', *ODNB*.
34. G. Borus, 'Political Parties in the Years Before and After the Glorious Revolution', *Hungarian Journal of English and American Studies (HJEAS)*, 13 (2007), pp. 121–30; H. Smith, 'The Court in England, 1714–1760: A Declining Political Institution?' *History*, 90 (2005), pp. 23–41; G. V. Bennett, 'English Jacobitism, 1710–1715; Myth and Reality', *Transactions of the Royal Historical Society*, 32 (1982), pp. 137–51.

35. Oates, 'Jacobitism and Popular Disturbances in Northern England, 1714–1719', p. 111; M. G. M. Pittock, *Jacobitism* (Aberdeen, 1998), p. 37.
36. On the importance of the Tudor and Stuart Calendar see Cressy, *Bonfires*.
37. Oates, 'Jacobitism and Popular Disturbances in Northern England, 1714–1719', p. 444. See also: https://www.rct.uk/collection/1110512/the-political-state-of-great-britain-v-49-jan-june-1735, accessed 23 November 2025; G. Gibbs, 'Boyer, Abel (1667?–1729)', *ODNB*.
38. Oates, 'Jacobitism and Popular Disturbances in Northern England, 1714–1719', p. 127, quoting: *The Flying Post*, 3716, 27–29 Oct. 1715.
39. Oates, 'Jacobitism and Popular Disturbances in Northern England, 1714–1719', p. 114, see (though Whig Newspaper) *The Flying Post*, 3548, 28–30 Sept. 1714; see York City Archives, F12a, p. 18. Violence erupted in mob form on the streets of Newcastle between Whigs and Tories in response to a bonfire celebration for George I, see: E. Hughes, 'Some Clavering Correspondence', *Archaeologia Aeliana*, 4th ser., xxxiv (1956), pp. 20–21.
40. Parliamentary Archives, HL/PO/PU/1/1714/1G1s2n7.
41. J. Cannon, 'George II (1683–1760)', *ODNB*.
42. S. Taylor, 'Wake, William (1657–1737)', *ODNB*.
43. See LPL, MS 1079b; see also Range, *Music*, pp. 137, 141–2.
44. J. Cannon, 'George III (1738–1820)', *ODNB*.
45. R. Sharp, 'Drummond, Robert Hay (1711–1776)', *ODNB*. See also Roberts, *George III: The Life and Reign of Britain's Most Misunderstood Monarch*, pp. 73–5; Black, *George III: America's Last King*, pp. 109–111; and J. Brooke, *King George III* (New York, New York, 1972), p. 85.
46. Strong, *Coronation*, pp. 407–8 – see LPL, MSS 1082 and 1719, fol. 35–43 (letter of Catherine Talbot); *Annual Register or a view of the History of Politics ..., 1761,* 7th edn (1800), pp. 229–35; W. S. Lewis, *et al.* (eds), *Horace Walpole's Correspondence* (Oxford, 1960) V, pp. 534–7.
47. Roberts, *George III: The Life and Reign of Britain's Most Misunderstood Monarch*, pp. 74–5. J. Lemay, 'Franklin, Benjamin (1706–1790)', *ODNB*.
48. E. Smith, 'Caroline [Princess Caroline of Brunswick-Wolfenbüttel] (1768–1821)', *ODNB*. See also, M. Solly, 2 May 2023, https://www.smithsonianmag.com/history/a-not-so-brief-history-of-british-coronations-180982088/, accessed 23 November 2025; J. Robins, *The Trial of Queen Carline: The Scandalous Affair that Nearly Ended a Monarchy* (New York, New York, 2006), pp. 307–12; F. Fraser, *The Unruly Queen: The Life of Queen Caroline* (London, 1996), pp. 456–7; Laqueur, 'The Queen Caroline Affair: Politics as Art in the Reign of George IV', pp. 417–66; & On Queen Caroline's contribution to Art and Culture, see J. Marschner, *Queen Caroline: Cultural Politics at the Eighteenth-century*

Court (New Haven, Connecticut, 2014); See also S. G. 'Westminster Abbey', p. 286.
49. Cockin, 'Queen Caroline's Pains and Penalties: Silence and Speech in the Dramatic Art of British Women's Suffrage', p. 50. See also M. Levy, 'Fitzherbert [née Smythe; other married name Weld], Maria Anne (1756–1837), unlawful wife of George IV by a marriage invalid under the Royal Marriages Act of 1772', *ODNB.* George IV as Prince of Wales in 1785 had married clandestinely the Roman Catholic widow Maria Fitzherbert without George III's permission and against the law (the Royal Marriages Act 1772). His marriage in 1795 to Queen Caroline was an effort to produce an heir to the throne and clear his exponential debts.
50. M. Brock, 'William IV (1765–1837)', *ODNB.*
51. See LPL, MS 1083b: Service for George III, revised for William IV. Archbishop Howley noted that William IV's service 'was printed from this copy: but some farther alterations were introduced as it passed through the press'; *TLG*, 13 September 1831, Issue 18848, pp. 1861–1875 (https://www.thegazette.co.uk/London/issue/18848/page/1861, accessed 23 November 2025); V&A, 38041016058729 (R. Hyde, Paper Peepshows. The Jacqueline and Jonathan Gestetner Collection (Woodbridge: The Antique Collectors' Club, 2015), cat. 224 (The Coronation in the Abbey of St Peter's Westminster, of His Majesty King William IVth and Queen Adelaide, Essex, C., ca.1831); London Museum, A16163 (G. Cattermole, 'Coronation Procession of King William IV and Queen Adelaide' (1831). See also: Torrance, 'The coronation: History and ceremonial', p. 15 (n.) 42; Van Der Kiste, *William IV: The Last Hanoverian King of Britain*, pp. 122–6; Poole, 'Collins in Context: William IV, Affability and the Reform Crisis, 1830–37', pp. 163–4; Shenton, *Mr Barry's War: Rebuilding the Houses of Parliament After the Great Fire of 1834*, pp. 83–84; Ward, *Writing the Victorian Constitution*, pp. 1–2.
52. H. Spooner, & M. Chapman, 'Temple, Frederick (1821–1902)', *ODNB.*
53. *The Church Times* (August 15th 1902).
54. H. Matthew, 'Edward VIII [afterwards Prince Edward, duke of Windsor] (1894–1972)', *ODNB.*
55. H. Matthew, 'George VI (1895–1952)', *ODNB.*
56. S. Bradford, *The Reluctant King: The Life and Reign of George VI, 1895–1952* (New York, New York, 1990), pp. 25–6. See also *TLG:* 28 October 1902, Issue 27489, pp. 6859–6892 (https://www.thegazette.co.uk/London/issue/27489/supplement/6859, accessed 23 November 2025); H. Matthew, 'George V (1865–1936)', *ODNB.*
57. RA/GV/PRIV/GVD, 9 August 1902 diary entry from York House, London, of George, Prince of Wales (later King George V), pp. 336–8.

58. https://www.rct.uk/collection/2301735/the-kings-coronation-dinner-to-the-people-5-july-1902, accessed 23 November 2025; See also D. Starkey, *Crown and Country: The Kings and Queens of England* (London, 2010), p. 473. See also R. Strong, *Coronation*, p. 466; and M. Carter, *The Three Emperors: Three Cousins, Three Empires and the Road to World War One* (London, 2009), p. 275; Wollaston, *Coronation ... The Court of Claims*, *passim*.
59. Anon., *A Proclamation* [6 July 1603] *Signifying the Kings Maiesties Pleasure, Touching the Resort of People to his Coronation* (London, 1603); Cf. FSL, MS X.c.20 (Matthew Hutton to his son, 18 July 1603), excusing his son's attendance at the reduced coronation solemnities and suggesting that 'verie few will go' given plague; and FLS, L.a.1060. Cf. KA, MS U951 C261/15; *ibid.*, MS NR/CPh1/2 (Edward Kelke's circular letter to Cinque Ports, 11–13 July 1603). Cf. *ibid.*, MSS NR/CPh1/3 (Circular letter, 12 July 1603) and NR/CPh1/4 – which references the 'sickness [in] London'. See also Cressy, *Charles I*, p. 66.
60. F. Prochaska, 'Mary [Princess Mary of Teck] (1867–1953)', *ODNB*.
61. Owens, *The Family Firm*, p. 138.
62. M. Soames, *Clementine Churchill: The Biography of a Marriage* (rev. edn., New York, New York, 2003), p. 82.
63. R. S. Wortman, *Scenarios of Power: Myth and Ceremony in Russian Monarchy, from Peter the Great to the Abdication of Nicholas II* (Princeton, New Jersey, 2006), p. 343.
64. V. Gilyarovsky (trans. B. Kiernan), *Moscow and Muscovites* (original 1935, this edition 2013, Montpelier, Vermont), p. 334.
65. *Authorised Liturgy ... Coronation Rite ... Charles III*, p. 28.
66. For examples: https://www.theguardian.com/uk-news/2023/may/06/coronation-homage-of-the-people-toned-down-after-criticism#:~:text=The%20suggestion%20of%20the%20homage,holds%20the%20people%20in%20contempt%E2%80%9D, 6 May 2023, accessed 23 November 2025; T. Jones, 6 May 2023, https://www.standard.co.uk/news/london/king-charles-coronation-homage-people-queen-consort-b1079274.html, accessed 23 November 2025; S. Bradley, 2 May 2023, https://theweek.com/news/royals/960690/homage-of-the-people-should-public-pledge-allegiance-to-new-king, accessed 23 November 2025; V. Ward, 30 April 2023, https://www.telegraph.co.uk/royal-family/2023/04/30/public-homage-charles-coronation-voluntary-lambeth-palace/, accessed 23 November 2025; V. Ward, G. Swerling and S. Bird, 6 May 2023, https://www.telegraph.co.uk/royal-family/2023/05/06/coronation-service-changed-after-allegiance-backlash/, accessed 23 November 2025.

67. J. Crew, 5 May 2023, https://www.bbc.co.uk/news/uk-65493188, accessed 23 November 2025.
68. *Ibid.*, https://www.bbc.co.uk/news/uk-65493188, accessed 23 November 2025; H. Williams, 3 May 2023, https://www.churchtimes.co.uk/articles/2023/5-may/news/uk/archbishop-welby-defends-people-s-homage-in-the-coronation#:~:text=THE%20Archbishop%20of%20Canterbury%20has,a%20command%E2%80%9D%20but%20an%20invitation, accessed 23 November 2025; N. Duffy, 2 May 2023, https://inews.co.uk/news/public-refuse-allegiance-king-coronation-archbishop-canterbury-2312629?srsltid=AfmBOopqKC26220rvgRWGlqd3akdfCrkfrsHMGIipNK679e_T6eDKEij, accessed 23 November 2025.

CHAPTER 9

Impact, Education, and Conclusion

The year 2023 was a momentous one in Royal History, with the coronation in May at Westminster Abbey, a Scottish Investiture in July and an Abdication announcement in Denmark on New Year's Eve. In both cases, the monarch taking on the mantle of kingship—Charles III in the United Kingdom and Frederik X in Denmark (on 14 January 2024) —have been bequeathed their thrones on the back of extraordinary legacies of duty, longevity, and public respect. The late Queen Elizabeth II's approval ratings and those of Queen Margrethe II were unrivalled in their respective countries, regularly exceeding 80%. Elizabeth II reigned for 70 years, longer than any other monarch in British history, and Margrethe II ended her reign after 52 years on the Danish throne.

Since Charles III's succession, there have been a number of polls conducted looking at the future of the monarchy and what 'young people' think, with so-called 'deep generational divides'.[1] The findings of a further poll in the late summer of 2023 continued to show this pattern: of 18–24-year-olds, just 30% saw monarchy as 'good for Britain', in contrast to 77% of those over 65. The survey of 2000 adults was conducted to time with the anniversary of the passing of Queen Elizabeth II. Overall 62% of respondents wanted to retain the monarchy.[2]

At the end of 2022, with the coronation date already set for 6 May 2023, The British Coronations Project 2023, led by King's College London (KCL)[3] —with the University of Roehampton, Arts Projects for

G. W. C. Gross, *Crown and People*,
https://doi.org/10.1007/978-3-032-20786-9_9

Schools, the British Association for Local History, and the New Museum for the Stone of Scone—published a range of educational resources for schools telling the history of coronations. The British Coronations Project was set up to document the story behind many of the traditional elements from these momentous royal ceremonies, from why the king or queen is invested with a Coronation Ring, to how the monarch decides what food and wines will be served at a coronation banquet. As well as curriculum-based resources, structured lessons, and a wealth of historical information, schools were welcomed to contribute to two surveys, one before the coronation and one after for the KCL project, and with the support of Arts Projects for Schools, they were encouraged to create a commemorative coronation mug or yearbook.

The British Coronations Project 2023 featured on the government website for the coronation as part of the educational resources and opportunities for children across the United Kingdom (and beyond) to learn more about the occasion.[4] More than 2000 schools from across the United Kingdom registered to download the resources in the build-up towards King Charles III's coronation, leading to tens of thousands of pupils engaging with the KCL project. The project was free, and suitable for children in Key Stages 1 and 2 (P2–7 in Scotland & Northern Ireland), and included lesson packs, activity ideas, and presentations.

Children were presented with educational material based on previously unstudied and underused eye-witness accounts of, for instance, the 1661 coronation of Charles II, to changes in the way in which state portraits of monarchs have been painted; to how a fake version of the coronation oath was almost used by King Henry VIII.

As part of this project, the British Coronations Project set out to examine for the first time in British Coronation history what 'young people', that is children, think about the monarchy. Children were given the opportunity to express their views in the form of two surveys, in quiz style format—in essence polls. This chapter presents the first detailed analysis of those findings and asks important questions about identity and the impact of a coronation in the twenty-first century. With these questions in mind, there are clear indications for further avenues for exploration in future publications—not least extending the age range of the polls.

In 1953 Edward Shils and Michael Young sought to discuss the 'meaning' of the coronation. On the basis of 'a survey of street parties in East London', there was surprise that 'nothing was more remarkable than the complete inability of people to say why they thought important the occasion they were honouring with such elaborate ritual'.[5] Their conclusion was that a

> Coronation provided at one time and for practically the entire society such an intensive contact with the sacred that we believe we are justified in interpreting it as we have done in this essay, as a great act of national communion.[6]

That 'may' have been true for 1953 (and arguments have been equally made of 'social collectivity' around Queen Victoria's coronation and marriage celebrations),[7] but in the first such exercise in study of coronations, the KCL project attempted to discover what children think about such momentous events. How far did the project reach in terms of impact? What was their interpretation of a coronation? Did it—in a so-called secular age—continue to raise sacred ideas? What was prominent in their minds?

West Ham Church of England Primary School in London provides an exemplar of how our research informed discussion and learning around the coronation. The children there spent time discovering about the history of the king's crown and throne, whilst creating their own versions of these objects. The pupils also got involved with planning a re-enactment of the events of the coronation, which they performed in front of their family and friends at a local church (Fig. 9.1).

One pupil noted: 'I made a portrait of King Charles, it was really hard to draw. I don't come from London so I've been learning about a different culture'. Miss Gilliland, Art & Design & Technology Lead at the school explained that 'by incorporating The Coronations Project's resources into our curriculum, all the children at West Ham Primary schools have had their learning impacted both creatively and academically. They really enjoyed learning about this historic event through a creative and multisensory approach'. Dr Robert Watts, senior lecturer in Art and Design Education at the University of Roehampton, commented that 'the fact so many schools have welcomed the project is evidence that creativity has a future in children's education'. The British Association for Local History put great emphasis on the opportunity the project gave for children to 'explore' the history behind this 'momentous' event[8]; and CEO of Art Projects for Schools, Dan Dickey, stated: 'to have the chance to work with King's College London and the University of Roehampton, and to be part of the Government website's resources for schools, has been a real thrill. To have over 200,000 children benefitting from the wonderful ideas

Fig. 9.1 Pupils from West Ham Church of England Primary School used the resources to inform a re-enactment of the coronation ceremony

of those institutions is testament to the quality of their knowledge and stimulating ideas'.

Work on Quiz (or Poll I) began on 14 March 2023 and concluded at the end of the coronation festivities. This was then followed by Quiz (or Poll II) which began on 8 May 2023 and concluded on 6 July 2023.

Our first poll sample included 1,996 respondents with an average age of 10 years old (aged between 6 and 12). We picked these informative years when children are typically undertaking important assessments in English and Mathematics (KS2 for instance), and these are benchmarks for measuring aptitude/attainment. The poll was sent out to schools across the United Kingdom. Respondents had the chance to complete the poll online or in paper format (99% completed online), and this could be done in the classroom or at home. 97% of entries were completed in school and 3% from home.

Our second poll included 413 respondents with an average age of 10 years old (aged between 6 and 17). This followed a similar focus as with the first sample. The poll was again sent out to schools across the United Kingdom. 83% completed the poll in school, with 17% from home (Tables 9.1 and 9.2).

In Poll I, just under 88% of respondents came from schools in the State sector with just over 12% from the Private sector. 23% of pupils studied at Faith schools. Of all the schools responding, 22% were eligible for free school meals at those schools. In terms of gender split, 73% of children answered the poll as part of a class/group (girls and boys); 15% as girls only; and 13% as boys only.

Table 9.1 Poll I respondent information

Poll I	
Respondents	1996
Average Age	10
Answering at school or at home	97% at school; 3% at home
Answering online or on paper	99% online; 1% on paper
Answering as a group (girls and boys)	73%
Girls only	15%
Boys only	13%
State school	88%
Private school	12%
Faith school	23%
% Eligibility for Free School Meals	22%

Table 9.2 Poll II respondent information

Poll II	
Respondents	413
Average Age	10
Answering at school or at home	83.29% at school; 16.71% at home
Answering online or on paper	100% online
Answering as a group	75.54%
Girls only	16.22%
Boys only	8.23%
State school	77.2%
Private school	22.8%
Faith school	50.5%
% Eligibility for Free School Meals	26%

Table 9.3 Poll I monarchy question

Poll I	
Question	Many countries do not have kings or queens; they are republics. The United Kingdom is rare in having a monarchy—where the king or queen is Head of State—that (apart from 1649–1660) stretches back into the Middle Ages. How do you feel about having a monarchy in the United Kingdom?
Proud / Happy / Excited	64.7%
Annoyed / Bored / Sad	14.9%
Confused / Indifferent	20.4%

When children were asked 'how having a monarchy made them feel in the United Kingdom?'— 64.7% felt proud, excited, or happy, while just 14.9% felt sad, bored, or annoyed about the monarchy. A higher percentage of 20.4% were confused or indifferent rather than expressing negative views or feelings (Tables 9.3 and 9.4).

When asked, 'when you think of the fact that we still crown our new kings and queens, how does that make you feel?' 70.4% felt proud, excited or happy, while just 13% felt sad, bored or annoyed, and again there was a higher percentage of indifference rather than negativity with 16.6% confused or indifferent.

Table 9.4 Poll I coronation question

Poll I	
Question	Even where other countries have kept their monarchies, most do not hold Coronations. When you think of the fact that in the United Kingdom we still crown our new kings and queens in a big ceremony, how does that make you feel?
Proud / Happy / Excited	70.4%
Annoyed / Bored / Sad	13%
Confused / Indifferent	16.6%

It is clear that a substantive majority of children with an average age of 10 years are in favour of the monarchy. This is in marked contrast to those 18–24-year olds polled by yougov.[9] It is possible that it has ever been thus, that children are more traditionalist, but in their later teenage years and early adulthood turn to more liberal ideas and then as they move towards retirement age, we see the reverse and a reversion to traditionalist ideas. It is equally possible that this is new and that children were excited by the coronation events of 2023 with the build-up and planning to May. The figure is higher for those proud, happy, or excited by the idea of crowning kings or queens at 70.4% than those expressing their feelings about the monarchy more generally at 64.7%. A further possibility is that children polled had parents hugely in favour of the monarchy, and they therefore reflected the views of their parents, though that in itself would test the findings of the yougov polls. Likewise, it might have been possible that children were influenced by their teachers, but that again would suggest an interesting story about what those in the education sector (across the full educational cross-section of State, Private, and Faith schools) think of the monarchy and of the idea of a coronation. These polls certainly challenge the idea *or consensus* that the monarchy lacks support amongst younger people, and these findings indicate that the picture is significantly more nuanced than has been reported to date.

We then assessed the data in Poll I more closely, in terms of the school background, for these responses to both monarchy and the question of a coronation (Table 9.5).

Table 9.5 Poll I monarchy question breakdown by school background

Poll I	
Question	Many countries do not have kings or queens; they are republics. The United Kingdom is rare in having a monarchy—where the king or queen is Head of State—that (apart from 1649–1660) stretches back into the Middle Ages. How do you feel about having a monarchy in the United Kingdom?
State sector	
Proud / Happy / Excited	65.9%
Annoyed / Bored / Sad	14.4%
Confused / Indifferent	19.7%
Private sector	
Proud / Happy / Excited	55.7%
Annoyed / Bored / Sad	18.6%
Confused / Indifferent	25.8%
Faith schools	
Proud / Happy / Excited	68%
Annoyed / Bored / Sad	14.2%
Confused / Indifferent	17.8%
Type of school	**% of Poll I**
State school	88%
Private school	12%
Faith school[a]	23%

[a]Faith schools as a category include both State and Private schools

It is worth noting that State School pupil responses made up 88% of the sample, whereas Private School entries amounted to just 12%, just over 200 pupils, so we are looking at a very small sample from the Private sector, and Faith School entries at just 23%. Nevertheless the findings are interesting in the greater support shown in the State sector and show considerable support across all educational sectors.[10] When the Private School data is broken down by region, we are able to see that those in London showed a higher degree of negativity and apathy, with a total of 52.62% than those out of London at 37.28%, and this may be explained by the number of international students in the London Private school system. Private school students out of London polled 62.72% in favour of monarchy against 47.39% within London. It is less than likely that a student with perhaps their own head of state is likely to feel such a personal connection to the question of monarchy in Britain. Some might have thought this was a London issue, not just within the Private sector, and it is true that the percentage of support for monarchy from state school pupils does rise out of London, but from a very high base in London of 60.88% to 67.65%. By contrast, the percentage of London state schools supporting the monarchy remains far higher than in the Private sector, with 60.88% in favour from the State sector within London schools polled, against 47.39% in the Private sector in London, again pointing to the international background of students within London Private schools (Table 9.6).

Across all sectors, it is clear that the coronation (and associated build-up) attracted more positive feelings from those children responding to this poll than even the question of monarchy itself. There are many potential reasons for this, but it seems that more exposure to ideas, to the event itself and to the history around the crowning of kings and queens may be possible factors in this marked approval, a sign perhaps that from a monarchical stand-point a coronation is an important element in maintaining the interest, imagination, and support of those in school education. The Private sector response is the highest in support, and here the London percentage of apathy towards monarchy more generally changes in this question, with far more support for the event of the coronation itself. This is yet further evidence it would seem, for the need 'to be seen to be believed' and the power of spectacle, even for those with more limited ties to the United Kingdom.[11] Whereas to the first question, London Private school pupils gave just 47.39% in support of monarchy, in the second question in terms of a response to the idea of a coronation, this figure rose to 56.86%.

National identity has been a central theme of the chapters in this book—and how a coronation projected ideas, politically and religiously. In Poll I, pupils were also asked, when they thought of a British Coronation, which of these words come to mind, relating to areas and identities: 'British'; 'Commonwealth'; 'English'; 'Northern-Irish'; 'Scottish'; 'Welsh'.[12] Table 9.7 presents the findings, with the highest percentage going to British, and then strikingly 'Commonwealth' appearing in third place, with as high as 51.60%.

Our second poll, which was conducted after the coronation—took in a smaller sample size as schools moved beyond the topic to refocus on their

Table 9.6 Poll I coronation question breakdown by school background

Poll I	
Question	Even where other countries have kept their monarchies, most do not hold Coronations. When you think of the fact that in the United Kingdom we still crown our new kings and queens in a big ceremony, how does that make you feel?
State sector	
Proud / Happy / Excited	69.7%
Annoyed / Bored / Sad	13%
Confused / Indifferent	17.3%
Private sector	
Proud / Happy / Excited	76.4%
Annoyed / Bored / Sad	12.8%
Confused / Indifferent	10.1%
Faith schools	
Proud / Happy / Excited	73.6%
Annoyed / Bored / Sad	8.4%
Confused / Indifferent	18%

Table 9.7 Poll I identity

Poll I	
Question: When you think of a British Coronation, which of these words come to mind?	
British	92.08%
Commonwealth	51.60%
English	70.14%
Northern-Irish	22.55%
Scottish	31.06%
Welsh	29.51%

core curriculum. Nevertheless, more than 400 children responded to our second survey from schools in England, Wales, Scotland, and Northern-Ireland, aged 5–17 and the 'before and after' nature of our polls, made for some fascinating findings. The data reveal several important points, a number directly relating to the impact of coronations, but also several conclusions indicating the impact of KCL research for schoolchildren across the United Kingdom.

Table 9.8 Poll II Coronation Oath connection

Poll II	
Question	Has learning about the Coronation Oath made you feel more or less connected to King Charles III because you now know what promises he has made to the people, including you?
More connected	56.17%
Less connected	7.02%
No change	36.8%

Within the survey we asked: 'Has learning about the Coronation Oath made you feel', (i) 'more of less connected to King Charles III because you now know what promises he has made to the people, including you?' and (ii) 'more or less aware of the values which the king and the people think are important to uphold?' (Table 9.8)

In response, a clear majority felt more connected to the sovereign because of the Coronation Oath and the promises made by the monarch to the people.

When asked if they felt more or less aware of the values which the King and the people think are important to uphold, 52.30% said 'more', 46.49% said 'no change', and 1.21% said 'less' (Table 9.9).

Responses to the above questions highlight the impact of the Coronation Oath, adding yet further weight to the importance of this key element of a coronation as discussed in Chap. 3. In addition, the quiz also asked what the Coronation Oath meant to participants of the survey, with various options in two lists of 'important' or 'not important', the findings are yet further evidence of the importance of the coronation as a contract and as a projection of what Britian is about, in terms of concepts of 'justice and mercy' so prevalent within the Oath. 42.28% chose the argument of contract, that the Oath remains important because 'it contains promises the King/Queen makes to us, so that there is a sort of contract or bargain'. Nearly 1/5 of the survey felt that 'it shows what values we as a nation think are important'. 58.84% of respondents when pushed on whether they felt the Oath was no longer important, actively chose to disagree, selecting 'We disagree. The oath remains important'. This is not necessarily an argument for a coronation, but it is an argument for a public Coronation Oath, made visible to the nation and importantly in this case

Table 9.9 Poll II Coronation Oath values

Poll II	
Question	Has learning about the Coronation Oath made you feel more or less aware of the values which the king and the people think are important to uphold?
More aware	52.3%
Less aware	1.21%
No change	46.49%

Table 9.10 Poll II Coronation Oath significance

Poll II	
Question: The Coronation Oath has a complicated history. Circle any of the following options (in either list) to show what you think about it.	
The Oath is important because	
It tells the King/Queen what we expect of him/her	10.53%
It has been in the Coronation service for a long time	27.39%
It contains promises the King/Queen makes to us, so that there is a sort of contract or bargain	42.28%
It shows what values we as a nation think are important	19.80%
The Oath is not important because	
We disagree. The oath remains important	58.84%
It keeps changing	8.23%
It does not apply today when the King/Queen has little real power	25.18%
It was once messed up, causing confusion, as when Henry VIII got hold of a fake text to alter, though his version was never used	2.91%
It is impossible to make Kings/Queens stick to it	4.84%

the next generation. Thus, in 2023, one of the most enduring elements of a Westminster Abbey coronation service still resonates, with in this case, children of the twenty-first century (Table 9.10).

In addition, we asked on the basis of three images of the Coronation Ring (and students had been provided with this information for our project and lesson plans), whether schoolchildren surveyed could identify the Coronation Ring, and asked what it represents? (Table 9.11)

It was clear that those involved with the study and more generally children that had engaged with the coronation event, whether *via* television,

Table 9.11 Poll II Coronation Ring identification

Poll II	
Question:	
What is this object called?	
The Tudor Rose	2.91%
The Engagement Ring	7.75%
The Prime Minister's Ring	0.24%
The Coronation Ring	89.10%

Table 9.12 Poll II Coronation Ring significance

Poll II	
Question:	
What does the ring represent?	
A union or contract between the King or Queen and the country	50.96%
The marriage of the King or Queen to the country	27.50%
The King or Queen is very rich and can afford a ring	7.71%
A special gift from another King or Queen	13.84%

or online, or *via* other formats, had picked up on the various elements of the regalia within the coronation, with nearly 90% recognition.

A further question asked, 'What does the ring represent?' (Table 9.12)

Again the themes of contract and marriage trump the other possibilities.

We then turned to St Edward's Crown, to see the significance of the crowning object of the regalia in the eyes of those surveyed (Table 9.13).

Both the continuity of the St Edward link, and the crowning moment, as the only time a sovereign wears the crown, are highlighted as the key points within the answers to this question.

In addition, the poll asked about religiosity (Table 9.14).

The responses here revealed that for pupils within our sample, the Westminster Abbey coronation service of 2023 still retained a religiosity that was apparent to them. This of course does not indicate a preference, negativity or approval, but rather an awareness. It will continue to raise questions as to the role of such a religious service in the twenty-first century, with calls for a greater debate on the role of Church and State and a

Table 9.13 Poll II St Edward's Crown

Poll II	
Question: About St Edward's Crown, select the answer with which you agree the most	
Because the Crown of St Edward the Confessor was destroyed, and we don't know exactly what it looked like, it is silly to use this name	1.21%
It is important, by using this name, to keep the link with St Edward going even though the actual Crown has changed	38.26%
The fact that St Edward's Crown is only worn at the Coronation makes it very special	51.09%
It is silly to have a Crown that is only worn once in each reign, at the Coronation	9.44%

Table 9.14 Poll II religiosity

Poll II	
Question: Some people say that the religious side of a British Coronation has disappeared. If it has disappeared, then when? If you think that it has not disappeared, then please tick the box 'Not yet'.	
In Tudor times (16th century)	8.96%
In Stuart times (17th century)	0.73%
In Victorian times (19th century)	8.47%
Not yet	81.84%

more secular approach from the National Secular Society, to those arguing that Christianity should be at the core of this crowning moment.[13]

In both polls, we asked whether taking the survey made children more or less interested in finding out further things about British coronations? Poll I (of 1996 respondents), found 75.85% 'more interested' and just 24.15% 'less interested'—no option was included for indifference. Following the coronation, our second survey, Poll II, found that this percentage had risen to 83.05% for 'more interested' (of the 413 respondents). These are very high percentages, indeed the largest majorities recorded in all of the questions asked. The British Coronations Project can take credit for fuelling this interest *via* the questions asked, and the free historical material provided to students, but all that rests on having the event itself (Table 9.15).

Table 9.15 Poll I & II, more or less interested

Question		
Does taking this quiz make you either more or less interested in finding out further things about British Coronations?	More interested	Less interested
Poll I	75.85%	24.15%
Poll II	83.05%	16.95%

From these findings, we can see that the coronation helped children in the United Kingdom feel more connected to King Charles III and more aware of his values. The majority of Poll II said they felt more connected to King Charles III, because they now know what promises he has made to the people. In the same survey, the majority also felt they were more aware of the values which the King and the people think are important to uphold, due to learning about the oath, which forms part of the coronation ceremony. A coronation plays to the core of the late Queen Elizabeth II's maxim that the monarchy must be 'seen to be believed', and it appears from these findings, that for children across the United Kingdom, the ceremony enabled them to connect with King Charles in a new way. For these school children and very probably thousands more across the country, hearing the promises he made to them and the values he would uphold was important in understanding the role of the monarch and the UK constitution. It seems to have created a stronger bond, which could be particularly important to the Royal family, given the recent health challenges they have faced, limiting their abilities (for much of 2024) to carry out some of their normal public duties. The King has returned to many of public duties, following cancer treatment, and this has been met by the British public with relief and enthusiasm, as has been the case down the centuries. It is perhaps easy to imagine that in an age of social media and 24-hour coverage, the excitement around a return to public duties and interest surrounding the health of a monarch or other members of the royal family, such as The Princess of Wales, is something new. Yet, history can provide examples of similar patterns, with the very difficult balance of public appearance against the grief or private health of a member of the royal family. As we have seen, Edward VII had to delay his coronation, and there was considerable public interest and relief when he made his recovery from appendicitis. When Queen Victoria's beloved husband Prince Albert died at the age of just 42 in 1861, she plunged into despair, and adopted mourning (dressing in black) for the rest of her reign. Her grief led to a retreat from public life, which lasted for over ten years. Such an absence from the public eye was disastrous for her public support and led to speculation and even the idea she was unable to do her job. Calls for the abolition of the monarchy grew in some quarters in reaction to her withdrawal behind Windsor Castle walls—acquiring the sobriquet—'the Widow at Windsor'.[14] However, Queen Victoria turned this around—chiefly by being seen. Her Golden Jubilee in 1887 was greeted enthusiastically, and the vast celebrations for her Diamond Jubilee in 1897 saw her popularity restored to new levels. Queen Victoria was also more confident of the affection of the people towards her and the monarchy more generally and by this time was seen as the 'Grandmother' of the British people (if not also of the ruling dynasties of Europe too). She was congratulated with letters and telegrams from across the world, a far cry from the reaction to her withdrawal in the 1860s.[15] The well-known and much documented 'madness of King George' also placed the crown in great difficulty—and in the end resulted in a Regency.[16] Going back yet further to the early modern world and the Tudor dynasty, just as in any age, illness in a family, brings to the forefront concern and anxiety to the patient and to those in their immediate circle, and this is magnified yet further and more acutely when that person in question is a member of the royal family. Elizabeth I, not long after taking on the throne was diagnosed with smallpox in 1562—the near-fatal illness at the time. This revealed the fragility of the monarchy in England at that moment and the Protestant succession with it, with a young female monarch without children. Just a few weeks into her illness saw chaos and confusion amongst her government and privy council. Elizabeth I, nevertheless, recovered and her return to royal duties was even celebrated with a special gold coin.[17] In both cases, the vacuum left by absence highlights the late Queen Elizabeth II's adage on visibility—as true now as it was ever thus—and the complexity of managing illness and grief for those in the public eye. In all these instances, their return to the public gaze was and has been greeted with widespread enthusiasm.

Yet, if one takes being seen as one part of the connection, and a public undertaking or oath as generating a further link to pupils across the United Kingdom, the context and wider ceremony seems also to have been critical. A coronation oath alone seems unlikely to have made such an impact, the context, was all important, within the framework of such magnificence in Westminster Abbey and also the chiming of ideas that resonate across a younger generation, for the coronation had an emphasis on sustainability and inclusivity. There were numerous references to the environment, from the invitations to the anointing oil, and the bringing together of different faith leaders from across the country in active coronation roles, beyond those of just the Church of England (Fig. 9.2).[18]

When the sovereign dies, the heir inherits the throne immediately, which might lead some to question the value of having a coronation. However, history shows that those who reigned without having a coronation such as Edward VIII, Lady Jane Grey, and Edward V are not seen as having been fully sovereign. When the king or queen inherits the throne,

Fig. 9.2 The 2023 Coronation Invitation (or Summons) © Royal Collection Enterprises Ltd 2025 | Royal Collection Trust

they can be seen to be engaged to the state, but when they are crowned, this is the formalisation or marriage of the sovereign to the country as explored in Chap. 1 and 3. A coronation fully legitimises an uncrowned head of state and provides a very public framework in which a monarch and a regime signal the new priorities of the reign about to unfold. Delivered with relevant priorities, it can strike a chord with the next generation in binding a nation from the youngest of citizens upwards, as the country steps forward to a new era.

Conclusion/Coda

As something of an epilogue, afterword or coda to this chapter, and indeed this book as a whole, it is worth considering that throughout the centuries in terms of interest, and confirmed in this instance, significantly, across all sectors of education, the coronation and associated build-up attracted widespread enthusiasm. In this case, Charles III's coronation itself achieved even more positive feelings from those children responding to Poll I, than even the question of monarchy. There are many potential reasons for this, but it seems that more exposure to ideas, to the event at Westminster Abbey, to the history around the crowning of kings and queens, to the discussion around the occasion, are possible factors in this marked approval. In both polls, we asked whether taking the survey made children more or less interested in finding out further things about British coronations? Poll I (of 1996 respondents), found 75.85% 'more interested' and just 24.15% 'less interested'—no option was included for indifference. Following the coronation, our second survey, Poll II, found that this percentage had risen to 83.05% for 'more interested' (of the 413 respondents). These are very high percentages, indeed the largest majorities recorded in all of the questions asked. The British Coronations Project contributed to this interest *via* the questions asked, and the material provided to the participants, but that all relies on the presence of such an occasion. Perhaps this is therefore also a sign, at least from those of a monarchical standpoint, that a coronation is an important element in maintaining the interest, imagination, and support of those in school education—the mystery and magic—of Walter Bagehot's terms, comes readily to mind. In 1953, the Gold State Coach was seen to evoke 'something out of a fairy tale' akin to 'Cinderella's'.[19] For many witnessing the event, the music, both traditional (Handel's 'Zadok the Priest') and newly commissioned pieces will have been highlights. For others, the costumes, the colour, the ritual of the ceremony, the crown jewels being used for the very purpose of their creation—released in all their jewelled glory from behind screens in the Tower of London, with for instance, the Coronation Spoon of medieval origin used in the sacred liturgy; or carried in the case of a much commented-on sword—will have bedazzled. Moreover, there will be some that will have seen the setting as utterly striking, with a service within the heart of Westminster Abbey, above the Cosmati Pavement, adjoining Parliament square with the constitution in physical form (Parliament, Church, and Supreme Court together), that will have made a powerful impression.

For those of us commentating or being asked questions on the event, it was striking how the media and public mood evolved over the course of the build-up to the occasion, from the beginning of 2023 to 6 May itself. Rather like the approaching months and days to the 2012 London Olympics, it was easy to lose count of the grumblings and discontent of cost, purpose and necessity of the event, in essence, why was this needed? Even as people gathered on the Mall, on the eve of the coronation, such tropes continued,[20] with the ongoing and unknown questions until the day itself of whether the public would watch or turn up in significant numbers? Yet, from the morning of 6 May, the atmosphere altered. For then, across radio stations, television platforms, and streaming media devices, those describing events, were themselves part of an occasion—an occasion that would be 'history'—written down and commented on for generations to come, a moment that mattered to vast numbers of the public. For those in UK media, and much of the public onlooking, this extraordinary service, resting in the medieval, but with elements from across the generations, a marriage of a monarch to the country, the British Constitution re-enacted throughout the steps of the service on the stage of Westminster Abbey, was an invisible thread linking us to our forebears, but echoing in a new era. A tapestry with yet more to be woven. The street-parties up and down the land, the Red Arrows fly-past, all these elements of people coming together to mark the event, just as generations have done going back to Tudor times and before, will be remembered in the sense of what one did, or saw, 'on this day'.

Our nation story has been developed by and within the story of coronations, an evolving identity confirmed and shaped by the playing out of our constitution at the succession of the new monarch. Throughout the UK's history, transitions of power, between sovereigns and even more so, between dynasties, have been complex to say the least. A coronation fully legitimises an uncrowned head of state and provides a very public framework in which a monarch and a regime signal the new priorities of the reign about to unfold—in 2023, an emphasis on sustainability and inclusivity. The Coronation Oath has bound the monarch to the Constitution in vows that have helped secure the liberties of the subject down the ages, and underlined the central importance of justice, a reaffirming necessity whether it be centuries ago, or in the twenty-first century. Given the dangers of arbitrary rule in the world today, this is something that remains a cornerstone of how the United Kingdom projects itself, as a country steeped and governed in and by the rule of law. Yes, the day was all about symbolism, but with war on European soil, and the rule of law threatened around the globe, to have the head of state swear to uphold the law with justice and mercy speaks to a wider sense of what the United Kingdom has been and continues to be about.

Notes

1. M. Smith, 3 May 2023, https://yougov.co.uk/society/articles/45654-where-does-public-opinion-stand-monarchy-ahead-cor?redirect_from=%2Ftopics%2Fsociety%2Farticles-reports%2F2023%2F05%2F03%2Fwhere-does-public-opinion-stand-monarchy-ahead-cor, accessed 23 November 2025. For wider discussion on monarchy, see J. M. T. Balmer, 'Scrutinising the British Monarchy: The Corporate Brand that was Shaken, Stirred and Survived', *Management Decision*, 47 (2009), pp. 639–75.
2. I. Kirk, 1 June 2022, https://yougov.co.uk/society/articles/42695-platinum-jubilee-where-does-public-opinion-stand-m?redirect_from=%2Ftopics%2Flifestyle%2Farticles-reports%2F2022%2F06%2F01%2Fplatinum-jubilee-where-does-public-opinion-stand-m, accessed 23 November 2025.
3. https://www.kcl.ac.uk/research/british-coronations-project, accessed 23 November 2025.
4. https://webarchive.nationalarchives.gov.uk/ukgwa/20230712215452/https://coronation.gov.uk/resources-for-schools/, accessed 23 November 2025.

5. E. Shils and M. Young (eds), 'The Meaning of the Coronation', *The Sociological Review*, 1 (1953), p. 63.
6. *Ibid.*, p. 80.
7. Plunkett, 'Of Hype and Type', p. 16.
8. https://www.balh.org.uk/coronation-share-your-findings, accessed 23 November 2025.
9. M. Smith, https://yougov.co.uk/society/articles/45654-where-does-public-opinion-stand-monarchy-ahead-cor?redirect_from=%2Ftopics%2Fsociety%2Farticles-reports%2F2023%2F05%2F03%2Fwhere-does-public-opinion-stand-monarchy-ahead-cor, accessed 23 November 2025; https://www.kcl.ac.uk/news/primary-school-children-favour-british-monarchy-more-than-adults, 16 February 2024, accessed 23 November 2025.
10. S. Coughlan, 16 February 2024, https://www.bbc.co.uk/news/uk-68283130, accessed 23 November 2025.
11. Queen Elizabeth II's famous dictum: J. Dymond, 8 September 2022, https://www.bbc.co.uk/news/uk-59761477, accessed 23 November 2025; S. Bates, 29 March 2022, https://www.theguardian.com/uk-news/2022/mar/29/we-have-to-be-seen-to-be-believed-the-endurance-of-the-royal-tour#:~:text=As%20the%20Queen%20says%3A%20%E2%80%9CWe,display%20their%20magnificence%20and%20power, accessed 23 November 2025.
12. E. M. Carlin, 9 May 2024, https://www.communications.gov.uk/blog/a-year-on-the-enduring-legacy-of-the-coronation/, Government Communications Service, accessed 24 November 2025: talks of a 'tapestry of national identity' with the 'incorporation of the UK's four national flowers … throughout the visual landscape. This subtle nod to the rich diversity and unity of the United Kingdom served as a powerful symbol of national pride and unity'.
13. https://www.secularism.org.uk/news/2023/05/coronation-should-trigger-debate-on-church-and-state-says-nss, 2 May 2023, accessed 23 November 2025; J. P. Burnside, 6 May 2023, https://www.spectator.co.uk/article/why-christianity-is-at-the-heart-of-the-kings-coronation/, accessed 23 November 2025; H. Sherwood, 4 May 2023, https://www.theguardian.com/uk-news/2023/may/04/defender-of-all-faiths-coronation-puts-focus-king-charles-religious-beliefs, accessed 23 November 2025; D. Campanale, 21 April 2023, https://www.premierchristianity.com/king-of-kings-the-christian-message-at-the-heart-of-the-coronation/15373.article, accessed 23 November 2025.

14. For instance Rudyard Kipling's poem, see H. M., 'Kipling as a Poet', *Poetry*, 48 (1936), pp. 32–36; and G. L. Kriewald, 'The Widow of Windsor and the Spinster of Jefferson: A Possible Source for Faulkner's Emily Grierson.' *Faulkner Journal*, 19 (2003), pp. 3–10. See also A. Somerset, *Queen Victoria and Her Prime Ministers: A Personal History* (London, 2024), pp. 191–4 (death of Prince Albert and Queen Victoria's reaction).
15. See Somerset, *Queen Victoria and Her Prime Ministers*, pp. 412–4 (Golden Jubilee celebrations), p. 480 ('Grandmother of Europe'), pp. 490–3 (Diamond Jubilee celebrations). See also, B. L. Pearce, *et al.*, 'QUEEN VICTORIA'S GOLDEN JUBILEE 1887', *Journal of the Royal Society of Arts*, 135 (1987), pp. 573–97; & W. L. Arnstein, 'HISTORY: Queen Victoria's Diamond Jubilee', *The American Scholar*, 66 (1997), pp. 591–97; & F. W. Knickerbocker, 'Victoria Invicta', *The Sewanee Review*, 45 (1937), pp. 168–79.
16. *The Madness of George III* (1991), a play by Alan Bennett, premiered at the National Theatre, London, in November 1991. See also: J. Ambrose, 'MADNESS AND MUSIC: HANDEL'S PORPHYRIC PATRON, GEORGE III', *Bach*, 27 (1996), pp. 57–65; J. Beard, Review of *The Madness of King George (1994 Movie), BMJ: British Medical Journal*, 334, (2007), p. 1117; R. Wilson, 'The Madness of King Charles III: Shakespeare and the Modern Monarchy', *Critical Survey*, 29 (2017), pp. 76–93; N. Seppa, 'King George III Should Have Sued', *Science News*, 168, (2005), p. 94; R. Brazier, 'Royal Incapacity and Constitutional Continuity: The Regent and Counsellors of State', *The Cambridge Law Journal*, 64 (2005), pp. 352–87; E. A. Smith, 'A POLITICAL PRINCE', in *ibid.*, *George IV* (New Haven, Connecticut, 1999), pp. 82–95. See also Roberts, *George III* ..., pp. 677–80: for a reassessment, if not debunking of the porphyria thesis.
17. See Science Museum Group (UK), Sir Henry Wellcome's Museum Collection, A108752 (gold medal of Elizabeth I commemorating her recovery from smallpox, note this medal dates from 1572, but the commemoration would have been for 1562): https://collection.sciencemuseumgroup.org.uk/objects/co72125/gold-medal-commemorating-the-recovery-of-queen-elizabeth-i-from-smallpox-1572, accessed 23 November 2025. See also: A. McLaren, 'The Quest for a King: Gender, Marriage, and Succession in Elizabethan England,' *Journal of British Studies*, 41 (2002), pp. 259–90; Sir A. S. MacNalty, 'Medicine In The Time Of Queen Elizabeth The First', *The British Medical Journal*, 1 (1953), pp. 1179–85.

18. See for examples https://ecosend.io/blog/why-highlighting-sustainability-was-the-real-jewel-of-the-coronation-crown, 9 May 2023, accessed 23 November 2025; K. Fuller, 6 May 2023, https://www.cisl.cam.ac.uk/news/close-association-cisl-celebrates-coronation-king-and-queen-and-his-work-drive-transformative, accessed 23 November 2025.
19. Bloch, *James Lees-Milne: Diaries, 1942–54*, p. 454.
20. https://www.rnz.co.nz/national/programmes/saturday/audio/2018888990/dr-george-gross-coronations-the-good-the-bad-and-the-ugly, 5 May 2023, accessed 23 November 2025.

Select Bibliography of Works Cited in Notes

Manuscript Primary Sources

Arundel Castle

MS BN
MSS GI/99–105
MS MD/1590

The Bodleian Library

Ballard MSS 1, 12
Carte MSS 73, 129, 217
MS Eng.letters.e.29
Rawlinson MSS B40, D663, Letters 63, Letters 94, Letters 108, Letters 110
Smith MSS 57, 65
Tanner MSS 31
Wood MSS F. 39, F. 42

Bristol Record Office

MS F/AC/Box/19/1
MS M/BCC/CCP/1/7
MS M/BCC/CCP/1/8

G. W. C. Gross, *Crown and People*,
https://doi.org/10.1007/978-3-032-20786-9

MS M/BCC/CCP/1/9
MS P/AS/Chw/3 (b)
MS P/xch/Chw/1 (c)
MS P/xch/Chw/1 (d)

The British Library
Additional MSS 4457, 4712, 58833, 6113, 6281, 6286, 6303, 6308, 6336, 70020, 15950, 17019 (Hyde Papers), 18669, 30195, 31043, 32717, 34321, 37998, 38861, 45716A, 39864 (Husk Papers), 44915 (Cole Papers), 47087 (Egmont Papers), 47184 (Egmont Papers), 61684 (Blenheim Papers), 70285 (Portland Papers), 78471 (formerly SJE 10)
Cotton MSS Julius E IV/3, Tiberius C VI, Tiberius E VIII, Titus D. IV, Vitellius A. XIII, Vitellius B IV/1, Egerton MSS 1995, 3320, 3336 (Leeds Papers), 3350 (Leeds Papers)
Hargrave MSS 497
Harleian MSS 4129, 5111, 6118
Harley MSS 2901, 6798, 41
Lansdowne MSS 865
Royal MSS 15 E IV/2, 18 A. LXIV, App. 89
Sloane MSS 3516
Stowe MSS 580

Cambridge University Library
Hengrave MS 90/98

Castle Howard
MS J8 1/647
MS J8 1/648

Chatsworth House
MS 29

Cheshire Record Office
MS DCH/K/15
MS ZA/B/3/219

The Clothworkers' Company, Clothworkers' Hall, London
MS CL/B/1/9

The Codrington Library, All Souls College, Oxford
MS 115
MS 147 Part 1
MS 155
MS 187
MS 222 (Owen Wynne Papers)

The College of Arms
MS 'Coronations – Charles II/ James II/ William & Mary'
MS L.19
MS Vincent 24 & 1.7

Cornwall Record Office
MS J/1/1959

Dorset History Centre
MS D/WLC/F66 (Weld of Lulworth Castle Papers)

East Sussex Record Office
Ashburnham Papers
MS ASH AMS3705, MS ASH AMS3715
Rye Corporation Records
MS RYE/47/164/23
Parish of Hartfield MS PAR 360/30/1/1

Edinburgh University Library
DC.5.30–31

Eton College Archives, Windsor
Political Miscellany Vol.

The Folger Shakespeare Library, Washington DC
L.a.1060
MS L.b.8 (Loseley Papers)
MS V.b.277
MS W.a.341
MS W.b.132 (Strozzi Papers)
MS W.b.661
MS X.c.20

MS X.d.30 (43)
MS X.d.428
MS X.d.433
MS Y.c.573
MS Y.d.353

Glamis Castle, Angus
Strathmore Papers
MS NRAS885/1/Box 70/Folder 1/Bundle 3
Strathmore and Kinghorne Papers
MS 59/3/11
MS 59/5/23

Glamorgan Record Office, Cardiff
MS DCL/2/86 (Clemenstone Estate, Vale of Glamorgan Collection)
MS DF/VOL/119 (Fonmon Castle Estate)

Gloucestershire Archives, Gloucester
MS D688/1 and 2

Herefordshire Record Office, Hereford
MS BG11/17/5/75

The Huntington Library, California
Ellesmere, 1222 (35/B/32)

Inner Temple Library, London
Petyt MS 531 Vol. A

The John Rylands Library, Manchester
MS EGR4/1/12/10

Kent Archives, Maidstone Branch
Confederation of the Cinque Ports Records
MS CP/C1
Knatchbull Papers
MS U951/C261/15
New Romney Borough Records
MSS NR/CPh1/2, NR/CPh1/3, NR/CPh1/4, NR/CPh3/11

Lambeth Palace Library London
Fisher (Geoffrey Francis Fisher, 1887–1972, papers)
Lang (Cosmo Gordon Lang, 1864–1945, papers)
MS 1079b
MS 1082
MS 1083b
MS 1719

Lancashire Record Office, Preston
Cunliffe Shaw Collection
MS DDS/acc 1175/41
Kenyon Papers
MS DDKE/HMC/711

Library of Congress, Washington DC
Stevenson Papers: Box 8

Corporation of London Records
COL/AC/13/004/10
COL/SD/01/002

The National Archives, Kew
AO 1: Auditors of the Imprest and Commissioners of Audit: Declared Accounts (In Rolls)
AO 1/410/151
AO 1/2055/40
AO 1/2368/146
AO 1/2448/148
C57: Chancery and Lord Chancellor's Office: Crown Office: Coronation Rolls
C57/5 (Charles II)
C57/9 (George I)
C195: Court of Claims: Coronation Proceedings
C195/7
Exchequer Records
E 40/6687
E 42/317
E 164: Exchequer: King's Remembrancer: Miscellaneous Books, Series I

E 164/2
E 351: Exchequer: Pipe Office: Declared Accounts
E 351/567
E 351/1874
E 351/2847
E 351/3140
E 351/3319
E 372: Exchequer Pipe Office: Pipe Rolls
E 372/16 (Henry II records)
E 403: Exchequer of Receipt: Issue Rolls and Registers
E 403/1761
LC 2: Lord Chamberlain's Department: Records of Special Events
LC 2/3/1 (Coronation of Edward VI, 1547)
LC 5: Lord Chamberlain's Department: Miscellaneous Records
LC 5/107
LS 9: Lord Steward's Department: Kitchen Books
LS 9/49 (bill of fare, coronation 23 April 1685)
MINT 6: Royal Mint: Accounts (General)
MINT 6/2
MINT 19: Royal Mint: Sir Isaac Newton Papers
MINT 19/3
PC 2: Privy Council Registers
PC 2/90
SC 13: Special Collections: Seals
SC 13/H 88 (Henry I: Great Seal)
SP 14: Secretaries of State, State Paper Domestic James I
SP 14/2 (Coronation of James I, 1603)
SP 15: Secretaries of State, State Paper Domestic, Edward VI–James I
SP 15/9 (Coronation text/details for Elizabeth I, Sir William Cecil)
SP 29: Secretaries of State: State Papers Domestic, Charles II
SP 29/33/73
SP 29/122/27
SP 34: Secretaries of State: State Papers Domestic, Anne
SP 34/1/15
SP 34/1/16
SP 38: Secretaries of State, State Papers
SP 38/20
SP 44: Secretaries of State, State Papers: Entry Books
SP 44/3

SP 44/7
SP 44/48
T 51: Treasury: Entry Books of Miscellaneous Early Warrants
T51/3
WORK 3: Office of Works, Miscellaneous Letter Books
WORK 3/1

The National Library of Ireland, Dublin
MS 49,034/1 (Headfort Papers)
MS 49,034/2 (Headfort Papers)
MS 38,811

The National Records of Scotland, Edinburgh
Campbell Papers (Breadalbane Muniments)
MS GD112/39/145/2
Clerk Papers
MS GD18/3151
Cuninghame Papers
MS GD149/265
Episcopal Church of Scotland Records
MS CH12/12/1019
Erskine Papers (Erskine family, Earls of Mar and Kellie)
MS GD124/10/486/3
Exchequer Records
MS E67/2
MS E31/19
Kennedy Papers (Ailsa Muniments)
MS GD25/9/13
MS GD25/9/30/2
Kerr Papers
MS GD40/2/19/1/22–25
Minutes of Parliament
MS PA3/2
MS PA7/23/2/76
Morton Papers
MS GD150/2949
Scott Papers (Scott family of Gala, Selkirkshire)
MS GD477/358
Strathallan Papers

MS RH15/123/71

National Army Museum, London
6510/146-2-59

National Art Library, Victoria and Albert Museum, London
English Non-Illuminated MSS 20, 25, 26
38041016058729 (R. Hyde, Paper Peepshows, *c.*1831)
MS WM.1-2003

The National Library of Scotland, Edinburgh
Adv. MS 33.2.26
MS 2051 (Barras Papers)
MS 2052 (Regalia Papers)
MS 9255
Wodrow MS 4 TO XX
Wodrow MS Quarto LXXXVI

National Archives, Australia
A3522, 8/33 (State Banquet Canberra Coronation dinner 1953)
A462, 821/1/119

New York Public Library, New York
MS 1214 (Auditors of the imprests records, Vol, I, 1683–1717)

Norfolk Record Office, Norwich
City of Norwich Records
MS NCR Case 6a/4/86
Townshend Papers
MS MC 1601/40862X8

Northamptonshire Record Office, Northampton
Finch-Hatton Papers
MS FH2411
MS 2647
Isham Correspondence
MS IC 2160

Northumberland Archives, Woodhorn
MS SANT/BEQ/4/12/97/A
MS ZBR/38

Nottinghamshire Archives, Nottingham
Borough of Nottingham Records
MS CA 1799
MS CA 3400
MS CA 3469
Portland of Welbeck Papers
MS DD/5P/7/1–12

Oxfordshire History Centre, Oxford
Borough of Oxford Records
MS C/FC/1/A1/03

Parliamentary Archives, Palace of Westminster
HL/PO/PU/1/1714/1G1s2n7 (The Riot Act)

Perth and Kinross District Archive, Perth
Perth Burgh Records
MS B59/33/6

The Pierpont Morgan Library, New York
MS MA Unassigned, Misc English
MS MA Unassigned, Rulers of England Box 10, Charles II, Part 3, No. 9
MS MA Unassigned, Rulers of England Box 10, James II, No. 50
MS MA Unassigned, Rulers of England Box 11B, Anne, No. 4
MSM.736 (Miscellany on life of St Edmund, *c.*1130)

Public Record Office of Northern Ireland, Belfast
MS D207/73/277
MS D638/ MIC573/19 (De Ros Papers)

The Royal Collection Archives, Windsor
GEO/ADD/1/39
MS 1047389
RA GV/PRIV/GVD

RCIN 443368

Royal Berkshire Archives
N/D52/1/12–13
D/EX2547/4/5/12

Scone Palace, Perth
Box 74, Bundle 3
Bundle 268
Vol. 1 (Miscellaneous Scone Palace accounts, 1650–1652)

Shakespeare Centre Library and Archive, Stratford-upon-Avon
Leigh of Stoneleigh Papers
MS DR18/5/811
Stratford-upon-Avon Corporation Records
MS BRU/5/3/142
MS BRU/5/4/163
MS BRU/5/4/193

Shropshire Archives, Shrewsbury
MS 1536/2/1/1–18 (Condover Hall Papers)

The Society of Antiquaries of London, Burlington House
MS SAL/MS/444/3
MS SAL/MS/455

Staffordshire Record Office, Stafford Branch
Legge of Sandwell and Patshull (Earls of Dartmouth) Papers
MS D(W)742/M/1/60
MS D(W)1778/I/i/1798
Leveson-Gower Papers
MS D868/4/93b

Westminster Abbey Library
MS 38 (*Liber Regalis*, *c.*1390)

Westminster Abbey Muniments
WAM, 51119

West Sussex Record Office, Chichester
ACC 454 (Winterton Coronation of George VI Papers)
Add MS 54975
MS PAR 45/8/1
MS PAR 106/9/1

The William Salt Library, Stafford
MS M.534
S.MS. 164/7
S.MS.169/14
S.MS.169/24

Wiltshire and Swindon Archives, Chippenham
Ailesbury of Savernake Papers
MS 1300/407

York Archives
Corporation of York Records
MS Y/COU/1/1/41
Y/ORD/5/2/1/13 or F12a

Printed Primary Sources (Texts)

Allen, S. J., *A Sermon, preached at Burnley Church, on Sunday, July 1, 1838, on occasion of the Coronation of Her Most Gracious Majesty, Queen Victoria* (London, 1838)

Annual Register or a view of the History of Politics ..., 1761, 7th edn (1800)

Anon., *A Collection Out of the Book Called Liber Regalis, Remaining in the Treasury of the Church of Westminster. Touching the Coronation of the King and Queen Together, According to the Usual Form* (London, 1661)

Anon. [sometimes attributed to John Evelyn], *A Poem Upon his Majesties Coronation* (London, 1661)

Anon., *A Proclamation* [6 July 1603] *Signifying the Kings Maiesties Pleasure, Touching the Resort of People to his Coronation* (London, 1603)

Anon., *A Proclamation* [8 May 1660], *of both Houses of Parliament, for Proclaiming of His Majesty King of England, Scotland, France, and Ireland, Defender of the Faith, &c.* (London, 1660)

Anon., *A Proclamation* [6 March 1684/1685], *Declaring His Majesty's Pleasure Touching His Royal Coronation, and the Solemnity Thereof* (London, 1684/1685)

Anon., *A Proclamation* [11 April 1689], *Declaring William and Mary, King and Queen of England, to be King and Queen of Scotland* (Edinburgh, 1689)

Anon., *An Exact Account of the Ceremonial at the Coronation of Their Most Excellent Majesties King William and Queen Mary, the Eleventh Day of this Instant April, 1689* (The Savoy, 1689)

Anon., *At the Court at Whitehall the Ninth of January 1683 … the Happiness of Their Sacred Touch … Kings-Evil …* (London, 1683[/4])

Anon., *A True Relation of the Manner of the Deposing of King Edward II Together With the Articles which were Exhibited Against Him in Parliament. As also, an Exact Account of the Proceedings and Articles Against King Richard II …* (London, 1689)

Anon., *Festa Georgiana, or the Gentries & Countries Joy for the Coronation of the King on St Georges Day* (London, 1661)

Anon., *Gloria Britanica: or, A Panegyrick on His Sacred Majesties Passage thorow the City of London, to his Coronation. On the 23 of April, 1661…* (London, 1661)

Anon., *Great Britain's Welcome to his Sacred Majesty King George: a Poem Occasion'd by his Successful Negotiations this Summer* (London, 1719)

Anon., *Relazione Dell'ordine Tenutosi Nella Marchia del Re Britannico* (Bologna, 1685)

Anon., *The Declaration of the Estates of the Kingdom of Scotland, Containing the Claim of Right, and the Offer of the Crown to Their Majesties, King William and Queen Mary: Together with the Grievances Represented by the Estates; and Their Majesties Oath at Their Acceptance of the Crown* (Edinburgh, 1689)

Anon., *The Form of the Proceeding to the Coronation of … King William and Queen Mary, etc.* ([London], 1689)

Anon., *The Form of the Proceeding to the Royal Coronation of Her Most Excellent Majesty Queen Anne, the Twenty Third Day of this Instant April, 1702* (The Savoy, 1702)

Anon., *The History of all the Mobs, Tumults and Insurrections in Great Britain* (1715)

Anon., *The Manner of the Solemnity of the Coronation of his Most Sacred Majesty King Charles* (London, 1660)

Anon., *The Whole Ceremony of the Coronation of His Most Sacred Majesty King George: on Wednesday the Twentieth Day of October, 1714* (Dublin, 1715)

Anon. (ed.), *Diary of Mary Countess Cowper, Lady of the Bedchamber to the Princess of Wales, 1714–1720* (London, 1864)

Anon. (ed.), *Holinshed's Chronicles of England, Scotland and Ireland*, 6 volumes (London, 1807–1808)

Anon. (ed.), *Journals of the House of Lords* (London, 1767–)

Anon. (ed.), *The Book of Oaths, and the Severall Forms Thereof, Both Antient and Modern. Faithfully Collected out of Sundry Authentike Books and Records, not Heretofore Extant, Compiled in One Volume. Very Useful for all Persons Whatsoever, Especially those that Undertake any Office of Magistracie or Publique Imployment in the Common-Wealth* (London, 1649)

Anon. (ed.), *The Book of Oaths and the Several Forms Thereof, Both Ancient and Modern Faithfully Collected out of Sundry Authenticke Books of Records, not Heretofore Extant. Very Useful for all Persons Whatsoever, Especially those that Undertake any Office of Magistracy or Publique Imployment* (London, 1689)

Anon. (ed.), *The Book of Oaths, and the Several Forms Thereof, both Ancient and Modern, Faithfully Collected out of Sundry Authentick Books of Records. To Which is Added an Appendix Compleating the Whole to this Present Year ...* (London, 1715)

Anon., *The History of all the Mobs, Tumults and Insurrections in Great Britain* (1715)

Anon., *The History of the Life and Reign of her Late Majesty Queen Anne: Wherein all the Transactions of that Memorable Reign Are faithfully Compil'd from the Best authorities, and Impartially Related* (London, 1740)

Ashmole, E. and Sandford, F., *The Entire Ceremonies of the Coronations of ... Charles II and ... Queen Mary, Consort to James II, ...* (London, 1761)

Banks, T. C., *History of the Ancient Noble Family of Marmyun; Their Singular Office of King's Champion, by the Tenure of the Baronial Manor of Scrivelsby, in the County of Lincoln: also, Other Dignitorial Tenures, and the Services of London, Oxford, &c. on the Coronation-Day. The Whole Collected at a Great Expense from the Public Records; Illustrated by a Variety of Notes and Remarks, and Embellished with Several Curious Engravings* (London, 1817)

Banks, T. C., *An Historical and Critical Account of the Institution of the Coronation Ceremony; its Indispensability; the High and Official Services of the Day; the Origin of Inunction* (London, 1830)

Bayly, T., *The Royal Charter Granted Unto Kings by God Himself* (London, 1682)

Beaulieu, L., *A Sermon on the Coronation-Day, April 23 1702. Preach'd in the Cathedral Church of Glocester, before the Mayor and Corporation* (London, 1702)

Beckingham, C., *A Poem on His Most Sacred Majesty King George the IId, his Accession to the Throne, etc* (Dublin, 1727)

Beer, E. S. de (ed.), *The Diary of John Evelyn. Now First Printed in Full from the Manuscripts* ..., 6 volumes (Oxford, 1955)

Bilson, T., *A Sermon Preached at Westminster Before the King and Queens Maiesties, at their Coronations on Saint Iames his Day* ... 1603 (London, 1603)

Bilson, T., *The True Difference between Christian Subjection and Unchristian Rebellion* ... (Oxford, 1585)

Blair, J., *Divine Providence, the Security of the Crown and Subject: Two Sermons Preach'd in London-Derry December 8 1714 Being a Day of Thanksgiving, Observ'd by the Presbyterians of Ulster for the Peaceable and Happy Accession of his Most Excellent Majesty King George to the Throne of these Kingdoms* (Belfast, 1715)

Bliss, J. and Scott, W. (eds), *The Works of the Most Reverend Father in God, William Laud*, 9 volumes (Oxford, 1847–1860)

Blomfield, C. J., *A Sermon preached at the Coronation of Their Most Excellent Majesties King William IV. and Queen Adelaide in the Abbey Church of Westminster September VIII. MDCCCXXXI* (London, 1831)

Bocalini, Junior, *Iö Carole: or, An Extract of a Letter sent from Parnassus, Wherein are Contained Severall Epigrames, Odes, &c. Upon his Majesty's Coronation* ([London], 1661)

Bold, H., *St. Georges Day Sacred to the Coronation of His Most Excellent Majesty Charles the II* (London, 1661)

Boyer, A., *The History of the Reign of Queen Anne, Digested into Annals*, 11 volumes (London, 1703–1713)

Boyer, A., *The History of the Life & Reign of Queen Anne. Illustrated with all the medals struck in this reign, ... and other useful ... cuts. To which is added, an appendix* ... (London, 1722)

Boyse, J., *A Sermon Preach'd on the First of March, 1714/15. Being the Day of Publick Thanksgiving to Almighty God, for the Peaceable Accession of his Sacred Majesty King George to the Throne; and for Disappointing the Designs of the Pretender, and all his Adherents* (Dublin, 1715)

Brewer, J. S. *et al.* (eds), *Letters and Papers, Foreign and Domestic, of the Reign of Henry VIII, Preserved in the Public Record Office, the British Museum, and Elsewhere in England*, 23 volumes in 37 parts (London, 1862–1932)

Brie, F. W. D. (ed.), *The Brut, or The chronicles of England. Edited from Ms. Raw. B171, Bodleian Library, &c., …* (London, 1906–1908)

Brown, K. M. *et al.* (eds), *The Records of the Parliaments of Scotland to 1707* (St Andrews, 2007–2016)

Brown, R. *et al.* (eds), *Calendar of State Papers and Manuscripts, Relating to English Affairs, Existing in the Archives and Collections of Venice, and in other Libraries of Northern Italy*, 38 volumes (London etc., 1864–1947)

Brown, R. L. and Bentinck, G. C. (eds), *Calendar of State Papers and Manuscripts, Relating to English Affairs Existing in the Archives and Collections of Venice, and in Other Libraries of Northern* Italy, Volume 7: 1558–1580 (This edition first published 1890; this compilation published Cambridge, 2013)

Browne, S., *Religion and Loyalty. A Sermon Preach'd January 30, 1715/16, etc.* (London, 1716)

Bryant, Sir Arthur (ed.), *The Letters, Speeches and Declarations of King Charles II* (London, 1935)

Brydall, J., *Jura Coronae. His Majesties Royal Rights and Prerogatives Asserted …* (London, 1680)

Burnet, G., *A Discourse of the Pastoral Care* (London, 1692)

Burnet, G., *A Sermon Preached at the Coronation of William III. and Mary II. King and Queen of England, … France, and Ireland …, April 11. 1689* (London, 1689)

Calendar of Patent Rolls Preserved in the Public Record Office: Philip and Mary (London, 1937)

Caulfield, R. (ed.), *The Council Book of the Corporation of Youghall, from 1610 … to 1800* (Guildford, 1878)

Cole, R. (ed.), 'Particulars Relative to that Portion of the Regalia of England which was Made for the Coronation of King Charles the Second,' *Archaeologia*, 29 (1842), pp. 262–6

C[okayne], G. E. C., et al. (eds), *The Complete Peerage of England, Scotland, Ireland, Great Britain and the United Kingdom, Extant, Extinct or Dormant*, 14 vols in 15 parts (2nd edn, London or Stroud, 1910–1998)

Cook, A., *Titus Britannicus: An Essay of History Royal: in the Life & Reign of His Late Sacred Majesty, Charles II, of Ever Blessed and Immortal Memory* (London, 1685)

Correspondence of Sir Robert Kerr; first Earl of Ancram and his son William, third Earl of Lothian 1616, 2 vols (Edinburgh, 1875)

Creed, W., *Judah's Return to their Allegiance and David's Returne to his Crown and Kingdom. A Sermon Preacht at St Mary Woolchurch upon June 28. 1660, Being the Day of Solemn Thanksgiving for the Happy Return of His Majestie* (London, 1660)

Dasent, J. R. (ed.), *Acts of the Privy Council of England*, New Series, 32 volumes (London, 1890–1907)

Dennis, J., *A Poem upon the Death of Her Late Sacred Majesty Queen Anne, and the Most Happy and Most Auspicious Accession of his Sacred Majesty King George ...* (London, 1714)

Dennis, J., *The Monument: A Poem Sacred to the Immortal Memory of the Best and Greatest of Kings, William the Third* (London, 1702)

Doble, C. E. *et al.* (eds), *Remarks and Collections of Thomas Hearne ...*, 11 volumes, Oxford Historical Society, 2, 7, 13, 34, 42, 43, 48, 50, 65, 67, 72 (Oxford, 1885–1921)

Doebner, R. (ed.), *Memoirs of Mary, Queen of England, 1689–1693, Together with her Letters and those of King James II. and William III. to the Electress Sophia of Hanover* (Leipzig, 1886)

Dominion, 4 (Issue 1161) (23 June 1911)

Donaldson, S., Taylor, B. *et al.*, (ed.), *The Works of Elizabeth Barrett Browning*, vol. 2 (London, 2010)

Douglas, D. C. (general ed.), *English Historical Documents*, 10 volumes in 11 parts (London, 1953–1977)

Douglas, R., *Sermon Preached at Scoone, January 1st 1651, at the Coronation of Charles the Second* (Edinburgh, 1651)

Douglas, R., *The Form and Order of the Coronation of Charles the Second, King of Scotland, England, France, and Ireland. As it was Acted and Done at Schoone, the First Day of January, 1651.* (Aberdeen, 1651)

Dryden, J., 'Threnodia Augustalis: A Funeral Pindaric Poem. Sacred to the Happy Memory of King Charles II', in J. Warton *et al.* (eds), *The Poetical Works of John Dryden; Containing Original Poems, Tales, and Translations* (London, 1862), pp. 94–9

Dryden, J., *To His Sacred Majesty* [Charles II], *a Panegyrick on his Coronation* (London, 1661)

Du Boulay, F. R. H. (ed.), *Registrum Thome Bourgchier Cantuariensis Archiepiscopi A.D. 1454–1486*, The Canterbury and York Society, LIV (Oxford, 1957)

Edwards, A. S. G. (ed.), *The Life of St Edmund, King and Martyr: John Lydgate's Illustrated Verse Life Presented to Henry VI: A Facsimile of British Library MS Harley 2278* (London, 2004)

Ellis, H. (ed.), *The New Chronicles of England and France, in Two Parts; by R. F., Named by Himself The Concordance of Histories …* (London, 1811)

Evelyn, J., *A Panegyric to Charles the Second, Presented to His Majestie … the Day of His Coronation …* (London, [1661])

Evelyn, J., *Numismata. A Discourse of Medals, Ancient and Modern …* (London, 1697)

Evening Post, 14–17 October 1727 (London)

Eyton, R. W., *The Court, Household and Itinerary of Henry II* (London, 1878)

Farrar, F. W. and Murphy, J. B. C. *et al.*, *Sermons for The Coronation of King Edward VII* (London, 1902)

Ferdowsi, A. (trans. D. Davis), *Shahnameh: The Persian Book of Kings* (New York, 2006)

Franklin, J. H. (ed. and trans.), Jean Bodin, *On Sovereignty: Four Chapters from The Six Books of the Commonwealth* (Cambridge, 1992)

G., S., 'Westminster Abbey', *The Aldine*, 8 (1877), pp. 285–6

Garnett, R. (ed.), *The Accession of Queen Mary: being the contemporary narrative of Antonio de Guaras, a Spanish merchant resident in London* (London, 1892)

[Gibbon, J.], *Edovardus Confessor Redivivus, The Piety and Vertues of Holy Edward the Confessor, Reviv'd in the Sacred Majesty of King James the II …* (London, 1688)

Given-Wilson, C. (ed. and trans.), *Chronicles of the Revolution 1397–1400: The Reign of Richard II* (Manchester, 1993)

Gloucester Journal, 24 October 1727 (Gloucester)

Grafton, R., *A Chronicle at Large and Meere History of the Affayres of Englande and Kinges of the Same …* (London, 1569)

Green, M. A. E. (ed.), *Calendar of State Papers, Domestic Series, of the Reign of Charles II, 1660–1661, Preserved in the State Paper Department of Her Majesty's Public Record Office* (London, 1860)

Green, M. A. E. (ed.), *Calendar of State Papers, Domestic Series, of the Reign of Charles II, 1661–1662, Preserved in the State Paper Department of Her Majesty's Public Record Office* (London, 1861)

Green, M. A. E. (ed.), *Calendar of State Papers, Domestic Series, of the Reign of Charles II, 1664–1665, Preserved in the State Paper Department of Her Majesty's Public Record Office* (London, 1863)

Gregory, F., *David's Returne from his Banishment, set forth in a Thanksgiving Sermon [on 2 Sam. Xix. 30] for the Returne of [...] Charles II* (Oxford, 1660)

Gurney, J. H., *A Sermon, preached in Lutterworth Church, on Thursday, June 28, 1838, being the Day of Her Most Gracious Majesty's Coronation* (Leicester, 1838)

Halfpenny, E., '*The Cities Loyalty Display'd*: A Literary and Documentary Causerie of Charles II's Coronation "Entertainment"', *The Guildhall Miscellany*, 1 (1959), pp. 19–35

Hardy, T. D. (ed.), *Rotuli Litterarum Clausarum, 1204–27* (London, 1833)

Hardy, T. D. (ed.), *Rotuli Litterarum Patentium* (London, 1835)

Heath, J., *The Glories and Magnificent Triumphs of the Blessed Restitution of His Sacred Majesty King Charles II from his Arrival in Holland 1659–1660 till this Present* (London, 1662)

Hertz, Dr. J. H., *King George VI: Coronation Sermon* (London, 1937)

Heylyn, P., *A Sermon Preached in the Collegiate Church of St Peter in Westminster, on Wednesday May 29th. 1661. Being the Anniversary of his Majesties Most Joyful Restitution to the Crown of England....* (London, [1661])

Historical Manuscripts Commission, JP5: *A Calendar of the White and Black Books of the Cinque Ports, 1432–1955* (London, 1966)

Historical Manuscripts Commission: *Eleventh Report*, Appendix, Part VII: The Manuscripts of the Duke of Leeds, The Bridgewater Trust, Reading Corporation, The Inner Temple, &c. (London, 1888)

Holinshed, R. *et al.* (eds), *The Firste Volume... Chronicles of En[gland]... Scotlande, and Ire[land]... Faithfully gathered and set forth* (London, 1571)

Howlett. R. (ed.), *The Chronicle of Robert of Torigni, in Chronicles of the Reigns of Stephen, Henry II and Richard I*, 4 vols (Rolls Series, London, 1884–1889)

Howlett, R. (ed.), William of Newburgh, 'Historia Rerum Anglicarum', in *Chronicles of the Reigns of Stephen, Henry II and Richard I*, 4 vols., RS 82 (London, 1884–1889), I–II

Hubert, Sir F., *The Historie of Edward the Second ...* (London, 1629)

Hughes, J., *The House of Nassau: A Pindarick Ode* (London, 1702)

Hume, M. A. S. (ed.), *Calendar of Letters and State Papers Relating to English Affairs, Preserved Principally in the Archives of Simancas* [title modified for Volume IV], 4 volumes (London, 1892–1899)

Hunt, T., *The Great and Weighty Considerations, Relating to the Duke of York, ...* (London, 1680)

Indian Court. Festival of Empire 1911. Guide Book and Catalogue (London, 1911)

Irish Manuscripts Commission: S. Pender (ed.), *Council Book of the Corporation of Waterford, 1662–1700, Together with Nine Documents of 1580–82* (Dublin, 1964)

James I, 'A Speach to the Lords and Commons of the Parliament at White-Hall, on Wednesday the XXI of March. Anno 1609 [1610]', in James I, *The Workes of the Most High and Mightie Prince, Iames by the Grace of God, King of Great Britaine, France and Ireland, Defender of the Faith, &c.* (London, 1616), pp. 527–48

[James I], *The True Law of Free Monarchy, or The Reciprocall and Mutuall Duty Betwixt a Free King and his Naturall Subjects* (London, 1642)

James I, *The Workes of the Most High and Mightie Prince, Iames by the Grace of God, King of Great Britaine, France and Ireland, Defender of the Faith, &c.* (London, 1616)

James I, 'Speech to parliament of 19 March 1604', in J. P. Sommerville (ed.) *King James VI and I: Political Writings* (Cambridge, 1995), pp. 132–146.

James I, *A Meditation Upon the 27.28.29. verses of the xxvii Chapter of Saint Matthew. Or a Paterne for a King's Inauguration* (London, 1620)

Jerdan, W. (ed.), *Rutland Papers. Original Documents Illustrative of the Courts and Times of Henry VII. and Henry VIII. Selected from the Private Archives of His Grace the Duke of Rutland*, Camden Society, Old Series, XXI (London, 1842)

Johnson, G. W (ed.), *The Fairfax Correspondence. Memoirs of the Reign of Charles the First*, 2 volumes (London, 1848)

Kincaid, A. (ed.), *The History of King Richard The Third (1619) by Sir George Buc Master of the Revels* (New edn, London, 2023)

Knowles, R. (ed.), John Ogilby, *The Entertainment of His Most Excellent Majestie Charles II in His Passage Through the City of London to His Coronation* [London, 1662] (New York, 1988)

Laing, D. (ed.), J. Nicoll, *A Diary of Public Transactions and Other Occurrences, Chiefly in Scotland, from January 1650 to June 1667* (Edinburgh, 1836)

Lamb, P., *Royal Cookery; or, The Complete Court-Cook. Containing the Choicest Receipts in all the Particular Branches of Cookery, Now in Use in the Queen's Palaces of St James's, Kensington, Hampton-Court, and Windsor. With Near Forty Figures (Curiously Engraven)* (London, 1710)

Latham, R. and Matthews, W. (eds), *The Diary of Samuel Pepys*, 11 volumes (London, 1971)

Laud, W., *A Commemoration of King Charles his Inauguration; or, a Sermon* [on Ps. LXXII 1] *Preached at Pauls Crosse* ... (London, 1645)

Laud, W., *The Works* ..., 7 vols (Oxford, 1854; reprint Hildesheim, 1977)

Legg, J. Wickham (ed.), *The Coronation Order for King James I* (London, 1902)

Legg, J. Wickham (ed.), *Three Coronation Orders*, Publications of the Henry Bradshaw Society, 19 (London, 1900)

Legg, L. G. Wickham (ed.), *English Coronation Records* (London, 1901)

Leland, J. and Hearn, T. (eds.), *Antiquarii De rebus Britannicis Collectanea* (London, 1774), IV

Lewis, W. S., *et al.* (eds), *Horace Walpole's Correspondence* (Oxford, 1960)

Lochner, J. H., *Samlung Merkwürdiger Medaillen* (Nuremberg, 1744)

Luard, H. R. (ed.), *Annales de Wintonia* in *Annales monastici*, 4 vols (Rolls Series, London, 1864–1869)

Macray, W. D. (ed.), *The History of the Rebellion and Civil Wars in England Begun in the Year 1641, by Edward, Earl of Clarendon*, 6 volumes (Oxford, 1888)

Madden, F. (ed.), *Matthaei Parisiensis monachi sancti Albani, Historia Anglorum*, 3 vols, Rolls Series (London, 1865–1869)

Mahaffy, R. P. *et al.* (eds), *Calendar of State Papers, Domestic Series, of the Reign of Anne, Preserved in the Public Record Office*, 4 volumes (London, 1916–2006)

Malfatti, C. V. (trans. and ed.), *The Accession, Coronation and Marriage of Mary Tudor as Related in Four Manuscripts of the Escorial* (Barcelona, 1956)

Manchester Guardian, 24 July 1821 (Manchester)

Menin, N., *The Form, Order and Ceremonies, Used at the Investiture of all the Sovereign Princes of Europe: With the Whole Ceremony of the Grand Anointing and Coronation of the Present King of France* ... (London, 1727)

Mercurius Publicus ..., 19–26 July 1660 (No. 30, London)
Mercurius Publicus ..., 18–25 April 1661 (No. 16, London)
Mercurius Publicus ..., 25 April–2 May 1661 (No. 17, London)
Mercurius Publicus, ..., 2–8 May 1661 (No. 18, London)
Milles, T., *Catalogue of Honour ... of all the free monarches ... kinges of England ... Scotland ...* (1610)
Milton, J., *Eikonoklastes in Answer to a Book Intitl'd Eikon Basilike* (London, 1649)
Morley, G., *A Sermon* [on Prov. XXVIII 2] *Preached at the ... Coronation of ... Charles II, King of Great Britain, etc.* (London, 1661)
Morris, C. (ed.), *The Journeys of Celia Fiennes* (revised edition, London, 1949)
Newton, I., *The Chronology of Ancient Kingdoms Amended* (London, 1722)
Nichols, J. G. (ed.), *Literary Remains of King Edward VI*, 2 volumes (London, 1857)
Ogilby, J., *The Entertainment of His Most Excellent Majestie Charles II, in his Passage Through the City of London to his Coronation: Containing an Exact Accompt of the Whole Solemnity; the Triumphal Arches, and Cavalcade, Delineated in Sculpture; the Speeches and Impresses Illustrated from Antiquity. To these is Added, a Brief Narrative of His Majestie's Solemn Coronation: with his Magnificent Proceeding, and Royal Feast in Westminster-Hall* (London, 1662)
Ogilby, J. (facsimile with introduction by R. Knowles), *The Entertainment of His Most Excellent Majestie Charles II, in his Passage Through the City of London to his Coronation*, Renaissance Triumphs and Magnificences, New Series, 3 (Binghamton, New York, 1988)
Ogilby, J., *The Kings Coronation: Being an Exact Account of the Cavalcade, with a Description of the Triumphal Arches, and Speeches Prepared by the City of London for His Late Majesty Charles the Second, in his Passage from the Tower to Whitehall. Also the Narrative of his Majesties Coronation, with his Magnificent Proceeding, and Feast in Westminster-Hall, April the 23th* (Edinburgh, 1685)
Ogilby, J., *The Relation of His Majestie's Entertainment Passing Through the City of London to his Coronation etc.* (London, 1661)
Pannier, L., and Meyer P. (eds), *Le Débat des Hérauts D'Armes de France et d'Angleterre suivi de The Debate between the Heralds of England and France by John Coke* (Société des Anciens Textes Français [xxi], Paris, 1877)

Pinkerton, J., *The Medallic History of England to the Revolution: with forty plates* (London, 1790)

Planché, J. R., *Regal Records: or, A Chronicle of the Coronations of the Queens Regnant of England* (London, 1838)

Prynne, W., *Canterburies Doome, or the First Part of a Compleat History of the Commitment, Charge, Tryall, Condemnation, Execution of William Laud, Late Archbishop of Canterbury* (London, 1646)

Rabbi Daiches, I. H., *Sermon on the Coronation of Their Gracious Majesties, King Edward VII. and Queen Alexandra … On Saturday, August 9th, 1902 …* (Leeds, 1902)

Redington, J. and Shaw, W. A. (eds), *Calendar of Treasury Papers Preserved in Her Majesty's Public Record Office*, 6 volumes (London, 1868–1897)

Riley, H. T. (ed.), *The Annals of Roger de Hoveden: Comprising the History of England and of other Countries of Europe from A.D. 732 to A.D. 1201*, 2 volumes (London, 1853)

Robertson, A. J. (ed.), *The Laws of the Kings of England from Edmund to Henry I* (Cambridge, 1925)

Robertson, J. and Gordon, D. J. (eds), *A Calendar of Dramatic Records in the Books of the Livery Companies of London, 1485–1640*, Malone Society Collections, III (London, 1954)

Robertson, J. C. and Sheppard, J. B. (eds), *Materials for the History of Thomas Becket, Archbishop of Canterbury*, 7 vols (London, Rolls Series, 1875–1885)

Rosewell, S., *The King's True Divine Right. The Flourishing of his Crown: and the Shame of his Enemies. A Sermon Preach'd upon Occasion of His Majesty's Coronation: the Lord's Day after; being October the 24th. 1714. …* (London, 1714)

[Rymer, T.], *A General Draught and Prospect of Government in Europe, and Civil Policy. Shewing the Antiquity, Power, Decay, of Parliaments with Other Historical and Political Observations Relating Thereunto* (London, 1681)

Rye, W. B., 'The Coronation of King James I, 1603', *The Antiquary*, 22 (1890), pp. 18–23

Sachse, W. L. (ed.), *The Diurnal of Thomas Rugg, 1659–1661*, Camden Society, 3rd Series, XCI (London, 1961)

Sancroft, W., *A Sermon Preached in S. Peter's Westminster … at the Consecration of … John* [Cosin] *Lord Bishop of Durham, William* [Lucy] *Lord Bishop of S. David's, Beniamin* [Laney] *L. Bishop of Peterborough, Hugh*

[Lloyd] *Lord Bishop of Landaff, Richard* [Sterne] *Lord Bishop of Carlisle, Brian* [Walton] *Lord Bishop of Chester, and John* [Gauden] *Lord Bishop of Exeter* (London, 1660)
Sanders, W., *The True and Wonderful Relation of the Dreadful Fighting and Groans That Were Heard and Seen in the Ayr, on the Fifteenth of this Instant January, in Carmarthen, in South-Wales* ... ([London], 1681)
Sandford, F., *The History of the Coronation of the Most High, Most Mighty, and Most Excellent Monarch, James II. By the Grace of God, King of England, Scotland, France and Ireland, Defender of the Faith, &c. and of His Royal Consort Queen Mary: Solemnized in the Collegiate Church of St. Peter in the City of Westminster, on Thursday the 23 of April, being the Festival of St. George, in the Year of Our Lord 1685* (London, 1687)
Sandford, F., *A Genealogical History of the Kings of England and Monarchs of Great Britain ... from the Conquest, Anno 1066, to the Year 1677* (London, 1677)
Sayle, R. T. D. (ed.), *Lord Mayors' Pageants of the Merchant Taylors' Company in the 15th, 16th & 17th Centuries* (privately published, Reading, 1931)
Scott, W. (arr.), *A Collection of Scare and Valuable Tracts, on the most interesting and entertaining subjects: But chiefly such as Relate to the History and Constitution of these Kingdoms. Selected from an Infinite Number in Print and Manuscript, in the Royal, Cotton, Sion, and other Public, as well as Private, Libraries, Particularly that of the Late Lord Somers* (London, 1809–1815)
Second Supplement (*c.*8 February 1952) to *The London Gazette Extraordinary*, 6 February 1952 (No. 39463, London)
Senhouse, R., *Foure Sermons Preached at the Court upon Severall Occasions, etc.* (London, 1627)
Sharp, J., *A Sermon [on Isa. xlix. 23] Preach'd at the Coronation of Queen Anne, in the Abby-Church of Westminster, April 23, 1702* (London, 1702)
Shaw, W. A. *et al.* (eds), *Calendar of Treasury Books ... Preserved in The Public Record* Office, 32 volumes in 64 parts (London, 1904–1957)
Stevenson, J., (trans.), William of Newburgh, 'Historia Rerum Anglicarum', in *The Church Historians of England*, 5 vols. (London, 1853–1858)
Shawcross, W. (ed.), *Counting One's Blessings: The Selected Letters of Queen Elizabeth The Queen Mother* (London, 2012)

Sponsler, C. (ed.), John Lydgate, "Soteltes at the Coronation Banquet of Henry VI," *Mummings and Entertainments,* (Kalamazoo, Michigan, 2010)

Stubbs, W. (ed.), *Gesta regis Henrici secundi Benedicti abbatis: The Chronicle of the Reigns of Henry II and Richard I, AD 1169–1192*, 2 vols (Rolls Series, London, 1867)

Stubbs, W. (ed.), *Chronica Magistri Rogeri de Houedene*, 4 volumes, *Rerum Britannicarum Medii Aevi Scriptores*, 51 (London, 1868–1871)

Stubbs, W. (ed.), *Opera Historica: The Historical Works of Master Ralph de Diceto, Dean of London*, 2 vols (Rolls Series, London, 1876)

Sutton, A. F. and Hammond, P. W. (eds), *The Coronation of Richard III: The Extant Documents* (Gloucester, 1983)

Swetnam, J., *David's Devotions upon his Deliverances: Set Forth in a Sermon [on Psal. xxiv. 3] June 28, 1660, Being the Day of Publique Thanksgiving for his Majesties Happy Restauration* (London, 1660)

Talbot, W., *A Sermon* [on Ps. cxviii. 24, 25] *Preach'd at the Coronation of King George, ... October the 20th, 1714* (London, 1714)

The Authorised Liturgy for the Coronation Rite of His Majesty King Charles III, Commissioned and Authorised by The Most Reverend & Right Honourable Justin Welby, The Archbishop of Canterbury [with commentary] (London, 2023)

The Church Times (August 15th 1902)

The Courier, 2 January 1801 (London)

The Flying Post, 3548, 28–30 Sept. 1714

The Flying Post, 3716, 27–29 Oct. 1715

The Form and Order of Service that is to be performed, and of the Ceremonies that are to be observed, in the Coronation of their Majesties King George III. and Queen Charlotte, in the Abbey Church ... Tuesday the 22[n]d of September 1761 ... (London, 1761)

The Form and Order of Service that is to be performed and of the Ceremonies that are to be observed in the Coronation of their Majesties King Edward VII. And Queen Alexandra ... (London, 1902)

The Form and Order of Service that is to be performed and of the Ceremonies that are to be observed in the Coronation of their Majesties King George V. and Queen Mary in the Abbey Church ... Westminster, on Thursday ... 22nd day of June, 1911 (London, 1911)

The Form and Order of Service that is to be performed and the Ceremonies that are to be observed in the Coronation of their Majesties King George VI and Queen Elizabeth ... (London, 1937)

The Form and Order of the Service. Coronation of Her Majesty Queen Elizabeth II, 2 June 1953 (London, 1953)
The Kingdomes Intelligencer ..., 29 April–6 May 1661 (No. 18, London)
The London Gazette, 23–27 April 1685 (No. 2028, London)
The London Gazette, 27–30 April 1685 (No. 2029, London)
The London Gazette, 30 April–4 May 1685 (No. 2030, London)
The London Gazette, 11–14 May 1685 (No. 2033, London)
The London Gazette, 11–14 February 1688/1689 (No. 2427, London)
The London Gazette, 13–16 May 1689 (No. 2453, London)
The London Gazette, 30 April–4 May 1702 (No. 3806, London)
The London Gazette, 24–28 May 1705 (No. 4126, London)
The London Gazette, 17–19 April 1712 (No. 4993, London)
The London Gazette, 28 February–3 March 1712/1713 (No. 5099, London)
The London Gazette, 16–20 February 1713/1714 (No. 5200, London)
The London Gazette, 28 October 1902, (Issue 27489, London)
The London Gazette, 12 February 1952 (No. 39467, London)
The London Gazette, 13 September 1831, (Issue 18848, London)
The Order of the Music, &c. to be performed at the Coronation, June 26, 1838 (London, 1838)
The Post Man, 951 (4 April 1702)
The Statutes of the Realm, 11 volumes (London, 1810–1828)
The Times, 24 July 1821 (London)
The Times, Exhibition Supplement, 23 April 1924
Thomson, R., *A Faithful Account of the Processions and Ceremonies Observed in the Coronation of the Kings and Queens of England; Exemplified in that of ... King George the Third and Queen Charlotte ...* (London, 1820)
Turner, F., *A Sermon Preached Before their Majesties K. James II. and Q. Mary, at their Coronation in Westminster-Abby, April 23. 1685. ...* (London, 1685)
Turnbull, H. W. *et al.* (eds), The *Correspondence of Isaac Newton*, 7 volumes (Cambridge, 1959–1977)
Tyler, R. (ed.), *Calendar of State Papers, Spain, Volume 11, 1553* (London, 1916)
Ullmann, W. (ed.), with a note on the music by D. H. Turner, *Liber Regie Capelle: A Manuscript in the Biblioteca Publica, Evora*, Publications of the Henry Bradshaw Society, XCII (London, 1961)

Valentine, H., *God Save the King. A Sermon Preached in St. Pauls Church the 27th of March 1639. Being the Day of his Maiesties Most Happy Inauguration, and of his Northerne Expedition* (London, 1639)

Venables-Vernon, E., *A Sermon preached at the Coronation of King George IV. in the Abbey Church of Westminster July XIX, M.DCCC.XXI* (London, 1821)

Walker, Sir Edward, *A Circumstantial Account of the Preparations for the Coronation of His Majesty King Charles the Second, and a Minute Detail of that Splendid Ceremony, with all the Particulars Connected with it; Including the Installation of Knights, Creation of Peers, &c., to which is Prefixed, an Account of the Landing, Reception, and Journey of His Majesty from Dover to London* (London, 1820)

West, R., *The True Character of a Church-Man, Shewing the False Pretence to That Name. Together With the Character of a Low Church-Man Drawn in Answer to It, With Remarks* (London, 1702)

Whitelock, A. and MacCulloch, D., "Princess Mary's Household and the Succession Crisis, July 1553." *The Historical Journal*, 50 (2007), pp. 265–87

Williamson, P. and Baldwin, E. (eds.), *Baldwin Papers: A Conservative Statesman, 1908–1947* (Cambridge, 2004)

Winter, J., *A Sermon Preached at East Dearham in Norf. May 29 1661. Being the Day of the Coronation of our Most Gracious Soveraign Lord King Charles the Second, &c.* (London, 1662)

Wodrow, R., *The History of the Sufferings of the Church of Scotland, from the Restauration to the Revolution, Collected from the Public Records ... and ... Well Attested Narratives*, 2 volumes (Edinburgh, 1721–1722)

Wood, A., *Athenae Oxonienses. An Exact History of all the Writers and Bishops Who Have Had Their Education in the Most Ancient and Famous University of Oxford, From ... 1500 to the End of ... 1690 ...*, 2 volumes (2nd edition, London, 1721)

Wordsworth, C. (ed.), *The Manner of the Coronation of King Charles the First ... at Westminster 2 Feb. 1626. (The Manner of the Coronation of the Kings of England, Anno Dni, 1625–6. The Coronation of King James and Queene Anne, 25 July 1603. The Coronation of King Charles I. at Holyrood, 18 June 1633. Account by Prynne of the Coronation of King James I)*, Publications of the Henry Bradshaw Society, 2 (London, 1892)

Wright, N. (ed.), *Historia Regum Britannie of Geoffrey of Monmouth: I Bern, Burgerbibliothek, MS 568* (Woodbridge, 1985)

Primary Sources (Electronic)

Brown, K. M. et al. (eds), *The Records of the Parliaments of Scotland to 1707* (St Andrews, 2007–2020), 1649/1/71

Brown, K. M. *et al.* (eds), *The Records of the Parliaments of Scotland to 1707* (St Andrews, 2007–2016), M1650/11/34

Brown, K. M. *et al.* (eds), *The Records of the Parliaments of Scotland to 1707* (St Andrews, 2007–2016), 1689/3/1

Brown, K. M. *et al.* (eds), *Records of the Parliaments of Scotland to 1707* (St Andrews, 2007–2016), A1567/12/7

Brown, K. M. *et al.* (eds), *Records of the Parliaments of Scotland to 1707* (St Andrews, 2007–2016), 1689/3/105–9

Brown, K. M. *et al.* (eds), *Records of the Parliaments of Scotland to 1707* (St Andrews, 2007–2016), 1689/6/6

Brown, K. M. *et al.* (eds), *Records of the Parliaments of Scotland to 1707* (St Andrews, 2007–2016), 1689/3/160

Printed Primary Sources (Loose Illustrations) & Material Objects

The British Library

Additional MSS

42044 (Drawing of Coronation Chair, 19th century)

The British Museum

E.3442 (Gold coin of Oliver Cromwell/Protectorate, 1656)

G3, EM.1 (Coronation medal, 1546/1547)

M.7336 (Gold coronation medal of Charles II, 1651)

M.7337 (Silver coronation medal of Charles II, 1651)

M.7396 (Gold oval medal of Oliver Cromwell, with tree on obverse, 1658)

M.7477 (Gold coronation medal of Charles II, 1661)

M.7742 (Coronation medal of William III and Mary II, 1689)

1857,0715.1 (The Battersea Shield, *c.*350 BC–*c.*50 BC)

Eton College Archives, Windsor
Aq.1.1.2 (Anon., *Ceremonial of the Coronation of His Most Sacred Majesty King George the Fourth in the Abbey of St. Peter, West-Minster, etc.*, Westminster, 1823)
BRXYZ-R BK.I.5 (Printed account of Elizabeth I's 1742 Russian coronation)

The Folger Shakespeare Library, Washington DC
ART: Vol. d105 no. 41 (Print: interior of Westminster Abbey, taken from Sandford, *c.*1689)
D 219 I8 (Print (Italian): coronation of James II, 1685 (*Relazione dell'ordine tenutosi nella marchia del re britannico, 1685*)

Glasgow University Library
GLAHM:38005 (The Huntarian Numismatics collection of Coronation coins going back to Edward VI at The Huntarian Museum and Art Gallery, at The University of Glasgow)

London Metropolitan Archives
Special Collections: Art
SC/PZ/WE/01/2904 (Coronation Chair, paper work of art, 19x27cms, *c.*1800s)
SC/PZ/WE/02/1373 (Engraving: interior from high altar to west end during coronation of James II, 1687, by Francis Sandford, engraver)
SC/GL/PR/L/22/2/P7488105 (Engraving: Anon., 'De prachtige wyze van praalstaatie gewoonlyk vertoond op het kroonen van koningen en koninginnen van Engeland' [The coronation of William III and Mary II], *c.*1700)

Museum of London
A16163 (G. Cattermole, 'Coronation Procession of King William IV and Queen Adelaide', 1831)

Museums Victoria, Australia Collection
NU 33094 (Coronation medal, King Edward VII & Queen Alexandra, 1902)
NU 42797 (Coronation medal, King George V & Queen Mary, 1911)

The Museum of the Order of St John, London
LDOSJ:44 (Coronation Medals 1902–1934)

National Maritime Museum, Greenwich, London
Caird Collection
MEC1108; BM, G3, EM.1

Oriel College Archives, Oxford
AH 5 D1 (25 cast silver medals of workshop of Simon van de Passe: 17 medals of English monarchs from Edward the Confessor to Charles I, with monarch on obverse and arms and place of burial on reverse; 8 medals of relatives of Charles I, namely Mary, queen of Scots; Henry, Lord Darnley; Queen Anne; Queen Henrietta Maria; Prince Charles; Elizabeth, queen of Bohemia; Frederick, count of the Rhine Palatinate and king of Bohemia; and Charles Louis, count of the Rhine Palatinate. The medals are stored in a silver casket, the lid of which shows Charles I in profile, and they were possibly produced as propaganda pieces during the Civil War)

The Parker Library, Cambridge
MS 171 (The Scotch Chronicle, 15th century, illumination of Alexander III crowned at Scone, 1249)

Science Museum Group (UK)
A108752 (Sir Henry Wellcome's Museum Collection, gold medal of Elizabeth I commemorating her recovery from smallpox, note this medal dates from 1572, but the commemoration would have been for 1562)

Printed Secondary Sources

Abels, R. P., *Lordship and Military Obligation in Anglo-Saxon England* (Berkeley, California, 1988)

Adamson, J., 'The Kingdoms of England and Great Britain: The Tudor and Stuart Courts 1509–1714', in J. Adamson (ed.), *The Princely Courts of Europe: Ritual, Politics and Culture Under the Ancien Régime 1500–1750* (London, 1999), pp. 95–117

Al-Azmeh, A., 'Monotheistic Kingship', in A. Al-Azmeh and J. M. Bak (eds), *Monotheistic Kingship: The Medieval Variants* (Budapest, 2004), pp. 9–31

Ambrose, J., 'MADNESS AND MUSIC: HANDEL'S PORPHYRIC PATRON, GEORGE III', *Bach*, 27 (1996), pp. 57–65

Anderson, B. R. O'G., *Imagined Communities: Reflections on the Origin and Spread of Nationalism* (1st edition, London, 1983; 2nd edition, London, *c.*2006)

Andersen, C., *The King: The Life of Charles III* (Waterville, Maine, 2022)

Andreev, A. I., 'Petr I v Anglii v 1698', in *Petr Velikii: Sbornik statei* (Moscow and Leningrad, 1947), pp. 63–103

Anglo, S., *Images of Tudor Kingship* (London, 1992)

Archer, I. W., 'City and Court Connected: The Material Dimensions of Royal Ceremonial, ca.1480–1625', *The Huntington Library Quarterly*, 71 (2008), pp. 157–79

Armstrong, C. A. J., 'The Inauguration Ceremonies of the Yorkist Kings and Their Title to the Throne', *Transactions of the Royal Historical Society*, 30 (1948), pp. 51–73

Arnstein, W. L., 'HISTORY: Queen Victoria's Diamond Jubilee', *The American Scholar*, 66 (1997), pp. 591–97

Asch, R. G., *Sacral Kingship between Disenchantment & Re-Enchantment: The French and English Monarchies 1587–1688* (New York and Oxford, 2014)

Ash, L., *The Baton and The Cross: Russia's Church from Pagans to Putin* (London, 2024)

Atherton, I., 'The Itch Grown a Disease: Manuscript Transmission of News in the Seventeenth Century', in J. Raymond (ed.), *News, Newspapers, and Society in Early Modern Britain* (London, 1999), pp. 39–65

Auden, W. H. (ed.), *The Oxford Book of Light Verse* (Oxford, 1938)

Auerbach, J., 'Empire under Glass: The British Empire and the Crystal Palace, 1851–1911', in *Exhibiting the Empire. Cultures of Display and the British Empire*, edited by John McAleer and John M. MacKenzie (Manchester, 2015), pp. 142–67

Axton, M., *The Queen's Two Bodies: Drama and the Elizabethan Succession* (London, 1977)

Aylmer, G. E., *The Crown's Servants: Government and Civil Service under Charles II, 1660–1685* (Oxford, 2002)

Backscheider, P. R., *Spectacular Politics: Theatrical Power and Mass Culture in Early Modern England* (London, 1993)

Baines, J. M., 'The Cinque Ports and Coronation Services', *Hastings Museum Publication*, No. 18 (3rd edition, 1968)

Balmer, J. M. T., 'Scrutinising the British Monarchy: The Corporate Brand that was Shaken, Stirred and Survived', *Management Decision*, 47 (2009), pp. 639–75

Barclay, A., 'The 1661 St Edward's Crown – Refurbished, Recycled or Replaced?', *The Court Historian*, 13 (2008), pp. 149–70

Barenboim, D. and Said, E. W. (ed. A. Guzelimian), *Parallels and Paradoxes: Explorations in Music and Society* (London, 2004)

Bak, J. M., 'Medieval Symbology of the State: Percy E. Schramm's Contribution', *Viator*, 4 (1973), pp. 33–64

Barker, H., *Newspapers, Politics and English Society, 1695–1855* (Harlow, 2000)

Bates, D., *William the Conqueror* (New Haven, Connecticut, 2018)

Bayne, C. G., 'The Coronation of Queen Elizabeth', *The English Historical Review*, XXII (1907), pp. 650–73

Bayne, C. G., 'The Coronation of Queen Elizabeth', *The English Historical Review*, XXIV (1909), pp. 322–3

Bayne, C. G., 'The Coronation of Queen Elizabeth', *The English Historical Review*, XXV (1910), pp. 550–3

Beaken, R., *Cosmo Lang: Archbishop in War and Crisis* (London, 2012)

Beard, J., Review of *The Madness of King George (1994 Movie)*, *BMJ: British Medical Journal*, 334, (2007), p. 1117

Beattie, J. M., *The English Court in the Reign of George I* (Cambridge, 1967)

Beaver, D., 'Conscience and Context: The Popish Plot and the Politics of Ritual, 1678–1682', *The Historical Journal*, 34 (1991), pp. 297–327

Bebbington, D. W., *The Dominance of Evangelicalism: the Age of Spurgeon and Moody* (Leicester, 2005)

Beech, R., 'The Hammer-beam Roof of Westminster Hall and the Structural Rationale of Hugh Herland', *Architectural History*, 59 (2016), pp. 25–61

Bennett, G. V., *White Kennett, 1660–1728, Bishop of Peterborough: A Study in the Political and Ecclesiastical History of the Early Eighteenth Century* (London, 1957)

Bennett, G. V., 'English Jacobitism, 1710–1715; Myth and Reality', *Transactions of the Royal Historical Society*, 32 (1982), pp. 137–51

Benson, A. C. and Esher, Viscount (eds), *The Letters of Queen Victoria: A Selection from Her Majesty's Correspondence Between the Years 1837 and 1861*, 3 volumes (London, 1907)

Bergeron, D. M., *English Civic Pageantry, 1558–1642* (London, 1971)

Bergeron, D. M., 'Charles I's Edinburgh pageant (1633)', *Renaissance Studies*, 6 (1992), pp. 173–84

Berry, C. L., 'The Coronation Oath and the Church of England', *The Journal of Ecclesiastical History*, 11 (1960), pp. 98–105.

Bertelli, S., '*Rex et Sacerdos*: The Holiness of the King in European Civilization', in A. Ellenius (ed.), *Iconography, Propaganda, and Legitimation* (New York, 1998), pp. 123–45

Bertelli, S. (trans. R. Burr Litchfield), *The King's Body: The Sacred Rituals of Power in Medieval and Early Modern Europe* (University Park, Pennsylvania, 2003)

Bertram, E. and Norton, R. E. (eds), 'Napoleon', in E. Bertram and R. E. Norton (eds), *Nietzsche: Attempt at a Mythology* (Champaign, Illinois, 2009), pp. 171–82

Bevan, B., *King William III: Prince of Orange, the First European* (London, *c.*1997)

Bingham, T., *The Rule of Law* (London, 2010)

Bilinkoff, J., 'A Spanish Prophetess and her Patrons: The Case of Maria de Santo Domingo', *The Sixteenth Century Journal*, 23 (1992), pp. 21–34

Black, J., *The Hanoverians: The History of a Dynasty* (London, 2004)

Black, J., *George III: America's Last King* (New Haven, Connecticut, 2008)

Blair, C. (general ed.), *The Crown Jewels: The History of the Coronation Regalia in the Jewel House of the Tower of London*, 2 volumes (London, 1998)

Blanning, T., *The Triumph of Music: Composers, Musicians and their Audiences, 1700 to the Present* (London, 2008)

Blatt, H., "Reading Materially: John Lydgate's 'Soteltes for the Coronation Banquet of Henry VI,'" in H. Blatt, *Participatory Reading in Late-Medieval England* (Manchester, 2018), pp. 105–27

Bloch, M. (trans. J. E. Anderson), *The Royal Touch: Sacred Monarchy and Scrofula in England and France* (London, 1973)

Blurton, H., 'Egyptian Days: From Passion to Exodus in the Representation of Twelfth-Century Jewish-Christian Relations', in S. R. Jones and S. Watson (eds), *Christians and Jews in Angevin England: The York Massacre of 1190* (Woodbridge, 2013), pp. 222–37

Bogdanor, V., *The Monarchy and the Constitution* (Oxford, 1995)

Bonnett, S., *The City and the Coronation ... Compiled Largely from Material in the Corporation's Records Office* (London, 1953)

Bonney, N., 'The Evolution and Contemporary Relevance of the Accession and Coronation Oaths of the United Kingdom', *The British Journal of Politics and International Relations*, 13 (2011), pp. 603–618

Boorsch, S., 'Fireworks!: Four Centuries of Pyrotechnics in Prints & Drawings', *The Metropolitan Museum of Art Bulletin*, New Series, 58 (2000), pp. 3–52

Borus, G., 'Political Parties in the Years Before and After the Glorious Revolution', *Hungarian Journal of English and American Studies (HJEAS)*, 13 (2007), pp. 121–30

Bowen, M., *Crowns and Sceptres: The Romance and Pageantry of Coronations* (London, 1937)

Bowers, R., 'The Chapel Royal, the First Edwardian Prayer Book, and Elizabeth's Settlement of Religion, 1559', *The Historical Journal*, 43 (2000), pp. 317–44

Bowett, A., 'George I's Coronation Throne', *Apollo*, CLXI (2005), pp. 42–7

Braddick, M. J., *Parliamentary Taxation in Seventeenth-Century England: Local Administration and Response* (London, 1995)

Braddick, M. J., *State Formation in Early Modern England, c.1550–1700* (Cambridge, 2000)

Braddick, M. J., *The Nerves of State: Taxation and the Financing of the English State, 1558–1714* (Manchester, 1996)

Bradford, S., *The Reluctant King: The Life and Reign of George VI, 1895–1952* (New York, New York, 1990)

Bradley, I. C., *The Call to Seriousness: The Evangelical Impact on the Victorians* (London, 1976)

Bradshaw, P., 'Introduction', in H. Everett *et al.*, *Coronations: Past, Present and Future* (Cambridge, 1997), pp. 5–6

Bray, G. (ed.), *The Reign of Henry IV (1399–1413): Records of Convocation* (Woodbridge, 2023), pp. 69–86

Brazier, R., 'Royal Incapacity and Constitutional Continuity: The Regent and Counsellors of State', *The Cambridge Law Journal*, 64 (2005), pp. 352–87

Brewer, J., *The Sinews of Power: War, Money and the English State, 1688–1783* (London, 1989)

Broad, C. L., *Queens, Crowns and Coronations* (revised edition, London, 1952)

Brogan, S., *The Royal Touch in Early Modern England: Politics, Medicine and Sin* (Woodbridge, 2015)

Brooks, C. W., *Pettyfoggers and Vipers of the Commonwealth: The 'Lower Branch' of the Legal Profession in Early Modern England* (Cambridge, 1986)
Brooke, J., *King George III* (New York, New York, 1972)
Brown, K., 'Courtiers and Cavaliers: Service, Anglicization and Loyalty among the Royalist Nobility', in J. Morrill (ed.), *The Scottish National Covenant in its British Context 1638–51* (Edinburgh, 1990), pp. 155–92
Brown, M., *The Wars of Scotland, 1214–1371* (Edinburgh, 2004)
Brown, R. A., Colvin, H. M., & Taylor, A. J., *The History of the King's Works, The Middle Ages* (London, 1963)
Brown, S. J., *Providence and Empire: Religion, Politics and Society in the United Kingdom, 1815–1914* (Harlow, 2008)
Buc, P., 'David's Adultery with Bathsheba and the Healing Power of Capetian Kings', *Viator*, 24 (1993), 101–20
Buchwald, J. Z. and Feingold, M., *Newton and the Origin of Civilization* (New Haven, Connecticut, 2012)
Bucholz, R. O., 'Queen Anne: Victim of her Virtues?', in C. Campbell Orr (ed.), *Queenship in Britain, 1660–1837: Royal Patronage, Court Culture, and Dynastic Politics* (Manchester, 2002), pp. 94–129
Bucholz, R. O., *The Augustan Court: Queen Anne and the Decline of Court Culture* (Stanford, California, 1993)
Burchard, W. and Edwards, S., 'A Very Royal Perquisite: The Eventful Life of George I's Coronation Throne', *Furniture History Society Newsletter*, No. 195 (August 2014), pp. 5–9
Burden, J., 'Re-writing a Rite of Passage: The Peculiar Funeral of Edward II', in N. F. McDonald and W. M. Ormrod (eds), *Rites of Passage: Cultures of Transition in the Fourteenth Century* (Woodbridge, 2004), pp. 13–29
Burgess, G., *British Political Thought, 1500–1660: The Politics of the Post-Reformation* (Basingstoke, 2009)
Burgess, G., 'The Divine Right of Kings Reconsidered', *The English Historical Review*, CVII (1992), pp. 837–61
Burrows, D., 'Handel and the 1727 Coronation', *The Musical Times*, 118 (1977), pp. 469–73
Bussby, F., 'George Morley: Bishop of Worcester, 1660–62', *Transactions of the Worcestershire Archaeological Society*, New Series, XXXVII (1961), pp. 11–23

Caldwell, D. H. and Ewart, G., 'Finlaggan and the Lordship of the Isles: An Archaeological Approach', *The Scottish Historical Review*, 72 (1993), pp. 146–66

Callow, J., *James II: The Triumph and the Tragedy* (Kew, 2005)

Campbell, E., 'Oaths and Affirmations of Public Office under English Law: An Historical Retrospect', *The Journal of Legal History*, 21 (2000), pp. 1–32

Campbell, M. W., 'Earl Godwin of Wessex and Edward the Confessor's Promise of the Throne to William of Normandy.' *Traditio*, 28 (1972), pp. 141–58

Cannadine, D., 'The Context, Performance and Meaning of Ritual: The British Monarchy and the "Invention of Tradition", *c.*1820–1977', in E. Hobsbawm and T. Ranger (eds), *The Invention of Tradition* (Cambridge, 1983), pp. 101–64

Cannadine, D., *History in Our Time* (New Haven, Connecticut, 1998)

Cantor, N. F., *Church, Kingship and Lay Investiture in England 1089–1135* (Princeton, New Jersey, 1958)

Carleton, K. W. T., 'The *Traditio Instrumentorum* in the Reform of Ordination Rites in the Sixteenth Century', in R. W. Swanson (ed.), *Continuity and Change in Christian Worship*, Studies in Church History, 35 (Woodbridge, 1999), pp. 172–84

Carlson, D., 'King Arthur and Court Poems for the birth of Arthur Tudor in 1486', *Humanistica Lovaniensia*, 36 (1987), pp. 147–183

Carpenter, C., 'Resisting and Deposing Kings in England in the Thirteenth, Fourteenth and Fifteenth Centuries', in R. von Friedeburg (ed.), *Murder and Monarchy: Regicide in European History, 1300–1800* (Basingstoke, 2004), pp. 99–121

Carpenter, D. A., 'King Henry III and Saint Edward the Confessor: The Origins of the Cult', *The English Historical Review*, CXXII (2007), pp. 865–91

Carpenter, D. A., 'Archbishop Langton and Magna Carta: His Contribution, His Doubts and His Hypocrisy', *The English Historical Review*, 126 (2011), pp. 1041–65

Carpenter, E. (ed.), *A House of Kings: The History of Westminster Abbey* (London, 1966)

Carter, M., *The Three Emperors: Three Cousins, Three Empires and the Road to World War One* (London, 2009)

Chaline, O., 'The Kingdoms of France and Navarre: The Valois and Bourbon Courts *c.*1515–1750', in J. Adamson (ed.), *The Princely Courts of*

Europe: Ritual, Politics and Culture Under the Ancien Régime 1500–1750 (London, 1999), pp. 67–93

Chandaman, C. D., *The English Public Revenue: 1660–1688* (Oxford, 1975)

Chandler, D. and Beckett, I. (eds), *The Oxford Illustrated History of the British Army* (Oxford, 1994)

Christian, W. A., *Apparitions in Late Medieval and Renaissance Spain* (Princeton, New Jersey, 1981)

Clark, J. C. D., 'Protestantism, Nationalism, and National Identity, 1660–1832', *The Historical Journal*, 43 (2000), pp. 249–76

Clark, J. C. D., *English Society 1660 –1832: Religion, ideology and politics during the ancien regime* (Cambridge, 2000)

Claydon, T., 'Latitudinarianism and Apocalyptic History in the Worldview of Gilbert Burnet, 1643–1715', *The Historical Journal*, 51 (2008), pp. 577–97

Claydon, T., *Europe and the Making of England: 1660–1760* (Cambridge, 2007)

Claydon, T., 'The Sermon Culture of the Glorious Revolution: Williamite Preaching and Jacobite Anti-preaching, 1685–1702', in P. McCullough *et al.* (eds)., *The Oxford Handbook of the Early Modern Sermon* (Oxford, 2011), pp. 480–494

Clermont-Ferrand, M., 'Joan of Arc and the English Chroniclers: Monstrous Presence and Problematic Absence in *The Chronicle of London, The Chronicle of William of Worcester*, and *An English Chronicle 1377–1461.*' *The Medieval Chronicle*, 7 (2011), pp. 151–66

Cockin, K., 'Queen Caroline's Pains and Penalties: Silence and Speech in the Dramatic Art of British Women's Suffrage', *Law and Literature*, 24 (2012), pp. 40–58

Colclough, D., "I have brought thee up to a Kingdome': Sermons on the Accessions of James I and Charles I', in P. Kewes, and A. McRae (eds), *Stuart Succession Literature: Moments and Transformations* (Oxford, 2018), pp. 205–221

Cole, T., *The Norman Conquest: William the Conqueror's Subjugation of England* (Stroud, 2018)

Colley, L., *Britons: Forging the Nation, 1707–1837* (New Haven, Connecticut, and London, 1992)

Collinson, P., *The Birthpangs of Protestant England: Religious and Cultural Change in the Sixteenth and Seventeenth Centuries* (Basingstoke, 1988)

Collinson, P., *This England: Essays on the English Nation and Commonwealth in the Sixteenth Century* (Manchester, 2011)

Colvin, H. M. (general ed.), *The History of the King's Works*, 6 volumes (London, 1963–82)

Condren, C., *Argument and Authority in Early Modern England: The Presupposition of Oaths and Offices* (Cambridge, 2006)

Cook, B. J., 'Stampt with your own *Image*': Numismatic Dimension of Two Stuart Successions', in P. Kewes and A. McRae (eds), *Stuart Succession Literature: Moments and Transformations* (Oxford, 2019), pp. 303–18

Cooper, J., *Four Scottish Coronations (The Coronation of James VI – The Coronation of Anne, Queen of James VI – The Coronation of Charles I – The Coronation of Charles II)* (Aberdeen, 1902)

Copland, A., *What to Listen for in Music* (New York, 1957)

Cowan, I. and Easson, D., *Medieval Religious Houses, Scotland* (2nd edition, London, 1976)

Craig, L. A., 'Royalty, Virtue, and Adversity: The Cult of Henry VI', *Albion*, 35 (2003), pp. 187–209

Craig, Sir J., *Newton at the Mint* (Cambridge, 1946)

Crankshaw, D. J., 'Ecclesiastical Statesmanship in England in the Age of the Reformation', in D. Wendebourg (ed.), *Sister Reformations: The Reformation in Germany and in England* (Tübingen, 2010), pp. 271–303

Crawfurd, Sir Raymond, *The King's Evil* (Oxford, 1911)

Cressy, D., *Birth, Marriage, and Death: Ritual, Religion, and the Life-Cycle in Tudor and Stuart England* (Oxford, 1997)

Cressy, D., *Bonfires and Bells: National Memory and the Protestant Calendar in Elizabethan and Stuart England* (London, 1989)

Cressy, D., *Charles I and the People of England* (Oxford, 2015)

Crick, J., '*Pristina Libertas*: Liberty and the Anglo-Saxons Revisited', *Transactions of the Royal Historical Society*, 14 (2004), pp. 47–71

Croft, P., *King James* (Basingstoke, 2003)

Cross, C., 'Churchmen and the Royal Supremacy', in F. Heal and R. O'Day (eds), *Church and Society in England: Henry VIII to James I* (London, 1977), pp. 15–34

Curry, A. D., 'King Arthur of England, count of Habsburg: the use of Arthurian imagery in Habsburg diplomacy', *Historical Research*, 96 (2023), pp. 473–88

Daly, J., 'The Idea of Absolute Monarchy in Seventeenth-Century England', *The Historical Journal*, 21 (1978), pp. 227–50

Dawson, C., *The Services of the Barons of the Cinque Ports at the Coronation of the Kings and Queens of England, etc.* (Lewes, 1901)

Dean, B. P., "Thoreau and 'The Celebrated Koh-i-Noor Diamond,'" *The Thoreau Society Bulletin*, 242 (2003), pp. 6–7

de Bellaigue, G., 'A Royal Mise-en-Scène: George IV's Coronation Banquet,' *Furniture History*, 29 (1993), pp. 174–83

De La Bere, Sir Ivan, *The Queen's Orders of Chivalry* (1st edition, London, 1961; 2nd edition, London, 1964)

Dicey, A. V., *Introduction to the Study of the Law of the Constitution* (9th edition, London, 1945)

Dickinson, H. T., *Liberty and Property: Political Ideology in Eighteenth-Century Britain* (London, 1977)

Dillon, P., *The Last Revolution: 1688 and the Creation of the Modern World* (London, 2006)

Ditmas, E. M. R., 'The Curtana or Sword of Mercy', *The Journal of the British Archaeological Association*, 3rd Series, XXIX (1966), pp. 122–33

Dobson, R. B., *The Jews of Medieval York and the Massacre of March 1190* (York, 1974)

Dixon, N., 'The Church of England and the Coronation Rite, 1761–1838', *Church History*, 90 (2021), pp. 98–116

Dixon, N., 'The Evolution of the British Coronation Rite, 1761–1953' in A. Kalinowska, J. Spangler and P. Tyszka (eds), *Power and Ceremony in European History: Rituals, Practices and Representative Bodies since the Late Medieval Age* (London, 2021), pp. 49–68

Doran, S., *From Tudor to Stuart: The Regime Change from Elizabeth I to James I* (Oxford, 2024)

Douglas, D. C., 'The Conquest of England January 1066–March 1067' in D. C. Douglas, *William the Conqueror: The Norman Impact Upon England* (New Haven, Connecticut, 1999), pp. 181–210

Doyle, Sir Arthur Conan, *The Complete Sherlock Holmes; With Illustrations by Sidney Paget* (London, 2005)

Driscoll, S. T., 'Picts and Prehistory: Cultural Resource Management in Early Medieval Scotland', *World Archaeology* 30 (1998), pp. 142–58

Duggan, A., 'The Coronation of the Young King in 1170', in G. J. Cumming (ed.), *Studies in Church History*, vol. 2 (London, 1968), pp. 165–78

Echard, L., *The History of England. From the First Entrance of Julius Caesar and the Romans, to the End of the Reign of King James the First. Containing the Space of 1678 Years*, 3 volumes (1st edition, London, 1707; 2nd edition, London, 1718)
Edie, C. A., 'The in of Royal Ritual: Sermons, Medals, and Civic Ceremony in Later Stuart Coronations', *The Huntington Library Quarterly*, 53 (1990), pp. 311–36
Edwards, J., *Mary I: England's Catholic Queen* (London, 2011)
Eeles, F. C., *The English Coronation Service. Its History and Teaching. With the Coronation Services of King Charles I. and of Queen Victoria* (Oxford, 1902)
Einbinder, S. L., *Beautiful Death: Jewish Poetry and Martyrdom in Medieval France* (Princeton, New Jersey, 2002)
Eliot, G., *Daniel Deronda* (1876)
Elmer, P., *The Miraculous Conformist: Valentine Greatrakes, the Body Politic, and the Politics of Healing in Restoration Britain* (Oxford, 2013)
Epstein, R., 'Eating their words: food and text in the coronation banquet of Henry VI,' *Journal of Medieval and Early Modern Studies*, 36 (2006), pp. 355–77
Evans, N., 'Royal Succession and Kingship among the Picts', *The Innes Review* 59 (2008), pp. 1–48
Everett, H., 'The English Coronation Rite: From the Middle Ages to the Stuarts', in H. Everett *et al.*, *Coronations: Past, Present and Future* (Cambridge, 1997), pp. 7–21
Fantoni, M., 'The Grand Duchy of Tuscany: The Courts of the Medici 1532–1737', in J. Adamson (ed.), *The Princely Courts of Europe: Ritual, Politics and Culture Under the Ancien Régime 1500–1750* (London, 1999), pp. 255–73
Farmer, D. H., *The Oxford Dictionary of Saints* (5th edition, revised, Oxford, 2011)
Fennell, J., *A History of the Russian Church to 1448* (London, 1995)
Figgis, J. N., *The Divine Right of Kings* (Cambridge, 1896)
Fincham, K. (ed.), *The Early Stuart Church, 1603–1642* (Basingstoke, 1993)
Fincham, K., 'William Temple and William Laud', *Theology*, 125 (2022), pp. 241–319
Fincham, K. and Tyacke, N., *Altars Restored: The Changing Face of English Religious Worship, 1547–c.1700* (Oxford, 2007)

Fishclin, D. and Fortier, M. (eds), *Royal Subjects: Essays on the Writings of James VI and I* (Detroit, Michigan, 2002)
Fisher, H. A. L. (ed.), *The Constitutional History of England: A Course of Lectures Delivered by F. W. Maitland* (Cambridge, 1908)
Fox, A., 'Rumour, News and Popular Political Opinion in Elizabethan and Early Stuart England', *The Historical Journal*, 40 (1997), pp. 597–620
Fraser, A., *King Charles II* (London, 1979)
Fraser, F., *The Unruly Queen: The Life of Queen Caroline* (London, 1996)
French, R. V., *Nineteen Centuries of Drink in England: A History* (2nd edition, 1884–1890, London)
Friedeburg, R. von, 'Reformation of Manners and the Social Composition of Offenders in an East Anglian Cloth Village: Earls Colne, Essex, 1531–1642', *Journal of British Studies*, 29 (1990), pp. 347–85
Fritz, P. S., 'The Trade in Death: The Royal Funerals in England, 1685–1830', *Eighteenth-Century Studies*, 15 (1982), pp. 291–316
Fulford, T., 'Cobbett, Coleridge and the Queen Caroline Affair', *Studies in Romanticism*, 37 (1998), pp. 523–43
Gaborit-Chopin, D., 'Le Trésor au temps de Suger', in *Le Trésor de St Denis, les dossiers d'archéologie*, 158 (1991), pp. 2–19
Galloway, P., *The Order of the Bath* (Chichester, 2006)
Gardiner, S. R. (ed.), *The Constitutional Documents of the Puritan Revolution 1625–1660* (3rd edition, Oxford, 1906)
Garnett, G., 'The Origins of the Crown', in J. Hudson (ed.), 'The History of English Law: Centenary Essays on "Pollock and Maitland"', *Proceedings of the British Academy*, 89 (1996), pp. 171–214
Garnett, G., 'Coronation', in M. Lapidge, J. Blair, S. Keynes and D. Scragg (eds.), *The Wiley Blackwell Encyclopedia of Anglo-Saxon England*, 2nd edn (Oxford, 2014), pp. 125–126
Garnett, G., 'Coronation and Propaganda: Some Implications of the Norman Claim to the Throne of England in 1066: The Alexander Prize Essay.' *Transactions of the Royal Historical Society*, 36 (1986), pp. 91–116
Garnett, G., *The Norman Conquest: A Very Short Introduction* (Oxford, 2009)
Gem, R. D. H., 'The Romanesque Rebuilding of Westminster Abbey', *Proceedings of the Battle Conference on Anglo- Norman Studies*, 3 (1980), pp. 33–60
Gerhold, D., *Westminster Hall: Nine Hundred Years of History* (London, 1999)

Gibb, A., 'The Coronation of James the First, King of Scotland, and Jane Beaufort, Queen of Scotland, His Wife, 21st May, 1424', *The Scottish Antiquary* 17 (1902), pp. 1–8

Ghuman, N., 'Elgar's *Pageant of Empire*, 1924: An imperial leitmotif', in *Exhibition the Empire. Cultures of Display and the British Empire*, edited by John McAleer and John M. MacKenzie (Manchester, 2015), pp. 220–56

Gilyarovsky, V., (trans. B. Kiernan), *Moscow and Muscovites* (original 1935, this edition 2013, Montpelier, Vermont)

Gillingham, J., 'Two Yorkshire Historians Compared: Roger of Howden and William of Newburgh', *Haskins Society Journal* 12 (2002), 15–37

Goldie, M., 'The Revolution of 1689 and the Structure of Political Argument: An Essay and An Annotated Bibliography of Pamphlets on the Allegiance Controversy', *Bulletin of Research in the Humanities*, 83 (1980), pp. 473–564

Goldish, M., 'Patterns in Converso Messianism', in M. D. Goldish and R. H. Popkin (eds), *Millenarianism and Messianism in Early Modern European Culture*, Volume 1: Jewish Messianism in the Early Modern World (Dordrecht and London, 2001), pp. 41–63

Goodall, J., *The Castle: A History* (New Haven, Connecticut, 2022)

Gosling, L., *Royal Coronations* (Oxford, 2013)

Greenberg, J., 'The Confessor's Laws and the Radical Face of the Ancient Constitution', *The English Historical Review*, CIV (1989), pp. 611–37

Gregg, E., *Queen Anne* (2nd edition, New Haven, Connecticut, and London, 2001)

Gross, G. W. C., '1651: The Last Coronation in Scotland — An Anomaly?' *The Court Historian*, 26 (2021), pp. 229–245. https://www.tandfonline.com/doi/full/10.1080/14629712.2021.1996947#:~:text=The%20last%20Scottish%20coronation%20occurred%20at%20Scone%20in%201651

Guy, J., *Thomas More* (London, 2000)

Haas, S. W., 'Martin Luther's "Divine Right" Kingship and the Royal Supremacy: Two Tracts from the 1531 Parliament and Convocation of the Clergy', *The Journal of Ecclesiastical History*, 31 (1980), pp. 317–25

Hackett, H., *Virgin Mother, Maiden Queen: Elizabeth I and the Cult of the Virgin Mary* (Basingstoke, 1995)

Hajkowski, T., *The BBC and National Identity in Britain, 1922–53* (Manchester, 2010)

Hall, J., *Queen Elizabeth and Her Church: Royal Service at Westminster Abbey* (London, 2012)

Hammarol, P., 'The King's Two Bodies: Representations of Charles II', in J. Black and J. Gregory (eds), *Culture, Politics and Society in Britain, 1660–1800* (Manchester, *c.*1991), pp. 13–48

Hardman, R., *Charles III: New King. New Court. The Inside Story* (London, 2024)

Harris, T., *Restoration: Charles II and his Kingdoms, 1660–1685* (London, 2005)

Harris, T., *Revolution: The Great Crisis of the British Monarchy, 1685–1720* (London, 2006)

Hart-Davis, D., *King's Counsellor, Abdication and War: The Diaries of Sir Alan 'Tommy' Lascelles* (London, 2020)

Hassam, A., 'Portable iron structures and uncertain colonial spaces at the Sydenham Cystal Palace', in *Imperial Cities. Landscape, Display and Identity*, edited by Felix Driver and David Gilbert (Manchester, 1999), pp. 174–93

Hatton, R. M., *George I* (New Haven, Connecticut, and London, 2001)

Haugaard, W. P., 'The Coronation of Elizabeth I', *The Journal of Ecclesiastical History*, XIX (1968), pp. 161–70

Hauptman, W., "'The Blood-Stained Brush': David and the British circa 1802." *The British Art Journal*, 10 (2009), pp. 78–97

Hawkins, E. (comp.) and Franks, A. W. and Grueber, H. A. (eds), *Medallic Illustrations of the History of Great Britain and Ireland to the Death of George II*, 2 volumes (London, 1885)

Hayward, M., 'William Green, Coffer-Maker to Henry VIII, Edward VI and Mary I', *Furniture History*, 36 (2000), pp. 1–13

Hazell, R. and Morris, B., *Swearing in the New King: The Accession and Coronation Oaths*, The Constitution Unit (London, 2022)

Heal, F., 'What Can King Lucius Do For You? The Reformation and the Early British Church', *English Historical Review*, 120 (2005), 593–614

Heal, F., *The Power of Gifts: Gift Exchange in Early Modern England* (Oxford, 2014)

Heinze, R. W., *The Proclamations of the Tudor Kings* (Cambridge, 1976)

Helstosky, C. (ed.), *The Routledge History of Food* (London, 2015)

Hendriks, F., 'George I: Coronation Celebration at Leghorn, 1714', *Notes and Queries*, 9th Series, X (1902), pp. 404–5

Hillaby, J., 'A Domus Conversorum at Bristol?', *Jewish Historical Studies*, 42 (2009), pp. 1–5

Hinds, P., *'The Horrid Popish Plot': Roger L'Estrange and the Circulation of Political Discourse in Late Seventeenth-Century London* (London, 2010)
Hoak, D., 'The Coronations of Edward VI, Mary I, and Elizabeth I, and the Transformation of the Tudor Monarchy', in C. S. Knighton and R. Mortimer (eds), *Westminster Abbey Reformed 1540–1640* (Aldershot, 2003), pp. 114–51
Hoak, D., 'The Iconography of the Crown Imperial', in D. Hoak (ed.), *Tudor Political Culture* (Cambridge, 1995), pp. 54–103
Hoak, D., 'Tudor Deborah? The Coronation of Elizabeth I, Parliament, and the Problem of Female Rule', in C. Highley and J. N. King (eds), *John Foxe and His World* (Aldershot, 2002), pp. 73–88
Holmes, M., 'New Light on St. Edward's Crown', *Archaeologia*, 2nd Series, 97 (1959), pp. 213–23
Holmes, M. and Sitwell, H. D. W., *The English Regalia: Their History, Custody & Display* (London, 1972)
Holmes, M. J. R., *The Crown Jewels in the Wakefield Tower at the Tower of London* (3rd edition, London, 1961)
Holmes, R., *Wellington: The Iron Duke* (London, 2003)
Holmes, R., *Redcoat: The British Soldier in the Age of Horse and Musket* (London, 2002)
Holmes, R., *Marlborough: Britain's Greatest General* (London, 2009)
Hone, J., 'The Last Stuart Coronation' in P. Kewes and A. McRae (eds), *Stuart Succession Literature: Moments and Transformations* (Oxford, 2019), pp. 132–145
Hone, J., 'Isaac Newton and the Medals for Queen Anne', *Huntington Library Quarterly*, 79 (2016), 119–48
Hone, J., 'Politicising Praise: Panegyric and the Accession of Queen Anne', *Journal for Eighteenth-Century Studies*, 37 (2014), pp. 147–57
Hope, St. John W. H., 'The King's Coronation Ornaments', *The Ancester*, I (1902), pp. 127–59
Höpfl, H. and Thompson, M. P., 'The History of Contract as a Motif in Political Thought', *The American Historical Review*, 84 (1979), pp. 919–44
Hosler, J. D., 'Henry II, William of Newburgh, and the Development of English Anti-Judaism', in *Christian Attitudes Toward the Jews in the Middle Ages: A Casebook*, ed. M. Frassetto (New York, New York, 2007), pp. 167–82
Houlbrooke, R., *Death, Religion, and the Family in England, 1480–1750* (Oxford, 1998)

Hoyle, R. W., 'Introduction: Aspects of the Crown's Estate, *c.*1558–1640', in R. W. Hoyle (ed.), *The Estates of the English Crown, 1558–1640* (Cambridge, 1992), pp. 1–57

Hoyt, R. S., 'The Coronation Oath of 1308', *The English Historical Review*, LXXI (1956), pp. 353–83

Hughes, A., 'The Origins and Descent of the Fourth Recension of the English Coronation', in J. M. Bak (ed.), *Coronations: Medieval and Early Modern Monarchic Ritual* (Berkeley and Los Angeles, California, *c.*1990), pp. 197–216

Hughes, E., 'Some Clavering Correspondence', *Archaeologia Aeliana*, 4th ser., xxxiv (1956), pp. 20–21

Hughes, L., 'Russia: The Courts at Moscow and St Petersburg *c.*1547–1725', in J. Adamson (ed.), *The Princely Courts of Europe: Ritual, Politics and Culture Under the Ancien Régime 1500–1750* (London, 1999), pp. 295–313

Hunt, A., *The Art of Hearing: English Preachers and their Audiences, 1590–1640* (Cambridge, 2010)

Hunt, A., *The Drama of Coronation: Medieval Ceremony in Early Modern England* (Cambridge, 2008)

Hunt, A., 'The Bright Star of the North: James I and his English Coronation', in M. Twycross, S. Carpenter *et al.* (eds), *Medieval English Theatre 38: The Best Pairt of Our Play. Essays Presented to John J. McGavin. Part II.* (Woodbridge; 2017), pp. 22–37

Hunting, P., *Royal Westminster: A History of Westminster Through its Royal Connections* ([London], *c.*1981)

Husk, W. H., *An Account of the Musical Celebrations on St Cecilia's Day in the Sixteenth, Seventeenth, and Eighteenth Centuries. To Which Is Appended A Collection Of Odes On St. Cecilia's Day* (London, 1857)

Hutton, R., *Charles the Second: King of England, Scotland and Ireland* (Oxford, 1989)

Hutton, R., *The Rise and Fall of Merry England: The Ritual Year 1400–1700* (Oxford, 1994)

Ives, E. W., *Anne Boleyn* (Oxford, 1986)

Ives, E. W., 'Tudor Dynastic Problems Revisited', *Historical Research*, 81 (2008), pp. 255–79

Ives, E., *Lady Jane Grey: A Tudor Mystery* (Chichester, 2009)

Jack, S. M., '"A Pattern for a King's Inauguration": The Coronation of James I in England', *Parergon*, New Series, 21 No. 2 (2004), pp. 67–91

Jackson, C., *Charles III: A King and His Queen* (New York, New York, 2023)

Jackson, R. A., *Vive le Roi! A History of the French Coronation from Charles V to Charles X* (Chapel Hill, North Carolina, 1984)
James, A., *Charles III: A Modern Monarch* (Solihull, 2023)
James, L., *'This Great Firebrand': William Laud and Scotland, 1617–1645* (Woodbridge, 2017)
Jankovic, V., 'The Politics of Sky Battles in Early Hanoverian Britain', *Journal of British Studies*, 41 (2002), pp. 429–59
Jenkyns, R., *Westminster Abbey* (revised edition, London, 2011)
Johnston, M. F., *Coronation of a King, or the Ceremonies, Pageants and Chronicles of Coronations of all Ages … With Illustrations, etc.* (London, 1902)
Jones, A., 'The Significance of the Royal Coronation of Edgar in 973', *Journal of Ecclesiastical History*, 33 (1982), pp. 375–90
Jones, E., 'Conservatism, Edmund Burke, and the Invention of a Political Tradition, *c.* 1885–1914', *The Historical Journal*, 58 (2015), pp. 1115–39
Jones, D. M., *Conscience and Allegiance in Seventeenth Century England: The Political Significance of Oaths and Engagements* (Rochester, New York, 1999)
Jones, E. A., 'Some Coronation Plate', *The Burlington Magazine*, 70 (1937), pp. 240, 244–7
Jones, R. W., *A Cultural History of the Medieval Sword: Power, Piety and Play* (Martlesham, 2024)
Kantorowicz, E. H., *The King's Two Bodies: A Study in Mediaeval Political Theology* (Princeton, New Jersey, 1957)
Keay, A., *The Crown Jewels* (London, 2011)
Keay, A., *The Magnificent Monarch: Charles II and the Ceremonies of Power* (London, 2008)
Kenyon, J. P., *Revolution Principles: The Politics of Party, 1689 – 1720* (Cambridge, 1977)
Key, N. E., 'The Political Culture and Political Rhetoric of County Feasts and Feast Sermons, 1654–1714', *Journal of British Studies*, 33 (1994), pp. 223–56
Keynes, S., 'Edgar, Rex Admirabilis', in D. Scragg (ed.), *Edgar, King of the English, 959–975: New Interpretations* (new edn) (Woodbridge, 2008), pp. 3–59
Keynes, S., 'Church Councils, Royal Assemblies, and Anglo-Saxon Royal Diplomas', in G. R. Owen-Crocker and B. W. Schneider (eds), *Kingship,*

Legislation and Power in Anglo-Saxon England (Woodbridge, 2013), pp. 17–182

Kidd, C., 'Protestantism, Constitutionalism and British Identity under the Later Stuarts', in B. Bradshaw and P. Roberts (eds), *British Consciousness and Identity: The Making of Britain, 1533–1707* (Cambridge, 1998), pp. 321–42

King, A. and Crewe, I., *The Blunders of our Governments* (London, 2013)

King, J. N., *Tudor Royal Iconography: Literature and Art in an Age of Religious Crisis* (Princeton, New Jersey, 1989)

Kinsey, C. D., 'Koh-i-Noor: Empire, Diamonds, and the Performance of British Material Culture,' *Journal of British Studies*, 48 (2009), pp. 391–419

Kipling, G., "'He that Saw It Would Not Believe It:' Anne Boleyn's Royal Entry into London," in Alexandra F. Johnston and Wim Hüsken (eds), *Civic Ritual and Drama* (Amsterdam - Atlanta, 1997), pp. 39–80

Kiryanova, E., 'Images of Kingship: Charles I, Accession Sermons, and the Theory of Divine Right', *History*, 100 (2015), pp. 21–39

Kishlansky, M., *A Monarchy Transformed: Britain 1603–1714* (Harmondsworth, 1996)

Kite, M. and Thomson, R., *Conservation of Leather and Related Materials* (Burlington, Massachusetts, 2006)

Knappett, G., *King Charles III* (London, 2023)

Knickerbocker, F. W., 'Victoria Invicta', *The Sewanee Review*, 45 (1937), pp. 168–79

Knoppers, L. L., *Constructing Cromwell: Ceremony, Portrait, and Print 1645–1661* (Cambridge, 2000)

Koziol, G., 'England, France and the Problem of Sacrality in Twelfth-Century Ritual', in T. Bisson (ed.), *Cultures of Power. Lordship, Status and Process in Twelfth- Century Europe* (Philadelphia, Pennsylvania, 1995), pp. 124–48

Kreitzer, L., 'Paying Gold with Chocolate: Thomas Simon and a Gift for the Swedish Ambassador in 1656', *The Medal*, 64 (2014), pp. 10–15

Kriewald, G. L., 'The Widow of Windsor and the Spinster of Jefferson: A Possible Source for Faulkner's Emily Grierson.' *Faulkner Journal*, 19 (2003), pp. 3–10

Kypta, U., "How to Be an Exchequer Clerk in the Twelfth Century: What the *Dialogue of the Exchequer* Is Really About," *History*, 103 (2018), pp. 199–222

Laborie, L., *Enlightening Enthusiasm: Prophecy and Religious Experience in Early Eighteenth-Century England* (Manchester, 2015)

Lacey, A., *The Cult of King Charles the Martyr* (Woodbridge, 2003)

Lake, P., 'The Laudian Style: Order, Uniformity and the Pursuit of the Beauty of Holiness in the 1630s', in K. Fincham (ed.), *The Early Stuart Church, 1603–1642* (Basingstoke, 1993), pp. 161–85

Lake, P., "The King (The Queen) and the Jesuit: James Stuart's 'True Law of Free Monarchies' in Context/s." *Transactions of the Royal Historical Society*, 14 (2004), pp. 243–60

Laqueur, T. W., 'The Queen Caroline Affair: Politics as Art in the Reign of George IV', *The Journal of Modern History*, 54, (1982), pp. 417–66

Lawson-Peebles, R., 'The Implications of the Accession of James VI and I', in *The Yearbook of English Studies*, 46, Writing the Americas, 1480–1826 (2016), pp. 56–74 (Modern Humanities Research Association)

Lee, M., Jr, *The 'Inevitable' Union and Other Essays on Early Modern Scotland* (East Linton, 2003)

Legg, J. Wickham, 'The Queen's Coronation Ring', *The Archaeological Journal*, 54 (1897), pp. 1–9

Le Hardy, W. H. C., *The Coronation Book. The History and Meaning of the Ceremonies at the Crowning of the King and Queen* (London, 1937)

Leneghan, F., "Royal Wisdom and the Alfredian Context of 'Cynewulf and Cyneheard.'" *Anglo-Saxon England*, 39 (2011), pp. 71–104

Lenman, B., 'The Exiled Stuarts and the Precious Symbols of Sovereignty', *Eighteenth-Century Life*, 25 (2001), pp. 185–200

Lenman, B., *The Jacobite Risings in Britain 1689–1746* (London, 1980)

Lenowitz, H., *The Jewish Messiahs: From the Galilee to Crown Heights* (Oxford, 1998)

Leonard, H. H., 'Distraint of Knighthood: The Last Phase, 1625–41', *History*, 63 (1978), pp. 23–37

Levine, M., *Tudor Dynastic Problems 1460–1571* (London, 1973)

Lightbown, R., 'The King's Regalia, Insignia and Jewellery', in A. MacGregor (ed.), *The Late King's Goods: Collections, Possessions, and Patronage of Charles I in the Light of the Commonwealth Sale Inventories* (Oxford, 1989), pp. 257–75

Loades, D., *The Reign of Mary Tudor: Politics, Government and Religion in England, 1553–58* (London, 1991)

Loades, D., *Mary Tudor: A Life* (Oxford, 1989)

Loades, D., 'The Origins of English Protestant Nationalism', in D. Loades, *Politics, Censorship and the English Reformation* (London, 1991), pp. 39–47

Lotz-Heumann, U., 'Confessionalization', in D. M. Whitford (ed.), *Reformation and Early Modern Europe: A Guide to Research* (Kirksville, Missouri, 2008), pp. 136–57

Loughlin, M., 'The State, the Crown and the Law', in M. Sunkin and S. Payne (eds), *The Nature of the Crown: A Legal and Political Analysis* (Oxford, 1999), pp. 33–76

Luckhardt, J., and Niehoff, F. (eds), *Heinrich der Löwe und seine Zeit. Herrschaft und Repräsentation der Welfen, 1125–1235*, 3 vols (Munich, 1995)

Ludington, C., *The Politics of Wine in Britain* (London, 2013)

Lyall, R. J., 'The Medieval Scottish Coronation Service: Some Seventeenth-Century Evidence', *The Innes Review*, 28 (1977), pp. 3–21

M, H.,'Kipling as a Poet', *Poetry*, 48 (1936), pp. 32–36

MacCulloch, D., 'Foxes, Firebrands, and Forgery: Robert Ware's Pollution of Reformation History', *The Historical Journal*, 54 (2011), pp. 307–46

MacCulloch, D., *The Boy King: Edward VI and the Protestant Reformation* (Berkeley, California, 2002)

MacCulloch, D., *Thomas Cranmer: A Life* (1st edn, New Haven, Connecticut, and London, 1996)

Mackay of Clashfern, Lord (ed. in chief), *Halsbury's Laws of England* (5th edition, London, 2008–)

MacNalty, Sir A. S., 'Medicine In The Time Of Queen Elizabeth The First', *The British Medical Journal*, 1 (1953), pp. 1179–85

Madway, L., '"The Most Conspicuous Solemnity": The Coronation of Charles II', in E. Cruickshanks (ed.), *The Stuart Courts* (Stroud, 2000), pp. 141–57

Mansel, P., *King of the World: The Life of Louis XIV* (London, 2022)

Mantell, Sir Thomas, *Coronation Ceremonies and Customs Relative to the Barons of the Cinque Ports as Supporters of the Canopy* (Dover, 1820)

Marcus, J. R. and Saperstein, M. (eds), 'The York Riots 1190', in J. R. Marcus and M. Saperstein (eds), *The Jews in Christian Europe: A Source Book, 315–1791* (Pittsburgh, Pennsylvania, 2015), pp. 103–8

Marsh, C., *Music and Society in Early Modern England* (Cambridge, 2010)

Marschner, J., *Queen Caroline: Cultural Politics at the Eighteenth-century Court* (New Haven, Connecticut, 2014)

Mason, E.,'"The site of king-making and consecration": Westminster Abbey and the Crown in the eleventh and twelfth centuries', in D. Wood (ed.), *The Church and Sovereignty c.590–1918. Essays in Honour of Michael Wilks* (Oxford, 1991), pp. 57–76

Matikkala, A., *The Orders of Knighthood and the Formation of the Honours System, 1660–1760* (Woodbridge, 2008)

Mayr-Harting, H., 'Charlemagne, the Saxons, and the Imperial Coronation of 800', *The English Historical Review*, 111 (1996), pp. 1113–1133

McCormack, M., 'Rethinking "Loyalty" in Eighteenth-Century Britain', *Journal for Eighteenth-Century Studies*, 35 (2012), pp. 407–21

McCullough, P., 'Preaching and Context: John Donne's Sermon at the Funerals of Sir William Cokayne', in P. McCullough *et al.* (eds), *The Oxford Handbook of the Early Modern Sermon* (Oxford, 2011), pp. 213–67

McCullough, P. *et al.* (eds), *The Oxford Handbook of the Early Modern Sermon* (Oxford, 2011)

McCullough, P. E., *Sermons at Court: Politics and Religion in Elizabethan and Jacobean Preaching* (Cambridge, 1998)

McLean, J., "The Crown in Contract and Administrative Law." *Oxford Journal of Legal Studies*, 24 (2004), pp. 129–54

McIlwain, C. H., 'Due Process of Law in Magna Carta', *Columbia Law Review*, 14 (1914), pp. 27–51, reprinted in C. H. McIlwain, *Constitutionalism and the Changing World: Collected Papers* (Cambridge, 1939), pp. 86–126

McKean, C., *The Scottish Chateau: Country Houses of Renaissance Scotland* (Stroud, 2001)

McKenna, J. W., 'The Coronation Oil of the Yorkist Kings', *The English Historical Review*, LXXXII (1967), pp. 102–4

McLaren, A. N., 'Delineating the Elizabethan Body Politic: Knox, Aylmer and the Definition of Counsel 1558–88', *History of Political Thought*, XVII (1996), pp. 224–52

McLaren, A., 'The Quest for a King: Gender, Marriage, and Succession in Elizabethan England,' *Journal of British Studies*, 41 (2002), pp. 259–90

Meikle, M. M., 'Anna of Denmark's Coronation and Entry into Edinburgh, 1590: Cultural, Religious and Diplomatic Perspectives', in J. Goodare and A. A. MacDonald (eds), *Sixteenth-Century Scotland: Essays in Honour of Michael Lynch* (Leiden, 2008), pp. 277–94

Metcalfe, W. C., *A Book of Knights Banneret, Knights of the Bath, and Knights Bachelor Made Between the Fourth Year of King Henry VI. and*

the Restoration of King Charles II. ... and Knights Made in Ireland Between 1566 and 1698, etc. (London, 1885)
Miall, L. (ed.), *Richard Dimbleby, Broadcaster, by his Colleagues* (London, 1966)
Miller, J., *James II* (New Haven, Connecticut, and London, 2000)
Miller, J., 'The Glorious Revolution: 'Contract' and 'Abdication' Reconsidered', *The Historical Journal*, 25 (1982), pp. 541–55
Miller, J., *James II: A Study in Kingship* (Hove, 1978)
Millar, O. (ed.), *The Inventories and Valuations of the King's Goods, 1649–51*, Walpole Society, 43 (1970–1972), (Glasgow, 1972)
Milton, A., 'Sacrilege and Compromise: Court Divines and the King's Conscience, 1642–1649', in M. J. Braddick and D. L. Smith (eds), *The Experience of Revolution in Stuart Britain and Ireland: Essays for John Morrill* (Cambridge, 2011), pp. 135–53
Mitchell, J. A., "Queen Katherine and The Secret of Lydgate's 'Temple of Glas.'" *Medium Ævum*, 77, (2008), pp. 54–76
Mitchell, R. J., *The Medieval Feast: The story of the coronation banquet of King Henry IV in Westminster Hall, 13th October, 1399* (London, 1958)
Mitchell, L. B., 'The Coronation of Henry IV,' *Social Science*, 6 (1931), pp. 130–33
Molyneaux, G., "Why were some Tenth-Century English Kings presented as Rulers of Britain? 'The Alexander Prize Essay.'" *Transactions of the Royal Historical Society*, 21 (2011), pp. 59–91.
Monod, P. K., *Jacobitism and the English People, 1688–1788* (Cambridge, 1989)
Monod, P. K., *The Power of Kings: Monarchy and Religion in Europe, 1589–1715* (New Haven, Connecticut, and London, 1999)
Moreno-Riaño, G., 'Marsilius of Padua on Rulership', in A. Al-Azmeh and J. M. Bak (eds), *Monotheistic Kingship: The Medieval Variants* (Budapest, 2004), pp. 277–89
Morrill, J., *'Uneasy Lies the Head that Wears a Crown': Dynastic Crises in Tudor and Stewart Britain 1504–1746* (Reading, 2005)
Mortimer, R., *Guide to the Muniments of Westminster Abbey*, Westminster Abbey Record Series, 7 (Woodbridge, *c.*2012)
Muir, E., *Ritual in Early Modern Europe* (2nd edition, Cambridge, 2005)
Murdoch, T., 'A Silver-Gilt Cup Commemorating the Coronation of James II and the Culture of Gifts and Prerequisites [*sic*] in Stuart and Hanoverian Coronations', *V&A Online Journal*, No. 2 (Autumn, 2009)

Murray, K. M. E., *The Constitutional History of the Cinque Ports* (Manchester, 1935)
Nelson, J. L., *Politics and Ritual in Early Medieval Europe* (London, 1986)
Nelson, J. L., 'Inauguration Rituals', in P. H. Sawyer and I. N. Wood (eds), *Early Medieval Kingship* (Leeds, 1977), pp. 50–71.
Nenner, H., *The Right to be King: The Succession to the Crown of England, 1603–1714* (Basingstoke, 1995)
Neuheiser, J., *Crown, Church and Constitution: Popular Conservatism in England, 1815–1867* (Oxford, 2016)
Neuschel, K. B., *Living by the Sword: Weapons and Material Culture in France and Britain, 600–1600* (Ithaca, New York, 2020)
Nevinson, J. L., 'The Robes of the Order of the Bath', *The Connoisseur*, 134 (1954), pp. 153–9
Nice, J. A., '"The Peculiar Place of God": Early Modern Representations of England and France', *The English Historical Review*, CXXI (2006), pp. 1002–18
Nichols, G. O., 'English Government Borrowing, 1660–1688', *Journal of British Studies*, 10 (1971), pp. 83–104
Nichols, J. G. (introductory remarks), *London pageants, I. Accounts of fifty-five Royal Processions and Entertainments in the City of London; chiefly extracted from contemporary writers. II. A bibliographical list of Lord Mayors' pageants* (London, 1831)
Nisse, R., 'Josephus, Jerusalem, and the Martyrs of Medieval England', in R. Nisse, *Jacob's Shipwreck: Diaspora, Translation, and Jewish-Christian Relations in Medieval England* (Ithaca, New York, 2017), pp. 19–48
Noll, M. A., *The Rise of Evangelicalism: the Age of Edwards, Whitefield and the Wesleys* (Nottingham, 2004)
Norrie, A., 'The Bishop and the Queen; or, Why did the Bishop of Carlisle crown Elizabeth I?', *Northern History*, LVI:1–2, 2019, pp. 25–45
Oates, J. D., 'Jacobitism and Popular Disturbances in Northern England, 1714–1719', *Northern History*, XLI (2004), pp. 111–28
O'Brien, B., "Conquest and the Law," in L. Ashe and E. J. Ward (eds), *Conquests in Eleventh-Century England: 1016, 1066*, (new edn) (Woodbridge, 2020), pp. 41–64
Oliver, C., *Dinner at Buckingham Palace: Secrets & Recipes from the reign of Queen Victoria to Queen Elizabeth II* (London, 2003)
Oman, C., 'Restoration Silver at the Royal Academy', *The Burlington Magazine*, 103 (February 1961), pp. 44–7

Owens, E., *The Family Firm: Monarchy, Mass Media and the British Public, 1932–53* (London, 2019)

Parker, G., 'The Place of Tudor England in the Messianic Vision of Philip II of Spain', *Transactions of the Royal Historical Society*, 6th Series, XII (2002), pp. 167–221

Parker Bowles, T., *Cooking and the Crown: Royal Recipes from Queen Victoria to King Charles III* (London, 2024)

Pearce, B. L., *et al.*, 'QUEEN VICTORIA'S GOLDEN JUBILEE 1887', *Journal of the Royal Society of Arts*, 135 (1987), pp. 573–97

Pečar, A., *Macht der Schrift. Politischer Biblizismus in Schottland und England zwischen Reformation and Bürgerkrieg (1534–1642)* (Munich, 2011)

Pennington, R., *A Descriptive Catalogue of the Etched Work of Wenceslaus Hollar 1607–1677* (Cambridge, 1982)

Pepinster, C., *Defenders of the Faith: The British Monarchy, Religion and the Next Coronation* (London, 2022)

Percival-Prescott, W., *The Coronation Chair. An Investigation into the History and Present Condition of the Chair* (London, 1957)

Perkins, J. H. T., *The Coronation Book … Illustrated by Mrs Temple Perkins, etc.* (2nd edition, London, 1911)

Perry, E., 'Gift Plate from Westminster Hall Coronation Banquets', *Apollo*, LVII (1953), pp. 198–200

Pettegree, A., 'Confessionalization in North Western Europe', in J. Bahlcke and A. Strohmeyer (eds), *Konfessionalisierung in Ostmitteleuropa: Wirkungen des Religiosen Wandels im 16. und 17. Jahrhundert in Staat, Gesellschaft und Kultur* (Stuttgart, 1999), pp. 105–20

Peyre, H., 'Napoleon: Devil, Poet, Saint.' *Yale French Studies*, 26 (1960), pp. 21–31

Phelps Brown, H., 'Gregory King's Notebook and the Phelps Brown-Hopkins Price Index', *The Economic History Review*, 2nd Series, XLIII (1990), pp. 99–103

Phelps Brown, E. H. and Hopkins, S. V., 'Seven Centuries of the Prices of Consumables, Compared with Builders' Wage-Rates', *Economica*, New Series, XXIII (1956), pp. 296–314

Phillips, S., *Edward II* (New Haven, Connecticut, 2010)

Picard, L., *Restoration London* (1st edn, London, 1997)

Pickup, D., 'John Croker and the Alehorne Manuscript', *The Medal*, 20 (1992), 19–31

Pilbrow, F., 'The Knights of the Bath: Dubbing to Knighthood in Lancastrian and Yorkist England', in P. Coss and M. Keen (eds), *Heraldry, Pageantry and Social Display in Medieval England* (Woodbridge, 2002), pp. 195–218

Pincus, S., *1688: The First Modern Revolution* (New Haven, Connecticut, and London, 2009)

Pincus, S., '"To Protect English Liberties": The English Nationalist Revolution of 1688–1689', in T. Claydon and I. McBride (eds), *Protestantism and National Identity: Britain and Ireland, c.1650 –c.1850* (Cambridge, 1998), pp. 75–104.

Pipes, R., *The Russian Revolution 1899–1919* (London, 1992)

Pittock, M. G. M., *Jacobitism* (Aberdeen, 1998)

Plumb, J. H. and Wheldon, H., *Royal Heritage: The Story of Britain's Royal Builders and Collectors* (London, 1977)

Plunkett, J., 'Of Hype and Type: The Media Making of Queen Victoria 1837–1845', *Critical Survey*, 13 (2001), pp. 7–25

Pocock, J. G. A., *The Ancient Constitution and the Feudal Law: A Study of English historical Thought in the Seventeenth Century* (Cambridge, reissue 1987)

Pollard, A. F., 'The Coronation of Queen Elizabeth', *The English Historical Review*, XXV (1910), pp. 125–6

Poole, S., 'Collins in Context: William IV, Affability and the Reform Crisis, 1830–37' in *ibid.*, *The Politics of Regicide in England, 1760–1850: Troublesome Subjects* (Manchester, 2000), pp. 162–76

Powicke, M. R., 'Distraint of Knighthood and Military Obligation under Henry III', *Speculum*, 25 (1950), pp. 457–70

Prebble, J., *The King's Jaunt: George IV in Scotland, August 1822* (Edinburgh, 2000)

Prochaska, F., *Royal Bounty: The Making of a Welfare Monarchy* (New Haven, Connecticut, 1995)

Purey-Cust, A. P., *Coronations: Their Rise and Development in England* (Leeds, 1911)

Ralph, E., 'Records of Coronation Celebrations in a Provincial Town', *Bulletin of the Society of Local Archivists*, 13 (1954), pp. 17–21

Range, M., 'Dei gratia and the 'divine right of kings': Divine legitimization or human humility', in E. Woodacre, L. H. S. Dean, C. Jones, R. E. Martin and Z. E. Rohr (eds), *The Routledge History of Monarchy* (Abingdon, 2019), pp. 130–145.

Range, M., *Music and Ceremonial at British Coronations: From James I to Elizabeth II* (Cambridge, 2012)
Range, M., 'The 1685 Coronation Anthem *I Was Glad*', *Early Music*, 36 (2008), pp. 397–408
Range, M., '"With Instrumental Musick of all Sorts"–The Orchestra at British Coronations Before 1727', *Acta Musicologica*, 82 (2010), pp. 87–104
Redford, D. B., *Akhenaten: The Heretic King* (Princeton, New Jersey, 1984)
Reedy, G., 'Mystical Politics: The Imagery of Charles II's Coronation', in P. J. Korshin (ed.), *Studies in Change and Revolution: Aspects of English Intellectual History, 1640–1800* (Menston, 1972), pp. 19–42
Reid, J. J., 'The Scottish Regalia, Anciently Styled the Honours of Scotland', *Proceedings of the Society of Antiquaries of Scotland*, 24 (1889–1890), pp. 18–48
Reinhard, W., 'Pressures towards Confessionalization? Prolegomena to a Theory of the Confessional Age', in C. S. Dixon (ed.), *The German Reformation: The Essential Readings* (Oxford, 1999), pp. 169–92
Reitan, E. A., 'From Revenue to Civil List, 1689–1702: The Revolution Settlement and the "Mixed and Balanced" Constitution', *The Historical Journal*, XIII (1970), pp. 571–88
Reitan, E. A., 'The Civil List in Eighteenth-Century British Politics: Parliamentary Supremacy versus the Independence of the Crown, *The Historical Journal*, IX (1966), pp. 318–37
Richards, J., 'The coronation of Queen Elizabeth II and film', *Court Historian*, 9 (2004), pp. 69–79
Richardson, H. G., 'The Coronation in Medieval England: The Evolution of the Office and the Oath', *Traditio*, 16 (1960), pp. 111–202
Richardson, H. G., 'The English Coronation Oath', *Transactions of the Royal Historical Society*, 4th Series, XXIII (1941), pp. 129–58
Richardson, H. G., 'The English Coronation Oath', *Speculum*, XXIV (1949), pp. 44–75
Richardson, H. G. and Sayles, G. O., 'Early Coronation Records', *Bulletin of the Institute of Historical Research*, XIII (1935–1936), pp. 129–45 and XIV (1936–1937), pp. 1–9, 145–8
Richardson, H. G. and Sayles, G. O. (eds), *The Governance of Mediaeval England from the Conquest to Magna Carta* (Edinburgh, 1964)
Ridley, J., *George V: Never a Dull Moment* (London, 2021)
Roberts, A., *George III: The Life and Reign of Britain's Most Misunderstood Monarch* (London, 2023)

Roberts, A., *Napoleon the Great* (London, 2016)
Robins, J., *The Trial of Queen Carline: The Scandalous Affair that Nearly Ended a Monarchy* (New York, New York, 2006)
Robinson, J. M., 'Patriotic Glory', *The Spectator* (May 2003), p. 42
[Robinson, W.], *Collections Relative to Claims at the Coronations of Several of the Kings of England, Beginning with Richard II* (London, 1820)
Robbins, C., 'Selden's Pills: State Oaths in England, 1558–1714', *The Huntington Library Quarterly*, XXXV (1972), pp. 303–21
Rodwell, W., *The Coronation Chair and Stone of Scone: History, Archaeology and Conservation* (Oxford, 2013)
Rodwell, W. and Tatton-Brown, T. (eds), *Westminster I & II. The Art, Architecture and Archaeology of the Royal Palace* (Abingdon, 2016–2017)
Rose, J., *Godly Kingship in Restoration England: The Politics of the Royal Supremacy, 1660–1688* (Cambridge, 2011)
Rose, T., *The Coronation Ceremony of the Kings and Queens of England and the Crown Jewels* (London, 1992)
Ross, G. L., 'Il Schifanoya's Account of the Coronation of Queen Elizabeth', *The English Historical Review*, XXIII (1908), pp. 533–4
Ross, T., 'Coronation Services of the Barons of the Cinque Ports', *Sussex Archaeological Collections*, XV (1863), pp. 178–210
Round, J. H., *The King's Serjeants and Officers of State: With their Coronation Services* (London, 1911)
Russell, C., *The Causes of the English Civil War* (Oxford, 1990)
Rymer, T. and Sanderson, R. (eds), *Fœdera* ..., 4 volumes in 7 parts (London, 1816–1869)
Ryrie, A., 'Divine Kingship and Royal Theology in Henry VIII's Reformation', *Reformation*, 7 (2002), pp. 49–77
Said, E. W., *Culture and Imperialism* (London, 1993)
Said, E. W., *Musical Elaborations* (London, 1991)
Said, E., *Orientalism: Western Conceptions of the Orient* (1st edition, London, 1978)
Sandquist, T. A., 'The Holy Oil of St Thomas of Canterbury', in T. A. Sandquist and M. R. Powicke (eds), *Essays in Medieval History, Presented to Bertie Wilkinson* (Toronto, 1969), pp. 330–44
Sauerberg, M. L., 'The Coronation Chair – Revisited', *Studies in Conservation*, 50 (2005), pp. 230–3
Sayles, G. O., *The King's Parliament of England* (London, 1975)
Scales, L. E., 'German Militiae: War and the German Identity in the Later Middle Ages', *Past & Present*, 180 (2003), pp. 41–82

Scarisbrick, J. J., *Henry VIII* (London, 1968)
Schilling, H., 'Confessionalization in the Empire: Religious and Societal Change in Germany Between 1555 and 1620', in H. Schilling, *Religion, Political Culture and the Emergence of Early Modern Society: Essays in German and Dutch History*, Studies in Medieval and Reformation Thought, L (Leiden, 1992), pp. 205–45
Schilling, H., 'The Reformation and the Rise of the Early Modern State', in J. D. Tracy (ed.), *Luther and the Modern State in Germany*, Sixteenth Century Essays & Studies, VII (Kirksville, Missouri, *c.*1986), pp. 21–30
Schilling, H., 'The Second Reformation - Problems and Issues', in H. Schilling, *Religion, Political Culture and the Emergence of Early Modern Society: Essays in German and Dutch History*, Studies in Medieval and Reformation Thought, L (Leiden, 1992), pp. 247–301
Schochet, G. J., *Patriarchalism in Political Thought: the Authoritarian Family and Political Speculation and Attitudes Especially in Seventeenth-Century England* (Oxford, 1975)
Schofield, R., 'Taxation and the Political Limits of the Tudor State', in C. Cross *et al.* (eds), *Law and Government Under the Tudors: Essays Presented to Sir Geoffrey Elton Regius Professor of Modern History in the University of Cambridge on the Occasion of his Retirement* (Cambridge, 1988), pp. 227–55
Schramm, P. E. (trans. L. G. Wickham Legg), *A History of the English Coronation* (Oxford, 1937)
Schwoerer, L. G., 'Images of Queen Mary II, 1689–1694', *Renaissance Quarterly*, 42 (1989), pp. 717–48, reprinted in G. J. Schochet *et al.* (eds), *Restoration, Ideology, and Revolution*, The Folger Institute Center for the History of British Political Thought Proceedings, 4 (Washington DC, 1990), pp. 419–44
Schwoerer, L. G., 'The Coronation of William and Mary, April 11, 1689', in L. G. Schwoerer (ed.), *The Revolution of 1688–1689: Changing Perspectives* (Cambridge, 1992), pp. 107–30
Schwoerer, L. G., 'The Transformation of the 1689 Convention into a Parliament', *Parliamentary History*, 3 (1984), pp. 57–76
Schwyzer, P., *Literature, Nationalism, and Memory in Early Modern England and Wales* (Cambridge, 2004)
Sebag Montefiore, S., *Jerusalem: The Biography* (London, 2011)
Seppa, N., 'King George III Should Have Sued', *Science News*, 168, (2005), p. 94

Seipel, W. (ed.), *A Brief Guide to the Kunsthistorisches Museum, II: Masterpieces of the Secular Treasury* (Vienna, 2008)

Seymour, W., *Sovereign Legacy: An Historical Guide to the British Monarchy* (London, 1980)

Shapiro, B., 'Political Theology and the Courts: A Survey of Assize Sermons c1600–1688', *Law and Humanities*, 2 (2008), pp. 1–28

Sharpe, K., *Image Wars: Promoting Kings and Commonwealths in England, 1603–1660* (New Haven, Connecticut, and London, 2010)

Sharpe, K., *Reading Authority and Representing Rule in Early Modern England* (London, 2013)

Sharpe, K., *Rebranding Rule: Images of Restoration and Revolution Monarchy, 1660–1714* (New Haven, Connecticut, 2013)

Shaw, I. and Nicholson, P., *The Dictionary of Ancient Egypt* (revised edition, New York, 2003)

Shaw, W. A., *The Knights of England: A Complete Record from the Earliest Time to the Present Day of the Knights of all the Orders of Chivalry in England, Scotland, and Ireland, and of Knights Bachelors*, 2 volumes (London, 1906)

Shenton, C., *Mr Barry's War: Rebuilding the Houses of Parliament After the Great Fire of 1834* (Oxford, 2016)

Shils, E. and Young, M., 'The Meaning of the Coronation', *The Sociological Review*, 1 (1953), pp. 63–81

Shore, C., 'The Crown as Metonym for the State?: The Human Face of Leviathan', in: C. Shore, and D. V. Williams (eds.), *The Shapeshifting Crown: Locating the State in Postcolonial New Zealand, Australia, Canada and the UK.* (Cambridge, 2019), pp. 53–74

Simonelli, D., '"[L]aughing nations of happy children who have never grown up": Race, the Concept of Commonwealth and the 1924–5 British Empire Exhibition', *Journal of Colonialism and Colonial History*, 10 (2009), pp. 23–46

Sitwell, H. D. W., 'The Jewel House and the Royal Goldsmiths', *The Archaeological Journal*, 117 (1960), pp. 131–55

Sitwell, H. D. W., *The Crown Jewels and other Regalia in the Tower of London* (London, 1953)

Skinner, Q., 'The State', in T. Ball, J. Farr and R. L. Hanson (eds), *Political Innovation and Conceptual Change* (Cambridge, 1989), pp. 90–131

Slaughter, T. P., '"Abdicate' and 'Contract' in the Glorious Revolution', *The Historical Journal*, 24 (1981), pp. 323–37

Slaughter, T. P., 'Abdicate' and 'Contract' Restored', *The Historical Journal*, 28, pp. 399–403

Smith, A., *George IV* (New Haven, Connecticut, 1999)

Smith, H., *Georgian Monarchy: Politics and Culture, 1714–1760* (Cambridge, 2006)

Smith, H., '"Last of all the Heavenly Birth": Queen Anne and Sacral Queenship', *Parliamentary History*, 28 (2009), pp. 137–49

Smith, H., 'The Court in England, 1714–1760: A Declining Political Institution?' *History*, 90 (2005), pp. 23–41

Smuts, R. M., 'Public Ceremony and Royal Charisma: The English Royal Entry in London, 1485–1642', in A. L. Beier *et al.* (eds), *The First Modern Society: Essays in English History in Honour of Lawrence Stone* (Cambridge, 1989), pp. 65–93

Snyder, H. L., 'The Circulation of Newspapers in the Reign of Queen Anne', *The Library*, 5th Series, XXIII (1968), pp. 206–35

Soames, M., *Clementine Churchill: The Biography of a Marriage* (rev. edn., New York, New York, 2003)

Somerset, A., *Queen Anne: The Politics of Passion: A Biography* (London, 2012)

Somerset, A., *Queen Victoria and Her Prime Ministers: A Personal History* (London, 2024)

Sommerville, J. P., *Politics and Ideology in England, 1603–1640* (1st edition, London and New York, 1986)

Sommerville, J. P., *Royalists and Patriots: Politics and Ideology in England 1603–1640* (2nd edition, London and New York, 1999)

Speck, W. A., *James II* (London, 2002)

Speck, W. A., *Reluctant Revolutionaries: Englishmen and the Revolution of 1688* (Oxford, 1988)

Speck, W. A., *Stability and Strife, England, 1714–1760* (1977)

Spencer, A., 'The Coronation Oath in English Politics, 1272–1399', in B. Thompson and J. Watts (eds), *Political Society in Later Medieval England: A Festschrift for Christine Carpenter* (Woodbridge, 2015), pp. 38–54

Spurr, J., '"The Strongest Bond of Conscience": Oaths and the Limits of Tolerance in Early Modern England', in H. E. Braun and E. Vallance (eds), *Contexts of Conscience in Early Modern Europe, 1500–1700* (Basingstoke, 2004), pp. 151–65

Spurr, J., 'A Profane History of Early Modern Oaths', *Transactions of the Royal Historical Society*, Sixth Series, XI (2001), pp. 37–64

Spurr, J., 'Perjury, Profanity and Politics', *The Seventeenth Century*, 8 (1993), pp. 29–50

Starkey, D., *Crown and Country: A History of England through the Monarchy* (London, 2010)

Starkey, D., *Elizabeth: Apprenticeship* (London, 2000)

Stephen, Sir Leslie and Lee, Sir Sidney (eds), *Dictionary of National Biography*, 22 volumes (original edition, reissued, London, 1908–1909)

Stewart, J. D., *catalogue raisonné: Sir Godfrey Kneller and the English Baroque Portrait* (Oxford, 1983)

Stone, L., *The Crisis of the Aristocracy, 1558–1641* (original edition, Oxford, 1965)

Straka, G., 'The Final Phase of Divine Right Theory in England, 1688–1702', *The English Historical Review*, LXXVII (1962), pp. 638–58

Strickland, M., *Henry the Young King, 1155–1183* (New Haven, Connecticut, 2016)

Strong, R., *Coronation: A History of Kingship and the British Monarchy* (London, 2005)

Strong, R. C., 'Queen Elizabeth I and the Order of the Garter', *The Archaeological Journal*, 119 (1962), pp. 245–69

Stuart, J. P. C., Marquis of Bute, *Scottish Coronations* (London, 1902)

Sturdy, D. J., '"Continuity" versus "Change": Historians and English Coronations of the Medieval and Early Modern Periods', in J. M. Bak (ed.), *Coronations: Medieval and Early Modern Monarchic Ritual* (Berkeley and Los Angeles, California, *c.*1990), pp. 228–45

Sturdy, D. J., 'English Coronation Sermons in the Seventeenth Century', in H. Duchhardt (ed.), *Herrscherweihe und Königskrönung im Frühneuzeitlichen Europa* (Wiesbaden, 1983), pp. 69–81

Sykes, N., *William Wake, Archbishop of Canterbury, 1657–1737*, 2 volumes (Cambridge, 1957)

Tabraham, C., *The Honours of Scotland: The Story of the Scottish Crown Jewels & The Stone of Destiny* (Edinburgh, 2019)

Tanner, L. E., 'Coronations in the Abbey', in E. Carpenter (ed.), *A House of Kings: The History of Westminster Abbey* (London, 1966), pp. 405–15

Tanner, L. E., *The History of the Coronation* (London, 1952)

Taylor, A., *The Glory of Regality: An Historical Treatise of the Anointing and Crowning of the Kings and Queens of England* (London, 1820)

Taylor, S. and Fincham, K., 'Episcopalian Identity, 1640–1662', in A. Milton (ed.), *The Oxford History of Anglicanism. I: Reformation and Identity c.1520–1662* (Oxford 2017), pp. 457–82

Taylor, S., 'State formation, political stability and the revolution of 1688', in T. Harris, & S. Taylor (eds.), *The final crisis of the Stuart monarchy. The revolutions of 1688–91 in their British, Atlantic and European contexts* (Woodbridge, 2013), pp. 273–304

Theilmann, J. M., 'Caught Between Political Theory and Political Practice: "The Record and Process of the Deposition of Richard II"', *History of Political Thought*, XXV (2004), pp. 599–619

Thomas, A., 'Crown Imperial: Coronation Ritual and Regalia in the Reign of James V', in J. Goodare and A. A. MacDonald (eds), *Sixteenth-Century Scotland: Essays in Honour of Michael Lynch* (Leiden, 2008), pp. 44–67

Thompson, A., *Britain, Hanover and the Protestant Interest, 1688–1756* (Woodbridge, 2006)

Thompson, A. C., *George II: King and Elector* (New Haven, Connecticut, and London, 2011)

Thompson, M. P., 'Significant Silences in Locke's *Two Treatises of Government*: Constitutional History, Contract and Law', *The Historical Journal*, 31 (1987), pp. 275–94

Thornbury, W. and Walford, E., *Old and New London: A Narrative of its History, its People, and its Places*, 6 volumes (London, [1873–1878])

Thrupp, G. A., *The History of Coaches* (London, 1877)

Todd, M., 'England After 1558', in A. Pettegree (ed.), *The Reformation World* (London, 2000), pp. 365–86

Torrance, D., 'The coronation: History and ceremonial', *Parliamentary Research Briefing*, Number CBP9412 (2023)

Toynbee, M., 'The City of Oxford and the Restoration of 1660', *Oxoniensia*, XXV (1961 for 1960), pp. 73–95

Tresidder, G. A., 'Coronation Day Celebrations in English Towns, 1685–1821: Elite Hegemony and Local Relations on a Ceremonial Occasion', *British Journal for Eighteenth Century Studies*, 15 (1992), pp. 1–16

Trowles, T., *Treasures of Westminster Abbey* (London, 2008)

Tudor-Craig, P., 'Henry VIII and King David', in D. Williams (ed.), *Early Tudor England*, Proceedings of the 1987 Harlaxton Symposium (Woodbridge, 1989), pp. 183–205

Tyacke, N., *Anti-Calvinists: The Rise of English Arminianism c.1590–1640* (Oxford, 1987; paperback edition, Oxford, 1990)
Uglow, J. S., *A Gambling Man: Charles II and the Restoration, 1660–1670* (London, 2009)
Ullmann, W., *Principles of Government and Politics in the Middle Ages* (2nd edition, London, 1966)
Ullmann, W., '"This Realm of England is an Empire"', *The Journal of Ecclesiastical History*, 30 (1979), pp. 175–203
Ullmann, W., 'Thomas Becket's Miraculous Oil', *The Journal of Theological Studies*, 8 (1957), pp. 129–33
Valente, C., 'The Deposition and Abdication of Edward II', *The English Historical Review*, CXIII (1998), pp. 852–81
Vallance, E., *The Glorious Revolution: 1688, Britain's Fight for Liberty* (London, 2006)
Van Der Kiste, J., *William and Mary: The Heroes of the Glorious Revolution* (new edition, Stroud, 2008)
Van Der Kiste, J., *William IV: The Last Hanoverian King of Britain* (Barnsley, 2022)
Van Houts, E. M. C., 'Le Roi et son historien: Henri II Plantagenêt et Robert de Torigni, abbé du Mont- Saint- Michel', *Cahiers de civilisation médiévale*, 37 (1994), pp. 115–18
Vilinbakhov, G., 'K istorii uchrezhdeniia ordena Andreia Pervozvannogo', *Kul'tura i iskusstvo petrovskogo vremeni* (Leningrad, 1977)
Vincent, N., 'A Queen in Rebel London, 1215–17', in L. Clark and E. Danbury (eds), *"A Verray Parfit Praktisour": Essays Presented to Carole Rawcliffe* (Woodbridge, 2017), pp. 23–50
Waddell, G., 'The Design of the Westminster Hall Roof', *Architectural History*, 42 (1999), pp. 47–67
Walsham, A., *Providence in Early Modern England* (Oxford, 1999)
Ward, I., *Writing the Victorian Constitution* (Cham, Switzerland, 2018)
Ward, P. L., 'The Coronation Ceremony in Mediaeval England', *Speculum*, XIV (1939), pp. 160–78
Watanabe-O'Kelly, H., *Projecting Imperial Power: New Nineteenth-Century Emperors and the Public Sphere* (Oxford, 2021)
Watson, J. R., 'Into the Twentieth Century', in J. R. Watson, *The English Hymn: A Critical and Historical Study* (Oxford, 1999), pp. 511–532
Weber, H., *Paper Bullets: Print and Kingship under Charles II* (Lexington, Kentucky, 1996)
Wedgwood, C. V., *The Trial of Charles I* (London, 1964)

Welander, R. *et al.* (eds), *The Stone of Destiny: Artefact and Icon*, Society of Antiquaries of Scotland, Monograph Series, 22 (Edinburgh, 2003)
Werrett, S., *Fireworks: Pyrotechnic Arts and Sciences in European History* (Chicago, Illinois, 2010)
Werrett, S., 'Healing the Nation's Wounds: Royal Ritual and Experimental Philosophy in Restoration England', *History of Science*, 38 (2000), pp. 377–99
Westfall, R. S., *Never at Rest: A Biography of Isaac Newton* (Cambridge, 1980)
Weston, C. C., 'The Theory of Mixed Monarchy Under Charles I and After', *The English Historical Review*, LXXV (1960), pp. 426–43
White, C., *Peter Paul Rubens: Man and Artist* (New Haven, Connecticut, and London, 1987)
White, G. H., 'Coronation Claims', *The Genealogists' Magazine*, 7 (1937), pp. 505–16
Whitman, J., 'National Icon: The Winchester Round Table and the Revelation of Authority', *Arthuriana*, 18 (2008), pp. 33–65
Wiliam, M. E., 'Monarchy and National Identity: Wales and the 1953 Coronation', *Cultural and Social History*, 19 (2022), pp. 301–322
Wilkinson, B., *The Coronation in History* (London, 1953)
Wilkinson, B., 'The Coronation Oath of Edward II', in J. G. Edwards *et al.* (eds), *Historical Essays in Honour of James Tait* (Manchester, 1933), pp. 405–16
Wilkinson, B., 'The Coronation Oath of Edward II and the Statute of York', *Speculum*, 19 (1944), pp. 445–69
Wilkinson, J. and Knighton, C. S., *Crown and Cloister: The Royal Story of Westminster Abbey* (London, 2010)
Wilkinson, J., *Louis XIV: The Real King of Versailles* (Stroud, 2019)
Will, K., 'When is a Panther not a Panther? Representing Animals in Early Modern English Heraldry', *Early Modern Culture*, 11 (2016), pp. 78–98
Williams, G., 'Manipulation and the Maid: Joan of Arc and the Siege of Orléans', *Medieval Warfare*, 4 (2014), pp. 25–32
Wilson, H. A., 'The Coronation of Queen Elizabeth', *The English Historical Review*, XXIII (1908), pp. 87–91
Wilson, R., 'The Madness of King Charles III: Shakespeare and the Modern Monarchy', *Critical Survey*, 29 (2017), pp. 76–93
Withington, R., 'Scott's Contribution to Pageantic Development: A Note on the Visit of George IV to Edinburgh in 1822', *Studies in Philology*, 17 (1920), pp. 121–25

Wollaston, G. W., *Coronation Claims: Containing a Full Report of all the Cases Argued Before the Court of Claims at the Coronation of King Edward VII., with Other Matter Relating to Coronation Services in General* (2nd edition, London, 1910)

Wooding, L., *Henry VIII* (Abingdon, 2009)

Wolffe, B., *Henry VI* (New Haven, Connecticut)

Woolgar, C. M., *et al.* (eds), *Food in Medieval England: Diet and Nutrition* (Oxford, 2006)

Wormald, J., 'James VI and I, *Basilikon Doron* and *The Trew Law of Free Monarchies*: The Scottish Context and the English Translation', in L. L. Peck (ed.), *The Mental World of the Jacobean Court* (Cambridge, 1991), pp. 36–54

Wortman, R. S., *Scenarios of Power: Myth and Ceremony in Russian Monarchy, from Peter the Great to the Abdication of Nicholas II* (Princeton, New Jersey, 2006)

Wren, M. C., 'The Chamber of London in 1633', *The Economic History Review*, 2nd Series, I (1948), pp. 46–53

Yorke, J., 'Archbishop Juxon's Chair', *The Burlington Magazine*, 141 (1999), pp. 282–6

Youngs, F. A., Jr, *The Proclamations of the Tudor Queens* (Cambridge, 1976)

Zaller, R., 'Breaking the Vessels: The Desacralization of Monarchy in Early Modern England', *The Sixteenth Century Journal*, XXIX (1998), pp. 757–78

Unpublished Material

Anon., 'Records of Coronation Celebrations in a Provincial Town', 20th century [unpublished typescript notes at Bristol Record Office, no call-number]

Barker, E., "The Coronation and Banquet of Henry IV" (University of Wisconsin unpublished paper): https://dc.uwm.edu/cgi/viewcontent.cgi?article=1064&context=rsso

Brückmann, J. J., 'English Coronations, 1216–1308: The Edition of the Coronation "*Ordines*"', PhD thesis, University of Toronto (1964)

Burden, J. F., *Rituals of Royalty: Prescription, Politics and Practice in English Coronation and Royal Funeral Rituals c. 1327 to c.1485,* (York Ph.D. thesis, 1999)

Goldie, M., 'Tory Political Thought, 1689–1714' (Cambridge Ph.D. thesis, 1977)
Hunt, A., ''What art thou, thou idol ceremony?': Tudor coronations and literary representations, 1509–1559', PhD thesis, Birbeck, University of London (2005)
Kilburn, M. C., 'Royalty and Public in Britain: 1714–1789', DPhil. thesis, University of Oxford (1997)
Samson, A., 'The marriage of Philip of Habsburg and Mary Tudor and anti-Spanish sentiment in England: political economies and culture 1553–1557', PhD thesis, Queen Mary, University of London (1999)
Shaw, D., 'The Coronation and Monarchical Culture in Stuart Britain and Ireland 1603–1661' (unpublished PhD dissertation, University of Cambridge, 2002)

Online sources

Adams, C., 18 May 2023, https://www.bbc.co.uk/news/uk-65636772#:~:text=Local%20News-,Queen%20Elizabeth%20II%3A%20Funeral%20and%2010%20days,mourning%20cost%20government%20%C2%A3162m&text=Queen%20Elizabeth%20II's%20funeral%20and,11%20days%20after%20her%20death, accessed 23 November 2025
AFP, 4 March 2023, https://jordantimes.com/news/region/coronation-oil-charles-iii-consecrated-jerusalem, accessed 22 November 2025
Anand, A., 20 April 2016, https://www.bbc.co.uk/news/world-asia-india-36095025, accessed 22 November 2025
Andreeva, N., 30 April 2011, https://deadline.com/2011/04/so-how-were-the-royal-wedding-ratings-126926/, accessed 6 March 2025
Avison, B., 4 March 2020, https://www.hostcity.com/news/city-development/economic-impact-cricket-world-cup-2019-revealed, accessed 23 November 2025
Bailey, M., (Radio Newcastle) & Lonsdale, J., https://www.bbc.co.uk/sounds/play/p0fl2s3z, accessed 22 November 2025
Bates, S., 19 November 2004, https://www.theguardian.com/uk/2004/nov/19/politics.france, accessed 22 November 2025
Bates, S., 29 March 2022, https://www.theguardian.com/uk-news/2022/mar/29/we-have-to-be-seen-to-be-believed-the-endurance-of-the-royal-tour#:~:text=As%20the%20Queen%20says%3A%20

%E2%80%9CWe,display%20their%20magnificence%20and%20power, accessed 23 November 2025

Berger, S., 21 May 2018, https://www.cnbc.com/2018/05/21/ratings-for-prince-harry-and-meghan-markle-royal-wedding.html, accessed 23 November 2025

Black, C., 21 November 2024, https://www.bbc.co.uk/news/articles/c9dl3v522xdo, accessed 22 November 2025

Bostock, J. (BBC Radio Leicester), 7 May 2023, https://www.bbc.co.uk/programmes/p0fly8z0, accessed 22 November 2025

Bradley, S., 2 May 2023, https://theweek.com/news/royals/960690/homage-of-the-people-should-public-pledge-allegiance-to-new-king, accessed 23 November 2025

Breiding, D. H., 1 October 2022, https://www.metmuseum.org/toah/hd/make/hd_make.htm#:~:text=The%20names%20of%20Passau%20and,it%20to%20their%20own%20blades, accessed 22 November 2025

Brie, F. W. D. (ed.), *The Brut, or The chronicles of England. Edited from Ms. Raw. B171, Bodleian Library, &c., …* (London, 1906–1908), p. 461: https://quod.lib.umich.edu/c/cme/APG1531/1:2.9?rgn=div2;view=fulltext, accessed 22 November 2025

Brown, T., 6 November 2024, https://lordslibrary.parliament.uk/house-of-lords-reform-government-policy-and-recent-developments/, accessed 22 November 2025

Burden, J. F., *Rituals of Royalty: Prescription, Politics and Practice in English Coronation and Royal Funeral Rituals c. 1327 to c.1485,* (York Ph.D. thesis, 1999), p. 199: https://etheses.whiterose.ac.uk/2497/1/DX212138.pdf, accessed 23 October 2024

Burnside, J. P., 6 May 2023, https://www.spectator.co.uk/article/why-christianity-is-at-the-heart-of-the-kings-coronation/, accessed 23 November 2025

Campanale, D., 21 April 2023, https://www.premierchristianity.com/king-of-kings-the-christian-message-at-the-heart-of-the-coronation/15373.article, accessed 23 November 2025

Campbell, Z., 5 May 2023, https://www.dailymail.co.uk/news/article-12050535/What-happens-King-Charles-anointed-screen-for.html, accessed 8 May 2023

Capurro, D., 8 January 2023, https://www.telegraph.co.uk/royal-family/2023/01/08/prince-harry-has-written-kings-coronation/, accessed 20 March 2023

Carlin, E. M., 9 May 2024, https://www.communications.gov.uk/blog/a-year-on-the-enduring-legacy-of-the-coronation/, Government Communications Service, accessed 24 November 2025

Carp, S., 4 March 2020, https://www.sportspro.com/news/2019-cricket-world-cup-uk-economy-impact-england-wales/, accessed 23 November 2025

Clarke, J., 14 September 2022, https://www.bbc.co.uk/news/uk-62875864, accessed 20 November 2025 https://www.parliament.uk/globalassets/documents/parliamentary-archives/Churchill-for-web-Mar-2014.pdf, accessed 20 March 2024 https://www.bbc.co.uk/pressoffice/pressreleases/stories/2002/11_november/25/greatbritons_final.shtml (Press Office release, 25 November 2002), accessed 20 March 2024

Cooper, J., 8 May 2023, https://www.telegraph.co.uk/news/2023/05/08/charles-iii-is-a-21st-century-philosopher-king/#:~:text=In%201994%2C%20he%20seemed%20to,the%20epithet's%20prior%20Anglican%20exceptionalism, accessed 10 May 2023.

Coughlan, S., 1 March 2023, https://www.bbc.co.uk/news/uk-64798077, accessed 22 November 2025

Coughlan, S., 11 October 2022, https://www.bbc.co.uk/news/uk-63172425, accessed 22 November 2025

Coughlan, S., 16 February 2024, https://www.bbc.co.uk/news/uk-68283130, accessed 23 November 2025

Coughlan, S., 19 April 2023, https://www.bbc.co.uk/news/uk-64856842, accessed 22 November 2025

Coughlan, S., 24 May 2023, https://www.bbc.co.uk/news/uk-65700045, accessed 22 November 2025

Coughlan, S., 3 December 2024, https://www.bbc.co.uk/news/articles/c791wr2e7nyo, accessed 23 November 2025

Coughlan, S., 9 April 2024, https://www.bbc.co.uk/news/uk-68769481, accessed 23 November 2025

Coyle, S., 6 May 2023, https://www.manchestereveningnews.co.uk/news/uk-news/what-anointing-king-charles-covered-26837280, 10 May 2023

Crew, J., 5 May 2023, https://www.bbc.co.uk/news/uk-65493188, accessed 23 November 2025

Davies, C., 11 April 2021, https://www.theguardian.com/uk-news/2021/apr/11/she-made-a-pact-with-god-why-the-queen-will-not-be-abdicating, accessed 20 May 2021

Davies, C., 9 April 2023, https://www.theguardian.com/uk-news/2023/apr/09/king-charles-iii-coronation-procession-route#:~:text=In%20keeping%20with%20the%20king's,about%205%20miles%2C%20taking%20in, accessed 22 November 2025

Diver, T., 1 April 2023, https://www.telegraph.co.uk/royal-family/2023/04/01/dress-down-coronation-peers-coronets-palace-king-charles/, accessed 23 November 2025

Dixon, H. and Narwan, G., 13 September 2022, https://www.telegraph.co.uk/royal-family/2022/09/13/charles-coronation-prince-king-monarchy-when-plans-cost-living/#:~:text=Sources%20have%20said%20that%20the,was%20only%20announced%20this%20year, accessed 22 November 2025

Douglas, T., 22 January 2012, https://www.bbc.co.uk/news/entertainment-arts-16671101, accessed 10 April 2023

Duffy, N., 2 May 2023, https://inews.co.uk/news/public-refuse-allegiance-king-coronation-archbishop-canterbury-2312629?srsltid=AfmBOopqKC26220rvgRWGlqd3akdfCrkfrsHMGIipNK679e_T6eDKEij, accessed 23 November 2025

Duffy, N., 5 June 2022, https://inews.co.uk/news/entertainment/platinum-party-palace-jubilee-becomes-most-watched-tv-event-of-the-year-thirteen-million-tune-in-2022-1669735, accessed 11 March 2023

Dymond, J., 8 September 2022, https://www.bbc.co.uk/news/uk-59761477, accessed 23 November 2025

Easton, M., 4 June 2013, https://www.bbc.co.uk/news/uk-22764987, accessed 20 May 2023

Fuller, K., 6 May 2023, https://www.cisl.cam.ac.uk/news/close-association-cisl-celebrates-coronation-king-and-queen-and-his-work-drive-transformative, accessed 23 November 2025

Gartenberg, C., 20 May 2019, https://www.theverge.com/2019/5/20/18633136/game-of-thrones-got-season-8-finale-hbo-most-watched-show-all-time-viewership-numbers-live, accessed 10 March 2023

Gross, G. W. C., '1651: The Last Coronation in Scotland – An Anomaly?' *The Court Historian*, 26 (2021), pp. 229–245: https://www.tandfonline.com/doi/full/10.1080/14629712.2021.1996947#:~:text=The%20last%20Scottish%20coronation%20occurred%20at%20Scone%20in%201651, accessed 22 November 2025

Gross, G. W. C., 'https://subscribe.worldoffinewine.com/product/issue80-june-2023/' (accessed 23 November 2025), in *The World of Fine Wine*, Issue 80 (June) (2023), pp. 134–41

Gross, G., 4 July 2023, https://www.telegraph.co.uk/royal-family/2023/07/04/king-charles-scottish-honours-coronation-st-giles-cathedral/, accessed 22 November 2025

Handlin, E., https://library.brown.edu/readingritual/handlin_jamesII.html, accessed 22 November 2025

Hatton, H. and Coughlan, S., 9 December 2024, https://www.bbc.co.uk/news/articles/cd75d47n34do, accessed 22 November 2024

Howard, J., 21–22 November 2024, https://www.bbc.co.uk/news/articles/c04lyddv2p5o, accessed 23 November 2025

Howells, K., 18 April 2023, https://blog.nationalarchives.gov.uk/celebrating-the-coronation-of-edward-vii/#return-note-61427-2, accessed 23 November 2025

http://foodhistorjottings.blogspot.co.uk/2012_04_01_archive.html, 28 April 2012, accessed 23 November 2025

http://news.bbc.co.uk/1/hi/england/1957421.stm, 29 April 2022, accessed 22 November 2025

http://www.westminster-abbey.org, accessed 22 November 2025

https://api.parliament.uk/historic-hansard/commons/1953/feb/25/coronation-oath-changes-1, accessed 18 November 2025

https://assets-learning.parliament.uk/uploads/2023/05/Coronation-Timeline.pdf, accessed 22 November 2025

https://avalon.law.yale.edu/medieval/ang10.asp#b43 (*The Anglo-Saxon Chronicle: Tenth Century*), accessed 13 March 2025

https://avalon.law.yale.edu/medieval/ang11.asp (*The Anglo-Saxon Chronicle: Eleventh Century*), accessed 13 March 2025

https://blogs.bl.uk/digitisedmanuscripts/2023/05/the-coronation-banquet-of-henry-vi.html, accessed 20 November 2023

https://collections.falkirk.gov.uk/objects/6540/medal-commemorative-coronation-george-v, accessed 23 November 2025

https://collections.museumsvictoria.com.au/items/75743, accessed 22 November 2025

https://ecosend.io/blog/why-highlighting-sustainability-was-the-real-jewel-of-the-coronation-crown, 9 May 2023, accessed 23 November 2025

https://en.numista.com/catalogue/mint.php?id=5136, accessed 22 November 2025 https://forteressechinon.fr/en/discover-fortress/its-great-characters/charles-vii, accessed 22 November 2025

https://hansard.parliament.uk/commons/1953-02-25/debates/8218c895-c62e-4918-b23c-0c4b83edd819/CoronationOathChanges, volume 511, debated on Wednesday 25 February 1953, accessed 18 November 2025

https://humanists.uk/2023/05/06/humanists-uk-to-attend-coronation/, 6 May 2023, accessed 21 November 2025.

https://hunterian.blog/coronation-coins-and-medals/, 4 May 2023, accessed 23 November 2025

https://johnbellcroyden.co.uk/blogs/about-us/who-we-are, accessed 22 November 2025

https://magpas.org.uk/a-token-of-thanks-clinicians-receive-the-coronation-medal/, 30 July 2024, accessed 23 November 2025

https://members.parliament.uk/member/4712/contact, Lord Carrington, accessed 22 November 2025

https://metseditions.org/read/7PVQMQqHB4eI4wZmsR2WWS2QR65rjZb, accessed 22 November 2025

https://perthmuseum.co.uk/the-stone-of-destiny/, accessed 22 November 2025

https://recherche-collection-search.bac-lac.gc.ca/eng/home/record?idnumber=2854828&app=fonandcol&q=KLEIN, accessed 26 August 2024

https://royalleicestershireregiment.org.uk/archive/medals-list-honours/commemorative-medals/230151-king-edward-vii-coronation-medal?#:~:text=This%20medal%2C%20designed%20by%20Emil,officers%20involved%20in%20the%20celebrations, accessed 23 November 2025

https://royal-needlework.org.uk/embroidered-anointing-screen/, 29 April 2023, accessed 22 November 2025

https://scone-palace.co.uk/, accessed 22 November 2025

https://tankmuseum.ca/blog-post/the-ontario-regiment-and-the-coronations/, accessed 1 August 2024

https://ukparliament.shorthandstories.com/spectacle-ceremony/index.html, accessed 22 November 2025

https://web.archive.org/web/20051122221448/http://www.bfi.org.uk/features/mostwatched/1960s.html, accessed 10 March 2025

https://webarchive.nationalarchives.gov.uk/ukgwa/20230712215452/https://coronation.gov.uk/resources-for-schools/, accessed 23 November 2025

https://www.archbishopofcanterbury.org/speaking-writing/speeches/archbishop-canterburys-sermon-coronation-king-charles-iii#:~:text=The%20unity%20you%20show%2C%20the,give%20our%20lives%20to%20others, accessed 22 November 2025

https://www.ashmolean.org/alfred-jewel, accessed 22 November 2025

https://www.balh.org.uk/coronation-share-your-findings, accessed 23 November 2025

https://www.bankofengland.co.uk/monetary-policy/inflation/inflation-calculator, accessed 22 November 2025

https://www.bankofengland.co.uk/news/2022/december/king-charles-iii-banknotes-unveiled, 20 December 2022, accessed 23 November 2025

https://www.bbc.co.uk/news/av/uk-65498600, 5 May 2023, accessed 24 November 2025

https://www.bbc.co.uk/news/uk-23265716, 12 July 2013, accessed 22 November 2025

https://www.bbc.co.uk/news/uk-42651950, reflections on the life of Prince Philip, 9 April 2021, accessed 22 November 2025

https://www.bbc.co.uk/news/uk-62872323#:~:text=People%20were%20told%20not%20to,to%20know%20about%20the%20queue, 19 September 2022, accessed 22 November 2025

https://www.bbc.co.uk/news/uk-65507435, 5 May 2023, accessed 22 November 2025

https://www.bbc.co.uk/news/uk-england-gloucestershire-33251481#:~:text=The, 24 June 2015, accessed 22 November 2025

https://www.bbc.co.uk/newsround/64451239, 1 February 2023, accessed 23 November 2025

https://www.bbc.com/historyofthebbc/anniversaries/july/wedding-of-prince-charles-and-lady-diana-spencer, accessed 6 March 2025

https://www.bbc.com/historyofthebbc/anniversaries/june/coronation-of-queen-elizabeth-ii/, accessed 23 November 2025

https://www.beehive.govt.nz/release/pm%E2%80%99s-international-travel-advance-nzs-economic-interests, 18 April 2023, accessed 22 November 2025

https://www.bibelotslondon.com/antique-coronation-banquet-menu-buckingham-palace-hosted-by-queen-elizabeth-ii-6037-p.asp, accessed 2 October 2024

https://www.bl.uk/collection-items/material-relating-to-the-coronation-of-queen-victoria, accessed 11 March 2023

https://www.british-history.ac.uk/old-new-london/vol3/pp544-560, accessed 22 November 2025

https://www.british-history.ac.uk/rushworth-papers/vol2/pp175-244, accessed 22 November 2025

https://www.britishnewspaperarchive.co.uk, accessed 6 March 2025

https://www.cbcew.org.uk/archbishop-stack-cross-of-wales-presentation/, 26 January 2024, accessed 22 November 2025

https://www.churchinwales.org.uk/en/news-and-events/cross-of-wales-kings-gift-to-church-to-be-officially-received/, 22 January 2024, accessed 22 November 2025

https://www.dailymail.co.uk/news/article-12050535/What-happens-King-Charles-anointed-screen-for.html, accessed 8 May 2023

https://www.dpmc.govt.nz/publications/kings-birthday-and-coronation-honours-list-2023, 5 June 2023, accessed 22 November 2025

https://www.economist.com/britain/2022/05/26/britain-celebrates-a-jubilee-again: 'The Platinum Jubilee: Land of hops and glory', 26 May 2022, accessed 6 March 2025

https://www.edenprojectcommunities.com/big-lunch/the-big-lunch-through-history, accessed 22 November 2025

https://www.edinburghcastle.scot/, accessed 22 November 2025

https://www.edinburghcastle.scot/see-and-do/highlights/honours-of-scotland, accessed 22 November 2025

https://www.fruitandvine.co.uk/cornwall-vineyard-receives-royal-warrant/, accessed 24 November 2025

https://www.gov.uk/guidance/medals-campaigns-descriptions-and-eligibility#:~:text=On%205%20May%202023%2C%20the,expected%20total%20of%20400%2C000%20recipients, accessed 23 November 2025

https://www.hrp.org.uk/tower-of-london/history-and-stories/the-story-of-the-tower-of-london/#gs.h01nm3, accessed 22 November 2025

https://www.kcl.ac.uk/events/the-british-coronation-oath-why-an-age-old-custom-still-matters-lecture-1, F. D. Maurice Lecture I, KCL, 2 May 2023, accessed 10 June 2023

https://www.kcl.ac.uk/news/primary-school-children-favour-british-monarchy-more-than-adults, 16 February 2024, accessed 23 November 2025

https://www.kcl.ac.uk/research/british-coronations-project, accessed 23 November 2025

https://www.laurencesternetrust.org.uk/sterne/life-and-times/sterne-in-coxwold-letters/, accessed 23 November 2025

https://www.legislation.gov.uk/ukpga/1931/4/pdfs/ukpga_19310004_en.pdf, accessed 10 March 2025

https://www.legislation.gov.uk/ukpga/1971/24, accessed 23 November 2025

https://www.londonmintoffice.org/blog/384-the-greatest-briton-24, accessed 20 November 2025

https://www.londonmuseum.org.uk/collections/london-stories/long-reign-queen-victoria/, accessed 11 March 2023

https://www.nam.ac.uk/explore/coronation-medals, accessed 23 November 2025

https://www.nationalarchives.gov.uk/currency-converter, accessed 23 November 2025

https://www.nationalgeographic.com/adventure/article/sir-edmund-hillary-tenzing-norgay-1953, 3 March 2013, accessed 22 November 2025

https://www.nationaltrustcollections.org.uk/object/557886, accessed 22 November 2025

https://www.nationaltrustcollections.org.uk/object/772308, accessed 22 November 2025

https://www.navy.gov.au/history/feature-histories/ships-named-anzac, accessed 22 November 2025

https://www.navy.gov.au/hmas-sydney-iii, accessed 22 November 2025

https://www.nlb.gov.sg/main/article-detail?cmsuuid=12d4e7ff-b08f-4372-864b-a5a1a84b7c64, accessed 22 November 2025

https://www.nms.ac.uk/discover-catalogue/anointed-with-oil-the-coronation-ampulla-of-charles-i#:~:text=The%20ampulla%20held%20the%20oil,Queen%20of%20Scots%2C%20in%201543, accessed 22 November 2025

https://www.nottinghamshire.gov.uk/council-and-democracy/get-involved/kings-coronation/the-coronation-big-lunch, accessed 22 November 2025

https://www.nytimes.com/2003/03/11/opinion/IHT-1953coronation-costly-for-uk-in-our-pages100-75-and-50-years-ago.html, 11 March 2003, accessed 23 November 2025

https://www.oed.com, accessed 24 November 2025

https://www.oxfordhistory.org.uk/mayors/government/coronation.html, accessed 22 November 2025

https://www.oxfordreference.com/display/10.1093/oi/authority.20110803095754366, accessed 23 November 2025

https://www.parliament.scot/about/history-of-the-scottish-parliament/the-path-to-devolution, accessed 22 November 2025

https://www.parliament.uk/about/living-heritage/building/palace/westminsterhall/architecture/the-hammer-beam-roof-/, accessed 20 March 2023

https://www.parliament.uk/about/living-heritage/building/palace/westminsterhall/other-uses/spectacular-coronation/, accessed 22 November 2025

https://www.parliament.uk/about/living-heritage/building/palace/westminsterhall/, accessed 22 November 2025

https://www.parliament.uk/about/living-heritage/building/palace/westminsterhall/other-uses/coronation-banquets/

https://www.parliament.uk/about/living-heritage/building/palace/westminsterhall/other-uses/coronation-banquets/#:~:text=From%201189%20to%201821%2C%20Westminster,Richard%20the%20Lionheart%20in%201189, accessed 22 November 2025

https://www.parliament.uk/about/living-heritage/evolutionofparliament/parliamentwork/offices-and-ceremonies/collections/parliamentary-collections-royal-weddings/princess-annes-wedding-/, accessed 5 March 2025, (Parliamentary Archives, PUD/15/4)

https://www.parliament.uk/about/living-heritage/evolutionofparliament/houseoflords/house-of-lords-reform/overview/hereditarypeersremoved/, accessed 22 November 2025

https://www.parliament.uk/about/living-heritage/evolutionofparliament/legislativescrutiny/act-of-union-1707/, accessed 22 November 2025

https://www.parliament.uk/about/living-heritage/evolutionofparliament/legislativescrutiny/act-of-union-1707/overview/union-of-the-crowns/, accessed 22 November 2025

https://www.pepysdiary.com/diary/1660/02/03/, accessed 22 November 2025 https://www.pepysdiary.com/diary/1661/04/22/, accessed 23 November 2025

https://www.pepysdiary.com/diary/1661/05/09/, accessed 23 November 2025

https://www.raf.mod.uk/our-organisation/stations/raf-cosford/news/coronation-medals-presented-to-our-personnel/, 29 March 2024 accessed 23 November 2025

https://www.rbo.org.uk/people/antonio-pappano, accessed 22 November 2025

https://www.rct.uk/collection/1005090/ceremonial-of-the-coronation-of-his-most-sacred-majesty-king-george-the-fourth, accessed 22 November 2025

https://www.rct.uk/collection/1110512/the-political-state-of-great-britain-v-49-jan-june-1735, accessed 23 November 2025

https://www.rct.uk/collection/2301735/the-kings-coronation-dinner-to-the-people-5-july-1902, accessed 22 November 2025

https://www.rct.uk/collection/31706/the-imperial-crown-of-india, accessed 23 November 2025

https://www.rct.uk/collection/31733/the-coronation-spoon, accessed 20 May 2023

https://www.rct.uk/collection/stories/the-crown-jewels/st-edwards-crown, accessed 18 November 2025

https://www.rct.uk/collection/stories/the-crown-jewels/the-ampulla, accessed 20 May 2023

https://www.rct.uk/collection/themes/exhibitions/the-queens-coronation-1953/buckingham-palace/coronation-banquets, accessed 2 September 2023

https://www.rct.uk/collection/themes/Trails/royal-jubilees/queen-victoria, accessed 22 November 2025

https://www.rct.uk/sites/default/files/null/Fact%20Sheet_The%20Coronation%20Banquet.pdf, accessed 1 October 2024

https://www.records.nsw.gov.au/image/NRS12160%5B4_8533-3%5D_003, accessed 22 November 2025

https://www.rhs.org.uk/plants/372820/vitis-sovereign-coronation-(b-s)/details, accessed 23 November 2025

https://www.rnz.co.nz/national/programmes/saturday/audio/2018888990/dr-george-gross-coronations-the-good-the-bad-and-the-ugly, 5 May 2023, accessed 23 November 2025 https://www.royal.uk/50-facts-about-queen-elizabeth-iis-coronation, accessed 22 November 2025

https://www.royal.uk/coronation-weekend-plans-announced, 21 January 2023, accessed 22 November 2025.

https://www.royal.uk/honours-scotland, accessed 22 November 2025

https://www.royal.uk/news-and-activity/2023-04-29/the-anointing-screen, 29 April 2023, accessed 22 November 2025

https://www.royal.uk/royal-archives-coronation, accessed 11 March 2023

https://www.royal.uk/the-coronation-quiche, accessed 18 October 2023

https://www.royalcollection.org.uk/collection/404951/charles-ii-1630-1685, accessed 23 November 2025

https://www.royalcwsociety.org/upcoming-events/commonwealthdayservice#:~:text=%E2%80%8BThis%20annual%20event%2C%20held,particularly%20amongst%20its%20young%20people, accessed 22 November 2025

https://www.royalmint.com/aboutus/press-centre/the-royal-mint-unveils-new-coins-of-the-nation/, 12 October 2023, accessed 23 November 2025

https://www.royalmint.com/aboutus/press-centre/the-royal-mint-unveils-remastered-henry-viii-coin-as-part-of-popular-british-monarchs-collection/#:~:text=This%20layer%20eventually%20wore%20away,nickname%2C%20'Old%20Coppernose, accessed 23 November 2025

https://www.royalmint.com/king-charles-iii/the-cross-of-wales/, accessed 22 November 2025

https://www.royalmintmuseum.org.uk/journal/curators-corner/crowned/medals/, accessed 23 November 2025

https://www.royalmintmuseum.org.uk/journal/people/isaac-newton/, accessed 20 August 2024

https://www.royalmintmuseum.org.uk/learning/teaching-resources-7-11/wildlife/, accessed 23 November 2025

https://www.royalwarrant.org/company/camel-valley, accessed 23 November 2025

https://www.secularism.org.uk/news/2023/05/coronation-should-trigger-debate-on-church-and-state-says-nss, 2 May 2023, accessed 23 November 2025

https://www.standard.co.uk/hp/front/boris-johnson-makes-barbara-windsor-capitals-street-party-queen-6575673.html, 12 April 2012, accessed 22 May 2025

https://www.stgeorges-windsor.org/news/edward-the-confessor/, accessed 22 November 2025

https://www.stgilescathedral.org.uk/, accessed 22 November 2025

https://www.swansea.gov.uk/article/22308/How-we-celebrated-the-coronation-in-times-gone-by, accessed 23 November 2025

https://www.tate.org.uk/art/artworks/martin-the-coronation-of-queen-victoria-n05753, accessed 23 November 2025

https://www.thegazette.co.uk/all-notices/content/104168, accessed 23 November 2025

https://www.theguardian.com/uk-news/2023/may/06/coronation-homage-of-the-people-toned-down-after-criticism#:~:text=The%20suggestion%20of%20the%20homage,holds%20the%20people%20in%20contempt%E2%80%9D, 6 May 2023, accessed 23 November 2025

https://www.therlws.com/grand-cru-events, accessed 10 October 2024

https://www.toronto.ca/explore-enjoy/history-art-culture/online-exhibits/web-exhibits/web-exhibits-culture-people/toronto-remembers-the-coronation-of-elizabeth-ii/, accessed 22 November 2025

https://www.trentbridge.co.uk/news/2020/january/2019-cricket-world-cup-confirmed-as-most-watched-ever.html, accessed 11 March 2023

https://www.vam.ac.uk/articles/the-festival-of-britain, accessed 22 November 2025

https://www.vatican.va/content/francesco/en.html, accessed 22 November 2025

https://www.wellingtoncollection.co.uk/wellington-stories/new-exhibition-coronation-robes/, accessed 5 March 2025

https://www.westminster-abbey.org/abbey-commemorations/royals/edward-the-confessor-and-edith/, accessed 22 November 2025

https://www.westminster-abbey.org/abbey-commemorations/royals/elizabeth-ii/, accessed 22 November 2025

https://www.westminster-abbey.org/abbey-news/canaletto-painting-display/, 2 March 2020, accessed 22 November 2025

https://www.westminster-abbey.org/abbey-news/stone-of-destiny-welcomed-to-the-abbey, 29 April 2023, accessed 22 November 2025

https://www.westminster-abbey.org/history/explore-our-history/the-coronation-chair/#:~:text=Origins%20and%20decoration,of%20the%20Abbot%20of%20Westminster, accessed 22 November 2025

https://www.westminster-abbey.org/visit-us/plan-your-visit/the-queens-diamond-jubilee-galleries (triforium), accessed 23 November 2025

https://www.westminster-abbey.org/worship-music/services-times/edwardtide/, accessed 22 November 2025

https://www.westminster-abbey.org/visit-us/the-queens-diamond-jubilee-galleries, accessed 2 December 2025

https://www.westyorksfire.gov.uk/news/coronation-medal-go-front-line-emergency-service-workers-fire-service, 5 May 2023, accessed 23 November 2025

https://www.yadvashem.org/righteous/stories/princess-alice.html, accessed 22 November 2025 https://www.westminster-abbey.org/abbey-commemorations/commemorations/grand-duchess-elizabeth, accessed 22 November 2025

https://x.com/KingsCollegeLon/status/1654788387058876416, 6 May 2023, accessed 7 May 2023

Hunneyball, P., https://historyofparliament.com/2023/05/11/1626-coronation-charles-i/, accessed 22 November 2025

Jackson, B. (BBC Radio Leicester), 5 April 2023, https://www.bbc.co.uk/programmes/p0ffl1hj6, accessed 22 November 2025

Jones, T., 6 May 2023, https://www.standard.co.uk/news/london/king-charles-coronation-homage-people-queen-consort-b1079274.html, accessed 23 November 2025

Khalil, H. and Foster, M., 4 March 2023, https://edition.cnn - Charles III coronation-oil, accessed 22 November 2025

Kirk, I., 1 June 2022, https://yougov.co.uk/society/articles/42695-platinum-jubilee-where-does-public-opinion-stand-m?redirect_from=%2Ftopics%2Flifestyle%2Farticles-reports%2F2022%2F06%2F01%2Fplatinum-jubilee-where-does-public-opinion-stand-m, accessed 23 November 2025

Kottasová, I., 2 May 2023, https://edition.cnn.com/2023/05/02/business/cost-of-living-doncaster-coronation-gbr-cmd-intl/index.html, accessed 23 November 2025

Leake, N., 11 May 2023, https://www.tatler.com/article/penny-mourdant-opens-up-about-her-star-role-at-king-charles-iiis-coronation, accessed 22 November 2025

Low, V., 13 February 2023, https://www.thetimes.com/article/kings-fleet-wont-sail-to-mark-coronation-n76j7rl8m, accessed 23 November 2025

Low, V., 3 March 2023, https://www.thetimes.com/uk/royal-family/article/king-charles-coronation-downton-abbey-herb-strewer-jkxw8g-zzf, accessed 4 March 2023

Maqbool, A., 18 September 2022, https://www.bbc.co.uk/news/uk-62942772, accessed 22 November 2025

McRae, I., 3 May 2023, https://www.bigissue.com/news/social-justice/how-much-kings-coronation-cost/, accessed 23 November 2025

Moran, J., 2 June 2013, https://www.radiotimes.com/books/why-elizabeth-iis-1953-coronation-is-the-day-that-changed-television/, accessed 23 November 2025

Murdoch, T., 'A Silver-Gilt Cup Commemorating the Coronation of James II and the Culture of Gifts and Prerequisites [*sic*] in Stuart and Hanoverian Coronations', *V&A Online Journal*, No. 2 (Autumn, 2009) http://www.vam.ac.uk/content/journals/research-journal/issue-02/a-silver-gilt-cup-commemorating-the-coronation-of-james-ii/, accessed 22 November 2024

Murray, C., 5 May 2023, https://www.forbes.com/sites/conormurray/2023/05/05/king-charles-iiis-people-of-all-faiths-pledge-why-theyve-introduced-new-inclusive-language-as-more-crown-critics-emerge/#:~:text=As%20Britain%20has%20become%20more,religions%20in%20the%20United%20Kingdom, accessed 5 May 2023

Nanji, N., 20 August 2024, https://www.bbc.co.uk/news/articles/c3ejnv74dwno, accessed 23 November 2025

Peachey, K., 13 October 2023, https://www.bbc.co.uk/news/business-67091137, accessed 23 November 2025

Potts, L., 20 April 2023, https://www.bbc.co.uk/news/uk-65031625, accessed 2 May 2023

Prescott, E., 19 May 2024, https://www.dailymail.co.uk/news/royals/article-13434187/prince-harry-king-charles-duke-norfolk-emily-prescott.html, accessed 22 November 2025

Queen Victoria Diary, http://www.queenvictoriasjournals.org/, accessed 23 November 2025

Quigley, E., 27 November 2021, https://www.bbc.co.uk/news/uk-scotland-59394186, accessed 22 November 2025

Rayner, G., 5 May 2023, https://www.telegraph.co.uk/royal-family/2023/05/05/queen-camilla-second-wedding-king-charles-coronation/#:~:text=According%20to%20the%20Liturgy%20for,to%20the%20public%20in%20service, accessed 10 March 2024

Reynolds, N., 19 November 2004, https://www.telegraph.co.uk/news/uknews/1476967/President-Chirac-faces-the-musical.html, accessed 22 November 2024

Rhoden-Paul, A., 6 May 2023, https://www.bbc.co.uk/news/uk-65510506, accessed 22 November 2025

Rhoden-Paul, A., 7 May 2023, https://www.bbc.co.uk/news/uk-65518360#:~:text=King%20Charles%20III's%20Coronation%20watched%20by%20more%20than%2018%20million%20viewers,-Published&text=The%20King's%20Coronation%20was%20watched,UK%2C%20overnight%20figures%20have%20shown, accessed 12 May 2023

Rotondi, J. P., 13 November 2009, https://www.history.com/this-day-in-history/september-6/some-2-5-billion-tv-viewers-watch-princess-dianas-funeral, accessed 10 March 2023

Sachdeva, M. and Muir, E., 9 May 2023, https://www.independent.co.uk/life-style/royal-family/penny-mordaunt-who-coronation-sword-dress-b2335333.html, accessed 22 November 2025

Science Museum Group (UK), Sir Henry Wellcome's Museum Collection, A108752: https://collection.sciencemuseumgroup.org.uk/objects/co72125/gold-medal-commemorating-the-recovery-of-queen-elizabeth-i-from-smallpox-1572, accessed 23 November 2025

Sherwin, A., 18 April 2021, https://inews.co.uk/culture/television/prince-philips-funeral-watched-more-than-13-million-uk-viewers-961811, accessed 11 March 2023

Sherwood, H., 4 May 2023, https://www.theguardian.com/uk-news/2023/may/04/defender-of-all-faiths-coronation-puts-focus-king-charles-religious-beliefs, accessed 23 November 2025

Sherwood, H., 9 September 2022, https://www.theguardian.com/uk-news/2022/sep/09/king-charles-to-be-defender-of-the-faith-but-also-a-defender-of-faiths, accessed 22 November 2025

Sleator, L., 11 May 2023, https://www.thetimes.com/article/penny-mordaunt-meme-sword-coronation-75h97n5g7, accessed 22 November 2025

Smith, M., 3 May 2023, https://yougov.co.uk/society/articles/45654-where-does-public-opinion-stand-monarchy-ahead-cor?redirect_from

=%2Ftopics%2Fsociety%2Farticles-reports%2F2023%2F05%2F03%2Fwhere-does-public-opinion-stand-monarchy-ahead-cor, accessed 23 November 2025

Solly, M., 2 May 2023, https://www.smithsonianmag.com/history/a-not-so-brief-history-of-british-coronations-180982088/, accessed 23 November 2025

Somerville, E., 30 May 2023, https://www.telegraph.co.uk/politics/2023/05/30/penny-mordaunt-mp-tory-members-coronation-sword-charles/, accessed 22 November 2025

Stewart, A., 6 May 2023, https://www.bbc.co.uk/news/uk-northern-ireland-65461480, accessed 22 November 2025

Supplement to The London Gazette, 26–27 September 1911 (referencing 22 June 1911), https://www.thegazette.co.uk/London/issue/28535/supplement/7077, accessed 22 November 2025

Syed, A., 6 May 2023, https://time.com/6277718/penny-mordaunt-king-charles-coronation/, accessed 22 November 2025

'The Coronation', *BBC* (2018) https://www.bbc.co.uk/programmes/b09plvdh#:~:text=Shedding%20an%20entirely%20new%20perspective,overwhelmed%20colleagues%20lost%20their%20voices, accessed 20 May 2024

The 2023 Coronation Roll, https://www.coronationroll.gov.uk, accessed 22 November 2025

The Australian War Memorial, Canberra, A04831, https://www.awm.gov.au/collection/C728, accessed 22 November 2025

The London Gazette, 1 June 1953: https://www.thegazette.co.uk/London/issue/39863/supplement/2939, accessed 22 November 2025

The London Gazette, 20 July 1838: https://www.thegazette.co.uk/London/issue/19637/page/1639, accessed 22 November 2025

The London Gazette, 24 July 1838https://www.thegazette.co.uk/London/issue/19639/page/1666, accessed 22 November 2025

The London Gazette, 28 October 1902, Issue 27489, pp. 6859–6892 https://www.thegazette.co.uk/London/issue/27489/supplement/6859, accessed 23 November 2025

The London Gazette, 29-30 December 2023: https://www.thegazette.co.uk/London/issue/64269/data.pdf, accessed 22 November 2025

The London Gazette, 13 September 1831, Issue 18848, pp. 1861–1875: https://www.thegazette.co.uk/London/issue/18848/page/1861, accessed 22 November 2025

The Museum of the Order of St John, London, LDOSJ:44: https://museumstjohn.org.uk/collections/king-edward-vii-coronation-medal-king-george-v-coronation-medal-and-service-medal-with-bars-awarded-to-mrs-e-denchfield/, accessed 1 August 2024

The National Archives, https://discovery.nationalarchives.gov.uk/details/r/D7730541, accessed 10 May 2023

The National Archives, https://webarchive.nationalarchives.gov.uk/ukgwa/+/https:/www.nationalarchives.gov.uk/jubilee/gallery/queen-elizabeth-second-highlights/coronation-oath/, accessed 18 November 2025

The Palais du Tau museum, https://www.palais-du-tau.fr/en, accessed 22 November 2025

Thomas, T., 11 May 2023, https://www.theguardian.com/politics/2023/may/11/penny-mordaunt-took-painkillers-before-sword-carrying-role-coronation, accessed 22 November 2025

Torrance, D., 19 April 2023, https://commonslibrary.parliament.uk/changes-to-the-coronation-oath/, accessed 20 May 2023

Tucker, H., 1 May 2023, https://www.bbc.com/travel/article/20230430-coronation-chicken-the-story-behind-the-royal-dish, accessed 22 November 2024

Tudor, G., 7 May 2023, https://www.bbc.co.uk/news/uk-england-shropshire-65518256, accessed 8 May 2023

Turner, L. and Coughlan, S., 8 May 2023, https://www.bbc.co.uk/news/entertainment-arts-65480420, accessed 10 May 2023

Ukrainian TV 1+1 - two episodes on the history of Coronations (1–2 May 2023): https://www.youtube.com/watch?v=x97CzPkglkQ, accessed 10 May 2023

Vickers, H., 5 May 2023, https://www.standard.co.uk/comment/charles-sacred-ritual-different-man-coronation-b1079086.html, accessed 20 May 2023

Ward, V. and Diver, T., 10 February 2023, https://www.telegraph.co.uk/royal-family/2023/02/10/peers-uk-ministers-lobbying-attend-king-charles-coronation/, accessed 23 November 2025

Ward, V., 30 April 2023, https://www.telegraph.co.uk/royal-family/2023/04/30/public-homage-charles-coronation-voluntary-lambeth-palace/, accessed 23 November 2025

Ward, V., Swerling, G. and Bird, S., 6 May 2023, https://www.telegraph.co.uk/royal-family/2023/05/06/coronation-service-changed-after-allegiance-backlash/, accessed 23 November 2025

Watt, G., 31 August 2017, https://www.cambridge.org/core/journals/ecclesiastical-law-journal/article/coronation-oath/F83079759125218B8D97BA1722954CBC, accessed 10 May 2023

Webber, E., 5 May 2023, https://www.politico.eu/article/my-part-in-the-pomp-meet-the-uk-minister-carrying-a-huge-sword-for-king-charles/, accessed 22 November 2025

Welsh, T. and Foster, A., https://www.bbc.co.uk/news/uk-england-london-65476887, accessed 23 November 2025

Williams, H., 3 May 2023, https://www.churchtimes.co.uk/articles/2023/5-may/news/uk/archbishop-welby-defends-people-s-homage-in-the-coronation#:~:text=THE%20Archbishop%20of%20Canterbury%20has,a%20command%E2%80%9D%20but%20an%20invitation, accessed 23 November 2025

Willsher, K., 25 May 2024, https://www.theguardian.com/world/article/2024/may/25/history-is-written-at-the-dining-table-what-4000-menus-tells-us-about-royals-politicians-and-society, accessed 22 November 2025

www.queenvictoriasjournals.org, accessed 23 November 2025

Musical Sources (Discography)

'Coronation Anthems: Anthems Composed and Sung at the Coronations of James II in 1685, William and Mary in 1689, Anne in 1702, George I in 1714, George II in 1727, and George III in 1761' (Decca, 2002)

'Coronation Music for King James II (1685) Choir of Westminster Abbey and Orchestra on Authentic Instruments' (Polydor International GmbH, Hamburg, 1987)

Index[1]

[1] Note: Page numbers followed by 'n' refer to notes.

G. William Cullen Gross, *Crown and People*,
https://doi.org/10.1007/978-3-032-20786-9

D

F

G

H

N

www.ingramcontent.com/pod-product-compliance
Lightning Source LLC
Chambersburg PA
CBHW070431080926
51106CB00029B/1110
* 9 7 8 3 0 3 2 2 0 7 8 5 2 *